19 Co-operative Change Management through Practitioner Inquiry 238
Susan Groundwater-Smith

PART III PERSONAL: SELF-AWARENESS,
DEVELOPMENT AND IDENTITY **249**

Introduction to Part III 250

20 Ethics and the 'Personal' in Action Research 254
Jane Zeni

21 Writing to Learn: A Process for the Curious 267
Mary Louise Holly

22 From Passionate Enquiry to Loving Detachment: One Researcher's
Methodological Journey 278
Marion Dadds

23 The Interconnections between Narrative Inquiry and
Action Research 290
Debbie Pushor and D. Jean Clandinin

24 Capabilities, Flourishing and the Normative Purposes of
Action Research 301
Melanie Walker

25 Demonstrating Quality in Educational Research for
Social Accountability 313
Jean McNiff and Jack Whitehead

26 Action Research and Pedagogy as Science of the
Child's Upbringing 324
Petra Ponte and Jan Ax

27 Developing Relationships, Developing the Self: Buddhism and
Action Research 336
Richard Winter

28 Teaching and Cultural Difference: Exploring the Potential for a
Psychoanalytically Informed Action Research 347
Terrance Carson

29 Complexity Theory and Action Research 358
Dennis Sumara and Brent Davis

30 Agency through Action Research: Constructing Active Identities
    from Theoretical Models and Metaphors   370
    Bridget Somekh

31 Existentialism and Action Research   381
    Allan Feldman

**PART IV   POLITICAL: POPULAR KNOWLEDGE,
DIFFERENCE, AND FRAMEWORKS FOR CHANGE**   **393**

    Introduction to Part IV   394

32 Elbows Out, Arms Linked: Claiming Spaces for Feminisms
    and Gender Equity in Educational Action Research   398
    Patricia Maguire and Britt-Marie Berge

33 Students' Participation in School Change: Action Research
    on the Ground   409
    Pat Thomson and Helen Gunter

34 Community Action and Agency in the Education of Urban Youth   420
    Peter C. Murrell Jr.

35 Social-Political Theory in Working with Teachers for Social
    Justice Schooling   432
    Marie Brennan and Susan E. Noffke

36 Rethinking Action Research: Commonsense and Relations of
    Freedom   442
    Andrew Gitlin

37 Participatory Action Research in Latin American Education:
    A Road Map to a Different Part of the World   453
    *Eduardo Flores-Kastanis, Juny Montoya-Vargas, and
    Daniel H. Suárez*

38 Teacher Development and Political Transformation:
    Reflections from the South African Experience   467
    Maureen Robinson and Crain Soudien

39 The Impact of Action Research in the Spanish Schools in the
    Post-Franco Era   481
    *Àngel I. Pérez Gómez, Miguel Sola Fernández,
    Encarnación Soto Gómez and José Francisco Murillo Mas*

CONTENTS

Contributors   x

Acknowledgement   xxvii

INTRODUCTION   1
Susan E. Noffke and Bridget Somekh

1. Revisiting the Professional, Personal, and Political Dimensions
   of Action Research   6
   Susan E. Noffke

**PART I   ACTION RESEARCH METHODOLOGY:
DIVERSITY OF RATIONALES AND PRACTICES**   **25**

Introduction to Part I   26

2   Building Educational Theory through Action Research   28
   John Elliott

3   Teacher Research as Stance   39
   Marilyn Cochran-Smith and Susan L. Lytle

4   Dialogic Inquiry as Collaborative Action Research   50
   Gordon Wells

5   Action Research and the Personal Turn   62
   *Sandra Hollingsworth, Anthony Cody, Mary Dybdahl, Leslie Turner
   Minarik, Jennifer Davis-Smallwood and Karen Manheim Teel*

6   Educational Action Research: A Critical Approach   74
   Wilfred Carr and Stephen Kemmis

7   Action Research for/as/mindful of Social Justice   85
   Morwenna Griffiths

**PART II PROFESSIONAL: KNOWLEDGE PRODUCTION,
STAFF DEVELOPMENT, AND THE STATUS OF EDUCATORS   99**

Introduction to Part II   100

8 A School District-Based Action Research Program in the
   United States   104
   *Cathy Caro-Bruce, Mary Klehr, Ken Zeichner and
   Ana Maria Sierra-Piedrahita*

9 Using Action Research to Support Students with Special
   Educational Needs   118
   Christine O'Hanlon

10 Renegotiating Knowledge Relationships in Schools   131
    Chris Bigum and Leonie Rowan

11 Lesson Study as Action Research   142
    Catherine Lewis, Rebecca Perry, and Shelley Friedkin

12 Practitioner Action Research and Educational Leadership   155
    Gary L. Anderson and Kathryn Herr

13 Educational Action Research as a Paradigm for Change   166
    Shoshana Keiny and Lily Orland-Barak

14 Practitioner Action Research: Building and Sustaining
    Success through Networked Learning Communities   178
    Christopher Day and Andrew Townsend

15 Action Research and Educational Change: Teachers as Innovators 190
    Lesley Saunders and Bridget Somekh

16 A School System Takes on Exhibitions through
    Teacher Action Research   202
    Marie Brennan

17 Action Research, Professional Development and Systemic Reform 213
    Herbert Altrichter and Peter Posch

18 Sustaining the Next Generation of Teacher-Researchers to Work
    for Social Justice   226
    Barbara Comber and Barbara Kamler

The SAGE
Handbook of
Educational Action
Research

The SAGE
Handbook of
Educational Action
Research

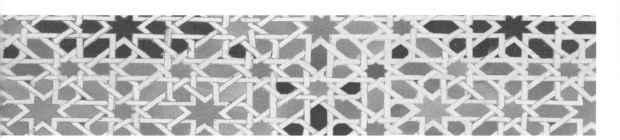

Edited by

Susan E. Noffke
and Bridget Somekh

Los Angeles • London • New Delhi • Singapore • Washington DC

First published 2009

SAGE Publications Ltd
1 Oliver's Yard
55 City Road
London EC1Y 1SP

SAGE Publications Inc.
2455 Teller Road
Thousand Oaks, California 91320

SAGE Publications India Pvt Ltd
B 1/I 1 Mohan Cooperative Industrial Area
Mathura Road
New Delhi 110 044

SAGE Publications Asia-Pacific Pvt Ltd
33 Pekin Street #02-01
Far East Square
Singapore 048763

Library of Congress Control Number: 2008928395

British Library Cataloguing in Publication data

A catalogue record for this book is available from the British Library

ISBN 978-1-4129-4708-4

Typeset by CEPHA Imaging Pvt. Ltd., Bangalore, India
Printed in India by Replika Press Pvt. Ltd.
Printed on paper from sustainable resources

40 Popular Education and Action Research   495
    Mary Brydon-Miller, Ismail Davids, Namrata Jaitli,
    M. Brinton Lykes, Jean Schensul, and Susan Williams

41 Partnership Action Research for Social Justice: Politics,
    Challenges and Possibilities   508
    Lew Zipin and Robert Hattam

    Conclusions   521
    Bridget Somekh and Susan E. Noffke

    Index   527

CONTRIBUTORS

Herbert Altrichter, is a Professor of Education at Johannes-Kepler-Universität Linz, Austria. Founding President of the Austrian Educational Research Association, training as organizational consultant. Research interests: school development, governance of schooling, evaluation, teacher education. Recent publications: *Teachers Investigate Their Work* (with Allan Feldman, Peter Posch, and Bridget Somekh; London, 2008, 2nd edition); *Educational Governance* (with Thomas Bruesemeister and Jochen Wissinger; Wiesbaden, 2007); *Lehrerinnen und Lehrer erforschen ihren Unterricht* (with Peter Posch; Bad Heilbrunn, 2007, 4th edition; translations in Greek and Chinese); *Images of Educational Change* (with John Elliott; Buckingham, 2000).

Gary L. Anderson is a Professor in the Steinhardt School of Culture, Education and Human Development at New York University. He is a former high school teacher and principal. He has co-authored two books and many articles on action research. The latest is *The Action Research Dissertation* (with Kathryn Herr). His new book, *Advocacy Leadership*, will be published by Routledge in early 2009.

Jan Ax is an Associate Professor in Educational Studies at the University of Amsterdam in the Netherlands. He has published and conducted research in educational policy and school organization, especially in the domain of secondary education and senior vocational education. His teaching subjects are instruction and curriculum, educational research methods, educational policy, and school organization.

Britt-Marie Berge is an Associate Professor and Senior Lecturer at the Department of Education and Umeå Centre of Gender Studies, Umeå University, Sweden. She has pedagogic experiences as a school teacher, university lecturer, and parent. Her main research interest is the construction of gender in educational settings and she has carried out research on pre-schools, compulsory schools, teacher training, and study circles. For the past 15 years she has also pursued action research on gender equity, which in English is published in articles and with Hildur Ve in the book *Action Research for Gender Equity* (Open University Press, 2000).

Chris Bigum is an educational consultant. His research interests include the implications of computing and bio-technologies for educational practice and policy. Specifically, these interests include read/write Web (or Web 2.0) environments, genomic literacy, new literacy studies, actor-network approaches to the study of educational innovation and change, digital epistemologies, schools as knowledge producers, and scenario planning in education.

Marie Brennan is a Professor of Education at the University of South Australia. She teaches curriculum and policy studies and has a long history of partnership research in the schooling sector in Australia, as well as work in early childhood, adult education, and higher education. Her main research interests are in participatory methodologies, political sociology of school reform, and in issues pertaining to democracy and educational injustice in globalizing times.

Mary Brydon-Miller directs the University of Cincinnati's Action Research Center and is an Associate Professor of Educational Studies and Urban Educational Leadership in the College of Education, Criminal Justice, and Human Services. She is a participatory action researcher who engages in both community-based and educational action research. Her current scholarship focuses on ethics and action research. Other publications include work on participatory action research methods, feminist theory and action research, refugee resettlement, elder advocacy, disability rights, and academic writing in the social sciences.

Cathy Caro-Bruce is currently working as an educational consultant to school districts with the Wisconsin Department of Public Instruction developing the Statewide System of Support (NCLB). For 30 years she has been a Staff and Organization Development Specialist for the Madison Metropolitan School District, and for 15 years has coordinated Classroom Action Research as part of the district professional development program. Cathy was a co-editor of *Creating Equitable Classrooms through Action Research* (Corwin Press, 2007). Cathy also works with school districts around the country helping them implement action research based on principles that drive high quality professional development.

Wilfred Carr is a Professor of the Philosophy of Education at the University of Sheffield. He is also an Honorary Professor in the Faculty of Education and Social Work at the University of Sydney, an Honorary Vice-President of the Philosophy of Education Society of Great Britain and a member of its National Executive Committee. His is interested in a range of philosophical questions concerning the nature of educational practice and their significance for the ways in which educational theory and research are currently conducted and understood. He is editor of *The Routledge Falmer Reader in the Philosophy of Education* (Routledge, 2005).

Terrance Carson is a Professor of curriculum studies and teacher education in the Department of Secondary Education at the University of Alberta in Edmonton, Canada. He is the former Chair of the Department and has taught post-graduate courses in action research since the mid-1980s. His publications include *Action Research as a Living Practice*, which he co-edited with Dennis Sumara. His recent research focuses on questions of diversity, teaching, and the internationalization of curriculum. He is currently a Vice-President of the International Association for the Advancement of Curriculum Studies.

D. Jean Clandinin is a Professor and Director of the Centre for Research for Teacher Education and Development at the University of Alberta. She is co-author with Michael Connelly of four books including *Narrative Inquiry. Composing Diverse Identities: Narrative Inquiries into the Interwoven Lives of Children and Teachers* (2006) drew on research with children and teachers in urban schools. She edited the 2007 *Handbook of Narrative Inquiry: Mapping a Methodology*. With AERA, she was a Vice-President of Division B; the 1993 winner of the Early Career Award; and she was awarded the 2002 Division B Lifetime Achievement Award.

Marilyn Cochran-Smith holds the John E. Cawthorne Millennium Chair and directs the Doctoral Program in Curriculum and Instruction at Boston College's Lynch School of Education. Cochran-Smith was 2005 President of AERA. Her seventh book, *Handbook of Research on Teacher Education: Enduring Questions in Changing Contexts* (co-edited with S. Feiman Nemser, J. McIntyre, and K. Demers), was published in 2008. Cochran-Smith is co-editor of the Practitioner Inquiry Series, produced by Teachers College Press. The book, *Inquiry as Stance: Practitioner Research in the Next Generation*, co-authored by Marilyn Cochran-Smith and Susan L. Lytle, will be published by Teachers College Press in the spring of 2009.

Anthony Cody is a National Board certified teacher who has worked for the past 21 years in the Oakland schools. He taught middle school science for 18 years, and is now the secondary science coach for the District. He is active in the Teacher Leaders Network and recently helped found the Forum of Accomplished California Teachers. His two sons are now 15 and 17 years old, and he lives in the Oakland hills with his partner and their two dogs and two cats.

Barbara Comber is an acting Director of the Hawke Research Institute for Sustainable Societies at the University of South Australia. Her interests include literacy education, social justice, teachers' work and identities, place and space, and practitioner inquiry. She has worked on a number of collaborative research projects with teachers in high poverty locations focusing on innovative and critical pedagogies which address contemporary social challenges. She has recently co-edited two books: *Literacies in Place: Teaching Environmental Communication* (Comber, Nixon & Reid, 2007) and *Turn-around Pedagogies: Literacy Interventions for At-Risk Students* (Comber & Kamler, 2005).

Marion Dadds is a Professor of Education at the University of Cumbria, UK. She has a distinguished background in the theory and practice of practitioner research, having conducted and published several of her own projects as well as supporting other professionals, especially teachers. Her particular contribution has been in the area of the emotional and spiritual dimensions of practitioner research.

Key publications include *Passionate Enquiry and School Development* and *Doing Practitioner Research Differently* (published jointly with Susan Hart).

Ismail Davids is the Executive Director at Foundation for Contemporary Research (FCR), a Cape Town-based action research NGO contributing toward poverty alleviation by promoting good local governance and municipal-community partnerships. His research interests include local governance and participatory democracy, inclusive citizenship, community development, poverty, and wealth. Ismail co-authored the South African university prescribed textbook *Participatory Development in South Africa: A Development Management Perspective* (2005, 2008), authored *Voices from Below: Reflecting on Ten Years of Public Participation of Democratic Local Government in the Western Cape Province* (2004), and has published numerous articles on issues of citizenship, democracy, and participatory development.

Brent Davis is a Professor and David Robitaille Chair in Mathematics, Science, and Technology Education at the University of British Columbia. His research is developed around the educational relevance of developments in the cognitive and complexity sciences, and he teaches courses at the undergraduate and graduate levels in curriculum studies, mathematics education, and educational change. Davis has published books and articles in the areas of mathematics learning and teaching, curriculum theory, teacher education, epistemology, and action research. His most recent book is *Engaging Minds: Changing Teaching in Complex Times* (2nd edition, 2008; co-authored with Dennis Sumara and Rebecca Luce-Kapler).

Jennifer Davis-Smallwood was a public school educator for 18 years. She taught in Waimea, Hawaii, as well as Vallejo and Berkeley, California. She is currently ranch manager and home schooling her third and sixth grade children.

Christopher Day is a Professor of Education and the Director of the Teacher and Leadership Research Centre (TLRC) at the University of Nottingham. He is an editor of *Teachers and Teaching: Theory and Practice* and co-editor of the *Educational Action Research Journal*. His books have been published in several languages and include *Teachers Matter* (2007), Open University Press; *Successful Principal Leadership in Times of Change: An International Perspective* (2007), Springer; *A Passion for Teaching* (2004), Falmer; *International Handbook on the Continuing Professional Development of Teachers* (2004), Open University Press; and *Developing Teachers: The Challenges of Lifelong Learning* (1999), Falmer Press.

Mary Dybdahl received her teaching credential and M.A. in Education from UC Berkeley's Developmental Teaching Education program in 1988. She started teaching in the Vallejo City USD that year and joined the Berkeley Group almost immediately. After 10 years in the classroom and four years as a categorical program coordinator, Mary returned to UC Berkeley to get her administrative credential through the Principal Leadership Institute, a program that focuses on educational leadership in urban schools. For the past six years she has been an elementary school administrator in Vallejo.

John Elliott is an Emeritus Professor of Education within the Centre for Applied Research in Education at the University of East Anglia. He is well known internationally for his role in developing the theory and practice of action research in the contexts of curriculum and teacher development. He was an Advisory Professor to the Hong Kong Institute of Education (2001–2006) and a *consultant* to the Hong Kong Government on the strategic development of its curriculum reforms from 2001 to 2006. His recent publications include *Reflecting Where the Action Is*: *The Selected Works of John Elliott in the Routledge World Library of Educationalists* (2007).

Allan Feldman is a Professor of Science Education and Teacher Education at the University of Massachusetts Amherst. His research is focused on what it means to teach and to be a teacher. This is tied to his study of action research, self-study of teacher education practices, and existential conceptions of teaching. He has published in the *Journal of Research on Science Teaching, Educational Action Research,* and *Science Education*. Professor Feldman taught middle and high school science and math for 17 years before obtaining his doctorate at Stanford University.

Eduardo Flores-Kastanis is an Associate Professor and coordinator of the research group called 'Schools as Knowledge Organizations' at the Escuela de Graduados en Educación (Graduate School of Education) at the Tecnológico de Monterrey, in Mexico. He belongs to the Mexican Council of Educational Research (COMIE), and has been appointed as National Researcher of Mexico's National Council of Science and Technology (CONACYT). His current research interests focus on the effects of organizational structures on the work of teachers, and how action research can contribute to improve administration in Mexican public schools. He lives in Chihuahua, Northern Mexico.

Shelley Friedkin is a Research Associate at Mills College in Oakland, California. Her current research interest focuses on teachers' use of data to improve classroom instruction. The co-authors are currently studying the impact of lesson study on teachers' content knowledge. Additional information and video of US and Japanese teachers engaging in lesson study are available at www.lessonresearch.net.

Andrew Gitlin holds a Chair in the Department of Social Foundations at the University of Georgia. He has focused his research efforts on trying to understand the intimate connections between knowledge and power. Looking at this issue, Gitlin has centered his latest work on the exploration of the political dimensions of aesthetics and the implications of this 'deep politic' for schooling. His current scholarship includes *Educational Poetics: Inquiry Freedom and Innovative Necessary* (New York: Peter Lang, 2005), and 'Inquiry, imagination, and the search for a deep politic', *Educational Researcher,* 34(3): 15–24.

Morwenna Griffiths is a Professor of Classroom Learning in the Moray House School of Education at Edinburgh University. She has taught in primary schools in Bristol; at the University of Isfahan, Iran; at Christ Church College HE in Canterbury; at Oxford Brookes, Nottingham; and Nottingham Trent Universities. Her recent research has included philosophical theorizing and empirical investigation, related to epistemology of auto/biography, social justice, public spaces, the nature of practice, feminization, and creativity. Her books include *Action for Social Justice in Education: Fairly Different*; *Educational Research for Social Justice;* and *Feminisms and the Self: The Web of Identity*.

Susan Groundwater-Smith is an Honorary Professor in the Faculty of Education and Social Work at the University of Sydney. She convenes the Special Interest Group that focuses on practitioner research within the Division of Professional Learning. She manages The Coalition of Knowledge Building Schools, a loose alliance of metropolitan and regional schools in New South Wales, Australia, all of whom have a common interest in and commitment to practitioner inquiry. She has published widely in the area of teacher professional learning both within the context of initial teacher education and continuing professional development. Her recent contributions have been in the area of the ethics that guide practitioner research and matters of quality.

Helen Gunter is a Professor of Educational Policy, Leadership and *Management* in the School of Education at the University of Manchester. Her particular interest is in the history of knowledge production in the field of educational leadership, and she has undertaken work around mapping theory and research. She is currently completing an ESRC-funded project on knowledge production and school leadership in England in the first decade of New Labour. Her most recent books are *Leading Teachers* (Continuum, 2005) and, co-edited with Graham Butt, *Modernising Schools: People, Learning and Organisations* (Continuum, 2007).

Robert Hattam is an Associate Professor in the School of Education and the Hawke Research *Institute* for Sustainable Societies at the University of South Australia. His research has focused on teachers' work, critical and reconciliation pedagogies, refugees, and socially just school reform. He has published in a range of journals and has been involved in book projects with others that include *Schooling for a Fair Go, Teachers' Work in a Globalising Economy,* and *Dropping Out, Drifting Off, Being Excluded: Becoming Somebody Without School*.

Recently he published a book entitled *Awakening-Struggle: Towards a Buddhist Critical Theory*.

Kathryn Herr is a Professor in the College of Education and Human Services at Montclair State University. She is a former social worker, middle school teacher, and counsellor. She has co-authored two books and many articles on action research. The latest is *The Action Research Dissertation* (with Gary L. Anderson). She also co-edited the three volumes of *Encyclopedia of Activism and Social Justice* (2007) with Gary L. Anderson.

Sandra Hollingsworth is a visiting Professor at the University of California, Berkeley, and a Professor of Teacher Education at San Jose State University. A former published historian and K-12 classroom teacher, Dr. Hollingsworth has studied *teachers'* understanding of the equity issues in minority students' literacy development since the beginning of her career. Dr. Hollingsworth has worked in developing countries in South Asia, the Middle East and western Africa. She is currently the co-editor of *American Educational Research Journal – Social and Institutional Analysis*. Dr Hollingsworth's after-hours passions revolve around gardening, visual arts, and her five grandchildren.

Mary Louise Holly serves as a founding Director of the Faculty Professional Development Center at Kent State University where she is a Professor in the department of Teaching Leadership and Curriculum Studies. Mary Lou's interest in human development began as she taught children art. In early research she worked with teachers using life history and biographical methods for AR. Current research explores learning communities using AR to improve science education and preserve wetlands in the Cuyahoga watershed. The 3rd edition of *Action Research for Teachers* (Prentice Hall) with colleagues Joanne Arhar and Wendy Kasten, was published in 2009.

Namrata Jaitli is currently a Fellow in PRIA Continuing Education, a division of PRIA, Delhi, India. She has a Bachelors in Psychology (Honors) from Lady Sri Ram College, Delhi University, and a Masters in Social Work from Delhi University. She has coordinated and participated in diverse projects, which include national coordination of women's empowerment project, research studies on monitoring participation in projects, capacity building interventions for development practitioners on participation and institutional development; and course development and teaching on themes of participation and civil society to diverse ranges of development of professionals and students.

Barbara Kamler is an Emeritus Professor at Deakin University, Australia. She has lifelong research interests in writing and identity, writing as social action and critical approaches to literacy. Recent books include *Relocating the Personal: A Critical Writing Pedagogy* (Kamler, 2001); *Helping Doctoral*

Students Write: Pedagogies for Supervision (Kamler and Thomson, 2006); and an edited collection *Turn-Around Pedagogies: Literacy Interventions for At-Risk Students* (Comber & Kamler, 2005). She continues to develop models of research that enhance the agency of participants and is currently doing consultancy work on academic writing and publishing for doctoral students and early career academics.

Shoshana Keiny is a Senior Lecturer (now in retirement) in the Education Department of Ben-Gurion University, where she has been engaged in research and teaching since its foundation. Her fields of activity include facilitating educational change processes by teachers, through collaborative Action Research; developing a new conception of Environmental Education, based on Ecological Thinking, and translating it to curricular units constructed by teachers in various national projects such as IPSTES; Science & Technology in Society, etc. She is a member of editorial boards for various international journals. *Ecological Thinking: A new approach to Educational Change*, published in 2002 by UPA has been translated to Hebrew.

Stephen Kemmis is a Professor of Education at Charles Sturt University, Australia. For over 30 years Stephen has been writing about educational research and evaluation. Among his publications are *Becoming Critical: Education, Knowledge and Action Research* (with Wilfred Carr; Falmer, London, 1986) and the chapter 'Participatory action research: Communicative action and the public sphere' (with Robin McTaggart; in Norman Denzin and Yvonne Lincoln, eds, *The SAGE Handbook of Qualitative Research,* 3rd edition, Thousand Oaks, California, 2005). He has also written numerous evaluation reports, chapters, and articles on professional practice, indigenous education, participatory action research, and qualitative methods in educational research.

Mary Klehr holds a joint Madison WI Metro School District/University of Wisconsin-Madison position supervising a Professional Development School elementary teacher education partnership program, which is designed to prepare skilled and caring teachers committed to working in culturally diverse, urban public schools. Mary has been involved in teacher research since 1996 as a practitioner and facilitator. She coordinates the school district's Classroom Action Research Program and recently co-edited an anthology of Madison studies, *Creating Equitable Classrooms through Action Research* (Corwin Press, 2007).

Catherine Lewis is a distinguished research scholar at Mills College in Oakland, California. She has conducted research in Japanese and US schools for 25 years, and written the first English-language articles about lesson study, the award-winning book *Educating Hearts and Minds: Reflections on Japanese Preschool and Elementary Education* (Cambridge University Press, 1995) and *Lesson Study: A Handbook of Teacher-Led Instructional Change* (Research for

Better Schools, 2002). Lesson study video, tools, and publications can be found at www.lessonresearch.net

M. Brinton Lykes, is a Professor of Community-Cultural Psychology and Associate Director of the Center for Human Rights and International Justice at Boston College. Her participatory action research with survivors of war and organized violence analyzes the causes and effects of gross violations of human rights and contributes to the development of community-based programs that aspire to rethread social relations and transform social inequalities. She has published extensively, co-edited three books, and co-authored a fourth with women of rural Guatemala. Brinton is a co-founder of the Boston Women's Fund and the Ignacio Martín-Baró Fund for Mental Health and Human Rights.

Susan L. Lytle is an Associate Professor of Education and Chair of the Language and Literacy in Education Division, Graduate School of Education, University of Pennsylvania, Director of the Master's and Doctoral Programs in Reading/Writing/Literacy, and founding Director of the 22-year-old Philadelphia Writing Project, a site of the National Writing Project and an urban school–university collaborative network. Lytle is co-editor of the Practitioner Inquiry Series, produced by Teachers College Press as well as a past President of the National Conference on Research in Language and Literacy (NCRLL) and the NCTE Assembly on Research. The book, *Inquiry as Stance: Practitioner Research in the Next Generation,* co-authored by Susan L. Lytle and Marilyn Cochran-Smith, will be published by Teachers College Press in the spring of 2009.

Patricia Maguire is a Professor of education and Chairperson of the Gallup Graduate Studies Center, Western New Mexico University. She has worked as a school and mental health counselor, international development worker and trainer (Africa, Jamaica), and community activist. For the past 20 years, Pat has been a member of a collaborative team developing transformative-oriented graduate education programs in a rural community on the edge of the Navajo Nation and Pueblo of Zuni. Her networking, research, and publication interests include the interface between feminisms and participatory action research and teacher action research, building on her 1987 book, *Doing Participatory Research: A Feminist Approach.*

Jean McNiff is an Adjunct Professor at the University of Limerick, Ireland; Honorary Professor at Ningxia Teachers University in the People's Republic of China; and Research Associate at the Nelson Mandela Metropolitan University in South Africa. She is also associated with York St. John University, UK, and the University of Pretoria, South Africa. She supports practitioners in a range of settings, including schools and universities, as they find ways of demonstrating their personal and social accountability in influencing processes of cultural and social transformation.

She writes about the need for practitioners to undertake their action enquiries as they critically engage with their own professional learning in demonstrating their claims to educational influence.

Leslie Turner Minarik has been a second grade teacher for 21 years, at the Highland Elementary School, West Contra Costa USD. She has studied at University of California, Berkeley, Teaching Credential, University of California, B.A. French and Portuguese and Universite de Bordeaux. She received District Teacher of the Year in 1996 and is builder of three school gardens. She is a nationally ranked orienteer. Prior to discovering teaching, she worked for 10 years in publishing for *Runner's World Magazine* and *Sunset Magazine*.

Juny Montoya-Vargas is an Associate Professor of Law and Education and Head of the Center for Research and Teaching on Education (CIFE) at University of Los Andes. She received her Ph.D. in Education from the University of Illinois. She teaches graduate courses in curriculum and pedagogy, qualitative research methods, and program evaluation. She is a member of the American Evaluation Association. Her work is on legal education, participatory evaluation, and education for democracy. The recent publication is 'Education in the Colombian Constitution of 1991 and in the Constitutional Court decisions', in Ibañez, J. (wd.) *The Right to Education and Democratic Citizenship*. Bogotá: Ediciones Jurídicas Gustavo Ibáñez.

José Francisco Murillo Mas is a Senior Lecturer at the University of Málaga. He is the second international award winner of innovative university teaching. His main interests in research are the innovation of the university teaching through Action Research, educational evaluation, and initial and in-service teacher training. He has participated in several research projects, such as Evaluación de la Educación Secundaria Obligatoria en Andalucía, Evaluación de los centros ICT and Evaluación de los Centros del profesorado. His most relevant publications include 'Comprehensiveness and diversity in secondary compulsory education in Andalucía', in *EARJ* and 'Innovación de la enseñanza universitaria en la formación de docentes: la relevancia del conocimiento', in *Investigación en la Escuela*.

Peter C. Murrell, Jr. is a Professor and Dean of the School of Education at Loyola College in Baltimore, Maryland. He teaches graduate and undergraduate courses in human learning, cognitive development, and identity development. His work in urban schools includes leadership development and the creation of learning communities. Dr Murrell's research focuses upon academic identity and racial identity development with respect to school achievement in urban schools and communities. His most recent book on identity and learning entitled *Race, Culture and Schooling: Identities of Achievement in Multicultural Urban Schools* was published by Lawrence Erlbaum.

Susan E. Noffke is an Associate Professor of Curriculum and Instruction at the University of Illinois – Urbana/Champaign and co-editor with R.B. Stevenson of *Educational Action Research* (Teachers College Press, 1995). She taught at the primary school level for a decade, and has led masters and doctoral level courses in action research for the past 20 years. She continues to work with many collaborative projects with schools and school districts.

Christine O'Hanlon is an Honorary Reader in Education at the University of East Anglia. She has developed the professional practice of teachers and other educational professionals through action research for many years. She has initiated, managed, and taught two university-based inclusive education programs for 'action research and inclusion' in education, and written extensively in the UK and worldwide about the benefits of action research for inclusive and special needs education. She has recently published a book, *Inclusive Education and Action Research* (Oxford University Press, 2004), and continues to publish and supervise students for higher degrees through action research.

Lily Orland-Barak is a Senior Lecturer and Head of the Department of Learning, Instruction, and Teacher Education at the Faculty of Education, The University of Haifa, Israel. Her research focuses on the areas of Mentoring and Mentored Learning, Action Research, Second Language Teacher Education, and Curriculum Development. She had led curricular innovations and reforms in the areas of Mentoring and EFL, and is currently involved in the design and implementation of various educational reforms in Teacher Education both nationally and internationally. She has published numerous articles in leading journals in these areas. She is also a member of the editorial board of *Educational Action Research* and *Teachers and Teaching: Theory and Practice*.

Ángel I. Pérez Gómez is a Professor at the University of Málaga, and previously in Salamanca, Madrid, and La Laguna. He is Deputy Vice-Chancellor at the University of Málaga and at the International University of Andalucía as well as an editorial board member of several national and international journals. Apart from the first award, National Educational Research, he has received several medals and awards of prestige. He has published 12 books and over 100 articles and chapters in books: *Las fronteras de la educación; La Comunicación didáctica; La enseñanza, su teoría y su práctica*; *Comprender y transformar la enseñanza*; *La cultura escolar en la sociedad neoliberal; Comprehensivenes and Diversity in Secundary Compulsory education in Andalucía; Desarrollo profesional del Docente*.

Rebecca Perry is a Senior Research Associate at Mills College in Oakland, California. Her research and writing focuses on teachers' professional communities, teacher learning, policy implementation, and education reform efforts at the national, state, and local levels.

Petra Ponte has a background in Pedagogiek and Educational Studies. She has published in the fields of special and inclusive education, cross-cultural collaboration, teachers' professionalism, and action research. She is a Professor at Utrecht University of Applied Sciences and Senior Researcher at ICLON, Leiden University (Graduate School of Teaching), both in the Netherlands. In addition to these roles, she is Adjunct Professor, RIPPLE, Charles Sturt University, as well as an Honorary Professor, Faculty of Education and Social Work, University of Sydney, both in Australia. She is an active participant in international networks and co-ordinating book editor of the *Educational Action Research Journal*.

Peter Posch Professional career: teaching degrees in English and Geography, Ph.D. in Education and Psychology; studies and research activities at the universities of Innsbruck (A), Konstanz (D), Vienna School of Economics (A); Professor of Education at the Institute of Education of the University of Klagenfurt in Austria from 1976 to 2000; visiting Professor in the School of Education of Stanford University, USA (1992) Retired in 2000. Present interests: (inservice) teacher education, school development, action research. Present positions: Chairman of the Advisory Board of the national project 'Innovations in Mathematics, Science and Technology Teaching' (IMST). He is a member of the Governing Board of the University College of Teacher Training, Carinthia.

Debbie Pushor is an Associate Professor in the Department of Curriculum Studies at the University of Saskatchewan. She is a former teacher, consultant, principal, and central services administrator. Debbie is engaged in research, funded by the Social Sciences and Humanities Research Council of Canada, which is exploring parent knowledge – what it is and how it is held and used. Debbie is a contributor to *The SAGE Encyclopedia of Qualitative Research Methods* and she co-authored, with D. Jean Clandinin and Anne Murray Orr, 'Navigating sites for narrative inquiry', recently published in the *Journal of Teacher Education*.

Maureen Robinson has been a Professor and Dean of the Faculty of Education at the Cape Peninsula University of Technology in Cape Town, South Africa, since 2002. She previously worked at the University of the Western Cape, in the fields of action research, materials development, teacher development, and curriculum studies. Her main area of interest is teacher education for a transforming society. She has published locally and internationally, and reviews for numerous journals. She has been active in South African teacher education policy fora for many years and is currently a board member of the International Council on Education for Teaching.

Leonie Rowan is a Senior Lecturer in the Faculty of Education at Griffith University. Her research interests range from early childhood environments through to university settings and relate to the broad fields of equity and social justice. She is particularly interested in the use of transformative pedagogies for disrupting traditional patterns of exclusion in diverse educational and cultural sites. Within this framework she has focused on areas, such as early childhood literacy development, boys in schools, girls and ICT, and the role of knowledge producing schools in disrupting traditional patterns of educational success and failure.

Lesley Saunders joined the General Teaching Council as a Senior Policy Adviser for Research at its inception in September 2000. Prior to that, she was a Principal Research Officer at the National Foundation for Educational Research where she headed the School Improvement Research Centre; she is also a qualified teacher. Lesley is currently a Visiting Professor at the Institute of Education, London, and has written extensively for policy, academic, and practitioner audiences; she recently edited *Educational Research and Policy-Making: Exploring the Border Country between Research and Policy* (Routledge, 2007).

Jean J. Schensul, an anthropologist, is a Senior Scientist and founding Director, Institute for Community Research, Hartford, CT. She is committed to popular inquiry by developing research approaches for community-based participatory and action research in urban areas of the USA and other countries. Her youth Participatory Action Research approach to addressing social injustices in the urban environment is being adapted in urban areas of the US. Recent publications include the seven volume NGO/CBO-friendly *Ethnographer's Toolkit*, and papers addressing action research, international and national health, mental health disparities, the role of CBROs, and local knowledge in the globalization of science.

Ana Maria Sierra-Piedrahita is a Ph.D. candidate in the Department of Curriculum and Instruction at the University of Wisconsin-Madison. She is also a professor in the School of Languages at Universidad de Antioquia in Medellin, Colombia. She is a member of the Action Research and Evaluation Group (GIAE) at Universidad de Antioquia, Medellin, Colombia. Her research interests are teacher professional development, linguistic policies, and autonomy in language teaching and learning.

Miguel Sola Fernández is a Senior Lecturer at the University of Málaga. He is an editorial board member of national and international journals, first award national educational reserch and second international award of innovative university teaching. His main interests in research are the innovation of the university teaching through Action Research, and the impact of ICT in curricular change. He has participated in international research projects and coordinated some nationally. His publications include 'Comprehensiveness and diversity in secondary compulsory education in Andalucía', in *EARJ*, 'La formación del profesorado en el contexto del EEES', in *Interuniversitaria de Formación del Profesorado,* and 'Evaluación de la jornada escolar', in *Revista de Educación.*

Bridget Somekh is a Professor of Educational Research at Manchester Metropolitan University. Her research interests are the process of innovation and the management of change. She is a founding editor of the journal, *Educational Action Research,* and a long-standing member and coordinator of the Collaborative Action Research Network. Her books include *Research Methods in the Social Sciences*, edited with Cathy Lewin (Sage, 2005); *Action Research: A Methodology for Change and Development* (Open University Press, 2006); and *Teachers Investigate Their Work: An Introduction to Action Research across the Professions* (2nd edition, Routledge, 2007, co-authored with Altrichter, Feldman and Posch).

Encarnación Soto Gómez is a Senior Lecturer at the University of Málaga. Her topics of research are innovation and educational evaluation, with particular emphasis on learning contexts and action research. She has participated in national and international research projects such as SIFKAL, BARIE and BARTIC, CHACO LEARN (Argentina). Her most relevant publications include 'El tiempo en la escuela', in *Cooperación Educativa*. 'Outros tempos para outra escola', in *Revista Pedagógica Patio* (Brazil), 'Objetos de aprendizaje y sujetos que aprenden', in *Andalucía Educativa*. And in collaboration, 'Comprehensiveness and Diversity in Secondary Compulsory Education in Andalucía', in *Educational Action Research, and* 'Innovación de la enseñanza universitaria en la formación de docentes: la relevancia del conocimiento', in *Investigación en la escuela.*

Crain Soudien is a Professor in Education and formerly the Director of the School of Education at the University of Cape Town. He teaches in the fields of Sociology and History of Education and has published over 100 articles, reviews, and book chapters in the areas of race, culture, educational policy, comparative education, educational change, public history and popular culture. He is also the co-editor of three books on District Six, Cape Town and another on comparative education and the author of *The Making of Youth Identity in Contemporary South Africa: Race, Culture and Schooling* and the co-author of *Inclusion and Exclusion in South African and Indian Schools.* He was educated at the Universities of Cape Town, South Africa and holds a PhD from the State University of New York at Buffalo. He is involved in a number of local, national, and international social and cultural organisations, and is the Chairperson of the District Six Museum Foundation, President of the World Council of Comparative Education Societies and currently the Chair of a Ministerial Committee on Transformation in Higher Education.

Daniel H. Suárez is an Adjunct Professor in the Department of Educational Sciences and Senior Researcher at the Instituto de Investigaciones en Ciencias de la Educación at the Universidad de Buenos Aires, in Argentina. He leads a research group that studies the relationship between pedagogical knowledge, teaching practice, and narrative research. Currently he leads the project: 'The knowledge of experience: Pedagogical experience, narrative and subjectivity in the professional trajectory of teachers'. He is also Director of the program 'Teacher memory and pedagogical documentation', at the Public Policy Laboratory of Buenos Aires, where he does action research with groups of teachers and pedagogical networks.

Dennis Sumara is the Professor and Head of the Department of Curriculum and Pedagogy at the University of British Columbia. His research areas include curriculum theory, teacher education, and literacy education, as oriented by conceptual interests in hermeneutic phenomenology, literary response theory, and complexity science. Specific topics of research include literary engagement and curriculum, problems and possibilities of learning and teaching, and normativity and counternormativity in teacher education. His extensive publications include *Why Reading Literature in School Still Matters: Imagination, Interpretation, Insight*, and he is recipient of the 2003 National Reading Conference's (USA) Ed Fry Book Award.

Karen Manheim Teel is a Professor in the Graduate Education Department at Holy Names University in Oakland, California. Her current research interests are urban education and teacher research. Karen Manheim Teel is on the faculty of the School of Education at the University of California at Davis. Her most recent publication is *Building Racial and Cultural Competence in the Classroom: Strategies from Urban Educators*, 2008, co-edited with Jennifer E. Obidah, published by Teachers College Press.

Pat Thomson is a Professor of Education and Director of Research in the School of Education, The University of Nottingham. A former headteacher in Australian disadvantaged schools, her research focuses on ways in which schooling can become more inclusive and just. Her current research interests are creative school change, the pedagogies of community arts, headteacher retention, and collaborative scholarship. Publications include *Helping Doctoral Students Write: Pedagogies for Supervision* (with Barbara Kamler, Routledge, 2006), an edited collection, *Doing Visual Research with Children and Young People* (Routledge, 2008), and *School Leadership – Heads on the Block?* (Routledge, 2009).

Andrew Townsend is an Assistant Professor in Educational Enquiry in the Institute of Education at the University of Warwick. This post is principally concerned with supporting action research conducted by education professionals studying for master's level programs. Before taking up his current post he worked as a consultant researching, supporting, and evaluating professional development and action research projects. This interest in change and development through action research was cultivated during a 10-year teaching career.

Recent work has included researching and publishing on the process and outcomes of collaborative and networked enquiry, and supporting student voice and research projects.

Melanie Walker is a Professor of Higher Education in the School of Education, University of Nottingham, UK, and extraordinary Professor at the University of the Western Cape, South Africa. Her research interests include higher education and human development, education and equalities, and pedagogies and identity formation. She is the author of *Higher Education Pedagogies: A Capabilities Approach* (Open University Press, 2006) and co-editor of *Amartya Sen's Capability Approach and Social Justice in Education* (Palgrave, 2007). She is an editor of *Educational Action Research* and co-editor of the *Journal of Human Development*. She is currently working with Elaine Unterhalter on a book on Martha Nussbaum, capabilities and education.

Gordon Wells is currently a Professor of Education at the University of California, Santa Cruz, where he researches and teaches in the fields of language, literacy, and learning; the analysis of classroom interaction; and sociocultural theory. As an educator, his particular interest is in fostering dialogic inquiry as an approach to learning and teaching at all levels, based on the work of Vygotsky and other sociocultural theorists.The rationale for this approach together with examples of it in practice are presented in *Dialogic Inquiry: Towards a Sociocultural Practice and Theory of Education* (Cambridge University Press, 1999). From 1969 to 1984, he was the Director of the Bristol Study of Language Development at the University of Bristol, UK (*The Meaning Makers*, Heinemann, 1986), and from 1984 to 2000, he was a Professor at the Ontario Institute for Studies in Education of the University of Toronto where, in addition to teaching and research, he was involved in several collaborative action research projects with educational practitioners in Canada. Books arising from this work are *Constructing Knowledge Together* (Heinemann, 1992), *Changing Schools from Within* (OISE Press and Heinemann, 1994), and *Action, Talk and Text: Learning and Teaching through Inquiry*, written with teacher colleagues (Teachers College Press, 2001). He is also co-editor of *Learning for Life in the 21st Century: Sociocultural Perspectives on the Future of Education* (Blackwell, 2002). His most recent paper is Semiotic mediation, dialogue and the construction of knowledge, *Human Development*.

Jack Whitehead has been a Lecturer in the Department of Education at the University of Bath since 1973. He originated the idea of practitioner-researchers generated their own living educational theories as explanations for their educational influences in learning. He is a former President of the British Educational Research Association, distinguished Scholar in Residence at Westminster College, Utah, and Visiting Professor at Brock University in Ontario. He is currently a Visiting Professor at Ningxia Teachers University in China. His award-winning web-site http://www.actionresearch.net makes available the living educational theories of practitioner-researchers from their masters and doctoral research programs.

Susan Williams has worked for 26 years as a community organizer and a popular educator in East Tennessee. She works as Education Coordinator at the Highlander Research and Education Center in Tennessee, currently coordinating the popular education work and organizing the library and resource center. She is working on an historical timeline for Highlander's 75th anniversary, to help record and share the history of Highlander's connection to many people who have helped to change the South and Appalachia.

Richard Winter is an Emeritus Professor of Education at Anglia Ruskin University. He became interested in action research in the mid-1970s, and his Ph.D. thesis was on the philosophical underpinning for action research. He has published a number of books and numerous articles on various aspects of action research, latterly on action research in nursing and social work settings and also on the writing of fiction as a tool for developing professional understanding. He became involved in Buddhism while working in Thailand in the 1990s and he is currently involved in Buddhist education for young children at the Cambridge Buddhist Centre.

Ken Zeichner is Hoefs-Bascom Professor of Teacher Education and Associate Dean of the School of Education at the University of Wisconsin-Madison. He is currently an editor of the international journal *Educational Action Research* and author of a soon-to-be-published book, *Teacher Education and The Struggle for Social Justice* (Routledge).

Jane Zeni is a Professor Emeritus of English Education at the University of Missouri-St. Louis. There, she has worked with pre- and in-service teachers as well as doctoral students doing qualitative research. Earlier, she taught secondary school in Philadelphia and Santa Fe. As founding Director of the Gateway Writing Project, Zeni collaborated with many action research groups; she also gathered data with her students to improve her own teaching (Singer & Zeni, 2004). Her books include *Writing Lands* (1990); *Mirror Images: Teaching Writing in Black and White* (Krater, Zeni and Cason, 1994); and *Ethical Issues in Practitioner Research* (2001).

Lew Zipin lectures in Sociology/Policy of Education at the University of South Australia, where he is a member of the Hawke Research Institute for Sustainable Societies. His research interests include critical analyses of power in educational institutions; issues of governance and ethics in schools and higher education; and education for social justice. His work has been published in various journals and book chapters, including a chapter in the *SAGE Handbook of Education for Citizenship and Democracy*. He is currently co-editing a book collection on changing dimensions of university governance and work in globalizing contexts.

ACKNOWLEDGEMENT

Chapter 27 is from R. Winter, 'Buddhism and action research toward an appropriate model of inquiry for the caring professions', *Educational Action Research Vol. 11:1* (2003) pp. 141–60, and is reprinted by permission of the publisher (Taylor & Francis Ltd, http://www.informaworld.com).

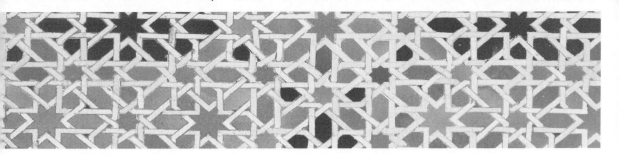

Introduction

Susan E. Noffke and Bridget Somekh

This Handbook provides a scholarly source book, presenting and critiquing the main traditions of educational action research throughout the world. It contains chapters by well-established and respected scholars whose work has been seminal in building knowledge and expertise in the field, as well as new voices from areas less often represented in educational research. Since one of the key features of educational action research is its participatory, 'grass-roots' quality, the Handbook also contains chapters exemplifying the work of key practitioner groups, often working outside universities.

The overall structure of the Handbook follows the analytical framework developed by Susan Noffke in her article, 'Professional, personal, and political dimensions of action research' published in the Review of Research in Education and edited by Michael Apple (1997, p. 2: 305–43). This structure reflects Noffke's scholarly analysis of the very wide range of work undertaken under the broad category of action research since the 1940s, including participatory action research, critical action research, classroom action research, action learning, etc. The categories 'professional', 'personal' and 'political' are fluid with porous boundaries rather than essentialist. They reflect orientations towards action research, which, to a degree that varies between authors, are also open to the other two orientations. By using the fluid categories Professional, Personal, Political, as the organizing framework, we seek to avoid simplistic divisions between different kinds of action research which always tend to produce a hierarchy of status/worth. For example, the critical, practical, technical categories of Carr and Kemmis (1986) and Grundy (1982) suggest that only AR which engages politically and follows a critical theory Marxist ideology is 'emancipatory'. This has been strongly contested by writers such as Elliott (1987) who draws on Gadamer's hermeneutics rather than Habermas' critical theory for an underpinning philosophy for action research.

Editing the Handbook has itself been a form of action research into the praxis of writing to represent an action research tradition. Over two years our understanding of the form of the individual chapters and their relationship to one another and to the book as a whole has been shaped and re-shaped through dialogue with the authors and inter-personal reflexivity. Now in their finished form, the chapters explain and explore key ideas in each strand, mapping their development, presenting new insights and illuminating their meaning through examples from action research practice. The aim has been to create texts that retain the creative energy and emergent character of educational action research, while also creating a unified text. The Handbook, as a whole, carefully references the very wide body of action research literature, from its origins in the early part of the twentieth century to the present day. We believe this has resulted in a book that does not 'inscribe' action research in stone, but allows diverse meanings to flourish and provides an opportunity for new coalitions to form.

There has been a huge growth of interest in action research in educational settings over the past 20 years across the Americas, Europe, Australia and Africa. Such growth has been particularly strong in those areas where the already well-established scholarly traditions of action research in education have provided a methodological base to support the development of research-based practice. Since the early 1990s, there has also been a big increase of interest in educational action research in Asia and Eastern Europe, where it fits well with growing interest in developing pedagogies which foster creativity, critical thinking and learning how to learn. In all these settings action research is a methodology exceptionally well suited to exploring, developing and sustaining change processes both in classrooms and whole organizations such as schools, colleges and university departments of education.

In response to this increase in interest, action research has become a prominent methodology taught to doctoral and masters level students in universities, and has gained full acceptance for doctoral research in many major institutions. As a result, in the past 10 years the action research literature has blossomed as part of the tertiary education textbook industry. It is widely accepted as a means of supporting school-based professional development, for example in teachers' unions' efforts to provide continuing professional development (CPD) for teachers, in the efforts of agencies to improve schools, communities, and as a part of certification schemes in many countries. Action research is also often incorporated in proposals for research funding to national, federal and local governments, international agencies and non-governmental agencies in developing countries. Accounts of a number of such research projects, their knowledge outcomes and impact on policy and practice, are given in chapters of this Handbook.

At the same time, in line with the development of neo-liberal ideologies in many countries, so-called scientific research in education – under the guise of 'evidence based practice' – has inscribed more deeply the old distinction between pure and applied research, where pure or 'blue sky' research belongs to the 'university' and other forms of research are seen as making a contribution to practice and social improvement but not to 'scientific robustness' (Furlong and Oancea, 2006). As a result, action research and kindred methodologies tend not to be treated as knowledge producing methodologies in themselves.

This unprecedented growth in interest in educational action research has spawned a large number of 'how to do it' books from major publishing companies, for example Altrichter et al. (2007), Hendricks (2008), McNiff and Whitehead (2006), Mills (2006), Stringer (2007), and there is an established refereed journal literature developed over the last 25 years on many aspects of action research. The international journal, *Educational Action Research,* has for 16 years provided a scholarly vehicle for publishing new work, and its policy of including articles from at least three countries in every issue has ensured coverage of a wide range of traditions. In 2003 a second journal, *Action Research*, was launched, which includes educational action research as well as work from many other fields. The Collaborative Action Research Network (CARN) has organized annual international conferences since 1978 and the Action Learning, Action Research Association (ALARA) and Practitioner Research networks have both consistently offered biannual conferences for more than 15 years. In the USA there has been an Action Research special interest group of the American Educational Research Association since 1994, and since 2005 the North American Action Research Alliance (NAARA) has held two summit meetings and is working toward creating resources across education and social service and university and community sites. There have been other organizations and meetings, some with longstanding and international traditions and others more local The networks of action research scholars and practitioners that have formed and re-formed and inter-collaborated across these groups have given a strong base to developing this Handbook.

The salience of action research in the educational academic literature as well as in programs of study for school personnel has drawn heavily on this existing literature. However, there has as yet been no Handbook to provide a scholarly reference text, an overview of this work, brought together to inform the development of the field. This *Handbook of Educational Action Research* fills this gap. It draws on the substantial body of scholarly work that has provided leadership in the field of educational action research since the 1970s; for example, among others Carr and Kemmis (1986), McNiff (1988), Altrichter et al. (1993), Hollingsworth (1997), Elliott (1993), but moves beyond it.

In Chapter 1, which precedes Part I, Noffke re-visits and further develops her original analysis (Noffke, op. cit.). The chapter opens with a reflective summary of the key characteristics of each 'dimension' as originally presented. This is followed by an exploration and development of the dimensions as analytic categories, focusing on action research developments since publication of the original article. The chapter ends by projecting possible directions for action research work in the multiple contexts (offering both opportunities and constraints) emerging through globalization. It provides a contextual framework and historical location for the Handbook chapters that follow.

The main body of the Handbook is divided into four Parts, covering Methodology and the Professional, Personal and Political 'dimensions'. Part I on methodology maps the diversity of rationales and practices that have developed over the years (often incorporating mixed methods) thus providing a 'way in' for the reader to see how different forms of action research proceed differently. Parts II–IV are organized around the categories of Professional, Personal and Political. The complexity of the categorization is signalled by their sub-titles – Part II: Professional: Knowledge production, staff development and the status of educators; Part III: Personal: Self-awareness, development and identity; and Part IV: Political: Popular knowledge, difference, and frameworks for change. Each of these sections begins with an overview and proceeds from the level of those working most closely with students, to teachers' professional development, school leaders/administrators working with organizational change, issues of professional voice, and practitioner knowledge production, ending with issues of policy and change issues. Thus the structure of the Handbook reflects the interrelationship between the categories. The heuristic power of the dimensions – Professional, Personal, Political – has been explored empirically by the Editors over the two years of working with the many authors writing the Handbook.

Parts II to IV each include chapters unique to their orientation, but also ones that address issues of epistemology and theoretical framework, ethics, data collection and analysis, facilitation, dissemination, and use of findings, including uses in teacher education. Through the titles of the chapters, these orientations are evident, giving the readers easy access to concepts and skills common to all approaches, but also those unique to each orientation group.

The final chapter, Conclusions, reviews the contents of this *Handbook of Educational Action Research* and draws out key messages for policy-makers and action researchers. It sets out a vision for using the Handbook as an opportunity to strengthen coalitions of action researchers with a shared purpose of educational improvements grounded in the construction of educational knowledge through inquiry. While it can be seen as an academic work, it is one that seeks opportunities for collaborative efforts, ones that highlight changes in the professional, personal, and political dimensions. It can also provide an intellectual opportunity for coalition building within and outside of education, and across international boundaries. We hope, in working on this book, that it provides an opportunity for building such coalitions.

REFERENCES

Altrichter, H., Posch, P. and Somekh, B. (1993) *Teachers Investigate Their Work: An Introduction to the Methods of Action Research.* London and New York: Routledge.

Altrichter, H., Feldman, A., Posch, P., and Somekh, B. (2007) *Teachers Investigate Their Work: An Introduction to Action Research Across the Professions* (2nd edn). London and New York: Routledge.

Carr, W. and Kemmis, S. (1986) *Becoming Critical: Education, Knowledge and Action Research.* London and Washington: Falmer Press.

Elliott, J. (1987) 'Educational theory, practical philosophy and action research', *British Journal of Educational Studies,* 35 (2): 149–69.

Elliott, J. (2007) *Reflecting Where the Action Is: The Selected Works of John Elliott.* London and New York: Routledge.

Furlong, J. and Oancea, A. (2006) 'Assessing quality in applied and practice-based research in education: a framework for discussion', *Review of Australian Research in Education: Counterpoints on the Quality and Impact of Educational Research,* 6: 89–104. Available online at: www.bera.ac.uk/pdfs/Qualitycriteria.pdf (accessed 06/05/108).

Grundy, S. (1982) 'Three modes of action research', *Curriculum Perspectives,* 2 (3): 23–34.

Hendricks, C. (2008) *Improving Schools Through Action Research: A Comprehensive Guide for Educators* (2nd edn). Boston: Allyn & Bacon.

Hollingsworth, S. (ed.). (1997) *International Action Research: A Casebook For Educational Reform.* London and Washington: Falmer Press.

McNiff, J. (1988) *Action Research Principles and Practice.* London Macmillan Education.

McNiff, J. and Whitehead, J. (2006) *All You Need to Know About Action Research.* London: Sage.

Mills, G. (2006) *Action Research: A Guide for the Teacher Researcher* (3rd edn). Upper Saddle River, NJ: Pearson Education.

Noffke, S.E. (1997) 'Professional, personal, and political dimensions of action research'. Review of *Research in Education,* 22 (1): 305–43.

Stringer, E. (2007) *Action Research in Education* (2nd edn). Columbus, OH: Pearson Prentice Hall.

1

Revisiting the Professional, Personal, and Political Dimensions of Action Research

Susan E. Noffke

Let us confess that the schools have never built a new social order, but have always in all times and in all lands been the instruments through which social forces were perpetuated. If our new curriculum revision is to do better, it must undertake an acceptance of the profound social and economic changes which are now taking place in the world. (Horace Mann Bond, 'The curriculum and the Negro child', 1935: 68)

This quote comes out of a tradition that seems quite disconnected from many common understandings of action research. Yet for me it raises issues that are at the core of action research practices. It demands recognition of the essentially 'conserving' function of schooling, and highlights the need for educational responses to profound structural changes in society. It also comes out of a long-standing tradition of African American academic literature that has refuted the dominant narrative of educational history which claimed education as a major vehicle for social advancement of disempowered peoples. It also embodies major questions that have haunted me for many years, as to what extent and in what ways action research in educational work can play a role in building a 'new social order' (Counts, 1932/1978) – one in which economic and social justice are central aims. A major part of this chapter addresses these issues, by examining the multiple practices of action research, both historically and conceptually.

Action research has long been part of research in education, as well as in multiple social science fields. But even a brief look at the literature reveals important differences in the processes as well as the purposes of the research. Some forms highlight new strategies for data collection and analysis which correspond to varied theoretical frameworks underpinning the research, while others look remarkably similar to 'traditional' forms of empirical/analytic or interpretive research. Some focus on relatively narrow aspects of classroom work, while others seek connections to larger social visions and social movements. In much of my work over the past 20 years, I have sought to understand these varied meanings and practices dimensionally, in terms of their histories and in terms of their underlying assumptions. In this effort, Sandra Harding's (1987) definitions of 'method', 'methodology', and 'epistemology' have been very useful. In her distinctions, a 'method' is a technique or process by which evidence is gathered. In contrast, a 'methodology', encompasses both the role of theory and the means of analysis that outline how we should proceed as researchers in addressing the data we collect via our varied 'methods'. The theories we use and the data analysis strategies we employ are not neutral means; they embody our relations to power through the arenas they center.

'Epistemology', in Harding's depiction, includes the usual interpretation of a 'theory of knowledge' (1987: 3), yet it takes us much further in ways very useful to understanding action research. She invokes the sociological sense of epistemologies as differing 'strategies for justifying beliefs' (p. 3), which in turn reminds us that all social research is a social construction, made possible through existing power relations. Harding's further emphasis on epistemology pushes toward examining assumptions about 'who can be a "knower"'?, about what strategies count as 'means to be legitimated as knowledge'?, and about 'what kinds of things can be known'? (p. 3). The varied forms of action research address these questions quite distinctly. Some assert a 'grassroots' form of knowledge production and challenge existing research methodologies while others reinscribe them and the existing power relations from which they emanate.

Over the past two decades, I have worked on field-based efforts as well as on conceptual research involving careful readings of both the literature on educational action research and various strands of relevant social research. The historical part of this research led to identifying 'professional, personal, and political' dimensions to action research. These dimensions, which I used in an extensive review of the action research literature more than 10 years ago (Noffke, 1997a), have formed, at my co-editor's suggestion, the framework for this book. An important caveat was noted then:

> These three areas – the professional, the personal, and the political – form the frames for this review of the literature on action research. They may seem to be distinct emphases; within the context of action research, however, all clearly deal with issues of power and control. In that sense, the public sphere of professionalism and the domain of the personal are also particular manifestations of the political. (Noffke, 1997a: 306)

As I worked through these dimensions, the long-standing feminist argument that 'The personal is political' (Hanish, 1970/2000) played a role. Also important was the recognition that the professional dimension, too, is an important part of the power structures of education, and as such, it, too, is political.

In what follows, I first trace out the dimensions and their various meanings. Especially important in this is the understanding that these 'dimensions' are not discrete categories, but reflect differing emphases. As I noted then, and reaffirm now: All forms of action research embody a political dimension. As action research works towards improvement of educational practice (the action part of the dual term's meaning), it does so with a vision of what might make the lives of children and those with whom they work, and indeed the larger society, 'better'. Such visions of change embody the political in that they all work through and often against existing lines of power.

I next look at what has transpired in the past decade. A prominent characteristic of this era of action research is tremendous growth, both in its conceptual and practical understandings and in the visibility of action research in prominent journals and texts emanating from the academy. But alongside that growth, in terms of the growing acceptance of action research in educational settings, has been increased visibility of action research in educational work in non-school settings.

Finally, I address work in action research in the current context. Part of this section addresses the impact of globalization alongside the growing recognition of action research as an international phenomenon, or social movement. Here too there are tensions, as work moves forward to recognize the local and often cultural needs of keeping action research flexible and responsive to differing contexts. The contradictory context of the huge growth in neo-liberal constructions of education alongside the growth in a form of research that emphasizes 'grassroots' knowledge will be explored.

UNDERSTANDING ACTION RESEARCH DIMENSIONALLY

The dimensions of 'professional, personal, and political' were derived from historical study of the field of action research (Noffke, 1997b). My primary concern in using the 'dimensions' construct was to find a way to explore the multiple layers of assumptions, purposes, and practices without creating an implicitly hierarchical set of categories which could be used to prioritize or even dismiss some forms of action research in comparison to others. Instead, I sought a way to see the complexities and interconnectedness across the dimensions. While all forms of action research (and indeed all research) embody the political, I felt that what was needed was a way to see the complexities of work in action research, rather than to find the form that is 'just right'.

THE PROFESSIONAL

From its early emergence in the early part of the 20th century, action research was part of an overall context of struggle in the social sciences over the nature of research. At the same time, feminists and scholars such as W.E.B. DuBois were working at creating a form of social research that was deeply connected to social struggles. In Europe and the U.S. scholars such as J.L. Moreno (Altrichter and Gstettner, 1993), John Collier, and Kurt Lewin worked at developing forms of research that were aimed at solving social problems. In emergent fields like education, action research was articulated in terms of its potential to enhance the 'science of education' as well as the status of the professionals who work in schools and colleges. Developing a 'knowledge base' for teaching has been tantalizing educational academics since the beginnings of their move into universities in the early 20th century. Research by and with teachers has been one way to advance that agenda, and clearly highlights action research as a 'knowledge generating' activity.

Action research projects have varied greatly in this area, though, ranging from some which have focused on technical skills to those which include teachers in the process of theorizing, through their research, the intended ends as well as means of educational work. In the U.S., the work of Stephen Corey in the early 1950s was clearly directed towards the latter. In the 1970s, the work of Lawrence Stenhouse (1975), and John Elliott in the U.K., developed a conscious and contrasting effort to reframe the nature of teaching as in itself a form of research, and to extend the concept of the professional to highlight careful deliberation over both the ends and means of educational work. Through projects such as the Humanities Curriculum Project and the Ford Teaching Project, they built not just a body of knowledge about educational practice, but also a conception of teaching that focuses on careful reflection on data from one's own practice as the basis for subsequent theorizing and actions. This work formed the foundation for the development of the Classroom (later Collaborative) Action Research Network and later on to the establishment of the journal *Educational Action Research* in 1993.

Action research in Australia was also developing in the late 1970s, partly influenced by the ideas of Lawrence Stenhouse, but also enhanced by a political context in which much curriculum work was being done around issues of educational equity. Many scholars at Deakin University, and elsewhere in Australia, worked on projects that were school-based and used action research to improve educational understanding and practice, as well as their context. The work used the Lewinian 'spiral' of planning, taking action, observing and reflecting as core elements to the action research process, typified in *The Action Research Planner* (Kemmis and McTaggart, 1981). Carr and Kemmis (1983) later developed some of the ideas into an important book, *Becoming Critical*, which richly explored the transformation of educational research in a way that embodied a new construction of the relationship between theory and practice, and also contributed to the professional development of teachers.

Action research in the U.S. also experienced a 'rebirth' during this same era. Beginning with federally funded projects aimed at familiarizing teachers with research methods and at building stronger university–school collaborations, there was a clear emphasis on enhancing the status of the profession of teaching, through recognition of the knowledge producing potential of teachers.

The 'teacher research movement', advanced through the efforts of many teacher education researchers such as Marilyn Cochran-Smith, Susan Lytle, Ann Lieberman, Marian Mohr, and Dixie Goswami, forms an important strand to the professional dimension of action research. Beginning in the early 1990s, their work led to an increased visibility of knowledge produced by teachers and a growing recognition of the importance of the teacher's voice in generating knowledge for educational practice.

An important point to considering the professional dimension of action research has to do with thinking through whether action research produces not only knowledge to add to a changing understanding of a 'knowledge base' for teaching, but whether it comprises a different 'way of knowing', one that can bridge theory and practice, but also thereby generate new ways of understanding practice. Action research has been seen as a means of adding to knowledge generated in the academy via traditional methods, but it has also been seen as a distinctive way of knowing. This point is directly related to whether action research is seen as producing knowledge for others to use, or whether it is primarily a means for professional development. Whether part of meeting the needs of changing demands for qualified teachers for an increasingly migratory world population, or part of a response to policy changes affecting the work lives of teachers, action research has been seen as one way to enhance the professional quality and status of the profession.

THE PERSONAL

The personal dimension, too, has had several distinct aspects. One part deals with the idea that action research has an impact on the personal growth and development of those who engage in it, another emphasizes the individual versus collaborative nature of the work, and a third addresses the involvement of individual university faculty in the action research process. First, much of action research work has been conceived of as a collaborative process. The early work of Corey and others at the Horace Mann Institute in New York involved a collaborative effort among university and school personnel. The goal was for teachers to learn about, and participate in, the knowledge-generating process.

At the same time, others were developing other perspectives on the purposes for engaging in action research. One is best noted in the work of Abraham Shumsky who (also in the 1950s) developed action research as a form of self-development, a way for teachers to understand themselves and their work better. At around the same time, Hilda Taba, perhaps in response to a then salient teacher shortage, found that action research not only could have an impact on professional problem solving, but it was also a way for teachers to become more skilful. While the context for learning to do action research was a group, the focus of attention was the individual teacher-learner. The role of university faculty changed as well, with attention to their expertise in the process of guiding the teachers.

In more recent years, the personal dimension has taken the form of working with teachers to explore closer connections between their personal beliefs about teaching and learning and their practice. This can be seen in the works supported by John Elliott in the 1970s, but is also salient in the subsequent work in the U.K. and Ireland supported by Jack Whitehead and Jean McNiff. In both, the strong theme is working toward making personal beliefs more congruent with practices, often involving ideals of social justice at the level of individual beliefs. The growth of the 'self study' in teacher education group in the early 1990s embodies the struggle for congruence between goals and actions. In many cases, it used life history and personal narratives of individual growth around teaching strategies or philosophical orientations, but in some instances engaged directly with political issues, such as the social relations of race, class and gender. Personal belief systems play into this, and issues of 'development' take on new aspects in looking at how individual teachers take into account their own life experiences as they explore these in relation to working with children whose experiences are different from their own. The professional is also salient, in that much of the work around individual growth and learning is aimed at furthering the status of teachers and teacher educators through educational action research.

THE POLITICAL

The political dimension, which is also embedded in the previous two dimensions, highlights a different purpose for action research work in education. As with the other dimensions, the political has many differing manifestations. In the 1930s–1950s, there was a strong concern for creating democratic processes in schools. The search for solutions to social problems, the development of collaborative processes, locally developed curriculum, and more socially conscious schooling processes represented a 'democratic impulse' in action research of that era.

Yet action research has other origins that speak to a different understanding of the role of research in politics, one that represents the struggles of marginalized peoples to use research methods to leverage social change. The works of W.E.B. Du Bois, Ida B. Wells, and Carter G. Woodson, for just a few examples, represent a tradition of various explorations of the uses of research methods to inform social actions, particularly ones directed at the redress of social inequalities. Work of early 20th century feminists also shows this tendency to see research as aimed at making changes directly, rather than waiting for someone else (a research consumer) to implement changes based on reading of research. Likewise, the work of Myles Horton and others at the Highlander Center in the Appalachian region of the U.S. gave birth to another 'stream' of work that shows the ways in which the generation and analysis of information were seen as deeply connected to work for social and economic justice in local communities. In this stream of work, action research was always deeply tied to work by, for and with marginalized peoples. In that sense, action research has always been deeply connected to social struggle.

The works of Paulo Freire and Orlando Fals Borda, and a large number of participatory researchers have also been important influences for action research in education. First appearing in the literature in the 1970s, these works present a challenge to the political economy of knowledge production similar to the earlier work of the Highlander Center. Knowledge generation, in these works, is not solely a tool of professional researchers; it is a tool for social struggle. Working in diverse communities in Asia, the U.S., Canada, Latin America, and Africa, participatory research projects emerged which highlighted the important role that knowledge generation plays in social and economic struggles (Park et al., 1993). In the 1980s, when action research was becoming increasingly visible in education, important connections were formed between the participatory research advocates who had been working for a decade with marginalized peoples around popular knowledge issues in Canada, Africa and South America, and action researchers in education in the Northern Hemisphere and Australia.

During the 1980s and 1990s, educational action research work in the political dimension included efforts developed around issues such as gender equity, or less frequently around racial equity, but showed few signs of connection to social struggles. In addition, beyond Carr and Kemmis's work in using the writings of Habermas to highlight the potential to transform understandings of professional practice, or Richard Winter's work on social inquiry (1987), there was scant attention to the ways in which newer social theories, especially those from feminist or post-colonial work, might inform the growth of action research in education. This is an important issue, as I move to considering the last decade of action research work. The local and communitarian processes often embodied in action research as a 'democratic impulse' still may be enhanced through the use of a wider body of social theory, one that has embraced a social justice agenda that takes into account both local and global manifestations of oppression.

UNDERSTANDING ACTION RESEARCH DEVELOPMENTS IN THE PAST DECADE

In the past decade, there has been a remarkable growth in the acceptance of action research. This can easily be seen in the publication of over two dozen textbooks aimed clearly at a market of university further development programs for teachers. In addition, action research has gained credibility through its inclusion in prominent texts and handbooks of research methodology, as well as through the publication of the Handbook of Action Research (Reason and Bradbury, 2001). It has achieved greater visibility in existing journals, as well as the host of new journals in education. In addition to the journal, *Educational Action Research*, noted earlier, another journal, *Action Research*, emanating from the handbook's authors, began publication in 2003 and continues to offer articles on action research from a wide variety of disciplines. Action research is recognized widely in the funding of projects by state agencies and in many places plays a significant role in teacher education. It has also become increasingly accepted as a legitimate research strategy for the doctoral degree. What is presented here is not a thorough review of the recent literature, but rather my 'reading', as a student of action research, of the noticeable changes. Many of the varied 'streams' of action research have flourished, with rich bodies of associated literature developed. Other areas have opened up, offering new ways to see salient issues in the field, especially those addressing equity and justice issues. Although the literature on the latter is smaller in growth than that of the overall new literature, it is nonetheless salient and important.

THE PROFESSIONAL

In the professional dimension, the dimension focused directly on issues related to developing the practices of schooling and the enhancement of the teaching profession, the growth has been very large. Action research has gained acceptance in prominent educational research venues, with active special interest groups in many national and international groups and their publications. There are many on-going national and international organizations with conferences and publications, and these are growing as more associations use the Internet for connections. Within traditional academic venues, journals, book series, and many textbooks aimed at guiding educators in their action research work have brought in new audiences for this kind of educational research, and play a role in many postgraduate certification programs for teachers. All of these show a very healthy 'market' for educational action research in the new information economy.

There has also been growth in parallel areas such as narrative inquiry and lesson study, which foreground the professional, but also show connections to the personal and political dimensions, and which highlight the 'educator's voice'. This is particularly important, given this era of global reliance on standardized tests to measure educational progress, and thereby professional quality. This salience of action research, as part of professional development, could be seen as aimed at ways to reinforce educational institutions, to justify current practices. Prominent professional organizations highlight action research as part of their professional development 'products', and many universities and ministries of education (e.g. Singapore and Hong Kong) have employed action research as part of their further education and 'improvement' strategies. Several electronic journals have sustained work in making the research of teachers available (e.g. *Networks*, and *Action Research Expeditions*), and teachers' unions (e.g. the British Columbia Teachers Federation) have promoted its use. There has been growth in the use of action research to create new interpretations of justice-oriented practice. One good example of this is the Teachers College Press 'Practitioner Research' series.

Since 1996, it now has published more than 30 volumes, showing educators taking on many socially critical issues.

Action research has been increasingly invoked in terms of work in teacher education (e.g., Hui and Grossman, 2008). Although this idea has long been part of the literature on action research, newer work has emphasized the role of action research in teacher education in developing nations and in terms of challenging notions of 'race' and gender. Although focused on the education of the professional, these efforts also clearly emphasize political dimensions. For example, much work has been done in several African nations, most notably in Namibia (Zeichner et al., 1998; Dahlström, 2003) but also in other areas. One prominent feature in this work is the conscious effort to not 'export' particular understandings of action research to these contexts, but rather to develop a form of research which addressed the specific context, namely one in which issues of the legacies of colonization and apartheid could be addressed in the process of developing educational programs (Dahlström and Mannberg, 2006).

Another area of teacher education in which action research is playing an important role is exemplified by the work of Alice McIntyre. Since her dissertation work, she has been using action research to work with preservice teachers (who are often primarily 'white') to explore the meaning of 'whiteness' within the context of a course in multicultural education (2002). Particularly noteworthy in this work is her use of innovative methods, drawn both from feminist and participatory research traditions. She has also applied this approach to looking at the whole of the teacher preparation process, arguing that improving teacher education, especially the ability of teachers to work with populations that are different from themselves, can be enhanced through the integration of action research strategies (McIntyre, 2003).

These works are rich in their implications for action research in the profession of education in many ways. First, they show the rich possibilities that can emerge when the 'methodologies' of action research, along with their underlying 'epistemologies' are not seen as fixed. Rather, these respond to the cultural contexts of the participants. In addition, these works are examples of how, in the process of action research, the 'facilitators' of teacher learning also problematize their own assumptions. Finally, they show ways in which concepts around 'the professional' are not taken for granted, but rather must be examined and redefined in relation to their cultural, and indeed, global contexts.

THE PERSONAL

In the personal dimension, too, there have been many substantive developments. As noted in the previous section, Alice McIntyre's work has focused attention to issues of whiteness in relation to teachers' identities (2002). That same sense of the personal as interconnected to issues of the self and identity is also evident in several of the Practitioner Inquiry series books. For example, in

'Is this English?': Race, Language, and Culture in the Classroom, Bob Fecho (2004) documents not only how the learning of his students of color changed, but how he, too, changed through his inquiry process. In *Because of the Kids: Facing Racial and Cultural Differences in Schools*, Jennifer Obidah and Karen Teel (2000) example the roles their own differing identities play in working in urban classroom settings.

Another body of work I associate primarily with the personal dimension is that of Jack Whitehead and Jean McNiff (Whitehead and McNiff, 2006; McNiff and Whitehead, 2006). In their work over the past two decades, attention to all three dimensions is evident. The profession of teaching is central to the work in two ways. First, Whitehead's work has continually highlighted the 'living educational theories' that are generated from practice, and change through the cycles of action research. Second, his work at developing masters and doctoral level programs for educators can also seen as a contribution to the professional dimension. Both McNiff and Whitehead have contributed greatly to the availability of information about action research for educators through their many texts, but also through the Internet. Whitehead's website (www.actionresearch.net), one of the earliest such resources on action research, contains a wealth of information and examples, and is regularly maintained. The position that teachers are generators of knowledge carries with it a sense of the political dimension, in that such a stance challenges hierarchies of knowledge production and the power relations they maintain.

But it is in the personal dimension that McNiff and Whitehead's strongest contribution continues to be made. The individual process of examining one's own practice is the core of this form of action research. Questions around individual actions, how one might do things differently to improve one's practice, initiate research with a central emphasis on the value of the teacher's own voice. Individual accountability, in the form of 'giving an account' of one's practice, is seen as crucial, along with being 'accountable' (in that same sense) to others. Appropriately, the most common form of these rich 'accounts' of practice is the personal narrative.

Another area of overall growth in the literature has been the work around 'self-study'. Scholars, including Tom Russell, John Loughran, Vicki LaBoskey, Allan Feldman, and others have worked hard to promote this area of educational research. The self-study Special Interest Group within the American Educational Research Association has been an international organization from its beginning in 1993, drawing members not only from North America, but also from the U.K., the Netherlands, Austria, Australia, New Zealand, and elsewhere. Self-study researchers have produced a Handbook (Loughran et al., 2004), a journal, *Studying Teacher Education*, as well as five volumes in a 'Self Study of Teaching and Teacher Education Practices' series. Tom Russell's chapter in the second volume of the series (2005) provides rich insights into the progress of the work. He recounts his long experiences working in teacher education, as well as working through self-study to change his teaching.

Loughran (2007) has pushed for understanding self-study as an individual experience, but argues that moving beyond the explorations of the 'self', to a process of 'reframing' through greater inclusion of alternative perspectives and more visible documentation is needed. Such efforts move self-study towards the capacity to create a knowledge base for teacher education, and are a strong manifestation of the professional dimension. One of the major agendas of self-study has been working to help others in education and in policy circles understand the complex and important work of teacher educators.

Work by Wade et al., (2008) seems to exemplify this approach to research. Their work focused on the examination of teachers' 'critically reflective problem solving' in pedagogical discussions in an online environment. One of the members of the research team was the teacher educator, while the other two participated in a 'self-study dialogue' and in the data analysis process (discourse analysis). In this article, another dimension is visible, that of the political. The work addresses issues around English Language Learners, with the expressed goal of furthering sociopolitical thinking in the problem-solving process. The intersections with the political dimension, including consideration of issues of cultural identity, language, gender, and race are also evident in several chapters of the book, *Just Who Do We Think We Are?* (Mitchell et al., 2005). Within the context of their self-studies, researchers take on issues of marginalization, queer identity, and whiteness. In another article Milner (2007) documents his work in the use of personal narrative as a means to address the importance of the consideration of race and racism in curriculum deliberations. Taken together, these works show the very personal nature of the work, as well as its inherently political qualities; they also point to the maturity of the field.

THE POLITICAL

As was apparent in the previous two sections, the political is in many ways evident even in action research that emphasizes the professional or personal dimension. Issues of inequities around race and gender matters are more frequently part of the literature than earlier, both in individual articles and chapters, and in whole books (e.g. Edelsky, 1999; Caro-Bruce et al., 2007). At least one text, aimed at pre-service teachers (Phillips and Carr, 2006) takes an explicitly 'critical' stance. In the sense of having a central commitment to exposing and working as part of a social movement against structural inequalities in power relations as a central aim, the political dimension in action research seems at best mixed. Mostly absent are serious considerations of theoretical resources emanating from outside of 'white' academicians, including epistemologies that have their origins in people of color or from women. By this I mean that these resources and 'standpoints' alter not just the topic of research or even the analytic framework; they alter fundamentally understandings of the 'methodology' itself.

Yet if we broaden the definition of education to include venues outside of schools and school personal, we see much work that shares assumptions and even points of origin with some forms of action research, even when not always using the term. Although much of the work I will describe is in some ways connected to universities or individual academics, it is often not centered in the academy.

There have been several long-term, effective projects aimed at school reform, where the impetus for reform has come from the community rather than the school authorities. In fact, the community groups are organizing research as a means to leverage change from the authorities. These local efforts emanate from the idea that action research is about local knowledge production for civic purposes, an idea not always seen as part of educational action research work, but very common in the forms of action research that have developed in health, human services, and the social sciences. Although some of this work is reported in the academic literature (e.g. Baum, 2003; Shirley, 1997), it is more widely available through the websites of the groups sponsoring the work, such as Research for Action (www.researchforaction.org), Justice Matters (www.justicematters.org), DC Voice (www.dcvoice.org) and Californians for Justice (www.caljustice.org). These groups bring together parents, and often students, in work that is directed at gathering information needed to provide evidence to be used towards change efforts. All of these projects serve communities of color and/or economically oppressed groups.

Another strand to this strategy of using research in the cause of social justice issues involves working with youth groups, assisting them in learning the skills of research, so that they can apply them to working for change in areas they identify as needs. Here, too, some of the works are available in the academic literature, through alliances with individual faculty members or university groups, while others are not. Some focused on gender issues, reflecting working with girls on body weight and shape (e.g., Piran, 2001), while others (e.g., McIntyre, 2000) attended to issues of violence, and still others involved youth who were in 'Government Care' programs (Rutman et al., 2005). Some work specifically engaged students within the context of specific courses in their high schools (e.g., Cammarota, 2007), while others have created curriculum to teach research skills that students can use to address their concerns but exist outside of conventional educational settings, for example the work of the Institute for Community Research (www.incommunityresearch.org). Still others are connected with university's graduate programs, but work for similar ends (e.g. Cahill, 2007; Cammarota and Fine, 2008).

All of these works share the sense that learning the skills of research provides not only means to deal with current issues, but also develops a sense of agency in dealing with life issues over the long haul. There is often also a sense that these efforts are part of the development of a sense of civic participation in the building of more democratic social and political relations. All address youth groups who are endangered by existing structures of inequality. These examples push beyond thinking about action research as within classrooms and schools, toward connecting with the communities they are intended to serve, as well as the students whose lives are deeply affected by the education they do (and do not) 'receive' and might instead 'construct'. They also push beyond constructions of action research in relation to usual notions of the professional, instead recognizing the wealth of knowledge in communities that can be used to educate young people. Collaboration, seen by many as central to action research methodologies, is not only within schools, but a process of both reaching out and allowing others to work toward change. Finally, the projects show not only the power of popular knowledge production, but also the power of taking on the political dimension as a central aspect to action research efforts in educational work. Taken together, they show what Jean Anyon (2005) has called 'Radical Possibilities', ones which if fully articulated (as opposed to commodified and marketed) could contribute to a cohesive, and resistant social movement.

UNDERSTANDING ACTION RESEARCH CONTEXTUALLY

The past decade has been one of substantive changes in educational policy in many locations in response to changing global economic conditions. These have had severe effects on the professional and personal dimensions of action research. Accountability processes, the role of the teacher in educational practice, as well as identity issues around teachers and students have been changing. Important among these has been the widespread influence of neo-liberal policies which have resulted in a culture of 'performativity' (Ball, 2003). One prominent example is the attempt to reduce the parameters of educational work to doing only that which results in gains in the narrow band of standardized achievement test, and the 'mapping' of curriculum and instructional strategies against that which is tested (Blackmore, 2007; Hursh, 2008).

The change in educational policy can be seen as an indication of a move toward a market discourse in which notions of education for the public good are reduced to a focus on individual and sub-group achievement. What students learn in schools is thereby positioned solely in terms of their preparation for a fluid and internationally competitive labour market, rather than in relation to some sense of their participation in building more socially and economically just global societies. Educational decisions seem to be increasingly based on goals of preparing students for a changing economy, rather than on debate over what might best be done 'in the public interest' (Ladson-Billings and Tate, 2006). The current professional context seems inconsistent with the remarkable growth in the breadth and depth of literature on action research described in this book.

Action research most often appears to be an inherently local activity – it derives its primary impulse from the needs of people in a locality (whether educators, community members, or students), and highlights the abilities of people within these contexts to use research to address local educational and social issues. Localities are always diverse in terms of 'race', gender, and social class, and a whole range of 'differences'. Those who seem to be absent physically are always present, nonetheless. This is more evident recently because of the interconnections between the global economy and culture. For example, gender issues may be hidden under local cultural norms, but are always a factor in human interactions. Regardless of whether 'difference' is the focus of local educational work, it is always an element of action research because diversity, rather than homogeneity, is the global norm (Rizvi, 1994). For example, even if there is scant attention to social class in a particular action research project, defined in terms of the huge gaps between the 'haves' and the 'have nots', local and global economics are influences on the issues addressed in the research.

The local intersects with both the professional and the personal dimensions. Action research is part of the process of constructing what it means to be an educator, and involves interconnections between the identities of the researcher and the researched. Some action research work directly addresses issues such as racial identity and how that works through school practices. There are examples of this in this Handbook and elsewhere (Peter Murrell, Chapter 34 this volume; Cahill and Collard, 2003). Most of the work around identity in action research is done within the framework of nation-states, rather than in relation to shifting global economies of the dispossessed.

By highlighting the overarching political dimension, action research can be better seen in its global context, one in which the production of local knowledge is viewed alongside the emergence of global knowledge economies. Professional knowledge and the processes of teaching and learning are transformed through action research, but they are also transformed through transnational policies driven by the growing emphasis on the knowledge industry. Professional knowledge is in a state of flux, along with the identities of those who are educators and those who are to be educated in the skills of 'life-long learning'. All of these changes are in relation to global shifts and 'flows' of people and discourses (Appadurai, 2006).

Given this context, it seemed appropriate to look at that literature for analyses that could juxtapose the 'local' nature of knowledge in action research within global issues. One useful work toward this end is Arjun Appadurai's (2006) argument for 'The right to research'. Appadurai defines research as 'a specialised name for a generalised capacity, the capacity to make disciplined inquiries into those things we need to know, but do not know yet' (p. 167). Historically, action research has provided a means by which those involved in education can investigate their practice in order to improve it. To many, it asserts research as 'systematic inquiry, made public' (Stenhouse, 1975). Both Appadurai and action research emphasize the capacity of those outside the academy to come to understand practices and their contexts, and to direct those understandings toward actions that will improve what Melanie Walker (Chapter 24 this volume) outlines as 'human flourishing'.

Appadurai emphasizes the global context: '... a world of rapid change, where markets, media, and migration have destabilised secure knowledge niches and have rapidly made it less possible for ordinary citizens to rely on knowledge drawn from traditional, customary or local sources' (pp. 167–8). He sees research as integrally connected not just to the production of knowledge for the knowledge industry, but to what he calls 'the capacity to aspire': 'the social and cultural capacity to plan, hope, desire, and achieve socially valuable goals' (p. 176). Importantly, he also conceives of research as a 'right' and links it to citizenship. Speaking about work with youth in India, he argues '... that developing the capacity to document, to inquire, to analyze and to communicate results has a powerful effect on their capacity to speak up as active citizens on matters that are shaping their city and their world' (p. 175).

Remarkably resonant with the emerging youth-oriented action research reported on in this chapter and elsewhere in the Handbook (Thomson and Gunter, Chapter 33; Murrell Chapter 34, this volume), what Appadurai invokes has long been part of the participatory action research (PAR) tradition. Information, and the processes by which forms of knowledge are legitimated (its epistemology), have long been linked to social struggle. The project that he notes is directly related to works that this volume highlights (e.g. Brydon-Miller et al., Chapter 40). What the PAR tradition emphasizes is that the gathering of 'information' can be dangerous. Myles Horton was once arrested for 'coming here and getting information and teaching it' (Lewis, 2001: 357). The links between action research and learning to become active citizens are clear. What is not clear is whether the furthering of the skills of democratic engagement are prerequisites for education action research efforts, or outcomes (see Robinson and Soudien, Chapter 38 this volume).

It seems to me vital that those using the term action research (and indeed those who use other terms for similar ideas) are clear in their assumptions about the kinds of knowledge(s) they seek to enhance, the traditions they feel are part of their work, the ends towards which their research efforts are aimed, and the social movements with which they articulate. This may be especially important for those who don't see ideology and politics as embodied in their professional and personal agendas, but is equally true for those who highlight the political dimension. Action research, unproblematized in terms of its goals, can act to reinscribe existing practices rather than create new forms which focus on social justice. In this current context we need to look for ways to create convergences (Fals Borda, 1992) in action research, rather than ways to legitimate it. When viewed as an accepted 'method' within the academy, the work is positioned as an iconoclastic commodity rather than something capable of sustained group work as part of a social movement.

In this chapter and in the overall book, we've worked to create an 'ecumenical' representation of action research, including research that highlights its different dimensions. It seems to me that rather than work solely within the academic norms of identifying, owning, and marketing the idea of action research, we need to be constantly looking for our 'traveling companions', our allies, our comrades with whom we can form coalitions around our shared interests. Appadurai (2006) notes that 'Research-produced knowledge is everywhere, doing battle with other kinds of knowledge (produced by personal testimony, opinion, revelation, or rumor) and with other pieces of research-produced knowledge' (p. 12). That battle needs to keep in mind the importance of locally produced knowledge, often narrative in style, which frequently exists in forms not recognized in traditional forms of research. Folks outside and inside of the action research tradition need to look at what has been done and not 'reinvent' action research, but rather look for coalitions for new forms of knowledge that allow for challenges, as well as additions, to the knowledge economy.

The dimensional analysis of action research offers a way to understand and thereby use action research as a means not solely for knowledge generation (which as a form of research it entails), but for personal and professional development (for which as a form of learning it is used), and for contributions to social justice (which its articulation to social movements and social change demonstrates). Across its varied forms, action research is a set of commitments (a methodology, in Harding's (1987) sense of the term), rather than a set of techniques for research (a method). It also embodies various epistemologies, varied ways of establishing its knowledge claims. While the strategies for data collection and the ideas that guide data analysis (method and methodology) across the various forms of action research vary, they share an epistemology that sees knowledge as essentially connected to practice. As such, the dimensional analysis is also a way to get beyond definitional struggles toward thinking about action research as embodied in many forms and looking toward more just educational practice.

REFERENCES

Altrichter, H. and Gstettner, P. (1993) 'Action research: A closed chapter in the history of German social science?' *Educational Action Research*, 1 (3): 329–60.

Anyon, J. (2005) *Radical Possibilities: Public Policy, Urban Education, and a New Social Movement*. New York: Routledge.

Appadurai, A. (2006) 'The right to research', *Globalizations, Societies and Education*, 4 (2): 167–77.

Ball, S. (2003) 'The teacher's soul and the terrors of performativity', *Journal of Education Policy*, 18 (2): 215–28.

Baum, H. (2003) *Community Action for School Reform*. Albany, NY: State University of New York Press.

Blackmore, J. (2007) 'How is educational research "being framed"? Governmentality, the (ac)counting of, and expertise in, educational research', in B. Somekh and T. Schwandt (eds), *Knowledge Production: Research Work in Interesting Times*. London: Routledge, pp. 42–78.

Brydon-Miller, M., Maguire, P. and McIntyre, P. (eds). (2004) *Traveling companions: Feminism, Teaching, and Action Research*. Westport, CN: Praeger

Bond, H.M. (1935, April) 'The curriculum and the Negro child', *Journal of Negro Education*, 4 (2), 159–68.

Cahill, C. (2007) 'The personal is political: Developing new subjectivities through participatory action research', *Gender, Place, and Culture*, 14 (3), 267–92.

Cahill, R. and Collard, G. (2003) 'Deadly ways to learn' ... a yarn about some learning we did together', *Comparative Education*, 39 (2): 211–19.

Cammarota, J. (2007) 'A social justice approach to achievement: Guiding Latino/a students toward educational attainment with a challenging, socially relevant curriculum', *Equity & Excellence in Education*, 40, 87–96.

Cammarota, J. and Fine, M. (eds) (2008) *Revolutionizing Education: Youth Participatory Action Research in Motion*. New York: Routledge.

Caro-Bruce, C., Flessner, R., Klehr, M. and Zeichner, K. (eds) (2007) *Creating Equitable Classrooms Through Action Research*. Thousand Oaks, CA: Corwin Press.

Carr, W. and Kemmis, S. (1983) *Becoming Critical: Knowing Through Action Research*. Geelong: Deakin University Press.

Counts, G.S. (1932/1978) *Dare the School Build a New Social Order?* Carbondale: Southern Illinois University Press.

Dahlström, L. (2003) 'Critical practitioner inquiry and the struggle over the preferential right of interpretation in the South', *Educational Action Research*, 11 (3): 467–77.

Dahlström, L. and Mannberg, J. (eds) (2006) *Critical Educational Visions and Practices – in Neo-liberal Times*. Global South Network. http://alfa.ped.umu.se/projekt/globalsouthnetwork/

Edelsky, C. (ed) (1999) *Making Justice our Project: Teachers Working Toward Critical Whole Language Practice*. Urbana, IL: National Council of Teachers of English.

Fals Borda, O. (1992) 'Convergences in theory and in action for research, learning and management'. in C. Bruce and A. Russell, *Transforming Tomorrow Today: 2nd World Congress on Action Learning* Brisbane: ALARPM, pp. 11–18.

Fecho, B. (2004) *'Is this English?': Race, Language, and Culture in the Classroom*. New York: Teachers College.

Hanish, C. (1970/2001) 'The personal is political', in B.A. Crow (ed.) *Radical Feminism: A Documentary Reader*. New York: New York University Press. pp. 113–16.

Harding, S. (1987) 'Introduction: Is there a feminist method?' in S. Harding (ed.), *Feminism and Methodology*. Bloomington: Indiana University Press, pp. 1–14.

Hui, M. and Grossman, D.L. (eds) (2008) *Improving Teacher Education Through Action Research*. New York: Routledge.

Hursh, D. (2008) *High-stakes Testing and the Decline of Teaching and Learning*. Lanham, MD: Rowman & Littlefield.

Kemmis, S. and McTaggart, R. (1981) *The Action Research Planner*. Geelong: Deakin University Press.

Ladson-Billings, G. and Tate, W.R. (eds) (2006) *Education Research in the Public Interest*. New York: Teachers College.

Lewis, H. (2001) 'Participatory research and education for social change: Highlander research and education center', in P. Reason and H. Bradbury (eds), *Handbook of Action Research: Participative Inquiry and Practice*. London: Sage, pp. 356–62.

Loughran, J. Hamilton, M. LaBoskey, V., and Russell, T. (2004) *International Handbook of Self-study of Teaching and Teacher Education Practices*. Dordrecht, The Netherlands: Kluwer Academic.

Loughran, J. (2007) 'Researching teacher education: Responding to the challenges, demands, and expectations of self-study', *Journal of Teacher Education*, 58 (1): 12–20.

McIntyre, A. (2000) 'Constructing meaning about violence, school, and community: Participatory action research with urban youth', *The Urban Review*, 32 (2): 123–54.

McIntyre, A. (2002) 'Exploring whiteness and multi-cultural education with prospective teachers', *Curriculum Inquiry*, 32 (1): 31–49.

McIntyre, A. (2003) 'Participatory action research and urban education: Reshaping the teacher preparation process', *Equity & Excellence in Education*, 36 (1): 28–39.

McNiff, J. (1988) *Action Research: Principles and Practice*. London: Routledge.

McNiff, J. and Whitehead, J. (2006) *All You Need to Know About Action Research*. London: Sage.

Milner, R. (2007) 'Race, narrative inquiry, and self-study in curriculum and teacher education', *Education and Urban Society*, 39 (4): 584–689.

Mitchell, C., Weber, S. and O'Reilly-Scanlon, K. (eds) (2005) *Just Who Do We Think We Are? Methodologies for Autobiography and Self-study in Teaching*. New York: RoutledgeFalmer.

Noffke, S.E. (1997a) 'Professional, personal, and political dimensions of action research', in M.W. Apple (ed.), *Review of Research in Education*, 22: 305–43.

Noffke, S.E. (1997b) 'Themes and tensions in US action research: Towards historical analysis', in S. Hollingsworth (ed.), *International Action Research: A Casebook for Educational Reform* London: Falmer Press, pp. 2–16.

Obidah, J. and Teel, K.M. (2000) *Because of the Kids: Facing Racial and Cultural Differences in Schools.* New York: Teachers College.

Park, P., Brydon-Miller, M., Hall, B. and Jackson, T. (eds) (1993) *Voices of Change: Participatory Research in the U.S. and Canada.* Westport, CN: Bergin & Garvey.

Phillips, D.K. and Carr, K. (2006) *Becoming a Teacher Through Action Research.* New York: Routledge.

Piran, N. (2001) 'Re-inhabiting the body from the inside out: Girls transform their social environment', in G. Tolman and M. Brydon-Miller (eds), *From Subjects to Subjectivities: A Handbook of Interpretive and Participatory Methods.* New York: New York University Press, pp. 218–38.

Reason, P. and Bradbury, H. (eds) (2001) *Handbook of Action Research: Participative Inquiry and Practice.* London: Sage.

Rizvi, F. (1994) 'The arts, education and the politics of multiculturalism', in S. Gunew and F. Rizvi (eds), *Culture, Difference and the Arts.* Sydney: Allen & Unwin, pp. 94–110.

Russell, T. (2005) 'How 20 years of self-study changed my teaching,' in: C. Kosnik, C. Beck, A. Freese and A. Samaras (eds), *Making a Difference in Teacher Education Through Self-study.* Dordrecht, The Netherlands: Springer, pp. 3–17.

Rutman, D., Hubberstey, C., Barlow, A. and Brown, E. (2005) 'Supporting young people's transitions from care: Reflections on doing action research with youth from care', in L. Brown and S. Strega (eds), *Research as Resistance: Critical, Indigenous, and Anti-oppressive Approaches.* Toronto: Canadian Scholars' Press, pp. 153–79

Shirley, D. (1997) *Community Organizing for Urban School Reform.* Austin: University of Texas Press.

Stenhouse, L. (1975) *An Introduction to Curriculum Research and Development.* London: Heinemann.

Wade, S., Fauske, J. and Thompson, A. (2008) Prospective teachers' problem solving in online peer-led dialogues, *American Educational Research Journal,* 45 (2): 398–442.

Whitehead, J. and McNiff, J. (2006) *Action Research Living Theory.* London: Sage.

Winter, R. (1987) *Action-research and the Nature of Social Inquiry: Professional Innovation and Educational Work.* Aldershot: Avebury.

Zeichner, K., Amukushu, A., Muukenga, K. and Shilamba, P. (1998) 'Critical practitioner inquiry and the transformation of teacher education in Namibia', *Educational Action Research,* 6 (2): 183–203.

PART I

Action Research Methodology: Diversity of Rationales and Practices

Introduction to Part I

The six chapters contained in Part I have been chosen to provide readers with a scholarly overview of methodological issues in the field of Educational Action Research. In selecting them we have conceptualized methodology in Sandra Harding's terms as 'a theory and analysis of how research should proceed'. This encompasses exploration of 'issues about an adequate theory of knowledge or justificatory strategy' (1987: 2) – the epistemological aspect of a methodology. By definition this rejects any sense of methodology being reduced to a prescription for data gathering and analyzing techniques. The chapters all exemplify a commitment to dialogue and reflexive engagement. They illustrate methodology that is a process of interaction between theories *about* social practices and theories emerging from inquiry *into* social practices. In so doing they map out the diversity of the territory of educational action research rationales and practices.

The first two chapters focus on action research as a means of constructing and elaborating teachers' professional knowledge. Elliott argues for action research as 'a form of practical philosophy', drawing on Aristotle's theory of phronesis. He draws no distinction between the development of 'educational theory' and the process of teachers-as-researchers. For him teachers conducting action research are 'developing their practical insights into the problems and dilemmas of realising their educational values in concrete teaching situations'. Cochran-Smith and Lytle focus on 'teacher research' as a form of practical inquiry, similar to action research. They reject the traditional boundaries between knowledge generation and the process of teaching, characterizing teacher research as a 'stance' that involves 'working the dialectic between research and practice'. Taken together these two chapters argue the case for 'educational praxis' that involves a dialectic relationship between critical theorizing and action as the rationale that drives teacher (action) research.

The next two chapters provide insights into ways that action research can generate and sustain personal growth and development. Both focus on processes of collaborative inquiry through which participants develop agency and generate educational knowledge that informs their practice. Wells starts with an account of how he learned from a teacher that, to be ethical, research needs to be engaged in collaboration with teachers. His vision is of transforming students' learning experiences in schools by creating 'dialogic communities' of learners and teachers. By inviting teachers to lead the inquiry into how their practice affected students' opportunities for dialogue, he was able to create the conditions to make it a reality. Hollingsworth et al. provide an account of the professional growth that has resulted from participating in such a collaboration over 20 years. Like Wells, Hollingsworth starts with a story of personal learning, in this case from her first cohort of K-12 student teachers. Having found that they needed to engage in 'a collaborative conversation' in order to learn, she set up a study group with her students during their first year of teaching and this has continued to exist ever since. The chapter is written by the six voices of this career-long partnership. It illustrates the group's continuous development as educators with a passion for social justice, through engaging with professional practice in the light of their developing knowledge of feminist theories and epistemologies.

The final two chapters in Part I address the political nature of action research in terms of its rationales and practices. Carr and Kemmis argue that 'it is precisely because "education" is always the subject of [a] process of contestation that it is intrinsically "political"' – to be 'educational' teaching practices need to be guided by ethical values. They argue the case for personal, professional and political approaches being necessarily integrated in critical action research. Critical action research engages with the interfaces between all three with commitment to transformation of self, the profession and educational institutions. Griffiths focuses on the different ways in which action researchers address issues of social justice. She engages with the nature of the 'political' in action research, going on to conceptualize social justice as 'a kind of action'. She discusses a range of theories on the relationship between individuals and community in search of a definition. The core of her chapter is a discussion of different orientations towards social justice in the theory and practice of action research. She suggests that the different orientations can be distinguished from one another by the extent to which they engage with 'questions to be asked frequently (QAF)'. These QAFs provide a flexible and powerful framework for engaging with social justice in the course of action research.

Taken together, these chapters provide an entrée into looking at the complex interconnections between the professional, personal, and political dimensions of action research which follow in the next sections. But it seems worth repeating that these are 'dimensions' rather than discrete categories or typologies. What follows, we hope, shows how the dimensions are interconnected, with some aspects foregrounded, but always keeping others in view.

REFERENCES

Harding, S. (ed.) (1987) *Feminism and Methodology: Social Science Issues.* Bloomington: Indiana University Press.

2

Building Educational Theory through Action Research

John Elliott

In this chapter I will offer an account of educational action research as a form of *practical philosophy* (see Carr 2004: 55–73) that unifies the process of developing theory and practice. This mode of reasoning aims to clarify universal conceptions of value in the process of reflecting in and on the actions taken to realize them. As such it poses an epistemological issue about the relationship between knowledge of universals and knowledge of particulars. The social sciences have tended to assume that these are discrete forms of knowledge and that each has their own distinctive methods of inquiry. *Nomothetic* methods yield universal knowledge while *ideographic* methods yield knowledge of particulars. Practical philosophy, on the other hand, does not draw a tight methodological boundary between these forms of knowledge. Indeed, I will argue that it should not be depicted as a *method* of reasoning.

EDUCATIONAL RESEARCH OR RESEARCH ON EDUCATION?

In 1978 I published a paper entitled 'Classroom Research: Science or Commonsense?' In it I coined a distinction between 'Research on Education' and 'Educational Research'. I was drawing attention to the difference between viewing research into teaching and learning as a form of ethical inquiry aimed at realizing the educational good, and viewing it as a way of constructing knowledge about teaching and learning that is detached from the researcher's own personal constructs of educational value. *Educational Research*, I argued, is carried out with the practical intention of changing a situation to make it more educationally worthwhile. Its sphere is that of ethically committed action, or what Aristotle called *praxis*. At the time I construed it as a form of *commonsense theorizing* in contrast to the kind of *scientific theorizing* that stemmed from research *on* education.

Some would claim that the notion of commonsense theorizing is a contradiction in terms, in as much as what marks out commonsense knowledge is its taken-for-granted nature (see Carr, 2004: 61–2 and Pring, 1976: Ch. 5). However, I argued that although much commonsense knowledge may partake of this taken-for-granted character, it is not necessarily so. What fundamentally characterizes such knowledge is that it can be expressed in the vernacular language, hence enabling people to co-ordinate their actions for the purposes of everyday living. Such knowledge may simply be transmitted on a tacit basis in the process of inducting individuals into a practical tradition. However, at times new knowledge may be needed to address contingencies and situations that arise in contexts of action, which the established way of doing things –the tradition – cannot adequately address.

The kind of commonsense reasoning that I have depicted involves discerning the particularities of a situation from the standpoint of an ethical agent, and in the process, discriminating its practically relevant features. Aristotle called this form of reasoning, which arises in the search for situational understanding or practical wisdom, *phronesis*. He regarded it as quite distinct from theoretical reason, which is aimed at the discovery of universally valid truths that are essential and unchanging and valued 'for their own sake' *(episteme)*.

'Case-based' reasoning in the context of *phronesis* should not be confused with the use of ideographic methods in the social sciences, such as *ethnography*. For example, the latter is a social anthropological method for generating knowledge about the activities of an unfamiliar society or group. Methodologically *ethnographies* aspire to interpret the social world without changing it. All methodology serves to distance the construction of knowledge from the domain of *praxis*. Methodology is inherently prejudiced against prejudice (see Gadamer, 1975: 239–40). *Phronesis,* on the other hand, is inevitably biased by the adoption of an evaluative standpoint. As Carr (2006) argues, practical wisdom can only 'be acquired by practitioners who, in seeking to achieve the standards of excellence inherent in their practice, develop the capacity to make wise and prudent judgements about what, in a particular situation, would constitute an appropriate expression of the good'. It should, he contends, be regarded as a 'moral and intellectual virtue that is inseparable from practice and constitutive of the moral consciousness', rather than the outcome of a method of reasoning that detaches 'knowledge' from 'action'.

In the context of phronesis there can be no discernment of the particularities of a situation or discrimination of its practically relevant features that are not conditioned by value-bias. Yet such discernment will be disciplined by a person's conversation with others, whose perspectives will draw attention to unanticipated features of the situation and challenge her to reconstruct her original biases. Phronesis is a naturalistic mode of reasoning that opens up a space for the reflective reconstruction of bias in conversation with others. This is because it does not separate means from ends as objects of reflection. It may be regarded as practical philosophy since changes in *praxis* will be accompanied by changing conceptions of the good to be achieved, and vice versa.

This kind of dialectical process is appropriately located in a community of practice for the purpose of securing the conditions for co-ordinated action amongst ethical agents. Any constraints on reasoning leading to modifications of bias and prejudice will stem, not so much from any methodological disciplining of inquiry, as from the constraints that are embedded in good conversation within the community of practice, and which might be described in terms that Dewey depicted as the *democratic virtues* (see Dewey, 1974: 182–92).

BEYOND METHODOLOGY

In my 1978 paper I claimed that one could either theorize from the standpoint of practice or from the standpoint of science. I had assumed that the standpoint of science was that of an impartial spectator freed from the prejudices that biased human understanding in the practical circumstances of everyday life.

However, in the wake of the post-modern deconstruction of all epistemologies that claim to specify conditions for grasping essential truth, I have found it increasingly difficult to draw a tight boundary between the standpoints of the scientist and the practitioner. I would now claim, following Rorty (1999), that all science is a form of practical reasoning and that all theories are practical tools. Hence, I no longer wish to draw a distinction between theorizing from the standpoints of commonsense and science. Rorty claims that in general 'To argue for a certain theory – is to argue about what we should do'. He is happy to use the term 'theory' in the context of the inexact as well as the exact sciences. For Rorty, 'whether we are arguing for a theory concerning the microstructure of material bodies or for one about the proper balance of powers between branches of government, we are arguing about what we should do to make progress'. The first argument, he points out, is about what we should do to make technological progress and will therefore take the form of instrumental reason. The second argument about what we should do to make political progress involves, I would suggest, something like *phronesis* as a form of reasoning. Rorty appears to imply that the term 'theory' has an intelligible use in the context of social practices like politics, and can accommodate *phronesis* as its mode of production.

The spectator theory of knowledge, embedded in so much of what has passed for 'science', is no longer philosophically sustainable. The revival of philosophical pragmatism has purged our picture of science of its essentialist assumptions. Hence we find Rorty contending that there are no methodological constraints on inquiry (1982: 165), 'derived from the nature of objects, or of the mind, or of language'. The only constraints are conversational ones, 'those retail constraints provided by the remarks of our fellow inquirers'. He argues that those of us engaged in inquiry 'have a duty to talk to each other, to converse about our views of the world, to use persuasion rather than force, to be tolerant of diversity, to be contritely fallibist' (1991: 67). Such are the democratic virtues that Dewey associated with the scientific method (see Dewey, 1974: 182–92), but which Rorty wishes to dissociate from the essentialist connotations of the term 'method'. In this sense he gives us an account of inquiry without method. It is one that puts methodology on the run, and supports an account of 'educational research' as a dialogical and democratic process of inquiry that is grounded in *phronesis*.

THE IDEAS OF 'TEACHERS-AS-RESEARCHERS' AND 'TEACHERS-AS-EDUCATIONAL THEORISTS'

The above account of educational research is rooted in my experience as a teacher researcher in a secondary school at the height of the school-based curriculum development movement in the UK during the mid-1960s, and further shaped by the experience of working with Lawrence Stenhouse on the Nuffield Foundation/Schools Council Humanities Curriculum Project. In the context of this project Stenhouse linked the idea of 'teachers as researchers' (see Stenhouse, 1975: Ch. 10) to the construction of a theory of education (1979: 19–20). From his point of view a theory of education is an articulation of teachers' shared practical understandings of how to make their practice in classrooms more *educational* through concrete and situated action. He was quite clear that it was the task of teachers conceived as researchers to construct a body of common knowledge – what he called *a tradition of understanding* – about how to effect educational change from their experimental actions in the particular contexts of their practice. A theory of education, for Stenhouse, constituted a tradition of understanding about how to effect educational change, and a condition of its construction was the collective engagement of teachers in researching their practice. On this view teachers have a central role in generating practically valid educational research findings that can be cast in the form of an educational theory. In the context of the Humanities Project the task was to build a tradition of understanding about how to teach controversial issues in classrooms. Stenhouse regarded the development of 'educational theory' as inseparable from the idea of the 'teacher as researcher'.

This link destabilizes the specialist domains of the educational philosopher and theorist, the empirical researcher, and the practitioner. It will be contested by those post-modern thinkers who associate theory with the claim to grasp essential and unchanging truth *(episteme)*. For such thinkers the concept of 'theory' is inextricably linked to foundationist and essentialist assumptions.

RECONTEXTUALIZING THE USE OF THE TERM 'THEORY' IN EDUCATION

I will now argue that there are practical reasons for trying to re-contextualize the use of the term 'theory' in the way Stenhouse did. The use of the term conveys meanings other than a claim to provide knowledge of essential and unchanging truth. Some of these, as I hope to show, are also implicit in the concept of practical reason linked to *phronesis*. By wrenching the term 'theory' out of its historical context of use and thereby divesting it of its essentialist connotations, and putting it into service as part of the practical discourses that arise in contexts of action one might strengthen the generative capacity of teachers (and other social practitioners) to effect change and to resist the domination of *techne* over their practical reasoning. A re-contextualized conception of educational theory – one that is fused with the concept of *phronesis* – may help teachers to reclaim their activities as having a space for *praxis*. It may also help social researchers based in higher education to construct better links between research and practice by demonstrating that knowledge, which carries many of the hallmarks of theory, can be generated in action contexts without the need for any methodological guarantees. Any unification of educational theory and practice through action research will depend on how successful attempts to fuse the concepts of *theoria* and *phronesis* are in terms of constructing meaning for action.

The meanings of *theoria* that educational action researchers need to integrate into their practical discourse are:

1   It is a process of reasoning that yields universal knowledge.
2   It constructs a clear and systematic view of its subject-matter.
3   It enables the prediction of future possibilities.

In modern culture the idea of universal knowledge became appropriated by the construction of a positivist science that served the practical interests of technical rationality. In this context it was understood as knowledge of the general laws of cause and effect governing events in both the natural and social world. Such knowledge is cast in the form of empirical generalizations that can be applied by human beings in choosing the best means for achieving a given end. It provides a clear and systematic view of what needs to be done to bring about certain states of affairs, and thereby promises to give human beings the power to predict and control the outcomes of their behaviour.

Dunne (2005: 373) characterizes the mode of rationality that underpins this conception of theory or universal knowledge as follows:

> It puts a premium on 'objectivity' and detachment, suppressing the context-dependence of first-person experience in favour of a third-person perspective which yields generalized findings in accordance with clearly formulated, publicly agreed procedures. These procedures give an indispensable role to operations of observation and measurement, modes of testing that specify precisely what can count as counter-evidence, replicability of findings, and the adoption of a language maximally freed from possibilities of misinterpretation by its being maximally purged of the need for interpretation itself. And through these procedures, knowledge is established that is both explanatory and predictive.

Dunne's account of technical rationality – a mode of reasoning that Aristotle called *techne* – appears to capture all of the meanings I attributed to *theoria* above. In this context theory provides the rational foundation for technical knowledge about how to achieve given ends. It leaves no space for context-dependent inquiry based on first-person experience. Hence, the view that one cannot generalize from the case studies of action researchers. I now want to show how *phronesis* as a mode of practical reasoning can also capture the meanings I attributed to *theoria*.

As Carr (2006: 7–8) has pointed out both *phronesis* and *techne* are alike, inasmuch as both subsume particular cases under general principles. However, he also points out that unlike *techne*, *phronesis* 'is not a deductive form of reasoning which issues in a prescription for action'. The judgements in which it issues are context-dependent and constitute understandings 'of what, in a particular situation, would constitute an appropriate expression of the good'. *Phronesis* therefore constitutes the relationship between the general and the particular in a form that is very different from the relationship that obtains in *techne*. In the latter one deduces what ought to be done in a particular situation from general propositions. In the former what actions might count as an instance of a general principle is a matter of interpretation that takes into account the particularities of the practical situation. *Phronesis* is a mode of reasoning in which general conceptions of the good and the actions taken to realize them in particular situations are mutually constitutive.

As such, it possesses the quality of deliberative reflection in which both 'means' and 'ends' are objects of inquiry in a process where 'the "means" are always modified by reflecting on the "end" just as an understanding of the "end" is always modified by reflecting on the "means"' (Carr, 2006: 7–8). The capacity to engage in Deliberative Case-based Reasoning *(phronesis)* is best depicted as a virtue rather than the mastery of a method. Dunne (2005: 376), for example, refers to it as 'a cultivated capacity' to make calls to judgement 'resourcefully and reliably in all the complex situations that they address'. Dunne, like Carr, is reluctant to depict such judgements as contributions to the development of theory. They assume that theories must take the form of empirical generalizations, which serve the interest of technical rationality in prediction and control (see Dunne, 2005: 384–86). However, I would argue that Dunne's model of theory, derived as it is from the natural sciences, does tend to blinker him to a different and more commonsense notion of 'predictability' as an anticipation of future possibilities for action. The latter is a notion that arises in the context of *praxis* conceived as ethically committed action. Indeed it is implicit in Dunne's own account of *phronesis* where he depicts 'general understanding' in very different terms to the grasp of the kind of general principles or 'generalizations' that are shaped by technical rationality. He writes of the need of *phronesis* 'to embrace the particulars of relevant action-situations within its grasp of universals' (p. 375), and argues for 'richly descriptive studies' that possess 'epiphanic power' by 'illuminating other settings' (p. 386). Such studies I would argue are a source of what Stake (1978) has termed 'naturalistic generalizations', whereby social practitioners are able to build a common tradition of understandings from their concrete experiences of particular situations. Such common understandings can be summarized as 'universal rules of thumb' (see Nussbaum, 1990: 67–8) that pick out those practically relevant respects in which particular situations are judged to be similar. Such universal rules, from which Nussbaum is careful to distinguish general causal rules, enable practitioners to anticipate if not exactly predict the consequences òf their actions in a particular concrete situation. This is why in the context of teachers' research I have tended to use the term 'hypotheses' to depict the universal rules of thumb being constructed through such research. As Nussbaum argues, 'universal rules of thumb' are open to the experience of surprise. Our capacity to recognize the unique and novel features of a case that are nevertheless ethically significant depends on their use. Becoming capable of recognizing the unanticipated when it occurs depends on the anticipations provided by universal rules of thumb or *action hypotheses*.

Alasdair MacIntyre has argued (1990: 59–61) that the standards of reasoning that characterize moral inquiry are universally valid, inasmuch as they are embedded in a tradition of understanding – about how to realize goods that are internal to a social practice in particular circumstances – that has withstood the test of time and circumstance. Such a tradition embodies the best standards developed to date. As such they express the shared experience of a community of practice situated in time and place, and are therefore not fixed and unchanging as if they were based on rational foundations that transcended the contingencies of human existence. *Universal* standards of non-instrumental practical reasoning, according to MacIntytre, are always open to revision in the light of new contingencies that challenge practitioners to find novel ways of expressing their values in action. The aspiration that underpinned the notion of 'teachers as researchers' was for teachers to respond to the challenge of curriculum change by building together through their action research new understandings of how to express their educational values in action.

I have tried to explain why the consensus of judgements that emerges in the course of educational action research might warrant the description of 'theories'. Such judgements constitute both a knowledge of particulars and of *universals,* and express a *clear and systematic* (unified) *view* of the practically relevant features of situations, and enable practitioners to anticipate if not infallibly predict future occurrences and to recognize unanticipated ones when they occur. As anticipations such judgements do not enable practitioners to exercise strong technical control over events, but by enabling them to recognize the ethical significance of the unexpected when it occurs they establish conditions for sustaining the practitioner as an ethical agent in the situation. In other words they enable the practitioner to exercise 'ethical control' of their conduct in unanticipated situations.

If one looks at the case study and generalization issue in the light of the distinction between universal and general rules governing the relation between means and ends, one can argue that case studies cannot yield general rules, but when constructed in action situations they are the means by which universal rules are both tested and developed. Any use of the term 'theory' in the context of action will differ from its use in a purely intellectual context that is dominated by a

Cartesian picture of the mind. Indeed John Macmurray (1957: 198–202) finds no use of the term beyond an *intellectual* mode of reflection where it takes the form of generalization. Within what he calls the *emotional* mode reflection is concerned with valuations of situations, i.e. discernments of their practically relevant features. Such 'situational understandings' provide descriptions of situations that are conditioned by the intention to change them for the better. 'Understanding' in this sense is not a claim to know a world that exists independently of the intention to change it. For Macmurray, it claims knowledge of the world 'as a system of possibilities of action'. As such, its development involves an increasing particularization of action possibilities in a given situation. The greater the particularization of descriptions of situations the more they take the complexities of making wise judgements and decisions into account. Yet at the same time, I would contend, such 'situational understandings' can also be of universal significance by throwing light on possibilities for action in other situations. Cannot such understandings be meaningfully described as 'theories'?

The practically relevant features of particular action contexts will tend to repeat themselves across contexts. Indeed one can argue that the discernment of practically relevant similarities across contexts is enhanced by more concrete, particularizing, descriptions of action possibilities in each. Hence, when communities of teacher researchers develop such descriptions in disciplined conversation with each other they will increasingly experience an 'overlapping consensus' about action possibilities, and with it a capacity for co-ordinating the development and testing of action-hypotheses across their classrooms. Such a process is what constitutes rigour in action research rather than any adherence to methodological dogma. As Rorty argues 'rigour' is something 'you can have only after entering into an agreement with some other people to subordinate your imagination to their consensus' (1998: 339).

Educational action research 'findings' will take the form of 'universal rules of thumb', which I would regard as elements in a theory of education. However, these rules are never fixed and unchanging, since their applicability to new and changing circumstances will need to be continuously tested. A theory of education is perhaps best depicted as a provisional summary of the common features of good practice across a given range of contexts.

It has been my experience that educational action research, which involves teachers sharing and developing their practical insights into the problems and dilemmas of realizing their educational values in concrete teaching situations, together with their judgements about how these are best resolved, can yield useful summaries of the universal significance of insights and judgements to guide further reflection and action. The diagnostic and action hypotheses developed in the contexts of the Humanities Curriculum and Ford Teaching Projects in the UK can be regarded as having this form and function (see Elliott, 1976: 14–17 and 1983: 114–16). They constitute both a *tradition of understanding* of educational action and a *theory of educational change*. It is clear that Nussbaum regards the development of universal rules to guide ethically committed action in particular situations as dependent upon the practical discourse of a community of inquiry rather than individuals acting and reflecting in isolation from each other. This is quite consistent with Aristotle's notion of *phronesis*. It is a form of reasoning that embodies a democratic and foundationless rationality (see Elliott, 2006), that is free from the constraints of methodology. Here we can discern a continuity of thinking about the nature of social inquiry, between the neo-Aristotelian philosophers like Nussbaum and MacIntyre and the philosophical pragmatism of Dewey, Rorty and Amartya Sen. From the latter standpoint all inquiry is practical and discursive, differing only with respect to the kinds of practical interests it serves. That which serves the interests of morally committed action in the form of *phronesis* is no less scientific than that which serves the interests of technical rationality. Moreover, from the standpoint of philosophical pragmatism, a practical social science may need to unify and harmonize instrumental and non-instrumental reasoning – *techne* and *phronesis* – within *a* single process of inquiry shaped by a discursive and democratic rationality that protects the integrity of each.

The work on social choice by the philosopher and economist, Amartya Sen, provides an interesting account of such a process. Sen (2002: 39–42), points out that a principle of instrumental reasoning couched in terms of the maximization of utility leaves no space for the rational scrutiny of goals and values. Not all our values, he contends, are goals. Some may rule out the pursuit of certain kinds of goals or at least impose restrictions on the means we adopt to bring them about. Hence our choice of behaviour may be based on reasons that qualify the maximization of utility principle. Sen argues that we need a broader conception of practical rationality that reaches beyond the maximization principle to include a 'critical scrutiny of the objectives and values that underlie any maximizing behaviour' and an acknowledgement of values that constitute '*self-imposed* constraints' on that behaviour. He casts such a conception in terms of a democratic process of *rational scrutiny* that is based on discussion of the reasons people might offer for their choice of actions. Such reasons will be various. They will include non-instrumental as well as instrumental considerations, and considerations of ends as well as the means of bringing them about. Sen (2002: 287), argues along similar lines to Rorty, that values are rationally established and validated through free and open discussion alone, and like Rorty, claims that rationality in the sphere of values does not require some set of Kantian-like transcendental rational principles for ordering people's values. He also shares with Rorty the view that the process of reasoning about values through discussion is a disciplined affair, and it is discussion itself that provides it rather than 'a favored formula, or an essentialist doctrine' (p. 46).

CONCLUDING REMARKS

What frankly disappoints me is the extent to which educational action research, originally conceived as a practical philosophy, has become distorted by the methodological discourse of the social sciences and sucked into the battle between the qualitative and quantitative paradigms. This has meant that published accounts of action research have tended to be dominated by descriptions of, and justifications for, the method of research as opposed to the representation and discussion of the understandings and insights it generated. Any vision of educational values and how they might be realized in action is often missing from such accounts and with it the capacity of action research to represent its findings in a form that might sustain *educational praxis* within the teaching profession. Such a capacity depends not on any particular method-ological standpoint but rather on a commitment to creating space for a community of inquirers to engage in a good conversation with each other about how best to express their educational values in action. Of course, this goes against the grain of an educa-tional system that has increasingly been shaped by the logic of technical rationality in which the ends of education are no longer treated as open to discussion and inquiry.

In order to reclaim their practice as a sphere of ethically informed action, teach-ers will need the support of teacher educators in higher education. The great chal-lenge for teacher educators is to integrate their dual roles as educational practitioners and researchers. Rather than seeing themselves as 'researchers on edu-cation' who find opportunities to disseminate the findings and methods of this kind of research through their teaching, teacher educators will need to see their teaching role as one of enabling teachers to develop and test a common stock of shared understandings about how to realize worthwhile educational ends. This will also involve them undertaking collaborative research with teachers into finding solutions to some of the most persistent problems the latter face in their classrooms and schools. The complexity of these problems is such that they defy many of the solu-tions proposed by conventional research carried out in accordance with the strictest methodological canons. Such research may secure publication in prestigious aca-demic journals, but is unlikely to support teachers to make worthwhile educational change in their classrooms and schools.

REFERENCES

Carr, W. (2004) 'Philosophy and education', *Journal of Philosophy of Education*, 38 (1).
—— (2006) 'Philosophy, methodology and action research', *Journal of Philosophy of Education*, 40 (4): 421–35.
Dewey, J. (1974) 'Science as subject-matter and as method', in R.D. Archambault (ed.), *John Dewey on Education: Selected Writings*. Chicago and London: University of Chicago Press.
Dunne, J. (2005) 'An intricate fabric: understanding the rationality of practice', *Pedagogy, Culture, and Society*, 13 (3).
Elliott, J. (1976) 'Developing hypotheses about classrooms from teachers' practical constructs: An account of the work of the Ford teaching project', *Interchange*, 7 (2). Republished in *Reflecting Where The Action Is: The Selected Works of John Elliott*, 2006, Ch. 2. Abingdon, Oxon: Routledge.
—— (1978) 'Classroom research: Science or commonsense', in R McAleese and D Hamilton (eds), *Understanding Classroom Life*. Windsor: NFER Publishing Company.
—— (1983) 'A curriculum for the study of human affairs: the contribution of Lawrence Stenhouse', *J. Curriculum Studies*, 15 (2). Republished in *Reflecting Where The Action Is: The Selected Works of John Elliott* 2006, Ch. 1. Abingdon, Oxon: Routledge.

——(2006) 'Educational research as a form of democratic rationality', *Journal of Philosophy of Education*, 40 (2).

Gadamer, H-G (1975) *Truth and Method.* London: Sheed & Ward.

MacIntyre, A. (1990) *Three Rival Versions of Moral Inquiry.* London: Duckworth.

Macmurray, J. (1957) *The Self as Agent.* London: Faber & Faber, pp. 198–202.

Nussbaum, M. (1990) 'An Aristotelian conception of rationality,' in *Love's Knowledg*e. Oxford: Oxford University Press.

Pring, R. (1976) Knowledge and Schooling. London: Open Books.

Rorty, R. (1982) *Consequences of Pragmatism.* Minneapolis: University of Minnesota Press.

—— (1991) 'Pragmatism without method', in *Objectivity, Relativism and Truth: Philosophical Papers Volume 1.* Cambridge: Cambridge University Press.

—— (1998) 'Derrida and the philosophical tradition,' in *Truth and Progress, Philosophical Papers.* Cambridge: Cambridge University Press.

—— (1999) *Philosophy and Social Hope.* London: Penguin Books.

Sen, A. (2002) *Rationality and Freedom.* Cambridge, MA: Harvard University Press (Belknap): Chs.1 and 8.

Stake, R.E. (1978) 'The case study method in social inquiry', *Educational Researcher*, 7: 5–8. Reprinted in Simons, H. (ed.) *Towards a Science of the Singular,* CARE Occasional Publications 10, pp. 64–7. (Norwich: Centre for Applied Research in Education, University of East Anglia).

Stenhouse, L. (1975) *An Introduction to Curriculum Research and Development.* London: Heinemann Educational Books.

Stenhouse, L. (1979) 'Research as a basis for teaching'. Inaugural Lecture at the University of East Anglia: Norwich. Subsequently published in Stenhouse, L. (1983) *Authority, Education and Emancipation.* London: Heinemann Educational.

3

Teacher Research as Stance

Marilyn Cochran-Smith and Susan L. Lytle

This chapter is about teacher research, a genre of practitioner inquiry that has unique potential to challenge common assumptions about knowers, knowing, and knowledge for the improvement of teaching and learning that are operating in schools in these acutely conservative times. We take practitioner inquiry as a conceptual and linguistic umbrella for an array of related educational research genres with distinctive features but also an underlying set of common assumptions. In this chapter we focus on one type of practitioner inquiry – teacher research – by exploring its theoretical and epistemological architecture and illustrating its grounding in a fundamentally dialectical relationship or stance. The current policy and political climate raises new questions about the viability of practitioner inquiry at the same time that it brings new meaning to questions that have been considered for some time. Despite the current emphasis on teaching as test preparation and learning as on-demand test performance, however, many educators and reformers still believe that deep changes in practice can only be brought about by those closest to the day-to-day work of teaching and learning. And, in fact, despite all of the forces working against it, teacher research and the larger practitioner inquiry movement are burgeoning in the United States and in many other parts of the world. We conclude by suggesting that teacher research has a distinctive potential for rethinking, resisting, and re-forming the ways we think about, and take action regarding, the arrangements and purposes of schools and schooling.

PRACTITIONER INQUIRY AS UMBRELLA

We take 'practitioner inquiry' as an umbrella for a number of its well-known versions and variants. In using practitioner inquiry as an umbrella, it is not our intention to blur the important ideological, epistemological, and historical differences that exist between them, but to identify features and assumptions that most versions share (see Cochran-Smith and Lytle, 2004).

Versions and Variants of Practitioner Inquiry

Under the umbrella of practitioner inquiry, 'action research,' which is the focus of this handbook, is commonly used to describe collaborations among school-based teachers and other educators, university-based colleagues, and sometimes parents and community activists. Their efforts center on altering curriculum, challenging common school practices, and working for social change by engaging in a continuous process of problem posing, data gathering, analysis, and action. Similar in some ways, but different in others, 'teacher research' refers to the inquiries of K-12 teachers and prospective teachers, often in collaboration with university-based colleagues and other educators. Teacher researchers work in inquiry communities to examine their own assumptions, develop local knowledge by posing questions and gathering data, and – in many versions of teacher research – work for social justice by using inquiry to insure educational opportunity, access, and equity for all students.

The term 'self-study,' is used almost exclusively to refer to inquiries at the higher education level by academics involved in the practice of teacher education, broadly construed. Often drawing on biographical, autobiographical, and narrative forms of data collection and analysis, self-study works from the postmodernist assumption that it is never possible to divorce the 'self' from either the research process or educational practice. Closely related to self-study are 'narrative inquiry' and/or 'autobiographical inquiry,' terms that are generally used to refer to the idea that the narratives produced through systematic reflections by teachers and teacher educators contain knowledge within them. The assumption here is that narratives make the practitioner's knowledge explicit and convey it to others outside the immediate context of the knower.

The term 'the scholarship of teaching' was originally coined by Ernest Boyer (1990), as part of a special report on the priorities of the professoriate. Lee Shulman and colleagues built on this term. They advocate making the scholarship of teaching public, accessible to critique by others, and exchangeable in the professional community (Shulman et al., 1999). Along somewhat similar lines, a form of practitioner inquiry is also sometimes carried out by university-based researchers who take on the role of teacher in a K-12 setting in order to conduct research on the intricate complexities involved in the problems of practice.

Cross-Cutting Aspects of Practitioner Inquiry

Although there are differences in emphasis and intention as well as different historical and epistemological traditions among these various approaches to practitioner inquiry, there are also general aspects that cut across all of them. With every form of practitioner inquiry, the practitioner himself or herself simultaneously takes on the role of researcher. This duality of roles makes it possible for the classroom teacher, the school principal, the community college instructor, the university faculty member, the adult literacy program tutor, and other stakeholders in given social situations such as parents, community members, and families to participate in the inquiry process as researchers. The common assumption here is that those who work inside particular educational contexts and/or who live inside particular social situations are among those who have significant knowledge and perspectives about the situation. This challenges the idea that knowledge can be generated only by those outside a given social or educational setting and then applied inside classrooms.

Practitioner inquiry across types is built on the assumption that the relationships of knowledge and practice are complex and distinctly non-linear, and that the knowledge needed to improve practice is influenced by the contexts and relations of power that structure the daily work of teaching and learning. A third common feature of the many varieties of practitioner inquiry is that the professional context is the site for inquiry, and the problems and issues that arise from professional practice are taken as the topic or focus of study. Questions emerge from the day-to-day experiences of practice and, often, from discrepancies between what is intended and what actually occurs. The unique feature of the questions that prompt practitioners' inquiry is that they emanate from neither theory nor practice alone but from critical reflection on the intersections of the two. Thus the boundaries between inquiry and practice blur when the practitioner is a researcher and a knower and when the professional context is a site for the study of problems of practice.

Another important feature shared by many forms of practitioner inquiry is that notions of validity and generalizability are quite different from the traditional criteria of transferability and application of findings (often, the identification of causes and effects) to other populations and contexts. All of the forms of practitioner inquiry referred to above share the features of systematicity and intentionality in terms of documentation, data collection, and analysis, which are also characteristic of many other forms of research. What distinguishes practitioner inquiry from other qualitative research that relies on similar forms of data collection and analysis, however, is that the former includes systematic examination and analysis of students' learning juxtaposed to, and interwoven with, systematic examination of the practitioners' own intentions, reactions, visions, and interpretations. Finally, almost all forms of practitioner inquiry are characterized by their emphasis on making the work public and open to the critique of a larger community.

TEACHER RESEARCH: THEORETICAL AND EPISTEMOLOGICAL FRAMEWORKS

For the remainder of this chapter, we elaborate the theoretical and epistemological underpinnings of one form of practitioner inquiry – teacher research, which has been the focus of much of our joint work with each other and with teachers, teacher candidates, and other colleagues for the last 20 years. We suggest that teacher research is a theoretical hybrid in that, although it has been influenced by several major theories and intellectual movements, it is grounded fundamentally in the dialectic of inquiry and practice rather than in one particular theoretical tradition or framework.

Theoretical Traditions and Intellectual Roots

As we have suggested elsewhere (Cochran-Smith and Lytle, 1999), the current North American teacher research movement was influenced by several major theories circulated in the U.S. and the U.K. during roughly the same time period. Influential writings about language, learning and literacy were grounded in the paradigm shift in researching, teaching and assessing writing that evolved in the 1970s and 1980s (e.g., Atwell, 1987; Berthoff, 1987; Bissex and Bullock, 1987; Goswami and Stillman, 1987; Heath, 1983; Mohr and Maclean, 1987; Myers, 1985; Wells, 1986). At about the same time, writings that shared a grounding in critical and democratic social theory focused on the role of teachers in research conceptualized as a form of social change (e.g., Beyer, 1988; Carr and Kemmis, 1986; Elliot, 1985; Kemmis and McTaggart, 1988; McNiff, 1986; Stenhouse, 1983; Stenhouse in Rudduck and Hopkins, 1985). A third influence on teacher research was the work of a loosely connected group of progressive educators, committed to social responsibility and to the construction of alternative modes of understanding students' learning and teachers' development (e.g., Bussis et al., 1976; Carini, 1979, 1982, 1986; Duckworth, 1987; Goodman, 1985; Perrone, 1989; Strieb, 1985; Traugh et. al., 1986). Finally, and also during the 1980s, a body of writing about teacher research rooted in an ethnographic research tradition and a multi-disciplinary understanding of language, literacy, and pedagogy began to juxtapose the possibilities of teacher research with the hegemony of an exclusively university-generated 'knowledge base' for teaching (e.g., Cochran-Smith and Lytle, 1987; Erickson, 1986; Florio-Ruane and Walsh, 1980; Lytle and Cochran-Smith, 1989).

Although these intellectual traditions were different in important ways, they were compatible with one another. Each constructed the role of teacher as knower and agent in the classroom and in larger educational contexts. They also had in common a critique of prevailing concepts of the teacher as technician, consumer, receiver, transmitter, and implementer of other people's knowledge as well as a critique of many of the prevailing social and political arrangements of schools and schooling. These agendas were shaped by teachers and teacher groups, some initiated and sustained by teachers themselves or by groups working to invent new collaborations and partnerships among teachers and university-based faculty. In this way, the North American teacher research tradition had from the beginning a distinctly grassroots character that has informed and been informed by a number of provocative intellectual approaches to educational change.

Theorizing Teacher Research: Working the Dialectic

Teacher research is informed by the intellectual traditions described above. Over the past 20 years, as university-based scholars and practitioners, we have worked with teachers, teacher candidates and many other school- and program-based practitioners, to explore teacher research as a way to rethink practice, question our own assumptions, and challenge the status quo – not only in schools but also in the university. Over time we came to use the term 'teacher research' as a kind of shorthand for a larger set of premises about: teachers/practitioners as knowers, reciprocal school-university relationships, teaching as both an intellectual and political activity, learning to teach as a process that occurs within inquiry communities and throughout the professional lifespan, schooling as deeply influenced by culture and history, and the need for parallel transformation of universities and schools. Fusing conceptual and empirical research, we have worked to theorize and take seriously the notion of teacher research and its underlying premises and to instantiate and act on those premises in our daily work. We think of these efforts collectively as 'working the dialectic.'

By 'dialectic,' we refer to the reciprocal, recursive, and symbiotic relationships of research and practice, analysis and action, inquiry and experience, theorizing and doing, conceptual and empirical scholarship, and being researchers as well as practitioners. We also mean the dialectic of generating local knowledge of practice while at the same time making that knowledge accessible and usable in other contexts and thus helping to transform it into public knowledge. When we 'work the dialectic,' there are not distinct moments when we are only theorizers or only practitioners. Rather these activities and roles are intentionally blurred. By 'working' we mean capitalizing on, learning from, and mining the dialectic as a particularly rich resource for new knowledge. Clearly this occurs when we study and theorize our practice as university-based faculty members and teacher educators. But in our teaching and program evaluation efforts, we also highlight and learn from the work of those who are engaged in teacher research. We also 'work' the dialectic by collaborating with others to develop the contexts that support the inquiries of student teachers, new and experienced school-based teachers and administrators, university-based fieldwork supervisors and teacher educators, community program-based educators, and many other educational colleagues and collaborators.

For us as university-based faculty members, working the dialectic has been an especially productive way to invent and direct teacher education and professional development initiatives and, at the same time, to theorize and analyze many aspects of those projects. Based on this work, we have theorized teacher research through a series of essays presented and published over a period of 20 years. In each of the theoretical essays we wrote about teacher research, we addressed a particular question or set of questions that had been problematic in our daily work as teachers, teacher educators, and researchers. Thus, in a very real sense, the contradictions in our own practice oriented our research just as much as did our reading of the wider literature related to teacher learning, inquiry, school and social change, and language and literacy. At the same time, the theoretical distinctions we made in our writing provided new lenses on our practice and on our interpretations of the theoretical and empirical literature. These experiences contributed to our growing discontent with the assumption that research by school-based teachers should be expected to follow the epistemological and methodological conventions developed in the university. At the same time, the theoretical frameworks we developed prompted us to formalize and rethink the kinds of inquiry opportunities available in our programs and projects.

Working the dialectic is a decidedly non-linear process – more like improvising a dance than climbing a set of stairs. As we theorized the relationships of inquiry, knowledge and practice based on critical analysis of others' work as well as systematic inquiry into our own practice, we saw many ways to reinvent practice, which prompted further nuances in our theoretical frameworks and posed new questions to analyze; these, in turn, suggested new interpretive frameworks and strategies. Over the years, working the dialectic changed our work, changed who we are, changed what we do and how we do it. In our location at research universities, it also challenged many of the formal and informal rules universities live by.

Inquiry as Stance: Teacher Research as a Way of Knowing

Below we discuss the notion of 'inquiry as stance,' a term we coined in the mid-1990s to make the point that teacher research is not simply a project or bounded activity that teachers and teacher candidates complete as part of their professional education, but rather a larger epistemological stance, or a way of knowing about teaching, learning and schooling that is neither topic- nor project-dependent. Theorized in this way, the notion of inquiry stance talks back to, and challenges, many of the assumptions that define teaching and research on teaching in the current era of acute educational accountability with its singular emphasis on test scores at the expense of other educational purposes, the resultant narrowing of the school curriculum and reduction of the roles of both teachers and students, and increased surveillance of teachers' day-to-day work.

In everyday language, 'stance' is used to describe body postures, particularly with regard to the position of the feet, as in sports or dance, and also to describe intellectual or political positions. We use the metaphor of stance to suggest both orientational and positional ideas, to carry allusions to the physical placing of the body as well as to intellectual activities and perspectives over time. Inquiry as stance is distinct from the commonly-occurring instantiation of inquiry (or action research or teacher research) as time-bounded project within a teacher education program or one of a number of effective strategies for staff development. Taking an inquiry stance means teachers and student teachers working within communities to generate local knowledge, envision and theorize their practice, and interpret and interrogate the theory and research of others. Fundamental to this notion is the idea that the work of inquiry communities is both social and political – that is, it involves making problematic the current arrangements of schooling, the ways knowledge is constructed, evaluated, and used, and teachers' individual and collective roles in bringing about change. In the remainder of this chapter, we out-line the dimensions of inquiry as stance as a theoretical construct and point to some of the significant ways it talks back to the operating assumptions of the cur-rent educational regime.

Generating Local Knowledge of Practice

In our theorizing of teacher research, we have broken with traditional formal-practical knowledge distinctions (e.g., Fenstermacher, 1994; Richardson, 1994), suggesting instead that teachers' inquiry communities generate knowledge that may be thought of as both local and public (Cochran-Smith and Lytle, 1998; Lytle and Cochran-Smith, 1992). Borrowing Geertz's (1983) term, we use 'local knowledge' to signal both a way of knowing about teaching and what teachers and communities come to know when they build knowledge collaboratively.

In the sense we mean it here, constructing local knowledge is understood as a process of building and critiquing conceptual frameworks that link action and prob-lem-posing to the immediate teaching context as well as to larger and more public social, cultural, and political issues. Implicit in this process are questions that guide practice, broadly construed: Who am I as a teacher? What am I assuming about this child, this group, this community? What sense are my students making of what's going on in the classroom? What are the implicit assumptions of the texts, tests, cur-riculum standards, and reporting mechanisms in place at my school? How do my efforts as an individual teacher connect to the efforts of the community and to larger agendas for school and social change?

These questions stand in stark contrast to the questions that are assumed to guide the work of effective teachers, from the perspective of the current account-ability regime (Cochran-Smith and Lytle, 2006). The 'Toolkit for Teachers' (U.S. Department of Education, 2004) that accompanies NCLB, for example, states that teachers are faced with three essential questions: How do I know what works? What intervention is best to support a student who lacks certain skills? How do I analyze a program's or intervention's effectiveness? (p. 31) Framed this way, the teacher's task is complicated chiefly by the array of educational inter-ventions that claim to be supported by evidence. According to NCLB and the var-ious policy tools of the current educational regime, good teachers are wise consumers of the reservoir of products for instructional decision-making created by experts in the field and certified by scientifically based research.

Inquiry Communities Across the Life Span

From the perspective of inquiry as stance, beginning and experienced teachers engage in similar intellectual work. Working together in communities, both new and more experienced teachers pose problems, identify discrepancies between theories and practices, challenge common routines, draw on the work of others for generative frameworks, and attempt to make visible much of that which is taken for granted about teaching and learning. From an inquiry stance, teachers search for significant questions as much as they engage in problem solving. They count on other teachers for alternative viewpoints on their work.

The idea of beginning and experienced teachers working together in inquiry communities talks back to the current emphasis on teacher 'expertise,' which implies certainty and state-of-the-art practice. The expert–novice distinction assumes that the expert is one who implements the formal knowledge base for teaching, which has been generated by experts outside schools, while the novice is one who learns effective practices by imitating the strategies of his or her more competent colleagues. The image of teacher as life-long learner, on the other hand, implies tentativeness and practice that is sensitive to particular and local histories, cultures, and communities. An across-the-life-span perspective on teacher development makes salient the role of communities and their intellectual projects over time and challenges the individual, in-the-head model of teacher development that highlights individual differences among teachers.

From an inquiry stance, teacher leadership and group membership look very different from what they might look like when teachers are 'trained' in workshops or staff development projects. Taking an inquiry stance on leadership means that teachers challenge the purposes and underlying assumptions of educational change efforts rather than simply helping to specify or carry out the most effective methods for predetermined ends, such as raising test scores. When inquiry is a stance on teaching, learning, and schooling, there is an activist aspect to teacher leadership. From this perspective, inquiry communities exist to make consequential changes in the lives of teachers and, as importantly, in the lives of students and in the social and intellectual climate of schools and schooling.

Critical Frameworks for Change

In teaching, the term practice has typically been used to refer to doing, acting, carrying out, and/or performing the work of the profession. From the perspective of inquiry as stance, however, teaching and teacher development are centrally about forming and re-forming frameworks for understanding practice: how students and their teachers construct the curriculum, co-mingling their experiences, cultural and linguistic resources, and interpretive frameworks; how teachers' actions are infused with multi-layered understandings of learners, culture, social issues, institutions, and materials; and, how teachers develop questions and interpretive frameworks informed by the immediate situation and multiple larger contexts.

The concept of inquiry as stance is intended to capture the nature and extent to which those who teach and learn from teaching by engaging in inquiry interpret and theorize what they are doing. More generative than regarding practice as primarily practical is the idea of 'teaching as praxis,' which emphasizes that teaching involves a dialectical relationship between critical theorizing and action

(Britzman, 1991; Freire, 1970). The key idea here is that teachers theorize all the time, negotiating between their classrooms and school life as they struggle to make their daily work connect to larger movements for equity and social change.

When inquiry is a stance on teaching, it is assumed that teacher development is inextricably linked to larger questions about the consequences and ends of education. This assumption clearly talks back to and challenges current initiatives to boost students' achievement through teachers' wholesale participation in mandated professional development based on scientifically researched or scripted curriculum and instruction. These do not substitute for grassroots change efforts, regardless of their labels. In fact, when teachers work from an inquiry stance, they often challenge fundamental practices such as tracking, teacher assignment, promotion and retention policies, testing and assessment, textbook selection, school-community-family relationships, administrator roles, personnel decisions, school safety, not to mention to raise questions about what counts as teaching and learning in classrooms. They critique and seek to alter cultures of collegiality, ways that school or program structures promote or undermine collaboration, ratios of teacher autonomy to teacher responsibility, norms of teacher evaluation, relationships among student teachers, teachers, and their university colleagues, and the ways power is exercised in teacher-to-teacher, mentor-to-teacher, and school-university partnerships.

The idea of teacher research as stance on practice is something of a paradox in these times. In very real ways, it is completely out of sync with the current emphasis on high stakes accountability and with narrow forms of evidence-based practice. At the same time, however, it offers a compelling framework for enacting change that is grounded in the everyday politics of practice. The multiple traditions that have informed teacher research have lent a kind of intellectual richness to the effort and have fostered ever-widening participation in this kind of practitioner-driven work. No matter what the policy frameworks (generally both impositional and potentially generative) in place in a particular school or district, teachers' questions arising from the daily dilemmas of practice can drive inquiries that reveal critical dimensions of what it means to be teaching and learning in these times. When teachers make the current arrangements of schooling problematic and use daily practice as critical sites of inquiry, they not only mirror the kind of curriculum that many agree is necessary for learning in this complex, global environment, but they position themselves as lifelong learners, people who interrogate and enact inventive pedagogies that address the real learning needs of particular students and that evolve over time. It is this kind of activism as teachers – who rethink, resist, and re-frame the problems of education – that marks the most engaged and productive school cultures.

REFERENCES

Atwell, N. (1987) 'Class-based writing research: Teachers learning from students', in D. Goswami and P.R. Stillman (eds), *Reclaiming the Classroom: Teacher Research as an Agency for Change.* Upper Montclair, NJ: Boynton/Cook, pp. 87–93.

Berthoff, A. (1987) 'The teacher as researcher', in D. Goswami and P.R. Stillman (eds), *Reclaiming the Classroom: Teacher Research as an Agency for Change*. Upper Montclair, NJ: Boynton/Cook, pp. 28–48,

Beyer, L. (1988) *Knowing and Acting: Inquiry Ideology and Educational Studies*. London: Falmer Press.

Bissex, G. and Bullock, R. (1987) *Seeing for Ourselves: Case Study Research by Teachers of Writing*. Portsmouth, NH: Heinemann.

Boyer, E.L. (1990) *Scholarship Reconsidered*. San Francisco, CA: Carnegie Foundation for Advancement of Teaching.

Britzman, D. (1991) *Practice Makes Practice: A Critical Study of Learning to Teach*. Albany, NY: State University of New York Press.

Bussis, A., Chittenden, E. and Amarel, M. (1976) *Beyond Surface Curriculum*. Boulder, CO: Westview.

Carini, P. (1979) *The Art of Seeing and the Visibility of the Person*. Grand Forks, ND: North Dakota Study Group on Evaluation, University of North Dakota.

Carini, P. (1982) *The School Lives of Seven Children: A Five-Year Study*. Grand Forks, ND: North Dakota Study Group.

Carini, P. (1986) *Prospect's Documentary Process*. Bennington, VT: Prospect School Center.

Carr, W. and Kemmis, S. (1986) *Becoming Critical: Education, Knowledge, and Action Research*. London: Falmer Press.

Cochran-Smith, M. and Lytle, S.L. (1987) *Research on Teaching and Teacher Research, Ethnography and Education Research* Forum. University of Pennsylvania, Philadelphia, PA.

Cochran-Smith, M. and Lytle, S.L. (1998) 'Teacher research: The question that persists', *International Journal of Leadership in Education,* 1 (1): 19–36.

Cochran-Smith, M. and Lytle, S.L. (1999). 'Relationship of knowledge and practice: Teacher learning in communities', in A. Iran-Nejad and C. Pearson (eds), *Review of Research in Education* (Vol. 24, pp. 249–306). Washington, DC: American Educational Research Association.

Cochran-Smith, M. and Lytle, S.L. (2004) 'Practitioner inquiry, knowledge, and university culture', in J. Loughran, M. Hamilton, V. LaBoskey and T. Russell (eds), *International Handbook of Self-Study of Teaching and Teacher Education Practices*. London: Kluwer, pp. 601–50.

Cochran-Smith, M. and Lytle, S.L. (2006) 'Troubling images of teaching in No Child Left Behind', *Harvard Education Review*, 76 (4): 668–97.

Duckworth, E. (1987) *The Having of Wonderful Ideas and Other Essays on Teaching and Learning*. New York, NY: Teachers College Press.

Elliot, J. (1985) 'Facilitating action research in schools: Some dilemma', in R. Burgess (ed.), *Field Methods in the Study of Education*. London: The Falmer Press.

Erickson, F. (1986) 'Qualitative methods on research on teaching', in M. Wittrock (ed.), *Handbook of Research on Teaching* (3rd edn) New York, NY: Macmillan, pp. 119–61.

Fenstermacher, G. (1994) 'The knower and the known: The nature of knowledge in research on teaching', in L. Darling-Hammond (ed.), *Review of Research in Education* (Vol. 20, pp. 3–56). Washington, DC: American Educational Research Association.

Florio-Ruane, S. and Walsh, M. (1980) 'The teacher as colleague in classroom research', in H. Trueba, G. Guthrie and K. Au (eds), *Culture in the Bilingual Classroom: Studies in Classroom Ethnography*. Rowley, MA: Newbury House.

Freire, P. (1970) *Pedagogy of the Oppressed* (M.B. Ramos, Trans.). New York, NY: Seabury Press.

Geertz, C. (1983) 'Blurred genres: The refiguration of social thought', in C. Geertz (ed.), *Local Knowledge*. New York, NY: Basic Books.

Goodman, Y. (1985) 'Kid watching: Observing in the classroom', in A. Jagger and M. Smith-Burke (eds), *Observing the Language Learner*. Newark, DE: International Reading Association.

Goswami, P. and Stillman, P. (1987) *Reclaiming the Classroom: Teacher Research as an Agency for Change*. Upper Montclair, NJ: Boynton/Cook.

Heath, S. (1983) *Ways with Words: Language, Life, and Work in Communities and Classrooms*. Cambridge, MA: Harvard University Press.

Kemmis, S. and McTaggart, R. (1988) *The Action Research Planner*. Geelong, New Zealand: Deakin University Press.

Lytle, S.L. and Cochran-Smith, M. (1989) 'Teacher research: Toward clarifying the concept', *National Writing Project Quarterly,* 11 (2): 1–3, 22–7.

Lytle, S.L. and Cochran-Smith, M. (1992) 'Teacher research as a way of knowing', *Harvard Educational Review,* 62 (4): 447–74.

McNiff, J. (1986) *Action Research: Principles and Practices*. London: Falmer Press.

Mohr, M. and MacLean, M. (1987) *Working Together: A Guide for Teacher-Researchers*. Urbana, IL: National Council of Teachers of English.

Myers, M. (1985) *The Teacher-Researcher: How to Study Writing in the Classroom*. Urbana, IL: National Council of Teachers of English.

Perrone, V. (1989) *Working Papers: Reflections on Teachers, Schools, and Communities*. New York, NY: Teachers College Press.

Richardson, V. (1994) 'Conducting research on practice', *Educational Researcher,* 23 (5): 5–10.

Rudduck, J. (1985) *Research as a Basic for Teaching: Readings from the Work of Lawrence Stenhouse*. London: Heinemann.

Shulman, L., Lieberman, A., Hatch, T. and Lew, M. (1999) 'The Carnegie Foundation builds the scholarship of teaching with K-12 teachers and teacher educators'. *Teaching and Teacher Education: Division K Newsletter, American Educational Research Association*: 1–5.

Stenhouse, L. (1983) *Authority, Education, and Emancipation*. London: Heinemann Educational Books.

Strieb, L. (1985) *A (Philadelphia) Teacher's Journal: North Dakota Study Group Center for Teaching and Learning*. Grand Forks, ND: North Dakota Study Group Center for Teaching and Learning.

Traugh, C., Kanevsky, R., Martin, A., Seletzky, A., Woolf, K. and Strieb, L. (1986) *Speaking Out: Teachers on Teaching*. Grand Forks, ND: University of North Dakota.

U.S. Department of Education. (2004) *No Child Left Behind: A Toolkit for Teachers*. Washington, DC: U.S. Department of Education, Office of the Deputy Secretary.

Wells, G. (1986) *The Meaning Makers. Children Learning Language and Using Language to Learn*. Portsmith, NH: Heinemann.

4

Dialogic Inquiry as Collaborative Action Research

Gordon Wells

About a quarter of a century ago I had a very salutary experience that changed my approach to research in schools and classrooms. At that time, I had newly arrived at the Ontario Institute for Studies in Education (now OISE/University of Toronto) and was just starting the second year of a longitudinal study; we were following 72 children from different ethnolinguistic backgrounds in order to investigate factors that might be responsible for these groups' differential educational success. At the end of the first year the children moved up a grade and we had to secure the cooperation of a new group of teachers into whose classes these children would be entering in the following year. In all but one case, the new teachers were willing to have us make observations in their classrooms. But one grade three teacher absolutely refused. Immediately I went to talk with her.

Firm in her refusal, this teacher gave the following explanation. Two years earlier she had attended a conference in Toronto at which I had been a guest speaker. Still excited about the longitudinal study I had just completed in England, where I and my colleagues had followed a representative sample of 32 children from 15 months to the age of 10, audio and video recording them in their homes and classrooms (Wells, 1986), I had played short extracts from some of the recordings and offered my comments on the opportunities for learning that each provided. About one particular teacher-whole class discussion I had been rather critical, pointing out how the teacher had engaged her grade one children in an extended episode of 'guess what's in teacher's mind'.

'You're not going to do that to me', she insisted. And as I listened to her, I knew she was right. The stance I had taken in the past was both unethical and unproductive. In effect, I had been exploiting my 'subjects', not only giving little in return for their participation but also criticizing them in public when they had no chance to put their own points of view. But my approach to research was also mis-guided as a way of trying to understand learning and teaching. Classrooms are communities that, over time, develop ways of acting and interacting that cannot be understood by an outsider who pays occasional visits to collect and take away for analysis limited stretches of observational data, extracted from their organic historical context.

IMPROVING THE QUALITY OF EDUCATION

It seems incontrovertible that the purpose of research in the field of education is to improve the quality of education that students receive. But how often does research actually improve the educational experiences of those who take part in the research? Clearly, there are many ways in which this goal can be served, including research on equitable provision of resources, modes of governance, and procedures for account-ability. However, since research on these issues is usually conducted on a very large scale, often involving statistical analysis of aggregated data from many schools or school districts, the beneficial results are likely to be diffused and spread over a long period of time. On the other hand, much research is more local in nature for, within whatever organizational framework students receive their education, it is widely rec-ognized that the quality of their experience is dependent on 'the company they keep and what they do and say together'.[1] A considerable amount of research, therefore, focuses on what happens in particular schools and classrooms and, to this end, teach-ers and students are asked to allow outsiders to observe, question and interview them and make recordings of these events.

The Ethics of Classroom Research

To ensure that those who are studied in school- and classroom-based research are not harmed as a result of their participation, Institutional Review Boards require that participants should be informed about the purpose of the research and about what their participation will involve; they are then asked to give their 'informed consent'. In practice, this simply means that they are guaranteed that any evalua-tions based on the data collected will be made in such a way that those evaluated cannot be identified, and where particular events or quotations are cited, real names will be replaced by pseudonyms.

From an ethical point of view, these practices are certainly necessary. But are they sufficient? If the purpose of such research is to lead to improvements in the quality of educational experiences, should not those who agree to be studied receive some benefit from their participation? Should they not at least have the right to know what conclusions the researchers drew from their analysis of the data and the opportunity to discuss how they might act on the basis of the find-ings? Indeed, should not benefiting the participants ideally be built into the over-all design as one of the aims of the research? (see Zeni, 2000).

Understanding What Happens in Classrooms

Researchers who make only occasional visits to classrooms for scheduled observations gain a very limited understanding of what they observe. While a lesson may appear to have a clear and specific goal that is (or is not) accomplished within the allotted time, no lesson is self-contained for those who participate in it, as is illustrated by the following anecdote.

Working on a curriculum project in England with Stenhouse in the 1970s, Walker and Adelman (1976) were making a classroom observation one day when a student uttered the word 'strawberries' and the whole class fell apart in laughter. The researchers, extremely puzzled by this event, decided to ask the teacher why the mention of strawberries had such an effect. Apparently, in a previous lesson, strawberries had been the subject of a well-remembered heated debate that, this student was suggesting, was relevant to the current situation.

What is made clear by this anecdote is that, as a teacher and a class of students spend time together, they construct shared knowledge, not only about the content of the curriculum but also about how they interpreted and acted upon that content. Each class thus has its own unique history, which provides a resource that participants draw on in successive lessons. Green and Dixon (1993) go so far as to argue that, as a result, in any classroom, 'what counts as knowledge' is what has been negotiated over the course of the time spent with their particular teacher. This strongly suggests that it is necessary to make regular visits over a considerable period of time to any classroom if one wants to gain a deep understanding of what happens in a particular lesson.

But simply making observations is still not sufficient. In order to win the trust and active collaboration of teacher and students, it is necessary to be an active participant oneself, joining in activities and treating students and teacher as experts about their own learning and teaching. This was what had been missing from my longitudinal study in Bristol; because I attempted to be a 'fly on the wall', observing but not participating, I never got to know the classrooms I observed from the perspectives of those I was observing. This limited the extent of my understanding of what was happening and put me at risk of misinterpreting the reasons for the behaviors that I observed. What I came to realize, therefore, was that, for a more complete understanding, one needs to become to some significant extent a participating member of the classroom community.

BECOMING A COLLABORATIVE ACTION RESEARCHER

It was with these ideas in mind that I decided to abandon my initial stance and to embark on collaborative action research. As I found, however, changing one's role as a researcher in mid-stream is not a simple matter. In the first place, teachers have little experience of collaboration across the school–university divide and many assumed that, despite what I said, I was still intent on evaluating what I observed. One step I took in an attempt to dispel this perception was to adopt the practice of giving copies of the videorecorded observations I had made to the teachers concerned. Then, when they had had a chance to watch them, we met together to view whichever extracts they wished to discuss. This often led to insights on both our parts about the dynamics of particular events and also to a recognition on the part of the teachers of ways in which they might try to improve an aspect of their practice. Reporting teachers' – as opposed to my – evaluations about learning and teaching in their own classrooms proved to be much more effective, for not only did I avoid the risk of antagonizing my audience by engaging in 'teacher bashing', but hearing about how colleagues had taken upon themselves to research their own teaching in order to improve it inspired others to do the same.

Not all the teacher participants in the study of children from diverse ethnolinguistic backgrounds referred to above took up the invitation to collaborate in this way. Nevertheless, by the end of the second year, some half dozen were enthusiastically conducting research in their own classrooms and sharing what they discovered with their colleagues. A forthcoming meeting in Toronto of the International Reading Association led to the further step of planning to offer a jointly prepared symposium on the importance of classroom inquiry.

The great insight we achieved together in this process was the close relationship that exists between teacher research and the adoption of an inquiry approach to curriculum. This was particularly well illustrated by an investigation of the value of revision that Ann Maher, a third grade teacher, conducted in her classroom. She herself started with an inquiry into how she could encourage her students to work on revising their written texts. However, it was during a unit on 'living creatures' she was teaching that the connection between her and her children's investigations became clear.

For this unit, she planned to include two forms of investigation. In the first, the children were to spend some days closely observing one of the assortment of living creatures – newts, crickets, a white rat, a Mexican land crab among others – that she had assembled. Believing that close observation of any of these creatures would awaken the children's interest, she had them pick straws to determine which they would study. Lucy, a Portuguese Canadian child, found herself assigned to the mealy worms. 'Yuk', she said. 'I hate mealy worms'. However, within a few days she had revised her initial opinion. See Figure 4.1 for what she wrote in her journal, and see Figure 4.2 for her witty accompanying illustration.

For the second investigation, the children were allowed to choose what living creature they would research. Some had difficulty in making up their mind so, in a whole class meeting, Maher decided to address this issue by asking them about their writing. 'What was most important in choosing what to write about?', she asked. After various suggestions, she insisted, 'You must care about your topic'. She then went on to remind them about the importance of revising, not only their writing, but also what they chose to investigate; they should revise if they did not feel committed to their original idea.

Fri, Jan, 8, 1988. Frist day

Hi my name is Lucy and I live at 97 Oxford St. Today at school we got assigned to an animal. We have lots of animals in are class room. She gave as numbers and I was number 5. I got to be a mely worm. I said I hated mely worms. But then I said to my self maybe it will be kind of fun!

Mon Jan 11 1988

Today I fil more better about the mealy worms and I studeyed it a lot and I did have fun I had lots of fun.

Tues Jan 12 1988/ - Wed Jan 13

Today I said I wonder if I feed the mealy worms some pizza and see if they will eat it. Anyway I tink thet they are going thro a stage my techer said she has a booklet and she is going to let me read it

Figure 4.1   Entries from Lucy's Journal.

Space does not allow me to go into further detail about the interesting presentations the children made on the basis of their investigations. But the success of this unit was highly significant for both Maher and myself (Wells and Chang-Wells, 1992). From this point on, I began to emphasize the importance of teacher as well as student inquiry in the courses I taught in our M.Ed. degree for practicing teachers.

THE CASE FOR DIALOGIC INQUIRY

From my earliest research on children's oral language development (Wells, 1986), I had been concerned by the restricted and restricting quality of interaction in the classroom as compared with that experienced in the homes of all the children

Figure 4.2   The Stage the mealy Worms are going through.

we had studied. Whereas, at home, children initiated conversation as often as adults, and adults showed interest in what they had to say and helped and encouraged them to extend their ideas, in the classroom it was the teacher who decided who might talk and what might be talked about. and rarely elicited or responded to children's own ideas.

The central role of language in children's intellectual, social and emotional development is captured in Vygotsky's (1978) metaphor of working in the zone of proximal development: It is in the course of interaction that occurs during jointly undertaken activities that children encounter the concepts, skills and values of the culture in which they are growing up and, with adult assistance, gradually make them their own. As Halliday puts it, 'Language has the power to shape our consciousness; and it does so for each human child, by providing the theory that he or she uses to interpret and manipulate their environment' (1993: 107). Furthermore, according to Bakhtin (1986), this process necessarily involves dialogue, in which individuals 'ventriloquate' the words and ideas of others on the way to making them their own.

In sum, from their different disciplinal perspectives, all these writers argue that it is in dialogue with others that children – and adults – extend their individual 'higher mental functions' by first learning to use the language of others through 'thinking together' (Mercer, 2002) and then gradually transforming this dialogue into a resource for solo thinking in the mode that Vygotsky (1978) called 'inner speech'.

Unfortunately, however, although common at home in the preschool years, dialogue of this kind occurs very rarely in the vast majority of classrooms (Nystrand and Gamoran, 1991; Galton, Hargreaves et al., 1999). Instead, lessons are enacted according to what Tharp and Gallimore (1988) call the 'recitation script', which takes the form of a series of relatively disconnected three-part exchanges (Initiation – Response – Evaluation) concerned to ensure that students show that they can reproduce the information delivered by the teacher or the textbook. Not surprisingly, therefore, there is little opportunity for students to ask questions about what interests them or to voice their own ideas and opinions.

To my mind, therefore, if we want to improve the opportunities for learning in school we must find ways to create the conditions for the dialogue of 'thinking together' to become the dominant mode of interaction. These conditions seem to include the following:

- The topic must be of interest to the participants.
- Individual students must have relevant ideas, opinions, or experiences that they want to share.
- Others must be willing to listen attentively and critically.
- The teacher must share control and the right to evaluate with students.

One way of creating these conditions, which has been taken up in a number of recent reform efforts, was first proposed by Dewey in *Experience and Education* (1938). In order for students to engage with a topic, he argued, it must be of interest to them. But it must also be one that poses problems or raises doubts that will motivate the student to explore further. This led Dewey to place great emphasis on inquiry, both as the motivation for engaging in, and as the organizing principle for the selection of, learning activities. These, he believed, should grow out of first-hand experience and be determined largely by the students themselves, with the teacher acting more as facilitator than as director. While more recent writers in this tradition have placed less emphasis on individual choice of topic for inquiry and, following Vygotsky, more on the guiding role of the teacher, they agree with Dewey in emphasizing that the key characteristic of investigatory activities should be that they take as their object significant and often problematic features of the students' experience and environment and have as their intended outcome a growth in the students' understanding, where this is taken to mean, not simply factual knowledge, but knowledge growing out of, and oriented to, socially relevant and productive action (Cohen, McLaughlin et al., 1993).

However, rather than treating the problem of how to create these conditions in contemporary classrooms as one to be resolved by university researchers and then handed over to teachers for implementation, I believe it is ultimately more productive to tackle it through collaborative action research with a group of interested and informed teachers. How I attempted to achieve this is described below.

THE DEVELOPING INQUIRING COMMUNITIES IN EDUCATION PROJECT (DICEP)

Most of the teachers who volunteered to join DICEP had already carried out inquiries in their own classrooms as part of the M.Ed. program at the university; they had also developed some familiarity with Vygotskian ideas about the importance of talk and of providing assistance to learners in their zones of proximal development. We thus had a shared theoretical orientation and some individual experiences of classroom research. What we did not have, at least initially, was a shared idea of how to bridge the university–school divide in order to become a cohesive, collaborating group.

The problem was not simply the difference in status between the members of the group; as principal investigator, I also had the responsibility for ensuring that the objectives set out in the grant proposal were achieved to the satisfaction of the funding agency, while also ensuring that decisions on how to proceed were jointly made.[2] In the early stages, our attempts at collective planning and decision making were not always easy, and there were occasions when we had difficulty in resolving the tension between individual autonomy and maintaining a common focus. However, two actions taken early in the project were important, in more than symbolic ways, in establishing this new form of school–university collaboration. The first was the decision to have a rotating chairperson for our monthly meetings, with the agenda for each meeting being constructed by the incoming chair on the basis of proposals received from all members of the group.

The second was the choice of a new name for the project, arrived at after an extended process of discussion in meetings and via our e-mail network. The name finally chosen, *Developing Inquiring Communities in Education Project*, also served as a form of manifesto, for it made explicit our conviction that inquiry was not only relevant to learning in schools; it applied equally to university classrooms, to preservice and in-service teacher development and, most important, to the work of our own group.

What ultimately gave greatest cohesion to the group, however, was presenting at conferences and writing together. In preparing for these events, we spent time not only in selecting and interpreting data from individual investigations but also in identifying values and practices that seemed to be common to the various inquiries that individual members were carrying out. We also engaged in a common program of reading and discussion of theoretical articles and of the work of other researchers. These collaborative practices led to a special issue of the OISE journal, *Orbit,* and to the founding of *Networks, an On-line Journal for Teacher Research.* At the end of the project we also produced a book together, *Action, Talk, and Text: Learning and Teaching through Inquiry* (Wells, 2001), which included reports of a variety of individual investigations as well as an overview of the development of the project. We also regularly reviewed our ways of working together, using our project listserv for email discussion and, on two occasions, conducting semiformal interviews with all members of the group.

As they came to be defined, the overall aims of the project were twofold: to explore different approaches to creating classroom communities of inquiry; and to investigate the quality of the discourse that occurred during inquiry-oriented curricular units. Evidence pertaining to the first aim was largely descriptive and appeared in the case studies of individual investigations carried out by project members.[3] Some of these also included reflections on the growth in the authors' own understandings of the value of inquiry in promoting greater student engagement and learning.

The following example of such reflection comes from an article written by two teachers and myself following a science unit in their combined grades one and two class, in which the children had experimented with elastic-powered vehicles to answer a number of questions that arose in the course of their experiments.

As classroom teachers, we felt a large responsibility for 'covering the curriculum'. However, what we came to recognize was that we had neglected the fact that we were not alone: that covering the curriculum also required students' active collaboration. The question we then began to ask ourselves was whether we trusted the students enough to guide us in fulfilling this responsibility. Over the preceding two years, we had observed many exciting and authentic learning situations develop when students had an active role in the direction and course of study, but we had been reluctant to trust the implications of these observations. As a result of the present investigation, however, we recognized that a major shift had occurred in our understanding of our curricular responsibilities. As Mary Ann [Van Tassell] wrote:

We have come to identify that the most important thing we do in our science class is listen. We listen in order to ask questions. Because our focus has shifted to assisting students in their zpds, we are able to listen to the students and to each other. We did not know this was the shift we needed to make, nor did we anticipate it at the outset, but it was the most significant learning for us. … And, as with all learning, [it has] carried over into all other areas of our teaching.

The change in us, as teachers, was reflected in our interactions with the children and in the changed climate of the classroom. Students' questions and knowledge were as valued in the learning process as those of the teachers. Consequently, the students were supported in their efforts to make sense of their world and were motivated to take risks to further their own understandings. Because of this act of being responsive, both to the students and to each other, the knowledge constructed over the course of the unit was much deeper and more meaningful than we had anticipated. (Galbraith, Van Tassell et al., 1997, quoted in Wells, 1999: 310–11)

Barbara and Mary Ann then went on to discuss the value to them of conducting the research in a collaborative team. Indeed, one of the most commonly reported benefits of taking part in DICEP was the support and encouragement that individual members experienced. Here is how Zoe Donoahue responded in the final interview:

Having a group with whom to talk, share my findings, hear about other people's inquiries, has kept me going with my research. Writing and presenting together, as well as presenting my current work at meetings, gives me a reason to analyze and think about my data on a regular basis. Getting feedback from others, answering their questions and hearing how my thinking links with other members of the group helps me to develop ideas and gives me ideas for future inquiries. (McGlynn-Stewart, 2001: 195–96)

DEVELOPING DIALOGUE IN THE CLASSROOM

The second major aim of the project was to investigate how adopting an inquiry orientation changed the quality of classroom interaction and, in particular, whether it became more dialogic. While this was of general concern to project members, it was not the focus of any of their individual inquiries. In fact, it was only at the end of the second period of funding that we began to address this question through analysis of data. In the preceding years, videorecordings had regularly been made during the teachers' inquiries and these had been transcribed so that the teachers could use them as data to answer their own questions. About half of the recordings that they contributed to the overall database involved small groups of students at work; the remainder involved episodes of teacher–whole class interaction. In all, there were 43 of the latter, spanning grades one through eight and recorded at different points in the teachers' participation in the project.

The first analysis we carried out was based on categorizing the episodes according to the overall function of each episode in relation to the curriculum unit in which it occurred. Here what we found was that the interaction became more dialogic when the class was engaged in such activities as planning, interpreting or reviewing student inquiries. By contrast, episodes of teacher-led instruction, classroom management, and checking on what had been learned tended to be characterized by shorter sequences of talk on a particular issue and a higher proportion of evaluative responses to student contributions (Nassaji and Wells, 2000).

The second analysis divided the recorded episodes according to when they occurred in each teacher's participation in the project. By comparing 'early' with 'late' episodes, we found a number of significant changes, which can be summarized as follows:

- Over the duration of the project, there was a sustained and successful attempt to adopt an inquiry orientation to curriculum and this, in turn, led to a more negotiatory and dialogic style of interaction.
- More specifically, comparing late with early episodes, there was a decrease in the proportion of sequences initiated by a teacher question and, correlatively, a significant increase in student initiation of sequences.
- When the teacher did initiate with a question s/he was more likely to request information that opened up discussion rather than calling for known information.
- Following student answers, there was a significant increase in the frequency with which teachers provided high level evaluation, either by taking up and developing the student's contribution or by inviting the same or a different student to do so. There was also a significant increase in the frequency with which the teachers did not take up the option of giving follow-up, thereby allowing the discourse to proceed in a more dialogic style.

On the basis of these results, we concluded that an inquiry orientation to curriculum does indeed make dialogic interaction involving exploratory talk more likely to occur. We also concluded that the single most important action a teacher can take to shift the interaction from monologic to dialogic is to ask questions to which there are multiple possible answers and then to encourage the students who wish to answer to respond to, and build upon, each other's contributions (Wells and Mejía Arauz, 2006).

One particularly exciting development occurred in the very last months of the project as a result of a student's objection to the amount of time that was being spent on class discussion in his classroom. Initially taken aback by this complaint, Karen Hume, his teacher, decided to invite this student and some of his grades six and seven peers to join in a co-investigation of how to make class discussions more productive (Hume, 2001). This project was so successful and inspiring that the DICEP group successfully sought another grant from the Spencer Foundation to explore how, in their different settings, they could each find ways of including their students as co-researchers. Their findings and conclusions can be found in a special issue of *Networks* (2003).

CONCLUSION

Looking back over the past 20 years, I have no doubt that my change of stance as a researcher was for the better. Not only have I learned a great deal more about the challenges that today's teachers face, and shared in finding ways to overcome at least some of them, but, more importantly, I believe that engaging in collaborative research has enabled my research colleagues in a variety of such projects to feel empowered to act as agents of change (Wells, 1994). By becoming action researchers in their own classrooms they have been successful in developing new ways of teaching that, based on their own experiences with particular groups of learners, have significantly enriched the learning of their students and, at the same time, given them the evidence to argue for similar changes in the schools and districts in which they work. Indeed, several members of the group have moved to positions as administrators and teacher educators in which they are now able to have an even wider influence.

One thing is clear: To prepare students to be able to act agentively, effectively, and responsibly in recognizing and tackling the problems that they will undoubtedly meet in the years ahead, they need to develop these dispositions and the necessary knowledgeable skills in their formative years at school. And for this to happen, there is a need for teachers to develop the same ways of thinking and acting and to model them for their students by making their classrooms communities of dialogic inquiry. On the evidence of the DICEP experience, collaborative action research is one powerful and empowering way in which this necessary change can be brought about.

What happens in schools today will have significant consequences for our society tomorrow and, indeed, for human life on our planet. Dewey recognized this nearly a century ago when he wrote in *Democracy and Education*.

> In directing the activities of the young, society determines its own future in determining that of the young. Since the young at a given time will at some later date compose the society of that period, the latter's nature will largely turn upon the direction children's activities were given at an earlier period. (1916/1966: 41)

It is time we took his advice seriously.

NOTES

1 In these words, I have tried to encapsulate the key ideas in Vygotsky's theory of learning and development (Wells, 1999).

2 Between 1991 and 1999 the project was funded by two grants from the Spencer Foundation, the second of which recognized that, if it were to be collaborative, the research to be carried out could only be planned in detail by all the participating members. We were very grateful for their generous and understanding support of this novel request for support.

3 See Wells (ed.) 2001: 213–15 for a full list of the project's publications.

REFERENCES

Bakhtin, M.M. (1986) *Speech Genres and Other Late Essays*. Austin: University of Texas Press.

Cohen, D.K., McLaughlin, M.W. and Talbert, J.E. (eds). (1993) *Teaching for Understanding: Challenges for Policy and Practice*. San Francisco: Jossey-Bass.

Dewey, J. (1938) *Experience and Education*. New York: Collier Macmillan.

Dewey, J. (1916/1966) *Democracy and Education.* New York: The Free Press.

Galbraith, B., Van Tassell, M.A. and Wells, G. (1997) Aprendizaje y ensenanza en la zona die desarrollo proximo (Learning and teaching in the zone of proximal development). *Hacia un curriculum cultural: La vigencia de Vygotski en educacion.* A. Alvarez. Madrid, Fundacion Infancia y Aprendizaje.

Galton, M., Hargreaves, L., Comber, C., Pell, T. and Wall, D. (1999) *Inside the Primary Classroom: 20 Years on.* London: Routledge.

Green, J.L. and Dixon, C.N. (1993) 'Talking knowledge into being: Discursive and social practices in classrooms'. *Linguistics and Education,* 5 (3–4): 231–9.

Halliday, M.A.K. (1993) 'Towards a language-based theory of learning'. *Linguistics and Education,* 5: 93–116.

Hume, K. (2001) 'Co-researching with students: Exploring the value of class discussions', in *Action, Talk, and Text; Learning and Teaching Through Inquiry.* G. Wells (ed.). New York: Teachers College Press, pp. 150–70.

McGlynn-Stewart, M. (2001) 'Look how we've grown!' *Action, Talk, and Text; Learning and Teaching Through Inquiry.* G. Wells (ed.). New York, Teachers College Press, pp. 195–200.

Mercer, N. (2002) 'Developing dialogues'. *Learning for Life in the 21st Century: Sociocultural Perspectives on the Future of Education.* G. Wells and G. Claxton (eds). Oxford: Blackwell, pp. 141–53.

Nassaji, H. and Wells, G. (2000) 'What's the use of triadic dialogue? An investigation of teacher-student interaction'. *Applied Linguistics,* 21 (3): 333–63.

Networks : An on-line journal for teacher research, 6 (1) (2003) (Accessed 2 October 2007) http://journals.library.wise.edu/index.phplnetworks.

Nystrand, M. and Gamoran, A. (1991) 'Student engagement: When recitation becomes conversation'. *Effective Teaching: Current Research.* H.C. Waxman and H.J. Walberg (eds). Berkeley, CA: McCutchan Publishing Corp, pp. 257–76.

Tharp, R. and Gallimore, R. (1988) *Rousing Minds to Life.* New York: Cambridge University Press.

Vygotsky, L.S. (1978) *Mind in Society: The Development of Higher Psychological Processes.* Cambridge, MA: Harvard University Press.

Walker, R. and Adelman, C. (1976) 'Strawberries'. *Explorations in Classroom Observation.* M. Stubbs and S. Delamont (eds). London: Wiley.

Wells, G. (1986) *The Meaning Makers: Children Learning Language and Using Language to Learn.* Portsmouth, NH: Heinemann.

Wells, G. (ed.) (1994) *Changing Schools from Within: Creating Communities of Inquiry.* Toronto, Portsmouth NH: OISE Press, Heinemann.

Wells, G. (1999) *Dialogic Inquiry: Towards a Sociocultural Practice and Theory of Education.* Cambridge: Cambridge University Press.

Wells, G. (ed.) (2001) *Action, Talk, and Text: Learning and Teaching through Inquiry.* New York: Teachers College Press.

Wells, G. and Chang-Wells, G.L (1992) *Constructing Knowledge Together: Classrooms as Centers of Inquiry and Literacy.* Portsmouth, NH: Heinemann Educational Books.

Wells, G. and Mejía Arauz, R. (2006) 'Dialogue in the classroom'. *Journal of the Learning Sciences,* 15 (3): 379–428.

Zeni, J. (ed.) (2000) *Ethical Issues in Practitioner Research.* New York, Teachers College Press.

5

Action Research and the Personal Turn

Sandra Hollingsworth, Anthony Cody,
Mary Dybdahl, Leslie Turner Minarik,
Jennifer Davis-Smallwood and
Karen Manheim Teel

The authors of this chapter are six members of a 20-year action research collaborative – self-named 'The Learning to Teach Collaborative' or the 'Berkeley Group' because of our initial formation as beginning teachers/researchers at UC Berkeley. We were invited to join our friends in this Handbook because of the personal 'results' we've had while engaging in two decades of collaborative research. In reflective conversations and emails preparing for this chapter, we posed some questions to help surface the major themes that braided our work.

1   What drew us together in the beginning – and kept us meeting for 20 years?
2   Which guiding principles, if any, did we follow?
3   What counted as evidence when we engaged in everyday action research – inside and outside of the collaborative?
4   How and what did we learn from each other?
5   What kinds of transformative turns have we experienced from the praxis of participating in our regular conversations, taking what we've learned into our lives and work, and bringing our revisited experiences back to the group for reflective analyses?

Characteristic of our group's processes, we won't address the questions in sequential order, but weave them through the narratives we're co-creating. We'll begin with a historical and theoretical reflection on our group's beginning, and Sam's (or Sandra Hollingsworth's) reflections on the ways our collaborative conversations compelled her (like the others) to re-examine long-held conceptions of both teaching and research. Then Leslie, Mary, Karen, Jennifer and Anthony will speak to how our conversational analyses played out in both formal and informal action research projects in their classrooms. Along the way, we'll integrate the personal, political and professional turns in our lives that this conversational journey encouraged. We'll close by highlighting the major themes that recurred through the years.

TEACHING AND LEARNING ACTION RESEARCH

Sam: My first academic job was at UC Berkeley. My first course was called 'Action Research' (AR). I hadn't heard of the concept in grad school, so I read everything I could starting with Lawrence Stenhouse (1975). Stenhouse's traditional research approach in a collaborative setting made good sense to me, given my cognitive psychology background.

That first AR class in 1986 had four international students. They developed rather formulaic action research proposals to take back to their countries and study education. They didn't learn much in that course and neither did I.

The last AR course I taught at Berkeley in 1991 was much different. I had gone through a sea change in the way I viewed research, learning, and living.[1] Here's how it happened. Along with the AR class, I also taught literacy to a K-12 cohort of student teachers – including four co-authors of this chapter. With the help of doctoral student Marsha, I studied the impact of my teaching on students' learning. Marsha observed my literacy classes, and then met with the students during the year-long course to find out what they were learning. We didn't discuss what she found until she gave me a paper reporting her study at the end of the year. I wasn't worried. I was an accomplished scholar and public school teacher of literacy, even though I was a beginning teacher at Berkeley. I knew I'd taught well.

Marsha wrote that my students didn't learn much at all about literacy. Their attention was focused on the immediate needs of the classroom management, exploring the political landscape, and trying to have a life beyond school. I was shocked. I wondered why they had learned so little of what I taught them. So I invited 12 of them, along with doctoral research assistant Karen and some of her peers, to engage in a collaborative conversation with me after they graduated and began their first years of teaching. After a year or so, the group size settled at six.

A COMMON PASSION

We wondered why the others didn't stay with us. We thought perhaps they were uncomfortable with our topics. The 'core group' was dedicated to and focused on teaching for social justice. We were very clear about the role school played in the disenfranchisement of people who happened to be poor. We knew that we could predict student achievement by zip code. We envisioned a different possibility and wanted to explore it through AR.

AND THEN THERE'S 'THE FOOD'

As we all know, great conversations and intellectual work need sustenance. As we talked we enjoyed Karen's salads, Leslie's soups, Anthony's pies and cookies, Mary's and Sam's entrées, Jennifer's ice cream, and California wine. Sitting over those pot-luck dinners once a month and free from the constraints of university course/evaluation systems, we began to do collaborative action research studies on topics we really wanted to learn: the inequities in urban school districts, the effects of poverty on learning, the false authority of high stakes testing. It was only at the end of their first year of teaching that these teachers felt the need to learn to teach reading.

THE POLITICAL JOURNEY

Sam continues: Politically, the move to the conversational format for support and research involved a shift in power from my previous role as these teachers' course instructor. I had to change my interactions so that I was no longer telling teachers what I knew (as the group's 'expert' on the topic of reading instruction) and checking to see if they learned it, to a process of working with them as a co-learner through non-evaluative conversation. To accomplish that shift, I had to get still and listen; I also had to struggle publicly with what I was learning. Our change in relationship now required that I look at changes in my own learning as a researcher and a teacher educator as equally important in determining the success of *teachers'* knowledge transformations (see Hollingsworth, 1992).

We found it was not only *knowing* about teaching and learning that led both to our transformational turns as teachers and individuals, but also our *enacted* and successful teaching of literacy to both children and adolescents. To accomplish such success, we had to go beyond traditional assessments of students' reading. We had to tackle underlying political issues even as we selected our curriculum and our evaluation modes. The action research stories we lived came from continuous questioning into the process of our actions as literacy instructors dedicated to educate for a more equitable society.

Mary told us about her action research project on fourth grade literacy comprehension in her poverty-laden classroom: I began to measure comprehension by looking to see if they were able to move from the topic of Rosa Parks into our own lives. Are they able to see the significance of political activity? Are they able to see the power of the individual in the bigger picture? Are they able to see how important cooperation is in something like the Montgomery bus boycott, so that children can see that's a skill, that's not just a school skill, but it's a life skill? Those are all ways that I would measure whether or not we were successful. (For more on this story, see Hollingsworth, et al., 1994.)

CONVERSATIONS IN A FEMINIST KEY

From Sam's perspective, the approach we developed to both facilitate and learn from collaborative conversation is but *one example* of feminist research – in which the impact of the method affects everyone involved. As summarized from a classic piece by Sandra Harding (1987), feminist inquiries ask questions that lead to changes in oppressive situations – usually those of women, but also applicable to men and children in underpowered life roles. The context of this research site, beginning teachers' worlds, encompassed the feature of 'women's experiences' in the broader sense.

Although we never all agreed that feminist theory could explain our interactions, Anthony summed up what we all did agree on. 'We shared a sense of dedication to social justice and the well-being of our students – and ourselves' (emailed comment on an earlier draft of this chapter, July 15, 2007). Leslie explained how our continuous conversation played out in her life as an educator: I have often said that I found my voice as a result of participating in this group. I was committed to teaching in the inner city. I was committed to being an advocate for students. But I see now that the system, in my experience, was and is set up to silence teachers. They are referred to as professionals, responsible for outcomes, but rarely listened to when they share their knowledge of ways to create better student learning and school environments. For many years I was able to be the advocate I wanted to be, to be the critical voice for school improvement. That happened because everyone in our AR group had the same commitment and supported me as I voiced concerns loudly to my school and my district.

Jennifer reported to us that the validation after validation that she felt from this group made her self-perceptions of her strengths as a teacher and person real: Our group reminds me of my son Asher's play group. I could see that the kids in the group developed at different rates – and Asher was more developed in some tasks and less in others. I knew my kid was great without the playgroup input, but seeing him in the playgroup and knowing that the other moms thought he was great too helped me have a more realistic perspective of his greatness. In a similar way, this group has had an incredible impact on each of us because we've all been validated in our different stages. It's OK that we're different in the tasks we can do. Like, I don't write – but I teach! and it's OK. What we each bring to the conversations and the respect that we have for each other makes us safe to express ourselves and make mistakes. Those kinds of conversations have scaffolded our thinking and given us permission to become the risk-taking practitioners that we have become (phone conversation on this chapter, Nov. 15, 2007).

RELATIONAL KNOWING

As we hope we're making clear, our sustained and deepening relationships with each other, our students and their families was the bedrock for our inquiries. We were fearless in tackling any injustice that came between the school and our students. However, in contrast with our teacher education experiences, we did not respond to issues raised by giving each other concrete solutions or 'answers', but by telling related stories (Connelly and Clandinin, 1990). In that way we both validated the importance of an issue, and heard varying practice-based analyses to incorporate into our own experiential understanding of the issues.

One of the most powerful examples came from an analysis of the inequitable power of high stakes testing. When reporting Parnessa's low standardized literacy test scores to her grandmother, Mary learned that 'success' inside and outside of school were viewed differently: The African-American grandmother brought the point home to me. She took righteous exception to the failing marks I reported for her granddaughter. She said, 'What does this say about my child – that she's a moron, she's stupid and slow? Does it say that I read to her every night? Does it say that her mother's in jail and her daddy died just last year? Does it tell you that she's getting her life together, slowly? Does it say that she's learning songs for Sunday school? Does it say she wants to be a doctor? What does this piece of paper say about my baby? I don't want it near her. She needs good things. She's had enough in her life telling her that she's no good. She doesn't need this and I won't have it. I refuse to sign a piece of paper that says my child is no good (see Hollingsworth et al., 1994: 29).

Sam: By listening to open-ended and complex verbalized analyses of the pressing problems of beginning teachers it seemed that such conversational processes could provide the scaffolding to support all of our goals – the researcher's need to study learning to teach and the beginning teachers' need for support to learn about complex classroom issues. I learned what teaching issues were raised, why they surfaced, how the teachers worked through and made sense of them – and the results of their sense-making. Consequently, I changed both my beliefs about the content and process of supporting teachers' learning, and my own pedagogical approach to teacher education courses (see Hollingsworth, et al., 1993).

To investigate the complex social processes that contributed to learning, we learned in a dynamic understanding of self in relationship to both self and others across multiple contexts. Good classical theoretical work has been done in this area, including that of Jean Clandinin and Michael Connelly (2000), Maxine Greene (1979), Arthur Jersild (1955), and Nell Noddings (1984). The heart of this work is that knowing through relationship to self and others is central to teaching the child. Maxine Greene (1979) wrote that teachers who are alienated to themselves are also alienated from their students. Good teaching requires relational knowing of self and others in changing dynamics. Relational knowing thus retains an element of selves and knowledge becoming, not 'learned and fixed'.

Mary reminded Sam of Maxine Greene's 'Shudders of identity' (1996) when she spoke at our November 15, 2007 meeting about the group support that accompanied her changes from teacher to union leader to principal.

Similar to Connelly and Clandinin's (1990) notion of personal practical knowledge – or narrative knowing, embodied in persons, embracing moral, emotional and aesthetic senses, and enacted in situations – the concept of knowing through relationship, or relational knowing, involves both the instantiation (or generation of thought) and the reflection on what is currently known in social and political settings. The narrative discourse that displays relational knowing is not the simple recall of mentally-indexed information, rather it suggests the characters' slippery representations of the world, which, kaleidoscope-like, change form as the scenes and settings change (see Nespor and Barylske, 1991). Selves who come to know in relationship enter a hermeneutic circle as conversational participants or persons whose paths through life have fallen together (Rorty, 1967). Relational knowing does not rest in contemplation but becomes clarified in action (see Hollingsworth et al., 1994).

Jennifer translated the theory of relational knowing into everyday language: Somebody in the group would be more articulate about it, but overall I'd say this group works because of how we all come together from different areas of life and education – the parts just fit. There's a word to describe it, like dynamics (that's not it) or something else, but I can't think of it (e-mailed communication, November 16, 2007).

Mary gave us an example of relational knowing from her classroom action on literacy in the Rosa Parks project: When children did not achieve the intended literacy goals, I didn't just question specific behaviors or understandings; I also investigated students' emotional relationship to the topic – and to me as teacher. Let me talk about the Rosa Parks project. Celeste had real resistance to the whole project and I speculated about that with her. I asked her whether it made her uncomfortable. She said no, she thought that Rosa Parks was boring; she was more interested in Dr. Martin Luther King. I … suggested to her perhaps that I was the one that chose the topic and that she was much more interested in choosing her own topic. She said yeah, that was it but … I doubt that because she really didn't have a replacement. And I wonder if the issues of the racial tension were such that it was hard for her. She was one of the kids who persisted in coming back to the issue of Martin Luther King's relationship with white people. It was of interest to her, it was a challenge to her, and I think she saw [resisting the study of Rosa Parks] as a challenge to me. 'Classroom resister' is an important function she plays in the classroom. I think that may have been part of it. Very complicated (Hollingsworth et al., 1994).

As it turns out, the importance of relationships in action research follows long-established traditions. Peter Reason (2005) quotes Stephen Kemmis:

> The first step in action research turns out to be central: the formation of a communicative space... and to do so in a way that will permit people to achieve mutual understanding and consensus about what to do, in the knowledge that the legitimacy of any conclusions and

decisions reached by participants will be proportional to the degree of authentic engagement of those concerned (p. 272).

Other contemporary work putting relationships at the center of action research comes from Rogers et al., (2006), Comber et al., (2001), and Moore (2005). In establishing the criteria for evaluating college students' learning about education, Mary Moore points to these outcomes:

- Relationships with self: Does education enhance critical self-awareness and character-development while it raises students' awareness of their deepest passions, values, and concerns and their relationship with a wider world?
- Relations with difference: Does education enhance knowledge, appreciation, understanding, negotiation, and even reconciliation across communities of difference? (p. 45)

It seems our attention to relational knowing puts us in good company.

INTIMACY

Sam: As our conversations continued and our trust grew, we began to interrogate even more personal and difficult issues for us: identities, loves, biases, power relations, and fears. We were developing a 'deep politic' (Gitlin, 2005) that went back into our lives and work. We were a varied group: female and male, heterosexuals, lesbians, mixed-race and Caucasian, parents or not, with varying levels of risk tolerance (depending on the day and the issue). Across three meetings in 2001, we fought each other about the racial characterization of Karen in her powerful book with Jennifer Obidah: *Because of the Kids: Facing Racial and Cultural Differences in Schools* (2001).[3] We frequently turned to Jennifer when we wanted a check-in on our own racist stances. We argued about power relations in our conversations: who speaks, who's silenced? Because we cared so intrinsically for each other, we wouldn't change a topic until the issues were articulated and received – even if it took several meetings.

Jennifer spoke to the differences in our group: The make-up of the group – how we are alike and different: our backgrounds – socioeconomic, racial, gender, family commitments, where we were raised, how we were raised, life experiences that brought us to teaching, the environments we teach/taught in (not the same as each other), probably other stuff – is key to why the group works for me. Then there's the respect for how those differences and alikenesses (like that word?) affect our teaching and our reasoning about teaching that develops over the years. Can't forget honesty in communication either (Phone conversation, Nov. 15, 2007).

Leslie summarized her thoughts: Although our goals have changed somewhat over 20 years, there have been several guiding principles that are foundational to the group. I personally think that these principles are responsible for keeping us together when our group goals and personal goals have changed, our educational roles have changed, our lives have changed, we have moved to other cities and schools, and our views about education itself have changed. As a group we have always been committed to being honest, capable of solving our own classroom problems together, and able to listen well and support each other as we've traveled through difficult personal and professional situations. Most importantly we have cared about each other, indicating a high level of trust that was critical to sustaining our 20-year relationship. Therefore, we could correct, question and push each other on uncomfortable issues while always feeling cared-for. The results of our learning were cast as powerful narratives that we lived together and differently. (Emailed communication, July 15, 2007).

Jennifer: This group has become an integral part of who each of us is – it's hard to articulate, but we have internalized the convictions and hopes and dreams of the group. (Phone conference discussing the chapter, Nov. 15, 2007).

THE IMPORTANCE OF NARRATIVE INQUIRY

Many others have found that conversational inquiries such as ours produce narrative text (e.g. Florio-Ruane, 1997; Clandinin and Connelly, 2000). MaryBeth Gasman and her colleagues (2004) conducted a narrative inquiry to understand how race and class impact learning in the academy. They cite Ellis and Bochner (2000) explaining that this kind of research 'breaches the conventional separation of researcher and subjects, highlights emotional experience, and thus challenges the absence of subjectivity in traditional forms of research. … [The] narrative text refuses the impulse to abstract and explain, stressing the journey over the destination' (p. 744 in Gasman et al., p. 692).

Most of the time, our action research narratives came from conversational analyses of our current questions about our work in education: Anthony's puzzles as he moved from the classroom to the District Office in Oakland, where he was now in charge of other teachers' professional development; Mary's politically and emotionally challenging first year as a Principal in Vallejo; Karen's evolving understanding of issues of race in her Richmond middle school classroom; Sam's struggle to survive as a first year Department Chair at San José State University; Leslie's recurring political issues of a primary teacher remaining in the same district for 20 years; and Jennifer's educational questions as she moved from construction work to teaching, to promoting farming in learning, and now as an infiltrator of a home school collaborative in Northern California. We didn't usually speak about, write or finalize the 'results' of our collaborative action research inquiries – we lived them. And in living those experiences, then bringing them back to the group, we all gained new insights into educational issues and actions.

Leslie reflected on her personal changes: This way of operating has become, over the years, the natural way I look at my classroom and my teaching practice. For example, the way in which I set my classroom up to encourage personal responsibility was a direct outgrowth of an action research project I did when the group was thinking of doing a new book. My understanding of the timing required for second grade students during creative writing was a result of having learned how to take field notes. A research project on gender discrimination in a classroom had most amazing and unexpected outcomes which caused me to make a huge change in my understanding of how my students think about their environments outside of the classroom and how I could better teach them to work with each other free of gender bias. Our action research conversations also had a profound impact on my understanding of how students learn. And the key to this process was that the issues we took on were so personal (being of real importance in my classroom at the time I was doing the research) that the lessons I learned have stayed with me for all these years (emailed communication on an earlier draft of this chapter, July 15, 2008).

PUBLIC READINGS OF OUR COLLABORATION

As we clarified and articulated our sense of power as teachers and researchers, our group decided to take professional action and reach out beyond the classroom to share our developing expertise with other audiences. Then our collaboration took the form of formal action research projects: Leslie's understanding of the role of gender on primary children's learning; Anthony's literacy-based efforts to get immigrant adolescents engaged in science; Karen's and my (Sam) learning to teach adolescents how to read their way out of poverty; Mary's quest to understand the nature of relationships in learning. None of us will ever forget Jennifer's debate with John Elliot on the language of action research at a conference in 1995.

Leslie reflected on our going public with our research: Over our years together we have done 'formal' action research that resulted in publications and presentations at conferences. In all of those cases we collected data in a variety of ways and spent many hours discussing what we did, how the research went and how we felt it changed our practice. I learned the 'tools' of action research: how to set a goal or define a problem, to take frequent and informative field notes, to set up assessments and collect data, to use taped conversations with students and be able to summarize my findings. I learned such skills from our collaborative as they were modeled by different members and as they were practiced and supported by our collaborative projects (emailed communication, July 15, 2007).

We've described our learning in many different venues (e.g., Hollingsworth, 1992; Hollingsworth et al., 1994; Hollingsworth and Dybdahl, 1995; Hollingsworth and Dybdahl, 2006; Hollingsworth et al., 1993; Hollingsworth, et al., 1992; Lock and Minarik, 1995). Sam reflected on our 'going public': For me, the presentations and publications were *essential* for my career. They weren't for most of the others (except Karen, who is now a university professor). The teachers had to take 'sick leave' to present their research at national conferences. I often worried about that – I was gaining professionally from our conversations, and they weren't – was that OK? Of course I knew (as others did), that it was the coming together to unpack and validate our changing selves that was the real reward of doing this kind of intensive work. Yet – I remained first author.

On the other hand, I now saw my role as a professor and scholar in many different ways. I stopped evaluating my students' learning (I turned that responsibility over to them.) I moved far away from psychologically based research. My new form of 'research' where I reflected on my own personal learnings along with others in the study – earned me the critique of 'navel gazing' at one professional conference. Yes, it hurt, but I had a conversational action research space where I could work it out and decide what action needed taking. In this case it was anticipating such reactions and learning how to express myself more powerfully.

SO WHAT?

So, we've come to the end of our allotted page length and our story. What was the 'outcome' of our 20 years together? Well, you've probably already determined that we didn't change public education in the direction of social justice. Topics raised at our meeting to discuss this chapter on Nov. 15, 2007 revealed our disappointment and anger at the educational system, but validation in our personal turns during our work together.

Leslie: The current oppressive accountability movement stands as a solid barrier to creating more equitable schools. When it's time, I'll leave the classroom being the teacher I wanted to be, not the way the system wanted me to become.

Anthony: We changed our classrooms and our roles, but that was not enough.

Mary: It's exhausting and aggravating work, but personally transforming because of this group.

Karen: There's something amazing about how deeply this group can go.

In fact, our 20-year collaboration did help all of us and many other teachers and students see schooling, learning and themselves in different perspectives. We have citations, letters and verbal feedback that strongly support that point. In summary, our collective action research was based on principles of education for social justice, and involved learning to teach through the support of on-going conversations, a passionate belief in ourselves and our students as knowledge creators and inquirers, a willingness to create eclectic approaches to teaching and action research characterized by relational integrity, and a propensity to look critically at both our students and ourselves in relationship to evaluate the results. We also hope, in some ephemeral way, that we've shaped the way others think about the importance of the personal turn in action research.

NOTES

1 This play on words refers to Rorty (1967) writing on the linguistic turn.

2 Karen was a member of that final class. In response to this chapter, she explained she'd rather refer to our work as Teacher Research rather than Action Research. 'Teacher Research is, of course,

specifically about educators investigating their own practice and then acting on their findings in an ongoing, cyclical way. That is the process you taught us in graduate school which empowered me so much and transformed my thinking about teaching'.

3 That was only one of Karen's many books. Her new one is forthcoming from Teacher's College Press: *Building Racial and Cultural Competence in the Classroom: Strategies From Urban Educators.*

REFERENCES

Clandinin, D.J. and Connelly, F.M. (2000) *Narrative Inquiry: Experience and Story in Qualitative Research.* San Francisco: Jossey-Bass.

Comber, B., Thomson, P. and Wells, M. (2001) 'Critical literacy finds a "place": Writing and social action in a low-income Australian grade *2/3* classroom', *The Elementary School Journal*, 101 (4): 451–64.

Connelly, F.M. and Clandinin, D.J. (1990) 'Stories of experience and narrative inquiry', *Educational Researcher,* 19 (5): 2–14.

Florio-Ruane, S. (1997) 'To tell a story: Reinventing narratives of culture, identity, and education', *Anthropology and Education Quarterly*, 28 (2): 152–62.

Gasman, M., Gerstl-Pepin, C., Thompkins, S.A., Rasheed, L and Hathaway, K. (2004) 'Negotiating power, developing trust: Transgressing race and status in the Academy', *Teachers College Record,* 106 (4): 689–715.

Gitlin, A. (2005) 'Inquiry, imagination, and the search for a deep politic', *Educational* Researcher, 34 (3): 15–24.

Greene, M. (1979) 'Teaching as personal reality', in A. Lieberman and L. Miller (eds), *New Perspectives for Staff* Development. New York: Teachers College Press.

Green, M. (1996) '*Shudders of identity'.* Paper prepared for a conference on Research on Women and Education, San José, CA.

Harding, Sandra (1987) *Feminism and Methodology.* Bloomington, IN: Indiana University Press.

Hollingsworth, S. (1992) 'Learning to teach through collaborative conversation: A feminist approach', *American Educational Research Journal,* 29 (2): 373–404.

Hollingsworth, S. and Dybdahl, M. (1995) 'The power of friendship groups: Teacher research as a critical literacy project for urban students', in J.E. Brophy (ed.), *Advances in Research on Teaching*, Vol. 5. JAI Press, Inc, pp. 167–93.

Hollingsworth, S. and Dybdahl, M. (2006) 'Talking to learn: The critical role of conversation in narrative inquiry' in J. Clandinin (ed.), *Handbook of Narrative Inquiry: Mapping a Methodology.* Thousand Oaks, CA: Sage.

Hollingsworth, S., Dybdahl, M. and Minarik, L. (1993) 'By chart and chance and passion: Learning to teach through relational knowing', *Curriculum Inquiry*, 23 (1): 5–36.

Hollingsworth, S., Teel, K. and Minarik, L. (1992) 'Listening for Aaron: A beginning teacher's story about literacy instruction in an urban classroom', *Journal of Teacher Education,* 43(2): 116–27.

Hollingsworth, S., Cody, A., Dybdahl, M., Minarik, L T., Smallwood, J. and Teel, K.M. (1994) *Teacher Research and Urban Literacy Education: Lessons and Conversations in a Feminist Key.* New York: Teachers College Press.

Lock, R.S. and Minarik, L.T. (1995) 'Gender equity in an elementary classroom: The power of praxis in action research', in C. Marshall (ed.), *Feminist Critical Policy analysis: Dismantling the Master's House.* London: Falmer Press.

Moore, M.E.M. (2005) 'The relational power of education: The immeasurability of knowledge, value and meaning', *Interchange*, 36 (1–2): 23–48.

Nespor, J. and Barylske, J. (1991) 'Narrative discourse and teacher knowledge', *American Educational Research Journal*, 28 (4): 805–23.

Noddings, N. (1984) *Caring: A Feminine Approach to Ethics and Moral Education.* Berkeley, CA: University of California Press.

Obidah, J.E. and Teel, K.M. (2001) *Because of the Kids: Facing Racial and Cultural Differences in Schools.* New York: Teachers College Press.

Reason, P. (2004) 'Critical design ethnography as action research' *Anthropology and Education Quarterly*, 35 (2): 269–76.

Rogers, D., Bolick, C.M., Anderson, A., Gordon, E., Manfra, M.M. and Yow, J. (2006) '"It's about the kids": Transforming teacher–student relationships through action research', *The Clearing House*, 80 (5): 217–221.

Rorty, R.M. (ed.) (1967) *The Linguistic* turn: *Essays in Philosophical Method.* Chicago: University of Chicago Press.

Stenhouse, L. (1975) *An Introduction to Curriculum Research and Development.* London: Heinemann.

6

Educational Action Research: A Critical Approach

Wilfred Carr and Stephen Kemmis

In advocating 'emancipatory action research' and in construing this as a form of 'critical educational science', our (1986) book *Becoming Critical* has often been viewed by the action research community as offering a 'political' approach to action research as opposed to those other methodological perspectives which focus more on the 'personal' and 'professional' development of educational practitioners. In this chapter, we will take the opportunity to expose and challenge a key assumption underlying this way of understanding emancipatory action research: the assumption that it is either possible or desirable for educational action research to be anything other than 'political'. In doing this, we will argue that education cannot be extracted from politics for the simple reason that, to paraphrase Carl von Clausewitz's famous dictum about diplomacy and war (2004), education is politics conducted by other means. In elaborating and defending this argument, we will explore what we mean by 'political' first in relation to 'education' and then in relation to 'educational action'. We will then try to show how, construed as a form of critical educational science, emancipatory action research is 'political' in the sense that it is constituted by and constitutive of the values and principles of the democratic form of social life it seeks to foster and achieve. Finally, we will try to expose the weaknesses of any attempt to classify different forms of educational action research by distinguishing those focusing on 'personal' and 'professional' development from those offering a 'political' approach.

WHAT IS EDUCATION?

Any view of educational action research presupposes views of 'education', 'action' and 'research'. In *Becoming Critical*, we adopted the relatively uncontroversial view that 'education' can only be adequately understood as an intrinsic part of the general process of social reproduction: the social process by which each new generation is initiated into the language, rituals, roles, relationships and routines which its members have to learn in order to become members of a society. At one time, this process of enculturation was not differentiated from the general process of childrearing through which the young would learn what they needed to know and understand in an informal and unstructured way. But as the significance and complexity of this process for the maintenance and continuity of society became more apparent, so it gradually became more formally recognized and more culturally defined. There therefore developed a range of distinctive *social practices* ('teaching', 'lecturing', 'tutoring'), distinctive *social roles* ('teacher', 'lecturer', 'tutor') and distinctive *social institutions* ('academy', 'university', 'school', 'college') all concerned with the pursuit of the human activity we now call 'education'. Walter Feinberg (1983: 155) outlined this way of understanding 'education' in these words:

> To speak of education as social reproduction is to recognize its primary role in maintaining intergenerational continuity and in maintaining the identity of a society across generations. … At the most basic level, the study of education involves an analysis of the process whereby a society reproduces itself over time such that it can be said of one generation that it belongs to the same society as did generations long past and generations not yet born.

The social identity of a society is rarely static or fixed. It is constantly evolving in response to changing historical circumstances and new cultural conditions. Although education has a necessary and conservative tendency to reproduce existing patterns of social life, it also serves a *transformative* function by equipping rising generations with the forms of consciousness and modes of social relationships necessary to participate in changed, and hopefully better, forms of social life. Neither the reproductive nor the transformative function of education is possible without the other: both are essential features of education in any society and there is always an unavoidable tension between the two.

The fact that education plays a major role in the process of social reproduction and transformation makes questions about the kind of society it should aspire to foster and promote unavoidable. To raise such questions is necessarily to raise political questions about the nature of the 'good society': questions about the kind of society that would best enable its members to live a satisfying and worthwhile form of life. It follows from this that it is always possible, and invariably desirable, to evaluate any educational policy or practice by evaluating the assumptions it makes about what constitutes 'the good society'. It also follows that the conventional demarcation lines drawn between 'education' and 'politics' are, to say the least, suspect. As Martin Hollis (1971: 153) put it:

> Education is a process of shaping society a generation hence. Whether that shape is well chosen is a question in public moral philosophy whose other name is political theory.

To recognize that the aims, forms and contents of education are an integral part of the general process through which a society's own definition of the 'good society' is reproduced and transformed is not to regard these aims, forms and contents as passive responses to societal demands. It is simply to recognize that practical educational questions about what to teach and how to teach are always themselves a particular expression of more fundamental political questions about which existing patterns of social life ought to be reproduced or transformed. Conversely, it is also to recognize that political questions about how society ought to be changed and improved always give focus and direction to practical questions about the kind of education that a more desirable form of social life presupposes and requires. To recognize that the relationship between 'education' and 'society' is always reciprocal is also to recognize why educational questions and political questions are always indissolubly linked.

Because individuals and social groups with different views about the future shape of their society will have conflicting views about which aspects of education should be preserved and which need to be changed, educational policy and practice is always the subject of intense processes of *contestation* engendered by the diverse range of values and interests that exist in any society. It is precisely because 'education' is always the subject of this process of contestation that it is intrinsically 'political'. Since 'politics' may, in Harold Laswell's famous (1936) phrase, be defined as 'being about who gets what, when, how', educational questions (not only about the aims, forms and content of education, but also about who should answer these questions) are always part of a wider political debate between those holding different views about the nature of the 'good society'.

Different views about the nature of the 'good society' always reflect different political ideologies – that is, the historically sedimented forms of consciousness through which individuals acquire their understanding of social life, including their beliefs about the relationship between education and society. It is for this reason that the kind of education dominant in a society at any one time can always be understood as the product of past political struggles through which the relationship between education and society has continually been modified and transformed. Insofar as these political struggles have shaped the process of contestation through which education is formed, contemporary education is – like contemporary society itself – always a product of history.

WHAT IS EDUCATIONAL ACTION?

Given this understanding of the role of education in the contested process of social reproduction and transformation, it should be obvious why, in *Becoming Critical*, we rejected those 'technical' forms of *educational* action research that construed 'educational action' as a form of politically neutral action that serves as an instrumental 'means' to some externally determined political 'end'. Instead, we took the view that the 'educational action' buried in the term 'educational action research' can be more appropriately understood as a species of those distinctive human practices that Aristotle (2003) termed *praxis*: ethically informed practices in which and through which some understanding of the individual good and the good society are given practical expression. This is not to say that an educational practice is explicitly based on some theoretically vindicated political theory about the nature of 'the good life' or 'the good society'. It is simply to make the point that to act educationally is always to act on the basis of an ethical disposition to practise in accordance with some more or less tacit understanding of what constitutes 'the good life' and 'the good society'.

Aristotle called this ethical disposition *phronēsis* – which we would today translate as practical wisdom. It is revealed by educational practitioners who, in striving to achieve the 'good' view of the 'good society' intrinsic to their practice, demonstrate a capacity to see the particularities of their concrete practical situation in the light of its general educational significance and, on this basis, to make an educationally principled decision about the most appropriate action to take. But *phronēsis* is not something that can first be learned 'in theory' and then applied 'in practice'. It can only be acquired by a process of initiating novice practitioners into a largely unarticulated and usually tacit body of practical knowledge and understanding endemic to the particular social context within which educational practices are conducted. Of course, the body of practical knowledge and understanding circulating in a community of educational practitioners at any given time and within any given culture is not simply 'given'. It is always constituted by, and constitutive of, those historically bequeathed traditions of educational thought and action within which practitioners' understandings of the good of their practice develop and evolve. In other words, the 'educational action' which educational action research aspires to develop and improve has a history and it is only possible to develop or improve understanding of this action by first acknowledging the historical traditions through which this practice develops and evolves and through which any understanding of the role of education in promoting the 'good society' has been reproduced and transformed over time. Understood as a species of *praxis*, 'educational action' is thus a form of political action aimed at realizing the view of the good society to which the educational practitioner is tacitly committed.

WHAT IS EDUCATIONAL ACTION RESEARCH?

What does it mean to describe the kind of emancipatory educational action research advocated in *Becoming Critical* as 'political'? On the one hand, it may mean that it offers a view of action research that is politically partisan or doctrinaire, implying that other views of action research are somehow apolitical or non-political. On the other hand, describing it as 'political' might mean that it self-consciously promotes a particular view of the good society. The kind of emancipatory action research we advocated in *Becoming Critical* embodies the latter understanding in that it is a form of educational research that embodies a view of the good society as a democratic society committed to extending opportunities for all citizens collectively to shape the future of their society by engaging in what Amy Gutmann (1987: 39) calls 'conscious social reproduction'. Understood in this way, what distinguishes emancipatory action research from other forms of action research is the recognition that there is no single vision of the 'good society' that can be put beyond rational dispute and hence that the arguments, disagreements and processes of contestation to which such disputes give rise should not be concealed or repressed. Emancipatory action research is not 'political' because it dogmatically espouses a fixed image of the 'good society' but because it seeks to provide the conditions that make processes of contestation through which debates about 'the good society' are conducted rational and democratic: 'rational' in the sense that such debates are conducted in accordance with principles of rational discourse; 'democratic' in the sense that everyone concerned is able to participate on equal terms. Far from promoting some partisan or doctrinaire image of the good society, emancipatory action research simply seeks to create and nurture the kind of democratic culture which fosters the processes of deliberative reasoning necessary for practitioners to collectively and self-consciously participate in the processes of contestation through which their society – including its system of education – is reproduced and transformed. But as well as promoting the aims and aspirations of a 'deliberative democracy', emancipatory action research is itself embedded in, and conducted in accordance with, the democratic values and deliberative processes of the kind of 'good society' it seeks to foster and promote. As such, it is nothing other than an elaboration of the democratic form of social life of which it would itself be an integral part.

The reasons why, in *Becoming Critical*, we located this approach to action research within the critical theory of Jürgen Habermas have more recently been described by Gutmann and Thompson (2004: 9–10):

> More than any other theorist, Jürgen Habermas is responsible for reviving the idea of deliberation in our time, and giving it a more thoroughly democratic foundation. His deliberative politics is firmly grounded in the idea of popular sovereignty. The fundamental source of legitimacy is the collective judgement of the people. This is to be found not in the expression of an unmediated popular will, but in a disciplined set of practices defined by the deliberative ideal. … What makes deliberative democracy democratic is an expansive definition of who is included in the process of deliberation – an inclusive answer to the question of who has the right (and effective opportunity) to deliberate or choose the deliberators and to whom the deliberators owe their justifications. In this respect, the traditional tests of democratic inclusion, applied to deliberation itself, constitute the primary criterion of the extent to which deliberation is democratic.

In *Truth and Justification*, Habermas gave a more sustained and updated account of his view of communicative action, including the kind of communicative action we find in everyday life and in wider public spheres of argument about contemporary issues (2003: 106–7; emphases in original). He writes:

> … the rational acceptability of validity claims is ultimately based only on reasons that stand up to objections under certain exacting conditions of communication. If the process of argumentation is to live up to its meaning, communication in the form of rational discourse

must, if possible, allow all relevant information and explanations to be brought up and weighed so that the stance participants take can be intrinsically motivated solely by the revisionary power of free-floating reasons. However, if this is the intuitive meaning that we associate with argumentation in general, then we also know that a practice may not seriously count as argumentation unless it meets certain pragmatic presuppositions.

The four most important presuppositions are (a) publicity and inclusiveness: no one who could make a relevant contribution with regard to a controversial validity claim must be excluded; (b) equal rights to engage in communication: everyone must have the same opportunity to speak to the matter at hand; (c) exclusion of deception and illusion: participants have to mean what they say; and (d) absence of coercion: communication must be free of restrictions that prevent the better argument from being raised or from determining the outcome of the discussion. Presuppositions (a), (b) and (d) subject one's behaviour in argumentation to the rules of an egalitarian universalism. *With regard to moral-practical issues*, it follows from these rules that the interests and value-orientations of every affected person are equally taken into consideration. And since the participants in practical discourses are simultaneously the ones who are affected, presupposition (c) – which in *theoretical-empirical disputes* requires only a sincere and unconstrained weighing of the arguments – takes on the further significance that one remain critically alert to self-deception as well as hermeneutically open and sensitive to how others understand themselves and the world.

We would now wish to argue that the inclusive principle of deliberative democracy suggested by Gutmann and Thompson, and the 'exacting conditions of communication' and 'pragmatic presuppositions' argumentation outlined by Habermas are principles and presuppositions 'crucial for the conduct of' emancipatory action research. In short, emancipatory action research is a form of research that seeks to create the kind of communicative space within which practitioners can participate in making decisions, taking action and collaboratively inquiring into their own practices, their understandings of these practices, and the conditions under which they practice. Such inquiries are conducted not only as a private matter for each person involved, but also in a shared 'communicative space' (Kemmis and McTaggart, 2005) – that is, a space created for communicative action (Habermas, 1984, 1987a, 1987b, 1996) in which co-participants consciously strive to reach intersubjective agreement, mutual understanding and unforced consensus about what, at any particular historical moment, they ought to do in order to realize the goods of their *praxis*.

But emancipatory action research is not just 'political' because of the political function of education in the process of social reproduction and transformation. It is also 'political' in the sense that the relationships between those involved and others affected are ones in which questions of morality and justice – questions of 'who gets what, when, how' – are in the forefront of participants' considerations. There is something slightly odd in this formulation, however: it suggests that there are or might be other 'non-political' views of, or approaches to, action research in which such questions are *not* in the forefront of people's considerations. For surely no one would want to defend an approach to action research in which questions of morality and justice were set aside. It is difficult to imagine that even a very pressing technical concern about how things might be done better than they are now, or about overcoming a current crisis or obstacle, could justify *not* attending to questions of morality and justice.

Describing only *some* kinds of action research as 'political' in the sense in which we understand action research to be political seems to imply, however, that other kinds of action research can legitimately proceed without being 'political' in this sense. We are at a loss to understand how this can be so without profound contradiction – that is, without risking being morally *unjustifiable* and thus, in principle, not an appropriate activity in which people should be involved.

EDUCATIONAL ACTION RESEARCH: 'PERSONAL', 'PROFESSIONAL' OR 'POLITICAL'?

In the foregoing sections, we have argued that education is indissolubly connected to notions of the good society; that educational action must therefore be political action aimed at realizing the tacit commitments of educational practitioners to ideas about how the good society is constituted; and that emancipatory action research is political because it engenders communicative spaces appropriate for a deliberative democracy. If these arguments are sound, are the distinctions between 'personal', 'professional' and 'political' forms of action research sustainable? Perhaps they are no more than distinctions between things put in the foreground and things left in the background – differences of emphasis rather than differences in kind. Might it be the case, however, that all forms of educational action research are simultaneously 'personal' *and* 'professional' *and* 'political'? Are the distinctions between action research as *either* 'personal' *or* 'professional' *or* 'political' coherent?

In our view, it is mistaken to think that action research can be other than *'personal'*. Participation in the research by those involved in the action has been a defining feature of action research for the whole of its history. In this sense, all action research is personal, and one of its fruits is always the *self-transformation* of participants through their developing understandings achieved through enquiry, investigation or research. Similarly, at least in the case of professional practitioners investigating the practices that are part of their professional conduct (their work as teachers or medical doctors, for example), action research cannot be other than *'professional'*. Forms of action research described as 'political', therefore, must always also be 'personal' and 'professional', at least insofar as they involve professional practitioners.

On this view, 'personal' action research cannot suspend the claims of 'political' or 'professional' action research (at least insofar as professional practitioners are involved); 'professional' action research cannot suspend the claims of 'personal' and 'political' action research; and 'political' action research cannot suspend the claims of 'personal' or 'professional' action research. To make any distinction between them can only mean, surely, that we are concerning ourselves *principally* with what is 'personal' or 'professional' or 'political' about them at some particular moment and for some particular reason. While of course one may speak of one topic more than another at any moment, we are not sure that the distinction really stands as a distinction between *types* or even *emphases* of different kinds of action research. For surely what we are interested in is the activity and conduct of action research, or a particular action research initiative, not just a way of looking at it at any particular moment (from a 'personal' or 'professional' or 'political' perspective, perhaps). If the activity itself is conducted in a way that loses sight of any one of these different aspects or perspectives, then that action research or action research initiative must surely risk losing coherence and justification.

The interdependence of 'the personal', 'the professional' and 'the political' in action research can be illustrated by reference to Alasdair MacIntyre's (1983) seminal text *After Virtue*. The *personal* in action research points towards what he describes as *'the narrative unity of a human life'*; *the professional* in action research points towards what he describes in terms of *institutions*; and *the political* in action research points towards what he describes in terms of *traditions*. MacIntyre argues that virtue depends upon the interdependence of these elements. Moral *conduct*, particularly in the context of a professional practice like the practice of education, simultaneously depends upon:

(a) the existence of a *practitioner* devoted to caring for the goods internal to the practice (actually doing education and not indoctrination, for example); *and*
(b) the existence of the *institutions* that support education and through which education is made available (like formal and informal schools, libraries, universities, professional associations of educators and many other institutions); *and*
(c) the existence of *traditions* that make certain practices comprehensible and valuable *as* education (and not something else, like indoctrination).

Virtues, the unity of practitioners' lives, the existence of institutions, and the orienting power of traditions are mutually necessary and mutually constitutive of *educational practice*. To have lost the knowledge and the sense of this mutual necessity is to have lost a sense of education as a practice. According to MacIntyre, this loss is characteristic of our late modern, bureaucratized age. For him, as for other critics of modernity, it is precisely our lack of consciousness of this loss that constitutes the greatest threat not only to the tradition of the virtues but also to our communal forms of life. What we have 'forgotten' is not only virtue, but the shared forms of life within which virtue was and still may be possible – for example, a form of life in which the integrity of *education* as a practice would be protected from the standardized, bureaucratized, instrumentalized, de-professionalized and *de-valued* activities of much contemporary *schooling*.

Construed in this way, the conduct of educational action research presupposes the existence of educators (the 'personal' dimension) with a commitment to practising education. It presupposes the existence of institutions for the conduct of education (the 'professional' dimension) in which and about which practical problems and questions about the conduct of education arise, and in which professional educators deliberate about what to do about these problems and questions. And it presupposes the existence of traditions of education (the 'political' dimension) in which successive generations of educators, and contemporary practitioners of education, reach contested and evolving understandings of what education is and how educational practice is and should be conducted under different circumstances, with different kinds and levels of learners, in different places and times. Action research ceases to be *educational* action research, however, when any of these elements is missing, because in the absence of any of these elements we are no longer concerned with the living practice of education, about which practical problems may arise. In the absence of educators, or of institutions or arrangements constructed (purportedly) for education, or of the intellectual and practical resources furnished by traditions of educational thought and practice, the particular kinds of problems that we recognize as *educational* cannot arise. Without each of these elements, moreover, problems of *educational practice* cannot and do not arise. Moreover, educational problems are practical problems and, as Gauthier (1963: 1) pithily remarks, 'practical problems are problems about what to do ... their solution is only found in doing something, in action. Practical problems may be contrasted with theoretical problems, whose solution is found in knowing something'. While many different kinds of practical problems might arise in educational settings, *educational* practical problems concern what to do in the 'doing of' *education*, that is, in *educational practice*.

If *educational* action research is a form of research that is not so much 'in' and 'about' education as 'for' education, then deliberating on and responding to problems of what to do in order to make one's practice *educational* is primarily (though not solely) a matter for educators. It is a matter for each educator as a person, for educators collectively as a profession, and for the institutions established in order to care for the goods that are internal to education – namely, the development of the capacity for good in and for each person being educated, and development of the collective capacity for good in and for humankind. What this has meant in past times, and what it will mean in the future, is a contested and thus necessarily political matter. The different educational practices, institutions and traditions that have developed and evolved in education in different times and places attest to the way different settlements have been reached among the diverse groups and contending interests involved in and affected by the character, conduct and consequences of education for different people and groups.

CONCLUSION

Writing in 1974, W.J.M. MacKenzie said:

> No one studies politics, no one seeks to learn it academically, unless he or she is in some sense 'committed', and all are committed except the *ideotai* – who are not necessarily idiots, but seek another way of life, in contemplation or pure mathematics or cultivating their gardens. And the committed would say that these also are political stances ... (p. 218)

Substitute 'education' for 'politics' and add that, in an educational context, being 'committed' simply means being bound by a particular view of the role of education in creating the good society, and this quotation expresses our position concerning the relationship between politics and educational action research. In other words, nobody 'studies' or 'researches' education without taking some stance towards its political purpose and goals. Although some action researchers may, and frequently do, conduct their inquiries without articulating any particular political stance, this should not be taken to indicate that their inquiries are 'apolitical'. However apolitical some action researchers may believe their research to be, it always conveys a political commitment, even if this is unintended and even though it remains unacknowledged and undisclosed. Choosing between 'personal', 'professional' or 'political' approaches to educational action research is thus never simply an expression of a methodological preference. It also and always reflects a political commitment as well. To take, as we do in *Becoming Critical*, a 'critical' approach is deliberately to explore the relationships between these three faces of educational action research – relationships between individual and collective self-transformation, the transformation of the educational profession and educational institutions, and the transformation of the society in which one participates as an educator and a citizen – and to realise the fruits of these explorations in conduct directed towards the good for each person and the good for humankind.

REFERENCES

Aristotle (2003) *Ethics*, trans. [1953] J.A.K. Thompson, revised with notes and appendices [1976] H. Tredennick, with an introduction [1976, 2003] J. Barnes, and preface [2003] A.C. Grayling. London: The Folio Society.

Carr, W. and Kemmis, S. (1986) *Becoming Critical: Education, Knowledge and Action Research*, 2nd edn. London: Falmer.

Clausewitz, C. von (2004, originally published in German 1832) *On War*, trans. J.J. Graham, revised F.N. Maude, introduction J.W. Honig. New York: Barnes & Noble.

Feinberg, W. (1983) *Understanding Education: Towards a Reconstruction of Educational Inquiry.* Cambridge: Cambridge University Press.

Gauthier, D.P. (1963) *Practical Reasoning.* London: Oxford University Press.

Gutmann, A. (1987) *Democratic Education.* Princeton, NJ: Princeton University Press.

Gutmann, A. and Thompson, D. (2004) *Why Deliberative Democracy?* Princeton, NJ: Princeton University Press.

Habermas, J. (1984) *Theory of Communicative Action, Volume One: Reason and the Rationalization of Society*, trans. T. McCarthy. Boston: Beacon.

Habermas, J. (1987a) *The Theory of Communicative Action, Volume Two: Lifeworld and System: A Critique of Functionalist Reason*, trans. T. McCarthy. Boston: Beacon.

Habermas, J. (1987b) *The Philosophical Discourse of Modernity: Twelve lectures*, trans. F.G. Lawrence. Cambridge, MA: MIT Press.

Habermas, J. (1996) *Between Facts and Norms: Contributions to a Discourse Theory of Law and Democracy*, trans. W. Rehg. Cambridge, MA: MIT Press.

Habermas, J. (2003) *Truth and Justification*, trans. Barbara Fultner. Cambridge, MA: MIT Press.

Hollis, M. (1971) 'The pen and the purse', in *Journal of Philosophy of Education*, 5 (2): 153–69.

Kemmis, S. and McTaggart, R. (2005) 'Participatory action research: Communicative action and the public sphere', In N. Denzin and Y. Lincoln (eds), *The Sage Handbook of Qualitative Research*, 3rd edn. Thousand Oaks, CA: Sage, pp. 559–604.
Laswell, H.D. (1936) *Politics: Who Gets What, When, How*. New York: P. Smith.
MacIntyre, A. (1983) *After Virtue: A Study in Moral Theory*, 2nd edn. London: Duckworth.
MacKenzie, W.J.M. (1974) 'Political science: Between analysis and action', *New Society*, x (x): 218.

7

Action Research for/as/mindful of Social Justice

Morwenna Griffiths

This chapter examines and explores the potential of action research to enhance social justice in education. It discusses different approaches and practices within the field of education in relation to epistemologies and principles underlying research for social justice. Implicit in many characterizations of action research is the potential to work for justice – in small-scale projects or for larger social and educational ends. At the same time, disquiet has been expressed by many action researchers about the co-option of action research for merely instrumental ends, or for purposes of social control rather than of social justice. The chapter addresses the question: when and how far is action research coherent with aims for social justice?

ACTION RESEARCH AND POLITICALLY COMMITTED RESEARCH

Arguments rage over the issue of politics in action research. The term 'politics' here means a concern with power relations, decision making and action in large- or small-scale social worlds. Thus a concern for social justice is a political one. All sides claim the moral high ground. There are those who would see particular kinds of politics as basic to good action research, and others who would not want their research to be political at all. I myself take the position that all research which enhances social justice is to be welcomed, and indeed that it is a moral and/or political obligation for action researchers at some (but not all) points in their action research careers.

One reason that arguments rage is that most proponents of action research have strong ethical and/or political commitments which underpin their reasons for espousing it. However, the array of commitments underpinning different approaches do not necessarily coincide, and even where they overlap there is a difference of emphasis. Noffke (1997) has usefully suggested one way of distinguishing different approaches. She distinguishes those that are primarily concerned with the professional, the personal and the political. She takes care to stress that each of these will inevitably include the other two, and indeed, should do so (Noffke and Brennan, 1997).

The 1980s saw a burgeoning of overlapping but distinguishable approaches to action research that are, broadly speaking, concerned with social justice. Cochran-Smith and Lytle (1999) provide a useful account of the different intellectual traditions within teaching and teacher education which gave an impetus to teacher research including action research. It is a movement which continues to refer to these traditions. Some of them are self-consciously rooted in intellectual movements that construct research as a form of social action related to democracy, the production of knowledge and social change. Accounts of such research include terms with highly political connotations, such as 'power', 'transformation', 'joint action', 'radical', 'social re-construction' and 'emancipation'.

SOCIAL JUSTICE AS A KIND OF ACTION

Some terms which attract general approval are what are called 'hurrah' words. Examples are 'freedom' and 'fairness'. Such terms mean different things to different people, depending on their various political and moral commitments. Therefore it is particularly important to be clear about their meaning.

In some ways, 'social justice' is bound to be a hurrah term because, put most simply, social justice characterizes a good society. It is an idea with a long history which influences its current meaning. Aristotle's conceptualization of social justice remains hugely influential on all subsequent Western political philosophy. Indeed his formulation remains relevant and useful today. In *Politics*, he first explains how individuals come to have a common interest, and then goes on to use the idea to define justice (Aristotle, 1980):

> People ... are drawn together by a common interest, in proportion as each attains a share in the good life. The good life is the chief end both for the community as a whole and for each of us individually. (III, 6, 1278b6)
>
> ...
>
> The good in the sphere of politics is justice, and justice consists in what tends to promote the common interest. (III, 11, 1282b14)

This he goes on to discuss in terms of distributive justice, that is, the right distribution of benefits in a society.

The themes of the individual and the community, and a fair distribution of benefits remain central to modern discussions of social justice. In contemporary philosophy and political theory, conceptions of social justice are dominated by John Rawls (1971) who provides a theory of justice as fairness. This theory is based on the social contract and distributive justice. His work remains an important source of modern thinking about justice. However, it is firmly rooted in a Liberal understanding of the legacy of the Enlightenment, especially its belief in rationally achieved consensus. This legacy has been subject to critique and reconstruction by other strands in political thinking during the latter half of the twentieth century.

Hannah Arendt introduces a focus on political action. For her the 'realm of human affairs' is not static. It is the sphere of actions, the *bios politicos* (1958: 13). The concept of 'natality' is central to her argument. As new people are born and enter the realm of human affairs, they ensure that society is never static. Rather, the situation changes in unpredictable ways. She says (1958: 190):

> Action ... always establishes relationships and therefore has an inherent tendency to force open all limitations and cut across all boundaries ... [which] exist within the realm of human affairs, but they never offer a framework that can reliably withstand the onslaught with which each new generation must insert itself.

Such action is never merely individual for Arendt. Actions need to be argued for and carried through by distinct individuals in 'a web of relation' with others. Action and speech are closely related because of human plurality, which, she says, 'has the twofold character of equality and distinction' (Arendt, 1958: 175). She continues:

> If each human being [were] not distinct, each human being distinguished from any other who is, was, or will ever be, they would need neither speech nor action to make themselves understood. ... With word and deed we insert ourselves into the human world. (Arendt, 1958: 175–6)

Arendt herself had a negative view of politics as action for social justice. We do not have to agree with this: her perspective on action illuminates the concept of social justice. First, her arguments show that social justice is dynamic: a kind of action rather than a static state of affairs. Second, they point up the significance of voice and empowerment, since both equality and speech are essential for action. Third, they signal that knowledge about the realm of human affairs is always provisional.

Lyotard's postmodern critique of Liberalism shows the significance of local context for justice. In *The Postmodern Condition* (Lyotard, 1984) he developed an argument for 'incredulity toward metanarratives' (xxiv). By 'metanarrative' he means narratives of legitimation, such as 'the progressive emancipation of reason and freedom ... [and] the enrichment of all humanity through the progress of technoscience' (Lyotard, 1992: 29). He argued that these are just one way of understanding the world. Attention should also be paid to other narratives, the 'little stories', which are 'continuing to weave the fabric of everyday life' (p. 31). These are always told in specific contexts and for specific purposes and cannot always be understood outside those contexts. Their existence challenges the grand narratives of universalizable, generalizable knowledge, and develops 'a practice of justice' (1984: 66) which respects local differences.

Lyotard developed this position in *The Differend* (Lyotard, 1989) where he addresses the question of communication and difference; this is a question which matters in relation to understanding voice and empowerment. He focuses attention on cases where different social groups have unequal power. He shows how the power of one side may mean that the experience and understanding of the less powerful become unsayable, and the only possibility becomes silence. He argues that justice requires that communication is continued, even though it is impossible to do it using the usual Liberal rules of rational argument.

Feminist theory has been a powerful source of critique and development of traditional perspectives on social justice. Different feminist epistemologies have significant philosophical differences but unite in pointing up the significance of perspectives in knowledge. Feminists have also theorized (and practised) the use of different expressive forms to communicate. For instance, Young (2000) criticizes the privileging of rational argument and deliberation and argues for more use of other forms of expression, such as narrative. In educational theory, Jane Roland Martin (1994) provides a critique of self-consciously rational discourse which silences other voices.

Nancy Fraser (1997) has shown that while an emphasis on redistribution is essential, it is only partial. Social justice also requires all members of a society to be given recognition. Some social groups are materially (dis)advantaged compared to each other. Redressing this requires redistribution. However, this is not enough to explain injustice. Some social groups are treated with (dis)respect – not given recognition. Iris Marion Young says there is a requirement for what she calls 'greeting' (2000: 58). As she points out, without acknowledgement of the other as a subject rather than an object, communication is distorted. Fraser (1997) has helpfully suggested using the analytical dimensions, 'cultural' and 'structural' to differentiate kinds of social groups. Some, like groups based on sexuality, tend to be cultural, of which some are in need of recognition. Others, like those based on social class, tend to be more structural, of which some are in need of redistribution. Race and gender score high on both dimensions and give rise to a need for both redistribution and recognition.

Fraser is careful to avoid fixing any group within its dimensions. She argues that any such descriptions remain fluid and provisional. Young explains the damaging, misleading effects of attempting to fix group identities (2000: 88–9):

> Everyone relates to a plurality of social groups; every social group has other social groups cutting across it … The attempt to define a common group identity tends to normalize the experience and perspective of some group members while marginalizing or silencing others.

Since each member of any group will also belong to other groups, no one solution will fit all.

Evidently social justice is a complex cluster of related concepts. I attempt to draw them together in a definition that includes redistribution, action, provisionality, locality, voice, recognition, and fluid identities. It is as follows:

> Social justice aims at the good for the common interest, where that is taken to include both the good of each and the good of all, in an acknowledgement that one depends on the other. The good depends on mutual recognition and also on a right distribution of benefits and responsibilities. It includes paying attention to individual perspectives and local conditions at the same time as dealing with issues of discrimination, exclusions and recognition, especially on the grounds of (any or all of) race, gender, sexuality, special needs and social class. As the situation changes, it is likely that identities will change too. So it could never be achieved once and for all. Any solutions remain provisional.

The discussion in this section has been dense and compressed. So I conclude by drawing out what is most relevant to the theme of this chapter.

1   Social justice could never be achieved once and for all. It is always subject to revision.
2   Therefore, action is central, especially joint action.
3   Voice and empowerment are for all. So both 'little stories' and 'grand narratives' need to be taken seriously.
4   Paying attention to a diversity of perspective is vital.
5   Therefore, recognition across difference is crucial …
6   … And so is redistribution: 'justice as fairness'.
7   The good for each person both affects and depends on the good for all in recognition of the reciprocal dependence of 'I' and 'we'.

ACTION RESEARCH AND PRACTICAL, REVISABLE KNOWLEDGE

The argument so far shows that there are ways in which social justice and action research may be coherent ways of understanding the world. Most obviously, both are centrally concerned with action and both expect any conclusions to be provisional and revisable. Both of them also acknowledge the personal and individual within the social world. In this section I argue that they have other common features.

In different forms of action research a number of features recur, but any one of them may not be present in any specific case. There is no specific method or epistemological position that characterizes all action research. To give just three examples, the research of Christianson et al. (2002) is informed by post-structural theories but Carr and Kemmis (1986) advocate critical theory. Whitehead (2007) proposes a new 'living epistemology' developed from dialectical theory. The different approaches are probably best described not as having any essential common feature but, rather, a family resemblance, in Wittgenstein's sense (1968).

Recurring features include:

1   Revisability and provisionality. Research takes place in spirals, in a process of continuing reflection and re-thinking.

2   Action taken together with others: collaboration.
3   Location in specific contexts, usually small-scale. So methods include case-study and narrative as well as other mainly qualitative techniques.
4   Openness to other perspectives. Sometimes this is described as attention to difference and diversity. In others it is in the concept of research as necessarily 'made public'.
5   Insider research and emotional involvement with the context. In the words of Marion Dadds (1995), action research is a passionate enquiry.

In short, the emphasis is on uncertainty, fallibility and risky judgements made in particular material, historical circumstances.

ACTION RESEARCH, SOCIAL JUSTICE AND QUESTIONS TO BE ASKED FREQUENTLY (QAFs)

Comparing the definition of social justice with the recurring features of action research it will be seen that one should fit easily with the other. Both of them depend on a view of practical knowledge as revisable and provisional. Both expect some kind of action as a part of the process. Both emphasize collaboration, the small-scale and context dependent, openness to other perspectives, and personal commitment. Some of the common features are tricky to implement in practice.

Collaboration is not easy, even when it is simply collaboration with like-minded colleagues. It becomes much harder to collaborate across real differences of perspective and background, as the relative paucity of reports of success in such research testifies. Similarly joint action is often tricky, requiring compromises and risks. For a successful joint action not only must there be agreement about at least some perspectives on, and understandings of, a situation, but also about what to do to improve it. It is not for nothing that politics is called the *art of the possible*.

Action research is always carried out in specific contexts. So 'little stories' are relatively easily constructed. However, it is harder to relate these little stories to grander narratives. Hollingsworth (1992) describes the process of a collaborative enquiry which was able to relate the little stories to some grand narratives (i.e. literacy education theory, and feminism) but only after a considerable period. Conversely there are many reports of action research which invoke theory but which do not relate their little stories to it in any detail and depth.

Dealing with diversity in action research is particularly difficult. There are many reasons for this. One is mentioned above, in relation to collaboration. It is much easier to work with the like-minded. Further, it can be difficult and painful to uncover and confront your assumptions of normality. Hollingsworth (1992) describes this both in relation to feminism (p. 377) and also to race and social class (p. 391). Ann Schulte (2005) reports an unsettling self-study into her 'white privilege' and how it affected her work as a teacher educator. It can be especially difficult to create ways of engaging with diverse perspectives when working and living in a homogeneous culture (Johnston-Parsons et al., 2007).

To summarize: some features of social justice appear in many action research projects. At the same time it is not surprising that action research does not often reach its full potential for enhancing social justice. There are many obstacles and constraints. But the potential is there: as well as obstacles and constraints, there are also openings and opportunities.

It may also be that researchers would like to include more features, but find the idea daunting. My proposal is that researchers ask themselves questions about their research and how it supports social justice (or does not). These questions would point up what researchers are doing well in terms of social justice as well as indicating what the next steps might be. Doing action research is hard: it is time-consuming, it puts one's own practice into question, and it is always uncertain. On the other hand, social justice is important. So asking questions that indicate a step-by-step approach gives researchers the opportunity to move at their own pace towards it rather than despairing or burning out while attempting perfection.

The questions to be asked are a set of questions to be asked of oneself (or of oneselves) in a reflective and exploratory frame of mind. While they can be approached at a depth manageable by the researcher, they are challenging. So they are not easily answered 'frequently asked questions' or FAQs. Rather, they are 'questions to be asked frequently': QAFs. The focus of some questions will be on the method and process of the research. Others focus on its substantive content. The precise way the questions become relevant changes with the research being questioned. Indeed, given the provisionality of all knowledge, QAFs themselves are fluid, emergent and always revisable.

QUESTIONS TO BE ASKED FREQUENTLY

Epistemology

Is there acceptance of continuing change, of no final answers, of provisionality? Is the end that the research was working for itself in question? How are conclusions presented?

Is there an openness to others' perspectives, however surprising or even unwelcome? Is there evidence of a willingness to put the selves of the researchers into question?

Is the research whole-hearted? Has it been personally enriching and exciting? Have there been tears and arguments? Despair and delight? What difference did these emotions make to the process and outcome of the research?

Action and Effects

Whose actions are they and for what ends? Is it a joint action or just that of single individuals? Is it specific changed behaviour and/or is it a transformation of perceptions? What will happen next? What are the effects of the research?

Have barriers and constraints to action been questioned and assessed? Do these include: local, internal, structural (e.g. school, department), and/or large-scale structures (e.g. gender, technical rationality)? What counts as action for this research – and why?

About Voice and Power

Who is included in the research? Was consideration given to including everyone with an involvement? So, for schools: not just the teachers, (say) but also the children, parents, cleaners, mid-day supervisors? For H.E.: not just the academic staff, but also support staff in various roles?

Was the research collaborative? In what sense? At what stage in the process? Why? Could anyone have done the research on their own? How did any collaboration make a difference?

Was everyone able to contribute confidently without compromising some part of their identity? Do the styles of communication take account of how the ground rules of communication vary by gender, cultural heritage, etc.? Do the modes of discourse (Chang-Wells and Wells, 1997) exclude some social groups? Is there an opportunity to have a say, using different modes of expression? What evidence is there about this?

Did the research take any unexpected directions when different perspectives were included? Were there misunderstandings and surprising differences of perception? How did they affect the process and outcomes of the research?

About Recognition and Redistribution

Has individual difference and social diversity been considered? Is attention paid to all the axes of difference (including race, ethnicity, religion, gender, social class, sexuality, (dis)abilities)? Is recognition given to all?

Is complexity acknowledged – or are some groups being stereotyped? Are material and human resources allocated fairly to all sectors – both during the research and as a result of it? Does the research treat anyone as especially important or insignificant? Why?

USING THE QAFs TO QUESTION APPROACHES TO ACTION RESEARCH

This section of the paper focuses on some major current approaches and practices in action research and how their underlying epistemologies and intentions relate to social justice. It uses a rough analysis of different approaches. But the discussion does not aim to provide an enduring categorization. Indeed it resists any such aim as tending to freeze previous creativity and to restrict it in the future. As Christine Battersby expresses it (1998: 13):

> The identities I describe emerge out of patterns of movement and relationality … in which the past is taken up into the present in ways that do not simply 'copy' a neutral 'real'.

The approaches I identify, I identify only for the sake of the argument of this chapter. They are 'temporary constructs' (Noffke, 1995: 323). They are (Battersby, 1998: 34):

> a kind of idealized image or snapshot – that is used to arrest the fluid and the manifold into a temporary stability of form.

To change the metaphor, they are like constellations or the different geometric shapes that can be read in complex patterns, such as can be found in Islamic decorations. They merge, overlap and share nodes.

Research which explicitly announces itself as political action research, or as prioritising social reconstruction and transformation, may conveniently be described under one category as political action research. It includes a number of different (though overlapping) approaches. They include:

1   The Habermasian and critical theory schools associated especially with Carr and Kemmis (1986) and inquiry-oriented social reconstruction drawing on Dewey and social movements. Both of these are associated with the well-known cycle of 'reflect, plan, act, observe'.
2   Attention to specific structural social issues, such as sexism, racism and, in some theoretical frameworks, disability. This may be a direct approach to one of these topics or it might be addressing other professional problems but noting the structural social issues that constrain them. Such concerns may be linked to professional and personal action research.
3   Conversational and dialogical approaches in which social justice issues are central. These approaches are often associated with learning communities, and activity theory. They are also associated with self-study approaches.
4   Research focused on general structural social issues, such as democratic procedures in the society as a whole – or the lack of them. This is particularly associated with Participatory Action Research.

The methods and methodologies of action research which is not primarily political are similar in broad outline to those of political action research. This set of methods and methodologies is complex in its relation to social justice and politics. Within each broad approach are subsets which have aspirations towards contributing to 'improvement', or towards a better, fairer society, but with the primary focus of the research being on other personal or professional issues. Sometimes these aspirations for social justice are explicitly stated. There is also action research which presents itself as being committed to being politically neutral in relation to the professional or personal issues being examined.

I have drawn attention to these subsets with italics. Approaches to action research which is not primarily political include:

1   Reflective practice in which practitioners inquire into what they see as issues for themselves. The rationale for this may be explicitly democratic (Elliott, 1987, 2006; Somekh, 2006). *Or it may be more neutral.* Reflective practice may include social justice issues as just one of many areas to be researched as part of 'effective and evidence-informed professional practice' (Pollard, 2002). Reflective practice, like critical action research uses the cycle of 'reflect, plan, act, observe'.
2   Research focused on specific professional technical problems. Some of these, like effective disciplinary procedures, are more amenable to a wider social or political development than others, such as the use of particular teaching and learning techniques or materials. But all technical and professional concerns can be the subject of personal and social analyses. *Researchers vary in their inclinations to consider such aspects.*
3   Learning communities and conversational inquiry. Such research may pay some attention to social justice issues (Somekh, 2006; Chang-Wells and Wells, 1997). *Or it may present itself as neutral* (Feldman, 1999; Higgins, 2006). There is considerable overlap between the third and fourth categories, since personal research is often carried out collaboratively and conversationally.
4   Research focused on the personal. This would include self-study. For these researchers, identity is central to professional practice. This research may address some social justice concerns such as freedom and agency (Feldman, 2002). McNiff et al. (1992) frame an individual's construction of a 'living educational theory', as taking account of a good social order, even when it is primarily focused on other issues. *Or it may work with a definition of the personal as against social or political.*

All of the political approaches to action research leave room for the QAFs to be asked explicitly. Indeed such researchers probably consider many of them explicitly. The different approaches, however, will highlight some questions while allowing others to be overlooked. A value of using the QAFs is that it shows this up, making it more difficult to ignore some aspects of social justice. Taking the set of 'epistemological' questions it can be seen that some approaches are thickly revisable or collaborative in comparison to others. For instance, the personal, conversational and collaborative approach proposed by Hollingsworth (1992) and Hollingsworth et al. (1997) demand the researchers' openness to revision of their dearest beliefs and attitudes. On the other hand, research focused on specific issues of gender and race may well leave most of the researcher's original values intact, especially if, as can happen, the research makes only one turn of the action research cycle. However, this latter research is far more likely to highlight issues of recognition and redistribution, which can be only thinly acknowledged in other approaches. Some researches have shown that they are willing to revise original ways of thinking radically, as well as specific revisions of action in successive cycles. One example is Carr and Kemmis's reappraisal of *Becoming Critical*, 20 years on from its original publication

(Car and Kemmis, 2005). But particular pieces of research using Carr and Kemmis's approach are rarely so radical.

Approaches to action research which are not primarily political may have considered some of the QAFs but are unlikely to have considered many of them explicitly. For instance approaches such as Elliott's (1991, 2006) that emphasize the democratic significance of teachers' views being central to educational knowledge, are less likely to consider all the QAFs about voice and inclusion, or those relating to recognition and redistribution. However, it is clear that this kind of approach is open to exploration using those QAFs. Some of the approaches which are not primarily political are unlikely to consider QAFs explicitly but might be open to exploring at least some of them. For instance, Higgins (2006) uses a learning community or activity theory approach to research. He remarks on the power relations between participating schools and the universities and on which sector 'owns' which decisions about the research. This is done in a very general way, but could easily be related to social justice issues of joint action, voice, recognition and redistribution.

There are plenty of examples of action research projects in which teacher's craft knowledge or professional self-identity are discussed without reference to such issues at all. All of these researchers *could* pay attention to QAFs, though no doubt finding only some questions readily in tune with some than their research focus. Only some of these researchers *would* consider doing so. Action research which is committed to political neutrality would not. For example, in their evaluation of teacher research, Furlong and Salisbury (2005) found a sizeable minority of teachers who were striving for strict neutrality in their research.

CONCLUDING THAT...

I come back now to the question posed in the introduction: what is the potential of action research to enhance social justice? The discussion in the previous section shows that all action research has potential but only some approaches will realize it. Just how they may (or will not) realize such potential is the subject of this section.

Action research can be focused directly on issues of social justice. These may be explicitly and reflectively related to the processes of research, such as the underlying epistemology, and its inclusivity in terms of collaborative practices and actions. This is *action research AS social justice*. On the other hand, it may be explicitly and reflectively focused on the outcomes of the research, in terms of voice, power, recognition and/or redistribution. This is *action research FOR social justice*. Research may be both of these, or it may move from one to the other over the course of time, especially if it is *MINDFUL OF* the whole range of social justice concerns. Action research may, however, be focused on other issues, yet be explicitly mindful of the social justice aspects of its processes and outcomes. This, too, is *action research MINDFUL OF social justice*.

Such research uses at least some of the QAFs to assess itself, and position itself in relation to social justice.

These three kinds of social justice action research do not form a hierarchy. All three kinds are important to educational practice and to enhancing social justice. A researcher may move from one to another and back over the course of their professional career. As long as it is clear that all three kinds of research are valuable and have a significant part to play in enhancing social justice, researchers who are more comfortable in one or the other kind and are disinclined to move will, nevertheless, be ready to learn from the others. This ought to work against the tendency of social groups to define themselves against each other. Rather than having 'social justice researchers' and 'others', it is surely better for all researchers to see their work as coherent with social justice, while at the same time be challenged to improve on this aspect of it. What Heikkinen et al. say about truth can be adapted to describe the possibilities for social justice within action research (2001: 22):

> The multi-paradigmatic situation [which] seems to exist among action researchers … could be regarded as a productive situation, rather than some undeveloped stage of science.

Although there is no hierarchy between these three kinds of social justice research, there is one between all three of them and action research which makes no explicit reference to social justice. Such research could be explicitly mindful of social justice, given the opportunity and reason to do so. Alternatively, while it could be, it would not be because of a commitment to political neutrality.

There are many reasons for researchers not being explicit about social justice concerns in their work, not least in reports to funders, such as the report by Higgins (2006). It may be that, to a different public, such researchers are fully explicit about their reasons, but other researchers may be less so. Where this is the case, it is unlikely that reflection will be challenging and coherent with social justice as a whole. In the latter case the research might be termed 'pre-mindful'. The difference is analogous to the difference between ordinary professional practice and reflective practice using a systematic research and evidence.

Of more concern are the researchers who take themselves to be good professionals only if they are politically neutral in their research and practice. They are not mindful of social justice and would not want to be. Furlong and Salisbury's (2005) evaluation of the 3,000 teacher research projects undertaken in the UK in the early 2000s was mentioned earlier. It shows clearly how many of the projects were focused on severely technical matters, such as the use of the interactive whiteboard. Whereas there was plenty of evidence of transformed technical practice there was much less evidence of transformed understandings of the political in professional practice. Of course, a focus on technicalities may be a very good starting point for wider reflection. A version of the QAFs would be useful here for critics of such a position. They would provide a framework for arguing in depth that action research is always to some extent, even when it aspires to be, neutral.

It has been the argument of this chapter that social justice is complex, and that this very complexity provides an opportunity to turn more action research into better research *for*, *as* and *mindful of* social justice. It is an argument for a range of approaches and emphases. It is more helpful and productive to see how far, and in what respects particular action research projects are coherent with aims for social justice, than proposing a single best methodology.

REFERENCES

Aristotle (1980) *Politics*. Oxford: Oxford University Press.
Arendt, Hannah (1958) *The Human Condition*. London and Chicago: University of Chicago Press.
Battersby, Christine (1998) *The Phenomenal Woman: Feminist Metaphysics and the Patterns of Identity*. Cambridge: Polity.
Carr, W. and Kemmis, S. (1986) *Becoming Critical*. London: Falmer.
Carr, W. and Kemmis, S. (2005) 'Staying critical', *Educational Action Research*, 13 (3): 347–57.
Chang-Wells, Gen Ling and Wells, Gordon (1997) 'Modes of discourse for living, learning and teaching', in S. Hollingsworth (ed.). *International Action Research: A Casebook for Educational Reform*. London: Falmer.
Cochran-Smith, Marilyn and Lytle, Susan L. (1999) 'The teacher research movement: a decade later', *Educational Researcher*, 28 (7): 15–25.
Christianson, Mary, Slutsky, Ruslan, Bendau, Shirley, Covert, Julia, Dyer, Jennifer, Risko, Georgene, Johnston, Marilyn (2002) 'The rocky road of teachers becoming action researchers', *Teaching and Teacher Education*, 18: 259–72.
Dadds, Marion (1995) *Passionate Enquiry and School Development: A Story about Teacher Action Research*. London: Falmer.
Elliott, John (1987) 'Educational theory, practical philosophy and action research', *British Journal of Educational Studies*, 35 (2): 149–69.
Elliott, John (1991) *Action Research for Educational Change*. Milton Keynes: Open University Press.
Elliott, John (2006) 'Educational research as a form of democratic rationality', *Journal of Philosophy of Education*, 40 (2): 169–85.
Feldman, Alan (1999) 'The role of conversation in collaborative action research', *Educational Action Research*, 7 (1): 125–47.
Feldman, Alan (2002) 'Existential approaches to action research', *Educational Action Research*, 10 (2).
Fraser, N. (1997) *Justice Interruptus: Critical Reflections on the 'Postsocialist' Condition*. New York and London: Routledge.
Furlong, John and Salisbury, Jane (2005) 'Best practice research scholarships: an evaluation'. *Research Papers in Education*, 20 (1): 45–83.
Heikkinen, H., Kakkori, L. and Huttenen, R. (2001) 'This is my truth, tell me yours: some aspects of action research quality in the light of truth theories', *Educational Action Research*, 9 (1): 9–24.
Higgins, Steve (2006) 'Learning to Learn Phase 3: Action Research Support 2003–2006', http://www.ncl.ac.uk/ecls/research/education/project/1605
Hollingsworth, Sandra (1992) 'Learning to teach through collaborative conversation: a feminist approach', *American Educational Research Journal*, 29 (2): 373–404.
Hollingsworth, Sandra, Miller, Janet and Dadds, Marion (1997) 'The examined experience of action research', in S. Hollingsworth (ed.), *International Action Research: A Casebook for Educational Reform*. London: Falmer.
Johnston-Parsons, Marilyn, Lee, Young Ah, Thomas Michael (2007) 'Students of colour as cultural consultants', *Studying Teacher Education*, 3 (1).

Lyotard, Jean-François (1984) *The Postmodern Condition: A Report on Knowledge.* (Trans. Geoff Bennington and Brian Massumi). Manchester: Manchester University Press.

Lyotard, Jean-François (1989) *The Differend: Phrases in Dispute* (Trans. George Van Den Abbeele). Minneapolis: University of Minnesota Press.

Lyotard, Jean-François (1992) *The Postmodern Explained to Children: Correspondence 1982–1985* (Trans ed. Julian Pefanis and Morgan Thomas). London: Turnaround.

Martin Jane Roland (1994) *Changing the Educational Landscape: Philosophy, Women and the Curriculum,* London, Taylor & Francis.

McNiff, Jean, Whitehead, Jack and Laidlaw, Moira (1992) *Creating a Good Social Order Through Action Research.* London: Hyde.

Noffke, Susan (1995) 'Action research and democratic schooling: problematics and potential', in S. Noffke and R. Stevenson (eds), *Educational Action Research: Becoming Practically Critical.* New York: Teachers College Press.

Noffke, Susan (1997) 'Professional, personal, and political dimensions of action research', *Review of Research in Education,* 22: 305–43.

Noffke, Susan and Brennan, Marie (1997) 'Reconstructing the politics of action in action research', in S. Hollingsworth (ed.). *International Action Research: A Casebook for Educational Reform.* London: Falmer.

Pollard, Andrew (2002) *Reflective Teaching: Effective and Evidence-informed Professional Practice.* London: Continuum.

Rawls, John (1971) *A Theory of Justice,* Oxford: Oxford University Press.

Schulte, Ann (2005) 'Assuming my transformation: transforming my assumptions', *Studying Teacher Education,* 1 (1): 31–42.

Somekh, B. (2006) *Action Research: a Methodology for Change and Development.* Maidenhead: Open University Press.

Whitehead, Jack (2007) 'Generating educational theories that can explain educational influences in learning: living logics, units of appraisal, standards of judgment'. Paper presented to BERA annual conference, London, http://www.jackwhitehead.com/jack/jwbera07sem.htm

Wittgenstein, Ludwig (1968) *Philosophical Investigations.* Oxford, Blackwell.

Young, Iris Marion (2000) *Inclusion and Democracy,* Oxford: Oxford University Press.

Professional: Knowledge Production, Staff Development, and the Status of Educators

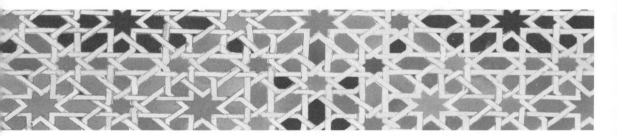

Introduction to Part II

The 12 chapters in Part II draw on the work of those who use action research to extend and develop their own professional practice and who engage in facilitating the work of teacher-researchers. In this sense their overarching focus is professional. Yet all show a deeply personal connection to their work, as they consider both their own learning and that of the communities and schools they serve. They also show the ways in which the focus on improving the lives of young people, their teachers and their communities embody particular political visions of social change. They are grouped, as in Parts III and IV, into three subsections to reflect a range of orientations within this broad category. The subsections are, of course, reflective of a particular emphasis. The chapters demonstrate the ways in which these primary foci permeate across categories.

The first four chapters focus on *'working with and for students and schools'*. The lead chapter, by Caro-Bruce et al., presents the work of the Madison Wisconsin teacher-research group which has developed and flourished over 18 years, led by the School District in close collaboration with teacher educators in the university. It provides an overview of the group's history and achievements. The Core Program Principles, and the outcomes of the two evaluations of the group's work, make an important contribution to knowledge about building, sustaining and benefiting from teacher action research in a School District. O'Hanlon's chapter has a specific focus on action research undertaken with students who have special educational needs (SEN). She draws on her wide-ranging experience of project work and teaching in many countries to show how action research makes a unique contribution to the education of SEN students and explores some of the complex ethical issues it raises. Both chapters show the importance of doing action research for particular groups of students.

With Bigum and Rowan's chapter the scope broadens to focus on students as knowledge producers undertaking projects on behalf of their local community. In the Knowledge Producing Schools students from diverse backgrounds carry out research and build knowledge that draws directly on their own cultural capital. In the fourth chapter in the group, Lewis et al. focus on Lesson Study (LS) as a particular form of action research. They emphasize that although the focus of LS is on improving classroom practice, it has a major impact on the personal-professional development of teachers, and in its original form, in Japan, is used to test out new policies in classrooms and contribute to the learning of all teachers with the potential for systemic change. The starting point for two of these chapters is the research of individual teachers. LS focuses attention on an individual teacher being observed by others, but the overall process is inherently collaborative. In the Lewis chapter the focus is on working with the professional community; in the Bigum and Rowan chapter the knowledge-producing projects of students working for, and with, the community and their school is the central focus of their practice.

The chapters in the second group focus on *'professional development, teacher voice and knowledge production'*. The opening chapter by Anderson and Herr explores the complexities – and important advantages – of action research carried out by administrators in their role as senior leaders in schools. Ethical issues relating to differences in power make it difficult for administrators to collect data by means of interviews and observation, and the chapter offers suggestions for new ways of collecting data that ensure high quality of knowledge outcomes. The chapter by Keiny and Orland-Barak provides a meta-analysis of four projects representative of the range of approaches to action research in Israel. The projects are drawn from different contexts: university teaching, a university–schools partnership, a community school engaged in collaborative work with local industry, and the facilitation of workshops aimed at reconciliation-transformation between Jews and Arabs. They argue that action research is 'a paradigm for change', emphasizing its hermeneutic orientation to combining research and the co-construction of new knowledge with the process of changing and improving one's own practice.

The chapter by Day and Townsend focuses on action research as a long-term process within a networked learning community. They begin by reviewing key publications on networking as a form of action research and then present, as an illustrative example, an eight-year-old network comprising of eight schools in England. The chapter provides an important body of knowledge in terms of kinds of networking activities, ways of resolving tensions that arise and an analysis of how such networks mature over time, enabling them to work at a deeper level. The final chapter in the group, by Saunders and Somekh, describes the collaboration between a university and a professional body for teachers in England, to support participatory action research with teachers and students into how technology might be used to transform students' learning. The authors describe how they drew for the design of the project on their common backgrounds in the Stenhouse tradition of 'teachers as researchers'. Like Stenhouse their aim was systemic reform and, by working within a partnership between a university and a teachers' professional body, they generated a means to feed the project's knowledge outcomes into policy development at the national level.

Taken together, these four chapters show the complex ways in which teachers' professional development enhances the voice of teachers. But they also show the complex ways in which the production of knowledge by teachers intersects with that of communities and students. Issues of partnership, tools for furthering this agenda, play significant roles as they work through professional development, teacher voice and knowledge production issues.

The last four chapters focus on action research relating to *policy and change*, within the professional dimension. All four are based on a meta-analysis of large-scale projects aimed at reforming the professional practices of schooling to give students better life chances. Brennan's chapter describes a project in Australia that tackled 'the intractable problem' of how to retain the motivation and commitment to education of adolescents so as to reverse the trend towards dropping out early from school. Students were given 'rich tasks' to carry out individual projects and present an exhibition of their work to a panel of community members. Like Saunders and Somekh, this project involved collaboration between the university and a teachers' professional body, and it also involved the policy-makers from the relatively small administrative region of the Australian Capital Territory. Brennan describes the long-term impact of the project as well as its important knowledge outcomes in terms of designing and implementing system-wide reform using action research.

The chapter by Altrichter and Posch starts by presenting the outcomes of a two-year action research programme developed by a university in Austria and refined over time to increase the involvement of participants' schools in an attempt to have a system-level impact. The chapter then goes on to analyse different approaches to innovation and conceptualizes action research as 'an adaptive-evolutionary innovation strategy'. It suggests that action research can be a successful strategy for effective school reform when it is allied with research into school governance leading to changes in structures that will enable innovation.

The following chapter, by Comber and Kamler, draws on a network of teacher-researchers across two states in Australia that engaged with the 'toughest equity challenges'. It describes how action research focused on respecting and valuing children's 'lifeworlds' outside school rather than expecting them to conform to 'schoolworlds'. The project worked through partnerships between 'early career teachers' and their mentors, with an emphasis on mutual learning and support. There was a particular emphasis on teachers as producers of knowledge, presenting and publishing their work.

The final chapter in the group, by Groundwater-Smith, describes a major programme for school reform in yet another Australian state. This was action research in the sense that knowledge creation and knowledge transfer were at the core of the schools' activities, starting from self-evaluation and the development of 'learning portfolios', supported by a meta-evaluation team from the university. The thread running through all four of these chapters is that knowledge generated by teachers and students has the potential to contribute to systemic reform of schooling if policy-makers and university partners collaborate with schools to support knowledge transfer.

The chapters in Part II begin to illustrate how the theories and methodologies presented in Part I are used in action research practice in this dimension and in the further sections. They all show how the professional is infused with learning at the individual (personal) level and has the potential to contribute to learning at the policy (political) level. While their locus of involvement is in professional practice, each shows the ways in which the navigation of systems of power is part of the landscape of changes that have personal as well as political dimensions. In the many references to individual teacher and student changes, they also pave the way for reading Part III with its focus on the 'personal', and for the Part IV explorations of the 'political'.

8

A School District-Based Action Research Program in the United States

Cathy Caro-Bruce, Mary Klehr,
Ken Zeichner and
Ana Maria Sierra-Piedrahita

When the first Classroom Action Research (CAR) opportunity was offered by the Madison, Wisconsin Metropolitan School District staff development department in 1990, it was conceived and presented as an isolated learning opportunity. It was not supported by the kind of deep thinking and planning that would ensure its sustainability, nor was there a sense for how it would fit into the larger context and goals of the district. In the years since its modest beginnings, it has grown to meet the needs of individual schools and the larger district, has become aligned with national professional development standards, and manages to survive despite numerous challenges related to the changing landscape of education in the district and the country.

From its inception, a set of core principles was identified to guide the program, resulting in a successful structural model that is grounded in foundational beliefs about how teachers learn and develop, and the important knowledge they produce. It is this focus on teachers' questions and their capacity to work on issues they have identified that has resulted in the success and longevity of action research in the Madison district. Nearly 20 years since it began, teachers, principals, and support staff perceive the CAR program to be one of the most valuable professional development opportunities offered by the district.

Between 30 and 100 teachers, support staff, and administrators participate voluntarily in the CAR program each year, and nearly 600 studies have been posted on the district website.[1]

In this chapter, we discuss the historical development of the Madison CAR program, the core principles at its foundation, and what we have learned from research that we have conducted on how teachers' participation in the program influenced themselves, their students, schools, and the school district. We also provide a critical view of the challenges the program currently faces in times of standards, accountability and budget cuts.

HISTORY OF ACTION RESEARCH IN THE MADISON WI SCHOOL DISTRICT

The Early Years: Building Interest and Support

The Madison Metropolitan School District (MMSD) currently serves approximately 25,000 students in 31 elementary schools, 11 middle schools, four large comprehensive high schools, and an alternative high school. The first school district-sponsored action research group began humbly, with eight teachers who came together in response to an informational flyer sent out by the district staff development team. Several years before, a staff development specialist had read about action research and thought that it would provide a stimulating opportunity for teachers to come together to find more effective strategies for helping students be successful. Two initial groups were formed, and evaluations were enthusiastic. The work was not yet connected to the larger picture of school improvement, however, and when this staff development specialist left the district, the initiative was not continued.

The remaining staff development team saw that there was something here that teachers found powerful, and decided to build on what had been begun. There were significant challenges ahead. Perhaps the most difficult issue was a lack of understanding about the need to help teachers become more reflective about their instructional practices. A number of people at the district level initially dismissed efforts to grow the action research program because they didn't think teachers would be interested in anything that had 'research' in its title, nor did they perceive it to be valuable since they did not see a strong enough connection to what they felt the district needed to accomplish.

It took two more years of hard work to convince district administrators to provide continued support and formally launch the CAR program. Attention to the long-term goals of the program and a clear focus on the link between action research and best practices in professional development made an appreciable difference. Efforts to clarify to district leadership why it was important for teachers to engage in action research and show how it would connect to the broader vision of staff development and school improvement increased awareness and developed strong pockets of support at the district level. Also important was the connection between action research and educational equity that continues in Madison to this day.

Finding a Focus

The past two decades have brought a significant increase in students of color, children living in poverty, and second language learners to the Madison schools. This dramatic shift in the student population was the impetus for starting the first action research group, and educational equity has been a continuing theme of teachers' studies since then. By the late 1980s, teachers who had felt successful working with a fairly homogeneous student population began to notice that the instructional strategies that they had used for years were no longer meeting the needs of this growing and challenging population, and improving minority student achievement became a district focus.

Once minority student achievement had been established as a priority for the district, it became clearer to district decision-makers that Classroom Action Research had the potential to provide teachers with the venue to more deeply explore ideas about cultural differences, try out new practices in a systematic way, and share the knowledge they were gaining with others. Given its now clear connection to the goals and priorities of the district, funding was found to support the coordination of action research groups.

In the spring of 1990, two staff developers, a staff developer and the coordinator for research and evaluation, Cathy Caro-Bruce and Jennifer McCreadie, sent a letter inviting elementary teachers to participate in a CAR group called 'Meeting the Needs of Diverse Learners'. When eight people responded, Cathy and Jennifer designed a year-long, reflective process for teachers to explore questions about their practice, collect and analyze data, and write about their findings. As program coordinators and facilitators of the group, they quickly saw how hungry teachers were for this kind of professional development and began to plan for sustaining action research in the district on a long-term basis.

The following year, Classroom Action Research was offered to both middle school teachers and to principals. Participants in both groups found the experience very powerful, and although situations periodically arose that required them to leave monthly meetings and return to their buildings, the principals appreciated the time away from their schools to reflect on their work as much as the teachers did.

Key learnings during these beginning years included how quickly that action researchers embraced the experience rapidly; that involving principals led to not only their own growth, but also their support of teachers' participation; and that practitioners had important issues that they wanted to address in their teaching and leadership and saw action research as a viable way to make that happen.

Growing the Program

Over the next several years, the Classroom Action Research program grew under the steady hand of Cathy Caro-Bruce, a staff developer whose responsibilities included overseeing the logistics of the groups (anywhere from 30–100 teachers participating annually); working with various stakeholders within and outside the district, e.g. district administrators, university staff, and school improvement teams to find funding so that teachers could be released from their classrooms and studies could be published; developing dissemination strategies; and mentoring the group facilitators. During this period of growth, action research groups focused on specific district priorities such as equity, smaller learning communities, math instruction, and working with English language learners.

In collaboration with area colleges and districts, MMSD hosted seven annual conferences where teachers, university students and staff from various action research programs discussed their studies. The Action Research of Wisconsin Network was formed to host the conferences and publish a newsletter. The Madison district also produced several shows on a local cable television channel highlighting the work. It was hard to keep up with the growth.

Key learnings during this time included: how quickly the program grew and how excited participants were about action research; the importance of having a coordinator to organize all facets of the program; the value of presenting work to colleagues beyond the comfort of the immediate action research group; and how efforts to develop direct connections to district priorities helped generate interest and commitment among administrative staff.

Partnership with the University of Wisconsin-Madison School of Education

From the earliest days, the Madison Metropolitan School District and the University of Wisconsin-Madison designed a unique partnership around the classroom action research program. Unlike many models that exist, program leadership came from the school district, with the university taking on a supportive role. Over the years, university faculty has sought ways to enhance opportunities for teachers and give them access to experiences not routinely available to them. Professor Ken Zeichner has also designed a course so that teachers can receive university credit for their work and use their action research study as part of a research requirement in some graduate programs. This healthy partnership resulted in a grant to study the impact of action research in the district from the Spencer and MacArthur Foundations (Zeichner et al., 1998), as well as a university–community partnership award from the UW-Madison chancellor in 2004. Most importantly, teachers and university staff see action research as a vehicle for collaboration, one that helps break down some of the educational research barriers that are often found between school districts and universities.

The Recent Years

Establishing action research as an ongoing district-wide professional development opportunity took more time and was more challenging than anticipated, and while significant progress has been made since 1990, many of the struggles to keep action research alive and well in the district persist. The last few years have been fraught with the challenges of dwindling resources and district decisions that have seriously impacted the CAR program. Faced with severe budget shortfalls, MMSD has eliminated most of the staff development money that supports teachers meeting to work on curricular and instructional issues. There is no longer a dedicated budget for CAR, even to cover supplies and printing, nor is there any longer a staff developer charged with coordinating the program, even as a small part of their position. (Currently, Mary Klehr, an elementary resource teacher, organizes the program beyond the responsibilities of her full-time position.) Although a few departments have continued to provide partial funding for substitutes, most CAR groups must now meet after school, which makes it difficult for teachers with families and other obligations to participate, and which, after a full day of teaching, is not the most productive time for the kind of deep thinking that action researchers find so valuable.

At this stage, with decreased resources and funding, it is uncertain how the program can continue to provide the same level of quality and access, and maintain its place in the larger vision and work of the district. But throughout the years, challenges like these have pushed the CAR program to evolve and adapt. The bright side of this stage in the CAR history is that despite pressures of the federal 'No Child Left Behind' education act, severe budget cuts, and equally severe reductions of ongoing district professional development, facilitators and participants feel strongly that they want action research to continue in the district, and demonstrate a willingness and energy to ensure its survival. What the program has done right from the very first group is to focus on a set of guiding principles that have not only sustained viability, but have ensured ownership by the most important stakeholders – the teachers. These new challenges will hopefully push it to grow even stronger and in new directions, as the program's history continues to unfold.

CORE PROGRAM PRINCIPLES

Possibly the most significant dimension in which educational action research programs vary is the orientation toward teachers, their learning, and the knowledge they produce that can be seen through differences in philosophy, structure, and interactions. Rather than recreating the hierarchical patterns of authority and disregard for teachers' capabilities found in some forms of professional development (including some action research programs), the teacher-driven classroom action research program in Madison is committed to supporting teachers in exercising their own professional judgment and leadership abilities to improve learning for themselves and their students. Annual program evaluations and recent studies of the Madison program (e.g. Zeichner et al.,1998; Zeichner, 2003; Bixby et al., 2001) highlight 10 essential principles that guide the MMSD CAR program and are critical to its long-term success.

1 Participation is Voluntary

A central tenet of this program is that action research is a voluntary endeavor, and participation is open to all kindergarten-grade 12 instructional and support staff. We strongly believe that classroom research should not be a requirement, nor should it be a tool that is used by policy makers or administrators to mandate particular changes on teachers' practices. Rather, we want the work to be driven by participants as much as possible in order to develop the kind of personal investment that is often missing from required professional development activities for teachers. This also lessens the concern about action research being an imposed 'add-on' to teachers' already busy workload; when action research is a voluntary activity, participants are trusted to recognize the work involved, and to make good judgments about their own time and energy.

2 Teachers Have Control over Research Questions and Methods

The Madison CAR program takes a constructivist stance toward pedagogical knowledge. Unlike researchers who take their questions out of existing literature, here teachers identify a central area of pedagogy to investigate, and go through a refining process similar to the practice in qualitative research. In some cases, teachers' questions change in focus completely in relation to evolving data, actions taken by the teacher, or unexpected developments in student interactions and current events.

MMSD action researchers also have autonomy in identifying data collection and analytical strategies that closely match individual contexts and interests. Participants learn from facilitators and other group members about a range of inquiry methods, and choose combinations of qualitative and quantitative approaches to observe, document, and analyze classroom culture and practice. Teacher journals are common data sources, as are quasi-experimental designs and naturalistic methods such as field observations, interviews, and document analysis. Triangulation – multiple and diverse sources, methods, and perspectives in data collection and analysis – is a key element of the process. As is the case with other research in academic settings, this open-by-design quality is intentional and pragmatic, allowing teachers to match method with situation, purpose, and philosophy.

3 Teachers Are Treated as Knowledgeable Professionals

In addition to having control over research content and process, recognition and respect for teachers as knowledgeable professionals are communicated in a number of other ways. Until recent budget cuts made it prohibitive, provision of release time and funding for substitute teachers allowed teachers to meet together during the workday, away from the hectic pace of school, to learn about and develop elements of the research process, share progress, and support each other's learning. Through connections with university faculty, action researchers have been provided with opportunities to publish in journals and present their work to larger audiences at conferences and workshops. Participants can also receive university or district professional advancement credit, and can use the experience as part of the state licensure requirements.

4 Research Group Meetings Take Place in a Nurturing and Supportive Environment over an Extended Period of Time

Monthly research group meetings provide teachers with emotional support and a chance to think deeply about their practice with colleagues. These meetings take place in a nurturing, non-judgmental environment over an extended period of time, creating a culture of inquiry that respects the voices of teachers and the knowledge they bring to the research experience. In annual evaluations of the CAR program, participants repeatedly report that the way in which the meetings are conducted honors their experience and struggles while providing intellectual challenge and collegiality.

MMSD action research groups typically are made up of 6 to 10 participants from across the district, promoting cross-school sharing about practices and ideas. When funding is available, groups meet monthly in the morning, with several additional afternoons provided during the year for individual writing. Meeting spaces are donated by community organizations, so that teachers have a physical and intellectual space away from school to focus and reflect about issues of teaching and learning. Attendance at all meetings is critical, since absences lead to loss of momentum and disconnection from the group. Working in a teacher-facilitated group in which all members are engaged in self-study, even if individual research projects differ in content and scope, helps participants develop new ways to work collaboratively.

5 Specific Rituals and Routines Provide a Structure for the Group Meetings

Although there is variation across research groups, monthly meetings are conducted according to a particular set of assumptions about how teacher learning is best supported. There is a general structure to the meeting activities over the course of the school year (see Caro-Bruce, 2000, for details), and a unique culture within each group is developed by the participants through agreed-upon ground rules for group interactions and shared ideas for research questions and data processes. The authentic nature of the communication (e.g., people 'really listening' to each other) is an important aspect of the group experience for teachers. Ample time for discussion is provided, which allows the researchers to more fully understand the context of each other's work, and become advocates for each other's success. This is not to imply that the goal is to create a collective, unified view; rather, individuals are pushed to be clear about their thinking in a public way, to be open with colleagues about their challenges, and thoughtfully engage with the diverse ideas and findings of other group members.

6 Facilitators Provide a Framework for the Research Process and Technical Assistance along the Way

Group facilitators, experienced action researchers who for the most part are classroom teachers themselves, provide an overall framework within which the research is conducted, help teachers locate literature and resources related to their research topic, offer technical assistance through each stage of the research process, and support teachers in writing research reports. Facilitators work in pairs, an experienced facilitator often mentoring a beginner. Because they have gone through the CAR process themselves, facilitators understand the subtleties of the process and empathize with the struggles that teachers experience in conducting classroom inquiry. Rather than positioning themselves as content experts or research instructors, CAR facilitators model a critical reflective stance, posing clarifying questions as opposed to suggesting actions or solutions, and sharing leadership with the whole group in providing feedback and support.

7 Group Facilitators Receive Regular Support

Regular support for the group facilitators is an important feature of the program. In addition to the co-facilitation model, the program coordinator provides an overall structure for the operation of the groups and material resources (see Caro-Bruce, 2000). Monthly seminars bring facilitators together to discuss issues related to adult learning and research facilitation. During these seminars, facilitators work with the coordinator to reflect on participant feedback, refine aspects of the action research process, analyze program effectiveness, and shape its direction.

8 Teachers Write Summary Reports that are Shared with Others

At the end of the school year, Madison action researchers present their findings at a district-wide forum and summarize their work in writing. Although the written studies vary in length, content, and tone, the reports typically lay out the teachers' research processes, tentative findings, the impact on themselves and their students, and speculations about where the research will lead. While some studies focus on developing a better understanding of current practice, most attempt to change and improve it. A majority of the nearly 600 studies between 1991 and 2007 focus on specific classroom concerns, but some move beyond to school-wide or district-level issues (e.g. Friend-Kalupa, 2001; Motoviloff, 2004;

Valaskey, 1999). Although initially feared by many participants, program evaluations show that most feel that the expectation to discuss findings with others and write a report for district publication are important vehicles for synthesizing what was learned, creating meaningful professional connections with other researchers, and inspiring continued inquiry work.

9 Reflective Practice Is at the Heart of Action Research

Madison's CAR program is guided by principles of rigorous reflective practice. It shares what Metz (2001) calls the 'common anatomy' of educational research – finding a research question of pedagogical importance, identifying prior knowledge, generating and analyzing data, and sharing the findings with others – but adds the catalytic step of action. As noted by Henry and Kemmis (1985), action research is motivated by teachers' determination to understand and improve practice, and is thus about problem-posing as much as it is about problem-solving. Because the process of reflection and action is typically ongoing and continually in flux, few Madison action researchers feel a sense of finality at the end of their research year.

10 The District-University Relationship Around CAR is Collaborative and Democratic

The relationship between teachers, staff developers, and University of Wisconsin-Madison faculty around action research is collaborative in nature. Rather than taking control of the program or serving as intellectual gatekeeper, the university's role is one of advocacy, access, and support. While the district 'owns' the program by designing, funding, and facilitating the work, the university has provided credit, opportunities for teachers to share their research on campus, periodic funding to present at national conferences, publication assistance, and sustained efforts to integrate action research knowledge into its teacher education programming. Several university faculty have also included MMSD action research studies as part of the required reading for both undergraduate and graduate courses.

Investing in teachers to do this kind of work and supporting them in taking control over the scope and nature of their research, a commitment reflected in these 10 core principles, demonstrates a regard and recognition of the role teachers ought to play in examining pedagogical questions that are relevant to classrooms and schools. Much of the passion Madison action researchers have for this work lies in its self-defining nature and the intellectual satisfaction that derives from having control over research agendas; making decisions about how to conduct, theorize, and share the research; and connecting research with the very real life of classrooms in ways that thoughtfully contribute to student learning and sustain interest in the profession.

RESEARCH ABOUT THE NATURE AND IMPACT OF THE PROGRAM

Since the inception of the MMSD classroom action research professional development program in 1990, there have been two systematic studies of the nature and impact of the program on the researchers, their students, and schools. These studies were conducted by a combination of researchers inside and outside of the district and were reported in a variety of publications (e.g., Bixby et al., 2001; Zeichner et al., 1998; Marion, 1998; Zeichner, 2003; Zeichner et al., 2000).

The first study focused on illuminating the nature and impact of the program on teachers and their students and involved interviews with 74 educators who had conducted action research in this program as well as with 10 individuals who facilitated research groups. The study also examined all the written reports and recordings of four television shows in which action researchers talked about their research. Another part of this study conducted by Marion (1998) involved the researcher co-facilitating and documenting what went on inside two research groups, the rituals and routines that were used to structure the meetings, and how the facilitation was enacted. This portion of the larger study sought to illuminate the particular aspects of the action research process that were linked to teacher learning.

The second study focused on the work of two CAR groups that were concerned with special education issues. These groups were organized in 1999–2000 by Jack Jorgensen, the district director of special educational services, following the introduction of a new service delivery model. Data were collected through a series of interviews with 15 teachers and four facilitators, analysis of written reports produced by the teachers at the end of the year, and a district-sponsored forum where teachers presented their research and district staff spoke about the impact on policy.

A number of significant things were learned about the nature and impact of the program from these two studies. For example, in the interviews, many of the teachers reported that engaging in action research had helped them develop more confidence in their ability to influence the circumstances in which they teach. They felt a greater sense of control over their work and thought that they were more proactive than before in dealing with difficult issues that arose in their practice. Many teachers also reported that they now looked at their teaching in a more analytic, focused manner, a habit they claimed to have internalized and applied beyond the research experience. These teachers stated that they were now more likely to step back and examine what they were doing and that they had become more concerned with the need to gather data to understand the impact of their teaching. The following statement from one of the interviews is typical of what teachers told us:

> I look at classrooms differently now. Prior to actually gathering data, I made assumptions as we all do about why particular students are acting the way they are. And one of the things I learned, not just through my research but by listening to other people's too, is that our

assumptions are wrong more often than they are right. And so I began to ask questions and by the time I finished my year as a classroom action researcher, I was very much in the habit of looking at things through questions.

Many teachers also reported that they were now more likely to talk with colleagues in their schools about their teaching and that engaging in what they perceived to be authentic dialogue convinced them of the importance of collaborative work with other teachers. Several teachers indicated that the research experience raised their expectations for how they should be treated by others in the district. Because they felt that they were treated with respect and trust within the action research program, they now expected other professional development activities to demonstrate this same respect for teachers and ambitious view of their capabilities.

There is also substantial evidence in the data that teacher practice became more 'learner-centered' as a result of conducting action research. Many of the teachers stated that they were now much more convinced of the importance of talking to their students and listening carefully to them, and that they had developed higher expectations for what their students know and can do. The following comment by a science teacher is typical of what we heard on this issue:

I gave them a list of all of the labs I did in my classes. What labs do you favor, which do you not like, why don't you like them, and how can I improve them for students next year? They gave me so much insight into where they were coming from that they really helped me. I was able to go back to a number of the labs and change them to reflect what they had suggested. It worked so much better the way that they had suggested. It was like oh wow. You know we should really spend more time talking to the kids.

It is important to remember that these and other similar outcomes are connected to an action research professional development program based on a particular set of principles and structural characteristics (see above), and are not the result of action research *per se*. Marion's (1998) insider study as a group co-facilitator illuminated some of the ways in which the core principles discussed earlier are enacted within the groups. For example, she describes the structures and routines that help build a collaborative research culture within the groups, achieving consensus on interaction norms and confidentiality, and certain procedures designed to help teachers question their assumptions and think more deeply about their research issues.

One of the most interesting findings from our studies of the CAR program is the impact that the research of the teachers in the two special education groups had on district-level policies. Contrary to common perceptions that teacher inquiry has limited impact beyond one's classroom, our research identified several specific aspects of the district's new professional development plan for special education staff that came directly from the findings of teachers' studies. For example, a number of the studies concluded that there was a need to provide training and support for teachers to work with students with disabilities that fall outside a teacher's specific certification area. Consequently, this training was built into the district's professional development offerings. Also, several of the action research studies uncovered the need for more professional development for special education assistants, and a new program for these paraprofessionals was subsequently developed and implemented. Using the findings of teachers' studies to inform the development of the school district's professional development plan was part of the intent of forming the groups in the first place and these effects were clearly documented the year following the completion of the work of the two CAR groups (Bixby et al., 2001). There are a few other examples in the literature of the action research studies of teachers influencing educational policies (e.g., Atkin, 1994; Grimmett, 1995; Meyers and Rust, 2003), but generally neither teachers nor policy makers have thought about the possibilities for drawing on the insights of teachers' action research to shape educational policies.

Our studies also revealed a number of complications and difficulties that were experienced by some teachers. For example, narrowing down an area of interest into a research question and finding the time to write were two of the most common challenges of the research process. Also, some teachers who were in large research groups were periodically frustrated by the lack of time for everyone to have the opportunity to share their research progress in depth.

At another level, teachers who were either trying to build more positive relations with their colleagues or were challenging things that were accepted by most of the staff in their schools uncovered and sometimes intensified tensions that made their lives more complicated. Although conducting action research was often difficult, complex and sometimes frustrating for teachers, most valued the intellectual challenges posed by the research experience in comparison with what they saw as the superficial nature of many of their other professional development experiences.

THE COMPLEXITIES OF SUPPORTING TEACHER ACTION RESEARCH IN AN ERA OF NARROW FORMS OF ACCOUNTABILITY AND DECLINING SCHOOL BUDGETS

Although this school-based classroom action research program has been built from the beginning on the belief that teachers and other educators who work directly every day with students can make important contributions to creating innovative solutions to the many problems that face public schools, there are several factors in recent years that have worked against the idea of investing in teachers as active contributors to creating solutions to educational problems.

One of the major factors that have worked against this vision of teachers as educational leaders is the pressure created by the national education law, the 'No Child Left Behind Act', to focus on standardized testing as the force that drives decisions in schools. With the increased pressure on staff to avoid the punitive sanctions imposed when standardized test scores do not measure up to federal standards, there has been a noticeable increase in the district in mandated professional development experiences tied to district standards and assessments and a decrease in the kind of teacher-initiated professional development opportunities like the classroom action research program that had been particularly prominent in this district for many years.

A second factor that has undermined the role of teachers-researchers who create and share innovative practices has been the consistent budget cuts in the school district that have resulted in the reduction and elimination of many programs and services, including funding for professional development activities for staff in addition to the required district-initiated professional development activities tied to standards and assessments. Because of the state of Wisconsin's school funding formula, the increased privatization of public schooling, and the federal government's underfunding of key programs related to providing extra support for students living in poverty, special education students, and English Language Learners, most districts in Wisconsin face severe financial difficulty every year. Professional development programs for staff have been particularly vulnerable during this time (Karp, 2003; Morales, 2006). This cutting of resources in public education systems is a phenomenon that has been occurring throughout the world (e.g., Carnoy, 2000; Samoff, 1996) and has resulted in a deterioration of teachers' working conditions almost everywhere (UNESCO, 1998).

Whether this school district-based action research program will be able to endure in the future remains to be seen. What has happened in Madison, Wisconsin with regard to the increasing centralization of control of teaching and learning into district hands and the corresponding reduction in teachers' abilities to exercise their judgments within their classrooms and about their own professional development is a phenomenon that is occurring in much of the world (Bottery and Wright, 2000; Tatto, 2007). The literature on school reform and teacher quality suggests that this deprofessionalization of the role of teaching through increased external accountability systems and reduction of teacher autonomy in relation to their work

> can deny teachers the very control and flexibility necessary to do their job effectively, can undermine the motivation of those doing the job ... and may end up contributing to turnover among teachers ... As a result such reforms may not only fail to solve the problems they seek to address, but also end up making things worse. (Ingersoll, 2003: 236–7)

A strong teacher-driven professional development system and working conditions for teachers that enable them to exercise their judgment and make continual adaptations to meet the ongoing needs of their students are essential to a successful public education system.

NOTE

1 The abstracts and studies can be retrieved at http://www.madison.k12.wi.us/sod/car/carhome page.html. Also see Caro-Bruce et al. (2007).

REFERENCES

Atkin, J.M. (1994) 'Teacher research to change policy: An illustration', in S. Hollingsworth and H. Sockett (eds), *Teacher Research and Educational Reform*. Chicago: University of Chicago Press, pp. 103–20.

Bixby, J., Klehr, M., Zeichner, K., Caro-Bruce C. and Lyngaas, K. (2001, April). 'From practice to policy: Using teacher action research to transform school district policies with regard to special education'. Paper presented at the annual meeting of the American Educational Research Association, Seattle, WA.

Bottery, M. and Wright, N. (2000) *Teachers and the State: Towards a Directed Profession*. London: Routledge.

Carnoy, M. (2000) 'Globalization and educational reform', in N. Stromquist and K. Monkman (eds), *Globalization: Integration and Contestation Across Cultures*. Lanham, MD: Roman & Littlefield, pp. 43–62.

Caro-Bruce, C. (2000) *Action Research Facilitator's Handbook*. Oxford, OH: National Staff Develop-ment Council.

Caro-Bruce, C., Flessner, R., Klehr, M. and Zeichner, K. (2007) (eds) *Creating Equitable Classrooms Through Action Research*. Thousand Oaks, CA: Corwin Press.

Friend-Kalupa, L. (2001) 'If we're all cross-categorical, why do we all think it means something different? Perceptions and satisfaction factors related to cross-categorical service delivery', (Vol *2000 Special Education I*). Madison, WI: Madison Metropolitan School District.

Grimmett, P. (1995) 'Developing voice through teacher research: Implications for educational policy', in J. Smyth (ed.), *Critical Discourse on Teacher Development*. London: Cassell, pp. 113–29.

Henry, C. and Kemmis, S. (1985) 'A point-by-point guide to action research for teachers', *The Australian Administrator*, 6 (4).

Ingersoll, R. (2003) *Who Controls Teachers' Work: Power and Accountability in America's Schools*. Cambridge: Harvard University Press.

Karp, S. (2003) 'Money, schools, and justice', *Rethinking Schools*, 18 (1). Retrieved from www.rethink ingschools.org. on August 18, 2006.

Marion, R. (1998) '*Practitioner research as a vehicle for teacher learning*'. Unpublished doctoral dissertation, University of Wisconsin-Madison.

Metz, M.H. (2001) 'Intellectual border crossing in graduate education: A report from the field', *Educational Researcher*, 30 (5): 12–18.

Meyers, E. and Rust, F. (eds) (2003) *Taking Action with Teacher Research*. Portsmouth, NH: Heinemann.

Morales, J. (2006) 'School board journey', *Rethinking schools*, 20 (3). Retrieved from www.rethinking schools.org on January 15, 2007.

Motoviloff, K. (2004) 'Inclusion: What practicing teachers say it take'. (Vol. *2004 Special Education*). Madison, WI: Madison Metropolitan School District.

Samoff, J. (1996) 'Which priorities and strategies for education?' *International Journal of Educational Development*, 16 (3): 249–71.

Tatto, M.T. (2007) (ed.). *Reforming Teaching Globally*. Oxford, UK: Symposium Books.

UNESCO (1998) *World Education Report: Teachers and Teaching in a Changing World*. Paris: UNESCO Publishing.

Valaskey, V. (1999) 'How can the science department and special education department heterogeneously group a wide variety of students in the same classroom and make it a successful experience for the students and staff?' (Vol. *1999 Teaching & Learning*). Madison, WI: Madison Metropolitan School District.

Zeichner, K. (2003) 'The nature and impact of teacher research as a professional development activity for P-12 educators in the USA'. *Educational Action Research*, 11 (2): 301–26.

Zeichner, K., Klehr, M. and Caro-Bruce, C. (2000) 'Pulling their own levers', *Journal of Staff Development*, 21 (4): 36–9.

Zeichner, K., Marion, R. and Caro-Bruce, C. (1998) *The Nature and Impact of Action Research in One Urban School District: Final Report*. Chicago: Spencer and MacArthur Foundations.

9

Using Action Research to Support Students with Special Educational Needs

Christine O'Hanlon

Educational reform continues apace with policy related to students with 'special educational needs' (SEN), reflecting the now familiar themes of quality, diversity, parental choice, greater school autonomy and greater accountability. The UK government and many others throughout Europe, Asia, USA, and South America have placed inclusion firmly at the centre of debate about the development of educational policy and practice. The UK government's commitment to inclusive education aligns educational policy with international initiatives worldwide (Ainscow, 1999; Pijl et al., 1997; O'Hanlon, 2003; Tomlinson et al., 2004). The basis of the initiatives is that mainstream schools can, and should, develop structures and practices to allow them to respond more fully to the diversity of learning need in the student population.

The everyday reality of schooling poses a particular set of complex dilemmas and problems for the inclusion of students with SEN into the mainstream and the implementation of inclusive educational practice more generally. International statistics (OECD, 2007; UNESCO, 2007; DfES, 2007) record that students who may have been previously separated into special education, with SEN, learning disabilities, additional educational needs, students with emotional and behavioural difficulties, and other numerous labels and syndromes, which vary between countries, are increasingly participating in mainstream or regular schools worldwide.

Because of the many dilemmas and problems resulting from inclusion worldwide, action research has become particularly attractive and successful as a school-based approach for better teaching and learning for students with SEN.

It is often chosen as a means of transforming existing practice and breaking traditional educational assumptions by creating new theories and practices unre-
strained by governments' erratic and changing agendas for raising school
standards. The following issues and concerns are consistently accepted as contemporary global issues for action research when governments' main priority is
to raise attainment for all students, and they are developed in more detail later:

- adaptation of the mainstream curriculum to meet the needs of students' diverse and wide
ability;
- the provision of support for students with SEN that is synchronized with mainstream subject teaching and provides equal opportunities for all;
- the social cohesion of classrooms and schools with students that are 'hard to reach' and
'hard to teach';
- relying upon teachers' judgements regarding the amount of SEN time, resources and
attention necessary for planning individual student learning needs.

Although much has been written on the topic of international policy developments in inclusion and special needs education, there has been little specifically
written about action research as a means of furthering the education of students
with SEN. One explanation is that action research for SEN has been modified
and developed into school improvement agendas (Ainscow, 1998), or lesson
studies (see CSNSIE website) in recent decades. Also, because of the movement
towards the inclusion of children and young people with special needs into mainstream schools worldwide, the action research that occurs for improved SEN
teaching and learning becomes subsumed into general educational journals and
is therefore difficult to specifically identify and access.

In addition, there is such a low percentage of children in special education
both nationally and internationally (1 to 3 per cent), action research carried out
with SEN students is often published as general school-based action research,
because of the small special education readership, or under the heading of inclusion, although individual studies can be found through networks and web
searches (Queen's University, 2000, Lloyd, 2002).

However, a small number of action research SEN case studies have been published in mainstream journals (see BERJ, 1995) and thus have reached a wide
readership. Also, a number of books directly address action research as a means
of supporting students with SEN (Bell, 1994; O'Hanlon, 2003; Armstrong and
Moore, 2004), and there are similar articles in international journals (Ainscow et
al., 2004; O'Hanlon, 2007a,b). However, much of what is written is focused on
the professional training of teachers for students with SEN (Buck and Cordes,
2005), and is merged within the general educational literature and thus difficult
to access specifically. Action research as a means of supporting students with
SEN can be evidenced from numerous action research networks (e.g., AERA,
2008 action research SIG). Also in Canada for example, the Alberta Teachers
Association and Chinook's Edge School Division have developed a project to use

collaborative AR to improve practice and knowledge of secondary teachers to aid in the integration of students with learning disabilities into the regular classroom (Alberta Teachers Association, 2008).

My main resource for this chapter is an archive of work on inclusion and SEN via action research, carried out at Masters and Ph.D. level and sustained by my examination of postgraduate research theses in a wide range of higher education institutions throughout the UK and Ireland. The issues and concerns listed earlier are gleaned from a growing body of knowledge in SEN through action research internationally, particularly from personal involvement in Spain, Italy, Greece, the Netherlands, France, Germany, Austria, Hong Kong and Africa which is now exemplified through the UK context.

THE UK CONTEXT

According to official UK figures for 2007 (Statistics DfES, 2007), there are 36 per cent of students with SEN placed in special schools or student referral units, and 61 per cent are placed in mainstream schools. There is an overall incidence of 2.8 per cent of all students who have statements of SEN, which indicates that these students are officially acknowledged, and entitled to, additional educational support. When the special needs focus in education moved away from child-centred problems to focus more on school environments and the social context, a greater responsibility was placed on mainstream teachers and schools to adapt and change to meet each child's needs.

The 1988 Education Reform Act introduced the National Curriculum and the devolvement of funding to schools, both of which have had a significant impact on the acceptance of students with SEN in mainstream schools. The Code of Practice on the Identification and Assessment of Special Educational Needs (DfES, 1994) provided a practical framework as a consequence of the 1993 Education Act. This legislation laid the foundations for the development of the role of the school special educational needs co-ordinator as it is today, because it set out the principles for SEN in school and the key areas of responsibility for the school SEN co-ordinator. The revised Code of Practice, published in 2002 (DfES), amended and reasserted the role of the school SEN co-ordinator as a manager and co-ordinator of SEN provision for all students within the school. Much of the action research carried out in UK schools is initiated and developed by the school SEN co-ordinator because funding is available for their continued professional development (CPD), which is often developed through action research.

Students with educational differences exist globally in every classroom, or school, without the necessity of official identification. The identification of different educational needs gives the UK student a statutory right to be 'statemented', i.e. with identified recorded specific need/s that should be met through schooling. The statementing process can be initiated by the parent or the school (with children of school age). When a child is 'statemented' there are legal obligations on the local education authority to provide for the child's educational needs, in school, or with additional help externally, as outlined in the statement. The professed aim of designating a child as 'special' or 'different', when he/she is experiencing school-related difficulties is to provide him/her with a better educational environment. Schools in the UK have sufficient learning support available to assist teachers and students with SEN. However, special and mainstream schools both share concerns about: management and organization; assessment and school placement; para/professional support; equality of treatment, and raising standards in literacy, numeracy and science subjects. Through action research, schools in the UK are able to assist teachers and students with SEN, in different learning environments, to create a variety of learning opportunities to meet the needs of children with unique and different learning and relational patterns. Educational differences, which formerly were seen as negative, are now seen as an educative opportunity. Every child is entitled to a school setting which provides the greatest growth potential for them.

Policies for 'inclusion' have ensured that children are no longer excluded from mainstream schooling because of perceived learning differences, language, cultural, racial, class, religious and behavioural differences. The consequent pedagogical adjustments require not simply the implementation of programmes of action but involve the negotiation of change in schools which requires an investigative structure with a sound basis for practical and planned action.

WHAT ARE THE MAJOR CHARACTERISTICS OF ACTION RESEARCH FOR SEN?

Action research for students with SEN is an investigatory strategy, which aspires to be inclusive in order to enable usually silenced, and excluded, individuals and groups, to be publicly heard, and to contribute to debates about their care and education. Action research is exploratory research where participants can be co-researchers and active partners in changing educational practice. In this sharing investigatory context, teacher/educational researchers are faced with the uniqueness of each student, and are challenged to find a means of representing them with respect and authenticity. Action research supports multiple perspectives gained from many data sources, such as interviews, discussions, research journals, and observations, to inform and reveal complexity and difference and bring about new understanding to inform future change and action, which is critical to the education of children with SEN and disabilities.

As in all forms of research, the validity of AR with students with SEN depends upon how carefully and accurately evidence is collected, interpreted and reported. But implicit in validation is the question of how the research methods themselves influence, and alter, observed behaviour and their accounts. How are these effects taken into account in explaining results and implementing change strategies? As in all research, AR should be checked for reliability, the subjectivity of the evidence, bias and accuracy, and the general motives and expectations for the research. Action research investigation in the field of SEN should be critical of, and concerned with deconstructing authoritative voices, those who speak for, and on behalf of others, while at the same time deconstructing the researcher's voice used to validate personal perceptions and explanations of what counts as good practice for students with SEN in any educational setting.

The key question is: *How does AR involving students with SEN differ from AR with children and young people generally?*

It differs primarily because it offers participants who are 'hard to reach' and 'hard to teach' equality as participants. In so doing, it poses a real challenge to the existing traditional and established educational institutions. The educational system perpetuates a hierarchical view of schooling and imposes controls on who manages and operates educational entitlement. Action research confronts the dilemmas and contradictions of the system in practice, and challenges the implicit assumptions which underpin school and examination systems, which are detrimental for the education of students with SEN.

ADDRESSING ISSUES IN PRACTICE

Students with SEN may not be in a position to give informed consent, they may be targeted by researchers because of their unusual or unacceptable school behaviour, or they may be seen as a challenge to teaching procedures, organization and programmes in schools. Often, because of the inclusion of children with SEN in mainstream schools there is a tendency for teachers to focus on students with SEN as the 'problem' rather than examine the educational, context and participants role within it. It is a challenge to teachers doing AR to view the student in the wider institutional context of school, and to examine the complex interplay of factors which lead to learning, behavioural or other school difficulties. Basic assumptions are often overturned by teacher/s reflection on their own role, behaviour and attitudes towards the student/s in specific school contexts. These issues are illustrated by the following case stories and summaries, which are recounted from archival material and action research data personally co-ordinated with the approval of the original investigators. Contributors to the case studies used in this chapter have asked not to be identified and have agreed to their work being used as exemplars.

For example, Barbara who taught a year four class in a mainstream school had chosen to research what she had initially considered to be some lazy, unmotivated, and difficult to reach students with SEN in classroom lessons. Several students in her class were problematic for her, and were not achieving as she would have hoped. She determined to look at this group, and at one student in particular, whom she thought was the leader/exemplar for much of the challenging behaviour. But she found when her action research advanced that the problems she was experiencing were related to the wider context of the curriculum and school, and that she was under pressure to ensure a high level of student performance, which put her and her students under great pressure. She reflects that:

> I had largely ignored the institutional aspect of the curriculum in that my students with SEN had rarely been given the opportunity to share, lead or co-operate with each other. I was often guilty of rewarding the good worker with more work and the less diligent, or lazy student got away with less effort. Only by examining my actions through my action research investigation I have come to realize how wrong I had been.

Barbara realized that she was part of the problem being examined and was willing to change herself and the situation to accommodate the learning needs of the 'difficult to reach' students. She was forced to examine her own practice and to reflect on the ethics of rewarding student work output with yet more work which became counterproductive and detrimental to students with SEN. Barbara was concerned with the whole class interaction and the role of 'work' as a criterion for reward. She viewed the classroom as an organic unit and her investigation encompassed the totality of student and teacher activities. By contrast, there are many action research investigations focused upon individual students, because of the tradition of individual case study in the field of special education and psychology.

Focusing on a single student with SEN as an action research case study can be problematic because of the instability of having only 'one' student, and also the ethical issue of selecting and acting differently, by possibly planning different teaching methods and techniques for just one student. When it is a group of students (with or without SEN) involved in the AR, there is an opportunity to understand wider student learning and behaviour in a group context, and to compare one or more students' development within the group. If there is no alternative course of action but to use a single student in the action research, great care must be taken to obscure the identity of the child, and to focus, as far as possible, on the implications of the action research to develop others' learning, beyond the single study, in order to support children with comparable learning needs in similar contexts. In the following example of a single student case study, Gemma, the teacher carrying out action research, finds her work with one student nevertheless benefits the learning of many other students in her class.

Gemma, a teacher in a mainstream primary school, noticed a boy in her classroom who was designated SEN, was not experiencing an inclusive schooling and wasn't taking advantage of the mainstream curriculum. She observed Ben for a period of three weeks in the classroom and school generally. He appeared to be withdrawn and did not interact in lessons except when Art was an activity. He was slow to start his work, he hated having to make decisions and panicked about time constraints. Colleagues in the school confirmed that Ben always had trouble with his work, was slow to start and wasted time sitting around instead of writing or engaging with the task. He was exceptionally good at Art, and spent most of his spare time drawing. Teachers felt he was of low average ability and he did not apply himself to school work. Gemma devised a research programme with new teaching techniques, involving multi-sensory approaches to learning for Ben. She talked to his parents and teachers and held discussions with Ben about his understanding of what he was doing and learning. Ben's primary sensory learning mode, she found out, was his visual ability, which was used intensively over the course of two months, to enable him to improve his attitude and engagement with school activities. Using a visual approach with Ben led to Gemma incorporating this method in her general teaching, which helped all the children in her class, because through this new approach their learning improved by visualizing problems before they started to work them out. All the students in the class have now grown in confidence and listen better to each other. On a recent problem-solving activity on a residential visit, Ben made himself heard, he put forward his own ideas, which were accepted and developed by the other students. He is now generally more confident about learning and able to access the full curriculum in school. His parents and other teachers are pleased with his progress, and the reduction in his anxiety and avoidance behaviour when doing school work. Gemma states that she is happy, that through the case study she has been able to step back and force herself to analyse her teaching styles and classroom ethos, which will benefit her students now and always.

The Policy Document on Inclusive Schooling (DfES, 2001) refers to the 'need to share good practice in supporting students who present challenging and disruptive behaviour' (20.49). Students who disrupt classrooms and are seen to have emotional and behavioural difficulties have a large representation among students with SEN and are often schooled separately in pupil referral units, with small teacher–student ratios and a more flexible curriculum. Nevertheless, mainstream teachers try hard to retain their existing students in school because they realize they often become disaffected in response to the school and its curriculum.

Students with SEN, in the UK and elsewhere, are increasingly being identified with Autism and Asperger's Syndrome. Depending on the severity of the condition, many children are placed in special educational provision in a special school. Lorraine worked in a special school, which did not want to segregate students with Autistic Spectrum Disorders or severe and challenging behaviours from other students with a range of learning difficulties, because of their behaviour. Such provision would not always provide appropriate social and communication role models for these students, but instead, would possibly reinforce stereotypical and isolating behaviours. There had been a recent trend to transfer 'problem children' to the school, and, however thorough the existing training for physical restraint, and its supporting philosophy, using physical intervention as a control was used too readily by school staff. It was decided that action research would be the best way to identify manageable methods for investigating situations that triggered challenging behaviour and to examine possible strategies that would help modify such student behaviour when it occurred. It was hoped that by researching other approaches to unacceptable behaviour, a model would be created which relied much less on physical handling. The research also highlighted the extent to which stress-related conditions diminished teachers' abilities to cope with challenging student behaviour, because it was found that many teachers involved in the study had significant periods of school absence. As a result of the changes brought about by the action research process, incident records are now monitored in great detail and show there have been clear decreases in the number of students' aggressive and challenging school incidents. Observations and questionnaires also indicate a reduction in the use of restraint. The changes have not only involved those students targeted for the project, but there has been a knock-on effect, which has impacted on all students in the school. The high profile nature of the action research project, and the wide-ranging involvement of many colleagues has influenced how all school staff (teachers and learning support assistants) are now reacting to challenging behaviours. The whole school staff perceived the focus of the research to be important and, in general, more positive management of students' behavioural difficulties has resulted. The strategies employed have made a real difference to how staff now manage students' behaviour, and consequently on how students behave, which has lessened staff stress.

The final conclusions indicate not only a positive impact on students' behavioural difficulties through new strategies employed by staff, but also on staff confidence and stress levels. None of the strategies employed were new or complex, and the questionnaire responses indicated that staff believed them to be effective.

As a result of the action research project the whole school development plan has been changed to ensure:

- increase in support for staff from the senior management team in relation to students with challenging behaviour; this is to include observation and feedback, support within class, leadership by example, and monitoring of staff well-being;
- in-service provision for behaviour management training sessions regularly every term or every half term; regular practical problem-solving sessions and peer support;
- ongoing monitoring of incident reports so that changes in behaviour and the management of behaviour are quickly identified and responded to;
- staff are encouraged, through group working, to become more self-reflective so that the action research process of working remains active within the school, and particularly in relation to what has been achieved in the last year;
- policy and practice is regularly reviewed within the school in the light of new guidance on the use of restrictive physical intervention, and its limited occasional use when absolutely necessary, for the protection of other students or staff.

The local education authority has written an action plan for the next four years and it is expected that this action research will be implemented on a wider basis to extend to mainstream schools through a clear plan of action based on the positive results of this project. The schools, both special and mainstream, targeted for the use of new behavioural strategies for students with Autistic Spectrum Disorders and behavioural difficulties, are now putting in place plans that were derived from the original action research project. The schools are being evaluated for the successful implementation of the new behavioural strategies in both settings.

Action research, because of its reflective nature, teases out the attitudes and motives held by professionals towards their roles and responsibilities, and encourages them to recognize why they work as they do, understand their actions and values, and appreciate their own worth when others often don't. Working to educate children with special needs is not a career chosen by all education professionals. It requires patience and above all a love of humanity, regardless of students' ability to respond and show appreciation for their care and education.

ETHICAL ISSUES

When all things are considered, action research with students and adults with SEN and disabilities is concerned with understanding that the research participants are vulnerable and susceptible to harm, because of their minority status or other stigmatizing factors. Ethical issues include confidentiality, anonymity, reporting abuse or neglect, conflict of personal and professional ethics, balancing demands and expectations of the participants, making the invisible visible, the interpretation of data, and the balance of power between the participants and the principal researcher/s.

Maureen was concerned when doing her action research, about the fact that her name alone could identify her in the context of the research if it were to be placed in the public domain. The student case study she was developing might have been identified via her professional place of work, as few children in this location had the specific syndrome or disorder she was investigating. The individualizing of the subject and persons in the inquiry would be identifiable to those close to the location and other research participants in the study. She assured the participants of their anonymity but found it difficult to guarantee.

Dolores was investigating home education in her research but uncovered what she suspected was child abuse with one particular home educator. The question was – how should she proceed? What action could she take … or should she exclude the family from her research sample? An informal research group comprised of colleagues and participants allowed her to resolve the issue through the sharing of data and rigorous debate.

Dominic worked in a care home and witnessed the sterilization of a young woman with learning difficulties who was viewed to be incapable of making decisions about her sexual activity. This issue was discussed in the group based on evidence and reflections recorded in his research journal. He finally confronted key personnel about the basis for the decision and its consequences, and concluded his action research with recorded entries from the group participants, the young woman concerned, and research colleagues.

When Christine was investigating the education of children with Down's Syndrome she realized that the families being interviewed expected some return for their co-operation in the research. It was difficult to deal with their demands, which were extraneous to the investigation, and the issues raised had to be resolved through informal research group debate and the advice of colleagues and co-researchers. The research report was partly compromised and re-written as a consequence, in order to protect a number of vulnerable research participants.

All participants in AR, especially involving students with SEN, must be alert about confidentiality and anonymity concerns. They need to reflect on whether or not to cover the identity of participants, because total anonymity may unwittingly deny a voice to vulnerable and invisible research participants. This issue involves the balance of power between participants and principal researcher/s and is often one of many issues taken for granted as a protective device for students with SEN and vulnerable people. Yet, because different situations bring their own complexities and realities, each context needs to be discussed openly and honestly to gauge the danger of exposure, or alternatively, the advantages to participants of being named in the research report. Being named can raise the status and self-esteem of participants, whereas if participants always remain anonymous, this can cause further invisibility and damage their self-identity. Each action research dilemma requires its own specific ethical deliberation and resolution.

CONCLUSION

In conclusion, action research has changed the teaching and learning for students with SEN by:

- establishing active participation of students, children and young people, as active partners in an active change process;
- enabling educational contradictions, ambiguity and change to be openly acknowledged and discussed in schools;
- allowing the main researcher/s to work reflexively and explain their understandings of SEN/inclusive situations which constitute school practice;
- seeking to help and support the child, or young person with SEN, to become more competent in school and daily life, by working with other professionals to find the best ways to advance education and development through shared decision making in practice;
- negotiating topics for research and the means of investigation with individual and groups of teachers in schools;
- agreeing guidelines and codes of practice about procedural activities during the research;
- encouraging regular discussion and negotiation with research participants about the recording and publication of the research;
- involving, and acknowledging all participants, especially young children and those with SEN in a respectful, democratic and fair manner.

Action research establishes new ways of working and includes students in new ways of learning. In any society aiming to be democratic and responsive to the needs of its citizens, a just, fair and inclusive culture can be demonstrated in practice through participation in research processes like AR which models the possibilities of inclusion.

As the case stories above illustrate, there are no simple formulae for the resolution of complex issues and concerns that arise as a consequence of inclusive practice and the advancement of better teaching practices for all students, particularly those with SEN. Challenging behaviour is only one issue facing schools which successfully include students with SEN, disabilities and other learning difficulties, but it is a critical one. A greater flexibility in curriculum delivery, an examination of 'how' as well as 'what' is delivered, may offer more positive student experiences and outcomes. Student disaffection and challenging behaviour will remain an ongoing problem in schools until new ways are found to successfully engage all students in learning.

It is critical that education opens up agendas for looking more deeply into professional activities aimed to help and support children and young people with SEN. Often this field of education, when it occurs separately, in special schools, is concerned with the care, support, development and teaching of children as individuals, whereas the education that takes place in mainstream schools is more concerned with national assessment, results, socialization and group learning. The professionals who work for the development of children with SEN share a commitment to their welfare and advancement as well as a genuine desire to make teaching and learning conditions more conducive for their general health, mental and emotional well-being, educational and social development.

Absolutely essential for success in AR is the interpretation of evidence, which inevitably creates a challenge for the principal researcher/s. However, when focused on students with SEN, the analysis of evidence should ideally be a shared, collaborative, professional activity, because AR and its associated change process can make a lasting impact on all schools, both mainstream and special, and affect the future educational opportunities for all students, particularly those with SEN. An informal research group can help to overcome the problems of possible individual misjudgements (in data interpretation or action planning), and encourage research participants and colleagues to share, and open up difficult and problematic ethical issues. It allows professionals to see that others share similar educational concerns and issues, and ultimately it enables them to reach supported understandings that would not have been possible on their own. Many impulsive and unwise interventions have been averted through this method (O'Hanlon, 2003).

In many ways the impact of action research on students with SEN depends on the teacher researchers' awareness of what they are doing and why. It depends on their reflective capacities and willingness to change and devise new strategies for teaching and learning. Students with SEN are increasingly being educated in ordinary schools where students live with, and share, the curriculum with other students. The small percentage of students who may be in special schools, for the most part are taught through individual teaching programmes, which often leads to teacher-researchers focusing on individual children for improved teaching and learning. In mainstream settings, AR is mainly focused on the observation and support of children in groups and classes, which provide the opportunity for long-term change in mainstream education. Because many more students with SEN are being educated in mainstream schools and are the focus of much AR, there is clearly a growing impact on the general education system through increased investigation and change, which challenges the existing status quo. Action research provides a professional impetus for school change, which is a necessary condition for the present and future educational success and inclusion of all young people in education and society.

REFERENCES

AERA (2008) American Educational Research Association, Action Research SIG. website: www.aera/net.

Ainscow, M. (ed.) (1991) *Effective Schools for All*. London: Fulton.

Ainscow, M. (1998) 'Exploring links between special needs and school improvement', in *Support for Learning*, 13 (2): 70–5.

Ainscow, M. (1999) *Understanding the Development of Inclusive Schools*. London, Falmer Press.

Ainscow, M., Booth, T. and Dyson, A. (2004) 'Understanding and developing inclusive practices in schools; a collaborative action research network', in *International Journal of Inclusive Education*, 8 (2): 125–39.

Alberta Teachers Association. http://www.teachers.ab.ca/quick+links. Accessed on 10.02.2008.

Armstrong, F. and Moore, M. (eds) (2004) *Action Research for Inclusive Education*. London: RoutledgeFalmer.

Bell, G. (1994) *Action Research, Special Needs and School Development*. London, David Fulton.

BERJ (1995) (ed. C. O'Hanlon), special issue entitled: *Teacher Research: Methodological and Empowerment Issues in Practical Research for Improved Teaching and Learning*, 21 (3).

Buck, G. and Cordes, J. (2005) 'An action research project on preparing teachers to meet the needs of underserved student populations', in *Journal of Science Teacher Education*, 16 (1): 43–64.

DfES (1994) *SEN Code of Practice*. London DfES/HMSO.

DfES (2001) *Inclusive Schooling: Children with Special Educational Needs*. London, DfES publications 0774/2001. *Special Educational Needs, Code of Practice*. London, HMSO.

DfES (2002) *The Revised Code of Practice* at www.dfes.gov.uk/sen/documents, accessed on 11th September 2007.

DfES (2007) http://www.dfes.gov.uk/statistics/DB/SFR/s0275/tab001.html, accessed 10th May 2007.

Lloyd, C. (2002) 'Developing and changing practice in SEN through critically reflective action research: a case study', in *European Journal of Special Needs Education*, 17 (2): 109–27.

OECD (2007) *Education at a Glance*. Annex 3, Chapter D. Paris: OECD.

O'Hanlon, C. (2003) *Educational Inclusion as Action Research: An Interpretive Discourse*. Maidenhead, Open University Press.

O'Hanlon, C. (2007a) 'A case-study in the eradication of ignorance and intolerance in child education through action research', in *Action Research in Education in Contexts of Poverty: A Tribute to the Life and Work of Professor Fals Borda*. Universidad de la Salle, Bogota, Colombia, pp. 15–33.

O'Hanlon, C. (2007b) 'Action research evaluation in a playcentre: staff training for children with SEN?' in *Hong Kong Journal of Education*, 6 (1): 1–11.

Pijl, S.J., Meijer, C. and Hegarty, S. (1997) *Inclusive Education: A Global Agenda*, London: Routledge.

Queen's University (2000) *Towards Meeting the Needs of all Learners: An Action Research Report.* Queen's University Ontario. Website http://educ.queensu.ca/-ar, accessed on 10.02.2008.

Tomlinson, K., Ridley, K., Fletcher-Campbell, F. and Hegarty, S. (2004) *Evaluation of UNESCO's Programme for the Inclusion of Children from Various Marginalized groups within Formal Education Programmes: Final Report.* Paris:UNESCO.

UNESCO (2007) UNESCO Institute for Statistics (UIS) @ http://uis.unesco.org/ev_en.php, accessed on 11.09.2007.

Contributors to the case studies used in this chapter have asked not to be identified and have agreed to their work being used as exemplars.

Renegotiating Knowledge Relationships in Schools

Chris Bigum and Leonie Rowan

I look to the future because that's where I'm going to spend the rest of my life.
(George Burns, 1983)

Commenting on the challenges associated with understanding and responding to the needs of contemporary children and youth, Douglas Rushkoff made the claim that:

> The degree of change experienced by the past three generations rivals that of a species in mutation. Today's 'screenager' – the child born into a culture mediated by the television and computer – is interacting with his [sic passim] world in at least as dramatically altered a fashion from his grandfather as the first sighted creature did from his blind ancestors, or a winged one from his earthbound forebears … what we need to adapt to, more than any particular change, is the fact that we are changing so rapidly. We must learn to accept change as a constant. Novelty is the new status quo. (Rushkoff, 1996: 3)

Rushkoff is neither the first nor the only theorist to draw attention to apparently dramatic differences between the worlds inhabited by past, current and future human generations. Authors from a wide range of backgrounds have commented on the changing environments, interests and capacities of contemporary youth, seeking to capture their distinctiveness through labels such as Generation X (Coupland, 1991), Generation Y,[1] the net generation (Tapscott, 1999), 'thumb culture'[2]; 'screenagers' (Rushkoff, 1996), millenials (Howe and Strauss, 2000) and so on. Many of these attempts at categorization are followed by attempts to draw attention to the specific challenges associated with providing meaningful educational opportunities for students who – to some teachers – almost appear to be 'aliens in the classroom' (Green and Bigum, 1993).

This chapter outlines one approach to contemporary schooling designed to help teachers move beyond a largely descriptive (and often pessimistic or nostalgic) acknowledgement of changed and changing circumstances (and the related gap between the experiences of teachers and students) towards more optimistic, pro-active educational programs that maximize opportunities for diverse students – no matter how alien they may at first glance appear to be – to cope productively with a future in which change is constant and novelty is the status quo.

This chapter is divided into three parts. In the first we acknowledge the range of challenges that the contemporary environment poses for educators and put forward the concept of 'future proofing' as a way of conceptualizing the purpose of education. In the second we link the aspirational goal of future proofing to philosophical ideas associated with participatory action research. In the third we draw upon both frameworks to analyse the transformative potential of a particular set of educational initiatives, known collectively as the *Knowledge Producing Schools* project or KPS.

PART ONE: EDUCATION, FUTURE PROOFING AND CHANGED AND CHANGING TIMES

The practical, economic, technological and ideological dimensions of this ceaseless change poses significant challenges. Educators are asked to provide not only the kinds of operational skills that may be meaningful in the employment, lifestyle and leisure activities of the future – how do we use technology X? what do we do with technology Y? – but also cultural skills necessary for understanding the different modes of behaviour and interaction that are valid and valued within particular contexts (behaviour A is appropriate in one context, but not in another) and finally the kinds of critical capacities which enable us to look at where particular patterns of behaviour have come from, and how we, ourselves, may contribute to either producing or contesting dominant ideological positions on a diverse range of topics.

The first challenge facing educators, then, is to acknowledge that we can no longer even pretend to be in the business of providing students with one particular set of skills which will equip them for a relatively stable and largely uninterrupted career in one particular industry and trade. With the possible exception of literacy and numeracy skills, there are few capacities that can now lay claim to an unproblematic alignment between the skill and a specific career path.

Such an acknowledgement has the immediate effect of shifting attention away from the kinds of *specific* skills that kids will need in the future towards the kinds of *dispositions* that will enable them to acquire and demonstrate whatever skills are demanded of them in their future work, personal and social lives.

We have argued elsewhere that these dispositions might include:

- a critical understanding of the changed/changing social, political and economic environments;
- a strong sense of self;

- the ability to live harmoniously in a community characterized by social and cultural diversity;
- a positive attitude to life-long and life-wide learning;
- the resultant potential to contribute to the intellectual, emotional and economic future well-being of the nation. (Rowan, 2007).

Underpinning this list is the belief that all students are entitled to develop a positive disposition towards knowledge work, which includes learning, teaching, producing and sharing knowledge. We use the term 'knowledge work' here to locate students with other, more commonly acknowledged knowledge workers, such as teachers (Kincheloe, 2006).

This brings us to the concept of future proofing. The term itself is derived from technology contexts where it refers to a technology possessing the greatest chance of remaining current into the future. We use the term in the context of educational debates to signal the responsibility that schools have to provide students with the kinds of robust and durable skills and dispositions that equip them to cope with increasing levels of change and uncertainty (as well as increasing political and ideological tension). This is not to suggest that schooling can function as some kind of guaranteed inoculation against whatever may await us in the future. Rather, a future proofing mindset emphasizes the importance of providing students with the kinds of meta-skills outlined above that are most likely to be useful to them regardless of what happens in the future.

Central to this mindset is a willingness to acknowledge that previous and dominant approaches to education have *not* offered all students access to successful futures. Indeed, despite years of equity-based reforms – focused on issues including gender, cultural background, disability, and socioeconomics – some groups of children remain more likely than others to experience educational failure. Attempts to move beyond this scenario require not the adoption of a new educational slogan – individualized learning, personalized learning, authentic learning – but rather some fundamental change in the way schools operate. Future proofing, in this sense, becomes an aspiration motivated by a belief in the need for, and possibility of change.

Any future proofing project, therefore, must be based on the core belief that schools *can* make a difference to how individual, and groups of, kids approach the future. This leads to the second key point. In order to take up the idea of future proofing as an educational aspiration, educators themselves must be willing to accept that the future is not a fixed reality out there that will come to us. We – teachers, parents, students, citizens – are not passive. Rather we have the capacity (albeit with different levels of authority) to contribute to the way that future develops.

To this end future proofing can be seen as aligned with an educational philosophy known as 'educated hope'. Ruth Levitas (1993: 257) describes educated hope as, 'the desire for a better way of living expressed in the description of a different kind of society that makes possible that alternative way of life'.

Extending this point, Henry Giroux (2003) describes 'educated hope', as a language:

> of resistance and possibility, a language that embraces a militant utopianism while constantly being attentive to those forces that seek to turn such hope into a new slogan or punish and dismiss those who dare look beyond the horizon of the given. Hope as a form of militant utopianism is one of the preconditions for individual and social struggle, the ongoing practice of critical education in a wide variety of sites – the attempt to make a difference by being able to imagine otherwise in order to act in other ways.

He goes on to say:

> Educated hope also demands a certain amount of courage on the part of intellectuals in that it demands from them the necessity to articulate social possibilities, mediate the experience of injustice as part of a broader attempt to contest the workings of oppressive power, undermine various forms of domination, and fight for alternative ways to imagine the future.

The key point made by Giroux here is that education is always, and inevitably, not only about providing students with particular skill sets, but also about demonstrating to students that futures are not fixed or already determined (regardless of how this may seem). For this idealistic sentiment to become a reality, however, all students need opportunities to see themselves as skilled, active, productive members of a community. The next question is how to move beyond this aspirational moment to new performances of schooling within which future proofing is a realistic goal. This leads us to the role of action research – more specifically, participatory action research – in shaping and re-shaping transformative educational agendas.

PART TWO: EDUCATED HOPE, FUTURE PROOFING AND PARTICIPATORY ACTION RESEARCH

Other chapters in this book illustrate a range of different enactments of action research. Here we are interested in the ways that the kind of philosophical disposition associated with participatory action research (hereafter PAR) can help to shape, reshape and, indeed, evaluate the kind of KPS initiatives outlined in the next section. Our purpose in drawing upon PAR is not so much to provide another articulation of what it looks like or how it might work. This is well documented in a large and diverse literature which takes in a broad family of approaches and practices (Bradbury and Reason, 2003). Our goal is to focus on the ways a genuine commitment to the principles underpinning PAR, taken alongside an awareness of the persistence of educational disadvantage *despite* so called changing times, supports educators seeking to focus on new kinds of questions. Specifically, we will look at the ways in which the mindset offered by PAR helps to foreground and justify a commitment within KPS schools to changing the *relationship* between students and their futures.

Clearly this constitutes a certain departure from the traditional uses of action research. In the following sections of this chapter we will explore the ways in which the ideological goals of PAR can be seen to shape a particular approach to schooling. Here it is necessary to identify the key principles of PAR that align with the future proofing agenda outlined above.

Firstly, Kemmis and McTaggart (1988) describe participatory action research as:

> ... a form of collective self-reflective enquiry undertaken by participants in social situations in order to improve the rationality and justice of their own social or educational practices, as well as their understanding of these practices and the situations in which these practices are carried out.

It is common for reflections on the various phases of action research to identify four key 'moments' in ongoing on spiral or cycle: planning, acting, observing and reflecting. The collaborative nature of PAR is, as Kemmis and McTaggart argue, a necessary condition:

> the approach is only action research when it is collaborative, though it is important to realise that the action research of the group is achieved through the critically examined action of individual group members. (1988: 5)

Central to this definition is the active role of participants in the pursuit of transformative educational agendas. As Grundy (1994: 35) puts it:

> Rather, what action research provides is a set of principles for procedure. One of these principles is clearly the principle of participation. It is not only experience in schools which has shown that real change is dependent upon 'ownership' of the change, which is in turn dependent upon participation in the decisions leading to the change by those most affected by that change. ...
>
> Participation brings with it, however, not merely autonomy but also responsibility. Action research is grounded in principles which allow for both autonomy and responsibility. These are the commitments to action and reflection. Action research does not simply mandate the taking of action by participants to bring about change, it also calls those participants to account by including the obligation for action to be grounded in and evaluated through research.

When the intent of a future proofing mindset is set alongside an articulation of the principles of action research, the synergies and consistencies are clear. Taken together, the concept of educated hope, and both the philosophical and methodological dimensions of PAR offer powerful lenses for reconceptualizing education. They acknowledge and prioritize the need to move beyond the reproduction of social inequities towards schooling and social systems that are genuinely able to meet the needs of diverse students into the, largely unpredictable, future.

In this chapter we are arguing that one way to disrupt the traditional relationship between 'at risk' students and schools and to achieve the kind of participant empowerment central to PAR is to look at the question of the relationships fostered within schooling more broadly. There are four kinds of relationships we see as particularly important: relationships between schools and knowledge work; between students and schools; between students and teachers; and between schools, students, teachers and their communities.

Schools have historically been situated as consumers of knowledge. In this context, the good teacher is one who transmits a set of knowledge, and a good student is one who can reproduce (at least in the short term) that same body of knowledge. An 'at risk' student is one who is unable or unwilling to achieve these outcomes. By extension, the role of community is generally limited. Parents and caregivers are called on predominantly as the audience for the various products produced by students, and, occasionally, as support staff to carry on or reinforce the work carried out at school.

For some students, these traditional relationships are undoubtedly more successful than for others. But even those students who possess the kinds of cultural capital that enable them to be good at 'doing school' are not necessarily being given the opportunity to develop the *capacities* that are essential to the contemporary context and its futures. In other words, traditional schooling positions students (and to some extent teachers) in a generally passive role as either the distributors or consumers of particular, authorized forms of knowledge. This passivity can make only limited contributions to the development of the capacities associated with future proofing outlined above. One of the key questions facing educators, then, is how to go about re-designing curriculum, pedagogy and assessment in order to change the relationships between schools, teachers, students, communities and knowledge work: how to achieve the transformative goals signalled both by PAR research, and critical analysis of educational successes and failures.

In the remainder of this chapter we are interested in exploring a particular way in which these aspirations can be used to shape a specific approach to curriculum, pedagogy and assessment. We are motivated here not by a desire to conduct an action research project *per se*, but rather to use the principles of PAR to reflect retrospectively on the transformative potential of the KPS initiative.

PART THREE: KNOWLEDGE PRODUCING SCHOOLS: FUTURE PROOFING IN PRACTICE

> *The important thing is not so much that every child should be taught, as that every child – and every adult – should be given the wish to learn.*
>
> *(John Lubbock, 1887)*

The KPS framework positions students' and schools' relationship to knowledge work as central in an era of increasingly unpredictable futures and rapidly changing contexts. In a challenge to this tradition, KPS projects are about building learning opportunities that address authentic *community* needs within *whole of community* contexts and under conditions that are as close as possible to the relevant mature versions of social practice. It is work that results in 'products' that approximate as closely as possible to *expert* productions in scope, approach and quality.

Under these conditions the classroom/school becomes the organizing base for learning, but is not the only site in which work occurs. Indeed, a lot of learning activity will spill into spaces beyond the school. In addition, the teacher is no longer the ultimate authority on the knowledge produced. S/he will draw on relevant expertise for the kind of production being undertaken at the time, much of which will come from people who are not school personnel. Within the KPS approach, education becomes a 'whole of community' responsibility, and schools become a knowledge-producing resource for their communities. As such, participation in real-world projects becomes an opportunity for *all* school members, and not merely for teacher researchers, or external researchers.

These interactions serve the dual purpose of supporting students in the development of knowledge that is relevant and useful within a particular context whilst simultaneously providing individual students with an opportunity to conceptualize themselves in a positive relationship with the community beyond the school. PAR reminds us of the importance of reflecting always on the question of whether it is possible to make a move from seeing students not as only consumers of other people's knowledge (or even as the beneficiaries of other people's research); but rather as *producers* of knowledge in their own right. To this end, the KPS framework emphasizes the value of real-world projects – developed and negotiated in conjunction with teachers, students and the community – for developing in students the positive attitude towards knowledge production that is essential to any future proofing project.

By extension, KPS projects do not stop at providing students with opportunities to undertake the research equivalent of 'busy work' where they may summarize information that no one really needs and communicate this back to a small audience (generally consisting only of the teacher and occasionally some other students). Instead, KPS projects go beyond these 'fridge door' tasks (assignments which are published on the refrigerator door at home) to involve students in work on authentic tasks in the real world with real audiences. These real-world tasks are meaningful to a diverse range of students and through KPS-type projects, children can understand themselves not only as people who are good at 'doing school' but as students – people! – who can be good at 'doing life'. The key point here is that, by employing a variety of real-world projects, schools have the opportunity to dramatically widen the kinds of skills and behaviours that are valued and rewarded in a schooling context. This means that children with diverse forms of cultural capital have a genuine opportunity to be associated with 'experts' who share their interests and thereby develop their own expertise as they learn to participate in specialist communities and experience knowledge work as it is practised by that community (Moore and Young, 2001).

Take for example the case of young Jake: Jake attends a small school in a working-class area. Although keen to begin school, Jake began prep with fewer formal pre-literacy skills than some of his peers. For some time, Jake was positioned in the lower groups for reading and numeracy activities. In a KPS project, however, students were involved in building recycling bags, and holders for the bags, to be distributed amongst the school community. This was a student initiative that was put to the local council when students observed that their town did not have a well-organized recycling programme. The commitment to authentic external collaborations gave Jake an opportunity to invite his uncle – a welder – into the school, to discuss with students the best design for the stand. With his uncle, Jake was able to demonstrate his own understanding of design. He felt himself, perhaps for the first time, to have been a leader in the school context and played a key role in the school's initiative to promote a recycling programme in the local community.

KPS work arises in a range of ways. One of us visited the Principal of Villa Primary School. The visit was punctuated by all kinds of interruptions and her trying to finish a presentation about her school's innovative approach to discipline. One of us, in an attempt to illustrate the kind of work that occurs in a KPS framework, told her the story of a Principal in a KPS site who was asked to give a presentation at a Principal's conference about the computing initiatives in her school. That Principal went to her year five students and offered them the task. Those students collected the data, shot video footage, edited, it, burned it to a CD and *gave* the presentation at the conference. At that point, the Principal to whom the story was being told leaped from her chair and hugged the story teller. Students from her school subsequently prepared and gave the presentation about the school's discipline programme at the Principals' conference.

In this broad mindset, it is not simply a matter of having students do work which might otherwise be carried out by teachers or other adults in the school, it is taking opportunities to promote new kinds of relationships between students, the school and various kinds of knowledge work. In so doing, students develop a sense of being able to act in the world. This is future proofing made as concrete as it is ever likely to be.

While KPS work occurs in single projects it is at its most interesting and empowering when it occurs in a school which has taken up this way of 'doing school'. For instance, such was the pervasiveness of this way of thinking in one of the schools with which we worked that students in the first year of primary school took business plans to the Principal about improving their recreational space in the school. On a later occasion Villa PS was invited, along with another school, to host a visit by OECD dignitaries to the state. Villa was the second school to be visited. At their first visit delegates had met with staff and the Principal, had morning tea and been given a tour of the school by teachers. When the bus arrived at Villa PS a line of year three students met and escorted each member of the delegation into the school, attended to their food, drink and bathroom needs and gave them a personal tour of the school.

In a different example, year one students are concerned for the health and well-being of a classmate who has to travel from their home town to a capital city for serious medical treatment. The school has a long history of KPS work that has created a climate of more or less spontaneous project development by students. These students invited the local press to their classroom to conduct a press briefing. Reporters and a photographer came to the class, sat on the tiny year one chairs and made notes as the students told of their classmate's plight. The story was front page in the local newspaper the next day and attracted television coverage which supported fund-raising events to support the family's travel.

There are many more stories that could be told. Some of them have been described in other places (Bigum, 2002, 2003, 2004). The key features that can be missed in these snapshots is that each real-world task is part of a broader school commitment to ensuring that students are able to see themselves as active participants in their learning and, through this process, as competent, motivated, valued producers of knowledge: knowledge about their community and knowledge about themselves. In other words, they are active participants in the research of, and responses to, their community. This knowledge has value not only because of the way it may help to address immediate tasks or problems but because it positions *diverse* children as equal participants in the kind of action research projects that are often done 'for' or 'to' or 'in spite of' them. And because these are real projects and thus multiple and varied in the issues they raise, children have multiple entry points. This means that kids, who may not yet possess the kinds of skills that position others to succeed in traditional written or oral tasks, can find other ways to experience success.

Thus, the central platform of KPS initiatives is the commitment to changing relationships: relationships between students and knowledge work, between students and school, between schools and their community. The real participation and involvement of students in reworking and *renegotiating relationships* is a key consideration in any KPS work. The autonomy and responsibility of which Grundy (1994) writes is commonplace in KPS work where students exhibit high levels of commitment and professionalism to completing their work. Further, participation in this work nurtures an agency not often found in schools. An agency which helps to be good at doing school, but, more importantly, contributes significantly to their learning to be good at doing life.

To sum up, then, KPS initiatives can be seen to combine the ideas and reflections associated with PAR and a range of equity-based educational writings through a commitment to offering students:

- authentic tasks, with authentic products, associated with the production of knowledge supported by experts and/or specialist communities,
- exposure to, and feedback from a real audience (beyond the school),
- meaningful use of contemporary technologies in achieving goals, rather than a focus on technological mastery for its own sake,
- fundamental and substantial interdisciplinary connections,
- multiple forms of student contributions allowing identification with the category 'good student' by diverse children.

There is one final point to be made about KPS frameworks: whilst working on authentic tasks and receiving feedback is a key platform of the KPS framework, this does NOT mean that students are expected to take on board the practices and dispositions of any particular field of endeavour without critically analysing them.

To be more specific, students may well discover environments or workplaces with problematic or dangerous attitudes towards particular topics, activities or whole groups of people. Students can be exposed to attitudes of sexism, racism, homophobia and the like. Clearly, KPS projects, and the teachers who pursue them, have a vital role to play in ensuring that just as students develop knowledge about tasks, and communities, they also develop their own knowledge about the production and reproduction of ideological positions, and the ways in which they – as individuals and as a group – can contribute to naturalizing particular views, particular options, particular political stances.

NOTES

1 The earliest citation according to WordSpy (http://www.wordspy.com/words/GenerationY.asp) is attributed to Scott L. Kuehl, 'Am I obsolete?', The Record (Kitchener-Waterloo, Ontario), July 22, 1992.

2 The earliest citation according to WordSpy (http://www.wordspy.com/words/thumbculture.asp) is Colin Joyce, 'Japanese give thumbs-up to silent mobiles,' *The Daily Telegraph*, August 7, 2000.

REFERENCES

Bigum, C. (2002) 'Design sensibilities, schools and the new computing and communication technologies', in I. Snyder (ed.), *Silicon Literacies: Communication, Innovation and Education in the Electronic Era*. London: Routledge, pp. 130–40.

Bigum, C. (2003) 'The Knowledge-Producing School: moving away from the work of finding educational problems for which computers are solutions', *Computers in New Zealand Schools*, 15 (2): 22–6.

Bigum, C. (2004) 'Rethinking schools and community: the knowledge producing school', in S. Marshall, W. Taylor and X. Yu (eds), *Using Community Informatics to Transform Regions*. London: Idea Group Publishing, pp. 52–66.

Bradbury, H. and Reason, P. (2003) 'Action Research: An opportunity for revitalizing research purpose and practices', *Qualitative Social Work*, 2 (2): 155–75.

Coupland, D. (1991) *Generation X: Tales for an Accelerated Culture*. New York: St Martin's Press.

Giroux, H. (2003) 'Public time and educated hope: Educational leadership and the war against youth [electronic version]. *The Initiative Anthology*, np. Retrieved 13th October 2007 Accessed from http://www.units.muohio.edu/eduleadership/anthology/OA/OA03001.html.

Green, B. and Bigum, C. (1993) 'Aliens in the classroom', *Australian Journal of Education: Special Issue: Media and Education – Guest Editors: Carmen Luke [Australia] and Keith Roe [Belgium]*, 37 (2): 119–41.

Grundy, S. (1994) 'Action research at the school level: possibilities and problems', *Educational Action Research*, 2 (1): 23–37.

Howe, N. and Strauss, W. (2000) *Millennials Rising: The Next Great Generation*. New York: Vintage Books.

Kemmis, S. and McTaggart, R. (1988) *The Action Research Planner* (3rd edn). Geelong: Deakin University.

Kincheloe, J. (2006) 'Introducing metropedagogy: Sorry, no shortcuts in urban education', in J. Kincheloe and K. Hayes (eds), *Metropedagogy: Power, Justice and the Urban Classroom*. Rotterdam: Sense Publishers, pp. 3–42.

Levitas, R. (1993) 'The future of thinking about the future', in J. Bird, B. Curtis, T. Putnam, G. Robertson and L. Tickner (eds), *Mapping the Futures*. New York: Routledge, pp. 257–66.

Lubbock, J. (1887) *The Pleasures of Life*. Retrieved 11th March 2008 from Project Gutenberg Online Book Catalog: http://www.gutenberg.org/dirs/etext05/8pllf10.txt

Moore, R. and Young, M. (2001) 'Knowledge and the curriculum in the sociology of education: towards a reconceptualisation', *British Journal of Sociology of Education*, 22 (4): 445–61.

Newmann, F.M. and Associates (1996) *Authentic Achievement: Restructuring Schools for Intellectual Quality*. San Francisco, CA: Jossey-Bass.

Newmann, F.M. and Wehlage, G.G. (1993) 'Five standards of authentic instruction', *Educational Leadership*, 50 (7): 8–12.

Newmann, F.M. and Wehlage, G.G. (1997) *Successful School Restructuring: A Report to the Public and Educators*. Madison, WI: University of Wisconsin, Center on Organization and Restructuring of Schools.

Rowan, L. (2007) *Why Future Proofing?* Retrieved 10th of October, 2007, from http://www.deakin.edu.au/arts-ed/efi/

Rushkoff, D. (1996) *Playing the Future: How Kids' Culture Can Teach Us How to Thrive in an Age of Chaos*. New York: HarperCollins.

Schrage, M. (2000) *The Relationship Revolution*. Retrieved 26th January, 2000, from http://www.seedwiki.com/wiki/yi-tan/the_relationship_revolution?wikiPageId=161143&searchresult=161143

Tapscott, D. (1999) *Growing Up Digital: The Rise of the Net Generation*. New York: McGraw-Hill.

11

Lesson Study as Action Research[1]

Catherine Lewis, Rebecca Perry and
Shelley Friedkin

Lesson study is *a system for building and sharing practitioner knowledge* that involves teachers in learning from colleagues as they research, plan, teach, observe and discuss a classroom lesson. Lesson study's inquiry cycle is consistent with the common, three-pronged description of action research (Noffke, 1997). Teachers seek to improve their knowledge and effectiveness (the *personal* component of the framework), by engaging in collaborative knowledge accumulation and theory-building (the *professional* component) thereby supporting changes in the goals and culture of instruction (the *political* component). This chapter provides a brief history and description of lesson study, reviews what has been learned about lesson study to date in North America, and identifies gaps in current knowledge.

LESSON STUDY: AN INTRODUCTION AND BRIEF HISTORY

Lesson study centers on cycles of inquiry (see Figure 11.1) designed to improve instruction and to build and share knowledge of teaching and learning. Lesson study is typically conducted by collaborative teams of three to eight teachers, but outside specialists may be involved as consultants, and additional colleagues may be invited to observe and discuss the 'research lesson' that is included in each cycle. The research lesson is designed to bring to life the team's thinking and study regarding the most effective ways to teach a particular topic, as well as their goals for students' long-term development (not just in the intellectual domain, but also socially, ethically, aesthetically, and so forth). The research

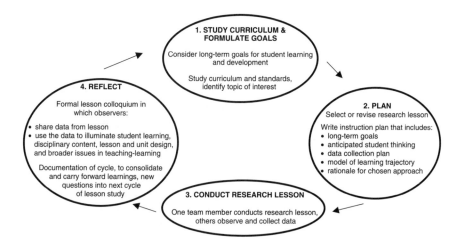

Figure 11.1   The lesson study cycle (based on Lewis, 2002b).

lesson is taught by one of the team members; other team members observe and collect data which are then discussed during a post-lesson colloquium, in order to draw out the implications for teaching and learning of the particular topic and for teaching and learning more broadly (Fernandez and Yoshida, 2004; Lewis, 2002a, 2002b).

Lesson study originated in Japan about 100 years ago (Ikeda, 2001) and became widely known to U.S. educators in 1999, when the Third International Mathematics and Science Study (TIMSS) brought existing ethnographic accounts of lesson study to light (Stigler and Hiebert, 1999). Several researchers credit lesson study for Japan's well-evolved and widely shared teaching methods (Lewis and Tsuchida, 1997; Matoba et al., 2006; Wolf and Akita, 2007; Yoshida, 1999). The term 'lesson study' is a translation of the Japanese words *jugyō* (instruction, lessons, or lesson) and *kenkyū* (research or study). Although the English word 'lesson' typically focuses on a single, discrete block of teaching that can be captured on paper (as when a teacher points to a document and says 'here's the lesson'), the Japanese word jugyō refers to *live interaction* between students and teacher that may occur over an *extended time period* (lessons or instruction). These differences are important lest lesson study be misunderstood simply as design of a lesson plan.

The term *jugyō kenkyū* (usually translated as 'lesson study,' but sometimes as 'lesson research') encompasses a large family of related instructional improvement strategies, the shared feature of which is observation of live classroom lessons by a group of teachers who collect data on teaching and learning and collaboratively analyze it. Within Japan and other countries, lesson study may take place in a variety of organizational contexts. It may be sponsored by a school, a department within a school, a district, an independent association of teachers (local or national), or outside of a specific organizational context, such as at conferences. (Lewis, 2002a, 2002b; Lewis and Tsuchida, 1997, 1998; Murata and Takahashi, 2002; Wang-Iverson and Yoshida, 2005).

Lesson study generally focuses on the personal, political, and professional (Noffke, 1997) but different varieties of lesson study differ in the strength of their emphasis on each domain. For example, the lesson study undertaken by teachers in their fifth and tenth years of teaching in many Japanese school districts involves teachers in *personal* identification of an aspect of their teaching they want to improve; team members help them to collect and analyze data targeted on that aspect, as well as to find relevant resources and think through that particular aspect of teaching. The *professional* dimension of lesson study is well-exemplified in the work of national subject matter associations and university-affiliated elementary schools in Japan, whose lesson study might focus, for example, on the relative advantages of two different ways of introducing multiplication. Findings from their lesson study work may travel through word of mouth, reports, and formal publications, influencing textbook treatment of the topic and broadly shared ideas about good instructional practice. Finally, the *political* dimension of lesson study is illustrated by school-wide lesson study in Japan, in which teachers use lesson study to bring to life their long-term goals for students (for example, to be self-motivated learners and enjoy friendships).

From its origin in Japan, lesson study has spread since 1999 not only to the U.S. but to other countries, including (at least) South Africa, China, England, Germany, Iran, Hong Kong, Korea, and Singapore (Lo et al., 2005, Matoba et al., 2006). Between 1999 and 2004, lesson study emerged at more than 335 North American schools across at least 32 states and became the focus of dozens of conferences, reports, and published articles (Lesson Study Research Group, 2004; Wang-Iverson and Yoshida, 2005; Watanabe, 2002).

A BRIEF EXAMPLE OF LESSON STUDY

Since 2000, we have followed the development of lesson study at an elementary school that is one of the first U.S. schools to adopt the practice (Lewis et al., 2006; Perry and Lewis, in press). The school, Highlands Elementary, serves just over 400 K-5 students in a suburban district in the western United States. One group of four teachers at the school tried out lesson study during the 2000–01 school year, and the following year nearly all school faculty decided to begin lesson study. By fall 2003, the faculty had voted to practice lesson study school-wide.

The school is currently in its seventh year of lesson study. In that time teachers have used lesson study to explore issues of particular concern to the district and school, including 'standards-based instruction,' 'differentiation,' and 'reducing the achievement gap.' Even staff members who initially chose not to participate in lesson study now participate actively: more than half of the staff members have taught research lessons, and many teachers have made presentations on lesson study outside the school. Teachers have conducted research lessons in mathematics, language arts, and science.

Each year, teachers organize themselves into small groups of three to six either by grade level or common interests. The groups rarely remain the same from year to year, offering teachers new opportunities to collaborate with various colleagues. Each group conducts a cycle of lesson study and shares their learning from lesson study with the entire faculty at an end-of-year meeting.

Teachers at the school are provided two hours per month during school time to collaborate in lesson study groups. Outside funding (from the district or through small foundation grants) has paid for small teacher stipends ($500) and substitute coverage during the research lessons. (The principal has reported that finding funding for substitute coverage is one threat to on-going lesson study.) A school-wide lesson study agenda developed by the principal and lesson study liaison (a classroom teacher designated to assist the principal with lesson study planning) and updated each month helps guide teachers through the year-long lesson study work. The agendas provide information on relevant research, suggestions on approaches to take during lesson study (e.g., quickly teaching a lesson to gather data on student thinking to use during planning), guidelines about time allocation for certain tasks (such as planning the lesson versus reflecting on the learning), and strategies for getting beyond challenges (e.g., methods for creating supportive collaborative norms).

An example from a group during the 2002–03 school year provides a window on lesson study as a form of action research. The principal asked lesson study groups to explore 'standards-based instruction,' an issue of concern to district and school administrators. Because the principal wanted teachers to explore issues of interest to them related to the standards, she asked each lesson study group to select one grade-level standard for in-depth investigation through lesson study. The grade 3 group selected a mathematics standard related to multi-step problem-solving, because standardized test scores revealed weakness in number sense and because multi-step problem solving was a particular emphasis of the third grade standards.

Examination of the teachers' discussions and the artifacts created during their group work reveals that these teachers studied students' difficulties with problem solving, and then located, tested, and integrated into their practice an approach to teaching problem-solving, after discovering that they had no shared or systematic approach for helping students learn to solve multi-step math problems. Their research helped them to identify (from the *Everyday Math* curriculum) a five-step process to help students become successful problem solvers: *(1) What do you know [about the problem]? (2) What do you want to find out? (3) What will you do? (4) Answer the question – Can you write a number sentence to show what you did? (5) Check to see if the answer makes any sense. How do I know?*

Figure 11.2 diagrams the events that occurred from discovery of the student difficulty to the decision to integrate the problem-solving idea into their own

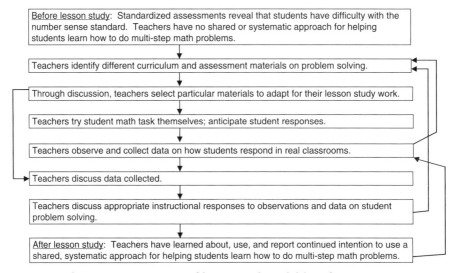

Figure 11.2   Sequence of lesson study activities of one group.

practice. Two conversations capture what teachers learned from the lesson study cycle:

Teacher 19: This is really interesting for me because I have not been doing this [teaching problem solving] routinely in teaching third grade. I have not been routinely taking kids through this five-step process. And now that we picked this as a standard, I mean, I would start the year next year … I'll be teaching it all year.

Teacher 67: I will too.

Teacher 19: I've done word problems with kids and I've done challenging parts. But I've never, like, taken them through these five steps and realizing that it isn't in the standards, really directly in the curriculum, and yet it's a critical mathematical skill that kids need to have. Although … this has been a difficult path to go down, I'm really glad that we have because it's going to change what I'm doing…. If I had started in September, [think] how many more strategies my kids would have now too. Like, now they just have whatever they brought from second grade. I haven't shown them new strategies. But now I'm realizing that it's an important thing – to be modeling so they have all those tools for ways to solve problems.

Teacher 69: Yeah, and that they recognize that there are different ways to do it.

* * *

Teacher 62: It's really important to teach that problem solving chart and embed it all the time into everything that we do, whether it's social studies, science, math, or whatever. Because there is an organizational part… We were talking about something in the class…. and I pulled this chart out and they went like … 'Oh, no. You have it too!' [Everybody laughs.]

And they go 'The guide to problem solving. It's in your room too?' I said, 'It's going to stay in my room. And we're going to refer to this…. You know what? It applies to every single thing. 'What do you know' and 'what do you want to find out?' And 'what will you do?' It's the same thing – answer the question. It applies to everything.
Teacher 111 [Teaches limited vision students]: I had mine laminated … and [put into] braille. I'm so into it.

EXEMPLARY TEXTS AND MECHANISMS

Much lesson study-related research and information is available only in Japanese. However, several English-language accounts of lesson study have been written by authors familiar with Japanese practice and able to use Japanese-language sources. These include Makoto Yoshida's extensive case study of mathematics lesson study in Hiroshima, Japan (Fernandez and Yoshida, 2004) on which *The Teaching Gap's* account of lesson study was based (Stigler and Hiebert, 1999); accounts of lesson study practices by experienced Japanese lesson study practitioners and researchers (Matoba et al., 2006; Takahashi, 2000; Tsubota, 2007; Watanabe, 2002); and a practical lesson study handbook by the first author based on extended observations of lesson study in Japan (Lewis, 2002b). In addition, several videos show research lessons or full lesson study cycles from Japan (Global Education Resources, 2002; Mills College Lesson Study Group, 2000).

U.S. teachers considering lesson study may want to start with a brief account of lesson study's development at Highlands Elementary school where, with strategic support from the principal, it grew school-wide (Lewis et al., 2006). A growing body of literature documents lesson study in settings outside Japan, illustrating features central to the Japanese model (such as collaborative planning, observation, and data collection and discussion) as well as adaptations that have been made to non-Japanese contexts, such as explicit setting and monitoring of norms for working together (Chokshi and Fernandez, 2004; Fernandez, 2002; Lewis 2002a; Lewis et al., 2006; Lewis, Perry, and Murata, 2006; Lo et al., 2005; Matoba et al., 2006; Wang-Iverson and Yoshida, 2005).

Lesson study has not been extensively theorized or studied in Japan, perhaps because it has been a traditional and therefore unquestioned feature of the educational environment (Isoda et al., 2007). Since the surge of interest in lesson study overseas, however, a number of non-Japanese and Japanese researchers and educators have proposed models to explain the connection between lesson study and instructional improvement. Tsubota, cited in Ikeda, 2001, uses the familiar triangle of learning in and from practice described in the book *Adding it Up* (National Research Council, 2001). Tsubota suggested that the three vertices of the triangle labeled 'students', 'teacher', and 'mathematics' are brought into closer relationship by lesson study – that, for example, teachers work with colleagues to make sense of student learning in response to curriculum and research findings used to re-design instruction. Lewis (2002b) proposed the model of lesson study's impact on instructional practice shown in Figure 11.3, and Lewis, Perry and Murata (2006) pointed out that North American lesson study users may start with a quite different set of assumptions about how lesson study works, i.e., that instructional improvement is due primarily to refinement of the lesson plan. Perry and Lewis (2008) document the changes in a lesson study effort that gradually shifted over time from viewing lesson study as lesson plan redesign and dissemination to viewing lesson study as a system for building and sharing knowledge about practice.

FINDINGS AND GAPS IN RESEARCH

Finding #1: Lesson Study Can Be Practiced and Sustained Outside of Japan

Initially, educators questioned whether lesson study could operate outside of Japanese culture and the Japanese educational system, citing collaborative culture, shared planning time, and subject matter knowledge of Japanese educators as important supports for lesson study (Cannon and Fernandez, 2003; Fernandez, 2005; Fernandez, Cannon et al., 2003). However, North American lesson study groups have shown considerable ingenuity in building these supports. For example, lesson study groups may spend some time in explicit development and monitoring of collaborative norms in order to build collaborative culture (Mills College Lesson Study Group, 2005), develop scheduling strategies that accommodate lesson study school-wide (Lewis et al., 2006; Liptak, 2002), and include university-based colleagues and study of research and curriculum materials as ways to amplify the subject matter knowledge available to lesson study group members (Perry and Lewis, 2007). The United States now has a number of lesson study efforts that have been sustained for more than five years,

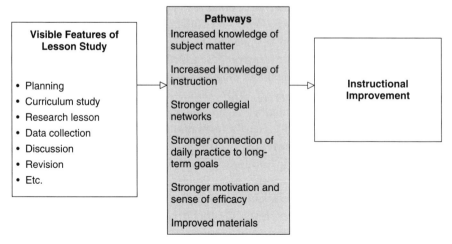

Figure 11.3   How does lesson study improve instruction?

often by practitioners who piece together funding with no guaranteed long-term funding stream (Education Development Center (EDC), 2002; Lesson Study Research Group, 2004; Lewis et al., 2006; Wilburg and Brown, 2006).

Accounts from North America also suggest that although early lesson study was heavily concentrated in mathematics (likely a function of its early introduction through *The Teaching Gap*), lesson study is spreading to other subject areas (Hurd and Licciardo-Musso, 2005; Ogden et al. 2008; Pesick, 2005), to many levels of schooling, including high schools and universities, where it is not common in Japan (Cerbin and Kropp, 2007; Oakland Unified School District, 2007), and to organizations other than schools, such as foundations and subject matter associations. Likewise, some U.S. teacher training programs have added a lesson study component (Cossey and Tucher, 2005; Finken et al., 2004; Hiebert et al., 2003; Perry et al., 2003; Taylor and Puchner, 2003).

Finding #2: Lesson Study may Initially be Conceptualized as a Program or Recipe, with an Understanding of Lesson Study as Research Emerging Later

North American educators are accustomed to educational reforms where they are expected to implement a blueprint or recipe. A view of lesson study as program implementation was evident in early lesson study efforts, as educators put in place the most easily visible features of lesson study without a full model of how their activities might improve instruction (Fernandez, 2005; Lewis et al., 2006; Perry and Lewis, 2006).

Data from a longitudinal U.S. case indicate that teachers can shift over time from a 'recipe' view of lesson study to a view of it as research on practice (Lewis et al., 2006; Perry and Lewis, 2008). Over time, the lesson study changed to include a closer connection between the research and action portions of the cycle, a stronger emphasis on data as a basis for action, greater emphasis on learning from practice, and greater recognition that what they may once have considered action – teaching a classroom lesson – may, through effective data collection, become research that informs the remainder of the cycle. Changes that helped support this shift to seeing lesson study as research included increased incorporation of teacher reflection and knowledge-sharing; increased use of protocols, tools and knowledge sources from outside the team; and increased focus on student thinking.

Finding #3: Lesson Study can Support Improvement of Teacher and Student Learning

During lesson study, teachers can improve their knowledge of content, pedagogy, and student thinking; ideally, lesson study builds teachers' capacity and commitment to learn from one another in daily practice (Fernandez, 2005; Lewis et al., 2006; Lo et al., 2006; Perry and Lewis, 2007). Student achievement data at Highlands Elementary School, where whole-school lesson study has been conducted since 2002, suggest that lesson study is paying off for students as well. Over 2002–05, the three-year net increase in mathematics achievement for students who remained at Highlands School was more than triple that for students who remained elsewhere in the district as a whole (an increase of 91 scale score points compared to 26 points), a statistically significant difference ($F = .309$, $df = 845$, $p < .001$). While a causal connection between the achievement results and lesson study cannot be inferred, other obvious explanations (such as changes in student populations served by the school and district) have been ruled out. School-wide lesson study appears to be a primary difference between the professional development at this school and other district schools during the years studied (Lewis et al., 2006).

The research literature documenting lesson study practitioners' activities and achievements is still young, and relatively little is known about lesson study practice and its potential benefit. One major difficulty of conducting research on lesson study is that lesson study groups may involve teachers from a wide range of experience levels who need (and want) to learn quite different things. For example, in one lesson study group we studied, a novice teacher sought information about various instructional tools mentioned by experienced teachers (e.g., asking what a KWL chart is), an experienced teacher sought information about recent approaches to teaching mathematics, and a teacher with a special needs class sought tools that would enable shared inquiry with mainstream teachers. Such varied backgrounds and interests result in different learning outcomes for teachers in the same group, challenging the use of standard research instruments to document teacher learning and instructional improvement.

Finding #4: Structures for Sharing Practitioners' Knowledge Are Underdeveloped

Japan's lesson study system is set up to promote the public sharing of lesson study processes and results, through large-scale public research lessons, educational networks, and written reports, articles, and books (Lewis and Tsuchida, 1997, Yoshida, 1999). U.S. lesson study practitioners have not yet widely shared the results of their work, although annual public research lessons sponsored by groups around the U.S. are becoming increasingly common. In order for the system to reap the benefits of the extensive amount of information that is generated through local lesson study efforts, some concerted effort must be paid to the issue of dissemination.

WHERE DO WE GO FROM HERE?

Despite the rapid spread of lesson study outside Japan from 2000 to 2006, many issues with respect to lesson study development and research remain largely unstudied.

1 Lesson Study Spread and Sustainability

Little is known about the number of sites outside Japan that have initiated lesson study, the percent of these that have sustained the lesson study work, or the factors that distinguish continuing sites from those that discontinue.

2 Impact on Teacher Community

A major goal of lesson study in Japan is the development of a teacher community in which teachers feel strongly accountable to one another and routinely work together to create a coherent program of instruction for students. Some evidence indicates that major lesson study initiatives undertaken by Japanese districts are indeed associated with such changes (Akita, 2007). To date, there appears to be little research outside Japan on the impact of lesson study on teacher community.

3 Connection to Policy and Curriculum

In Japan, lesson study practice is closely intertwined with curriculum and policy development. A system of *shitei kenkyūku* (designated research schools) allows schools to apply to use lesson study to test out recent policy directions, working together with university-based researchers and other interested schools. For example, when Japan shifted from science and social studies in elementary grades one and two to an interdisciplinary Life Environment Studies program, designated research schools tried out approaches to the new subject area. Their public research lessons, which included opportunities for the school faculty to talk about the approaches that had been tried and the rationale for the approach shown in the public lessons, attracted thousands of teachers. Lesson study also provides a forum for teachers to pioneer ideas that eventually influence national policy. For example, elementary teachers developed lessons on solar energy that resulted in the addition of this topic to the national curriculum and textbooks (Lewis and Tsuchida, 1997; Lewis et al., 2002).

4 Effective Tools, Interaction Styles and Collaborations

Little is known about the interaction processes within lesson study groups that lead to sustained learning and commitment to the processes of developing and spreading knowledge of teaching. Although many individuals who see video like 'How many seats?' comment on the supportive learning environment that group members create for one another and the apparent strengthening of teachers' identity as researchers of classroom practice (Mills College Lesson Study Group, 2005), a strong theoretical model of the kinds of interaction that build *teachers' learning and commitment to future inquiry* has not yet been developed. Models from other forms of professional development and action research may provide an important base on which to build.

Japanese groups often draw on outside expertise during portions of the lesson study cycle, a pattern that has been adopted by some non-Japanese groups as well (Takahashi, 2003; Watanabe, 2002). We know little about the interactions that make outside collaborators effective. In our experience, specialists can make or ruin a group, depending on their capacity to bring important intellectual resources without undermining the fundamentally teacher-led characteristics of the process. Likewise, little systematic research has been conducted on the tools and protocols that effectively support lesson study.

It seems appropriate to the increasingly global nature of our world that educators on several continents are working to use and adapt a form of action research that originated in Japan. We look forward to seeing whether the personal, political, and professional impact associated with lesson study in Japan can be replicated in other countries.

NOTE

1 This chapter is based upon research supported by the National Science Foundation under grants REC 9814967 and REC 0207259 and by the Mac-Arthur Spencer Meta-Study: Toward Producing Useable Knowledge for the Improvement of Educational Pratice. Any opinions, findings, and conclusions or recommendations expressed in this publication are those of the authors and do not necessarily reflect the views of the National Science Foundation.

REFERENCES

Akita, K. (2007) 'Japanese teachers' learning system in school: Collaborative knowledge-building through lesson study'. Paper presented at the Seoul University – University of Tokyo Joint Conference, Seoul, Korea.

Cannon, J. and Fernandez, C. (2003) 'This research has nothing to do with our teaching!: An analysis of lesson study practitioners' difficulties conducting teacher research'. Manuscript submitted for publication.

Cerbin, W. and Kropp, B. (2007) 'Lesson study project', University of Wisconsin-La Crosse [Electronic Version]. Retrieved 31 May, 2007 from http://www.uwlax.edu/sotl/lsp/.

Chokshi, S. and Fernandez, C. (2004) 'Challenges to importing Japanese lesson study: Concerns, misconceptions and nuances'. *Phi Delta Kappan*, 85 (7): 520–25.

Cossey, R. and Tucher, P. (2005) 'Teaching to collaborate, collaborating to teach', in *Teaching as Principles Practice: Managing Complexity for Social Justice*. Thousand Oaks, CA: Sage.

Education Development Center (EDC) (2002) 'EDC researchers explore innovative teacher program' [Electronic Version]. Retrieved 30 May, 2007 from http://main.edc.org/Newsroom/features/lessonstudy.asp.

Fernandez, C. (2002) 'Learning from Japanese approaches to professional development', *Journal of Teacher Education*, 53 (5): 393–405.

Fernandez, C. (2005) 'Lesson study: A means for elementary teachers to develop knowledge of mathematics needed reform-minded teaching?' *Mathematical Thinking and Learning*, 7 (4): 265–89.

Fernandez, C. and Yoshida, M. (2004) *Lesson Study: A Case of a Japanese Approach to Improving Instruction Through School-based Teacher Development*. Mahwah, NJ: Lawrence Erlbaum Associates.

Fernandez, C., Cannon, J. and Chokshi, S. (2003) 'A U.S.–Japan lesson study collaborative reveals critical lenses for examining practice', *Teaching and Teacher Education*, 19 (2): 171–85.

Finken, T., Matthews, M., Hlas, C. and Schmidt, J. (2004) 'Integrating lesson study for pre-service and in-service teachers'. Paper presented at the poster session of the National Council of Teachers of Mathematics (NCTM).

Global Education Resources (2002) *Lesson Study: An Introduction*. New Jersey: Global Education Resources.

Hiebert, J., Gallimore, R. and Stigler, J.W. (2003) 'Learning to learn to teach: An "experiment" model for teaching and teacher preparation in mathematics', *Journal of Mathematics Teacher Education*, 6: 201–22.

Hurd, J. and Licciardo-Musso, L. (2005) 'Lesson study: Teacher led professional development in literacy instruction', *Language Arts*, 82 (5): 388–95.

Ikeda, T. (2001) 'Japanese lesson study'. Paper presented at the International Council of Mathematics Educators (October 2001), North Carolina.

Isoda, M., Stephens, M., Ohara, Y. and Miyakawa, T. (eds) (2007) *Japanese Lesson Study in Mathematics: Its Impact, Diversity and Potential for Educational Improvement*. Singapore: World Scientific Publishing.

Lesson Study Research Group (2004) [LSRG maintains a central database of U.S. lesson study group]. Retrieved July 19, 2004, from http://www.tc.columbia.edu/lessonstudy/lsgroups.html

Lewis, C. (2002a) 'Does lesson study have a future in the United States?' *Nagoya Journal of Education and Human Development*, 1 (1): 1–23.

Lewis, C. (2002b) *Lesson Study: A Handbook of Teacher-led Instructional Change*. Philadelphia, PA: Research for Better Schools.

Lewis, C. and Tsuchida, I. (1997) 'Planned educational change in Japan: The case of elementary science instruction', *Journal of Educational Policy*, 12 (5): 313–31.

Lewis, C. and Tsuchida, I. (1998) 'A lesson is like a swiftly flowing river: Research lessons and the improvement of Japanese education', *American Educator* (Winter), 14–17, 50–2.

Lewis, C., Perry, R. and Hurd, J. (2004) 'A deeper look at lesson study', *Educational Leadership*, 61 (5): 18–23.

Lewis, C., Perry, R. and Murata, A. (2006) 'How should research contribute to instructional improvement? The case of lesson study', *Educational Researcher*, 35 (3): 3–14.

Lewis, C., Tsuchida, I. and Coleman, S. (2002) 'The creation of Japanese and U.S. elementary science textbooks: Different processes, different outcomes', in *National Standards and School Reform in Japan and the United States*. Columbia University: Teachers College Press, pp. 44–66.

Lewis, C., Perry, R., Hurd, J. and O'Connell, M.P. (2006) 'Lesson study comes of age in North America', *Phi Delta Kappan*, 88 (4): 273–81.

Liptak, L. (2002) 'It's a matter of time: Scheduling lesson study at Paterson, NJ School 2', *RBS currents*, 5 (2): 6–7.

Lo, M., Chik, P. and Pong, W. (2005) *For Each and Everyone: Catering for Individual Differences Through Learning Studies*. Hong Kong: Hong Kong University Press.

Lo, M., Chik, P. and Fai Pang, M. (2006) 'Patterns of variation in teaching the colour of light to primary 3 students', *Instructional Science*, 34: 1–19.

Matoba, M., Crawford, K.A. and Sarkar Arani, M.R. (eds) (2006) *Lesson Study: International Perspectives on Policy and Practice*. Beijing: Educational Science Publishing House.

Mills College Lesson Study Group (2000) *Can you lift 100 Kilograms?* [Videotape: 18 min.] Oakland: Lesson Study Group at Mills College.

Mills College Lesson Study Group. (2005) *How Many Seats?* Excerpts of a lesson study cycle [DVD]. Oakland, CA: Mills College Lesson Study Group.

Murata, A. and Takahashi, A. (2002) 'Vehicle to connect theory, research and practice: How teacher thinking changes in district-level lesson study in Japan', in D.L. Haury (ed.), *Proceedings of the Twenty-Fourth Annual Meeting of North American Chapter of the International Group of the Psychology of Mathematics Education*. Columbus, OH: ERIC Clearninghouse for Science, Mathematics, and Environmental Education, pp. 1879–88.

National Research Council (2001) *Adding it Up: Helping Children Learn Mathematics*. Washington DC: National Academy Press.

Noffke, S.E. (1997) 'Professional, personal, and political dimensions of action research', *Review of Research in Education*, 22: 305–43.

Oakland Unified School District (2007) 'History grows in Oakland: Teaching American history in an urban school district'. Lesson Study [Electronic Version]. Retrieved 31 May, 2007 from http://www.teachingamericanhistory.us/lesson_study/index.html.

Ogden, N., Perkins, C. and Donahue, D. (in press) 'Not a peculiar institution: Challenging students' assumptions about slavery in U.S. history'. *The History Teacher*.

Perry, R. and Lewis, C. (2007) 'Learning through lesson study: A case of proportional reasoning'. Manuscript under review.

Perry, R. and Lewis, C. (2008 book accepted). Building demand for research through lesson study. In M.K. Stein & C. Coburn (Eds.) *Research and practice in education: Building alliances, bridging the divide*. Lanham, MD: Rowman & Littlefield Publishing Group.

Perry, R. and Lewis, C. (2008) 'What is successful adaptation of lesson in the U.S.?' *Journal of Educational Change*, 9.10.1007/s10833-008-9069-7.

Perry, R., Tucher, P. and Lewis, C. (2003) 'Lesson study in pre-service education, Mills College'. Paper presented at the annual meeting of the American Education Research Association, Chicago, IL.

Pesick, S. (2005, Spring) '"Lesson Study" and the teaching of American history: Connecting professional development and classroom practice', *Social Studies Review*. Retrieved 11/07/07 from www.teachingamericanhistory.us/lesson_study/

Stigler, J.W. and Hiebert, J. (1999) *The Teaching Gap: Best Ideas from the World's Teachers for Improving Education in the Classroom*. New York: Summit Books.

Takahashi, A. (2000) 'Current trends and issues in lesson study in Japan and the United States', *Journal of Japan Society of Mathematical Education*, 82 (12): 15–21.

Takahashi, A. (2003) *Lesson study overview: Three major types of lesson study*. Paper presented at the Lesson Study Immersion Program, Japan.

Taylor, A. and Puchner, L. (2003) 'Learning from lesson study in Illinois'. *Illinois Mathematics Teacher*, 54 (1): 20–5.

Tsubota, K. (2007) 'Developing creative teaching strategies aimed at imparting diverse ways of thinking and fostering enjoyment of learning', in M. Isoda, M. Stephens, Y. Ohara and T. Miyakawa (eds) *Japanese Lesson Study in Mathematics: Its Impact, Diversity and Potential for Educational Improvement*. Singapore: World Scientific Publishing.

Wang-Iverson, P. and Yoshida, M. (2005) *Building Understanding of Lesson Study*. Philadelphia: Research for Better Schools.

Watanabe, T. (2002) 'Learning from Japanese lesson study', *Educational Leadership*, 59 (March): 36–9.

Wilburg, K.M. and Brown, S. (2006) *Lesson Study Communities: Increasing Achievement with Diverse Students*. Thousand Oaks, CA: Corwin Press.

Wolf, J. and Akita, K. (2007) 'Research lesson studies: Possibilities, emergent trends and three directions. *A preliminary analysis*'. Paper presented at the Tokyo University Conference on Lesson Study (May 21–2, 2007), Tokyo, Japan.

Yoshida, M. (1999) 'Lesson study: A case study of a Japanese approach to improving instruction through school-based teacher development'. Unpublished doctoral dissertation, University of Chicago.

12

Practitioner Action Research and Educational Leadership

Gary L. Anderson and Kathryn Herr

Action research that is initiated by practitioners, often called *practitioner action research*, is engaged in for the purpose of professional or organizational development/learning. This ongoing professional and organizational learning, it is hoped, will ultimately result in better teaching and learning in schools. What is learned through this inquiry on practice is generally recycled into one's professional practice or, if done collectively, into a growing spiral of understanding of the organizational and social context of teaching and learning. Thus, practitioner action research forms a reciprocal relationship between inquiry and action with the goal of acting with a greater understanding of how to design more effective and equitable actions. Some action research also aspires to generate new knowledge for dissemination beyond the practice site.

In this chapter we make the case that practitioner action research done by administrators and educational leaders in their own schools or districts brings its own challenges that have yet to be sufficiently addressed in the current literature on action research. We think there are unique barriers to administrators trying to research their own practices and sites and that, methodologically, we have much still to address in terms of making this effort feasible. Beyond this, there are unique ethical challenges that must be taken up, due to administrators' hierarchical roles and power, that will influence the methodological approaches taken to carry out the research. And yet, action research has great potential for: (1) transforming professional practices; (2) problematizing school reform efforts; and (3) contributing to the state of knowledge in education. Educational administrators who are willing to interrogate their own professional practices via practitioner action research can set the climate in their own settings for systemic inquiry that informs locally and beyond.

We will also attempt to provide some guidance for administrators and other school professionals struggling to use action research in their settings, as well as university faculty who teach in masters or doctoral degree programs in Educational Leadership. In doing so, we will pay particular attention to the unique problems experienced by those in positions of leadership. Because practitioner action researchers need validity criteria that fit their research context, we will discuss how thinking differently about validity may allow administrators to do research that more nearly fits their action-oriented needs. Finally, we will suggest that traditional social science approaches to qualitative and quantitative methods have not always served administrators well, and provide a brief description of some promising methods from the humanities and linguistics.

Given the large number of doctoral programs in Educational Leadership in which administrators are doing site-based dissertations, one might expect that these dissertations would be producing a significant body of professional knowledge. In an effort to document this growing knowledge base, Franklin Jones and I (Anderson) reviewed action research dissertations in the field of Educational Leadership (Anderson and Jones, 2000). We also read published accounts of administrator research either in academic or practitioner journals or book chapters. What we found was considerable confusion about what constituted an action research study. Many researchers engaging in studies at their own site used criteria and methods more appropriate to traditional forms of academic research rather than action research, creating problems associated with ethics and validity. These confusions seemed partly related to gaps in the doctoral programs' curriculum and, in many cases, their faculty's lack of experience with action research. Our study recommends greater attention to the many barriers that work against creating a significant body of professional knowledge via action research conducted by educational leaders.

We (Anderson and Jones, 2000) also found few studies moved outside of a fairly conventional view of school improvement and professional development. Few studies challenged current practices or explored issues of power, inequities, or controversial topics. This is problematic, but not surprising, since we point out:

> ... that both the threat of political controversy and personal and professional risk serve to distort both what is and isn't studied as well as the findings that are reported. There is, however, an even more subtle and insidious built-in tendency toward conservatism in administrator research. Administrators are immersed in a reified and naturalized world in which common sense is constructed. Furthermore, role expectations for legitimation of the status quo are embedded in administrators' work. (p. 449)

This problem is exacerbated by the fact that administrators occupy positions of hierarchical power over teachers and students, but are vulnerable themselves to those above them in the organizational hierarchy. This chapter will explore how action research by administrators might overcome these epistemological, methodological, political, and ethical barriers.

CHALLENGES FOR ADMINISTRATORS CONSIDERING PRACTITIONER ACTION RESEARCH

While we have written extensively about the problems of doing practitioner action research in both university and school contexts (Anderson, 2002; Anderson and Herr, 1999; Herr, 1999a; Herr, 1999b; Herr and Anderson, 2005), here we focus specifically on issues relevant to school and district administrators. Administrators share with teachers various struggles over doing research in their own sites: for example, time constraints, the fact that research is seen as an additional piece in an already heavy workload; conducting ethical research on or with those over whom they have authority. While these are puzzles shared in common with teachers, the answers may look different, given the different institutional positions of administrators. Ironically, teachers often name administrators in their list of obstacles to conducting action research, complaining that their principals do not set a tone that invites inquiry in the school or may view it with suspicion.

Argyris and Schon (1974) have elaborated on how organizations tend to be anti-learning and develop defensive routines that protect them from feelings of inadequacy. School districts may be dubious about allowing or supporting inquiry that could turn up or expose problems. Implicit in the role of an administrator is the management of a smooth running operation that publicly demonstrates its success. In schools, the need to 'look good' often drains action research of its ability to problematize or problem-pose, and instead it is used to problem-solve without an analysis of underlying causes or assumptions behind organizational problems. While our own view is that practitioner action research is a means to enhance organizational learning and support school improvement, its 'messiness' may not immediately look like it is contributing to school successes. It is the anti-thesis of defensive routines that protect institutions from their warts and, instead, invites close interrogations of business as usual. It is, simply, a pathway to authentic practitioner and organizational learning but it may not be comfortable or pretty.

Time constraints for practitioner action researchers are also a real and ongoing challenge. The multiple hats being worn – that of a full-time employee and a researcher, to name just two – compete for time and focus. At the same time, data gathering methodologies and approaches to analyses have too often been simply lifted from qualitative or quantitative approaches without a requisite reworking to fit the realities of practitioner action research. Practitioner action researchers have sometimes labored under an unrealistic expectation that they essentially can carry out their day-to-day roles as educators while simultaneously acting as ethnographers in their sites. Being an ethnographer is a full-time job in itself and the data-gathering approaches are labor intensive; it also implies being an objective outsider describing but minimizing any disturbance of the research on the setting. The task of a practitioner action researcher is to study the setting by acting in it and studying the effects of their actions. It is an intrinsically *disturbing* research. The different stance and roles of the action researcher require that we rework data gathering methodologies to account for this insider status. It means, for example, both acknowledging and appreciating the tacit knowledge about the site that an insider brings to the research while also devising research approaches to interrogate taken-for-granted analyses, that is, the things that everyone 'knows' in a site.

Any research that an administrator proposes and carries out on-site must factor in the hierarchical reality of schools and districts. Administrators 'administer' people as well as buildings and physical plants. While more power may be attributed to them than realities warrant, at the same time, when one's 'boss' decides to study day-to-day practices in a site, it sends reverberations throughout the system. Administrators face particular challenges in gaining voluntary participation for their research without those who might contribute to it feeling pressure to cooperate; can they freely turn down the boss without a fear of retaliation?

Research designs must factor in the realities outlined above. For example: how can the study be workable in terms of the time commitment? What steps can be taken to minimize or account for the power relations which are a part of the setting? What data gathering approaches both welcome and appreciate the insider knowledge the researcher(s) brings while also problematizing the taken for granted?

QUALITY CRITERIA FOR ACTION RESEARCH

While taking into account the constraints and ethical questions outlined above, administrators will also want to demonstrate that their research is of high quality, that is, can meet criteria for what researchers call *validity* or *trustworthiness*. We have outlined some tentative validity criteria for action research elsewhere (Anderson, Herr, and Nihlen, 2007; Herr and Anderson, 2005) so we will not discuss them in detail here. Briefly, (1) *Outcome validity* or *workability* is the extent to which actions occur which lead to a resolution or deeper understanding of the problem that led to the study; (2) *Process validity* asks to what extent problems are framed and solved in a manner that permits ongoing learning of the individual or system. It also asks whether traditional research methods have been appropriately modified to fit the realities of action research; (3) *Democratic, local* or *ecological validity* refers to the extent to which research is done in collaboration with the parties who have a stake in the problem under investigation. If not done collaboratively, how are multiple perspectives and material interests taken into account in the study? For example, is the researcher using action research to find solutions to problems in such a way that benefits the researcher but at the expense of other stakeholders?; (4) *Catalytic validity* is 'the degree to which the research process reorients, focuses, and energizes participants toward knowing reality in order to transform it' (Lather, 1986: 272); (5) *Dialogic validity* addresses what Myers (1985: 5) calls 'goodness-of-fit with the intuitions of the practitioner community, both in its definition of problems and in its findings'. Dialogic validity requires that researchers be able to demonstrate how they came to the conclusions they are drawing and how they have been and are open to alternative explanations that might be more useful or accurate.

The conception of action research implied in the quality criteria above recommends complex, ongoing learning, hopefully at both the individual and systemic levels; this conception asks that the researcher move beyond the implementation of a single solution strategy and engage instead in reflective cycles that include ongoing problematization. At the same time, it asks that the study be workable in terms of the time commitment and the multiple demands on the administrator/researcher's energies and time. This call that asks for rigorous reflection and inquiry and the need to fit such research into the busy professional lives of administrators may at first seem like a contradiction. But unlike the demands of traditional ethnographic methods that often guide administrators' studies, action research frames research in a way that makes it congruent with what we are asking administrators to do in schools: engage stakeholders in inquiry to frame and solve organizational problems.

NEW METHODS AND METHODOLOGICAL ADAPTATIONS FOR ADMINISTRATORS

Whereas it has become clear to many that traditional qualitative and quantitative research methods have not served action research well, there has been little discussion of how administrators (or teachers, for that matter) might either adapt traditional methods to their needs or develop alternative methods. Although not wishing to suggest closure to this ongoing debate, we will provide three methods that have generally not been used by administrators doing action research and discuss some adaptations of traditional qualitative and quantitative research methods.

Considering Qualitative Methods

Action research in education has long been under the influence of academic versions of qualitative and ethnographic methods. We believe this is because practitioner action research in education gained legitimacy around the same time that qualitative methods were gaining legitimacy in the academy (Anderson, Herr, and Nihlen, 2007). The notion of teachers as classroom ethnographers appealed to many academic researchers, and ethnographic methods were often taught to students in teacher education programs as a way to map their school's community and its cultural characteristics. While this may have worked well for teachers in training who were observing in classrooms and schools prior to their actual teaching, it soon became apparent that as classroom teachers they could not teach and take field notes at the same time. Wearing both the hats of researcher and colleague also led to political and ethical quandaries in the workplace. These problems were even more pronounced for administrators. Adaptations of qualitative methods were clearly necessary, and there are a number of books that help practitioners do this (Anderson, Herr, and Nihlen, 2007; Cochran-Smith and Lytle, 1993; Hubbard and Power, 1993).

For administrators the adaptations may be more complex because of their positions of power in their schools. For example, when administrators try to use interviews with faculty members as a data gathering strategy, they find it is fraught with problems. Interviews are never neutral; they are a social construction between the interviewer and interviewee. When bosses interview subordinates, regardless of the perceived level of trust, the data will be suspect. Beyond this, instances of perceived coercion, where an interviewee may not feel free to turn down an administrator's request for an interview, raise ethical issues. A related ethical issue arises in classroom observations: administrators may be genuinely interested in collecting classroom data, but when they step into a teacher's classroom to observe, they are still in a position in the school hierarchy of evaluator.

Both interviews and observations are time-honored data gathering approaches in qualitative studies, but for administrators doing action research they may be impractical, not only because of the time constraints involved, but also because of the administrator's position in the school. The task then becomes one of gathering data efficiently while using methods that honor subordinates' comfort zones in offering their responses as data. Methods such as anonymous surveys and questionnaires, where faculty members' responses are not provided face to face, may be more useful.

Sometimes administrators decide to study their own practices as administrators, essentially asking the question: 'How am I doing?' Here the data gathering could be much less intrusive. They might, for example, analyze their daily calendars, asking the question 'How am I spending my time? Does the way I spend my time reflect the values I espouse as an administrator?' Or, when looking at their budgets, similar questions can be posed: 'What values undergird the way money is spent here? Are they the values we publicly espouse?' Minutes of a meeting can be revealing in terms of how much decision-making power rests in the hands of an administrator and how much is shared. A content analysis of any of these documents can be the beginning of making some valuable shifts to administrative practices. Self-study methods will be further discussed below.

The point here is that it is always important for practitioner action researchers to question their multiple positions and roles in relation to the inquiry they are undertaking. Qualitative methods typically rely on face-to-face techniques for data gathering but these are questionable practices for administrators in terms of data gathering in their own sites. For administrators, probably the most important issue to factor in is their position of power within the school hierarchy. For the research to be successful, the issue is usually one of how to acknowledge that power and work around it via the design of the research. It is for this reason we suggest strategies such as self-study, collaborative action research, document analysis or data gathering methods that offer anonymity to participants.

New and Emerging Qualitative Methodologies

In this section, we will discuss some methodologies that are only beginning to find their way into action research studies. Some of these methods are drawn from the humanities and linguistics, and may better fit the realities of practitioners' lives. *Narrative action research* redefines the notion of 'data' as it draws less from the social sciences and more from the humanities. There are various iterations of narrative with perhaps the most common in education being the self-study. Self-study shifts the focus from the school and its programs to the practitioner's own beliefs and actions. *Critical discourse analysis* allows administrators to focus attention on the language and discourses – both oral and written – that are the substance of administrators' work and that surrounds them at all times. *Critical incident analysis* allows the administrator to focus on a specific incident or event and unravel the multiple contexts and perspectives that converge on it. Such incidents can be dramatic ones that catch an administrator's attention or they can be mundane routines that have gone unanalyzed for so long that they may need to be problematized. We briefly discuss each of these approaches below.

Narrative Action Research

School administrators may be more inclined to use narrative methods drawn from the humanities than research methods drawn from the social sciences. Many administrators have had some experience with journaling as teachers; others may have backgrounds in language arts, and literature or languages that provide them with an understanding of narrative and the writing skills needed to produce them effectively. Such methods are not mere story-telling (the 'how I turned my school around' articles that appear in some practitioner journals). While such accounts are of some utility, and they contain the seeds of narrative action research, they often lack the kind of critical self-reflection that rigorous narrative requires. Such accounts tend to focus on events the writer views as successful and on a 'how to' approach to replicating it. Narrative action research is more about sharing what has been learned through struggling with the dilemmas of administrative practice and what other administrators can learn from this struggle. In a sense, it shifts the notion of research as contributing to an academic knowledge base to sharing professional wisdom. Whereas academics often complain that school practitioners do not sufficiently use the findings of formal research, practitioners often find such research fails to address their particular dilemmas.

There are many different approaches to narrative research, not all associated with action research. Narrative action research can use autobiographical data or can be more focused on critical reflection on professional practice. Some may mix both approaches. A focus on one's own personal and professional selves is a form of action research usually called *self-study* (Bullough and Pinnegar, 2001) or *auto-ethnography* (Reed-Danahay, 1997). Connelly and Clandinin (1990) have ventured some tentative validity criteria for narrative research.

In a similar vein, Jack Whitehead (Whitehead and Lomax, 1987) seeks to replace traditional theories of educational practice based on propositional knowledge with what he calls 'living theories' that are derived through a dialectical process. He states, 'What I have been searching for is a way of moving educational theory from its propositional base onto a dialectical base and into a living form' (p. 181). He sees practitioners as 'living contradictions' who daily confront situations that negate their own educational values. For Whitehead, it is the experience of contradiction that provides the incentive for practitioners to resolve the contradiction through inquiry.

Critical Discourse Analysis

Schools are mostly about language in its many forms. Teaching and leading are largely verbal endeavors. Schools are also full of written texts; textbooks, worksheets, notes home to parents, email communication, policy manuals, contracts, budgets, etc. In fact, Peter Gronn (1983) did a study entitled, *Talk as the work: The accomplishment of school administration.* While language or discourse is an ever-present part of daily school life, it is seldom studied systematically and critically. By gathering samples of oral and/or written texts, administrators can approach data that is 'objectified' in the sense that it can be systematically studied as a cultural artifact – even when the language is one's own.

While there are numerous approaches to discourse analysis, we have chosen more critical approaches for the reasons discussed above. That is, administrators inhabit a reified and naturalized world in which much is taken for granted or treated as common sense. Critical approaches force administrators to look at language in terms of the work it does beyond that of utilitarian communication. That is, discourses are often attempting to accomplish such things as reinforcing certain cultural norms or ideological biases. A simple example is the use of the passive voice to mask agency, as when an administrator tells teachers 'we are being required to code our lesson plans to state standards,' instead of drawing attention to the individual or agency that is insisting on the coding. With reference to written texts, Fairclough (1992) suggests a three-dimensional structure for discourse analysis. The most immediate dimension is *textual analysis*, a close linguistic analysis of the text itself. The next dimension is an analysis of what Fairclough calls *discursive practices* which include the production, distribution, and consumption of the text. Discursive practice draws upon conventions that naturalize particular power relations and ideologies. Finally, he suggests an analysis of the text as a *social practice*, which includes a broader analysis of the macro-structural context within which the text is embedded.

There are several approaches to discourse analysis and insufficient room to discuss them here. For examples of studies in education that employ critical discourse analysis, see Rogers (2004) and Anderson (2001).

Critical Incident Methodology

Critical incident methodology can be a succinct way to document an event or incident in a school that could merit further examination. Typically critical incidents are written in a few pages as a narrative text. The author of the text tries to capture on paper the event as it occurred or was observed. Following the write-up of the incident, it is probed for meaning.

The naming of an event as a critical incident can come from any individual in an institution and signals that an event has occurred that potentially becomes the stimulus for reflection (Schon, 1983). It is essentially pushing the pause button on daily school life and signaling that something has occurred that needs further thought; with reflection and interrogation, the critical incident can be a vehicle that offers data on school practices that could be useful to examine further. Definitions of critical incidents vary from those who see them as 'surprises' or problematic situations' (Schon, 1983) to 'mostly straightforward accounts of very commonplace events that occur in routine professional practice' (Tripp, 1994: 25). The analysis of a critical incident can be done by individuals or in a group. It is assumed that critical incidents are not 'things' that happen independently of the norms of the institution but rather are a manifestation of the institutional culture; their analysis potentially unearths assumptions that remain largely unexamined or outside the realms of public awareness. Analysis allows for a probing into workplace norms that help construct institutional realities and can stimulate reflection on institutional practices, exposing underlying motives and structures. The naming of an event as critical potentially interrupts institutional meaning management and invites reflection on business as usual.

Typically the reflection on a critical incident is done through a series of questions posed. We have found Smyth's (1991) suggestions helpful in this regard; he poses the following to probe critical incidents: Whose interests are served or denied by the actions taken? What conditions sustain and preserve the actions? What power relations are involved? What structural, organizational, and cultural factors keep alternatives from arising? This probing can be done by a single administrator, with a critical friend trusted by the administrator, and/or in a group of stakeholders.

UTILIZING QUANTITATIVE METHODS

In an age of high stakes testing and annual yearly progress, administrators and teachers spend hours pouring over test data, looking for patterns. This type of quantitative data has always been available to administrators, but only since the

No Child Left Behind legislation has it become so ubiquitous in the USA. This is in part because of a largely non-reflective transfer of methods appropriate to business, but often inappropriate to education. For instance, many business models – Total Quality Management being the best known – use models of statistical control or product quality aimed at the elimination of variance. For most products – hamburgers, jet engines, blue jeans – the elimination of variance through statistical control is highly appropriate. However, these assumptions in education have fed an already engrained tendency to standardize instruction and use statistical test data to measure student outcomes, driving a one size fits all curriculum.

A more benign form of quantitative data widely used in schools is inventories, particularly those that measure school climate, safety, equity, and other issues. Surveys and questionnaires with closed-ended questions that are easy to quantify are also increasingly used. Surveys and questionnaires have the advantage for action researchers of anonymity and efficiency. For instance, Johnson (2002) has developed a comprehensive collection of surveys, questionnaires and other instruments that can be used to systematically gather school-wide data focused on equity. Quantitative data used in correlational and quasi-experimental designs have been less useful to practitioners. This is in part because the kinds of controls on the environment that such studies require are difficult to achieve in schools. Furthermore, such studies require a level of expertise in research design and inferential statistics that few administrators may possess.

CONCLUSION

In this chapter, we have taken up the challenge of suggesting methodological adaptations to action research practice that administrators might find useful in confronting the unique challenges they face, not only as insiders to their study site, but also because of their unique location within the hierarchy of the organization. Another entire chapter could be written on political and ethical issues that arise in such studies. Zeni's (2001) collection addresses these in some detail. Most ethical issues have to do with placing participants at risk, and we have tried to suggest methodological approaches that help to address some of these risk issues. Administrators doing action research may also have to decide how comfortable they are with controversy as action research often makes visible those dark corners of the organization in which power and privilege hide. Tracking practices by race or class, excessive referrals of students of color to special education, more access by low-income students to military recruiters than to college recruiters and a plethora of other unethical practices often go unchallenged but could be taken up in action research. As with all research, when done well, practitioner action research will challenge what we think we know rather than confirm it. This is why it has the potential to help us constantly rethink our practices to create schools that are more educationally sound, caring, and just places for our children and youth.

REFERENCES

Anderson, G.L. (2002) 'Reflecting on research for doctoral students in education', *Educational Researcher*, 31 (7): 22–5.

Anderson, G.L. (2001) 'Disciplining leaders. A critical discourse analysis of the ISLLC national examination and performance standards in educational administration', *International Journal of Leadership in Education*, 4 (3): 199–216.

Anderson, G.L. and Herr, K. (1999) 'The new paradigm wars. Is there room for rigorous practitioner knowledge in schools and universities?' *Educational Researcher*, 28 (5): 12–21.

Anderson, G.L. and Jones, F. (2000) 'Knowledge generation in educational administration from the inside-out: The promise and perils of site-based, administrator research', *Educational Administration Quarterly*, 36 (3): 428–64.

Anderson, G.L., Herr, K. and Nihlen, A. (2007) *Studying Your Own School: An Educator's Guide to Practitioner Action Research*. Thousand Oaks, CA: Corwin Press.

Argyris, C. and Schon, D. (1974) *Theory in Practice: Increasing Professional Effectiveness*. San Francisco: Jossey-Bass.

Bullough, R.V. and Pinnegar, S. (2001) 'Guidelines for quality in autobiographical forms of self-study research', *Educational Researcher*, 30 (3): 13–22.

Cochran-Smith, M. and Lytle, S. (1993) *Inside/Outside: Teacher Research and Knowledge*. New York: Teachers College Press.

Connelly, F.M. and Clandinin, J. (1990) 'Stories of experience and narrative inquiry', *Educational Researcher*, 19 (5): 2–14.

Fairclough, N. (1992) *Discourse and Social Change*. Cambridge, UK: Polity Press.

Gronn, P. (1983) 'Talk as the work: The accomplishment of school administration', *Administrative Science Quarterly*, 28 (1): 1–21.

Herr, K. (1999a) 'Unearthing the unspeakable: When teacher research and political agendas collide', *Language Arts*, 77 (1): 10–15.

Herr, K. (1999b) 'The symbolic uses of participation: Co-opting change', *Theory into Practice*, 38 (4): 235–40.

Herr, K. and Anderson, G.L. (2005) *The Action Research Dissertation: A Guide for Students and Faculty*. Thousand Oaks, CA: Sage.

Hubbard, R. and Power, B. (1993) *The Art of Classroom Inquiry: A Handbook for Teacher Researchers*. Portsmouth, NH: Heinemann Press.

Johnson, Ruth S. (2002) *Using Data to Close the Achievement Gap. How to Measure Equity in our Schools*. Thousand Oaks, CA: Corwin Press.

Lather, P. (1986) 'Research as praxis', *Harvard Educational Review*, 56 (3): 57–77.

Myers, M. (1985) *The Teacher-Researcher: How to Study Writing in the Classroom*. Urbana, IL: National Council of Teachers of English.

Reed-Danahay, D. (ed.) (1997) *Auto/Ethnography: Rewriting the Self and the Social*. New York: Berg.

Rogers, R. (ed.) (2004) *An Introduction to Critical Discourse Analysis in Education*. Mahwah, NJ: Lawrence Erlbaum.

Schon, D.A. (1983) *The Reflective Practitioner: How Professionals Think in Action*. New York: Basic Books.

Smyth, J. (1991) 'Problematising teaching through a "critical" approach to clinical supervision', *Curriculum Inquiry*, 21: 321–52.

Tripp, D. (1994) *Critical Incidents in Teaching: Developing Professional Judgement*. London: Routledge.

Whitehead, J. and Lomax, P. (1987) 'Action research and the politics of educational knowledge', *British Educational Research Journal*, 13 (2): 175–90.

Zeni, J. (ed.) (2001) *Ethical Issues in Practitioner Research*, New York: Teachers College Press.

13

Educational Action Research as a Paradigm for Change

Shoshana Keiny and Lily Orland-Barak

Our conceptual orientation stems from living in the pluralistic/multiethnic society of Israel, characterized by decades-long social and political change and friction and by rapid, ever-changing reforms at policy levels. Within this complex reality, the practice of action research in the context of educational change has gradually gained a prominent platform in the discourse of pre- and in-service education. Specifically, educational action research is regarded as a channel for voicing multiple educational perspectives and ideologies and for managing divergence and duality in differing teaching contexts. At a broader, communal level, action research constitutes a framework for extending boundaries of collaboration between schools, universities, colleges and the community.

In this chapter, we describe four action research projects in Israel, two of which the authors were involved in, that illustrate how practitioners manage emergent discrepancies in their work as they play out in an ever-changing reality. We regard these cases as reflective of action research as a paradigm for change, rather than solely as a research methodology. Such a conception calls for an inquiry stance that is flexible and open to a variety of strategies and methodological modalities according to the diverse needs of the context.

The selected cases are situated in four different contexts: (1) Action research in the university to develop teacher education curriculum; (2) Action research within projects of 'partnership'(between colleges of education and schools) to integrate theory and practice in teacher education programs; (3) Action research within a whole community, to enhance systemic or ecological change; and (4) Action research in cross-cultural settings, aiming toward co-existence between Arabs and Jews in Israel. We chose to construct our chapter in accordance with the grounded and reflective nature of action research, namely, to start with practice (i.e., the cases) and draw our 'lessons from the field' as they emerge from each case. Finally, we discuss our emergent insights to consolidate our conception of action research.

LESSONS FROM THE FIELD

Action Research in University Teacher Education: A Curricular Journey

Our first case focuses on how a course professor (one of the authors, so it's described in the first person) manages emergent discrepancies and dilemmas that arise when teaching an action research course at university level (Orland-Barak, 2004). The course, 'Action Research in Education' was a one-semester seminar course. The student participants were involved in educational practices at school or community levels, both in the Jewish and Arab sectors. My first years of teaching were guided by traditional views of action research, emphasizing a more technical, problem-solving approach to reflection on action. I realized that it was a course *about action research, rather than an action research course.* In the students' final action research projects there was almost no indication of an ongoing process of reflection 'on action', evident of how reflection and theory informed subsequent actions as the cycles developed. Likewise, the theoretical basis for the research project constituted one separate section, with no evidence of ongoing dialogue between theory and action or of theories as emergent from practice.

The changes introduced in the following years grew out of the insights gained from the first year. I was explicit about using the sessions as spaces for students to interact on their respective action research projects and to examine the assumptions underlying their practice. I began to put more emphasis on documenting and representing the process that students were going through questions such as: What would you like to gain a better understanding of in your educational practice? and, What does your choice of topic reveal about your educational approach and beliefs?

The changes did, indeed, contribute to a more integrative conception of reflection and action. Many papers included introspective accounts of how reflection on action had informed subsequent actions; several were autobiographical, connecting students' personal histories to their particular action research project. However, students expressed their discomfort with becoming too 'autobiographical' ('I don't feel I want to share anything personal in a university course'), and they felt there was too much vagueness and that not knowing exactly 'where they were going' had blocked them ('I really don't understand where I am going ... I'm lost!'). At that point, I began to wonder whether I was imposing demands which I didn't have the right to impose. I became particularly alert to those students who had gradually become resistant to the nature of the course, students who found it difficult to cope with the uncertainty brought about by the constructivist nature of the course. The process-oriented nature of the course was at odds with their product-oriented approach to teaching. This called for a re-examination of the emphasis that I was placing on process over product.

Since then, I have been trying to look for ways of establishing a balance between a discourse that encourages the raising of dilemmas and, at the same time, the solving of problems. I have also tried to provide closer guidance to students in terms of exposing them to different models of writing and representing the AR process of inquiry.

Lessons Learned: Reflecting on the Case

The above story illustrates how second-order action research (Elliot, 1993), .ie., the process by which the researcher/s attend to the insights gained as they engage in a critically reflective process before, during and after a situation they are facilitating, can shape a curricular journey, uncovering the challenges and tensions of teaching and evaluating action research in Israel. A major insight gained from the inquiry pertained to the tensions surfaced by the encounter between two rigid competing discourses: One was the professor's constructivist discourse, pushing toward a deeper understanding of one's action, prioritizing the articulation of dilemmas over the solving of problems, and re-examining assumptions that underlie participants' stance. By contrast, the participants' discourse pushed toward a more technical, problem-solving orientation to action research, stressing the need to arrive at clear-cut answers about 'what to do', to evaluate performance as 'right' or 'wrong', and included background reflection at personal and autobiographical levels (Rearick and Feldman, 1999).

These implications point in important directions: Being aware of potential dangers when pushing students from different cultural backgrounds into becoming personal and autobiographical in their reflections; and the importance of keeping a balance between divergent and convergent reflective processes. Another aspect pertained to the importance of providing models for representing process, i.e., how one cycle of action grows out of the other to generate personal theories. The process entails helping students to move from a positivistic paradigm of representing research, to a qualitative, interpretive one.

Action Research within Projects of 'Partnership': A Suggested New Venue for Teacher Education

Contrary to traditional views which establish a dichotomy between the academy as a theoretical context and the school as locus of practice, 'partnership' suggests merging the theory–practice divide by establishing a framework of collaboration between university and school. Its underlying conception is that teaching is a practical-reflective profession, and that pre- and in-service educations are two inter-related dimensions along a continuum of life-long professional learning (Slonim, 2007). In this vein, partnership creates a community of learners which generates a new discourse based on authentic dialogue and mutual learning, one that bridges the Cartesian split between theory and practice.

Our case tells the story of a seven-year partnership between one elementary school and a college of education. The leading figures were the school principal and the pedagogical mentor from the college. Participation in the partnership gradually expanded to include the whole school-teaching staff and student-teachers. Regular weekly meetings were scheduled after school hours, to identify and reflect on emergent problems, and for expanding on theoretical issues.

Gradually, the group developed into a self-organized community-of-learners, turning their weekly meetings into a 'school based in-service course' and assuming responsibility for the process as well as the products (Herbst, 1976). Typified by an egalitarian climate, participants were encouraged to voice dilemmas, conflicts and hesitations without fear of being ridiculed.

Discourse analysis of the various encounters and of field notes of classroom observations indicated that all participants had undergone some degree of conceptual change in terms of their roles. Shifting from 'instrumental' toward 'developmental' teachers (Keiny, 1993), participants acquired new understandings of pupils as autonomous learners and of the principal as a pedagogical figure. Yet, we should examine whether learning within the partnership was reciprocal and how the college benefited from the partnership.

The initiative to introduce the partnership came from the college's deputy. Three of the pedagogical mentors who worked with student-teachers were paired with schools to form three partnerships, and they were supported by the deputy and the rest of the pedagogical mentors through regular discussion meetings in the college. This new focus on partnerships meant that, in addition to classroom teaching, student-teachers had to spend whole days at school, gaining a wider exposure to the interactional aspects of the school culture but leaving less time for developing personal relationships with individual students – a crucial dimension of the learning to teach process. A major change was, thus, introduced in the college syllabus. Accordingly, each student-teacher would accompany two classroom students throughout their first year. The focus in the second year would be on strategies of group work, and only in the third year students would practice whole class management. This reconstructed syllabus was implemented by all college student-teachers.

Unfortunately, with the extension of the project toward developing and implementing a new curriculum for teacher professional learning, it failed to attract more pairs of college mentors and schools in order to spread the scope of partnership more comprehensively. The report (Margolin, 2007) portrays a serious theoretical learning endeavor on the part of the 24 colleges' teacher educators involved, yet it somehow backgrounds the *practical aspect* of students' learning within the partnership.

Lessons Learned: Reflecting on the Case

The community of learners developed as a self-organized group at the school. Typified by high-relationship, high-equality and high-freedom, 'community' facilitated the emergence of a medium in which participants could 'be themselves' (Fielding, 1995). The twin commitment to freedom and equality enabled the participants to be exploratory, inventive, and to develop their uniqueness; not as a static state but as an expression of growth and potential, inviting dialogue (ibid.). Put differently, the personal relationship climate best served the epistemological goal of the community of learners: to construct knowledge. As constructivist teachers, they were able to develop their students' inquiry stance as knowledge constructers. As compared to the school 'community of learners', which was encored in the participants' dialectical reflection on practice and construction of new pedagogy, learning in the teacher educators' group was primarily intellectual, based on predetermined objectives. Their idea of partnership tended to be hierarchical devoid of mutual learning since it was mainly the college who prescribed the change in the schools. We regard this as illustrative of educational change initiatives that manifest an AR orientation but, in actual fact, are predicated on an agenda of change established elsewhere.

Action Research within a Whole Community: Enhancing Systemic Change

The following is an account of a case study based on the 'Yerucham Comprehensive-Community School' Project, led by one of the authors (Keiny, 1993, 2002), so it is described by 'we'. Our metaphor for 'community school' is a school that extended its boundaries to include its natural and socio-cultural environment, as learning resource. Yet, our idea was not to impose the metaphor of a community school in a 'top-down' fashion, but rather to have the school staff construct their own model of a community school.

Yerucham is a small developing town in the Negev desert, situated within a unique landscape, populated by immigrants from different countries. It is also an industrial town, boasting of a number of factories. The case illustrates an action research initiative of teachers taking responsibility for their curriculum restructure and change. The principal's first step was to assemble the whole staff, the parents and some community representatives, calling for those interested to join the project. Four collaborative teams, consisting of teachers and community representatives, were formed, each engaging in a process of School-Based-Curriculum-Development (SBCD) with the aim of constructing new curriculum units that link the learning process to different institutions or other resources of the community.

To illustrate the learning process, we shall focus first on the industrial team, which consisted of teachers of Math, Technology, Sociology, Management and Secretarial Studies, and of community representatives from two industrial plants. The teachers' prior conception of the school–industry relationship was purely instrumental, i.e., that the factory should provide the best opportunity for applying what students had learned at school. We termed this conception an 'apprentice model' of learning. Yet, an alternative 'system-model' was suggested by one of the industry participants, which he demonstrated by a ceramic tile in his hand (quotations are all taken from the audio-recording of the meeting):

> When you look at the product, it is just a ceramic tile? very simple ... but just think how many processes are involved in its production: the basic materials; their transportation; weighing, grinding, and modeling; checking or quality-control at each stage; then wrapping, parceling, and storing, and finally marketing and shipping...

After a visit to the Negev Ceramics factory, the team facilitator opened a discussion with the following question:

What can we learn from this factory? How can we use it as a learning medium?

By juxtaposing the apprentice and system models, a new joint concept of 'school–environment relationship' was constructed. Teachers began to revise their prior assumptions about learning and plan new ways of teaching:

> We plan to open the curricular unit with a visit to the industrial plant. Only then, judging mainly by the students' reaction, by their level of involvement, will we be able to know where their interests lie.
> Let's not decide for them. Let them decide for themselves, otherwise we would be regressing back to our conventional framework, where teachers make decisions for the students on how to act.

Encounter with the factories led the group participants to realize the inter-relatedness among different aspects of their working reality, thereby raising their awareness of the impact of global changes on local factories, on community institutions (including schools) and on individual welfare.

The integrative curriculum units helped to bridge the classical rift between theoretical and practical knowledge, between school as a place for theoretical learning and the industrial plants as sites for practice. Learning was no more conceived as the transmittance of knowledge but rather as a complex process of construction of subjective knowledge (Glasersfeld, 1989).

A similar process of mutual learning was exhibited in the social team, which consisted of the staff of a day-nursery and teachers of home-economics, entailing 14 eleventh grade girls. The curriculum unit opened with a visit to the day nursery, which yielded many inquiry questions (such as 'why do babies cry'). Each girl chose a question as basis for the inquiry, collected data (both theoretical and practical) and triangulated it. The concluding chapter of their assignment was: What have I learned from my research study? Thus, their process of learning was reflected in their individual action research studies, which stemmed from their own question.

Lessons Learned: Reflecting on the Case Study

The community of learners is seen here as a *prerequisite* for collaborative action research. Within the community, each participant is exposed to two different loci: a practical and a social. As teachers, they practice new ways of teaching in the classroom; reflecting on their practice to reconstruct pedagogical knowledge. Simultaneously, within a reflective social locus, each is exposed to a variety of ideas and perspectives, engaging in a dialectical process of reflection-on-conceptions. This process liberates participants from narrow 'tunnel vision', leading them toward conceptual change. The heterogeneous nature of the social-reflective teams, which consisted of teachers from different disciplines and community people, helped expose participants to a wide scope of conceptions.

The case of the social curricular unit illustrates a second-order conceptual change. The teacher of home economics is herself involved in a process of curriculum development by experimenting with her implicit ideas, and conceptualizing them into a curriculum. The process clearly entails an interaction between practice and theory, and the curriculum achieved is not a package of learning materials but rather an open-ended process of learning of both the teacher and the students. By assuming responsibility for their assignment, the girls shifted from a conception of knowledge acquisition as rooted in objective and external sources toward a more subjective conception of knowledge construction.

Action Research in Cross-cultural Settings: Aiming toward Peace between Arabs and Jews

'Reconciliation-transformation workshops' for Jews and Arabs have been taking place in Israel since the early 1980s, focusing on the conflictual relations and the possibility of co-existence between the two nationalities in Israel (Bar and Bargal, 1995). Workshops based on reconciliation-transformation, which lasted one academic year, were designed for university students. They were elective courses and the students chose them as part of their regular course schedule. All group discussions during the workshop were audiotaped, transcribed and analyzed, using a typology for discourse classification based on seven categories (Steinberg and Bar-On, 2002). The lowest level identified in the analysis of the conversations was 'ethnocentric discourse'– monologues which do not meet, while the highest level was 'dialogical moments'– dialogues involving emotional and cognitive understanding.

A comparison between two workshops, one held in 1996/7 during the peace talks and the other in 2002/3 during the days of 'Intifada', yielded unexpected results. (The peace talks were held in Oslo, Norway, between Israeli and Palestinian delegates in an effort to arrive at a comprehensive peace agreement between the two nations.) The dominant speech category was the lowest level, i.e., ethnocentric discourse during the peace talks and, paradoxically, the highest level, i.e., dialogical moments, was recorded during the Intifada. The latter were characterized by making an effort to understand how reality was perceived and felt from the respective idiosyncratic perspectives of the participants. The researchers' interpretation was that a new group identity began to evolve, one which did not erase the national group identities but succeeded in reducing them, enabling the expression of feelings (ibid.).

Our case study, which was composed of eight Arab Israeli and eight Jewish Israeli students, draws on the above reconciliation transformation action research workshops. The facilitator was a graduate Jewish Israeli student who had been involved in educational action research frameworks. The following excerpt is taken from the audio-recording of one group session. It opens with the facilitator voicing her difficulties in trying to change the participants' conception of the 'other':

> Sitting together, they realize we are all nice human beings, but once they separate, and each party is back in their different contexts, they tend to make logical adjustments declaring, for example that: '... some Arabs are nice, but in general Arabs want to kill us... .

And she concludes:

> As I see it, there is a rationale but there are things that contradict it...' .

When asked to elaborate on how she deals with such situations, she responds:

> I believe in disclosing the conflicts rather than hiding them ... I try to expose them to a different world-view, not merely to different knowledge ... Once I accept the Arab narrative, I am then able to regard our 'Day of Independence' from their point of reference, as Nakba (disaster), but it then undermines my narrative, my identity. And [paradoxically] with no identity undermined, there is no conceptual change, merely a change in knowledge...

The excerpt reflects the facilitator's idea of conceptual change. She emphasizes the shortcoming of cognitive rational knowledge, as a lever for change and instead discloses their deep values and ingrained beliefs, as a possible platform for deeper change.

Lessons Learned: Reflecting on the Case

The above case of action research in cross-cultural settings underscores the power of action research *beyond* its scope for helping participants reconstruct prior knowledge. Transformation in this case is much deeper, touching participants' existential core, feelings, beliefs and identities.

The reflective action research cycles were guided by the facilitator's strong belief in the power of the workshop to touch the participants' identity. Adopting this transformative orientation to action research, she assists each party in learning to accept and legitimize the 'other's' identity, by encouraging reflection on their conceptions, and thereby building a basis for reconciliation and co-existence of the two nationalities in peace.

A prerequisite for the above process of deep change entails the formation of a 'cultural island' (Lewin, 1945), or of a 'community of learners' (Keiny, 2002), as context for significant activity (Oers, 1998). In this context, participants are not merely involved in an intellectual discussion but also engaged in activity as whole persons. The new understanding which emerges from this mutual learning activity is, in turn, formative of their identity (Wenger, 1995).

As a cultural-historical phenomenon, activity integrates human actions into a coherent whole, forming the basis for meaningful interpretations and actions of the learner. This creates a dialectical relationship between the individual learner as subject, and the ecology of the learning situation as context (Davis and Sumara, 1997).

EDUCATIONAL ACTION RESEARCH AS A PARADIGM OF CHANGE

A historical anecdote relates how Kurt Lewin, when he was conducting a supervision gathering, where each facilitator reported on the encounters in their last group meeting, noticed a participant of one of the groups raising his hand. Retrospectively, he notes that luckily he did not disregard him but nodded his head asking him to speak up, and his report of the same group interaction gave a completely different perspective: 'This was for me an illuminative moment', notes Lewin, 'with respect to the 'Rashomon' effect. I realized the power of a group to mirror diversive descriptions to one common experience' (Adelman,1993).

Years later, Donald Schön, in his book *The Reflective Practitioner* (1983), coined the term Reflection-on, and in-Action, connecting Kurt Lewin's group dynamics with the personal practical knowledge that practitioners develop as they reflect on their practice.

Since the early days of Kurt Lewin, action research has developed and spread out, taking different forms, such as individual AR in the classroom, collaborative AR and participatory AR. The latter draw on recent theorizing on the potential of collaborative dialogic-oriented models for engaging teachers in the sharing and co-construction of knowledge (Clark, 2001; Cochran-Smith and Lytle, 1993; Darling-Hammond and McLaughlin, 1996). These socio-cultural and social constructivist orientations to action research take the form of reflective, situated and transformative views to teacher knowledge development (Tillema, 2005).

We opened our chapter with an example of individual AR ('AR in the classroom'), grounded in a more reflective view of knowledge construction, addressing a major question in educational action research, namely, how to teach AR. The first case highlights AR as a tool and channel for professional growth. It illustrates how a reflective view of knowledge construction (Gilroy, 1993) is constantly structured and restructured to allow for voicing diverse and multiple perspectives in contexts which are ideologically inconsistent with practices that legitimize uncertainty and self-scrutiny.

The other three examples portray different cases of collaborative, participatory action research, whereby action research becomes a framework for extending boundaries of collaboration between schools, universities, colleges and the community. As such, they suggest a more situated and transformative view of knowledge construction (Bereiter, 2002; Engestrom, 1994). A central issue underlying all three is the generation of a 'community-of-learners' – a self-organized group that assumes responsibility for its processes (agenda) and products (knowledge), yielding both personal understandings and group knowledge. Each participant in the community became both an individual learner interacting with the other participants and an outside reflector, reflecting on the group process of knowledge construction. This double transformational role of the participant, which ultimately generates new theories of action, is consistent with our notion of 'ecological thinking' (Keiny, 2002).

A group becomes a community of learners by developing personal relationships toward equality and freedom, thereby allowing participants to 'be themselves' and explore their individuality (Belenkey et al., 1986). Indeed, the partnership action research project illustrates an egalitarian framework of community of learners between colleges and schools, thus offering a new model of teacher education. Based upon a real dialogue between the two institutes (school and college), it yields reconstructed shared knowledge that becomes explicit through social exchange and distributed as professional knowledge.

The 'Yerucham Comprehensive-Community School' project highlights the potential of extending the boundaries of community to reach natural, industrial and socio-cultural environments as learning resources. It is also consonant with an ecological or system paradigm, which emphasizes the connectedness and mutual dependence of the various subsystems that constitute our reality. This case also illuminates the 'action' dimension of AR, i.e., the activity intrinsic in each encounter (as compared to conventional intellectual group interaction). The concept of 'action' as the highest manner of being human was clearly expressed by Hanna Arendt (Arendt, 1958: 179) who emphasized the priority of action over thought:

> Action is a full concrete activity of the self in which all our capacities are employed, while thought is ... a withdrawal into an activity which is less concrete and less complete.

The power of the activity is also depicted in the cross-cultural Arabs and Jews case study, illustrating the transformational dimension of AR and professional knowledge construction (Bereiter, 2002), illuminating the potential of collaborative activity across populations and cultures, to challenge and reify knowledge and beliefs (Kelleher, 2003). This transformational aspect is consistent with Arendt's (1958) idea of action as a liberating activity which requires 'plurality or the presence of others'. Accordingly, 'people define themselves and create their identities in relationship, through dialogue with others'. From this point of view, we could regard the communities of learners that emerged in the above cases as optimal media for identity change.

The cases presented in this chapter indicate that within the complex reality of the Israeli society, educational action research has positioned itself as a practice which attends to the dilemmatic and multicultural composite of participants and their respective cultural settings. As such, it has served as a channel for voicing multiple perspectives and ideologies and for managing divergence and conflict. The four cases exemplify the extension of boundaries of collaboration beyond a single institution and beyond a particular culture. As such, they position the practice, as the title of our chapter suggests, as a paradigm for change rather than as solely a methodology of inquiry. Within this paradigmatic conception, the researcher participants, as depicted in the cases, are not merely involved in the process of researching their own field of practice, but also become the focus of the inquiry. A paradigmatic conception of change, in this context, highlights a hermeneutic orientation to action research, stressing the overriding goal of co-constructing new knowledge, along with a search for change and improvement of one's own practice. The different cases also depict idiosyncratic forms and meanings that shape the practice of educational action research in a pluralistic, multiethnic and conflictive society such as Israel. We welcome this sociocultural grounding to action research which is particularly consonant with agendas for promoting social change, giving action research a political character.

REFERENCES

Adelman, C. (1993) 'Kurt Lewin and the origins of action research', *Educational Action Research*, 1 (1): 7–24.

Arendt, H. (1958) *The Human Condition*. Chicago: University of Chicago Press.

Bar, H. and Bargal, D. (1995) *Living with Conflict: Encounters among Jewish and Palestinian-Israeli Youth*. Jerusalem Institute for Israeli Studies (in Hebrew).

Belenky, M.F., Clinchy, B.M., Goldberg, N.R. and Tarule, J.M. (1986) *Women's Ways of Knowing: The Development of Self, Voice and Mind*. New York: Basic Books.

Bereiter, C. (2002) *Education and Mind in the Knowledge Society*. Mahwah: Lawrence Erlbaum Associates.

Clark, M.C. (2001) *Talking Shop*. Columbia University, NY: Teachers College Press.

Cochran-Smith, M. and Lytle, S. (1993) *Inside/Outside: Teacher Research and Knowledge*. New York: Teacher's College Press.

Darling-Hammond, L. and McLaughlin, M.W. (1996) 'Policies that support professional development in an era of reform', in M.W. McLaughlin and I. Oberman (eds), *Teacher Learning: New Policies, New Practices*. New York: Teachers College Press, pp. 202–18.

Davis, B. and Sumara, D.J. (1997) 'Cognition, complexity, and teacher education', *Harvard Educational Review*, 67 (1): 105–24.

Elliot, J. (1993) 'Academics and action research: The training workshop as an exercise in ideological deconstruction', in J. Elliott (ed.), *Reconstructing Teacher Education*. London: Falmer Press.

Engeström, Y. (1994) 'Teachers as collaborative thinkers', in I. Carlgren (ed.), *Teachers' Minds and Actions*. London: Falmer Press.

Fielding, M. (1995) 'Beyond collaboration: On the importance of community', in D. Bridges and C. Husband, (eds), *Consorting and Collaboration in the Education Market Place*. London: Falmer Press.

Gilroy, P. (1993) 'Reflections on Schon, an epistemological critique', in P. Gilroy and M. Smith (eds), *International Analysis of Teacher Education*. London: Carfax.

Glasersfeld, E. von (1989) '*Cognition, construction of knowledge and teaching*', *Syntheses,* 80: 121–40.

Herbst, P.D. (1976) *Alternatives for Hierarchy*. Holland: Nijhoff.

Keiny, S. (1993) 'Four environmental cognition dimensions as criteria for the evaluation of conceptual change and development in teachers', *Cybernetics and Human Knowing*, 2 (l): 40–53.

Keiny, S. (2002) *Ecological Thinking: A New Approach to Educational Change*. University Press of America (UPA).

Kelleher, M. (2003) 'Sponsoring communities of practice; an innovative approach to delivering public policy', *The Learner*, 17: 20–5.

Lewin, K. (1945) 'Behavior, information and adopting new values', in D. Bargal (ed.), (1989) *Resolving Conflicts*. (in Hebrew) pp. 111–22.

Margolin, I. (2007) 'Creating a collaborative school-based teacher education program', in M. Zellermayer and E. Munthe (eds), *Teachers Learning in Communities*. Sense Publications, pp. 113–27.

Oers, B. van (1998) 'From context to contextualization', *Instruction and Learning*, 8 (6): 473–88.

Orland-Barak, L. (2004) 'What have I learned from all this?: Four years of teaching an Action Research course: insights of a second order', *Educational Action Research,* (1): 33–59.

Rearick, M.L. and Feldman, A. (1999) 'Orientations, purposes and reflection: A framework for understanding action research', *Teaching and Teacher Education,* 15 (4): 333–49.

Schön, D.A. (1983) *The Reflective Practitioner.* London: Temple Smith.

Slonim, S. (2007) 'A community of learners in the framework of "Partnership" between school and teachers college'. A paper presented in the symposium: A community of learners as medium for alternative teacher education: Developing teachers 'Ecological Thinking'. Mofet conference on Teacher Education, Tel-Aviv, September 2007.

Steinberg, S. and Bar-On, D. (2002) 'An analysis of the group process in encounters between Jews and Palestinians, using typology for discourse classification', *International Journal of Intercultural Relations,* 26 (2): 199–214.

Tillema, H.H. (2005) 'Collaborative knowledge construction in study teams of professionals', *Human Resource Development International,* 8 (1): 47–65.

Wenger, I. (1995) *Communities of Practice: Learning Meaning and Identity.* Cambridge: Cambridge University Press.

14

Practitioner Action Research: Building and Sustaining Success through Networked Learning Communities

Christopher Day and Andrew Townsend

This chapter explores the nature of networked action research and the benefits and challenges for school-based action researchers in sustaining their work together in such networks. Whilst the eight-year-old network, discussed here, places its emphasis upon face-to-face meetings, training, dissemination and debate rather than on similar forms of interactions online, there are, we believe, lessons to be learned about sustainability which are applicable to both.

The Characteristics of Action Research

Amongst the characteristics which are regarded as 'identifiers' of action research there are three which have particular relevance to networking: those dealing with participation and voice; collaboration and ownership; and the interface of these with change. The participatory and emancipatory nature of action research as a form of reflective inquiry has been emphasized by, amongst others, Carr and Kemmis, 1986, who define action research as:

> a form of collective self-reflective inquiry undertaken by participants in social situations in order to improve the rationality and justice of their own practices, their understanding of these practices, and the situations in which the practices are carried out. (Carr and Kemmis, 1986: 162)

In this respect the action researcher is seen as one who collaborates with others in individual and cooperative work which benefits both the individual and collective enterprises. In addition to action research being a mechanism through which participants can better understand and change practices within their social context, it also, it is claimed, enables them to understand better the nature of the influence of that social context. Kurt Lewin, often identified as the originator of action research, utilized this approach to involve communities regarded as underprivileged, in developments which would directly impact on their life and work (Lewin, 1946, 1948). His explicit intention was to encourage groups who were the most likely to be influenced by potential change to have a voice in saying exactly how proposed changes should be designed and implemented. Thus, crucial to success in undertaking collaborative action research are (1) the quality of the interpersonal relationships with other action researchers and with other participants in the same social context; and (2) the distribution of power and influence. This is especially the case for those engaged in so-called networked learning communities.

THE NATURE OF NETWORKS AND NETWORKING

A networked learning community may be defined as consisting of groups of individuals from different schools (or other organizations) voluntarily working together over time to inquire into their thinking and practice, and the contexts which influence these, for the purpose of deepening their understandings. Through this it is claimed that their capacities to contribute better to their working (and wider) contexts is enhanced, in the case of those who work in schools to the improvement of the well-being and achievement of students.

Action research networks are based upon principles of voluntarism (you only join if you want to); choice (you inquire into matters which are of significance to you); agency and ownership (what you learn belongs to you and those with whom you learn and change); and it is you who take decisions about change (there is an expectation that things will be better as a result of the engagement). It has, therefore, more than a utilitarian function, and is more than simply a 'group of organizations working together to solve problems or issues of mutual concern that is too large for any one organization to handle on its own' (Wohlstetter, et al., 2003). The principles also emphasize that the work of such networks will only be in the service of policy development where this is judged to be appropriate to the area of improvement identified within the network as a focus for change. Indeed, research conducted into action research networks has identified three main purposes to this networking:

- To enhance teachers' professional development
- To achieve school improvement
- To create knowledge (McLaughlin et al., 2007)

These emphasize the personal and institutional benefits of networking. One of the claims for successful networked learning is that it enhances self-reflection and that, as an essential intra-personal quality of those who work with others, this enables participants to cope better with rapid changes to the social contexts in which they work:

> In important ways education reform and professional development networks appear to be uniquely adapted to the rapid socioeconomic changes taking place in … society. (Lieberman and Wood, 2003: 4)

Thus, there is a direct connection claimed between engaging in systematic inquiry into practice, alone and with others, learning more about self, and learning how to be better at one's work and more critically aware of its social, political and policy contexts. A further and less well-evidenced claim made by some relates to the social and ideological position taken by a number of action research writers who suggest action research as an antidote to changes in society as a whole. Posch, for example, suggests that recent changes in society tend towards greater individualization but argues that these forces for greater separation between individuals must not be allowed to erode their need for interdependence – a need which networks are believed to be able to satisfy (Posch, 1994). According to this argument, the effects of the individualizing influence of societal change can be countered by creating sustainable social structures through which the trust and close relationships required for collaborative work and well-being can develop. Even in this conception of networking, however, the relationships which arise from interdependence need not necessarily cross institutional boundaries, or organizational divisions within institutions (such as department teams in schools).

Social networks emphasize the complex interactions of individuals in communities, exploring the relationships that they build with each other, and the effects that these have on the community as a whole. Bearing in mind the social dimension of education, it is unsurprising that the development of networks has also been of interest to many educational practitioners, policy makers and academics (see for example: Hite et al., 2005, Rauch and Schrittesser, 2003, Rauch and Steiner, 2006). With its concern for the ways in which participants in social situations interact there is also a complementarity between the promotion of social networks and the aspirations of action researchers who hope to implement change through participatory methods of inquiry.

In other words, ideally, networks are made up of volunteers who, in sometimes different configurations, collaborate to inquire into practice within a value led improvement ethic. They may emphasize critical sociological or neo-Vygotskian driven agendas and discourses, but all have change of some kind as their purpose. Action research in networks which consist of members from different organizations, whether these are connected in real or virtual time or space, may be individually or collectively designed and conducted. In the case of the networked learning community described here, both individual (school) and collective (networked) projects are undertaken in order to preserve and nurture the key principles of volunteerism, choice, agency and ownership which are so closely related to building capacity for change and reinforcing commitments to improving learning in the classroom and workplace.

THE ROLE OF THE INDIVIDUAL AND COLLECTIVE IN NETWORKED LEARNING COMMUNITIES

The Primary School Learning Network (PSLN), an eight-year-old network that we are using to illustrate this work, is composed of eight schools in a geographically coherent region of England. This network is supported internally by an infrastructure of school inquiry groups (SIGs), the leaders of which meet twice each school term, and a strategy group which includes representatives from SIGs, a network coordinator (drawn from a network school), head teachers of participating schools and two 'critical friends' from higher education. It is governed by key principles, one of which is respect for teachers' voices. Whilst there is a strategic management group which oversees the development of the network, decisions about particular inquiries are driven by a process of need identification in each school, related to shared interests across the network. Over the years there have been a whole network focus (e.g. student voice), sub-group foci (e.g. children's writing, well-being), and occasionally, individual school foci.

Throughout this work, the driving force has been the inquiry groups established in each school. Membership of these groups varies in size from two or three committed members of staff to all of the staff in the participating school (in some cases as few as three members of staff). The nature and extent of the participation of SIGs are the result of strategic decisions made by participating institutions and individuals. In many cases where schools have grown in confidence as inquirers, have aligned their inquiries to whole school improvement planning and, most importantly, have experienced good leadership, they have decided to include all members of staff as members of the school inquiry group. These inquiry groups, along with other network members, engage with each other through a series of network actvities, some of which are outlined below.

1 Writing Days

Writing days bring together action researchers from across the network to write accounts of the conduct and outcomes of their projects with similar aspirations to the writing aspects of the national writing project in the USA (Lieberman and Wood, 2003). Whilst one aim is for participants to communicate their work to each other, the act of writing is seen, in itself, as a part of the process of inquiry (Holly, 1989). This process stimulates reflection, encourages a creative examination of the experiences of the action researcher, and requires network members to think of how, and what, they want to communicate to each other about their work. This not only enables them to keep each other informed about their work but also stimulates writers to review their own experiences and perceptions in light of their conversations with fellow action researchers (see for example Harrington et al. 2006).

2 Milestone Conferences

Regular conferences are held which provide opportunities for network members to meet beyond the confines of their institutions in order to share work, celebrate progress, engage in further learning at a network level, and build, through informal networking, the trusting relationships from which they draw support to interrogate their work and the influences to develop new thinking and practices. Conferences are intended to provide a variety of stimuli to enhance the development of action research throughout the network, including presentations from invited guests and other network members, and informal socializing opportunities, from which much of the social cohesion of the network is derived.

3 Newsletters

Newsletters build on networking events in sharing the work of individual inquiry groups and the network as a whole. These newsletters are distributed to educational institutions outside the network and to colleagues in all participating schools, keeping all members of each participating school informed of inquiry work across the network, celebrating the commitment and work of network members and advertising the network to others.

4 Website

The network website was intended to provide a public face for the network and a resource for network members. This website contains basic network information, resources produced by SIG members and inquiry reports. However, our own experience, and those of related research projects, is that these websites are less successful as tools for network and individual development than the sustained dialogue resulting from the face-to-face elements of networking (Thomson et al., 2005).

5 The Directory of Enquiries

The directory of enquiries provides a mechanism for members to stay informed of the inquiry interests of other network members. The directory provides details of the members of the network along with projects with which they are currently (or have been) involved, allowing network members to make direct contact with others who have similar interests.

6 Annual Audits

These have been conducted by the external consultants since 2005 at the request of the network and have been key to sustaining the level of challenge in inquiry which has been set by schools over the past three years of its existence. Further details of these audits are outlined below.

CHALLENGES TO SUSTAINING NETWORKED INQUIRY COMMUNITIES

Networks are intended to provide systems, structures and cultures which can support the development of thinking and practices through collaborative action research which allows for varying levels of involvement from participants and differing forms of interdependence, from individual (but shared) action research, to close, collaborative relationships in working in shared projects. There are, however, challenges in sustaining networks (indeed any action research) in contexts of increased external demands which add to the normal busyness cultures of schools and classrooms by intensifying teachers' work and challenging existing professional identities. In England, for example, the intervention of central government policies into life in classrooms, curriculum, assessment and conditions of service of teachers has added to these pressures in imposing 'cultures of compliance'. These have had an impact upon the leadership and teaching agendas of schools and the charge, in some quarters (Ball, 2003; Elkins and Elliott, 2004; Elliott, 2002) that action research itself has been hijacked by policy makers and is being supported as a means of achieving a more efficient, effective, and unquestioning implementation of policy. Some of the other challenges that networks face in sustaining their work include:

- large number of meetings involved;
- difficulty in moving cooperative activity beyond headteachers, senior management teams and designated teachers with specific time release to work on projects;
- lack of involvement of pupils and parents;
- failure to collect adequate documentation of network activities which then hampers formative and summative evaluations;
- problems associated with establishing and maintaining communication within the network (Thomson et al., 2005: 7).

In the PSLN we were concerned about these challenges and those posed by the differing agendas of each of the partners, along with the influence of the policy context in which this work was conducted. We identified, also, five tensions which affect those who support action research networks (Day and Townsend, 2007):

1 *Individual vs group*: This highlights the tension that can evolve between the aspirations of individuals and the reality of trying to negotiate a common foci for the inquiry group of which they are a part.
2 *Individual and SIG vs the Community*: Networks of the type described here bring together groups of inquirers from different institutions. Tensions can occur between the inquiry

groups, and individual members, and the need for cohesion across the network, in particular where this requires conformity to common sets of practices or interests.

3 *School vs National Policy*: Change resulting from networked inquiry is implemented in a political environment in which there may well be tensions between policy makers, practitioners, and the schools within which they work.

4 *Individual vs Higher Education*: Debates about the nature and relevance of action research within academia may cast doubts, in contradiction with the views of the network action researchers themselves, on the quality of their work. This can create a tension between the outcomes focused aspiration of action researchers and academics who tend to be more critical of the conduct and outcomes of action research.

5 *Development programmes vs Higher Education*: The funded creation of networks through national programmes makes requirements of networks to report on the success of their work. The time pressures of these programmes can create a tension between short-term, easily measurable conceptions of improvement and academics who tend to problematize such simplistic perceptions of change.

These tensions operate on many of the network members differently, but there are two themes, in particular, which run throughout the tensions listed above:

Tensions Around Sustaining Continuity

The pace of inquiry, and indeed its timing, must follow the uncertain 'rhythms' of the professional learning lives of teachers and schools. For example, if a school were to be faced with external inspection and perceive preparation for this to be a priority, it might delay the start of an inquiry. It is not for those outside schools who facilitate action research in networks to judge whether such decisions are 'right' or 'wrong', but rather to ensure that teachers and schools which experience difficulties are able to remain in the network, if necessary playing a minimal active role in its work over the short term, returning to full participation once the time and energy once more become available.

Tensions Around Changing Identities

Often when teachers engage in action research, they do so without a clear understanding of its potential implications for their own classroom identities. For example, whilst work on 'student voice' in the classroom may be acceptable where 'voice' is taken to mean feedback on learning and engagement in assessing their own progress (as in 'assessment for learning'), it may have less appeal when it means that the teacher must change their role from expert holder of knowledge to mediator of knowledge which pupils themselves generate. There may, therefore, be limits in the extent to which participants in networked learning communities are prepared to change where such change threatens current practices and long-held identities.

THE MEANING OF MATURITY IN NETWORKED
LEARNING COMMUNITIES

In reviewing teacher research programmes in the USA, Zeichner (2003) suggested three key conditions or 'working hypotheses' related to their chances of success:

(i) creating a culture of inquiry that respects teachers' voices;
(ii) collaboration over a substantial time period in safe and supportive environments;
(iii) intellectual challenge and stimulation. (Zeichner, 2003: 318)

The PSLN has moved from the challenges of learning how to collaborate and to inquire systematically to a phase where relational trust (Bryk and Schneider, 2003) has been established, confidence has grown, and the intellectual and practical challenges of inquiry in school and network initiated learning have increased. It has become a 'mature' learning community. This has taken time, the journey has not always been smooth and progress has not ended. Maturity itself should not be associated with stasis. Indeed, to be mature and to stop growing is to invite the onset of decay. Moreover, what is a major development for one school's inquiry may be minor for another. In other words, networks and networked learning communities consist of individuals and organizations with a range of development needs and with different aspirations, capacities for and rates of progress. These are influenced or mediated by the commitment to inquiry, educational histories and quality of staff, the conditions in which they work, and the leadership and cultures of their schools. Together these contribute to the degree of confidence and trust in themselves and others which network members have. Thus 'maturity' is a relative concept. In the case of PSLN, we will define maturity as being sufficiently self-confident to choose to extend the opportunities to challenge one's thinking and practices, to share openly with other members of the network the nature of those challenges, to invite external as well as internal audit as a means of considering how the challenges have been met, and to share the results.

In the case of PSLN it was not until the fourth year of its life that a whole network theme of 'student voice' was embraced, other than the existing shared commitment to action research. Simultaneously, at the request of the network, we began to conduct annual audits of progress in meeting the challenges of inquiry, i.e. of enhancing pupil voice. This was audited against a framework developed from our own experiences and from the work of other authors (Fielding, 2001, 2007; Flutter and Ruddock, 2004, Leitch et al., 2007; Robinson and Taylor, 2007). In this framework we identify three 'levels' of pupil voice: student consultation, enhancing student agency and students as radical change agents. Although this is a hierarchy, inasmuch as we believe the higher levels represent a more intensive form of involvement, we do not regard activities at lower levels being less worthwhile; indeed, in most cases, schools aspired to have elements of all levels of pupil voice work. The framework is outlined below:

Level 1 Student consultation

Students' commitment to learning is enhanced in a climate of trust and openness in which:

(i) Students are listened to and taken seriously about some (specified) aspects of their educational experience.
(ii) Views have a (limited) impact on action.
(iii) Students are encouraged to have greater participation in and control over how they learn.
(iv) All students' voices are heard.

Level 2 Enhancing student Agency

Taking students seriously means giving them serious things to do in which:

(i) Teaching and learning issues are routinely discussed in the classroom.
(ii) Students are members of governing bodies.
(iii) There is a student-run school council.
(iv) There are community development projects, e.g. cross-age peer mentoring/community newspapers.
(v) There is community research and action.

The curriculum must include the capacity and willingness of students to act upon their learning – to value themselves as people who can 'make a difference' in ways that go beyond the teacher and classroom.

Level 3 Students as radical agents of change
(i) Students conduct research within organizational structures and cultures which enact teaching and learning as interdependent, a shared responsibility.
(ii) Students are sources of data, active respondents, co-researchers, and researchers.

The audit draws on a number of data sources, including pupil and staff interviews (group and individual), observations and an analysis of school and SIG documentation. In this respect we act as a conduit for the voices of the network participants, often pupils, reporting against an agreed framework and providing individuals and schools with the opportunity to comment on the nature, processes and outcomes of their work, and to identify and plan new ways to develop it further. An example of this is shown in the following extract of an audit reporting on some pupil comments.

> Pupils liked it when teachers consolidated what they had learned. What got in the way of their learning were 'people interrupting', 'when the teacher confuses you by suddenly changing the topic', and 'when the teacher starts talking when you're doing your work'... These confirmed the dominance of teachers' agendas in the classroom. Whilst in almost all

of the ten classes observed (albeit for short periods of time) teachers were clearly connected and genuinely interested in the pupils, most of the work was of the traditional whole class, 'I ask the question, you provide the answer' kind. Key words were 'clear learning intentions', 'colourful physical environments', 'uniformity', 'order', 'praise', 'knowledge of pupils/close personal engagement' and 'acceptance of teachers' responsibility of learning'. In one or two classes, also, there were examples of more teacher-learner equity through joint problem-solving activities, 'bridging' conversations which connected present learning to past learning … In relation to the intentions to involve pupils more in classrooms as co-researchers and researchers beyond active participation in their work, there was little evidence, and this was confirmed in the interviews. (Pupil voice audit, 2007)

A number of developments have been made in response to this and other audits. An example of this is a school which, having previously consulted pupils about their views on developing reading, aspired to implement a strategy to integrate classroom forms of representation with a school-wide representative body for pupils. This was based around circle time sessions, conducted in all classes, as a strategy for engaging the views of all children (Mosley, 1996). From these sessions each class identify three issues to take to the school (pupil) council via their two elected representatives. They then discuss the issues raised and make their representations to school management, which is in turn fed back to all children at school assemblies. This has resulted in tangible change, such as in the organization of the school day and the redevelopment of the school playground. This change in pupil voice strategy was supported by the network in a number of ways. Firstly, the stimulus for this change came from the pupil voice audit. Secondly, support was provided by other network members in developing these consultative structures with very young children. Finally, the idea for this approach was supported by similar models for student involvement shared at network conferences.

This is just one example of change made to the methods used to engage with pupil voice through consultation. Smaller changes have also occurred, for example altering the dynamics of school councils, with staff either absent entirely, or present by invitation only (having previously chaired and managed all meetings). The part that pupils play in school inquiry projects has also altered in response to this focus on pupil voice and the auditing process which underpinned it. This is most marked in projects where pupils have taken responsibility as researchers, rather than participants in others' research. And whilst there are concerns about establishing pupil researchers in more privileged positions than their peers, this greater involvement of pupils in strategic decision making and in conducting research does represent a development from the previous, adult centred, work of the network.

CONCLUSION: MANAGING COMPLEXITY IN NETWORKED LEARNING COMMUNITIES

Those who undertake inquiries into practice, as research and experience show repeatedly, live, at least temporarily, with levels of discomfort; for example, the ambiguity and uncertainty of attempting to change practices; gaining new (and sometimes disturbing) insights into the provisional nature of knowledge; or experiencing difficulties in seeking to create communities of inquiry in school and classroom where none have previously existed. Courage is needed in professional development work of this kind. Networked learning communities, in which participants support each other in confronting experience and practice in order to take decisions about change, provide a culture which can foster the collaborative relationships to which many action researchers aspire, but which also extends the remit of that collaboration beyond active involvement in one particular project. It is not necessary, for example, to require all network members to be active action researchers, or for all action researchers to address the same topic, or use the same approaches.

Thus, whilst networks may foster collaboration between members, not all relationships in a network are necessarily collaborative; and whilst one might aspire for active participation in action research projects, participation in the network can vary from passively observing developments to actively engaging in them. This can be of considerable benefit in encouraging involvement of individuals who, for a variety of reasons, may not always have the confidence or capacity to be able to engage actively at particular times. In cases where this is because of reservations over the relevance or potential of action research to them, networks can provide an opportunity to test the water, to attempt to understand the potential benefits and obligations of action research without having to engage fully in the process. In addition, networks can provide the systems and structures through which different communities facing similar challenges can engage in sustained, participant led, dialogue from which change can be implemented which reflects the collective interests and desires of all participants.

Building and sustaining successful networks means bringing together individuals with diverse interests, respecting these and working with them in ways which stimulate connections, build trust and open minds. Building and sustaining successful networked learning communities demands skilled leadership in the management of ambiguities, discontinuities and tensions. It is not an enterprise for the fainthearted, nor for the fulfilment of temporary interests of those from outside the communities of schools. To be successful is to make a long-term commitment to all those within the network, to be prepared to learn alongside network members in their interests. It means, also, bringing to the network a sense of focus which is appropriate not only to present needs and aspirations but which relates to an assessment, through close knowledge of the participants and consultation with them, of their current motivations and capacities for engaging in levels of action research which will continue to challenge current understandings and practices over the lifetime of their existence. Sustaining the work of networks, in other words, is likely to rely upon the growth of relationships and relational trust which are difficult to promote electronically and over a distance. Whilst some "virtual" relationships may survive over a relatively long period of time, most require regular face-to-face contacts to grow in depth and maturity.

REFERENCES

Ball, S.J. (2003) 'The teachers soul and the terrors of performativity', *Journal of Education Policy*, 18 (2): 215–28.

Bryk, A.S. and Schneider, B. (2003) *Trust in Schools: A Core Resource for School Improvement*. New York, Sage.

Carr, W. and Kemmis, S. (1986) *Becoming Critical, Education, Knowledge and Action Research*. London: RoutledgeFarmer.

Day, C. and Townsend, A. (2007) 'Ethical issues for consultants in complex collaborative action research settings: Tensions and dilemmas', in A. Campbell and S. Groundwater-Smith (eds), *An Ethical Approach to Practitioner Research: Dealing with Issues and Dilemmas in Action Research*. London: Routledge.

Elkins, T. and Elliott, J. (2004) 'Competition and control: the impact of government regulation on teaching and learning in English schools'. *Research Papers in Education*, 19 (1): 15–30.

Elliott, J. (2002) 'The impact of intensive "value for money" performance auditing in educational systems' *Educational Action Research*, 10 (3): 499–506.

Fielding, M. (2001) 'Students as radical agents of change', *Journal of Educational Change*, 2 (2): 123–41.

Fielding, M. (2007) 'Beyond "Voice": New roles, relations, and contexts in researching with young people' *Discourse*, 28 (3): 301–10.

Flutter, J. and Rudduck, J. (2004) *Consulting Pupils, What's in it for Schools?* London: Routledge.

Harrington, P., Gillam, K., Andrews, J. and Day, C. (2006) 'Changing teaching and learning relationships through collaborative action research: learning to ask different questions', *Teacher Development*, 10 (1): 73–86.

Hite, J.M., Williams, E.J. and Baugh, S.C. (2005) 'Muiltiple networks of public school administrators: An analysis of network content and structure', *International Journal of Leadership in Education*, 8 (2): 91–122.

Holly, M.L. (1989) 'Reflective writing and the spirit of inquiry', *Cambridge Journal of Education*, 19 (1): 10(71–80).

Leitch, R., Gardner, R., Mitchell, S., Lundy, L., Odena, O., Galanouli, D. and Clough. P. (2007) 'Consulting pupils in assessment for learning classrooms: the twists and turns of working with students as co-researchers', *Educational Action Research*, 15 (3): 459–78.

Lewin, K. (1946) 'Action research and minority problem', *Journal of Social Issues*, 2 (4): 34–46.

Lewin, K. (1948) *Resolving Social Conflicts*. New York: Harper.

Lieberman, A. and Wood, D.R. (2003) *Inside the National Writing Project, Connecting Network Learning and Classroom Teaching*. New York: Teachers College Press.

McLaughlin., C., Black-Hawkins., and K., McIntyre., D. with Townsend, A. (2007) *Networking Pracititoner Research*. London: Routledge.

Mosley, J. (1996) *Quality Circle Time*. London: LDA.

Posch, P. (1994) 'Changes in the culture of teaching and learning and implications for action research', *Educational Action Research*, 2 (2): 153–61.

Rauch, F. and Schrittesser, I. (2003) *Networks as Support Structure for Quality Development in Education*. Enschede: CIDREE.

Rauch, F. and Steiner, R. (2006) 'School development through education for sustainable development in Austria', *Environmental Education Research*, 12 (1), 115–27.

Robinson, C. and Taylor, C. (2007) 'Theorizing student voice: values and perspective', *Improving Schools*, 10 (1): 5–17.

Thomson, P., Brown, L., Day, C and Townsend, A. (2005) *Developing a Networked Learning Community with ICT–Learning the Hard Way*. London: Becta.

Wohlstetter, P., Malloy, C.L., Chau, D. and Polhemus, J. (2003) 'Improving schools through networks: A new approach to urban school reform', *Educational Policy*, 17 (4): 399–430.

Zeichner, K.M. (2003) 'Teacher research as professional development for P-12 educators in the USA', *Educational Action Research*, 11 (2): 301–25.

15

Action Research and Educational Change: Teachers as Innovators

Lesley Saunders and Bridget Somekh

Our starting point for this chapter is the work of Lawrence Stenhouse whose Humanities Curriculum project in England, in the early 1970s, confirmed the central role that teachers necessarily play in curriculum development (Stenhouse, 1975). Stenhouse believed that even the most detailed curriculum specification has no power of itself to bring about change, because learning in classrooms is a process resulting from the enacted interactions of teachers and students, rather than the aspirations set out in a curriculum document. He realized, in the course of the Humanities project, that to develop curriculum effectively and embed it in changes in practice depended on involving *teachers as researchers* in the development work.

This chapter brings together two narratives, drawing on the authors' own backgrounds and professional biographies, both energized by a passion for changing schools to make them better places for students and teachers. Bridget was an early teacher-researcher in the Stenhouse tradition. Lesley had drawn heavily on Stenhouse's ideas in the course of developing the GTC's position on teaching as a research-informed profession. Our shared commitment to supporting teachers in leading curriculum reform led us to work together in the Developing Pedagogies with E-Learning Resources Project (PELRS) which was led by Bridget at Manchester Metropolitan University (MMU) between 2003 and 2006 and sponsored by the General Teaching Council for England (GTC) where Lesley was Senior Policy Adviser for Research. PELRS was a curriculum development project in the tradition of Stenhouse, that explored how ICT (information and communication technologies) – conceived *pedagogically* rather than as hard/software or as a subject – might be able to transform students' learning. The two narratives trace the antecedents of the project and its development. They take it in turns to describe its theoretical and policy rationale and impact and to discuss its implications for teachers' professional learning and development through engaging in action research. The chapter is played out in four Acts and a Finale.

ACT ONE – BRIDGET'S NARRATIVE

My first action research was carried out in 1978–79 when, as a student of John Elliott on secondment for one year from my teaching post, I carried out research on behalf of Dave Henderson, a teacher at Redbourne School in Bedfordshire. I was learning the techniques of data collection and analysis; Dave was introducing the Nuffield innovative science curriculum to his advanced level students (aged 17); together we explored his questions, including why were the students reluctant to engage in discussions about Physics in the way the new curriculum specified? Our work over nine months involved me observing his classes and making notes, tape-recording and transcribing classroom verbal interactions, interviewing Dave, interviewing his students, and facilitating two discussion sessions Dave held with his students to talk about his teaching and their learning. This work was strongly influenced by my use of 'pattern analysis' to carry out preliminary analysis of observation and interview transcripts and set the agenda for discussions/interpretations of the data, first with Dave and later his students. Pattern analysis is a technique that draws on symbolic interactionist theory to uncover the routinized nature of human interaction and the ritual performances played out by students and teachers in classrooms (Ireland and Russell, 1978). From symbolic interactionism I learnt that our actions are often not in harmony with our espoused values and intentions; in other words that we often create impressions in others that we do not intend. From an early interest in Freud I was also well aware of the complexity of human action, the mix of emotional, rational and unconscious motivations. By analyzing the patterns of interaction, Dave and I were able to understand how students were inhibited from participating in discussion, partly because of their strong prior assumptions (e.g. that teachers' questions were intended to 'catch them out' rather than enable them to show their knowledge) and partly because of his own routines of practice (e.g. following up answers to questions with a further question 'why?' with a raised voice and forward body movement that students described as 'pouncing'. David Ireland and Tom Russell's short paper was published by the Classroom Action Research Network, set up by Elliott in 1976 to support teacher action research. The paper was important in giving me practical strategies for analyzing teacher–student interaction and opened my eyes to features of human behaviour I had never previously been able to see. It gave me a taste of classroom-based research that was to stay with me over the following 30 years. Both Elliott and

CARN (www.did.stu.mmu.ac.uk/carnew/) were to remain strong influences on my development as a teacher-researcher when I returned to my own classroom.

Between 1988 and 1990, shortly after I ceased to be a full-time teacher, I led an action research project called Pupil Autonomy in Learning with Microcomputers (PALM). PALM worked with around 100 teacher-researchers in East Anglia to explore how computers in classrooms could give pupils greater control and responsibility for their own learning, either working on their own or in groups. The teachers' research was published in the Teachers' Voices series. A meta-analysis of their case studies, carried out by the teacher-researchers and university-based facilitators at a residential weekend conference, was used to develop the PALM Dynamic Model for a Transforming Pedagogy for Information Technology (Somekh and Davies, 1991). It was clear from the PALM Project that a computer in a classroom intervened strongly in the interactions between teacher and students: this was primarily because it shifted the focus of students' attention away from the teacher to the computer screen, and also helped to support students' activities (individually and in groups) with less need for the teacher's intervention or surveillance: hence the computer, by disrupting the routines of classroom practice, opened up possibilities for changing pedagogy to transform students' learning through action research. PALM showed that computers *could* be used to give students more autonomy in learning, but the crucial factor in making this happen was *how* the teacher integrated computer use with other classroom activities, using what we called 'framing tasks'.

Between 1990 and 2002 I was involved in a number of evaluations of innovative technology programmes funded by the UK government. All showed that, despite very considerable investment in hardware, software and teacher professional development, there was little or no transformation of pedagogy or positive impact on students' learning (Somekh, 2007, pp. 109–112). I found myself torn between frustration, as a teacher and advocate, at the waste of expensive resources on relatively trivial activities (mainly the teaching of skills in using technology) and fascination, as a researcher, with the resilience of patterned and routinized classroom practices and the power of barriers-to-change in school structures, particularly secondary schools. Meanwhile there was considerable evidence that, although little was changing in schools, young people were using technology at home in ways that were radically changing their access to information and music, their ability to create and publish their own work, their sense of identity and their social lives (Lewin, 2004).

What could be the reasons for this extraordinary difference between the impact of technology on young people's lived experience at home and in school? Between 1998 and 2001 I had the good fortune to be involved in a series of seminars on sociocultural research methods and became immersed in a whole new (for me) set of theories that explained the relationships between human agency, motivation and cultural tools, and how these are constructed and re-constructed by organizational rules and divisions of labour (Cole, 1996; Engeström et al.,

1999). These theories mesh extremely well with action research methodology and shed light on the reasons why changes to teaching and learning practices with technology are peculiarly difficult to bring about in schools. I think that one of the great benefits I have gained from being an action researcher is a habit of *active* reading in which theory plays the part of research data and is both tested out in action research and integral with analysis of action research data. Action research for me is about looking for ways to make things happen in line with one's vision, never accepting that anything is impossible, and acting strategically and politically to make new alliances and gain leverage on organizational inertia. I like to use theories to inform the design of action research. The focus in sociocultural research is on setting up prototype practices or models and working collaboratively with participants to understand and theorize about them (Langemeyer and Nissen, 2005). Activity is analyzed in terms of how cultural tools mediate human actions, and actions are shaped by contexts and diffused between actors rather than the results of individual endeavour (Engeström and Middleton, 1996). These new theoretical tools, which Langemeyer and Nissen call 'a form of action research that stresses the integration of basic theoretical work with empirical-practical engagement' (op. cit: 190), were the inspiration for the design of the Developing Pedagogies with E-Learning Resources project that is the subject of the rest of the chapter.

The PELRS project was born from my desire to build on young people's transformative experiences with technology outside school – to see if the barriers of school and classroom culture could be overcome. Drawing on sociocultural theories I envisaged this project as involving a wide range of partners: teachers, school leaders (administrators), students, their parents and if possible policymakers. I needed external funding, but this broad scope was not attractive to sponsors who generally favoured focused studies on one subject or one age group. It was when I approached the General Teaching Council that I found the first potential sponsor who understood my vision; specifically I met Lesley and we worked on the initial design of PELRS together.

ACT TWO – LESLEY'S NARRATIVE

At the time I met Bridget, the General Teaching Council for England (GTC) was still relatively new. The GTC was established by the 1998 Teaching and Higher Education Act as an independent professional body and came into existence in September 2000. Advisory staff like myself were, with Council Members, tasked with shaping a strategy for policy work that could influence government and command credibility with the profession.

From 2000 to 2003, the GTC focused much of its policy and research effort on teachers' professional learning and development, in order to help create a climate of entitlement, quality and progression. The Council also recognized the potential of new technologies to generate a virtual learning environment that would engage both pupils' and teachers' interest and commitment. We realized that these fast-developing means of accessing, generating and interacting with an unprecedented range of information and issues were often not being brought fully through into the day-to-day reality of schools; and that this was partly due to a lack of confidence on the part of teachers about the pedagogical approaches that were necessary.

As Bridget outlined her ideas for a project on the pedagogical shifts that teachers' reflective use of ICT could bring about, it quickly became obvious to me that its most relevant and cogent aspects for the GTC were these:

- the specific focus on innovative pedagogies with e-learning resources, rather than pedagogies in which a range of ICT tools fit in, if only by default, to already-existing practice;
- development of 'generic' pedagogic strategies, based on explicit theories about learning, and their subsequent adaptation and tailoring by teachers to specific curriculum and/or learning contexts;
- participation of pupil-researchers to gain their unique insights on the learning processes and to extend the research into home and community contexts;
- involvement of school leaders in developing an organizational culture to enable pedagogic change;
- curriculum innovation (as envisaged by the Education Act 2002) in line with what research suggests is necessary to enable transformative learning;
- use of specialist software as a tool for collaborative knowledge building.

The project was offering an alternative paradigm of pedagogy, in which students' internalized and informal learning about new technologies would work in conjunction with teachers' own research-led development. The principles of action research were, and are, fully consonant with the concepts and values that inform the GTC's Professional Learning Framework and the Teacher Learning Academy: http://www.gtce.org.uk/cpd_home/ and http://www.gtce.org.uk/tla/.

At this stage in its evolution, the GTC was developing a strategy for research involving funding partnerships rather than relying solely on GTC-commissioned research – we did not have sufficient financial resources to commission directly the scale and scope of research we ideally wanted. We were able to enter into a partnership with Manchester Metropolitan University which allowed us to contribute to the project financially over three years, and of course to benefit from the emerging issues and findings in 'real time'.

The project began in earnest in September 2003. It is part of the GTC's research strategy to set up an advisory group for each research project in order to provide critical appraisal of, and also a 'champion' for, the work as it progresses; importantly, such a group can frame and guide the research within a rapidly changing national policy context. The PELRS Advisory Group included representatives from the British Educational Communications and Technology Agency (BECTA), the National College for School Leadership (NCSL) and the

Qualifications and Curriculum Authority (QCA), as well as academics and GTC Council Members. Its terms of reference were to:

- act as a critical friend to the research project by supporting the research team and ensuring constructive feedback;
- comment on and contribute to draft research instruments, documentation and reports;
- provide guidance on the design and direction of the project, including dissemination;
- offer support and feedback on progress;
- identify others who can contribute to the Group and/or the research;
- ensure discussions and papers remain confidential until approved.

The Advisory Group was very active throughout the project, but it was in terms of the dissemination of PELRS that its work was crucial, as is discussed in Act 4. For myself, I found it tremendously rewarding to be involved in helping to shape and secure the policy receptiveness for the work from its early days, which was quite different from the traditional role of research managers as contract-chasers on the one hand and rather passive receivers of eventual research findings on the other. And, as time went on, I had to think hard about the ways in which the project, and its Advisory Group, could address the policy challenges of 'scaling up' and 'transferability' in the context of this small-scale, deeply-engaged R and D project. Bridget takes up the description of PELRS in more detail in Act 3.

ACT THREE – BRIDGET'S NARRATIVE

Matthew Pearson[1] and I led PELRS together from the Centre for ICT, Pedagogy and Learning at Manchester Metropolitan University. Matthew combined expertise in facilitating teachers' and students' action research with considerable technological expertise; he and I shared an interest in sociocultural research and activity theory. During the first two years of PELRS we worked with teacher-researchers and student-researchers in four schools, two primaries, one secondary and a special school.[2] These schools were chosen because they were already known for innovative work with technology; two were in an inner city area of socioeconomic deprivation, the other two had mixed catchments in suburban areas. The schools were invited to take part in a research project which would involve brainstorming possibilities for using technology to make radical changes to pedagogy to transform students' learning; we were explicit that this would not be a project 'starting from where teachers are'. The teachers accepted our invitation to join a research partnership with enthusiasm.

The first term was spent observing how technology was already being used in order to capture current practice before we began to construct a prototype. Technology was being used to create additional excellence within traditional pedagogical methods, that is, teachers were in control of what was being learned and how it would be learned; learners were largely using instructions set down by teachers; opportunities for learners to make decisions about how to learn were limited and they were prevented by existing organizational routines from using technology to help them learn in subjects other than ICT.

The overarching PELRS research question was: 'Could we teach and learn in radically different ways now we have the internet, internet-look-alike CD/DVD materials, digital imaging and video, etc.?' Teachers told us they found this question gave them opportunities to develop new ways of teaching with the project's support. It helped that PELRS was *timely*, coming at a moment when the political process was shifting towards giving students more choice and responsibility in 'learning to learn'. It was agreed that our working definition of transformative learning would be when pupils were able to:

- achieve specified learning outcomes (e.g. from the national curriculum);
- learn creatively (e.g. contributing, experimenting, solving problems);
- learn as active citizens (e.g. acting autonomously, taking responsibility);
- engage intellectually with powerful ideas (e.g. using thinking skills, grappling with ideas/concepts);
- reflect on their own learning (e.g. evaluating own learning through metacognition).

To ensure that the prototype practices could directly access the levers for change revealed by sociocultural theories, we developed a generic pedagogic framework (GPF) to be used for planning learning events and as the interface for the PELRS website. This was drafted by the university-based research team, discussed with the teacher-researchers at a team meeting, and later refined (see Figure 15.1):

The GPF incorporated a key idea from the PALM project: that pedagogy with ICT involved a three-way interaction of teacher, pupils and ICT, rather than two-way teacher–pupil interaction: in practice, this developed the symbolic interactionist theories that had underpinned PALM towards the sociocultural theory that research into activity should incorporate agents (motivated towards an object) and their mediating cultural tools in a single unit of analysis (Wertsch, 1998). The GPF was customized to produce four PELRS Thematic Frameworks (Pedagogic Strategies) with more specific ideas for planning learning events: 'Pupils as Teachers'; 'Pupils as Producers of Media'; 'Pupil Voice'; and 'Learning Online'. These themes served to stimulate ideas; they also resonated with policy discourses current at the time, so that teachers could use them to gain leverage to carry out innovative work.

Key ideas embedded in the PELRS innovative pedagogies were:

- that learning should take place across contexts (home, school and online), and students should involve their parents and other adults at home and at school, as well as teachers;
- that teachers should negotiate the curriculum focus with students at the beginning of each learning event in plenary discussion sessions, following the national curriculum but allowing students to decide 'how' they would learn;

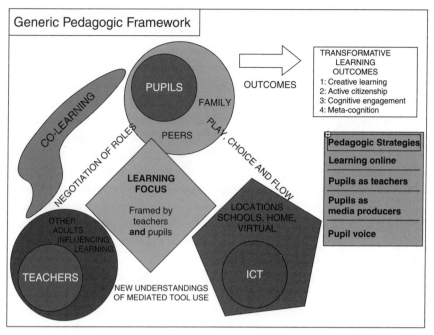

Figure 15.1   The PELRS generic pedagogic framework.

- that teachers should be co-learners with students and both their roles and students' roles should be renegotiated to allow students to take much more control and responsibility for their learning;
- that students should have choice over what technology (and other) tools to use to help them, and the chance to become totally focused on their learning so that they experienced the high levels of engagement known as 'flow' (Csikszentmihalyi, 1996).

PELRS worked in a participatory way with all students. Matthew was a frequent visitor in classrooms and filmed hours of digital video, interacting easily with teachers, stopping to talk to students about their work (i.e. informal interviewing recorded on the video), answering their questions, and sometimes passing the video camera to students themselves. Six students in each class were selected to participate more specifically as student-researchers. They were chosen for their facility with ICT from frequent use at home, by means of Matthew sitting beside them and asking them to 'show me what you can do with this computer'. Their role was to advise teachers on 'how what we do with ICT at school could be more like what we do at home'.

PELRS set out to involve teacher-researchers in all aspects of research activity without weighing them down with a heavy additional workload. These were not teachers who were enrolled on post-graduate study at a university; they were participating in action research as part of their normal teaching. In the PALM project, about a quarter of the teachers in the same position wrote up their own research reports and said that this had been one of the most exciting aspects of participating in the project, but PELRS teachers were working within a much more demanding education system, with a specified national curriculum and many more requirements to produce formal records, as well as a high stakes regime of testing (at age 7, 11 and 14) and formal inspections with published reports (including the possibility of being categorized as having 'serious weaknesses' or needing 'to be put in special measures'). The PELRS teachers planned their learning events and decided with Matthew what data should be collected. To prepare for analysis and interpretation Matthew and I made selections from the data and these were shown first to teacher-researchers and then student-researchers and recordings made of their comments and discussion. Differences in the students' interpretations and comments were discussed with the teachers after the students had given permission. We took a lead in writing up the action-research, critiqued by teachers, and they played a leading role in co-presenting with us at workshops and conferences.

PELRS demonstrated teachers' facility, through action research, to develop new pedagogical practices that unlocked the affordances (latent possibilities) technology offered for students to work more actively and creatively, with higher levels of engagement. Case studies of learning events in the four schools were published on the PELRS website, within a password-protected area (which has now, several years later, been made open to the public) www.pelrs.org.uk. In the third year, the PELRS project was opened up to 12 new schools who were interested in trialling the strategies and models and developing customized versions in their own schools.

The four PELRS themes provided realizable aspirations that gave teacher-researchers 'permission' within the traditional culture of their schools to change their routine practices, supported by university researchers and the GTC. The PELRS GPF – because it was intriguing and semiotically pleasing – made a good starting point for discussions of sociocultural theories between teacher-researchers and their university research partners. These theories explained the importance of negotiating the 'object' of learning events with students (in introductory plenary sessions), and giving them more control over their use of ICT and other resources. Introductory plenary sessions at which students decided *how* they would learn and *what resources (including ICTs) they would use* greatly increased their motivation. Giving students new roles as 'teachers' or 'producers of media' allowed them to take greater agency in their own learning. Analysis of video-recordings showed extraordinary changes in classroom discourse, with students (including some previously considered 'difficult') initiating discussions with teachers of information downloaded from the internet, and teachers rarely issuing instructions or reprimanding students. Teacher-researchers' assessments of students' learning showed that their learning gains (in traditional terms) were good, and in cases where teachers re-assessed these gains after several months they were surprised by students' high levels of retention of key vocabulary and conceptual understanding.

PELRS also showed that some features of school culture constituted serious barriers to using technology effectively and creatively. For example, the fragmentation of the school day into short timeframes made it impossible for students to engage in exploratory learning with ICT; and aggressive internet filters sometimes made it impossible for pupils to use the internet to access anything other than sites pre-determined by the school's technicians. These problems were much more evident in secondary schools than primary schools: hence, work is currently ongoing to establish further research in which secondary students will have their own 'digital learning companions' working in schools with an 'umbrella' of wireless connectivity and carrying their DLCs home for both learning and social uses. As in PELRS, the focus of this new research will be on changing roles and relationships so that students learn to use ICT tools, creatively and responsibly, to transform their learning.

ACT FOUR – LESLEY'S NARRATIVE

The GTC takes the view that good theory can be highly practical, an agent of change. PELRS developed a persuasive methodology for elaborating and strengthening theory through the practice of teachers and pupils in different contexts researching their own classrooms. We were very impressed with the ease and eagerness with which teachers unfamiliar with the academic discourse of cultural-historical activity theory grasped what this means when they saw the PELRS pedagogic diagrams, and worked through its implications for the way teaching and learning could be organized in their classrooms. The organizational apparatus of schools as institutions – timetables, rules, structures – can come to be substituted for the fundamental aims of education, and even make pupils feel they themselves are not part of those aims. PELRS encouraged teachers to question the relationship between schooling and learning, and to offer learners a more equal part in decision-making about their learning, without in the least undermining their pedagogical authority.

The Advisory Group worked with Bridget's team and the GTC to secure wider interest in the aims, processes and findings of PELRS. Towards the end of the funded work, the Advisory Group helped to design a dissemination strategy, which included working with journalists, integrating PELRS with the NCSL's Senior Leaders and ICT (SLICT) programme and Becta's research strategy, and presenting PELRS messages to the Government's Chief Adviser on School Standards.

As we argued in an earlier paper (Somekh and Saunders, 2007), PELRS by that point was no longer a bounded 'project' in the usual sense. When I look back, I can see that there was some important, contextualized, learning for the way we go about policy; most of all, in trying to re-formulate the issues and challenges of 'dissemination' and 'scaling up'. Among other things, this meant taking the risk that other agencies and organizations wanted and were able to make the PELRS principles and practice their own. This exchange of ideas between researchers, practitioners and policy advisers took place at meetings of the Advisory Group, interactive seminars, conversations, presentations and papers, and through the PELRS website.

This model of dissemination does not rely on the performative production of a text, the 'final report', but instead on a whole range of loosely related tools in the Vygotskyan sense operating in real time, which allows a continual re-invention, rather than a closing-down, of the research.

The PELRS work went on to have further applications to the policy environment. Its ideas and practices spoke directly to the government agenda on 'personalized learning' – an agenda which the GTC supported but which we also wished to strengthen and deepen. The GTC has used the ideas and evidence from the PELRS project for several of its public policy pronouncements, including:

- response to the Gilbert Review 'Teaching and Learning in 2020', August 2006;
- formal advice to government on personalized learning, March 2007;
- submission of evidence to the Primary Review, March 2007;
- response to the QCA Secondary Curriculum Review, May 2007

– all of which can be accessed on the GTC's website. At the time of writing, the GTC continues to draw heavily on PELRS material for conferences, seminars and colloquia around the theme of personalization. This all suggests that the 'return on investment' in PELRS has been high – for the schools and teachers involved and for the wider professional and policy communities. The GTC is therefore hoping, through support for a possible further project, to assist in the further refinement and evaluation of the PELRS 'tools' for pedagogical transformation in secondary schools, where the need is still great.

FINALE – LEARNING FROM PELRS ABOUT ACTION RESEARCH

The lessons that the PELRS work offers are, we think, new ones; at any rate, we believe they are useful to debate and develop further. We would summarize them like this:

I. Given that (i) learning is socially constructed and (ii) ICT is a tool in a Vygotskyan (as well as a conventional) sense, research into technology (ICT) and learning is inevitably an exploration of innovations that are social as well as technological.

II. Radically new and different social practices in schools (and elsewhere) are necessary to unlock, as well as to understand, the possibilities of ICT as a pedagogical innovation.

III. Schools need external support to develop such practices, because school routines (timetables, structures, etc.) quickly default to the status quo.

IV. To transform teaching and learning in education systems that are strongly regulated by central government, it is not appropriate to use a model of action research that 'starts

from where teachers are': instead, a prototype new practice needs to be designed, introduced and evaluated; it needs to be based on explicit theoretical principles, which teacher-
researchers and university-based researchers reconstruct, interrogate, develop and modify.

V. One consequence of all this is that a partnership approach is needed, with – for example
– a mixed team of teachers, school leaders, academic researchers and local authority
advisers all contributing their expertise and perspectives; such an approach is fully in
accordance with recent research on continuing professional development.

NOTES

1 We would like to thank Matthew Pearson, who now works for Steljes Limited, for his enormous contribution to the work of the PELRS project.

2 We would like to thank teachers and students who were partners in the research at the four
PELRS case study schools: Sandilands Junior School, Seymour Road Primary School, Medlock Valley
High School, all in Manchester, and Westhoughton High School Specialist Technology College,
Bolton.

REFERENCES

Cole, M. (1996) *Cultural Psychology: A Once and Future Discipline*. Cambridge, MA, and London, UK:
The Belknap Press of Harvard University Press.

Csikszentmihalyi, M. (1996) *Creativity: Flow and the Psychology of Discovery and Invention*. New York:
Harper Perennial.

Engeström, Y. and Middleton, D. (eds) (1996). *Cognition and Communication at Work*. Cambridge,
New York and Melbourne: Cambridge University Press.

Engeström, Y., Miettinen, R. and Punamäki, R.-L. (eds) (1999) *Perspectives on Activity Theory*.
Cambridge, UK, New York and Melbourne: Cambridge University Press.

Ireland, D. and Russell, T. (1978) 'Pattern analysis'. *CARN Bulletin, Cambridge Institute of Education*, 2:
21–5.

Langemeyer, I. and Nissen, M. (2005) 'Activity theory', in B. Somekh and C. Lewin (eds), *Research
Methods in the Social Sciences*. London and Thousand Islands, CA: Sage, pp. 188–96.

Lewin, C. (2004) 'Access and use of technologies in the home in the UK: implications for the curriculum', *The Curriculum Journal*, 15 (2): 139–54.

Somekh, B. (2007) *Pedagogy and Learning with ICT: Researching the Art of Innovation*. London and
New York: Routledge.

Somekh, B. and Davies, R. (1991) 'Towards a pedagogy for information technology', *The Curriculum
Journal*, 2 (2): 153–70.

Somekh, B. and Sounders, L. (2007) 'Developing knowledge through intervention: meaning and definition of "quality" in research into change', *Research Papers in Education Special Issue*, 22 (2): 83–97.

Stenhouse, L. (1975) *An Introduction to Curriculum Research and Development*. London: Heinemann
Educational Books.

Wertsch, J.V. (1998) *Mind as Action*. New York and Oxford: Oxford University Press.

16

A School System Takes on Exhibitions through Teacher Action Research

Marie Brennan

SYSTEMIC USES OF 'ACTION RESEARCH' AS COOPTION OR COMPLIANCE

Action research does not automatically emerge as a logical choice of methodology: it needs people who advocate for its use, who might know something about its methodologies, and who can make careful connection to where its potential can be embodied in lived projects. Sometimes, of course, activists find ready-made projects that can add dimensions of action research; more commonly, however, action research is built into projects as they develop. In the past two decades of educational action research in Australia, after a flowering of the approach in a range of educational settings in the 1970s and 1980s (Kemmis, 1980), a number of projects under the 'action research' label have been sponsored in the field of schooling by employer authorities and policy sponsors. Too often in such projects, the 'name' of action research has been used as a ploy as part of 'selling' the initiative to teachers, suggesting they will have some say over the project, that their professional judgement will be needed and that the outcomes are open to investigation (Kemmis, 2006). Such approaches became relatively common in the later 1990s in Australia. While there was sometimes opportunity to salvage needed local action and knowledge production through projects, compliance-directed projects from government were becoming the norm for teacher professional development.

This chapter, however, considers one of the exceptions to this trend: a large-scale project covering all 19 high schools in the Australian Capital Territory (ACT) that was able to develop in ways that were not totally defined by the marketized, individualized and compliance-driven context. A key feature of the conditions of possibility for this large project was the nature of the partnership among those who funded, sponsored and conducted it. The partnership among the Australian National Schools Network (ANSN), the ACT school system and the University of Canberra drew on history of all three and created a new space for action. The ACT, as a small territory with only 19 secondary schools, compared to large state systems such as Victoria or New South Wales with hundreds of secondary schools, had a progressive history of teacher participation in school governance, in curriculum development, and moderated cross-school assessment for 25 years from its inception in the mid-1970s. The University of Canberra ran teacher education programs in the Territory and its academics had worked closely with the school sector on a wide range of projects over many years. As a relative newcomer to the university and the ACT, I had already worked with the ANSN in earlier national projects in middle schooling. Prior to this particular project, I had also been commissioned to provide a discussion paper on revitalizing secondary high schooling (Brennan, 2000). The ANSN had a recognized history of innovative curriculum and partnership projects, and the ACT school system as a whole was a member of ANSN.

The ANSN had been established in the early 1990s as part of a federal Labor government approach to increase teacher knowledge and positioning through partnership projects between schools and systems and universities and school 'Roundtables' (Yeatman and Sachs, 1995). (Something of the history and activities of the network can be seen on the ANSN website: http://www.ansn.edu.au/.) Although de-funded by the incoming conservative Coalition government in 1996, ANSN survived through individual and school system membership and through tendering for commissioned projects. In particular, ANSN had worked on a wide range of projects on curriculum and teaching in the middle years (roughly grades 5–9, or 10–15 year olds) over a decade. Through its wide range of professional development activities – including national conferences with major speakers and key players from the USA and Canada, professional development kits arising from conferences, workshops, school-based and state-system-supported school projects and commissioned research projects – ANSN produced most of the knowledge in Australia about middle years innovation and a focus for teacher professional development nationally.

Despite progressive antecedents, ACT teachers by the end of the 1990s had become accustomed to professional development and training that was directed towards encouraging compliance with new policies and programs. In the first year of this project, for example, high schools had approximately 39 other projects in which they were engaged, on top of their ordinary work. These were as varied as new forms of sex education, driver education, new testing regimes for year 9, new compulsory year 10 computing competencies, and service classes.

All had required centralized, compliance-oriented professional development of teachers. This was, indeed, the only form of centrally provided professional development, since the schools, under 'global budgeting' of local school-based management approaches, were responsible for teacher professional development. This tended to mean that professional development was individualized – a teacher might be funded to attend a conference – or a speaker might be engaged to talk to the whole school. The project reported in this chapter can thus be seen as an exception: funded by the central school authority of the Territory but with a significant level of control left to the project and the teachers participating. The project, of course, did not exist outside the time and space of its conception and conduct: participating schools were heavily involved in developing marketing plans, providing standardized data and complying with the wide range of other projects. Nevertheless, as will be argued later, this project was able to build a space that provided both resources and legitimacy: something of an umbrella under which the teachers could develop their projects, make mistakes, redevelop, innovate and work together across schools and specializations in directions not foreseen at the start of the project.

THE ACT EXHIBITIONS PROJECT IN OVERVIEW

The project was conducted as a large 'research circle', funded by the education authority of the ACT and facilitated by Viv White of the ANSN and Marie Brennan of the University of Canberra. The 19 high schools of the ACT, teaching grades 7–10, participated, commencing, over the year 2000, with teachers consulting one another on students' work, the findings of which became available as *Student Work: The Heart of Teaching* (ANSN & Coalition of Essential Schools, 2000). Many of the same teachers continued in 2001, which focused on year 9 classes, including at least two teachers from each school. The focus of the second year of the project was on teachers developing units of work, which would culminate with students presenting their work at public 'Exhibitions'. The teachers were resourced with materials from Australian and international research, particularly emanating from the Queensland New Basics (Lingard et al., 2001), working together to investigate ways to develop 'rich tasks' for students, and criteria for the new units and assessment activities. The project was well documented, producing a professional development kit that could resource the participating schools and other schools to continue the learning from the project (ANSN *Assessment by Exhibition*, 2002) as well as a final report (Brennan et al., 2001). The action research focus was thus at two levels: each pair or team of teachers at each school had a focus for developing and working through the practice of an innovatory new unit of work, and the project as a whole investigated the parameters and resourcing needed for teachers to increase their professional judgement and expand practices in a major curriculum innovation to improve student learning.

ADDRESSING 'INTRACTABLE PROBLEMS' OF SCHOOLING RESEARCH

It is not just the context of neoliberal marketized reforms, permeating much school reform, that can arrest the development of good action research projects. Often, action research projects are too small in scale to make a significant enough dent in the 'intractable problems' of schooling. Many problems in schools are long-term and have been built into the design of mass schooling from its inception. The stratification of student outcomes from schooling in Australia, as with the USA and England, is one such problem. It is quite marked, tied in Australia particularly to socio-economic status, Indigeneity and rurality (Connell et al., 1982), and has strong consequences in terms of future education opportunities, health and employment for those at the 'tail end' of the stratification. In 1981 only 30% of students finished senior secondary schooling, a situation that was addressed strongly through policy in the 1980s, with the result that 79% retention to the end of senior secondary schooling was achieved by 1991 (Dwyer and Wyn, 2001). However, the retention rate has continued to fall since that peak, as Indigenous, rural and poor students see lack of outcomes in their communities from the restructuring of the labour market and a hollowness to the promises of future rewards from staying at school.

Understanding stratification has long been a focus of many efforts of research and of reform, from head start in the 1960s to the development of comprehensive high schools and literacy intervention programs. In recent years in Australia there have been several strands of research that focus on strategies for redressing relative disadvantage. One set of research and school reform has focussed on the post-compulsory years of schooling, particularly the years 11 and 12 curriculum and assessment regimes (e.g. Teese, 2000). Another has focussed on middle years (Brennan and Sachs, 1998), where alienation of students from schooling becomes salient, after which reattachment is difficult to achieve. A third strand has been to delineate the classroom teaching strategies by which students are included or marginalized (Luke et al., 1998; Comber and Hill, 2000). Drawing on this research, a 'middle schooling movement' developed in the 1990s that carried a strong teacher professional development focus and social justice ethic, endeavouring to make a difference for those typically disengaged from schooling.

The 'Exhibitions' project that is the focus of this chapter drew on the middle schooling movement and recent Australian research, taking a teaching and curriculum focus in year 9 (around 15 years old). A key question was whether enough significant reform could occur in curriculum and teaching in year 9 to begin to improve academic success for students, particularly those who were alienated from schooling and unlikely to achieve well enough to transit to senior college years 11 and 12. Is it possible for an action research project to address, even in part, such a large-scale problem, found intractable over generations of schooling? This is an educational policy problem as much as a methodological one for action research, so that much was at stake for the school system in sponsoring an action research approach to middle schooling reform with a key role for classroom teachers.

The high schools in the ACT included a nationally active group of teachers concerned with middle school curriculum initiatives. Several schools were seen as 'lighthouses' for their innovative developments in student-centred school organization and teaching; but other schools were clearly acting as 'sump' schools and their staff were significantly demoralized. By the end of the 1990s, innovations on middle schooling in Australia had largely stalled. As Luke and colleagues were to find (Luke et al., 2003), there had not been enough deep or 'structural' change, with middle schooling initiatives often treated as 'adjunct' to the ordinary work of schools. Despite significant investment by teachers and systems, not enough had changed in mainstream teaching strategies to alter the outcomes for target groups from educationally diverse backgrounds.

To make a difference that might start to redress the stratification of school outcomes,

- projects in each school had to engage at least one class, in two subject areas, with real room for student negotiation and research in a lengthy unit of work;
- teachers had to take the risk of teaching differently;
- student presentations at their Exhibition had to be rigorously assessed, involving parents, teachers, the school community and wider members of the community;
- the project as a whole had to succeed in convincing the policy makers that teacher-led innovations in curriculum could address significant problems and that there would be community, student, principal and teacher support.

Thus, the action research methodology needed to be highly reflexive among the group as a whole, with an eye to both the classroom and the policy makers.

THE PROJECT METHODOLOGY

The project worked on the basis of teachers as researchers and used group norms developed through a range of ANSN projects. Fifty teachers were involved, although the central school system provided funding for only two per school, i.e. 38. Some schools added other teachers to their initial team in order to ensure a greater chance of success, paying for their replacement back at the school. The project was able to draw on the extensive experience of 'Research Circles' which ANSN and partner universities had developed as a common feature of the early 1990s. The principles of operation of research circles were explicit and included commitments to examining work organization and student learning, social justice, collaboration and democratic research processes, with precedence given to questions derived from schools, and group ownership of the results. Research circle meetings of all participating teachers were held over seven days: two in

March, three in May and two in July, to develop and plan the rich task and the assessment by Exhibition. The Exhibitions project in classrooms was designed to occur throughout term 3 (July–September), a much longer period than most classes were accustomed to using for a single unit. The teaching and learning work was to culminate in a common week of Exhibition assessment panels in the third week of September, the second-last week of term. An extra day to reflect on and evaluate the project occurred in October. Meetings included reading time, research summaries and discussion, consultation with teachers and external experts over draft materials, identification of barriers to the work at the school and system level, reflection on progress, clarification of emerging criteria for tasks, and interpretation of the project.

The key question underpinning the Exhibitions project, as collectively derived, was: Does this process of developing, conducting and evaluating task development, implementation and exhibitions through the year 9 project create:

- conditions for teacher learning about curriculum, pedagogy, and assessment, and about their own capacity for curriculum change in school?
- conditions for good learning processes and outcomes for the full range of students?

All participants reflected explicitly on this overall question, helping to formulate it and feeding in the results of their own cycles of data gathering to address other questions specific to their interests and location in order to help address the question of the project as a whole. What was critical in this project was the core role for teachers themselves as researchers in developing the criteria for the units of work, and the processes of continual investigation into curriculum design and pedagogical invention. Rather than a group of outside 'experts' developing the units and their assessment, the participating teachers were able to call on the resources needed for 'upskilling' themselves, including access to the latest research and to researchers, and systematic exploration of the research materials cited above. The criteria and the materials developed through the project were particular to the historical conditions of these teachers and this school system, acknowledging both past and current conditions for school reform efforts.

The facilitators and colleagues in the Department visited each school several times, meeting with the principal and key senior staff as well as with participating teachers in each school. They also documented all discussions and gave the documentation back to teachers for discussion, pinpointing areas of disagreement and agreement across schools or sub-sets of teachers. The facilitators also provided reading materials and sourced relevant consultants upon teachers' requests.

The Exhibitions took significant organization to ensure that each of the hundreds of students participating in the teachers' classes received a good panel. Only two students did not complete their work and present at an Exhibition. Participants in the Exhibitions included parents, other students, teachers, interested community members, university, politicians and members of the head office education system staff. This ensured that each student had a varied audience who could ask questions, and contribute to the evaluation of this public presentation of learning and products.

THE PROJECT IN SCHOOLS

The project was largely successful in all dimensions. Many teachers noted that it reactivated their earlier investments in activist teacher curriculum work and offered a new style of classroom-focussed professional development through research for both relatively new as well as experienced classroom teachers. Teachers enjoyed their new skills and higher self-expectations about their role in making a difference to student learning outcomes. The project was also very successful in engaging the full range of students in rigorous work; and, given the wide audience, assessment through Exhibitions proved to be important politically as well as in educational terms.

The Research Circle developed a range of materials, taught and worked through key curriculum and teaching methodology issues, and was able to set out areas of agreement, and areas where disagreement was accepted. Specifically, there were a range of topics that linked two different subject areas, a set of criteria for the design, scope and focus of the units of work; and generated materials were presented to the group of schools as a whole, for use not only by participating teachers but by others in their school settings. The topics were very varied, ranging from researching salinity in the environment, lifestyle choice and its impacts, developing a youth health campaign, nutrition and youth lifestyle, art in two cultures, waste management, and choosing books in a library. Teachers consulted with each other, helped plan, co-taught units, and organized Exhibitions for each of the almost 800 students who participated in their classes. The findings from the project as a whole were taken up by the relevant government department and used as the basis for policy development on curriculum for year 9 across the school system. A subsequent independent evaluation found that all stakeholders believed this to be a successful initiative, still in effect some years later (Martin, 2002).

The practical parameters for designing units of work, or tasks, that could engage students in rigorous learning were developed after much paired discussion, school-based trialling, teacher consultation with colleagues and formal consultation in the research circle. Consultants who had been involved in developing the Queensland 'rich tasks' were brought in to give feedback on the quality and creativity of the tasks under construction by the teachers. Three-page overviews of each unit of work were made available to the school system and all participating schools.

Final parameters for the task and assessment were decided by the group as a whole. Requirements included a major piece of student work, lasting normally a full term, involving outcomes that are trans-disciplinary, in at least two learning areas, and designed around important, worthwhile areas of knowledge involving both depth and breadth. The projects aimed to inculcate significant student capacity to negotiate or design research, project directions and extension activities, and make connections with their own interests and the broader world. They aimed also to recognize and encourage diversity among the student body, and to be achievable by the full range of students. Assessment of the Exhibition entailed feedback on student achievements, from a panel of three to five members that would normally include a student, a teacher, and parent or community representatives. Prior to the Exhibition, students wrote covering letters to panel members outlining the work. Their portfolio of work and a reflective journal were to form the basis of the Exhibition. Assessment included coverage of student as researcher, as active learner, as reflective learner and as presenter.

The exhibitions process was highly valued by students. Absenteeism was significantly reduced across the whole term and most students completed a very significant project. The focus on the presentation process at the end of the unit gave them, as one student put it, 'dignity'. Students appreciated the opportunity to negotiate elements of the project with the teacher, and the presence of outsiders at the roundtable meant that others took their work seriously.

SIGNIFICANCE FOR SCHOOL REFORM

As a school-system initiative, as well as for those directly participating, this action research project has had long-term impact. In comparison to more typical, top-down, mandated efforts, this approach gained support from teachers, principals and students, as well as recognition by parents and the wider community. Because Exhibitions were then mandated for all year 9 students, indicating the Education Department's acknowledgement of the feedback, other teachers may not necessarily have welcomed the initiative – but at least what was mandated had been developed and trialled by colleagues in their own system. Energy spent on communicating within the schools, though varied in uptake, also alleviated usual complaints about imposed reform; and the language of 'exhibitions', 'student researcher', and 'negotiation' had already entered the schools, largely because of the public nature of the Exhibitions. Perhaps more importantly for winning acceptance, hundreds of students were directly involved and participated in the development, negotiating at different points of the curriculum process, and presenting to a wide range of community members who participated in their assessment.

The scale of this project was unusual for action research, involving roughly 50 teachers and classrooms, 800 students, support staff from the ACT department, university and ANSN people, and hundreds of parents and community members on Exhibition panels. Teachers reported that they had done more 'teaching', especially one-to-one, relative to 'classroom management', and that they had learned new ways of organizing activities and planning for longer-term work, and of working with their students as partners in curriculum. Almost all teachers reported that this was an effective form of professional development, with real time allocated and supported for them to participate. This is not to say there was no additional workload; but the teachers felt supported to participate through time release, meeting release and by their colleagues in the project and, eventually, back in their schools. Time for development of curriculum units, and for re-development over two full terms, meant that the normal 'rush' to produce was slowed down sufficiently for real investigation, consultation and gathering of resources. This space and time for teacher renewal allowed them to grow in professional judgement, curriculum development expertise, and teaching and learning methodologies, particularly in providing options for student negotiation and research.

The 10-week duration of classroom units was initially seen as a huge challenge by teachers accustomed to shorter units; but it was afterward seen as central to academic achievement by the full range of students. Except for two students who did not complete their work, all the students passed, many with stronger results than previously experienced. This suggests that the 'intractable problem' of systemic alienation and lack of success was addressed in ways that were effective; and that this was recognized widely among students, parents, school staff, and school system actors. These successes gained political mileage through roles in Exhibitions for senior policy people, administrators and political representatives. Student involvement in building curriculum, through research, was publicly noted as key to the success of the project. Documentation of the project, particularly through a Summerhill Films DVD, meant that the project's methodologies could spread into and through professional development of other teachers (ANSN, 2002).

In his discussion of graduation by exhibition, Joe McDonald (1993) suggests that one of the most important outcomes of that process of assessment is the food for thought it provides the school. Since the students present their work publicly, the school is more publicly accountable and many more people, including other teachers and students, begin to understand just what students can do. McDonald argues that public presence of students' work allows a school to see its 'products' in a different light. It requires people to go beyond the usual numbers games and traditional measures of school success to grapple with the underlying challenge of ensuring that schools teach all students. 'A school must dare to inquire what really exists as well as what might be', he comments (1993: 49). Yet inquiry or 'research' doesn't bring certainty: it brings more capacity to deal with uncertainty.

PARTNERSHIP CREATING SPACES

Looking back at this project, its hopes and challenges, we see substantial partnership – between schools and system, and between system, university and

ANSN – as the most important ingredient for effectiveness of all other design aspects. Partnership created new spaces, previously lacking in a relatively centralized school system undergoing significant 'restructuring' that, as with other Australian school systems, had emphasized marketization, corporate management and competition. That the project was sponsored by the school system, conducted by a national body, in conjunction with a university, gave it significance beyond the single classroom or school, and even the particular school system. The partnership broke up typical relations, based on compliance, between head office of the school system and its high schools. The other partners had a history of working collaboratively with teachers to build teacher production of knowledge about schooling. The commissioning of those partners for the project shows that, despite the broader conservative policy context, the ACT education department carried a corporate memory of other ways of operating and a commitment to building teacher expertise, along with recognition that 'intractable' problems of student disengagement could not be addressed without teachers in a core role. Albeit contradictory to many other initiatives on school management and curriculum operating for these schools, the ACT school system was a member of ANSN. The requirement that all schools participate may also have been a sign of the significant hope the school system had for the project to make a difference for students in their crucial high school years. Still, without the new space and momentum created by partnerships, it is doubtful whether the level of investment over the timeframe could have been sustained. Each element of partnership – principals, school system, University of Canberra, the National Schools Network and the teachers – themselves could find new opportunities as well as demands and constraints in the project space. The project could not have been accomplished without these partnerships.

Key officers of the Department understood that such a long-term 'intractable' problem as systemic student alienation would require increased provision for teachers, inclusion of their professional judgement, and explicit attention to their role in curriculum development and classroom innovation. They supported the project with secondment of key teachers and time release for participating teachers to attend Research Circles for two consecutive years. Thus, the project was not planned and implemented merely by one group, but necessarily involved teachers as active researchers and curriculum developers. To commission such a project in times of 'corporatized' school governance shows that contradictory spaces can be invented even within the confines of 'new public management'. Ironically, the discourses of privatization and marketization worked in favour of commissioning external groups such as the ANSN and the university to buttress state agency work, enhancing the role of teachers.

Perhaps the biggest lesson of the project is that it was possible to redesign curriculum and teaching development methodologies such that teachers, as researchers, have strong roles. Also, the project's inclusiveness enabled it to gain support from many middle class parents, as well as those of more marginalized social position, even in a climate dominated by 'corporate managerial' rationales.

Whether or not the strong role for students as producers of knowledge and teachers as curriculum developers lasted beyond this project remains an open question.

REFERENCES

ANSN and Coalition of Essential Schools (2000) *The Heart of Teaching: Protocols Kit.* ANSN and the Coalition of Essential Schools.

ANSN (2002) *Assessment by Exhibition.* Australian National Schools Network.

Brennan, M. and Sachs, J. (eds) (1998) *Integrated Curriculum for the Middle Years.* Canberra: Australian Curriculum Studies Association.

Brennan, M. (2000) *A New Generation of High Schools for the ACT.* Discussion paper produced for the ACT School system, Department of Education and Community Services.

Brennan, M., White, V. with Owen, C. (2001) *Year 9 Student Exhibitions Pilot Project: A Report to ACT Department of Education and Community Services.* Canberra: ACT DECS.

Comber, B. and Hill, S. (2000) 'Socio-economic disadvantage, literacy and social justice; learning from longitudinal case study research', *The Australian Educational Researcher*, 27 (9): 1–19.

Connell, R.W., Ashenden, D., Kessler, S. and Dowsett G. (1982) *Making the Difference: Schools, Families, and Social Division.* Sydney: Allen & Unwin.

Dwyer, P. and Wyn, J. (2001) *Youth, Education and Risk: Facing the Future.* London & New York: Routledge/Falmer.

Kemmis, S. (1980) *Action Research in Retrospect and Prospect.* Paper presented to the Annual Meeting of the Australian Association for Research in Education (Sydney, Australia, November 6–9, 1980).

Kemmis (2006) 'Participatory action research and the public sphere', *Educational Action Research,* 14 (4): 459–76.

Lingard, B., Ladwig, J., Luke, A., Mills, M., Hayes, D. and Gore, J. (2001) *Queensland School Reform Longitudinal Study: Final Report.* Brisbane: Education Queensland.

Luke, A., Elkins, J., Weir, K., Land, R., Carrington, V., Sole, S., Pendergast, D., Kapitzke, C., van Kraagenoord, C., Moni, K., McIntosh, A., Mayer, D., Bahr, M., Hunter, L., Chadbourne, R., Bean, T., Alverman, T., Stevens, L., Marks, G.N. and Fleming, N. (2003) *Beyond the Middle: A Report About Literacy and Numeracy Development of Target Group Students in the Middle Years of Schooling.* DEST Clearinghouse: Nathan: Griffith University.

Luke, A., Ladwig, J., Lingard, B., Hayes, D. and Mills, M. (1998) *School Reform Longitudinal Study (SRLS).* St Lucia: University of Queensland.

McDonald, Joseph P. (ed.) (1993) *Graduation by Exhibition: Assessing Genuine Achievement.* Alexandria, VA: ASCD.

Martin, A. (2002) *Every Chance to Learn: Summary and Analysis of High Schools for the New Millennium.* www.decs.act.gov.au/schools/pdf/curr_EveryChanceToLearn-EvaluationReport.pdf

Teese, R. (2000) *Academic Success and Social Power. Examinations and Inequality in Victoria, 1944–96.* Melbourne: Melbourne University Press.

Yeatman, A. and Sachs, J. (1995) *Making the Links: A Formative Evaluation of the First Year of the Innovative Links between Universities and Schools for Teacher Professional Development.* Perth: Murdoch University, WA.

17

Action Research, Professional Development and Systemic Reform

Herbert Altrichter and Peter Posch

The globalization of markets and the results of international student performance assessments have heavily increased the pressure on education systems. The public opinion in many countries calls for reform. The authorities search for instruments to govern the school system more quickly and more economically towards 'world standards'. In this climate we have recently seen in many developed countries new initiatives for system-wide school innovation.

Action research has some reputation as a powerful strategy for professional development of teachers and other professional practitioners. In the action research tradition instruments and social settings have evolved which help individuals or small groups of professionals who are keen on learning about and changing their practice to do just this: to develop aspects and instances of their practice in order to better understand them and to elaborate their professional knowledge and competences. And action research has stimulated such practitioners to build up supportive networks which give them some backing when they try to bring their improved knowledge and competences to their home organization, to change styles and conditions of work in their school, in their school system, etc.

But what could be the role of action research in system-wide change? What chances and pitfalls are offered to action research in this climate of increased pressure for system reform? How is action research equipped to contribute productively to systemic change without giving up its core values?

Starting with an example, the first part of the chapter suggests a conceptual tool which might be helpful in understanding the complex route to institutionalization of innovations. Its second part describes two general approaches to innovation, their strengths and weaknesses and in somewhat more detail characteristics of action research as an evolutionary-adaptive innovation strategy. The chapter concludes with a cautionary note. Institutionalization of action research needs more than professional development.

ACTION RESEARCH IN IN-SERVICE PROFESSIONAL DEVELOPMENT

In view of increasing demands on teachers, a professional development program 'Education and subject matter didactics for teachers' (PFL was used as acronym) was initiated by the Institute of Instructional and School Development of the University of Klagenfurt in 1982. One of several aims of the program is to enable and stimulate teachers to continuously improve the quality of their work through systematic reflection on action. The program has been offered for secondary school teachers of Mathematics, Science, English, History and the Arts as well as for elementary school teachers (Krainer and Posch, 1996; Altrichter and Posch, 1998). Its *main characteristics* are:

- *Long duration*: Each program lasts for two years. In this time span three one-week seminars and five so-called regional group meetings are organized (see Figure 17.1).
- *Location of learning is the school*: Besides more distanced learning situations (at seminars and regional groups) the individual school situation is an explicit learning site of the course.
- *Starting points are professional challenges*: Current professional challenges in the perception of the participants, *not* current issues of the relevant disciplines, are starting points of the course. The practitioners choose an issue of their own practice which they consider important for their work.
- *Research and development*: Action research philosophy and methodology is an integral element of the course: The central task of the participants is to plan a developmental project for their own classroom practice, to implement it in the time between the seminars, to do research assisted by collaborative support and advice in regional groups and to present experiences and findings in a case study. They reflect on their practical development work through, e.g. notes in a research diary, pupil interviews, observations by critical friends, etc., and on this basis they develop new ideas for action.
- *Cooperative learning and exchange*: The participants are invited to offer their research and development experiences in mini-workshops of 'collegial in-service training' during the seminars. Thereby, they are provided with an opportunity to acquire qualifications in teacher education.
- *Support system and constitution of a 'professional community'*: Through the seminars and regional groups individual action research is integrated in a consultancy structure which offers ample opportunities for both discussion of problems regarding contents and methods of teaching, and on the other hand for critical feedback and assistance (e.g. for pupil

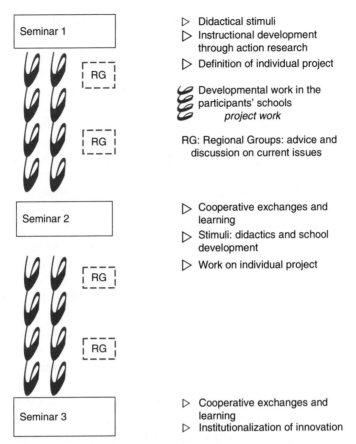

Figure 17.1   Organizational structure of the professional development program 'Education and subject matter didactics for teachers' (PFL).

interviews) with respect to their development and research work. Partners in this process are researching colleagues as well as academics who support the teachers' research as critical friends.

- *Interdisciplinary teams*: The courses are planned and led by an interdisciplinary team composed of course leaders from the subject matter disciplines, subject didactics, school practice and education. On the one hand, they act as traditional teacher educators, giving lectures and didactical stimuli. On the other hand, they moderate participants' working groups and offer advice and support for the teachers' developmental projects. The teachers have full control over their research process. This principle is assured through an agreed ethical code.

So far, more than 300 case studies have been written by participating teachers and published online as contributions to professional teacher knowledge (http://ius.uni-klu.ac.at/publikationen/praxisforschung). The program is institutionalized in the sense that there is a general understanding on the side of the university that the program belongs to its main 'services' and on the side of the ministry that the contribution of the courses to professional development of teachers and to competences needed for building a quality culture at school level are worth the investment.

PFL is obviously a modern and very comprehensive initiative for professional development. It is in-line with what empirical research has unearthed about conditions of teacher learning, and it was so even before in this research had been done. For example, Lipowsky (2004) concludes in his research survey finding that the following features may be typical of successful professional development:

- *long-term formats* allow intensive work with the issues to be developed;
- a *variety of learning and work methods* (alternation between input and work phases, between sequences of practical experimentation, trainings, and reflection);
- a *clear focus on the participants' classrooms* and practical issues of teaching;
- critical *questioning of basic assumptions of teachers* as a basis for sustainable changes of teachers' educational views and practice;
- making opportunities for *teacher collaboration* also beyond the times of the seminar (collaborative task in the back home situation);
- *integrating more teachers of a school* and promoting in-school dissemination of PD-learning results;
- *offering external support* for implementing PD-issues in individual schools.

The PFL programs provided professional development of individual teachers in many cases with remarkable effects on their individual practice. They helped individuals to make professional careers as principals, in-service trainers and schools inspectors. However, with a few remarkable exceptions, they have not had any observable effects on whole schools – not to speak of school systems.

In the meantime, a number of other programs have emerged. In order to extend the range of effects to the school as institution, a new course 'Professionality in Teaching' (PROFIL) was developed. Its general educational philosophy and organization is in many respects similar to PFL; however, it provides an academic degree ('Master of Arts in Education – Instructional and School Development') for PFL graduates after two years of further study. New is the focus on a combination of classroom *and* school development. To be accepted, participants need a declaration from their principal to support their work for the course. They are required to write three reflective papers and a final thesis on issues which potentially have structural implications for their schools. The case studies written in this course have produced institutional effects in the schools of some of the participants, such as the institutionalization of project days (Leopoldseder, 2005), and a new form of introducing youngsters to the elementary school (Engleitner, 2005), etc.

In a second program, a fund has been created to support teachers to initiate, study and analyze innovations in math and science education. If necessary, teachers are assisted in writing the proposal and in preparing their report. At the end they are required to present their studies at a conference. A program has also been developed and implemented to train teachers to provide professional development for other teachers in math and science subjects. A central element of this course is the systematic reflection on their present support activities and the exchange of experiences. All of these programs are coordinated by a university institute and are financed by the Ministry of Education, and, to a small extent, also by participants' fees.

These programs all provide contexts for systematic reflection on action by participating teachers. Although there is considerable teacher demand for the courses, this does not mean that action research is institutionalized at school level. There are several factors which impede such a development, factors relating to actors (their competences and professional values) as well as to structures such as regulations (e.g. regarding presence at school outside teaching) or resources (such as time and space for communication). These factors favour a culture of teaching and learning in which reflection and development are low in status. In this culture the main tasks of a teacher are to offer information, to keep pupils attentive and to test learning results. Information and tasks are prepared for a virtual pupil of assumed average ability (with some deviations up and down the scale). The learning process and the specific competences and values of the individual pupil, by which he or she has to cope with the subject matter, are of only marginal concern.

In the following section we want to sketch a conceptual model which may help to better understand the conditions which appear to be necessary for an innovation to be institutionalized.

FROM INITIATION TO INSTITUTIONALIZATION: CHANGING THE GOVERNANCE OF A SYSTEM

The pathway from a good idea to a new social practice may be a lengthy one. Fullan and Stiegelbauer (1991) distinguished three sub-processes in which an innovation is made to work (or not) in order to produce outcomes. The processes that eventually lead up to, and end with, the decision to take up a specific innovation proposal have been called *initiation phase* (also mobilization or adoption). In the *implementation phase* (in a more narrow sense) participants attempt to use the innovation proposal (e.g. a 'new curriculum') in order to change their practice. Frequently, extra support for translating the innovatory ideas into reality is offered on a project basis. Thus, while the initiation phase is concerned with the *nominal use* of a curriculum, the implementation phase focuses on the *actual* use. In the *continuation phase* (also called institutionalization, incorporation, or routinization) the innovation (or what has been made out of the innovation during implementation) is built into the routine organization, and extra support (if there had been any during the implementation phase) is withdrawn. Thus, while implementation is concerned with initial use of the innovation under project conditions, continuation deals with mature use under standard conditions.

What are the conditions which enable and facilitate the process from initiation to institutionalization? Institutionalization can be conceptualized as changing the governance of a system. Only recently the concept of governance was taken up in educational research, in particular, for analyzing changes in the university system and in the school systems. Research into governance studies issues of social coordination between (social) actors in multi-level systems in order to understand how social order and social performance is achieved (see Schimank, 2007; Altrichter et al., 2007a).

This approach is based on Giddens' (1992) view that structure and action must be seen as a 'duality'; they have to be seen in relation to each other, complementing each other. Action takes place in a structured space and structures it again. Structures are (re)produced by action and offer options for further action (see also Ortmann et al., 1990: 14). The *structural elements* of this complementarity (in relation to characteristics of the actor) are (see also Kussau and Brusemeister, 2007: 21ff.):

- *Rules and regulations,* which may be institutionalized or not, such as laws, administrative circulars, contracts, informal rights, 'unwritten laws', comme il faut-rules, customs, etc. Actors can (explicitly or implicitly) refer to them in order to legitimize their action.
- *Material and immaterial resources,* such as money, time, knowledge and competence, space, meaning, etc. They put actors in the position to shape their action.

These elements provide the opportunities and limits for action. The other elements are characteristics of the actor (in relation to the structural elements):

- *Intentions, motives, value judgments, world views of the actors.* Thereby actors position themselves in relation to structural rules and norms.
- *Competences, knowledge, instruments and means of actors.* Thereby actors are able to make use of the structural resources.

Very similarly, Strittmatter (2001) has distinguished three types of *conditions for the institutionalization of innovations:*

- *'Have to do' conditions (necessity)* which (more or less) enforce innovation, such as legal and other kinds of regulations or societal demands which cannot be overlooked;
- *'Want to do' conditions (volition),* such as accepted aims, benefits, ethical responsibilities, professional pride, positive experiences;
- *'Am able to do' conditions (ability),* such as competences, resources, and support.

In his view, none of these conditions can be dispensed with if innovations are to be institutionalized. The neglect of this 'multiplicative' relationship between these conditions can explain the failure of attempts to move innovations from initiation to institutionalization.

Systems are composed of several levels (e.g. individual teacher, school man-agement, regional educational authority, etc.) providing actors with different chances for participation and influence within and across levels. Changes in such a multi-level system can be described as changes in the social coordination between actors. They depend on specific places and instruments for coordina-tion. Lange and Schimank (2004: 20) distinguish three modes of coordination:

- coordination by observation (e.g. by observing others in action);
- coordination by exertion of influence (e.g. through power, money, knowledge, moral authority, etc.);
- coordination by negotiation (e.g. bilateral arrangements).

This conceptual model highlights that the process of institutionalization of innovations is a multi-faceted process.

GENERAL APPROACHES TO INNOVATION

Two *general approaches* to innovation (see Fullan, 1983: 493) may be con-trasted with respect to the way they deal with the 'implementation problem', i.e. the gap between a 'good plan' and its institutionalization in practice: The *programmed approach* (or 'fidelity approach') aims to solve the 'implementation problem' by concentrating on flaws in the *specification of the 'product'*, e.g.:

- gaps in the existing specification of innovation practices;
- failure to articulate the innovation's implication for teachers behavior;
- theoretical inadequacies with respect to identified means for achieving the intended out-comes of an innovation. (Leithwood and Montgomery, 1980: 23)

A contrasting conceptualization of the implementation problem is provided by the *adaptive-evolutionary approach*. It accepts that the innovation as it has been devised will be modified in the course of its implementation. This is not only seen as just a feature of mundane circumstances wise and realistic persons have to accept, but as an essential characteristic of implementation. This resonates with a central finding of the classic Rand Change Agent Study: 'The primary feature of effective implementation could be called "mutual adaptation" in which the project is adapted to its institutional context *and* organizational pat-terns are adapted to meet the demands of the project'. (Berman and McLaughlin, 1977: 5).

Particularly with complex innovations, this approach claims that it is concep-tually unsound, socially unacceptable, and empirically impossible to solve the implementation problem by programming the persons concerned to put the innovation into reality through detailed elaborations of the desired practice and step-by-step specifications for the process of implementation. Rather, innovators are required to present their innovation to their audience as 'intelligent hypotheses' (Stenhouse, 1975), but invite practitioners to rethink it and further develop it for the specific circumstances they are working in. They expect, and even invite, negotiation and transaction. Their aim is to stimulate practitioners to use their practical situational knowledge for implementation and for modifying the original models according to the demands and resources of the specific locality.

The *programmed approach* has certain strengths: It takes care to communicate its intentions and ways of implementation as clearly as possible and, thus, its evaluation criteria are unambiguous. However, it also has some weaknesses. Firstly, it is only suitable for such innovations which are actually programmable. Many researchers claim that curricula for more complex educational goals are not easily programmable because our knowledge about the conditions of application is not sufficient. Secondly, needs and characteristics of persons and organizations in different regions may vary so much that some leeway is desirable in order to cope with situational implementation problems. The *adaptive-evolutionary approach* is strong in adapting an innovation to situational characteristics. It also claims that complex changes necessitate relearning and, thus, invites participants to participate actively in the process of implementation which is seen as a prime opportunity for internalizing the main characteristics of the innovation. The main weaknesses of the adaptive-evolutionary approach are: firstly, problems may arise because of ambiguous objectives, variation of ways of implementation, and shifting evaluation criteria. Secondly, evaluation of success is difficult and may vary between different persons and constituencies because no common criteria are available from the outset (Fullan, 1983: 496).

Similarly, Berman (1980) has argued that both approaches have their merits and that the implementation approach should be chosen according to its fit to the specific implementation situation (Table 17.1). Thus, the programmed approach is appropriate if the amount of change intended is small or orchestrated in a gradual manner; if the innovation may be specified according to tested and widely known teaching methods; if the persons concerned by the implementation agree to its objectives and methods; if the school is comparatively integrated and its environment (e.g. the community) comparatively stable. Where these conditions are not met, an adaptive strategy may be more appropriate (Fullan, 1983: 498).

In practice, any practical implementation project will be situated somewhere between the extremes of the dichotomy just introduced. Innovations which demand substantial changes in the understanding of professional tasks of teachers, such as

Table 17.1   Characteristics of Innovation Approaches

	Programmed Approach	Adaptive-Evolutionary
Amount of change	Small, step by step	Big
Curriculum technology	Fixed, tested and known methods	Adaptive, open methods
Attitude of participants	Agreement	Conflict
Integration of the organization	High integration	Diversity
Stability of environment	Stable	Unstable

the acceptance of systematic self-evaluation, are unlikely to be institutionalized through programmed approaches only, but need adaptive-evolutionary strategies to be effective.

According to Fullan (1994: 2843) there is a small number of powerful themes which, in combination, describe *key process characteristics of successful institutionalization*. Among these are quite a number of themes which are more than familiar for action researchers, e.g. participation and empowerment, evolutionary development, intensive communication, monitoring, evaluation and problem-coping, staff development and resource assistance. The key theme 'vision building' indicates that a concrete and lively perspective of value and purpose is necessary to give direction and driving power for development (see Fullan, 1994: 2844). In our view this may well link in with the central role attached to the organizing power of educational values in action research (see Elliott, 1998: 157).

The key theme, 'pressure and support', points to a crucial point for those action researchers who are primarily used to working with voluntary teacher groups. Usually, they support such groups in their developmental aims as long as they are willing to engage in a process of collecting feedback from different persons concerned and to reflect on the educational value in the light of such data. When one works with whole organizations or systems, one will encounter differences in goals and value orientation which very often are not to be reconciled in the short run. To move forward necessitates negotiation about action plans which invariably will involve compromises between the main actors in the face of external pressure and opportunities. Such a compromise must be binding for some agreed span of time in order to avoid one party dropping out of an agreement when the difficult part of the contract comes for them. The same situation may also happen with external actors such as the school administration or the inspectorate. Various arrangements of interaction between the different actors involved, such as meetings, collaborative working groups, presentation meetings, etc., serve 'to integrate both pressure and support. One of the reasons that peer coaching works so effectively is that it combines pressure and support in a seamless way' (Fullan, 1994: 2846).

Another key theme – which action researchers who concentrate on actors and their research and development are in danger of losing sight of – is 'restructuring'. Innovation is always restructuring to some extent (Fullan, 1994: 2845). In practice, the need for revised timetabling, shuffling resources, time for individual and team planning, time for visiting other colleagues or joint teaching, staff development policies and practices, new roles such as mentors and coaches, etc. may surface during implementation. Where this task of restructuring is taken up explicitly and proactively in the course of the implementation (instead of waiting for the pressure to be so high that rearrangements cannot be avoided any longer), the chance of producing sustainable results will be higher. This links in with the last key theme to be mentioned here, with 'relationships to external agencies'. Phases of innovation must not only intensify the richness and variety of communication *within* an organization (Reinmann-Rothmeier and

Mandl, 1999: 73); clear and proactive information and communication with the organization's environment and the interested public is also important in order to avoid adverse reactions, to make the innovative changes understood, and, at times, to invite alternative perspectives (op. cit, 1999: 76).

ACTION RESEARCH AS AN ADAPTIVE-EVOLUTIONARY INNOVATION STRATEGY

Educational reform aims at a change of social coordination which will involve altered rules and resources. This change will extend in time and will involve numerous processes of negotiation and re-negotiation between social actors in the field. Those who want to influence these processes will need a strategy for contributing to this negotiation process, and the more complex the intended changes are, the more this strategy will resemble an 'adaptive-evolutionary' strategy in Fullan's sense.

It seems quite obvious that action research is a member of the adaptive-evolutionary 'family' of innovation strategies (Altrichter et al., 2007b). Implementation of innovation is seen as a reflective development of practice pushed forward by responsible professionals in negotiation with relevant stakeholders. This does not preclude that 'external ideas' (introduced by policy, administration, research, some sections of the public, or by teachers of other schools) are taken up, however; they must undergo some process of reflective transformation fuelled by the participants' close observation of the implementation process (see e.g. Stenhouse, 1975: 25). This reflective transformation is slow and consumes much precious (student, teacher, administrator, etc.) time; it cannot guarantee that pre-specified aims will be reached in a given time, and it is, in many senses, a counter-model to the image of 'quick fixes'. Stenhouse has provided convincing arguments against the notion of achieving quality changes of educational practice by 'programming' teacher behavior (maybe to the extent of 'teacher proof curricula'). To by-pass collaboration of teachers meant for Stenhouse to by-pass their rationality and their ingenuity, and this would not solve the implementation problem, but, on the contrary, make it worse. It is the practitioners who must bring a curricular idea to life in their concrete interaction with specific students under local circumstances.

The traditional formats by which action researchers contribute to change in the education system are descendants of Stenhouse's great idea: they build on some combination of practice development, research into this practice and professional development through research and with respect to the issues which are to be developed.

We may distinguish a 'project or issue-focused' branch which emphasizes the 'issue' to be developed as the starting point and main focus of the project, from a 'professional development-focused' branch which directs most attention to the learning situation of participating teachers, sometimes at the expense of a clear thematic focus (e.g. participants choose issues which are important in their individual classroom resulting in a diversity of topics in a course). The latter type has – as action research matured and won respectability in institutions of higher education – become more and more important as dozens of action research-based award-bearing courses indicate. We want to discuss some characteristics of this latter approach and start, again, with a case example.

PROFESSIONAL DEVELOPMENT AND SYSTEM-WIDE REFORM

In a 'governance view' of the education system, the 'professional development'-sub-system is an 'intermediary actor'. The main task of those with responsibility for professional development is to contribute to coordination between politics (with its claim to govern) and schools and classrooms which are to produce the performance typical for the system. The main function of the system of professional development seems to impart *knowledge and competences* to teachers which have not been acquired by their pre-service training and by work experience. Beyond this function, professional development certainly also communicates (formal and/or informal) *norms (rules)* from other system levels and – the longer an in-service event lasts, the more likely – builds up norms internal to the respective program (e.g. we would assume that the view 'asking for feedback from different viewpoints and reflecting on it is important' will be a socializing result of participation in an action research course). Thus, schools and teachers are to be supported by maintaining action and social coordination in a system-specific way. Both, new competences and norms are particularly important when it comes to system reform. Professional development may be used to support reform, e.g. by offering courses for new competences.

Traditionally, institutions of professional development, such as universities, cater for individual teachers. If they are successful, they help teachers build up new competences and norms. Teachers may use them, if their classrooms and schools offer structural conditions to exercise them; but if no special measures are taken (e.g. by the principal, by the district, by teacher networks, etc.) to embark on a transformation of these conditions and to overcome the time span characterized by frictions between old and new structures, teachers will put their new competences in storage or even do away with them.

Or to put it another way: Traditional professional development is most successful when teachers and schools are hungry for innovation. However, it has some problems when it is supposed to promote reforms for which the readiness of the field is an open question. This is because its main modus of operation – both organizationally and didactically – is offering competences and norms to individuals. Traditional professional development institutions are usually not in the position to complement this by inserting structural rules and resources which might stabilize the practice of these new competences and norms.

Additionally, these institutions (which are – at least in the centralist bureaucratic traditions of the German-speaking schools systems – keen on keeping up as much institutional autonomy from external authorities as possible) are usually not very experienced in joining forces with national/state administration in long-term complex alliances.

Likewise, action research-based in-service programs are a promising approach to professional development of individual teachers keen on reflecting and developing their practice. However, they are far from sufficient to develop a professional culture at school level in which innovations are welcome, in which they are tested and – if found useful – are transformed into everyday practice. For this to happen, the school needs structures (rules and resources) which provide reason, legitimacy and resources for innovation, and which, at the same time, enforce and facilitate those coordination activities which are necessary among staff and between teachers and students for an innovation to take roots, e.g.:

- internal positions with responsibilities for coordination of development and evaluation;
- time and space for team work;
- mechanisms to obtain data on quality issues;
- mechanisms for negotiation between staff, students, parents, and other constituencies;
- procedures for documentation and public accountability.

REFERENCES

Altrichter, H. and Heinrich, M. (2007) 'Kategorien der Governance-Analyse und Transformationen der Systemsteuerung in Österreich', in H. Altrichter, T. Brüsemeister and J. Wissinger (eds), *Educational Governance – Handlungskoordination und Steuerung im Bildungssystem*. VS: Wiesbaden, pp. 55–103.

Altrichter, H. and Posch, P. (1998) 'Einige Orientierungspunkte für "nachhaltige Lehrerfortbildung"', in H.-J. Herber and F. Hofmann (Hrsg.): *Schulpädagogik und Lehrerbildung*. StudienVerlag: Innsbruck, pp. 245–59.

Altrichter, H. Brüsemeister, T. and Wissinger, J. (eds) (2007a) *Educational Governance – Handlungskoordination und Steuerung im Bildungssystem*. VS: Wiesbaden.

Altrichter, H., Feldman, A., Posch, P. and Somekh, B. (2007b) *Teachers Investigate their Work. An Introduction to Action Research Across the Professions*. London, New York: Routledge.

Berman, P. and McLaughlin, M. (1977) *Federal Programs Supporting Educational Change*, Vol. VII: Factors Affecting Implementation and Continuation. Washington, D.C.: US Office of Education, Dept. of Health, Education and Welfare.

Berman, P. (1980) 'Thinking about implementation design: Matching strategies to situations', in D. Mann and H. Ingram (eds), *Why Policies Succeed or Fail*. Berkeley: Sage.

Engleitner, M. (2005) *Wie können wir Lehrer/innen die Schülereinschreibung an unserer Schule neu organisieren? Implementierung eines "Einschreibefestes' mittels Stationen statt formaler Einzeltests*. Klagenfurt: Institut für Unterrichts- und Schulentwicklung.

Elliott, J. (1998) *The Curriculum Experiment. Meeting the Challenge of Social Change*. Buckingham: Open University Press.

Fullan, M. (1983) 'Implementation und Evaluation von Curricula: USA und Kanada', in U. Hameyer, K. Frey and H. Haft (eds.), *Handbuch der Curriculumforschung*. Weinheim: Beltz.

Fullan, M. (1994) 'Implementation of Innovations', in T. Husen and T.N. Postlethwaite (Hrsg.): *The International Encyclopedia of Education* (2nd edn). Oxford: Pergamon, pp. 2839–2847.

Fullan, M. and Stiegelbauer, S. (1991) *The New Meaning of Educational Change.* London: Cassell.

Giddens, A. (1992) *Die Konstitution der Gesellschaft.* Frankfurt/M.: Campus.

Krainer, K. and Posch, P. (eds.) (1996) *Lehrerfortbildung zwischen Prozessen und Produkten.* Bad Heilbrunn: Klinkhardt.

Kussau, J. and Brusemeister, T. (2007) 'Educational Governance: Zur Analyse der Handlungskoordination im Mehrebenensystem der Schule', in H. Altrichter, T. Brüsemeister, and J. Wissinger, (eds.), *Educational Governance – Handlungskoordination und Steuerung im Bildungssystem.* Wiesbaden: VS. 15–54.

Lange, S. and Schimank, U. (2004) 'Governance und gesellschaftliche Integration', in S. Lange and U. Schimank (eds), *Governance und gesellschaftliche Integration*: Wiesbaden: VS, pp. 9–46.

Leithwood, K.A. and Montgomery, D.J. (1980) 'Evaluating program implementation', *Evaluation Quarterly*, 4: 193–214.

Leopoldseder, M. (2005) *Der kleine Unterschied – Initiativen zur Abgrenzung von anderen Schulen.* Klagenfurt: Institut für Unterrichts- und Schulentwicklung der Universität.

Lipowksy, F. (2004) 'Was macht Fortbildungen für Lehrkräfte erfolgreich? Befunde der Forschung und mögliche Konsequenzen für die Praxis', in *Die Deutsche Schule*, 96. S, pp. 463–79.

Ortmann, G.,Windeler, A., Becker, A. and Schulz, H.-J. (1990) *Computer und Macht in Organisationen.* Opladen: Westdt. Verlag.

Reinmann-Rothmeier, G. and Mandl, H. (1999) 'Implementation konstruktivistischer Lernumgebungen – revolutionärer Wandel oder evolutionäre Veränderung?' in H.-E. Renk (Hrsg.): *Lernen und leben aus der Welt im Kopf.* Neuwied: Luchterhand, pp. 61–78.

Stenhouse, L. (1975) *An Introduction to Curriculum Research and Development.* London: Heinemann.

Schimank, U. (2007) 'Die Governance-Perspektive: Analytisches Potenzial und anstehende konzeptionelle Fragen', in H. Altrichter, T. Brüsemeister, and J. Wissinger, (eds), *Educational Governance – Handlungskoordination und Steuerung im Bildungssystem.* Wiesbaden: VS, pp. 231–60.

Strittmatter, A. (2001) 'Bedingungen für die nachhaltige Aufnahme von Neuerungen an Schulen', *journal für schulentwicklung*, 4: 58–66.

18

Sustaining the Next Generation of Teacher-Researchers to Work for Social Justice

Barbara Comber and Barbara Kamler

When we met Judy Painter, she was in her thirtieth year of teaching, at a *Learning Centre* for elementary-aged students who had been temporarily excluded from their regular school because of violent or extreme anti-social behaviour. Her research focussed on Terry (also called 'Thunderface' by Judy) because he visibly resisted her normally successful approaches to re-engage troubled students and had the potential to disrupt the entire social fabric of the group. Her early career partner, Cherie Pickering, was in her fourth year of teaching the *Area Resource Class*. Her research focussed on improving the communication between her students by using popular cultural media. Despite the euphemistic naming of their classes, as a *Learning Centre* and the *Area Resource Class*, Judy and Cherie were teaching some of the most disadvantaged young people in South Australia, children growing up in poverty, in families struggling with homelessness and ill-health, in the outer southern suburbs. Additionally, their particular children were struggling with intellectual, emotional and social difficulties which were extreme enough for them not to be included in a mainstream class.

These teachers became part of a network of teacher-researchers in two states of Australia (South Australia and Victoria) exploring how to tackle some of the toughest equity challenges their teaching situations created. Like Judy and Cherie, the other teacher-researchers who joined the three-year project were teaching culturally and linguistically diverse student populations in a variety of schools and classrooms, city, rural and regional. While they brought different professional and personal histories to the research, different theories of literacy and pedagogy, what they had in common from the outset was a desire to make a positive difference to young people's literacy learning. This shared commitment to the potential of literacy education for social justice underlined their some-times painful investigations into some 'unwelcome truths' (Kemmis, 2006) about schooling for their students.

Importantly, they joined the project at a time when the Australian federal gov-ernment's approach to educational policy was marked by a conservative back-lash and public attack on the teaching and teacher education professions with respect to literacy standards (Doecke et al., 2006). In this accountability policy environment, what is recognized as valid research is increasingly dominated by a 'scientific' paradigm; hence our project could be seen as going against the grain of the contemporary authorized policy scene with its one-size-fits-all solu-tions to literacy as a basic skill (Cochran-Smith and Lytle, 2006). Given the dominance of accountability agendas internationally, we were committed to linking our teachers beyond local networks and sectors in order to problematize how translocal managerial discourses (Smith, 2005) impact on teachers' work in particular ways. Long-term theorist of critical action research, Stephen Kemmis deplores the decreasing discretionary space that teachers have to exercise their professional judgement.

> Increasingly states regulate the conduct of schooling through regimes of curriculum, assessment and pedagogical prescription that limit the reach and grasp of the educational practice of educational professionals, making them instruments of legislators and adminis-trators. (Kemmis, 2006: p. 462)

Kemmis (2006) bemoans the fact that a great deal of contemporary action research in education simply serves the interests of the state, in terms of the effi-ciency and effectiveness of teacher practices or focuses upon professional devel-opment, without critically questioning the nature of education or the potential of schooling to domesticate students and teachers. However, the teachers with whom we worked were prepared to 'unsettle' themselves (Kemmis, 2006: p. 462), and sometimes their colleagues, in the educational interests of their students.

Our research project made two crucial interrelated moves to support teachers to tackle this tough work. First, the project had an explicit social justice agenda. We were not simply researching literacy outcomes, but literacy pedagogies for the students teachers were most worried about. And we wanted to understand how the material conditions of students' everyday *lifeworlds* impacted on the working conditions of teachers' *schoolworlds*. We sought to open up a discursive space where teachers could talk about poverty, violence, racism and classism in ways that would take them beyond despair and into new imaginings and positive action. Second, the project was designed to start from the urgent questions of early career teachers and to draw on the accumulated practice wisdom of their chosen mentors. Hence we designed not only a teacher-researcher community, but cross-generational networks. Our aim was to build the capacities of both generations to address long-standing educational problems in new ways that drew overtly on their different and complementary resources.

A key outcome was that early career teachers were able to access the thinking and experience of late career teachers who had developed literacy pedagogies over several decades. Together, they came to understand the collective need to keep researching practice; that working for social justice is never solved once and for all; that teaching requires ongoing inquiry and sustenance in order to risk going beyond normative scripted pedagogies.

UNEQUAL LITERACY OUTCOMES

Many reports indicate that young people's unequal performances on standardized tests of literacy relate to class, race, and gender (Alloway and Gilbert, 1997; Organisation for Economic Co-operation and Development, 2004), but few studies have investigated this pervasive problem *with* teachers. From 2002 until 2004 we worked on a project entitled *Teachers Investigate Unequal Literacy Outcomes: Cross-Generational Perspectives*.[1] This research brought together teacher-researchers and university researchers to investigate the shared problem of inequitable literacy outcomes among school students. It also examined the way early career teachers (in the first five years of their career) and late career teachers (with at least 25 years' teaching experience) built professional knowledge about literacy and educational disadvantage.

In order to understand this phenomenon with fresh eyes we worked *with* teachers to take an ethical approach that starts with a commitment to social justice. We wanted the project to make a sustainable positive difference to the teachers and their students. We started with what teachers say about their work and used narrative methodologies and teacher practitioner research as legitimate forms of knowledge production. These methodologies 'give voice' to teachers, retrieve the local and particular and construct and reconstruct teachers' practical knowledge. Research done on or without teachers, by contrast, can have limited or even negative effects on practice and increase the rift between university and school-based educators.

By positioning teachers 'inside' research as tellers and knowers – both producers and builders of professional knowledge (Cochran-Smith and Lytle, 1993) – the project aimed to build new insights on the intractable problem of inequitable outcomes in literacy. But our secondary aim was to build new approaches to teacher induction and renewal, and indeed to teacher-research. Australia is not alone in facing the problem of recruiting and retaining high quality teachers, especially in high poverty schools (Johnson and Project on the Next Generation of Teachers, 2004). The late career teachers in the project were baby boomers, born in the decade or so after the Second World War. The early career teachers were more mixed in ages (mostly born in the 1970s and 1980s), on the cusp of generations x and y. Given dramatic demographic shifts in the teaching profession (with the impending retirement of baby boomers) and an estimated one-quarter of all beginning teachers leaving teaching within their first four years (Benner, 2000), our project sought to develop a new model of cross-generational teacher research to make the teaching profession more self-sustaining.

Teacher research has a long tradition internationally and in Australia (Carr and Kemmis, 1985; National Schools Network (www.nsn.net.au/research/ladwig.html). Teacher research communities have thrived particularly in relation to English language arts and literacy education in North America (Cochran-Smith and Lytle, 1993; Green et al., 1992) where in the past they have enjoyed support from prestigious research foundations, such as the Spencer Foundation.

We have noted, however, a worrying decline in literacy practitioner research and a tendency to reduce action research to data collection or a trialling of techniques (Kemmis, 2006) and to hijack it for a teacher improvement agenda (Somekh, 2006). Our approach was to make teachers *full* participants in the research, who in collaboration with university researchers, would assemble the required intellectual tools to conduct systematic, scholarly inquiry. Such cooperation allows new knowledge to be constructed and new mentoring relationships to emerge, particularly when teachers work across generations.

In sum, the twin innovation of the project was to encourage the formation of cross-generational mentoring relationships within teacher research communities and to directly address the shared problematic of unequal literacy outcomes by:

- making teachers central to the project of researching literacy education with the goal of improving outcomes for socioeconomically disadvantaged and marginalized children;
- improving knowledge in the field by producing a highly distinctive account of the dynamics of teaching literacy from the perspective of literacy teachers;
- developing new cross-generational research methodologies with implications for professional renewal and development;
- forging closer links between the outcomes of educational research and the work of teachers in schools.

DESIGNING PRODUCTIVE RESEARCH COMMUNITIES

The study recruited five early career teachers (under five years of teaching experience) in two states (hence 10 early career teachers altogether) who were interested in exploring the problem of unequal literacy outcomes in their classrooms. The teachers ranged from kindergarten to high school. We asked these teachers to select an experienced teacher (over 25 years teaching experience) to act as their mentor (hence 10 late career teacher mentors). The teachers mostly taught in working-class and poor areas where student populations included Aboriginal children, linguistic and culturally diverse groups of first or second generation refugees, as well as white working-class young people. These groups – Aboriginal, poor, some ESL learners and rural students – are those most statistically at risk of achieving the lower levels of literacy performance on standardized tests in Australia.

Careful attention was given to creating design conditions that fostered respectful, critical dialogue about professional practice and explicitly inducted teachers into various research practices – interviewing, reading scholarly literature, conducting curriculum audits and case studies, analyzing transcripts and students' work.

In the first part of the project we read selected international research and theory about teaching that made a difference to 'at-risk' children. In the second part of the project, all teachers conducted an audit of their literacy curriculum, using various heuristics to consider what their teaching made available and its effects on different students.

Teachers then identified a case study student who they were particularly concerned about. The challenge was to learn more about the students' 'funds of knowledge' (Moll et al., 1992), their family resources (McNaughton, 2002) and their investments in popular culture (Dyson, 1997). In other words, we asked the teachers to turn to their 'problem students', those with the lowest outcomes for normative literacy, and learn about them as 'children of promise' (Heath and Mangiola, 1991). Teachers engaged in a variety of data-producing activities, including home visits, informal chats with parents, informal interviewing and surveying of students. The key move was that they turned to students and their families to listen and watch.

Their research revealed not students 'in deficit' (Comber and Kamler, 2004), but young people whose potential resources remained invisible in the school context. Teachers discovered parents who cared, children with talents, networks of family and community practices in which young people were being inducted into important aspects of their cultures (including fishing, camping, family practices, sports, media, popular culture and so on). Armed with their new knowledge and new recognition of these young people, they then re-designed an aspect of their curriculum and pedagogy to incorporate what young people carried in their 'virtual school-bags' (Thomson, 2002). Importantly, in so doing, they realized that when they made the curriculum better for their 'at-risk' students, they were improving it for all their students.

RECIPROCAL INTERVIEWING: FIRST STEPS TOWARDS A RESEARCHER COMMUNITY

Reciprocal interviewing was the first stage of our research design. We invited early and late career teachers to interview one another about their understandings and experiences of unequal literacy outcomes in their current workplaces and across their careers. Crucially, the interviews maximized the agency of novice teachers in at least two ways. First, as interviewers, they played a key role in building the project archive. Their questioning of more experienced teachers gave them access to both the wisdom and the vulnerabilities of their mentors, and enabled them to understand 'new' curriculum initiatives and current demands in the context of the past. Second, as interviewees, they were positioned as people with knowledge and ideas to offer their more experienced colleagues. As recent graduates, they were given respectful dialogic space to articulate their different understandings, thus countering the hierarchic assumption that it is always experienced teachers who know best.

We prepared teachers to conduct their interviews in the first workshop, and developed a critical frame on the practice of interviewing as a co-construction (Freebody, 2003). We introduced an interview protocol and invited teachers to modify and add to these questions. Teachers then conducted hour-long interviews in the quiet after-hours spaces of their schools and homes. Their words were captured on tape recorders provided by the project in order to give material respect to their dialogue about professional practice.

From the start, we were explicit that these conversations should address issues of social justice and literacy; in retrospect, they also played a pivotal role in establishing a trusting base for all subsequent early and late career teacher dialogue. A significant move here was producing transcripts from the interviews and subjecting these to public analysis in the workshops. The interviews were not just a data set for the research team, but became a rich conceptual resource to be scrutinized and revisited by the whole community. So, for example, in one workshop we examined key metaphors in teacher transcripts, such as late career Judy Painter's metaphor of the *path* (**bold** highlights the path-related metaphoric language).

Judy: The **path** of a kid's learning can take so many **detours** that as a teacher you have to be prepared to know where the **detour** is, and in the old days you used to bring them back to the **main road**, there was just no variation everyone had to do it. These days you tend with some students, particularly the students I work with now, to follow their **detours** and let them lead you to their learning, particularly for the students with mental health issues … Over the years, there are still lots and lots of kids I can recall that have done amazing things, and it's that feeling that 'what I am doing is helping kids along the **path**, and we're taking a **step forward**' that keeps you there.

Workshop discussion centered on Judy's dogged insistence that it is never possible to abandon difficult students. Her image was teased out, argued over and the counter-tendency to blame students or their families dismissed as untenable in this project. Together teachers worried about how to live up to their responsibility to engage the most disaffected and disadvantaged students, to follow the detours, to find a way forward no matter how difficult or hopeless the material circumstances of students' lives might be.

A great deal of pedagogical work was achieved in these cross-generational interviews and their subsequent analysis, and the learning was reciprocal.

Some of the early career teachers were very vocal about impediments to making a difference in their schools, and their interview commentary fostered further group analysis of social justice issues. Kerry Rochford, for example, an Aboriginal Education and Year 12 English teacher, articulated her deep worries about colleagues who dismissed at-risk students as 'past the effort'.

Kerry: It bothers me a lot that there is that stuff and I hear it every day … I mean I heard a teacher saying one day, 'We don't have to worry about PES subjects.[2] If we don't get enough enrolments we'll just scrap them, because let's face it, these kids aren't going to go to university', and I mean that is such terrible stereotyping. 'If you live in this area you will not go to university', and it made my blood boil quite frankly. I just thought 'How can you do that?' and I mean as somebody who grew up in a Housing Trust home, in a working class family, I found that personally insulting. I know it can be done, people do do it.

Kerry's transcript stimulated discussion about how to contest the deficit discourses that all too often circulate in schools and are so resistant to change (Comber and Kamler, 2004). These kinds of research conversations allowed early career teachers, who themselves had working-class childhoods, safe spaces to articulate positions which could not easily be uttered in some school cultures. For older teachers the dialogic space of the interview allowed a similar opportunity to raise questions that might be unsayable in other contexts – and then to address them. In our project all teachers had problems to solve. The way we structured the cross-generational interviews allowed a kind of vulnerability, analysis and reciprocity that laid the foundation for all future interactions. Older teachers struggled as did younger ones – the struggles were different but no less distressing or pressing – especially in disadvantaged schools.

ASSEMBLING ETHNOGRAPHIC REPERTOIRES AND RESEARCHER DISPOSITIONS

Just as the cross-generational interviews created discursive space to consider questions of social justice, the opportunity to develop an ethnographic perspective provided critical, analytic distance on teachers' everyday practices. We introduced teachers to a range of ethnographic research practices, as our second design move, including home visits, interviewing parents and young people, observing students in different activity settings and learning contexts, analyzing various kinds of data and producing case studies. These inquiry activities and the data they produced were as important to the late career teachers as the early career teachers, in opening up their interpretive repertoires, and in allowing them to recognize student potential where previously thcy had seen deficit.

Taking a researcher standpoint was pivotal in challenging teachers' assumptions about children and seeing them as complex and socially situated. It enabled Rob Fuller, for example, in his first year of teaching, to re-think his view of Bill, a 7-year-old Aboriginal boy with school learning and literacy difficulties. Meeting Bill's parents and observing him in different contexts beyond classroom literacy events enabled Fuller to re-design the curriculum based around Bill's 'funds of knowledge' (Fuller and Hood, 2005, following Moll et al., 1992).

Whereas some psychological models of development and some sociological models of populations render young people to particular *grids of specification* (Foucault, 1979), our teachers' research investigations allowed them to recognize the relational nature of learning, literate practices and identity. Fuller initially saw Bill in terms of a list of diagnostic conditions (including 'dyslexia', 'speech and articulation difficulties', 'poor auditory memory', 'refusing to speak publicly'); but his research helped him recognize Bill's positive engagement in a range of learning beyond schooling (including his family's indigenous knowledges of the environment and commitment to supporting refugees). Once Bill was known differently, Fuller could move beyond the limits of mainstream diagnoses and associated individual forms of remediation to design a truly educative, inclusive curriculum with new kinds of curriculum and pedagogical encounters.

Developing a research repertoire not only made a difference to teachers' immediate professional practice, it also shaped their teacher-researcher dispositions and social justice standpoint. Like Carr and Kemmis (2005: 348) we see long-term payoffs when educational research plays 'an intrinsic role in the professional development of teachers'. But it is critical that we properly resource and support new generations of teacher-researchers to become critical professionals who can act ethically to work for social justice; who can envision, design and carry out ambitious educational projects which tackle contemporary social and environmental problems. They cannot do it on their own.

The ways in which we conceptualized 'turnaround pedagogies' (see Comber and Kamler, 2005) in our project was centrally about finding new ways to resource such long-term change. Thus, we as university researchers turned to teachers as collaborators, teachers in turn made multiple moves, towards families and students as informants, towards school-based colleagues and towards us as university-based researchers. On a more abstract level together we turned to the literature – theory, related research, methodologies. As we worked on multiple fronts we turned to each other as co-participants in interpreting data, suggesting responses and reviewing what happened. The turnaround pedagogies metaphor signifies a continual looking beyond and towards others, not a one-off move but a reciprocal and iterative process of learning from and with each other.

KNOWLEDGE GENERATION: WRITING LIKE A RESEARCHER

While the workshops, interviews and school-based research projects created space for serious dialogue that generated new pedagogical approaches to literacy for social justice, writing and publishing about this research was a crucial final move in our research design. We designed our writing workshops on the premise that research is writing, not separate from it; and that to help teachers write like researchers involves both text work and identity work (Kamler and Thomson, 2006). It requires learning particular genre and textual conventions of journal articles, but also learning how to assert oneself confidently and with authority in broader educational conversations. It is through this writing that teachers engage in additional analytic work, generate new knowledge and further develop their researcher dispositions.

Despite our commitment to this work, it needs to be said that encouraging our early and late career teachers to write like researchers was not easy. While they skilfully adopted an ethnographic lens on teaching, their early written drafts about that teaching were flat, unfocused recounts of practice. Their texts failed to include any of their detailed observations or insights as researchers; they were reluctant to name their contribution or elucidate the ways in which their pedagogic designs actually 'turned-around' student literacy performance.

We were somewhat at a loss initially as to what to do, as we had found the teachers to be confident arguers and evidence-based thinkers throughout the project. So we explored and experimented with a number of workshop strategies to reactivate their obvious strengths as speakers in the context of their writing. We read drafts and held conferences to get them to speak about what was *not* on the page. We scaffolded sentences and modelled how to frame an argument more confidently – almost like a cloze exercise. We held long distance teleconferences to get teachers to articulate issues they had omitted in their texts. Then we taped and transcribed these conversations and asked teachers to insert parts into their writing.

We also created multiple opportunities for teachers to present their scholarship and meet production deadlines. Some publications were more academic than others, some led more by the university researchers. In the end, we produced three kinds of publications, including:

- six chapters written by teachers for an edited collection titled *Turn-around Pedagogies: Literacy Interventions for at-risk Students* (Comber and Kamler, 2005);
- two international refereed peer-reviewed articles for *English Teaching: Practice and Critique*, jointly written with three late career teachers (Comber et al., 2004) and with one early career-late career pair (Boyer et al., 2004).
- three articles written by teachers for the journal *Practically Primary* (2005, volume 10, number 2) published by the Australian Language and Literacy Association.

These publications documented the multiple kinds of research-based knowledge and intellectual work generated by our cross-generational research collective. Teachers wrote about the innovative ways they engaged disaffected literacy learners, but they did not just offer good news stories. They wrote hopeful, agentic texts which examined their own problematic assumptions and misreadings as well as the ways they reconnected students with literacy. Publishing this work allowed teachers to reach the wider profession and engage broader disciplinary conversations about literacy, social justice and practitioner inquiry. Discursively, it moved them out of the confines of the classroom to stand in the wider global community of teacher-researchers.

Nonetheless, it is important to state that teacher research, or practitioner inquiry more broadly, continues to be frequently under-valued in academia and seen as of low status. Often it is not cited as much as it should be, as academics in particular traditions fail to appreciate the significance of such work, or even think of it as knowledge in its own right.

CONCLUSIONS

In retrospect, we believe there were five key aspects that made this research design for cross-generational mentoring successful:

- a persistent and serious social problem with no apparent solution;
- an equal valuing of the knowledges of both generations;
- greater agency than normal for younger teachers;
- a cross-institutional partnership, where the status of the more powerful institution is used to offer training, and foster analytic research-based conversations that value the perspectives of teachers;
- public textual accountability, where occasions are created to present teachers' research findings to the wider profession.

For early career teachers, joining a cross-generational research collective was a significant move in building a professional identity and assembling new repertoires of practice. Having people with insider institutional knowledge and years of practice wisdom, virtually on-tap, plus sympathetic yet critical outsiders from the university proved an ideal set of resources. For more experienced teachers, participating in a research community resulted in rejuvenation, renewed feelings of professional self-respect *and* renewed motivation for serious critical analysis of what they know and do. Participating in extended, research-based conversations over three years created dialogic space for both early and late career professionals to ask questions, check assumptions, test the limits of the constraints and their own potential for inventiveness and innovation.

Such models of practitioner inquiry hold great promise for the professional renewal of the teacher workforce. Elsewhere (Kamler and Comber, 2005) we have noted how frequently teacher-researchers move on to become school leaders, advisers, curriculum writers. In this project we have seen how much difference practitioner inquiry can make to teachers' ability to articulate their beliefs and practice and to become catalysts for school and policy change. Not surprisingly, many took up key leadership and promotional positions as a consequence of participating in the project.

Creating a mutually satisfying, reciprocal research enterprise requires that we make time and space for educative inquiry and conversation. There need to be genuine opportunities for in-depth investigations of children's learning, because ultimately that is what must inform teaching. Time is needed to induct teachers into research repertoires – interviews, audits, case studies, observation, analysis and writing. Schools and systems need to authorize such research activities as part of the infrastructure of professional in-service learning. The importance of institutionalizing safe research spaces for interrogating teaching practice in these times cannot be underestimated. It is a fundamental move in sustaining teacher innovation and improving *all* children's learning.

NOTES

1 The *Teachers Investigate Unequal Literacy Outcomes: Cross-Generational Perspectives* research project (no. DP0208391) was funded by the Australian Research Council Discovery Grants Program (2002–2004). The views expressed in this chapter reflect the views of the authors.

2 PES means that the subject is a 'publicly examined subject'. PES subjects have been understood as academic and of higher status in terms of university entry.

REFERENCES

Alloway, N. and Gilbert, P. (1997) 'Boys and literacy: Lessons from Australia', *Gender and Education*, 9 (1): 49–58.

Benner, A.D. (2000) *The Cost of Teacher Turn-over* (Austin, Texas: Texas Center for Educational Research). Available online at http://www.sbec.state.tx.us/SBECOnline/txbess/turnoverrpt.pdf, accessed May 15th, 2007.

Boyer, I. and Maney, B. with Kamler, B. and Comber, B. (2004) 'Reciprocal mentoring across generations: Sustaining professional development for English teachers', *English Teaching: Practice and Critique*, 3 (2): 139–50.

Carr, W. and Kemmis, S. (1985) *Becoming Critical: Knowing Through Action Research*. Geelong: Deakin University.

Carr, W. and Kemmis, S. (2005) 'Staying critical', *Educational Action Research,* 13 (3): 347–57.

Cochran-Smith, M. and Lytle, S. (1993) *Inside/Outside: Teacher Research and Knowledge*. New York and London: Teachers College Press.

Cochran-Smith, M. and Lytle, S. (2006) 'Troubling images of teaching in No Child Left Behind', *Harvard Educational Review*, 76 (4): 668–97.

Comber, B. and Kamler, B. (2004) 'Getting out of deficit: Pedagogies of reconnection', *Teaching Education*, 15 (3): 293–310.

Comber, B. and Kamler, B. (eds) (2005) *Turn-around Pedagogies: Literaccy Interventions for at-risk Students*. Newtown, NSW: Primary English Teaching Association.

Comber, B., Kamler, B., Hood, D., Moreau, S. and Painter, J. (2004) 'Thirty years into teaching: Professional development, exhaustion and rejuvenation', in *English Teaching: Practice and Critique*, 3 (2): 74–87.

Doecke, B., Howie, M. and Sawyer, W. (eds) (2006) *Only Connect: English Teaching Schooling and Community*. Kent Town, SA: Wakefield Press.

Dyson, A.H. (1997) *Writing Superheroes: Contemporary Childhood, Popular Culture, and Classroom Literacy*. New York and London Teachers College Press.

Freebody, P. (2003) *Qualitative Research in Education: Interaction and Practice*. London, Thousand Oaks, New Delhi: Sage Publications.

Foucault, M. (1979) *Discipline and Punish: The Birth of the Prison*. Trans. A. Sheridan. London; Peregrine.

Fuller, R. and Hood, D. (2005) 'Utilising community funds of knowledge as resources for school literacy learning', in B. Comber and B. Kamler (eds), *Turn-around Pedagogies: Literacy Interventions for at-risk Students*. Newtown, NSW: Primary English Teaching Association, pp. 63–76.

Green, J., Dixon, C., Lin, L., Floriani, A. (1992) 'Constructing literacy in the classroom: literate action as social accomplishment', in H. Marshall (ed.) *Redefining Learning: Roots of Educational Change*. Norwood, NJ: Ablex, pp. 119–51.

Heath, S.B. and Mangiola, L. (1991) *Children of Promise: Literate Activity in Linguistically and Culturally Diverse Classrooms*. Washington: National Education Association of the United States.

Johnson, S.M. and Project on the Next Generation of Teachers (2004). *Finders and Keepers: Helping New Teachers Survive and Thrive in our Schools*. San Francisco: Jossey-Bass.

Kamler, B. and Comber, B. (2005) 'Turn around pedagogies: Improving the education of at risk students', *Improving Schools*, 8 (2): 121–31.

Kamler, B. and Thomson, P. (2006) *Helping Doctoral Students Write: Pedagogies for Supervision*. London and New York: Routledge.

Kemmis, S. (2006) 'Participatory action research and the public sphere', *Educational Action Research*, 14 (4): 459–76.

McNaughton, S. (2002) *Meeting of Minds*. Wellington, NZ: Learning Media.

Moll, L.C., Amanti, C., Neff, D. and Gonzalez, N. (1992) 'Funds of knowledge for teaching: Using a qualitative approach to connect homes and classrooms', *Theory and Practice*, 31: 132–41.

Organisation for Economic Co-operation and Development (OECD) (2004) *Learning for Tomorrow's World: First results from PISA 2003*. Paris: OECD Publications.

Smith, D.E. (2005) *Institutional Ethnography: A Sociology for People*. Lanham: Alta Mira Press.

Somekh, B. (2006) *Action Research: A Methodology for Change and Development*. Maidenhead: Open University Press.

Thomson, P. (2002) *Schooling the Rustbelt Kids: Making the Difference in Changing Times*. Sydney: Allen and Unwin.

19

Co-operative Change Management through Practitioner Inquiry

Susan Groundwater-Smith

In his challenging and provocative interpretation of contemporary Australian society, Boris Frankel (2004) seeks to dismantle many of the shibboleths surrounding our characterization of schooling provision, as equitable and socially just. He argues that the political ecology of the continent of Australia is:

> particularly hospitable to three odd and troubling species: the zombies, stalking the political landscape like the walking dead; the Lilliputions, tiny in mind and timid in their expectations … and finally the sadists, prowling our workplaces, bureaucracies and parliaments. (p. 9)

He argues that, contrary to the myths we tell about ourselves, there continues in Australia to be deep educational and social inequality both in terms of participation in schooling and the nature of the experienced curriculum. His line of reasoning is supported by, among others, Richard Teese (2006) who makes the case that schools should be pursuing a rigorous agenda of equal outcomes for their students. In addition, he suggests that schools facing challenging circumstances should be ready and willing to be risk takers and innovators and that they should be provided not only with resources, but also an environment where their efforts are recognized and applauded.

Frankel's rather bleak analysis of Australian society is not one that stands alone. More than a decade ago Elliott and MacLennan (1994) pointed to striking similarities between Canadian, British and United States' policies that have been critical of 'educational progressivism and have concentrated upon business values, market discipline and market relations in schools and colleges' (p. 165). These policies, too, have brought about distortions in schooling, particularly when it comes to matters of equity and social justice.

It is in this context that somewhat surprisingly the Priority Action Schools Program was developed in the Australian state of New South Wales. This chapter will discuss the genesis of the program and its intention to improve the learning opportunities of young people. The Priority Actions Schools Program (PASP), a joint venture between the NSW Department of Education and Training (DET) and the NSW Teachers Federation (the local teachers union to which almost all teachers in government schools in the state belong) was designed to trial intensive assistance to 74 schools serving communities with deep needs. This group represented approximately one-quarter of those schools in the state who are in receipt of additional funding on the basis of issues around poverty, ethnicity and Aboriginality (a term employed to indicate the proportion of Indigenous students attending a given school). The trial aimed to build school and individual capacity to improve student engagement in learning and student learning outcomes, reduce disruptive behaviour and suspensions and improve attendance and retention in the context of fostering co-operation between schools, the Tertiary and Further Education Sector (TAFE) and other agencies and community organizations.

PASP was conceived of as a knowledge-based program in that schools were required to create and share professional knowledge. The program aimed to model for schools a culture of collaborative enquiry with opportunities for dissemination and the nurturing of teacher professional learning. The evaluation strategy, articulated in the guiding principles for evaluation, placed knowledge creation and knowledge transfer at its core.

DESIGNING A PROGRAM WITH AN EQUITY OF EDUCATIONAL OUTCOMES FOCUS

Currently educational policy development in Australia is primarily a matter for the individual states and territories, although, increasingly the federal government is seeking to intervene in relation to the development of a national curriculum, national testing and standards for teachers as they progress through their careers. Frankel (2004), whose colourful quotation opened this chapter, observed that social justice and equity concerns were not prominent in the policies of the then federal government; however, they remained of primary concern at the state level in all jurisdictions. This balance may change with the recent change of federal government; however, it is too early to make a determination in relation to any such change.

The objectives of the Priority Actions Schools Program were to support schools to build their capacity to:

- improve students' educational outcomes;
- improve student behaviour and attendance;
- support teachers through mentoring and induction programs;

- support whole school approaches to improved teaching practice;
- reduce high student turnover and increase retention to complete schooling;
- reduce the impacts of socioeconomic disadvantage; and
- maximize interagency and community support. (NSW Department of Education and Training, 2002)

Schools identified on a number of criteria were invited to submit expressions of interest, outlining strategies they would use in pursuit of these objectives. Each school's set of strategies was to be designed as a 'local solution' to local problems and issues. Funding was delivered to schools at the start of 2003 after negotiations with the state team managing the Program to identify how these additional resources to the schools might be used – including for additional teaching, executive or support staff.

The Priority Action Schools Program was structured as a 'knowledge building program'. Each school was required to conduct a systematic evaluation of its own work, assisted by an academic partner experienced in school-based research. Each school would build a *school learning portfolio* documenting its work. The meta-evaluators worked in a co-operative relationship with the state PASP team in a similar way to the academic partners who worked with each PASP school.

Together with their academic partners, schools explored a variety of strategies in pursuit of the objectives of the Program, including strategies aimed at developing:

- pedagogy;
- improved learning outcomes for students;
- whole school vision and culture building;
- staffing solutions;
- organization for learning;
- interagency work and parent and community involvement;
- student well-being and student support; and
- teachers' professional development.

The program was underpinned by the notion of 'pressure and support' (Beveridge et al., 2005). Where schools were expected to undertake action inquiry by first identifying the particular challenges they faced and then designing an appropriate means of addressing them. They were then to document their findings in partnership with an academic associate who would act as a practitioner research facilitator.

The pressure element was not in relation to an expectation that schools would conform to a 'one size fits all' solution, but rather that they were expected to be able to explain what they were doing, why and how they were doing it and how effective their strategies were. The pressure was intended to provide a form of professional accountability. Schools were supported to develop a culture of collaborative enquiry by engaging in a range of professional learning opportunities implemented by the NSW Department of Education and Training State Team.

Each learning portfolio was analyzed by the author of this chapter, Susan Groundwater-Smith, and by Stephen Kemmis. As well, the evaluators made a number of site visits and attended all team meetings at which the senior DET officers and union officers were present. The evaluators engaged with practitioners at all levels: in the classrooms, in the schools, in the communities, in the universities from which the academic partners came, and in the bureaucracy itself. Thus PASP was both a knowledge-building program and one that contributed to teacher professional learning in the context of an inquiry that has a social justice focus – that is a normative concern about what *should be*, as well as what *is*, where teachers are enjoined to be courageous learners as encouraged by Newman (2006).

ESCAPING OLD BONDS OF PRACTICE: TWO EXAMPLES

Changing educational practices is never an easy matter. In spite of being faced with often quite extraordinary challenges, it is the case that bringing about effective change in entrenched behaviours is difficult. Richardson and Placier (2001) have gone some way to assisting us in understanding this conundrum by offering two contrasting strategies for change, one they describe as an 'empirical-rational approach' (p. 905) where teachers are instructed by consultants, academics and bureaucrats about how they ought to go about their practice; the other is a 'normative-reeducative' approach (p. 906) that gives the practitioner agency in developing improvement strategies based upon systematic practical inquiry (Richardson, 1994). The PASP was clearly founded upon the latter.

In offering two examples from the case record of the PASP, the writer is mindful of respecting the confidentiality that has been required by the study. Therefore each example, is in effect, a composite of the work of several schools. In the first case, Moorok Central School is located in a remote area of the state and caters for children from Kindergarten to Year 10; in the second case Garrick Public School is on the metropolitan fringe and provides education for young people from Kindergarten to Year 6. The composites were formed by examining the portfolios of several schools located in similar areas and dealing with similar challenges.

Moorok Central School

One must first be appreciative of the fact that rural New South Wales has been subject to a prolonged drought that has placed great pressure on the social resilience of its most remote communities. As economic pressures increased those most able to leave have done so, leaving behind those who are increasingly impoverished and marginalized, many of whom are Indigenous Australians. The Human Rights and Equal Opportunities Commission (HREOC) conducted a national inquiry into rural and remote education (HREOC, 2000) and found that a range of social and structural factors limited access to quality education, among them: town size, distance to the nearest school, quality of roads and limited curriculum breadth due to school size; staff turnover, and student alienation resulting in participation, attendance, retention and achievement far below the national average. These conditions prevailed during the first year of the PASP and continue to this day.

In common with many small towns in remote New South Wales, Moorok has experienced the closure of a number of its businesses and services, including the local motel, pharmacy and real estate agency. Tradespeople such as plumbers and electricians have left, or are in the process of moving out. Many of the students experience significant learning difficulties, partly exacerbated by irregular attendance and health problems. All the same, the school is seen by a majority of its students as a place of safety, shelter and sustenance. All of these matters were documented carefully and poignantly in the school's learning portfolio. Indeed, it was suggested that this was itself a new experience, that is to say an opportunity to articulate the complex social challenges faced by the school in the context of being located in a remote community.

A major challenge for the school has been to retain its teachers and provide them with opportunities for professional learning. With no readily available relief teachers who could come in when called upon on an irregular basis, it was decided that the school would use some of its PASP funding to appoint additional staff to the school's complement. This has been no small achievement. Staffing government schools in New South Wales has been highly regulated. Because the program was undertaken in consultation with the New South Wales Teachers Federation it was possible to reach working agreements on variations that went outside the normal procedures. As a result of additional staff, teachers were able to be relieved from their classes and be engaged in examining the scope and sequence of the curriculum, seeking for greater integration and relevance. This is a particularly important strategy in a context of high staff turnover in such schools and a number of relatively inexperienced teachers, which means that much planning is of a stop-start nature, and much of it not integrated. Having additional staff also meant that a program that would mentor and nurture early career teachers could be put into place.

In relation to its community, the school sought to have closer links with ways in which local Indigenous culture could be better understood, acknowledged and incorporated into the practices of the school. Not only were local Indigenous elders consulted, but also local identities such as artists and musicians were invited into the school to share poetry and music.

While in this first year of the PASP the school concentrated upon its teachers' learning, particularly with respect to more inclusive and relevant pedagogy, it also acknowledged that students needed assistance in developing study habits that were more likely to lead to improved learning. Many of the young people had circumstances at home that made sustained study very difficult. Moorok Central School established a learning centre that was a quiet and congenial space, staffed by a teacher who would act as a facilitator for learning rather than engaging directly in instruction. As well, as a means of overcoming the limited curriculum choices of a relatively small school, arrangements were made to increase distance education opportunities through the learning centre.

Much of the evidence collected by the school to inform its learning portfolio related to descriptions of processes and documents that had been developed. Importantly the program provided opportunities for teachers to be professionally engaged with one another, returning to first principles as they reflected on practice. In summing up the impact of one year of PASP upon teaching and learning at Moorok Central School practitioners were rightly suspicious of 'silver bullets', and right to caution that significant changes may not occur in complex organizations like schools over several years, let alone a single year.

Garrick Public School

Whereas Moorok Central School faced the challenges attendant upon its physical isolation, Garrick Public School suffered an isolation of a different kind, that of being spurned and shunned especially by media representations. Located on the metropolitan fringe it was a school serving a community described by Vinson (2003) as one of those 'so concentrated in their degree of disadvantage of life opportunities ordinarily available to most people [that they] are crushed by the negative social spiral' (p. 1). He later continues:

> There are causal associations between poor neighbourhoods and other social problems that are more than the consequences of macroeconomic forces and individual or household characteristics. The larger and longer running the area health problems, the stronger the cumulative impact becomes causing a drain on services with resultant lower quality outcomes such as educational performance, housing services and health care ... neighbourhoods affect life chances during early childhood and late adolescence, the very times when a just society would be most anxious to open up life opportunities to children and young people. (p. 56)

Vinson conducted a study of entrenched social disadvantage by tracing the circumstances of neighbourhoods by postcode and found it to have become more concentrated in fewer areas in the last 25 years. Garrick is one such area.

Garrick Public School, catering for the first six years of schooling, draws its student body from the surrounding Department of Housing estate that predominantly provides for families in crisis. A large proportion of the families are under the care of a single parent who most likely is not in the paid workforce. Both mental and physical health difficulties plague the community with a notable number of its adult members suffering the consequences of substance abuse. As well as a number of families with Indigenous backgrounds many come from those where English is a second language. Breaking through to literacy is particularly problematic in that few children had any experience of early child-hood education prior to attending school.

In developing its first solutions to what seemed like intractable problems the whole staff withdrew for a weekend conference. Its first emphasis was to reor-ganize staffing with the appointment of a male teacher's aide; additional staff responsible for assisting in literacy development and a change in the work organ-ization of assistant principals who would undertake mentoring of the many early career teachers in the school. As well, a community liaison officer was appointed with a brief to keep in contact with families at risk. Also the school recognized that it had a small cohort of talented students who were often overlooked within a context of crisis management. It was decided that some extension programs should be provided for these students.

Working on a premise that students learn best when they feel safe, secure and have their basic nutrition needs met, the school instituted a breakfast program in conjunction with local providers of health and well-being services. Previously a number of children had come to school both tired and hungry. Providing breakfast appeared to reinvigorate the children and made for a pleasant start to the day.

An interesting development was that of seeking for a common, agreed lan-guage that students and teachers would employ when faced with a learning difficulty or block; students have been encouraged to 'self talk' about how they might tackle a problem, saying to themselves such things as 'have I tried to remember what I have been told?' 'can I help myself before I ask someone else?'. In reference to this development teachers wrote of 'not keeping learning as secret business; we explain not just the "what" of learning; but the "why" as well'.

In their reflections teachers not only noted increased academic engagement, but also wider community engagement. They had not been fully appreciative of the ways in which their former communication patterns had failed. The practice of sending notes home to parents who themselves suffer significant literacy problems is unlikely to be helpful. Phoning and visiting in a blame-free context appeared to have much more productive results. As one entry put it:

> We have found as the year has progressed that the only way to ensure constant contact and cooperation is to keep up the level of contact by phone or house visits as many of the com-munity cannot read, so written attempts at communication are futile. We have learnt that it is a community-wide problem. We now view the way in which we communicate in a differ-ent light. We have become far more sympathetic to the needs of our parents.

As well as recording drops in student absenteeism, the school has also been able to document reductions in staff absenteeism. Not only have the students been more engaged, but teachers have evidently also been more professionally engaged. In the past the school believed its teachers to be experiencing significant burnout; as a result of their sense of their own efficacy it would seem that they are finding their work more satisfying and rewarding. A major learning for teachers has been that consistency in approaches to student learning pays dividends.

'Children are very perceptive and have a well-established sense of what is fair and just'.

TOOLS AND STRATEGIES

It is clear from these case studies that the tools and strategies adopted by the PASP were critical to its implementation. The key concept was that of the *School Learning Portfolio* as a professional learning and accountability mechanism that could document processes of professional knowledge creation.

The school as a knowledge-building organization has been discussed widely, notably by David Hargreaves (1999) who argued that schools have within them significant professional knowledge, much of which is tacit and unexamined. But the great fund of knowledge held by practitioners can scarcely be drawn upon if it remains buried beneath the surface. Hargreaves (2003) has since developed his argument, making the case for mobilizing and developing the intellectual and social capital held by practitioners into a more coherent and integrated whole. Furthermore, he has argued for drawing upon organizational capital in the form of networks and external links in order to inform and improve at both local and regional levels. Importantly, he believes that moving beyond incremental innovation (swimming with the tide) to radical innovation (swimming against the tide) cannot be achieved by central direction, but requires the school itself to be a learning professional life form.

How then is knowledge created in a school, with its many participants, factions and territories? PASP believed that the school itself needs to be seen as an intelligent organization. MacGilchrist et al. (2004) have focused upon schools as institutions that are dynamic and organic in their nature. Drawing on notions of multiple intelligence and recent thinking about the nature of organizations, they offer a way of looking at schools as living systems through the exploration of the concept of the *'intelligent school'*. For them, intelligent schools are 'human communities that are continuously developing their capacity for improvement. The School Learning Portfolio required the schools to conceive of themselves as just that. Each school examined its history, its philosophy, the challenges that it was currently facing and the strategies that it chose to employ to ameliorate these. Each provided evidence of the ways in which successes had been achieved and which barriers continued to stand in their way.

The pressure and support that was provided by senior officers of the DET, the academic partners and the meta-evaluators ensured that schools stayed on track. This was not a draconian process but nevertheless was relentless. It was important that agreement had been reached with the teachers' union who endorsed the processes and also provided resources in the form of a seconded official who worked closely with the DET team and the meta-evaluators.

The insights that evolved did not develop through change mechanisms that tell teachers what they should do and how they should do it; but rather have come about as a result of coherent, school-based inquiry that has identified what is required and sought to develop appropriate interventions. It is action research writ large.

ACTION RESEARCH ON A LARGE SCALE

Lawrence Stenhouse, the founder of the Centre for Applied Research in Education at the University of East Anglia, is one who struggled long and hard with the question of 'what counts as research?' Stenhouse's minimal definition of research is that it is systematic self-critical inquiry, based upon a stable and deep curiosity (1981). As well, he has written of research as 'systematic inquiry made public' (1979). Stenhouse has argued that curiosity is both powerful and dangerous because it has the potential to lead to social change. It proposes heresy, is transgressive even, and threatens that faith in those embedded and enduring practices which conspires to keep so many of our institutions and professional practices so little changed. At the same time it gives a better informed context for action than just a belief in change would lead us to. It is for this reason that the Stenhousian position accords so well with the principles of the Priority Actions Schools Program.

Importantly, the processes that have been adopted are not individualistic. They have informed collegial professional learning about current conditions, past histories and future prospects. It is a co-operative process of problem solving by those who are participating. Together they seek to get a grip on the action processes and develop new action scripts through co-operative reflection. The notion of the 'script' is a dramaturgical one and is used here metaphorically. Thus the schools in the program worked together to construct scenarios of what exists and what needs to change and from these develop their action scripts. For example, in the case of Moorok Central School scenarios evolved around the concern for providing ways to relieve staff so that they might engage in more substantive professional learning in a context where short-term substitute staff was hard to find. The proposed script was to appoint a full-time teacher to the school who would be accepted by the students and could move in and out of classrooms as the need arose. Such new action scripts are tried out in practice, evaluated and adjusted or rejected. Furthermore, action and reflection are seen to reinforce each other, which results in a cyclical or narrative development. Reflection must not be disconnected from action; otherwise one runs the risk of estrangement, utopianism, dogmatism, scientism or fundamentalism. Reflection in and on action in the context of practice can be said to be a form of practical philosophy. Those 74 schools participating in the PASP may not have seen themselves thus engaged, but indeed they were.

> Practical philosophy aims at being a philosophy that engages with the conditions of all people, women and men, poor and rich, Others and us. It is a kind of philosophy that is interested in the empirical world as a way of grounding its conclusions in interaction between thinking and acting. (Griffiths, 2003: 21)

The action research basis of PASP assumed that those involved in it would constitute a group with common objectives and goals, interested in a problem that emerges from a given context. It has been research that has at its heart the public good (Jenson, 2006) in the development of professional knowledge. What has been argued for is a continuous process of testing theories in action and pursuing questions of significance. In some respects it can be counted as experiential learning where the experience is that of undertaking the inquiry. Fenwick (2003) points out that experiential learning

> … focuses on the messy problems and tenacious practices of everyday life which run counter to the logic, language and disciplines of the academy, particularly those privileging the rational and, increasingly, the linguistic and discursive … We need ask, is there a more generative way to meld educative intents with non institutional experience? To promote fuller participation of people in learning experience without normalizing it? (p. 13)

There can be no question that PASP schools have been pursuing 'messy problems and tenacious practices'. What was unusual about the program was its reach and scope, all conducted in a national, indeed international, context: where professional work is increasingly fragmented through work intensification; where detailed guidelines, procedures and checklists are created to circumscribe professional autonomy and discretion; and, where public trust is constantly eroded as governments and the media conspire to strip teaching of its professionalism by ever burgeoning surveillance in the form of standards development, audit measures and unrealistically high expectations.

As Mulford (2005) argued in terms of school leadership, organizational and student learning in schools:

> To have these advances [for school reform] fall to the same fate as the latest gimmickry, short-term political opportunism or impossibly high expectations benefits no one, especially the practitioners, those in and responsible for schools, for they are the people most likely to ensure the long-term improvement of schools, the children in them and the communities they serve. (p. 321)

In their conclusion to the report upon the Priority Action Schools Program, Groundwater-Smith and Kemmis (2005) quoted a participating school:

> Almost without exception, teachers spoke eloquently and passionately about their concept of teacher professionalism; the challenges they were confronting in their everyday work, the efforts to address these challenges and their re-invigoration as a result of the directions of their school, generally since 2001 and specifically under the PASP of 2003.
>
> As one noted: 'I used to think of teaching as a trade; you came to work, did your job and went home. Now I am treated as a professional and I act accordingly. This has been liberating for me'.
>
> And another observed: 'Teachers are feeling free and able to take risks to such an extent that the openness has led to people working more together. (p. 103)

Returning to Teese (2006) and his invocation that schools facing challenging circumstances should be ready and willing to be risk takers and innovators and that they should be provided not only with resources, but also an environment where their efforts are recognized and applauded, it can be argued that the

Program, as a large-scale action research project, has clearly met this test. With few exceptions, teachers who have participated should feel that they can walk tall and that they have made a difference in what might otherwise be seen as an indifferent world.

REFERENCES

Beveridge, S., Groundwater-Smith, S., Kemmis, S. and Wasson, D. (2005). 'Professional learning that makes a difference', *Journal of In-Service Education*, 31 (4): 697–710.

Elliott, B. and MacLennan, D. (1994) 'Education, modernity and neo-conservative school reform in Canada, Britain and the United states', *British Journal of Sociology of Education*, 15 (2): 165–185.

Fenwick, T. (2003) 'Community based learning and the development of really useful knowledge'. Conference paper presented at the International Conference of the Centre for Research in Lifelong Learning. Glasgow, June, 2003.

Frankel, B. (2004) *Zombies, Lilliputians and Sadists: The Power of the Living Dead and the Future of Australia*. Fremantle, WA: Curtin University Books.

Griffiths, M. (2003) 'Action for social justice in education', Open University.

Groundwater-Smith, S. and Kemmis, S. (2005) *Knowing Makes a Difference: Learnings from the NSW Priority Action Schools Program*. Report presented to the New South Wales Department of Education and Training, Sydney, NSW. Available on the web https://www.det.nsw.edu.au/reviews/pasp/index.htm Accessed 12 June, 2007.

Hargreaves, D. (1999) 'The knowledge creating school', *British Journal of Education Studies*, 47: 122–44.

Hargreaves, D. (2003) 'From improvement to transformation'. Keynote address presented to the International Conference of the *International Congress for School Effectiveness and Improvement (ICSEI)*. Sydney: Sydney Convention Centre, Darling Harbour, 5th–8th February.

Human Rights and Equal Opportunity Commission (2000) *Emerging Themes. National Inquiry into Rural and Remote Education*. Canberra: Commonwealth of Australia.

Jenson, J. (2006) 'Research and the public good', *Social Work Research*, 30 (4): 195–7.

MacGilchirst, B., Myers, K. and Reed, J. (2004). *The Intelligent School* (2nd edn). London: Sage Publications.

Mulford, B. (2005) 'Quality evidence about leadership for organisational and student learning in school', *School Leadership and Management*, 25 (4): 321–330.

Newman, M. (2006) *Teaching Defiance: Stories and Strategies for Activist Educators*. San Francisco: Jossey-Bass.

NSW Department of Education and Training, Initial briefing to District Superintendents and Teachers' Federation Organisers, 9th August, 2002.

Richardson, V. (1994) 'Conducting research on practice', *Educational Researcher*, 23 (5): 5–10.

Richardson, V. and Placier, P. (2001) 'Teacher change', in V. Richardson (ed.) *Handbook of Research on Teaching* (4th edn). Washington, DC: American Educational Research Association, pp. 905–47.

Stenhouse, L. (1979) 'Research as a basis for teaching. Inaugural lecture, UEA', in L. Stenhouse, (1983) *Authority, Education and Emancipation*. London: Heinemann Educational Books.

Stenhouse, L. (1981) 'What counts as research?' in *British Journal of Educational Studies,* 29 (2). Reprinted in J. Rudduck and D. Hopkins (eds) (1985) *Research as a Basis for Teaching*. London: Heinemann Educational Books, pp. 8–24.

Teese, R. (2006) 'Getting smart: The battle for ideas in education', *Griffith Review*, February.

Vinson, T. (2003) *Black Holes of Entrenched Disadvantage in Australia*. http:///.jss.org.au/media/pdfs/black_hole_address.pdf (accessed 20th May, 2007).

Personal: Self-Awareness, Development and Identity

Introduction to Part III

Part III contains 12 chapters that focus on the work of those whose action research places special emphasis on reflexivity and exploration of the self. In this sense their overarching focus is personal. All the chapters in the Handbook raise ethical issues, but here the focus on ethics is more specific to the personal commitments that both drive and serve to monitor educational action research. Some of the chapters draw on philosophical or psychological theories that shape how action researchers construct ontological knowledge – the nature of being in the world. Others address issues of personal development and growth in teachers and learning communities, as well as issues around educators' identities. All push at the interconnections between personal beliefs and practices and the social practice of education.

The first four chapters focus on *'working with and for students and schools'*. They raise important issues of values and identity in relation to the practice of educators and illustrate these with rich examples from lived experience. Zeni's chapter maps the territory of ethics, clarifying why the personal dimension of action research demands important and different qualities in ethical practice than in other forms of research. Action researchers engage with participants more intimately than other researchers, almost always playing dual roles. Zeni exposes the resulting tensions, for example showing how an assumption that anonymity is always 'right' can lead to stealing a participant's intellectual property. The chapter ends with 'questions for ethical reflection by action researchers working in the schools' that take the issue of ethics far beyond that of addressing institutional review boards.

Holly's chapter also pushes beyond traditional understandings of academic work, conceptualizing writing not as a 'product', but as a process of learning and discovery, a way of seeing and experiencing the world, 'a way to grow'. Her argument is grounded in examples from her research into writing over nearly 30 years. Preparing the way for Part IV, she shows how writing is always a political process because in writing we are forced to 'take a view'. Thus writing becomes a form of action through research with the power to make the lives of teachers and children better.

The chapter by Dadds explores the affective dimension of action research. She begins with reflections on her personal learning from the teacher whose work was the central focus of her book, *Passionate Enquiry* – about the autobiographical factors that shape action research and the emotional and attitudinal transformation that often results. She then goes on to explore the role of both positive and negative emotions in action research, drawing on Buddhist thought to develop concepts of 'objective subjectivity' and 'loving detachment' which we can use in our lived experience as professionals and researchers.

The final chapter in the group, by Pushor and Clandinin, provides an exploration of the interconnections between research in the narrative inquiry tradition and action research. When narrative inquiry is conceptualized as an educative process resulting in actions or change, it has shared epistemological and ontological commitments with action research. The educative process of 'resonant reading' of narrative inquiries has reciprocal resonances with Holly's notion of personal growth through writing.

The second group of chapters focuses on *professional development, teacher voice and knowledge production*, in each case through the lens of a theoretical framework for exploring and understanding human relationships and educational practice. Walker begins by showing how our cultural background and life history shape our action research practice. Her chapter draws on Sen's capability theory to uncover the normative assumptions that guide human behaviour. Educational action research is about finding ways of promoting human flourishing, by uncovering the social and cultural factors that limit human choices and finding ways of circumventing them to build students' capabilities.

The chapter by McNiff and Whitehead details a method for carrying out action research according to quality criteria that ensure social accountability, but as a way 'to make sense of personal and social practices'. The chapter is organized around a series of questions to guide enquiries, providing a new way of conceptualizing the cyclical process of action research. Quality in action enquiry, they argue, is manifest in social transformation and legitimated through others' critical evaluation. Their persistence in pushing for demonstration of the connections between one's personal beliefs and values, and one's commitments to others is an important aspect to their work.

The third chapter in the group, by Ponte and Ax, argues for the importance of grounding action research in the European tradition of pedagogy as 'the science of the child's upbringing'. To the action research principles of justice, critique and professionalism they add pedagogy, suggesting that enquiries should 'start with what children have in common' rather than focusing on tailoring education to the individual child. The human science of pedagogy provides a 'conceptual framework for questioning, analyzing and acting in the pedagogical praxis', a process which they suggest is somewhat similar to the Anglo-American notion of education as a moral endeavour. In the final chapter in the group, Winter argues that the core pursuit of action research is the transformation of relationships and the self-in-relation to others. He illuminates his argument by drawing analogies and parallels with Buddhism. As well as demonstrating the strong sim-ilarities between the two in terms of their emphasis on core values, dialectical processes, reflexivity and enlightenment/emancipation, he describes some of the 'value-based practices to change behaviour' offered by Buddhism. This chapter provides a bridge between the explorations of self in the previous group and the greater emphasis on self-in-community in the final group.

The final four chapters explore personal approaches to action research in the light of psychological, transdisciplinary and philosophical theories for under-standing self in relation to others. In this sense they are oriented towards *policy and change*. Carson's chapter starts by noting that action research always involves commitment to personal and collective action, and he gives a brief his-tory of the theories of identity which have been used by action research theorists to understand the nature of commitment. Illustrating his argument through an account of an action research project to prepare students to meet the needs of the diverse cultures of contemporary Canada, he argues that psychoanalytic theory provides a powerful and practical framework to allow self-exploration of teacher identities. Above all it re-directs the attention of action researchers to identity transformation in relation *with* others, informed by knowledge of the complexi-ties in both inter-psychic and intra-psychic relationships arising from the role of the subconscious.

The chapter by Sumara and Davis explores the contributions to their own action research resulting from 20 years of using complexity theory as a heuris-tic framework. Their focus is on the collective rather than the individual; on complex systems which they conceptualize as 'systems that learn'. The chapter moves back and forth between explanatory theory and illustrations from an action research project involving teachers, students and parents coming together to discuss a novel that challenged the assumptions embedded in their cultural traditions and roles. They suggest that action research and complexity theory share three crucial features: both are action-oriented, fluid and open to elabora-tion, and inherently trans-disciplinary.

Somekh's chapter presents a personal narrative of exploring models and metaphors for shaping the identity of the self-as-research-instrument to enable agency. Her approach to theories of the self is eclectic, each theory being tried out in practice and interpreted as a form of research data. She traces shifts in her understanding of her own identity over time: from the unique self whose authen-tic voice should be nurtured and privileged; to the multiple self able to position herself strategically and politically to gain leverage in an organization; to the 'mind as action' participating in social practices that can be transformed by adopting new tools and changing contextual parameters; to the playful postmod-ern self able perhaps to 'choose not only what research methods to use but even what researcher identities to perform'.

In the fourth chapter in the group, Feldman explores the inter-relationship between action research and existentialism. Through the 'existential lens' the focus of action research shifts to an exploration of the nature of the teacher's being and personhood, and how this affects relationships with others. He explains the key existential concepts of situatedness, the emergence of self, and freedom, and argues that existentialism is a profoundly educational philosophy because 'it is a theory of human becoming'. Feldman provides a brief history of existential practices in action research, such as T-groups in the early days and self-study more recently. The chapter ends with a discussion of the key features of existential action research: its focus on one's own being in relation to others; growth in one's sense of responsibility for the exercise of freedom; and freedom to act responsibly and care for self and others.

The chapters in Part III extend and enrich the theories and methodologies presented in Part I, opening up new possibilities for action research practice. They encompass the professional and the political within an over-arching personal orientation. In many ways, they invoke the inherent interconnections with values that are both part of personal growth, and of growth and change in relation to particular social agendas. In this way, they infuse complexity to the personal dimension of action research and lead toward the political dimension.

20

Ethics and the 'Personal' in Action Research

Jane Zeni

Action research is intrinsically engaged. Those conducting action research are insiders and stakeholders – working alone or in partnership with outside consultants – and it should be their questions that drive the inquiry. As action research has assumed a larger role in education, the need for appropriate ethical guidelines has become evident. However, the personal engagement and insider stance that are central to action research have complicated the effort to develop workable standards for research ethics.

The ethical challenges specific to engaged, insider research have become clearer to me over the years as I have collaborated with teachers doing classroom inquiry and researched my own practice as a teacher educator.

Some projects I have initiated and directed. In the mid-1980s, through my work in the National Writing Project, I wrote a grant and recruited a dozen secondary teachers whose students were writing with computers. We documented what happened to the writing and the teaching process in classrooms equipped with the new tools (Zeni, 1990). Although I was an insider to the Writing Project, the data I gathered came from other teachers' classes – because at that time my own writing classes at the university did not have access to computers. This first study raised few ethical dilemmas, but when I proposed a similar grant to the St. Louis Public Schools, the questions exploded: 'What are you going to say about our teachers? If it's bad news, who will you tell? If it's good news, who will get the credit?' At the time I was shocked. Later I came to see the possible dangers and distortions of action research.

In other projects, I was hired by teacher groups or schools as a consultant. Here, the power relations were different; the grants and the leadership rested with the school people. I was not a true insider – I was not examining my own practice – but often I developed close, collaborative relationships with my research partners (Krater et al., 1994).

In still other projects (many unpublished, a few published), I too gathered data to address problems in my own classrooms or in the English Education program I directed at the University of Missouri-St. Louis. Some 'projects' involved the thin data that many teachers collect routinely: as I puzzled over the small but disturbing number of student teachers who withdrew before completing their practicum in the schools, I kept track of their ages, prior work experience, academic records, and anything else that might help me anticipate or prevent their failure. A few projects were complex and longitudinal: a colleague and I analyzed the online conversations of student teachers, leading to improvements in the personal and academic support we provided during this stressful apprenticeship (Singer and Zeni, 2004). Often my projects were fully interwoven with my teaching. For example, my English methods students felt some urgency to root out their own usage errors before they would be marking the papers of their own students. I assigned an error analysis log, offering people with substantial usage problems a chance to earn course credit by addressing them; for my part, I analyzed the logs and reported the results at our last class meeting. Student feedback suggested that many came to see error correction more as academic inquiry than as punishment.

Despite my efforts to behave in a fair and respectful way, and to guide my research students accordingly, ethical dilemmas, questions, and roadblocks have emerged, usually catching me by surprise. Gradually, I realized that action research calls into question the ethical norms that guide the academic modes of inquiry, both quantitative and qualitative. The norms of quantitative research have defined the ethical researcher as an outsider; any personal involvement with the people or engagement with the events in a research setting is considered bias. The norms of qualitative research have allowed for the ethical researcher who is involved with participants, and who affects and is affected by events in the research setting; however, those relationships are limited, kept in check by anonymity and informed consent.

Neither quantitative nor qualitative guidelines offer a good fit for action research. It is no surprise, therefore, that research textbooks and mentors often cite universal principles that hamstring the action researcher, while ignoring real ethical dangers to students, colleagues, or others. I have found that analyzing exemplary cases (Mitchell, 2004; Smith, 1990) is a better route to understanding the ethics of the local, situated dilemmas of action research.

NEGOTIATING DUAL ROLES

Rather than focusing on methods or paradigms, I would define action research by the 'insider' stance: The researcher also plays another professional role in the research setting, with relationships and responsibilities that continue after a specific project ends. Each role – researcher and practitioner – brings its own ethical standards, and untangling these roles can present knotty challenges. I will illustrate with two cases.

Wanda Clay's dissertation was a self-study of her work as an instructional coordinator in an urban school. She reflected in her journal after her coaching sessions, triangulated by asking teachers to write the minutes of team meetings, and questioned her own actions – was she trying to improve instruction or enhance her data? Some of her journal entries even represented her thoughts as a dialogue between her Researcher self ('R') and her Practitioner self ('P'). In an essay revisiting this experience, Clay (2001) writes, 'Facing these dilemmas in my role as practitioner-researcher, I sometimes felt torn in two.' The following research memo captures the duality:

R: OK, so the second year is over. How do you feel?
P: I don't know, kinda funny. I know that the changes we made had a profound impact on the people who left, yet I don't feel responsible in the same way I did last year.
R: How so?
P: Well, last year I wanted small miracles. I mean I thought everyone would buy into the changes, and our context would be transformed. But this year I knew we were engaged in a struggle. I mean people were fighting change left and right, and I accepted that I was seen as the maker of the change.
R: And you are okay with that? ....
P: I have to accept that it isn't easy and there will be casualties of reform. My so-called power doesn't afford me the opportunity to work miracles. (p. 33)

Now consider the dual role when the 'insider' is a parent. Although many educators have written case studies of their own children's learning, to untangle one's ethical requirements as parent and as researcher may prove daunting. Puchner and Smith (2006) had discussed their own efforts to raise a son and a grandson, each with an ADD diagnosis. Accustomed in their professional work to writing careful documentation, each kept a log and noted how their actions affected the child. Soon, however, they were asking, 'How much does this child understand of what we're doing?' and 'How is my increased focus on this child going to affect others in the family?' Listening to their concerns in our Action Research Collaborative study group, I suddenly pictured a dilemma from Gilbert and Sullivan. After checking the musical reference, I messaged them:

> Your 'consent' dilemma reminds me of the Lord Chancellor in *Iolanthe*, who is legally responsible for all the 'Wards of Court.' He spends much of his time 'giving agreeable girls away' to various young suitors, but eventually finds himself more than a little attracted to a ward named Phyllis. Here he contemplates his predicament (hypothetically, of course, in the third person) –
>
> Can he give his own consent to his own marriage with his own Ward? Can he marry his own Ward without his own consent! And if he marries his own Ward without his own consent, can he commit himself for contempt of his own Court? And if he commit himself for contempt of his own Court, can he appear by counsel before himself, to move for arrest of his own judgment! Ah, my Lords, it is indeed painful to have to sit upon a wool-sack which is stuffed with such thorns as these! (*Iolanthe*, Act I)

After analyzing their own predicament, Puchner and Smith chose to set aside their research, at least temporarily. They could not foresee the potential impact of those 'thorns' on their families. In this ethical dilemma, the parent or grandparent role took precedence over that of researcher.

IN SEARCH OF AN ETHICAL BASIS
FOR ACTION RESEARCH

Even in less dramatic stories, the action research stance violates conventional norms. While pursuing an inquiry, the researcher usually exercises some power over other participants – whether through grades, allowance, diagnoses, or performance reports. Decisions about ethical principles such as anonymity or informed consent, if made in advance, must often be revised or renegotiated with other stakeholders in response to unforeseeable events.

This is our reality, but I would argue that the power and interpersonal complexity of the 'insider' role do not necessarily create an ethical threat. In fact, the bonds of caring, responsibility, and social commitment that engage action researchers with other stakeholders may be the most appropriate basis of ethical decision-making.

The rest of this chapter will explore ethical issues by foregrounding Noffke's (1997) 'personal' dimension and building on the engaged insider stance. I will frame my discussion with the themes of *responsibility/accountability*, *action/social justice*, and *caring/respect*. These themes will intertwine as I reflect on some ethical decisions and dilemmas in my own experience with action research.

RESPONSIBILITY AND ACCOUNTABILITY

The ethical standard of *responsibility* – the special trust that teachers or other professionals must exercise while investigating issues in their own schools – most clearly distinguishes action research from traditional modes. In 1987, high school teachers Marian Mohr and Marion MacLean published *Working Together: A Guide for Teacher-Researchers*, based on a decade of experience in the Northern Virginia Writing Project. In *Teacher-Researchers at Work*, they went on to articulate an ethic of research as an integral part of good teaching:

> [Teacher research] is enmeshed in the context of the classroom. It is designed so as not to expose students to harm in any way but rather to include them as participants in the process through which they and their teacher learn about learning. It offers students the model of an adult learner at work. (MacLean and Mohr, 1999: x–xi)

Lincoln and Denzin propose 'professional ethics' for the current 'moment.' Although their own work is not action research, they echo MacLean and Mohr: researchers should focus on their 'responsibility and obligation to participants, to respondents, to consumers of research, and to themselves as qualitative field-workers' (2000: 1117–18).

In classroom action research, the daily activities of teaching assume a dual role, as research activities. Several good handbooks (MacLean and Mohr, 1999; Hubbard and Power, 1999) illustrate this sleight-of-hand. Meetings with individual students become informal interviews; discussion circles and projects become focus groups; the full range of student work becomes data as well. One ethical question is central: 'Do the research methods support or interfere with my primary professional role?' (I recall the brilliant middle-school math teacher who became so enamored with writing field notes that he sat at his computer during class, observing and writing rather than engaging with students.) The challenge in planning action research is to make the methods transparent. When successful, the inquiry involves students as co-researchers and contributes both to student and to teacher learning.

Although *responsibility* is now widely cited as an ethical standard, many teacher researchers, universities, schools, and grant agencies still regard anonymity as the norm for student participants in classroom inquiry. However, if the research is shared with a wider audience through conferences or journals, anonymity is almost impossible. The child described in a good case study will be recognized by others from the community; most action research is written, not in the traditionally abstruse style of scholarship, but in a literary or journalistic voice that really might be read by parents or friends.

Ironically, when researchers discuss anonymity with their students, from primary school through university, most say they prefer their real names. (When told they must have pseudonyms, many children ask to create their own fanciful names, thereby reclaiming their stories.) As van den Berg comments:

> The qualitative research community thus seems basically to have decided that the subjects of its enterprises need protecting, and that there are certain ways in which this is to be done (which apparently seldom, if ever, involve consulting the researched).... The notion of protection, then, presupposes an unequal relationship between the researcher and the people she or he claims to be researching *with* .... (2001: 84–5)

A further irony is that anonymity may violate another ethical principle: credit for intellectual property (Anderson, 1998). Teachers admonish their students to cite sources accurately and to credit the ideas of others. Meanwhile, research manuals admonish those teachers to use a pseudonym when quoting from their students. Suppose the student work cited is a prize-winning poem? Suppose the 'student' is an adult in college? At what point does a student deserve credit more than protection?

To resolve such dilemmas, van den Berg (2001) proposes the principle of *accountability*. If action research draws on personal and professional relationships, open communication with participants should be the norm unless there is real evidence of risk. Consulting other stakeholders is especially important as the teacher tries to draw interpretations. To study his own program at a South African university, van den Berg referred draft reports back to his students for comments, corrections, or questions. And when their views differ? Instead of uncritically accepting the students' version of the story, or stubbornly maintaining the original, he wove multiple voices and interpretations into the text. Such a narrative, I believe, can better represent the lived experiences of participants.

ACTION AND SOCIAL JUSTICE

Action should be an ethical standard for action research, reminding the professional to risk naming the big social issues and not to ignore injustices simply because they have always existed. I see the emphasis on 'action' as a broad difference between the British tradition (including Australia and South Africa) and that of North America. Teacher research in the United States tends to minimize the political edge, the concern with large social issues. Some fine analyses in the American tradition (Cochran-Smith and Lytle, 1993; Zeichner, 2001) do incorporate the political with the personal and the professional. However, the popularized U.S. version of teacher research can be merely a small-scale trial of a new instructional method with no social context. In my own work I prefer the term 'action research' to signal my engagement with building a just, caring community inside and outside the classroom.

I see 'engaged action' as broader than radical political activity. (I began my teaching career in an alternative school of the 1960s, where we took field trips to participate in Civil Rights and peace marches.) Instead, I believe that the 'personal' is essential to engaged 'action.' To tease out some of the ethical issues, I will discuss my experience with an action research team in Webster Groves, Missouri.

For seven years (1987–1994), these secondary English teachers grappled with the big question, 'Why are the African American students in our community still underperforming in comparison with their White classmates?' (The 'achievement gap' was not yet a catchphrase.) Team leader Joan Krater, an eighth grade teacher, recalls: 'We wanted to believe that we educated ... all our students equally – but each year's writing assessment told a different story.' Everyone saw 'the dismal performance of too many African-American students in our integrated suburban schools,' but nobody took action. 'The problem lurks in the corners of department meetings and backyard barbecues. Teachers speak of it in whispers or shake their heads and change the subject' (quoted in Krater et al., 1994: 15–16). Minnie Phillips, team member and high school teacher, adds:

> College professors point to secondary teachers, secondary teachers point to elementary teachers, and elementary teachers to parents. Our hands are tied, we insist, by administrative policies or state and federal mandates. Television, of course, remains the universal culprit, as are on occasion the state of youth, the state of the economy and the state of the world in general. (quoted in Krater et al., 1994: 17–18)

Finally a new teacher – a year out of college and not yet schooled in the 'blame game' – voiced the question. As the faculty discussed the assessment results,

Theresa Wojak raised her hand. 'Why do Black writers score lower than Whites?' Krater and Wojak wrote a small Missouri Incentive grant to support a teacher study group, and a dozen colleagues joined them.

That summer, the predominantly White team read extensively in the emerging scholarship by African-American educators. They also analyzed 500 essays by Black and by White student writers, seeking to understand the error patterns as well as the strengths teachers might build on. During the school year, they tried out some recommended approaches that seemed to fit the issues they had identified in student writing. To keep the documentation manageable, I suggested each teacher focus on just a few of their African-American students as case studies. Teachers agreed to keep research logs, collect writing samples, and attend a monthly team meeting.

As I consider this project's origins, the 'inside/outside' design, and our action research process, I am especially proud of how we handled the power relations. Krater was coordinator of the annual assessment as well as team leader. During the first two years I rarely attended the monthly meetings; the teachers had hired me to advise them on research design, synthesize their logs, and meet with them for a week in June as they planned their next steps. Gradually, seeing the energy and commitment of the teachers and the progress of their students, I was drawn more fully into the project. In year 3 I asked to be considered a team member. In year 4, Joan Krater suggested that we write a book together. *Mirror Images: Teaching Writing in Black and White* was published by Heinemann in 1994.

Writing a 500-page book with 15 contributing researchers was the most challenging scholarly task I had undertaken. Chapters were planned in after-school meetings, circulated for comments, and revised repeatedly. (As the only team member with a prior publication record, I wondered about dominating the group. My worries ended when my draft of Chapter 2 was rejected by middle-school teacher Cathy Beck, who then spent an hour on the phone talking me through a – much improved – revision.) Negotiating authorship meant defining each person's stake in the project (including mine as an assistant professor nearing a tenure review). Eventually, we created a title page listing 15 authors in three tiers. Joan Krater, Nancy Cason (her successor as team leader), and I were named as primary authors; we actually wrote the text. Cathy Beck, Minnie Phillips, and Sandra Tabscott were reviewing authors; they commented on every chapter and proposed revisions. Nine contributing researchers are also listed; they shared their stories, field notes, and annual reports along with insights expressed orally in team meetings.

Just as the book seemed complete, some unexpected feedback caused me to rethink my view of action research. The Heinemann reviewer asked why, in 500 pages, *Mirror Images* told readers so little about the teachers. There were wonderful stories about kids, but where were the stories showing what their teachers brought into the project and what they learned? At first we were shocked and defensive. The book quoted extensively from team members' logs and research journals; it was full of teacher voices. But no, there was nothing about our personal histories, our experience (or lack of it) with African-American people, our history of activism (or apathy). After a disgruntled team meeting, eight of us agreed to draft a personal, cultural story. Writing these pieces brought new understandings – along with tears and laughter – among teachers who had worked closely together for years.

Since then, I have guided many people through their initial experiences with action research, and I always incorporate autobiographical writing. Although reflexivity is an accepted principle in qualitative inquiry, researchers need to tell their readers more than their actions and expectations. Nobody is culturally neutral; I believe that researchers should not only report but also discuss the implications of their own race, class, and gender whenever they apply such categories to others. Telling one's own story in a research group reveals many unstated cultural assumptions. From the shared recognition may come the individual commitment to take action.

Noffke acknowledges the 'limited ways in which issues of social justice have been addressed' in practitioner studies that 'highlight subjectivity' (1997: 329–30). The 'cultural,' however, can be the link between the 'personal' and 'political' dimensions, since personal growth does not occur in a vacuum and individual identity is shaped by social experience. I see personal and cultural self-awareness as central – both epistemologically and ethically – to action research that addresses social issues inside and outside the classroom.

CARING AND RESPECT

What I learned through *Mirror Images* has shaped the way I embarked on later projects. The team believed the most powerful principle identified in their research with African-American students was 'personalizing' their teaching. While studying my own practice as a university teacher educator, I have tried to build an environment that is emotionally safe as well as just.

Meyer et al. (2006) propose *caring* as an ethical standard for action research. Although rarely cited in guidelines for research in education and labeled an ethical risk in traditional outsider research, an ethic of *caring* tells me that doing action research should support rather than compromise our relationships.

To illustrate, I recall my struggle to communicate to future teachers my values of cultural diversity and social justice. My direct (preachy?) style had alienated my more conservative students and bored the others. So I asked my Methods class to write 'The Culture I Will Bring to My Classroom,' modeled on the personal writings in *Mirror Images*. The next term, as student teachers, they would relate these essays to their own classrooms. Where and how were they already cultural insiders in this setting? Where and how would they need to stretch their cultural boundaries in order to connect with this student population? I was thrilled by the response to the assignment. Students were engaged in sharing their personal stories and polishing their essays, often choosing them for the end-of-program portfolio. Unlike previous groups, they initiated discussions of culture in my class.

But was my action helping them connect with their own students as culturally responsive teachers (Gay, 2000)? My colleague Nancy Robb Singer and I had developed a student teaching listserv seminar to allow for communication between our monthly on-campus meetings. We became intrigued with the talk we were seeing online – a deeper, more personal, more intellectually challenging conversation than we typically heard in class (Singer and Zeni, 2004). Our norms for the listserv emphasized student voice and choice. Although the faculty took part, we did not set questions and we tried to keep a minimal presence. If we sat on our hands, another student teacher would usually respond to a colleague's issue, and we decided that the experience of collaborating in a professional group was more valuable than the wisdom we might impart.

Watching the listserv, Singer recognized more fully the new teachers' vulnerability, the roller-coaster of emotions. Early in the semester, Andrea wrote:

> I thought I would be scared out of my wits at this point, wanting to hide in a corner. But now that has passed .... I am ready to teach – I feel like a dog straining on a tether. I want those students. I want to teach....

Six weeks later, Andrea's emotional tone had changed:

> I am not really sure how things are going. I still feel kind of lost. I thought I would have a better sense of balance by now .... I think I still want to be a teacher, and I know that I am learning incredible amounts, but .... I'm tired of feeling like I am screwing up. I am too much of a perfectionist to enjoy watching myself make mistakes when people with real lives and futures are at stake.
>
> Hangin' On,
>
> Andrea (quoted in Singer and Zeni, 2004: 42–3)

In another month, Andrea found her balance. She finished the semester, signed a contract, and began her teaching career. Like most of her peers, she told us the listserv had offered valuable support that was there when she needed it.

In each cohort, one student teacher seemed to adopt the role of nurturer, responding quickly with comfort and affirmation as well as advice. (Having determined not to be the source of all wisdom, we discovered that we also did not have to be the source of all caring.) During certain points in the semester, we noticed a pattern of intense listserv activity. Singer restructured the seminar at those points, adding face-to-face meetings and tailoring assignments to the hot issues (such as classroom management) that were threatening new teachers' survival.

We tried in our seminar to build mutual trust, modeling the safe-yet-challenging climate of a teacher study group. We talked openly about our methods, our goals, and our interpretations.

> There are ethical risks in exploring the personal writing of a vulnerable population, so we keep the 'teaching' goal at the center of our 'research'... Our student teachers know that we are analyzing their messages, and they know why.... We believe it is an ethical responsibility in teacher action research to refer our tentative findings to the community about which we are writing. (Singer and Zeni, 2004: 34)

We handed out drafts of our paper, asked students for feedback, and credited their insights in our text. Later, we circulated revisions as email attachments.

I like the terms 'pastoral' or 'covenant' relationships to describe the personally engaged teaching and collaborative research that has been my goal. I cringe when teachers describe their students as subjects in an experiment: 'I am doing action research on Bobby.' In this statement, power and agency reside in the teacher; there is no hint of a personal relationship, of mutual learning, of respect; students have been transformed into data.

Conversely, in a case reported by Cohn and Kirkpatrick (2001), experienced high school teachers were transformed into data by student observers. In their school–university partnership, student teachers collaborated with their mentors in teaching and in action research. An ethical crisis arose when a few students gave presentations at a research conference painting their mentors in an unflattering light. After the embarrassment and soul searching, the team leaders' solution was quite simple: to their action research criteria they added *respect* – 'The tone of the report is professionally respectful.... It does not make its point by criticizing or negatively presenting one's colleagues. The focus of the report is a study of the actions of the researcher, not the actions of one's colleagues' (p. 143).

Respect as an ethical standard seems related both to *caring* and to *accountability*. I agree that when conducting, sharing and publishing classroom inquiries, a research partner should minimize the risk to other professionals' reputations. Kemmis (2006) argues instead for the public's right to know what happens in the classroom, for 'telling unwelcome truths' in order to transform practice. Certainly if an observer finds abuse or discrimination or other illegal behavior, the responsibility is to report. Otherwise, however, I view respect and confidentiality as paramount when I am a guest in someone else's professional world. Fishman and McCarthy (2000) show readers the back-story, the interweaving of caring and respect, truth and transformation in their research partnership.

A PERSONAL ETHIC FOR ACTION RESEARCH

Drawing together the three themes in this chapter, I will offer some questions for ethical reflection by action researchers working in the schools.

Responsibility and Accountability

A teacher researcher is first of all a teacher – responsible to students, administrators, parents, and the community (Mohr, 2001).

> Who else among the stakeholders has an interest in my question?
> To whom am I accountable professionally?
> How will I refer my interpretations back for comment so that my work has more than my own perspective?

Whose permission should I seek to pursue this inquiry?

If I publish or present my work, should I protect others with pseudonyms OR credit them by name?

Action and Social Justice

While focusing on a micro-society such as a single classroom, action researchers should consider forces in the larger society that play out in school and work toward more democratic classroom communities.

Where is the 'action' in my research?

If I am trying a new teaching technique, what are its assumptions about learners, learning, and society?

Will my research aim to interpret the experience of students or others who differ from me in culture (including gender, race, class)?

How can I prepare myself to better 'read' their experience?

If I publish or present my work, can I incorporate the voices of participants whose backgrounds differ from mine?

If the report is collaborative, how should we negotiate authorship?

Caring and Respect

Action research should enhance the personal, covenant relationships that connect the researcher and other participants for their mutual benefit.

How will my research activities come across to students, parents, others? Will they feel interested, bored, honored, annoyed? (How can I find out?)

Will the research be a learning experience for others, or just for me?

Can I involve my students (colleagues, parents, others) as my co-researchers?

If I publish or present my work, who might be hurt or embarrassed? Can I justify such damage by the public's right to know?

Can the stakeholders read, understand, and critique my report? (Voice is an ethical as well as a rhetorical choice.)

What About Institutional Ethics Boards?

In most universities and in many schools, an ethics committee reviews and approves all research proposals. While the composition and authority of these boards vary across the international scene, they raise concern among action researchers because of their grounding in traditional scientific models of inquiry (Pritchard, 2002). Looking for common ground, I have served on my university's institutional review board, and also on an ethical review committee of teacher researchers in a nearby school district. Elsewhere I have described some promising approaches to such reviews (Zeni, 1998; Zeni, 2001). Here I will simply urge that action researchers not allow external reviews to constrict our thinking about insider research ethics. We should resist the temptation to seek universal, 'yes/no' protocols and keep our ethical theorizing 'close to the settings, the decisions, and the actions [we] have taken' (Smith, 1990: 272).

Today, when public money and status are again linked with large-scale impersonal research, we need action researchers to tell the human stories. We need them to insist that research to improve one's own practice is a professional responsibility, part of good teaching. We need them to show that good research can aim higher than gains in test scores, and that democratic classrooms are possible. We need them to insist that any research in the schools treat persons with caring and respect, and to demonstrate the power of personal commitment.

REFERENCES

Anderson, Paul V. (1998) 'Simple gifts: Ethical issues in the conduct of person-based composition research', *College Composition and Communication*, 49 (1): 63–89.

Clay, Wanda (2001) 'Coming to know my place', in J. Zeni (ed.), *Ethical Issues in Practitioner Research*. New York: Teachers College Press, pp. 24–34.

Cochran-Smith, Marilyn, and Lytle, Susan (1993) *Inside/Outside: Teacher Research and Knowledge*. New York: Teachers College Press.

Cohn, Marilyn M., and Kirkpatrick, Suzanne (2001) 'Negotiating two worlds: Conducting action research within a school-university partnership', in J. Zeni (ed.), *Ethical Issues in Practitioner Research*. New York: Teachers College Press. pp. 136–48.

Fishman, Stephen, and McCarthy, Lucille (2000) *Unplayed Tapes: A Personal History of Collaborative Teacher Research*. New York: Teachers College Press.

Gay, Geneva (2000) *Culturally Responsive Teaching: Theory, Research, and Practice*. New York: Teachers College Press.

Hubbard, Ruth Shagoury, and Power, Brenda Miller (1999) *Living the Questions: A Guide for Teacher-Researchers*. York, ME: Stenhouse.

Kemmis, Stephen (2006) 'Participatory action research and the public sphere', *Educational Action Research*, 14 (4): 459–76.

Krater Joan, Zeni Jane, Cason Nancy, and Webster Groves Action Research Team (1994). *Mirror Images: Teaching Writing in Black and White*. Portsmouth, NH: Heinemann.

Lincoln, Yvonna S. and Denzin, Norman K. (2000) 'Epilogue: The eighth and ninth moments – Qualitative research in/and the fractured future' in N.K. Denzin and Y. Lincoln (eds.), *Handbook of Qualitative Research*, 2nd edn. Thousand Oaks, CA: Sage, pp. 1115–18.

MacLean, Marion, and Mohr, Marian (1999) *Teacher-Researchers at Work*. Berkeley, CA: National Writing Project.

Meyer, Julienne, Ashburner, Charlotte, and Holman, Cheryl (2006) 'Becoming connected, being caring', *Educational Action Research*, 14 (4): 477–96.

Mitchell, Ian J. (2004) 'Identifying ethical issues in self study proposals', in J.J. Loughran, M.L. Hamilton, V.K. LaBosky, and T.L. Russell (eds.), *International Handbook of Self Study of Teaching and Teacher Education Practices*. Dordrecht: Kluwer.

Mohr, Marian M. (2001) 'Drafting ethical guidelines for teacher research in schools', in J. Zeni (ed.), *Ethical Issue in Practitioner Research*. New York: Teachers College Press, pp. 3–12.

Mohr, Marian, and MacLean, Marion (1987) *Working Together: A Guide for Teacher-Researchers*. Urbana, IL: National Council of Teachers of English.

Noffke, Susan (1997) 'Personal, professional, and political dimensions of action research', in M. Apple (ed.), *Review of Research in Education,* 2: 305–43.

Pritchard, Ivor (2002) 'Travelers and trolls: Practitioner research and institutional review boards', *Educational Researcher,* 31 (3): 3–13.

Puchner, Laurel, and Smith, Louis M. (2006) 'The ethics of researching those who are close to you: The case of the abandoned ADD project'. Paper presented at the September 2006 meeting of the Action Research Collaborative, St. Louis.

Singer, Nancy Robb, and Zeni, Jane (2004) 'Building bridges: Creating an online conversation community for preservice teachers', *English Education,* 37 (1): 30–49.

Smith, Louis M. (1990) 'Ethics, field studies, and the paradigm crisis', in E. Guba (ed.), *The Paradigm Dialog.* Thousand Oaks, CA: Sage, pp. 139–57.

van den Berg, Owen (2001) 'The ethics of accountability in action research', in J. Zeni (ed.), *Ethical Issues in Practitioner Research.* New York: Teachers College Press, pp. 83–91.

Zeichner, Kenneth (2001) 'Educational action research', in P. Reason and H. Bradbury (eds.), *Handbook of Action Research.* Thousand Oaks, CA: Sage, pp. 273–83.

Zeni, Jane (1990) *WritingLands: Composing with Old and New Writing Tools.* Urbana, IL: National Council of Teachers of English.

Zeni, Jane (1998) 'A guide to ethical issues and action research', *Educational Action Research,* 6 (1): 9–19.

Zeni, Jane (ed.) (2001) *Ethical Issues in Practitioner Research.* New York: Teachers College Press.

21

Writing to Learn: A Process for the Curious

Mary Louise Holly

The idea of the search comes to me ...

What is the nature of the search? you ask.

Really, it is very simple, at least for a fellow like me; So simple that it is easily overlooked.

The search is what anyone would undertake if he were not sunk in the everydayness of his own life. This morning, for example, I felt as if I had come to myself on a strange island. And what does such a castaway do? Why, he pokes around the neighborhood and he doesn't miss a trick.

To become aware of the possibility of the search is to be onto something. Not to be onto something is to be in despair.

(Walker Percy, 1961, 112–13)

When I first began using writing as a tool for inquiry, it was in 1969 in a second grade classroom where children were definitely onto *the search*. We wrote stories and documented their experiences in science. Together we reconstructed stories of exploring the old mill on the edge of the schoolyard; of pet day, when John Coffman brought his (large) spotted cow to school. One day Jonathan and Michael found a small reddish-brown field mouse in a science beaker and made a home in the recently dead fish's bowl with borrowed chips from the hamster's flat. We documented growth of plants and visits by the fire chief and policemen. This same writing process later found its way into the college classroom where students in child development classes documented their interactions and study with children in laundromats, libraries, green spaces, and living rooms.

The first research project where I used writing as a tool for inquiry began in 1980 in a study entitled *Teacher Reflections on Classroom Life: An Empirical Base for Professional Development* (1983). The purpose of this phenomenological study was to find out from seven classroom teachers their perceptions: How *do* teachers grow and learn? What do they perceive as supporting their professional development and what do they perceive as constraining it? New questions evolved over time. What happens when teachers use diaries to reflect on their teaching? What happens to teachers as they together reflect on their work?

What started out as diaries for the researcher to look into classrooms from the teacher's perspective, became notebooks that the teachers returned to for their own purposes. These we later described as journals (Holly, 1989).

A more recent action research (AR) project – *Igniting streams of learning in science* (2008) – involves high school students, their teachers, near-peer mentors (undergraduate students), graduate students, faculty, field scientists, and environmental agency staff in science education.

What happens to students, teachers, and others when they are active participants in an intense field-based science program that evolves with them and their learning communities? What happens to individuals and what happens to the learning communities over a 12-day immersion in wetlands science? What happens when students take responsibility for creating curricula and environments for learning in their schools and communities?

In each of these stories – life in the early childhood classroom (1969), the college classroom (late 1970s), in public school classrooms (early 1980s), in field-based environmental science (2008), the spirit of inquiry was *in* the action of the people involved; learning with others is also key to the search and determines to a large extent what can be learned and created.

The focus of this chapter is on writing as a process *for* inquiry, and, as a process *of* inquiry in AR. First we'll investigate the neighborhood as it has evolved between the 1969 and 2008 stories. In writing this chapter, I used writing to explore how my ideas about writing have evolved, and what these stories might have in common including their theoretical roots.

Some of the lessons learned are presented here in the form of a framework for writing as a critical component of inquiry. The chapter concludes with a few speculations as to why writing and stories are important to AR.

POKING AROUND THE NEIGHBORHOOD

Much has happened over the last four decades to give inquiry a more central role in education. With the growth of AR, and our understanding of how people learn, the rise of neuroscience with its 'decades of the brain,' and an explosion of technology, there have been many improvements for those engaged in the scholarship of learning and teaching. Along with these improvements have come unintended consequences, or 'exaptations' (Gould, 1991) and 'axemaker's gifts' (Burke and Ornstein, 1995). In coining the term exaptations, Stephen Jay Gould referred to adaptations that went beyond initial purposes. Birds, for example, likely evolved feathers for warmth, not for flight. The first 'wing attempt' may have arisen as birds hopped from branch to branch looking for food.

Gradually their appendages evolved into wings. Writing as a tool has evolved its own wings, at least for the curious. The axemakers' gift refers to innovations that make life better (an alphabet, philosophy, microscope, the world-wide-web, journal writing) but bring with them long-term and unintended consequences that have the power to change minds and environments.

The evolution of 'the teacher as researcher' (Stenhouse, 1975) is slowly becoming a condition of educational practice. Journal writing, while relatively little used in the 1970s and 1980s, has increased in use to such an extent that many educators point to widespread abuse (O'Hanlon, 2006) – an axemaker's gift.

What are some of my 'learnings' (Pierre, 2003) about writing and from where did they come? Early on they came from young children, from carefully observing children express themselves, where in interaction and engagement with people and materials children told their tales. I saw and heard stories evolve in conversations the children had with media and each other. In a film about Paul Klee (*Child of Creation*), he marveled at how a child's picture came into being with one line suggesting another. The child didn't set out knowing where the lines might go – they developed in exploration. For young painters it wasn't long before their pictures became stories they narrated. As a wise teacher learns, one can learn a lot about children from listening.

Later in conceptualizing the *Teacher Reflections* study, I took a phenomenological approach, seeking to listen to teachers as they wrote and talked about their practice. I took to heart an excerpt from a novel given to me by Lucila Recart.

> The best way to find out things, if you come to think of it is not to ask questions at all. If you fire off a question, it is like firing off a gun; bang it goes, and everything takes flight and runs for shelter. But if you sit quite still and pretend not to be looking, all the little facts will come and peck around your feet, situations will venture forth from thickets and intentions will creep out and sun themselves on a stone; and if you are patient, you will see and understand a great deal more than a man with a gun. (Elspeth Huxley, 2000: 264)

Early in the study we realized that writing was a powerful intervention as teachers wrote about their experiences. There was a slow process of moving from writing to record to writing to inquire. Writing became a tool to 'figure things out,' even 'becoming a contract with myself.' Exaptations both! The more teachers wrote, the more they explored different topics and kinds of writing and the more comfortable they became with writing, until, 'When I found out that the only way to go was deeper – I stopped writing.' Judy wrote 'How much should we be questioning ourselves? ... all this self-evaluating stuff!' Jerry put it bluntly: 'Teaching is like breathing. You just do it.' Writing became unsettling, and writing a lot didn't necessarily clarify anything. Sometimes it made things worse. While writing was a great place to put down all those things that built up inside over the years, 'Now I had a place to tell them,' there was an unintended consequence of spinning around and around and going nowhere: 'Justine, Justine, Justine. I'd rather drink prune juice for a week than talk any more about that child.'

Memory. What do we know and how do we know it? There are two kinds of memory that we use to reconstruct experience: semantic (factual) and autobiographical (involving self and time). In both cases, our memories are reconstructions shaped by our present circumstances. '... our experiences directly shape the structure of the brain and this creates the mind that defines who we are' (Siegel and Hartzell, 2003: 22).

One of the researcher's challenges is implicit memory, memories that are present at birth and shape our experiences throughout life yet for which we have no recollection or conscious processing. Implicit memory, being outside of awareness colors our perceptions: 'emotions, behaviors, bodily sensations, perceptual interpretations, and the bias of particular non-conscious mental models may influence our present experience (both perception and behavior) without our having any realization that we are being shaped by the past' (Siegel and Hartzell, 2003: 26).

Emotion. Emotions, along with implicit memories that sometimes evoke them, can be used to our advantage when writing observations. Writing under strong feelings can be therapeutic, and more. While the limbic system sounds off in alarm or delight, it isn't an ideal time to judge what is (or will be) significant, but it offers a unique opportunity for learning once the brain's executive functioning comes back on line. Walking into my first research-related observation in a kindergarten classroom, unsure of myself as a researcher, Craig, the teacher, announced that he was so glad I had an early childhood background and couldn't I teach the children art? He handed me an apron. There I was with 32 eager children and lots of paint. My recollections of Craig, the focus of my observation, were quite different than they might have been had I not been teaching that day. *What helps teachers grow? What is teaching like for Craig?* Without planning, this experience showed me how it might feel to be the kindergarten teacher in this school.

Inside and outside perspectives. Writing offers the scholar ways to traverse personal insider and outsider perspectives in at least two ways: what happens on the inside when something changes on the outside, and what happens outside when the inside changes? One can also take insider and outsider perspectives in the classroom. Robert Kegan (1982, 1994) provides insights into what can happen developmentally when one puts distance between the doing, recording, and later revisiting. Judy, a second grade teacher, revisits her journal and finds an important absence of attention to a child:

> ... if I devoted as much time (written time) to him as I did to the other two boys – he'd be with second grade ... They're saying... that because he was LD [learning disabled] we were hoping for more tutoring time – that's why he went on. But that's only an excuse. Actually, I've been using it too because I feel as if I need something to fall back on, when what I really need is to be honest... (Holly, 1989: 35)

At first Judy uses the excuse (or it uses her). In the process of writing about the experience and returning to it later Judy moves into the observer perspective where she has options. When upset, we can *be* the upset; later with critical reflection we can *have* the upset.

LEARNING COMMUNITIES: UNIQUELY LOOKING OUT TOGETHER

Support for learning communities as incubators for stepping into the unknown comes from a diversity of adherents, from higher education (Cox, Richlin, 2004), technology (Palloff and Pratt, 1999), from communities of practice (Wenger et al., 2002), business (Surowiecki, 2005) and even biology (Seeley, 1996), to say nothing of participatory action research in this volume. Salient factors point to the aggregation of a rich diversity of ideas and the timely integration of the best ideas for practice. From the *Teacher Reflections* and *igniting streams of learning* LCs, people found it easier to write in an environment of trusted others; the students learned from each others' responses and the teachers felt empowered to look more carefully into their own practice.

In *Closely Observed Children: The Diary of a Primary Classroom* (Armstrong, 1980), researcher Michael Armstrong, kept daily diaries that 'were the heart of our research' that he shared weekly with Stephen Roland, the teacher. Over time he began to incorporate Stephen's comments into his diary. By the end of the project 'the daily notes represented less my own independent judgment than a common viewpoint established in our seemingly endless conversations' (p. 8). Conversations included another teacher, Mary Brown, who with Michael and Stephen developed the study's central argument.

WRITING AS A PROCESS OF INQUIRY

Writing is a political process. We write from a point of view, and our words have the power to transform others and ourselves, as Thomas Merten pointed out many years ago. 'Finding the right words at the right moment, quite apart from the information or communication they may convey, *is* action' (Arendt, 1958: 26, emphasis added). Some action researchers find it useful to frame writing as a flexible three-phase process. Capturing information is the *writing down* phase. Once you have secured data, next comes *writing up* the report which entails making sense of what you have *written down* and constructing an account. Although each phase is a tantalizing part of the search, most people find *writing about* the project to be the most creative part of the research.

Writing Down

Confucius dictum: A common man marvels at uncommon things; a wise man marvels at the common place.

The tongue, a boneless water balloon controlled only by squeezing, which can loosen food from a back tooth or perform the ballet that articulates words like thrilling and sixths. (Steve Pinker, 1997: 12)

> ... I recorded in them [diaries] what seemed to me on reflection to have been the most significant events of the day, together with my observations, interpretations, and speculations... particular incidents, children, pieces of work: whatever seemed to bear most directly on the character of the children's learning. Although I tried to make my notes detailed and objective, I did not seek to avoid subjective impression or judgment. (Michael Armstrong, 1980: 8)

> Man without writing cannot long retain his story in his head... without writing, the tale of the past rapidly degenerates.... (Loren Eisely, 1978: 41–2)

Writing down includes observations, field notes, analytical memos and personal thoughts and feelings, pictures, student work, any artifacts that seem relevant (see Altrichter and Holly, 2005 for a fuller treatment).

Get it down as close to 'it' as possible – in time and substance. There are many forms of writing. Take the reader – it will be you – there. Naturalist poet Mary Oliver keeps small notebooks in which she writes entries that are a foundation for her poetry and prose.

> What I write down is extremely exact in terms of phrasing and cadence... The words do not take me to the reason I made the entry, but back to the felt experience, whatever it was. This is important. I can, then, think forward again to the idea – that is, the significance of the event – rather than back upon it. It is the instant I try to catch in the notebooks, not the comment, not the thought. (Oliver, 1995: 46)

Use all your mental faculties. While the left hemisphere of the brain is concerned with the facts, the right hemisphere is more concerned with feelings and tone, with the meaning of experience.

Thick description. Since we often 'don't know what I think until I say it' saying it richly and evocatively gives us more to work with.

Commitment-attachment. Commit to capturing what you observe. The natural inclination is to see what we want to see, yet one of the most exciting parts of AR is discovering what we don't expect; putting together clues that don't add up, until ... all at once they do (and sometimes don't).

Identification/dis-identification. Jane Zeni, in this volume, presents a dialog where a teacher takes two perspectives (the researcher and the practitioner) and has a conversation with herself in her journal. *Writing down* conflicting thoughts, feelings, and multiple perspectives, is a highly useful way to converse, to document the researcher's perspectives, often leading to a richer data set and perhaps psychological integration.

Energy – emotion. The journal is the place (and space) to make friends with the sensitive, unruly, irascible, irrational, over-excitable, neuronal connections referred to as the limbic system, as well as the systems that observe more slowly and calmly. Leave no brain system behind, including those that want only to record the facts who can be quite helpful capturing details.

If the foundation of AR is making life better; 'valuation is integral to this mode of reflection' (Elliott, 2001: 28). While no one would deny the intellectual aspects of scholarship, it would be as egregious to neglect the affective; 'emotional reflection constructs knowledge aesthetically' (ibid. 29) and it can serve to keep the scholar anchored in the values that initiated the research.

Goldberg (1986) advises, go where your energy takes you: be specific, and often, strange as it might seem, don't think.

Narrate the journey. While carefully describing the context within which a study takes place, the scholar rarely focuses adequate attention on their own perspectives. This was called to my attention at a conference at the Centre for Applied Research in Education at the University of East Anglia in the late 1980s. I remember little other than a question that smacked me. After presenting my paper, Alan Marr asked: 'Where is the researcher in the story of those seven teachers?'

In the *Igniting Streams of Learning* project, we kept changing the protocols. For example, the high school students' journals started out with questions from the co-directors, then from the teachers, then from the students themselves. Someone looking at the 'data' needs to know that, especially since the richness of responses has a direct correlation to who asked the questions.

Writing Up

What you *write up* depends in part on the audience and what you have to work with, what you have *written down* and what you make of it. In *Teacher Reflections* much of the learning came from *writing up* the findings, especially case studies of the teachers. Assembling the data, and bringing it together in separate cases meant attempting to assume the teacher's perspective and also taking an outsider's perspective for 'Action reveals itself fully only to the storyteller' (Arendt, 1958: 192). Students and teachers in *Igniting Streams of Learning* found that *writing up* their projects to share with others enabled them to see their work in new ways.

Multiple perspectives. What perspectives does a researcher take? Is it the perspective of a chronicler, biographer, or historian? Or is it the perspective of a connoisseur and critic (Eisner, 2001)? Perhaps one takes the point of view of a poet or an impressionist with a more dramatic form (Van Maanen, 1988). The issues-oriented perspective of Robert Stake (1995) is especially well suited for AR as it develops the salient issues and draws on experiential data. Robert Coles, award winning author of *Children of Crisis*, is particularly facile at weaving quotations of the people studied into the text.

Assertions. Working on moving ground makes certainty less comfortable. 'In narrative thinking, interpretations of events can always be otherwise. There is a sense of tentativeness ... uncertainty, about an event's meaning' (Clandinin and Connelly, 2000: 31). Yet once a claim is made there is the opportunity for discussion. 'For assertions, we draw from understanding deep within us, understandings whose derivation may be some hidden mix of personal experience, scholarship, assertions of other researchers...' (Stake: 12).

Perspectives of those portrayed. This may be one of the most challenging parts of *writing up* an account: 'We try hard to understand how the actors, the people being studied, see things. Ultimately, the interpretations of the researcher are likely to be emphasized more than the interpretations of those people studied, but the qualitative case researcher tries to preserve the multiple realities, the different and even contradictory views of what is happening' (Stake: 12). Sharing portraits with those portrayed, as a check on the sense of what is written, on accuracy of information, and for ethical reasons is an important practice.

Portraiture. Portraiture, according to Sara Lawrence-Lightfoot, 'is a genre whose methods are shaped by empirical and aesthetic dimensions, whose descriptions are often penetrating and personal, whose goals include generous and tough scrutiny.' It involves 'a sensitive kind of work that requires the perceptivity and skill of a practiced observer and the empathy and care of a clinician' (1997: 369). The telling is not only of the portrayed '... our written pieces would reveal at least as much about their authors as they did about the school settings' (ibid).

Technology. With technology and multimodal forms of representation available, portraits and reports can be written, illustrated and narrated using rich media that were not even on the drawing board in 1982. Digital stories by researchers – and stories within stories in interactive websites and blogs – can bring accounts to life in ways that take the audience there literally and figuratively.

In *writing up* case studies of the *Igniting streams of learning* project, we are using multiple data sources, many of which are electronic. While some teachers didn't want to write case studies, four months later their attitudes had changed: 'Boy, I am glad I wrote those case studies! I can't thank you enough for the assignment.'

Coherence. There is no objective 'there' to call forth. The past is fiction, as is the future we imagine. We hold our lives together with the narratives we construct to give them meaning. Can it be different with our research? How does the account we construct hold together? What do others make of the evidence? When a learning community constructs a report there is a built-in check on coherence. 'This process of social correction of the coherence furnished by an individual is an extremely important aspect of discourse as a socially constructed rather than individually constructed phenomenon: (Linde, 1993: 17).

Writing About:

> The world isn't just the way it is. It is how we understand it, no? And in understanding something, we bring something to it, no? Doesn't that make life a story?
>
> I know what you want. You want a story that won't surprise you. That will confirm what you already know. That won't make you see higher or further or differently. You want a flat story. An immobile story. You want dry, yeastless factuality. (Yann Martel, 2001)

Once the *writing up* takes form, the real adventure begins. The storyteller can become more playful and more serious, can make different interpretations, take alternative points of view; a part, an issue, a portrait, a moment can become the focus; what was background becomes foreground. Laurel Richardson's evocative forms of telling could be explored. These include ethnographic fictional representations, poetic, ethnographic drama, narratives of the self, and mixed genres where one can draw on 'literary, artistic and scientific genres, often breaking boundaries of each of those as well' (1998: 357). With each imaginative casting of a research project, new learning is possible.

WHY STORIES ARE IMPORTANT

> The light that illuminates processes of action... reveals itself fully only to the storyteller, that is, to the backward glance of the historian, who indeed always knows better what it was all about than the participants... What the storyteller narrates must necessarily be hidden from the actor himself, at least as long as he is in the act or caught in its consequences. (Hannah Arendt, 1958: 192)

This is one reason why creating stories is important – it's how we hold our lives together. It is what we, as the storyteller, make of our lives – of our socially situated, culturally constructed, imaginationally rich, collaboratively lived lives. It is the third process, the *writing about*, that enables one to see breadth and depth in experience – and to portray this in such a way that new possibilities are created in the process.

The footprints of stories help us to see what other stories could be told. Each provides its own vantage points and possibilities.

- We say what we can't say with stories; they wiggle into our consciousness – unawares, to touch us where direct statements rarely can.
- We relate to stories on multiple levels and with different parts of our knowing and our brains.
- Stories touch our emotional life and weasel us into understanding.
- Writing stories focuses our attention – it hones our eyeballs – gets them working together and connects us to larger stories.
- When we write our research stories, our voices come through so even we can hear.

Self-awareness, development, and identity are sticky issues at best.

One, we don't really want to know ourselves.

Two, we share this complicity with others who don't really want to know us either.

Three, the 'complicitous' people around us don't want to know themselves.

Four, knowing ourselves (and others) isn't possible to begin with. *Know thyself*, while still a necessary aspiration, needs to be tempered with humility. 'Be careful what you pretend to be' said Kurt Vonnegut, 'for you are what you pretend to be.'

Concluding Thoughts

The reason we do action research is because we want to make something better; whether it's making the environment safer or providing the best possible education for all our children. The energy that drives us grows exponentially with colleagues and a recording device. The tools we have to capture the evidence have speeded up and are multiple, but the motivation is the same. To be onto something that matters and know it, writing can help. If it's all fiction, we might as well create the best of all possible worlds.

REFERENCES

Altrichter, H. and Holly, M.L. (2005) 'Research diaries', in B. Somekh and C. Lewin (eds.) *Research Methods in the Social Sciences*. Thousand Oaks, CA: Sage.

Arendt, H. (1958) *The Human Condition*. Chicago: University of Chicago Press.

Armstrong, M. (1980). *Closely Observed Children: The Diary of a Primary Classroom*. London: Writers and Readers.

Brookfield, S. (1995) *Becoming a critically reflective teacher*, San Francisco: Jossey-Bass.

Burke. J. and Ornstein, R. (1995) *The Axemaker's Gift: A Double-edged History of Human Culture*. New York: Penguin Putnam.

Clandinin, D.J. and Connelly, F.M. (2000) *Narrative Inquiry*. San Francisco: Jossey-Bass.

Coles, R. (1989) *The Call of Stories*. Boston: Atlantic Monthly Press.

Cox, M. and Richlin, L. (eds) (2004) 'Building faculty learning communitie', in *New Directions for Teaching and Learning* San Francisco: Jossey-Bass.

Dunne, J. (1993) *Back to the Rough Ground*. Notre Dame: University of Notre Dame.

Eisely, L. (1978) *The Star Thrower*. New York: Times Books.

Eisner, E. (2001) *The Educational Imagination: On the Design and Evaluation of School Programs* (3rd edn) New York: Prentice Hall.

Elliott, J. (2001) *Action Research for Educational Change*. Philadelphia PA: Open University Press.

Elliott, J. (2003) 'The struggle to redefine the relationship between knowledge and action in the academy: Some reflections on action research'. *Doctor Honoris Causa*, Universitat Autonoma de Barcelona.

Goldberg, N. (1986) *Writing Down the Bones*. Boston: Shambhala.

Gould S.J. (1991) 'Exaptations: A crucial tool for evolutionary psychology', in *Journal of Social Issues*, 47: 43–65.

Hamilton, D., Jenkins, D., King, C., MacDonald, B. and Parlett, M. (eds) (1977) *Beyond the Numbers Game: a Reader in Educational Evaluation*. London: McCutcheon.

Holly, M.L. (1983) *Teacher Reflections on Class-room Life: An Empirical Base for Professional Development*. Report to the National Institute of Education, Knowledge Use and School Improvement, Educational Research and Practice Unit.

Holly, M.L., Arhar, J. and Kasten, W. (2009) *Action Research for Teachers: Traveling the Yellow Brick Road*. Upper Saddle River, NJ: Prentice-Hall.

Holly, M.L. (1989) *Writing to Grow: Keeping a Personal-Professional Journal*. Portsmouth, NH: Heinemann.

Horton, M. and Freire, P. (1990) *We Make the Road by Walking*. Philadelphia: Temple University Press.

Huxley, E. (2000) *The Flame Trees of Thika: Memories of an African Childhood*. London: Penguin Classics.

Kegan, R. (1982) *The Evolving Self*. Cambridge, MA: Harvard University Press.

Kegan, R. (1994) *In Over Our Heads: The Mental Demands of Modern Life*. Cambridge, MA: Harvard University Press.

Linde, C. (1993) *Life Stories*. New York: Oxford University Press.

Lawrence-Lightfoot, S. (1997) *The Art and Science of Portraiture*. San Fransisco: Jossey-Bass.

Lortie, D.C. (1975) *Schoolteacher: A Sociological Study*. Chicago: University of Chicago Press.

Mallon, T. (1984) *A Book of Ones Own: People and their Diaries*. New York: Ticknor & Fields.

Martel, Y. (2001) *Life of Pi*. New York: Harcourt.

Nussbaum, M. (1986) *The Feeling of Goodness*. Cambridge: Cambridge University Press.

O'Hanlon, C. (2006) 'Personal witness, voice and representation in action research'. Paper presented at Collaborative Action Research Network 30th Anniversary Conference, Nottingham, November.

Oliver, M. (1995) *Blue Pastures*. New York: Harcourt, Brace.

Parlett, M. and Hamilton, D. (1972) 'Evaluation as illumination: A new approach to the study of innovatory programmes'. Occasional Paper of the Centre for Research in the Educational Sciences, University of Edinburgh. Mimeographed.

Palloff, R. and Pratt, K. (1999) *Building Learning Communities in Cyberspace: Effective Strategies for the Online Classroom*. San Francisco: Jossey-Bass.

Pierre, D.B.C. (2003) *Vernon God Little*. London: Faber & Faber.

Pinker, S. (1997) *How the Mind Works*. New York: W.W. Norton.

Richardson, L. (1998) 'Writing: A mode of inquiry', in N.K. Denzin and Y.S. Lincoln (eds), *Collecting and Interpreting Qualitative Materials*. Thousand Oaks, CA: Sage.

Seeley T. (1996) *The Wisdom of the Hive*. Cambridge, MA: Harvard University Press.

Schon, D. (1983) *The Reflective Practitioner: How Professionals Think in Action*. New York: Basic Books.

Siegel, D. and Hartzell, M. (2003) *Parenting From the Inside Out*. New York: Jeremy P. Tarcher/Penguin.

Stake, R. (1995) *The Art of Case Study Research*. Thousand Oaks, CA: Sage.

Stenhouse, L. (1975) *An Introduction to Curriculum Research and Development*. London: Heinemann.

Surowiecki, J. (2005) *The Wisdom of Crowds*. New York: Anchor Books.

Van Maanen, J. (1988) *Tales of the Field: On Writing Ethnography*. Chicago: University of Chicago Press.

Walker Percy (1961) *The Moviegoer*. New York: Knopf.

Wenger, E., McDermott, R. and Snyder, W. (2002) *Cultivating Communities of Practice*. Boston: Harvard Business School Publishing.

22

From Passionate Enquiry to Loving Detachment: One Researcher's Methodological Journey

Marion Dadds

PASSIONATE ENQUIRY IN ACTION RESEARCH

In the late 1980s and early 1990s, I undertook an action research project which I came to call 'Passionate Enquiry' (Dadds, 1995). This work changed, and deepened irrevocably, my understanding of the role of emotions and subjectivity in action research. It challenged profoundly an attachment to 'objectivity' and 'detachment' that I had inherited from a traditional education and from experience as a researcher in traditional research projects.

Passionate Enquiry was an exploration into the affective, lived experiences of the action researcher that lay beneath the seemingly tidy, logical lines and arrows of the classical action research cycle diagrams (e.g. Kemmis and McTaggart, 1981). When I first encountered these models in the 1980s, nothing could have seemed more straightforward as a set of guidelines directing one along a clear path from unknowingness to new action. The seeming comfortable logic was compelling, if somewhat clinical.

Yet my own action research and that of the many teachers I was supporting in higher education at the time, suggested that whole dimensions of the human experience were missing from the prevailing models and theories. As I described it at the time, 'I had a daily urge to lift the flaps and corners of the action research arrows, spirals and boxes; to take a closer look at the embroiled underworlds below the clean theoretical diagrams' (Dadds, 1995: 3).

The case study of Vicki that emerged from my project taught me lessons at a number of levels. First, and most powerfully, it showed me how crucial Vicki's autobiographically rooted drive was in identifying a significant focus for her major project. It powered her motivation. Vicki negotiated with her school colleagues to research the gendered nature of their curriculum and pedagogical practices. Here was an issue she cared about deeply enough to want to make a difference. This strong sense of caring arose from her own gendered socialization in which she experienced strong family support as an only daughter with brothers – but then suffered later discrimination as a wife and mother in the workplace. These contrasts coloured her desire as an educator to work for a more gender fair world. She accessed, and made public, these dimensions of her subjectivity through detailed autobiographical writing. This helped her to know herself within her project.

Far from distancing or eliminating it, Vicki capitalized on her historically rooted passion in a way that was crucial to the productive outcomes of her research. Her history was the affective and intellectual fuel that drove her along. But her conviction was not blind. As she studied gendered practices in her school, she developed a range of views from pupils, parents and colleagues. This enriched the evidence base and also ensured Vicki did not colour the study heavily with her own biases. Rather, in courting others' perspectives, she opened her own ways of seeing to scrutiny and change. This enhanced the subjective validity of her research (Dadds, 1995).

The second lesson from this research for me was of emotional and attitudinal transformation. In one of her projects, Vicki researched with two pupils with severe physical disabilities in her class. Vicki's attitudes towards her pupils grew in a positive and productive way as a result of what she learned through the enquiry. Her searching brought a deepening understanding of the challenges the children faced daily and the courage with which they dealt with them. The research drew her closer to the children. From the enhanced regard that evolved, she related to the children with greater respect and love. This positive change of attitude mirrored a similar change I experienced myself as I came to understand Vicki more deeply through my own case study of her work. I became more fully aware of the commitment she and other teachers brought to doing and sharing their action research in their schools. The complicated processes they worked through with children, colleagues, parents and their own family commitments were emotionally challenging. Sharing her research with the school audience added an additional highly charged emotional experience for Vicki. Yet, she struggled with, and transcended, her nervous, anxious sense of self in order for her research to have a wider impact. She took this step willingly in order to see her commitment through to new levels of action. In seeing all of this, my own attitudes changed and deepened. My heart developed greater respect for Vicki and other action researching teachers with whom I was working. My support practices changed too.

There were other emotional moments and trials for Vicki; for example, fear and panic in learning to deal with a child's fit for the first time; extreme tiredness and stress, trying to do good research in an already overcommitted life;

strained relationships with a colleague who could not validate Vicki's approach. The research process was well peppered with such emotional challenges.

FROM PASSIONATE ENQUIRY TO LOVING DETACHMENT

It was clear from Vicki's story that a range of feelings was involved in doing and using action research and that emotional transformation was both inevitable and necessary for success. In Vicki's case study, however, I did not look particularly closely at the processes involved in managing such transformations: this did not come under my microscope at the time. The later project, *Emotional intelligence in the workplace*, which I started in 2002 and which is still in progress, raised this imperative for me, clarifying the role of positive and negative emotions, how they could help the research, how they could hinder and, especially, how we might manage and use them wisely. This work added a new dimension to my understanding of subjectivity in action research. It linked, almost spontaneously, to my growing understanding and practice of Buddhism which presented a creative framework for thought and action. Buddhism also brought values of compassion and loving kindness more sharply to the fore, as well as a commitment to peaceful, non-violent forms of conflict resolution (Nhat Hahn, 1998).

Also, despite the passionate enquiry research, a belief in the validity of 'objectivity' as dispassionate and detached from self had not left me entirely and I was tentative about replacing it uncritically with a total reverence for the notion that inner subjective reality was the only truth we can have. In my mind and heart, I knew I was searching for a balanced marriage, rather than a contest, between the inner and outer. This merging came, for me, in the 'Emotional intelligence in the workplace' project. In this work, I have re-visited notions of objectivity and subjectivity, outer and inner, seeking to unite them with Buddhist ideas of 'non-attachment' (Nhat Hanh, 1998: 20/21) and 'loving kindness'. Thus blended, they offer what I am calling, *objective subjectivity.* This work has shown me how objective subjectivity can form a Buddhist-type practice which I have called *'loving detachment'* and which I explore in the rest of this chapter. I have been looking at how these blended ideas might harmonize with processes of action research that seek to bring head and heart together with validity.

Change is often a long, slow process. These two action research projects, 'Passionate Enquiry' and 'Emotional intelligence in the workplace', set some 20 years apart, have helped me to grow new ideas which have provided the key foundations on which I have built my understanding and action research practice today.

EMOTIONAL INTELLIGENCE, LOVING DETACHMENT AND ACTION RESEARCH

Emotional intelligence in the workplace is a collaborative action research project. In the first phase (2001–2004) I worked with two women colleagues,

Vanessa Champion and Heather Johnson, in a critical incident, self-study mode – a form of action research in which one's own self becomes the focus of enquiry (e.g. Dadds, 2003, also see websites[1]). Our purpose was to research, and try to improve, our emotional intelligence as we operated daily at work. We hoped that in studying lived critical incidents collectively, understanding ourselves within them, how we acted and why, that we would gradually develop a wiser basis for our daily decisions and actions with our colleagues and students.

As we drew upon others' research, literature and conceptual frameworks, to support and enrich our critical incident analysis, I found myself drawing more and more spontaneously on aspects of Buddhist psychology and philosophy. Three aspects have been particularly important.

First, as Richard Winter points out (Chapter 27, in this volume), Buddhism devotes itself to practices and beliefs that uphold a search for self-knowledge as a basis for self-transformation, in a world where personal struggles are part of everyone's lives. So, I drew on the framework of the Buddha's Four Noble Truths. The first Noble Truth acknowledges the existence of suffering in everyone's lives (The Dalai Lama, 1997). We do not have to translate this only as tragic suffering but, for the purposes of action research, can link it to experiences in which we identify discomfort, dissonance or concerns which we want to investigate and change. The second Noble Truth relates to understanding the causes of suffering by looking deeply into it and seeing it more clearly. This involves asking questions, seeking evidence, making sense in new ways, finding new 'truths'. The third Noble Truth celebrates the cessation of suffering and offers a positive belief that, through self-understanding and self-management, we can transform situations by changing ourselves within them. The fourth Noble Truth claims that we can draw enlightenment from our learning and travel more clearly a path that enables us to transcend suffering, applying new spiritual practices. We can design a more effective way of being. Together, the four Noble Truths describe a journey from a state of unknowing or ignorance, to one of learning and enlightenment, one that can improve life for oneself and those around. This is a compelling model of change and transformation that echoes the lines and arrows of the action research cycle whilst offering a deep psychology, philosophy and a set of practices for the journey.

Second, I referred my critical incident analysis to central values in Buddhism of understanding, loving kindness and compassion within the context of a belief in interconnectedness between all beings, in which there is no self separate from others. Buddhism is an ecological philosophy. It argues that we are in a state of 'interbeing' (Nhat Hanh, 1991) in which the experience of one affects the experience of the other. In this light, development of loving kindness and compassion makes individual as well as social sense for, in making experience better for oneself, one makes it better for others. In addition, Buddhism is a very practical philosophy offering many examples of meditation practices that can lead one along 'paths of enlightenment' and that can, as such lead to greater interconnectedness (Nhat Hanh, 1998).

Third, therefore, I drew on practical approaches to meditation that I found invaluable on this journey through the four Noble Truths: breathing meditation, the cultivation of an inner observing mind, and compassion meditation.

Critical Incidents as Our Data

We shared many workplace critical incidents, some of which gave rise to fairly strong negative emotions – anger, frustration, resentment, disappointment, regret, guilt, even despair. Other incidents were less severe yet still in need of emotional work. Some were short-lived; others were in a longer-term state of resolution. The incidents included disagreements, discord, conflicts, antagonism, bullying, aggression, injustice and abuse directed towards one or another of us, as we saw it. My own portfolio also included examples of occasions when I had acted negatively, unmindfully or precipitously towards others.

In sharing our data publicly, critical incidents are fictionalized for obvious ethical reasons, though we have kept to the basic dimensions and structure to present a kind of 'truth' that corresponds with the 'real' experience. The following fictionalization gives a flavour of some of the experiences we have encountered and researched.

> This incident told of a good relationship I had with a junior colleague that went badly wrong when I had, as her mentor, to give critical feedback on her failing practice. During a series of four meetings with her, her anger and hostility towards me turned progressively into behaviour that verged on bullying. She denied the validity of the feedback, blamed my mentoring style (which, to that point, she had appreciated) and also blamed a third colleague, Colin, who was involved in supporting her. My difficulties in dealing compassionately with her anger were compounded by struggles in my personal life between members of a closely knit group of which I was a member. Two members were in conflict with each other and, as I refused to 'take sides', each saw me as betraying their friendship. In this, therefore, I also became the target of abuse and aggression. These two parallel experiences, in which I felt I had become the depository into which others were projecting their negative feelings, gave rise to high levels of personal anxiety, sometimes depression, anger and a heart that seemed to turn to stone in a bid to protect myself. Was this inevitable and would I ever survive this overwhelming emotional period of my life?

Unhelpful Practice and 'Getting Stuck'

In the more severe circumstances such as this, I discovered that my responses were sometimes locking me into a most unhelpful emotional and mental strategy – what I have called the action replay response. This happened when I replayed and replayed the critical incident scenario in my mind and heart that had given rise to the negative emotions, as though that, in itself, would solve the problems 'out there'. In replaying the tape, so to speak, again and again, I was unable to do any productive emotional work that could move me forward. I was stuck, trapped inside my own strong negative responses which I re-cycled time and again. The mental formations (Nhat Hanh, 1998) that were foremost in my mind were not helping me. They sometimes gave rise to a cold and unyielding heart, sometimes to confusion, often to emotional exhaustion. More than that, I some-times re-wrote the script in my imagination as I re-played the tape, giving myself new lines in the drama that would confront the villain of my piece, express in no uncertain terms my wrath and ultimately wreak revenge. I was, to use a Buddhist metaphor, watering the negative seeds in my store consciousness – and they grew. Metaphorically, I was chasing the arsonist (Nhat Hanh, 2001: 24), who I believed had set fire to my house, rather than stopping to put out the flames. Hence, the house was in danger of being burned to the ground.

Critical incidents that gave rise to these re-plays and re-writes were few and far between and usually occurred when both my work and professional lives were simultaneously stressed. However, the whole action re-play response, when it happened, harmed me and disabled me from improving the situation for, and with, others. In the process, I was expending valuable emotional energy that was draining my resources – without producing any benefit. Interconnectedness through loving-kindness was a no go.

In the group, we came to see that we tended to operate with less emotional intelligence when we were under the most stress and, thus, at our most vulnera-ble. This, paradoxically, was when we needed to be more emotionally intelligent than ever, in order to transcend the suffering, understand the dimensions of the experience and find a productive way forward. However, at such times I was, in Buddhist terms, stuck at the first Noble Truth – the existence of suffering. Creating a 'path' to enlightenment and the fourth Noble Truth was far beyond my reach in these emotionally dead-end circumstances.

Loving Detachment as Helpful Practice

In contrast, there were many critical incident occasions when I was able to draw upon breathing meditation (Nhat Hanh, 1991) to 'cool the flames' (Nhat Hanh, 2001) and calm both mind and body, rather than leave the fire to rage. Breathing meditation, in which one attends to, and follows, the breath to slower and calmer states of being, happened sometimes during the incident but also afterwards, in my office or at home, if the scenario came back to haunt me and stir the flames. When I was out of the situation, I was able to meditate on my breathing in a more concentrated and sustained way. Thus, I touched the third Noble Truth, cessation of suffering, as I breathed my way slowly to a more tranquil state of being. Sometimes, however, the effect was temporary. Breathing meditation helped to calm negative emotions, sometimes helping me to find a 'softer' inner space but did not deepen my understanding of the problem which had arisen, since it focused only on the breath and not the critical incident. Mindful breathing some-times needed to be linked to a practice that allowed a more analytical approach in order to achieve deeper understanding of what was happening and why. It was helpful to calm the emotions but the mind needed to see the dimensions of the situation more clearly as well. Without this, the second Noble Truth of under-standing the causes of suffering – my own and others – could not be achieved.

For this, I found that two approaches, used in conjunction with each other, helped – critical friendship analysis together with observer mind in compassion meditation.

The critical friendship group – what we might see as the Buddhist equivalent of the Sangha, or practice community (Lawlor, 2002) – was invaluable. Collaborative discussion helped to identify and name aspects of the problem and offered a way into Buddhist mindfulness. Jack Kornfield suggests that 'the naming of our experience is the first step to bringing (it) to a wakeful conscious attention. Mindfully naming and acknowledging our experience allows us to investigate our life' (Kornfield, 2002: 89). The collaborative discussions that allowed this helped with the investigation and developed understanding of the potential causes of others' behaviour. More importantly, they helped in beginning to see oneself more clearly in the situation and to name the causes of one's own emotions and behaviour. Collaborative discussions helped to cultivate new aspects of self-awareness, painful though that sometimes was. In the case of the fictionalized critical incident, for example, I discovered, through collaborative analysis and searching, that I was extremely prone to defensiveness such as this as a consequence of being bullied in the workplace myself many years previously. Yet I had never named this experience to myself. The suffering the bullying caused at the time, and the defences I tried to build, were brought forward from my personal history to the events of the critical incident without my consciously knowing it. Once the personal bullying history was named, it was then clear to me where the emotional work needed to be done. I needed to override and transform defensiveness into a more productive response in such circumstances, rather than to continue to repeat the pattern embedded in this history. This transformation took a long time but was, of course, worth the effort.

On its own, the critical friendship analysis did not always lead to cessation of suffering in the most emotionally charged incidents. Whilst new understanding of others in the critical incident tempered the emotions to an extent, the discussions did not always put out the fire. Paradoxically, the flames were sometimes fanned by the telling of the stories which could easily slip into action replay mode. So, alongside critical friendship discussions, structured meditation became a more and more helpful partner.

The most helpful meditation practice combined, what I have called, observation meditation with compassion meditation (see Winter, Chapter 27, in this volume, for an account of compassion meditation). In this meditation, one's inner eye acts as a kindly observer, trying calmly to watch one's own thoughts and feelings as they arise – not becoming caught up in them, not *being* them or grasping at them but, rather, allowing them just to be there and letting them go. 'One is both the mind and the observer of the mind' (Nhat Hanh, 1991: 40). Also, there is a conscious decision from the outset to focus one's mind and heart on transformation through loving kindness. So, one focuses on the critical incident and the actors in it, watching the drama and players from a distance but now with the crucial help of an empathetic inner observer as part of the self. In this mode, the inner eye can, thus, objectify the scenario of the critical incident, observing it benignly as though it were 'out there' even though it is 'in here' as part of the mind over which one is gaining emotional control. With the help of focused breathing, one stands back, as it were, and observes one's thoughts and feelings more calmly and kindly in the imagination. This can lead to a growing awareness of one's own consciousness and mental formations: one can begin to familiarize oneself with one's mental and emotional territory and, therefore, with one's self. 'Through meditation, we're able to see clearly what's going on with our thoughts and emotions, and we can also let them go' (Chödrön, 1997: 13). As well as letting go of thoughts, there is a letting go of the negative emotions that have been blocking a constructive way forward, and this allows a better way of seeing and feeling. Hence, this meditation can be seen as a form of ***objective subjectivity***: the self steps outside of itself to watch itself and its responses to others in a detached but loving way. Object and subject inevitably become part of the same self, brought into the inner world and connected better through inner loving kindness. Some Zen masters advise smiling gently to one's thoughts during this process, seeking the softness and kindness within oneself – and directing it to one's unattached thoughts (Nhat Hanh, 2001; Kornfield, 2002). The smiling, observing mind is thus better disposed for cultivating loving kindness towards the protagonists in the critical incident play, including the self. Buddhism is quite clear about the need to be as kind to oneself as to others, for if the self does not care for the self, one is not in the strongest spiritual frame to be of use to others – 'to look after oneself is to look after both of us' (Nhat Hanh, 1991: 64).

As this approach can soften the heart whilst strengthening understanding, the scenario no longer possesses and overwhelms the self, even though it is part of the self. One can relate to one's inner drama (for that is where we play out our dramas) with a kinder heart and a clearer perception. One can achieve, what I have called, this state of ***loving detachment*** in which there is an emphasis on seeing more clearly and responding more kindly to self and others in a non-judgemental way, with Buddhist equanimity. This state allows us to acknowledge, not deny or reject, the difficult, negative thoughts and emotions that are part of us, at the same time as helping to transcend them. We accept ourselves more gracefully, warts and all, and move to better ground, having achieved valuable self-knowledge. 'We should treat our anxiety, our pain, our hatred and passion gently, respectfully,' writes Thich Nhat Hanh, 'not resisting it, but living with it, making peace with it, penetrating into its nature' (Nhat Hanh, 1991: 61/62).

In its powerfulness, this process has some of the qualities of creativity (Spender, 1946; Poincare, 1924) in that the mind can, in this meditative state, be propelled forward mysteriously into new perspectives and understanding once one stops grasping at one's thoughts and feelings to inhabit them. It is as though the deeper forces of being, which we can barely understand, are freed to do the creative work of positive reconstruction for us, once we loosen our grip. They help us to see a better way to act.

Regular practice of this form of meditation can help to develop what I see as the inner parent, an aspect of one's own mind that takes charge, gently controlling and managing one's thoughts and feelings. One becomes a good sovereign over one's own mental territory, ruling one's thoughts and feelings with more clarity, kindness and compassion (Nhat Hanh, 2003).

Keep Practising

Lest this all seems straightforward and achievable in the wink of an eye, it should be said that sometimes developing compassion and loving kindness through meditation is easier said than done. Sometimes, one struggles, seemingly interminably. There have been times when the desire to keep chasing the arsonist – and a parallel desire to catch him and give him a good piece of one's mind, or worse – have almost overcome the inner desire for cultivating a more tranquil and kind heart. Also, in a busy workplace existence, there is not always the time and space for sustained meditation, when one feels the need – nor access to the Sangha for support and an analytical context. So, constant practice-in-action is needed to become more skillful, especially when time and support are scarce. Fortunately, there is no shortage of practice opportunities: 'We don't have to go hunting.... They occur all by themselves, with clockwork regularity' (Chödrön, 1997: 12). Yet, in contrast to the action replay response, these meditation practices and loving detachment, if applied, bring rewards and can bear positive fruit. In the action replay response, one is trapped as the suffering actor in the drama and there is no kindly parenting, observer mind to help. One is alone and disabled as a result. In loving detachment mode, one benefits from cessation of suffering and is able to feel, as well as see, a path forward, one that benefits oneself and other protagonists, for in this calmer state of compassion and greater understanding, we can act more kindly and wisely. 'Serenity is the most important ingredient in being able ... to concentrate the mind. Concentration is an act of cherishing a chosen object' (Salzberg, 2002: 44).

Although these meditation practices grew out of the imperative of strong negative emotions, they also became effective in managing less stressful situations, wherever one had need of subjectively objective thinking. They are as helpful for the more straightforward everyday explorations as they are for the extremes – and practice brings benefits. In the project, we discovered that we were experiencing fewer critical incidents as time went on – and concluded that this was because we were becoming more practised in parenting our own thoughts and feelings in a range of potentially difficult situations. The world 'out there' was not necessarily changing. Rather, through practice, the world 'in here' was becoming better equipped. Nor should we despair when competence seems to evade us – as it does. This, in itself, can be a source for learning if we look deeply at it and seek the wisdom it offers. Buddhism encourages us always to start anew and to use these moments: 'The source of wisdom is whatever is happening to us right at this very instant.... If there's any possibility for enlightenment, it's right now, not at some future time ... how we relate to this mess will be sowing the seeds of how we will relate to whatever happens next' (Chödrön, 1997: 144). Our daily lives are our data base (Marshall, 2001).

REFLECTIONS

Through these two projects, 'Passionate enquiry' and 'Emotional intelligence in the workplace', I have learned, and tried to show that there are many dimensions to the subjectivity we bring to our action research. In studying our practice it is inevitable that we are a central part of the enquiry, since there is no practice independent of the practitioner. In order to research with transparency and validity, therefore, we need to acknowledge and account for our subjectivity. We also need to manage it well if our project is to bring benefit. Objectifying our subjectivity in a loving way, as though it were 'out there', can aid the investigation. Buddhist meditation can be particularly helpful, for it is not a cold, distancing objectification; it is a warm, compassionate observing, a form of loving detachment that can create positive transformation of thoughts and feelings.

One is always reticent about putting oneself in the frame, a cultural phobia, perhaps, in which foregrounding the self is considered to be 'showing off', privileging the 'I'. Yet, in self-study action research, knowing oneself is crucial. To know and change ourselves, we have to be self-aware (Goleman, 1996), to study our thoughts, actions, feelings, biographies, motivations, for if we do not know ourselves, we cannot take control, and gain sovereignty, of our minds and hearts in a way that is essential for transformation. As well as gently holding our inner world 'out there' for study, we need to bring the outer world 'inside', to familiarize ourselves with it and understand our responses. 'To the extent that we do not notice both inner and outer aspects of our passage through life, then our capacity for voluntary, deliberate, and purposeful action is commensurately diminished' (Elgin, 2002: 245). It is difficult to see how one can engage in reflective practice without this meta level of the self in which the 'I' observes and guides the 'I'. It is hard to see how it could be omitted from a self-study action research methodology, for we cannot manage what we do not know. So, we need methods for doing this. Critical friendship analysis, multiple perspective data, autobiographical writing, Buddhist meditation, as used in these two projects – these can all help.

Ken Zeichner has written of his wish to see action research making a contribution to 'building more humane and compassionate societies' (Zeichner, 1993: 203). An overtly Buddhist framework that helps to strengthen subjectivity can contribute to this aspiration since it offers a set of values that are consistent with those of action research (see Richard Winter's Chapter 27). Challenging though it is, Buddhist practice can transform heart and mind by looking deeply in order to bring new understanding. It can reach into richer, unspoken powers of our creative hearts and imagination, breathing compassion and kindness into our work, moving us to a better mental and emotional state to seek non-violent forms of conflict resolution, having first dealt with our own negativity. In these small ways, we may contribute to a more peaceful world by attaining our small moments and actions of equanimity.

We might see action research, woven into a Buddhist framework, as a form of 'spiritual revolution' (Heelas and Woodhead, 2005), in which people seek deeper human meaning in their enquiries. A more positivist objectivity in research separates people in cold detachment – a kind of research atheism devoid of the spirit of interconnectedness. Objective subjectivity and loving detachment, on the other hand, aspire to draw us closer together through research in more humane, understanding and compassionate ways. They marry head, heart and values, telling a different story of the 'out there' in a way that surely is good for the human credibility of research. They keep the spirit alive in a positivist world.

NOTE

1 http://www.ku.edu/sstep
www.bath.ac.uk/~edsajw/writings/livtheory.html
http://www.jeanmcniff.com/books.html

REFERENCES

Chödrön, P. (1997) *When Things Fall Apart: Heart Advice for Difficult Times*. Boston: Shambala.

Dadds, M. (1995) *Passionate Enquiry and School Development: A Story About Action Research*. London: Falmer.

Dadds, M. (2003) 'Dissidence, difference and diversity in action research', '*Educational Action Research*', 11(2): 265–82.

Dadds, M. (2006) 'Empathetic validity in practitioner research'. Paper presented to the annual conference of the British Educational Research Association.

Elgin, D. (2002) 'Voluntary simplicity', in A.H. Badiner, '*Mindfulness in the marketplace*', Berkeley: Parallax Press.

Goleman, D. (1996) *Emotional Intelligence,* London: Bloomsbury.

Heelas, P. and Woodhead, L. (2005) *The Spiritual Revolution: Why Religion is Giving way to Spirituality*. Oxford: Blackwell.

Lawlor, J. (ed.) (2002) *Friends on the Path*. Berkeley: Parallax Press.

Kemmis, S. and McTaggart, R. (1981) *The Action Research Planner*. Geelong: Deakin University Press.

Kornfield, J. (2002) *A Path with Heart*. London: Rider.

Marshall, J. (2001) 'Self-reflective inquiry practices' in P. Reason, and H. Bradbury (eds), *Handbook of Action Research: Participative Inquiry and Practice*. London: Sage.

Nhat Hanh, T. (1991) *The Miracle of Mindfulness*. London: Rider.

Nhat Hanh, T. (1998) *The Heart of the Buddha's Teaching*. London: Rider.

Nhat Hanh, T. (2001) *Anger: Buddhist Wisdom for Cooling the Flames*. London: Rider.

Nhat Hanh, T. (2003) *Returning to our Kingdom,* Dharma talk, 28 June, St Andrew's, available on CD, Plum Village Productions.

Poincare, H. (1924) 'Mathematical creation', in P.E. Vernon, (ed.) 1970, *Creativity*. Harmonds-worth: Penguin.

Salzberg, S. (2002) *Loving-kindness: The Revolutionary Art of Happiness*. Boston: Shambala.

Spender, S. (1946) 'The making of a poem' in P.E. Vernon, (ed.) 1970, *Creativity*. Harmonds-worth: Penguin.

The Dalai Lama (1997) *The Four Noble Truths*. London: Thorsons.

Zeichner, K. (1993) 'Personal renewal and social reconstruction', *Educational Action Research Journal*, 1 (2).

23

The Interconnections between Narrative Inquiry and Action Research

Debbie Pushor and D. Jean Clandinin

Writing a chapter on the interrelationships between narrative inquiry and action research may seem to be a contradiction for some people. Many authors (Rosiek and Atkinson, 2005; Creswell et al., 2007; Hara, 1995) cite narrative inquiry as distinct from action research and refer to them as two genres of qualitative research. Partly this contradiction about whether action research and narrative inquiry are distinct genres of research relates to the broad range of what counts as narrative inquiry. Reissman and Speedy (2007) note that '[n]arrative inquiry in the human sciences is a 20th-century development' (p. 428) and that the field 'has "realist," "modernist," "post-modern," and "constructionist" strands, and scholars disagree on origins and precise definition' (p. 428).

Clandinin and Rosiek (2007) who also note distinctions between narrative inquiry and other forms of qualitative research; see, however, 'real differences of opinion on the epistemological, ideological, and ontological commitments of narrative inquirers as well as real differences with those who do not identify as narrative inquirers' (p. 37). This provides an entry point into our (Debbie and Jean's) argument that, for some narrative inquirers, there is an interrelationship with action research, at least there is if we understand action research as research that results in action or change in the practices of individual researchers, participants, and institutional practices. In this chapter we take on the task of exploring these interconnections between narrative inquiry and action research understood from this perspective. Also, we draw on Jean's earlier theoretical conceptualizations of narrative inquiry undertaken with Michael Connelly. We then move on to exploring other views of narrative inquiry where the links with action and change are less apparent. Drawing on our own and others' studies we make explicit the changes in inquirers, in participants, and on landscapes through narrative inquiry.

AN ARGUMENT FOR SHARED EPISTEMOLOGICAL AND ONTOLOGICAL COMMITMENTS

Connelly and Clandinin (1990, 2006) observed that arguments for the development and use of narrative inquiry are inspired by a view of human experience in which humans, individually and socially, lead storied lives. We begin with Connelly and Clandinin's (2006) definition of narrative inquiry:

> People shape their daily lives by stories of who they and others are and as they interpret their past in terms of these stories. Story, in the current idiom, is a portal through which a person enters the world and by which their experience of the world is interpreted and made personally meaningful. Narrative inquiry, the study of experience as story, then, is first and foremost a way of thinking about experience. Narrative inquiry as a methodology entails a view of the phenomenon. To use narrative inquiry methodology is to adopt a particular view of experience as phenomenon under study. (p. 375)

In their definition we may, at first, see narrative inquiry as pointing toward a static, interpretive view of experience, one that would not easily align with action research. There appears, in that definition, little attention to the sense of narrative inquiry as involving a narrative understanding of experience as more than lived and told stories. Narrative inquiry also involves the retelling of stories through the relational inquiry process that may result in subsequent reliving of stories in changed practices and actions. It is in moving beyond the definition of narrative inquiry to the idea of the shared relational narrative inquiry space that the connections to action become sharper. Relationships live at the heart of narrative inquiry.

> Narrative inquiry is the study of experience, and experience, as John Dewey taught, is a matter of people in relation contextually and temporally. Participants are in relation, and we as researchers are in relation to participants. Narrative inquiry is an experience. It is people in relation studying with people in relation. (Clandinin and Connelly, 2000: 189)

Clandinin and Connelly (1998) develop these ideas as they explore the inter-relationships of narrative inquiry and educative experiences. They situate their ideas of story living and story telling as central in

> [o]ur collaborative work because we see the pursuit of these activities as directly connected with life and education. Narrative and storytelling allow us to link teachers' and children's lives with a concept of education. It is *education* that is at the core of our enterprise and not merely the telling of stories. We see living an educated life as an ongoing process. People's lives are composed over time: biographies or life stories are lived and told, retold and relived. For us education is interwoven with living and with the possibility of retelling our life stories. As we think about our own lives and the lives of teachers and children with whom we engage, we see possibilities for growth and change. As we learn to tell, to listen and to

respond to teachers' and children's stories, we imagine significant educational consequences for children and teachers in schools and for faculty members in universities through more mutual relations between schools and universities. No one, and no institution, would leave this imagined future unchanged. (pp. 246–47)

In their narrative conceptualizations of experience and education they make it clear that:

[t]he promise of storytelling in education emerges when we move beyond regarding a story as a fixed entity and engage in conversations with our stories. The mere telling of a story leaves it as a fixed entity. It is in the inquiry, in our conversations with each other, with texts, with situations, and with other stories that we can come to retelling our stories and to reliving them. (p. 251)

These ideas of story living and telling, retelling and reliving are central features in their, and our, particular view of narrative inquiry. For them, the inquiry into narrative, stories lived and told, creates spaces, gaps, which allow for change. Within their conceptualization, there are clear connections between narrative inquiry and a broad view of action research. Our (Jean and Debbie's) work picks up and builds from their conceptualization.

Not all approaches to narrative inquiry see this connection to growth and change. In the opening paragraph we noted the range of methodological strands within narrative inquiry. We use Clandinin and Connelly's (1995) metaphor of a professional knowledge landscape to describe social context or milieu. They see the landscape metaphor as allowing us 'to talk about space, place, and time ... and the possibility of being filled with diverse people, things, and events in different relationships... Because we see the professional knowledge landscape as composed of relationships among people, places, and things, we see it both as an intellectual and moral landscape' (pp. 4–5). Some people who work in narrative inquiry would see their work as descriptive or analytic and, while the findings might point toward the importance of change in person, action or 'landscape', undergoing the research in and of itself does not lead to change. For example, Atkinson (1995) sees narrative inquiry through life story interviews as helping the storyteller, listener, reader, and researcher to understand how life stories serve psychological, sociological, spiritual and/or philosophical functions. Change may not be involved. Elbaz-Luwisch (2007) makes a different, more context dependent point, as she notes that:

One of the central questions that arises when one considers the development of narrative inquiry in K-12 settings concerns the possibility of establishing narrative inquiry as part of the ongoing development work of the school and as a format for the continuing professional development of teachers. (pp. 373–4)

She notes, 'I would argue that collaborative inquiry is an important goal and ideal to be held up, but that each particular inquiry may fall short in different ways, depending on the unique situation' (p. 374). In Elbaz-Luwisch's view, while the connection between narrative inquiry and change is an ideal, context may not support such work.

Mattingly (2007), arguing from a different stance, also points toward the connection between stories, both lived and told, and change. She sees the nature of experience, including therapy, as narrative construction. Although she does not say so explicitly, we see in her work the possibility that while studying experience, including therapy, as narrative construction enables her to change her practice in more therapeutic healing ways, there is not change for the participants through the inquiry. Change occurs for the patients because of the therapy, not because of the patients' participation in the research. There could, however, be change in the landscape as these ways of understanding therapy become a more dominant aspect of how we understand experience.

In the next sections, we make explicit the ways in which narrative inquiry leads to change: change in the researchers; change in the participants; change in the institutional, social or cultural landscapes; change in the readers of the narrative inquiry.

CHANGE IN THE NARRATIVE INQUIRERS

McNiff (2007) makes explicit the links she sees between narrative inquiry and action research. For her, narrative inquiry and action research are linked as research 'that enables practitioner researchers to tell their stories of how they have taken action to improve their situations by improving their learning. They explain how reflecting on their action can lead to new learning, which can inform future learning and action' (p. 308). Drawing on Whitehead's (1989) ideas of living educational theories of practice, she notes that practitioner researchers' 'stories comprise their description and explanations of practice' (p. 308) and, through these stories, these living educational theories of practice, 'they are able to show how they hold themselves accountable for what they are doing and why they are doing it' (p. 308).

Pushor's (2001) narrative inquiry into the positioning of parents in relation to school landscapes provides an example of a practitioner researcher holding herself accountable for an alignment of her beliefs and knowledge with her lived practice. Pushor began her year-long narrative inquiry having lived an educator's story of schooling. Positioned as teacher, consultant, principal and central services supervisor, and in various places, she believed she knew school landscapes well. When her oldest son began school, her sense of knowing was disrupted as she was awakened to the apparent lack of voice and place for parents on school landscapes. Entering Gardenview School, Pushor lived alongside educators and parents both in and outside of the school – in meetings, professional development sessions, special events and day-to-day activities, sometimes a character in the stories being lived out, sometimes an audience to, and a recorder of, them. In research moments in which practices and policies in the school which positioned parents on the landscape of the school – or in the margins of it – were foregrounded, Pushor was often drawn backward in time to her own educator stories.

In the midst of her inquiry, she was called to re-imagine and retell her own stories in ways which shifted her sense of the educator she wanted to be in relation to parents. Pushor writes:

> In response to Evelyn's [the principal's] reading of my story of [my son's] first day of school, we shared stories of our experiences as principals with the first day of school. ... With pictures of [the school in which I had been principal] vivid in my mind, I shared my recollections of moving from classroom to classroom, welcoming back returning students and getting to know new students. I had to admit to Evelyn that parents were not a significant part of my recalled images. (p. 53)

While Pushor (2001) storied herself as an educator who had good relations with parents and who valued their shared conversations, she now asked herself hard questions about the absence of parents in her recalled images. She turned to Greene's (1995) conceptualization of seeing big and seeing small, of viewing human beings 'in their integrity and particularity' (p. 10) rather than 'from a detached point of view, ... from the perspective of a system' (p. 10). She asked, 'In my role as educator, who and what did I see big? Who and what did I see small?' (p. 10).

> As a teacher, I always planned extensively for that first day of school for children. ... As a principal, I always planned extensively for that first day of school for staff and for students. ... Yet, now I wondered, who plans that first day of school for parents? (p. 5)

She recognized she saw parents small; that she viewed them from a distance, as a given presence in the lives of children. In her retelling she awakened to the fact she did not see or attend to parents in their integrity and particularity in the same way in which she saw and attended to children and staff. As she retold her stories, she saw possibilities for reliving these stories in new ways in the future. She began to attend to many aspects of the taken-for-grantedness of school landscapes and of her work on these landscapes: the welcoming of parents and families and the hospitality extended them; the assumptions underlying parent involvement practices; and the implications of policies around such things as homework. She retold her experiences of these policies and practices in new ways, ways in which she saw parents big – as integral to the life of the school, as on the school landscape rather than in the margins of it.

Her retold stories, stories in which she re-imagined her experiences as an educator in relation to parents, began to be relived by her work as a teacher educator. In graduate and undergraduate courses, Pushor includes content related to working with parents. She and teacher candidates engage in conversation about their knowledge and beliefs regarding parents and how their knowledge and beliefs may be lived out in their practice. In this reliving, she foregrounds ways to work alongside parents and families and to honor parents' knowledge in program decisions as an integral consideration in what teachers do.

Engaged in narrative inquiries with epistemological and ontological commitments shared with action research, researchers often experience shifts in their stories of themselves as told and lived in their practices, shifts which create changes in themselves as researchers (Murray Orr, 2005; Pearce, 2005; Steeves, 2000) and changes in their 'claim to knowledge.' 'A claim to knowledge is the term used for when we say we have learned something, or now believe something to be the case, or when we reconfigure existing knowledge to create new knowledge' (McNiff and Whitehead, 2005: 2). Through living and telling, retelling and reliving stories of parents and parent stories in her narrative inquiry, Pushor's knowledge of parents and parents' knowledge on school landscapes was reconfigured, and extended and deepened. As Dewey (1938) states, 'Every experience,' and we would add the study of that experience, 'is a moving force. Its value can be judged only on the ground of what it moves toward and into' (p. 38). Pushor's experience moved her toward, and into, a restorying of her identity as an educator with and alongside parents and into reliving her knowledge as a teacher educator in ways educative to herself and others.

CHANGE IN PARTICIPANTS AND NARRATIVE INQUIRERS

Holding central Dewey's (1938) conception of experience as 'characterized by continuous interaction of human thought with our personal, social, and material environment' (Clandinin and Rosiek, 2007: 39), we see rich possibilities for shifts and changes in participants' identities, and in their knowledge and practices, as a result of their engagement in narrative inquiry. The inquiry 'generates a new relation between a human being and her environment – her life, community, world' (p. 39). Nelson (2003) studied the experiences of five Canadian teachers, including herself, as they participated in a professional development program with Kenyan teachers. We see in Nelson's narrative inquiry, as in action research, a starting place situated in teachers' experience, and in their stories of experience. When we return to those experiences at the close of her inquiry, we see a retelling of both participants' and researchers' experiences in the present which reflects shifts and changes in their identities and in their subsequent reliving of their experiences as they move into the future in new relation with the world.

Rather than focus on the 'other' as many suggested, Nelson focused on the experiences of the Canadian teachers and narratively inquired into their experiences in Kenya, experiences of what she calls 'the borderlands', to understand how moving to a different social, cultural landscape might shift their ever-evolving teacher identities, their 'stories to live by' (Connelly and Clandinin, 1999). Nelson used Steedman's work (1986) to characterize, what Nelson described as, stories from the borderlands as stories that serve as 'disruption and essential counterpoint' (p. 22), 'stories that serve to interrupt and dislocate our life's continuity' (Nelson, 2003: 86). Nelson notes that:

> borderland-traveling happens in the space before one gets to the destination. ... It is the space in between which has been created by the recognition of difference, the recognition that my present identity has not yet been allowed but is about to be formed by this new encounter. (p. 2)

Nelson emphasizes that 'borderland' travel has the potential to shift someone 'from being one person to being a different person' (Lugones, 1987: 11). Nelson's narrative inquiry began in the midst of her own work and her own storied identity. She then engaged each of the other four teachers in telling their stories of experience prior to the experience of going to Kenya. Based on their stories, Nelson wrote and negotiated narrative accounts that represented something of each participant's necessarily incomplete (Miller, 1998), fluid, multiple and changing stories to live by (Connelly and Clandinin, 1999).

In the following months, the five teachers went to Kenya and worked in a professional development situation with Kenyan teachers, living in a compound together with them, sharing meals, sharing classrooms. Nelson described the borderland space as, ' ... a space that allowed us to tell and retell our "stories to live by," a telling that was triggered by the experience we were living in that place at that time' (p. 34). Subsequently, the teachers told stories to each other, to themselves and to Nelson. She wrote, 'Some of the stories we told after our experience were the same ones we had told previously. But this time, they were told a little differently because we had been in the borderlands' (p. 34).

Nelson makes visible that by coming to the metaphorical borderland spaces in wide awake ways and by telling and retelling stories of experience, that is, by engaging in narrative inquiry, there was change in the individual participants' stories to live by as well as in her own. The narrative inquiry, a living out of change in who the participants were and were becoming, draws attention to how each of the participants experienced what Clandinin and Connelly (2000) note:

> We retell our stories, remake the past. ... To do so is the essence of growth and, for Dewey, is an element in the criteria for judging the value of experience. Dewey's reconstruction of experience (for us the retelling and reliving of stories) is good in that it defines growth. Enhancing personal and social growth is one of the purposes of narrative inquiry. (p. 85)

With the shared epistemological and ontological commitments between those engaged in narrative inquiry and those engaged in action research, we see the changed actions of both participants and researchers through the living out of the research. In Hollingsworth et al.'s (1994) long-term narrative inquiry, we clearly see the changed action of participants and researchers in how they lived their practices in teaching, teacher education and research.

CHANGING THE LANDSCAPES OF RESEARCHERS AND PARTICIPANTS THROUGH THE INQUIRIES

What became clear in Pushor's (2001) and in Nelson's (2003) work is that narrative inquiry can shift and change the identities and practices of researchers and participants. Narrative inquiries can also shift the landscapes on which the inquirers and participants are situated. The concept of 'story constellations'

(Craig, 2003) provides a way to understand the changes that occur in the land-scapes of researchers and participants in narrative inquiries.

> 'Story constellations' has the capacity to make visible the complexities that shape school landscapes [and teacher education landscapes], influence the nature of educators' experiences, and determine who knows and what is known both within, and about, the educational enterprise. The approach enables multifaceted studies to be framed that take into account multiple clusters of stories, and many versions of stories narrated by multiple tellers. Broad-grained shifts in school landscapes [and teacher education landscapes] are subsequently constructed and reconstructed alongside individual and collective accounts of change. (p. 11)

As the identities of inquirers and participants are shaped through the retelling and reliving of their stories of experience in the narrative inquiry, the landscapes on which they are situated also begin to change.

Nelson calls for a shift in the landscape of teacher education, a shift that would change the discourse of teacher education. Drawing on the work of Vinz (1996) and Scott and Freeman-Moir (2000) she echoes their call for attending to teacher identity formation in all discussions on teaching and learning. She writes, 'By paying attention to the shifting nature of teacher identities, we will have a greater chance that the reproductive shifts we desire in society will occur because teach-ers will be more committed to ensuring that the shifts take place – a commitment that comes from having been made aware of the benefit of the shifts that have occurred in their own "stories to live by"' (Nelson, 2003: 159). Story constella-tions of both individual and collective accounts of shifts in the teachers' stories to live by, and the resulting commitment of teachers to the benefit they have experienced because of these shifts, invite Nelson to call for a reconstruction of the teacher education landscape to position identity formation as central in a teacher education curriculum.

Desrochers (2006) picked up Nelson's call for shifting the discourse of the landscape of teacher education by conducting a further narrative inquiry with preservice teachers registered in a Canadian faculty of education. Desrochers, interested in Nelson's work because of the possibility it offered for enriching the way that service learning could be seen as a site for attending to the shifting nature of teacher identities, 'involved participants in volunteer work with children in after-school clubs located in culturally diverse and socially disenfranchised communities' (p. 4). She used these experiences to create 'states of disequilibrium' for herself and the preservice teachers in order to engage them in reflections on their stories to live by in relation to diversity. Desrochers writes:

> Using a concept of dispositioning participants' knowledge, I inquired into shifts in participants' personal practical knowledge. Four key considerations emerged: learning about diversity begins with experience, occurs in dispositioning contexts, occurs through relationships and occurs through reflection over time. Inquiry-based service learning in the community with a reconcep-tualized teacher education curriculum for diversity opens possible borderland spaces within which preservice teachers can engage in learning though collaborative, on-going reflection on experience, for their own and future learners' benefit. (p. 5)

In Desrochers' (2006) research, story constellations, again both individual and collective, around shifts in preservice teachers' personal practical knowledge of diversity, prompt her to create borderland spaces within teacher education landscapes where a curriculum for diversity can promote new stories to live by. We see that these narrative inquiries shift not only researchers' and participants' lived and told stories but they may also cause shifts in the landscapes of both participants and others who live on similar landscapes.

Another compelling example of a narrative inquiry that not only shifted the lived and told stories of participants, both children and a teacher, and the researcher but also the landscape of schools in Kenya becomes visible in the work of Mwebi (2005). Engaging in a narrative inquiry with Kenyan children and their teacher, Mwebi studied their experiences of working in an experiential inquiry approach to HIV/AIDS. The narrative inquiry shifted the landscape to a more open conversation around the pandemic.

RESONANT READINGS LEADING TO CHANGE

In the foreword to Craig's book on narrative understandings of school reform, Davis (2003) writes:

> Through [Craig's] narratives, she invites readers to think beyond the text, never unproductively just to do something like someone else did. On the basis of their own reflections and pondering only, her readers can imagine the prospects of how they might work in their own totally different situations, with altogether different colleagues and leadership, and with utterly different resources. Craig's narratives are grist for intellectual imagination and wonderment, neither a script to be followed nor plans to be implemented. (p. viii)

Davis, using Craig's work as an example, captures the possibility for resonant readings of the research texts composed through narrative inquiries. Through resonant reading of Craig's, Pushor's, Nelson's, Desrochers' and others' research texts, the storied qualities of the texts invite readers to pull forward their own stories of experience and to retell and relive them in newly imagined ways. For example, Pushor reports that readers of her text often say to her, 'You've written my story!' Her parent stories and her stories of parents call forward their own stories. Keats Whelan, a teacher, after reading Pushor's story of her first Meet the Teacher Night as a parent, exclaimed she would not think of that school practice in the same way again. She spoke of how her fear, as a new teacher, of being unable to answer questions parents may ask her about curriculum prompted her to fill the time allotted with her own talk (Personal communication, 1999). Seeing through a parent's lens, feeling the silencing and exclusion of parents' knowledge in relation to curricular and program decisions, Keats Whelan began to plan for a new structuring of that event. Pushor's story evoked change in Keats Whelan's lived and told stories. Through a process of resonant reading, readers of narrative inquiries begin to re-imagine themselves and their landscapes in new ways.

CONCLUDING THOUGHTS

While some might argue that narrative inquiry and action research are distinct genres of research, we see the interrelatedness through the ways both can lead to change and action. Clandinin and Rosiek (2007) wrote:

> Beginning with a respect for ordinary lived experience, the focus of narrative inquiry is not only a valorizing of individuals' experience but also an exploration of the social, cultural and institutional narratives within which individuals' experiences were constituted, shaped, expressed, and enacted – but in a way that begins and ends that inquiry in the storied lives of the people involved. Narrative inquirers study an individual's experience in the world and, through the study, seek ways of enriching and transforming that experience for themselves and others. (p. 42)

We see in this conception of narrative inquiry, the possibility for making more explicit the action and change through narrative inquiry. Calling on narrative inquirers to explicate more carefully the change that unfolds through and in the inquiry will help others to be more attentive to possibilities for action.

REFERENCES

Atkinson, R. (1995) *The Gift of Stories: Practical and Spiritual Applications of Autobiography, Life Stories, and Personal Mythmaking.* Westport, CT: Bergin and Garvey.

Clandinin, D.J. and Connelly, F.M. (1995) 'Teachers' professional knowledge landscapes: Teacher stories. Stories of teachers. School stories. Stories of schools', *Educational Researcher*, 25 (3): 24–30.

Clandinin, D.J. and Connelly, F.M. (1998) 'Asking questions about telling stories', in C. Kridel (ed.), *Writing Educational Biography: Explorations in Qualitative Research*. New York: Garland. pp. 245–53.

Clandinin, D.J. and Connelly, F.M. (2000) *Narrative Inquiry: Experience and Story in Qualitative Research*. San Francisco: Jossey-Bass.

Clandinin, D.J. and Rosiek, J. (2007) 'Mapping a landscape of narrative inquiry: Borderland spaces and tensions' in D.J. Clandinin (ed.), *Handbook of Narrative Inquiry: Mapping a Methodology*. Thousand Oaks, CA: Sage. pp. 35–75.

Connelly, F.M. and Clandinin, D.J. (1990) 'Stories of experience and narrative inquiry', *Educational Researcher*, 19 (5): 2–14.

Connelly, F.M. and Clandinin, D.J. (1999) *Shaping a Professional Identity: Stories of Educational Practice*. New York: Teachers College Press.

Connelly, F.M. and Clandinin, D.J. (2006) 'Narrative inquiry' in J. Green, G. Camilli and P. Elmore (eds.), *Handbook of Complementary Methods in Education Research* (3rd edn). Mahwah, NJ: Lawrence Erlbaum. pp. 447–87.

Craig, C.J. (2003) *Narrative Inquiries of School Reform: Storied Lives, Storied Landscapes, Storied Metaphors*. Greenwich, CT: Information Age Publishing.

Creswell, J.W., Hanson, W.E., Clark Plano, V.L. and Morales, A. (2007) 'Qualitative research designs: Selection and implementation', *Counselling Psychologist*, 35 (2): 236.

Davis, O.L. (2003) 'Foreword', in C.J. Craig, *Narrative Inquiries of School Reform: Storied Lives, Stories Landscapes, Storied Metaphors*. Greenwich, CT: Information Age Publishing.

Desrochers, C. (2006) 'Towards a new borderland in teacher education for diversity: A narrative inquiry into preservice teachers' shifting identities through service learning'. Unpublished doctoral dissertation, University of Alberta.

Dewey, J. (1938) *Experience and Education*. New York: Collier Books.

Elbaz-Luwisch, F. (2007) 'Studying teachers' lives and experiences: Narrative inquiry into K-12 teaching', in D.J. Clandinin (ed.), *Handbook of Narrative Inquiry: Mapping a Methodology*. Thousand Oaks, CA: Sage. pp. 357–82.

Greene, M. (1995) *Releasing the Imagination*. San Francisco, CA: Jossey-Bass.

Hara, K. (1995) 'The significance of teacher-based forms of enquiry', *Research in Education*, 54: 93–4.

Hollingsworth, S., Cody, A., Dybdahl, M., Minarik, L.T., Smallwood, J. and Teel, K.M. (1994) *Teacher Research and Urban Literacy Education: Lessons and Conversations in a Feminist Key*. New York: Teachers College Press.

Lugones, M. (1987) 'Playfulness, "world"-travelling, and loving perception', *Hypatia*, 2 (2): 3–19.

Mattingly, C.F. (2007) 'Acted narratives: From storytelling to emergent dramas', in D.J. Clandinin (ed.), *Handbook of Narrative Inquiry: Mapping a Methodology*. Thousand Oaks, CA: Sage. pp. 405–25.

McNiff, J. (2007) 'My story is my living educational theory', in D.J. Clandinin (ed.), *Handbook of Narrative Inquiry: Mapping a Methodology*. Thousand Oaks, CA: Sage. pp. 308–29.

McNiff, J. and Whitehead, J. (2005) *Action Research for Teachers: A Practical Guide*. London: David Fulton Publishers.

Miller, J. (1998) 'Autobiography and the necessary incompleteness of teachers' stories', in W. Ayers and J. Miller (eds.), *A Light in Dark Times: Maxine Greene and the Unfinished Conversation*. New York: Teachers College Press.

Murray Orr, A. (2005) 'Stories to live by: Book conversations as spaces for attending to children's lives in school'. Unpublished doctoral dissertation, University of Alberta, Alberta.

Mwebi, B.M. (2005) 'A narrative inquiry into the experiences of a teacher and eight students learning about HIV/AIDS through a child-to-child curriculum approach'. Unpublished doctoral dissertation, University of Alberta, Alberta.

Nelson, C. (2003) 'Stories to live by': A narrative inquiry into five teachers' shifting identities through the borderlands of cross-cultural professional development'. Unpublished doctoral dissertation, University of Alberta, Alberta.

Pearce, M. (2005) 'Community as relationship: A narrative inquiry into the school experiences of two children'. Unpublished doctoral dissertation, University of Alberta, Alberta.

Pushor, D. (2001) 'A storied photo album of parents' positioning and the landscape of schools'. Unpublished doctoral dissertation, University of Alberta, Alberta.

Reissman, C.K. and Speedy, J. (2007) 'Narrative inquiry in the psychotherapy professions: A critical review', in D.J. Clandinin (ed.), *Handbook of Narrative Inquiry: Mapping a Methodology*. Thousand Oaks, CA: Sage. pp. 426–56.

Rosiek, J. and Atkinson, B. (2005) 'Bridging the divides: The need for pragmatic semiotics of teacher knowledge research', *Educational Theory*, 55 (4): 421–42.

Scott, A. and Freeman-Moir, J. (eds.) (2000) *Tomorrow's Teachers: International and Critical Perspectives on Teacher Education*. Christchurch, New Zealand: Canterbury University Press.

Steedman, C. (1986) *Landscape for a Good Woman: A Story of Two Lives*. London: Virago.

Steeves, P. (2000) 'Crazy quilt: Continuity, identity and a storied school landscape in transition. A teacher's and a principal's work in progress' . Unpublished doctoral dissertation, University of Alberta, Alberta.

Vinz, R. (1996) *Composing a Teaching Life*. Portsmouth, NH: Boynton/Cook Publishers.

Whitehead, J. (1989) 'Creating a living educational theory from questions of the kind, "How do I improve my practice?"' *Cambridge Journal of Education*, 19 (1): 137–53.

24

Capabilities, Flourishing and the Normative Purposes of Action Research

Melanie Walker

We ask you to make society's problems your laboratory. We ask you to translate data into direction – direction for action.

(Martin Luther King)

BACKGROUND

I first became drawn to action research in the early 1980s when, catapulted from working in poor, mixed race secondary schools in Cape Town as a history teacher, I found myself working at the University of Cape Town and required to do research. Like many other school to university boundary crossers I searched out forms of research which addressed practices in real schools and classrooms and which had something to say about improving schooling in the volatile and politically charged context of South African schools at that time. Emancipatory action research held strong appeal with its claim to promote 'a critical consciousness which exhibits itself in political as well as practical action to promote change' (Grundy, 1987: 162), underpinned by ideals of freedom, equality and justice. This turned out to be rather more complicated in practice in the first action research study I undertook, working with teachers in Black primary schools in poor townships outside Cape Town (Walker, 1996a) and in a further collaborative study with academic colleagues at the University of Glasgow to explore how we did critical professionalism (Walker, 2001). This is not surprising. After all, one of the things action research investigates is these kinds of gaps between what we hope for in our educational aims and values, and what we actually achieve practically in complex, human situations.

In both these projects, action research was for me about the critical *doing* of education aimed at better forms of educational life and better individual lives in education. The driving force for my own action research studies had been an impetus for positive change and innovation through deepening my understanding of educational processes and developing strategies to bring about improvements consistent with my normative purposes. By normative I mean statements about education and about action research which go beyond descriptions of what education and/or action research is in a particular case, to considering what they ought to be in relation to assumptions about what makes education or life good for us. Such normative assumptions will inform the practical choices we then make to act in this way rather than that. What we take to be normative will also be deeply influenced by what our society considers to be a 'good education' and this is likely to differ in Cuba, Ghana and New Zealand for example. We might expect that comparative action research projects may have some descriptive features in common, but differ with regard to their normative purposes. In Country A this might involve normative concerns with inclusive political participation; in Country B there might be a normative concern with developing young people's skills for the marketplace. As action researchers we need to be critically aware of the norms that shape our own society and how these influence education and different approaches to action research. Our inquiries ought to (here I am being normative again!) generate dialogue which brings assumptions out for reflection. They would go beyond descriptions of change to ask why the change worked in the way it did with what effects for learning and our freedom and opportunity to become and to be.

What Noddings (2003) calls 'aims-talk' is surely fundamental then to action research – what are we trying to accomplish, for whom and why? Education affects our continuing journeys through adult life and having a full life. It matters therefore what it is that people are learning, and what they are learning to be in education. The key issue, then, as I see it, is that aims-talk is essential but also that not any old aim will do. I could point to examples of 'education' which involve a version of the good life in which girls and women or disabled people are denied full human flourishing on account of their gender or disability. The kind of education that constrains rather than enhances is captured in Laurel Richardson's moving ethnographic poem:

'Educational Birds'
(found poem, Raptor Barn, Felix Neck Widlife Sanctuary)

The Raptor Barn Houses
Various Birds of Prey
They are being Rehabilitated
for release. Those that
cannot be released

successfully
are kept
as Educational Birds (1994: 206)

This melancholy poem hardly needs a commentary. Its crucial point is that 'education' can train and confine and kill curiosity.

FOR EDUCATION AND FLOURISHING

Therefore I suggest that action research ought to be oriented in some way or the other, explicitly or implicitly, to fostering human flourishing and well-being, and democratic and inclusive forms of learning and education. To say this is to argue for foregrounding explicit normative purposes in action research studies, which at one and the same time bound what the research is about – for social justice, or for equality, or for democracy – but also expand hugely the possibility of lives in education being good lives which go well for the individuals concerned. A good definition of well-being is provided by the Wellbeing in Developing Countries Research Group: 'Well-being is a state of being with others, where human needs are met, where one can act meaningfully to pursue one's goals, and where one is able to enjoy a satisfactory quality of life' (McGregor, 2007: 11). We then need to think about how such a definition of well-being would look in education.

It is also to foreground education and the educational values that originally inspired me to use action research to investigate my own practice. As John Elliott (2007) has argued, what makes research *educational* is its practical intention to realize educational values in action. In taking up questions of practice, we cannot avoid, he says, taking an evaluative stance on the aims of education. Thus the importance of education, rather than 'training' or 'schooling' or even 'learning', must be central. Being educational, I suggest, involves:

> engaging live human beings in activities of meaning-making, dialogue and reflective understanding of a variety of texts, including the texts of their social realities. Growing, becoming different, becoming informed and articulate. (Greene, 1992: 285)

Elsewhere Maxine Greene writes that education, 'signifies an initiation into new ways of seeing, hearing, feeling, moving. It signifies the nurture of a special kind of reflectiveness and expressiveness, a reaching out for meanings, a learning to learn' (2001: 7). 'We are', writes Greene, 'interested in openings, in unexplored possibilities, not in the predictable or the quantifiable' (2001: 7).

'AIMS-TALK'

We might also argue that education ought (normatively) to promote 'a life that is worthy of the dignity of human being' (Nussbaum, 2000: 5), and that dignity would be fundamental in a process we named as education. Central to the idea of human dignity is the Kantian perspective that human beings should be treated 'never simply as means, but always at the same time as an end' (cited in Liebenberg, 2005: 6). Each of us has intrinsic worth as a human being and not simply as an economic producer. To value human dignity is then to put in place the social and pedagogical arrangements for the development of students' intellectual and social capabilities and learning environment in which they might flourish. To value human dignity is 'to constitute positive social relationships which both respect autonomy and foster the conditions in which it can flourish' (Liebenberg, 2005: 11). Dignity, argues Liebenberg, is a relational value so that both individual and social identities are at stake. In relation to education, we would be asking ourselves what is required for people to lead dignified lives? It would of course not be the only pedagogic value at stake – dignity without knowledge for example would seem somewhat hollow; dignity without satisfying economic opportunities, insufficient.

All this inflects towards the importance of human flourishing and of 'each person as worthy of regard, as an end and not just as a means' [to some other end] (Nussbaum, 2000: 32). Thus Noddings (2003) has argued for the importance of 'happiness' as an aim for education. While acknowledging the part resources play in having a good life, she reminds us that resources are a means not an end:

> A good society will make sure that its people do not suffer from a lack of those resources that constitute objective happiness, but its educational system will encourage them to explore and appreciate a full range of possibilities for promoting happiness. Education, by its very nature, should help people to develop their best selves – to become people with pleasing talents, useful and satisfying occupations, self-understanding, sound character, a host of appreciations, and a commitment to continuous learning (2003: 23).

While we might agree or not with all the items on Noddings' list, the point is rather to understand flourishing or happiness as a core aim of education.

On these understandings action researchers would be critical of the dominant contemporary view that market exchange is an ethic in itself and a guide for all human action, including in education (Harvey, 2005). Market fundamentalism assumes that economic growth and development mean the same thing, and that both equal well-being. Arising from this has been the domination of education policy by human capital theory, viewing education as merely an instrumental investment in the productive capacity of human beings (human capital) through education (Little, 2003). The effect of human capital theory for education has been to ascribe its primary value to the extent investment in individual students gives rise to increased economic productivity and higher incomes, and augmented national wealth. But human capital cannot, as Robeyns (2006) explains, account for any non-economic goods from education, such as someone wanting to learn poetry for its own sake, while evidence from economists shows that increased GDP and individual wealth does not make people any happier (Gaspar, 2004). While I would not seek to discard human capital – after all, having economic opportunities enables us to flourish in diverse ways – I would want to suggest that it should not be the sole measure of success and achievement in education.

FOR CAPABILITY FORMATION[1]

Instead, I want to propose that if we are concerned about education as a rich and complex endeavour of 'cultivating humanity' (Nussbaum, 1997) and our deep critical and imaginative faculties, we need to pay attention to the fundamental worth of each human being and to equality of some sort. The specific form of equality I advocate is not that of monetary equality but rather to ask about people's capabilities, that is their substantive freedom to rationally choose to be and to do what they value being and doing for their flourishing and agency (Sen, 1999). 'Capabilities' has both a normative dimension in that it is a framework for justice, and an evaluative dimension in that 'capabilities' is the space we compare and evaluate quality of life and well-being. Normatively the achievement of key education capabilities (or their non-achievement) by individuals, groups and countries would frame our action research studies.

Capability and human development are closely aligned conceptually in that the latter means 'an expansion of human capabilities, a widening of choices, and enhancement of freedoms and a fulfilment of human rights' (Fukudo-Parr and Kumar, 2003: xxi). 'Education is a key to all human capabilities' Nussbaum (2006: 322) argues. To argue for capabilities as central to opportunities and processes of education is to locate action research as an integrated process of research, of education practices and of human development processes and outcomes.

The capability approach has been developed by Nobel Laureate economist Amartya Sen (1992, 1999, 2002), and by philosopher Martha Nussbaum (2000, 2006), who has expanded and deepened the philosophical basis for capabilities. The key idea of the capability approach is that social arrangements should aim to expand people's capabilities – their freedom to promote or achieve 'functionings' which are valuable to them. 'Functionings' are the activities and states that make up people's well-being, such as becoming literate, having good friendships in school, being healthy, being able to appear in public without shame, and so on. They are related to goods and income, but they describe what a person is able to do or be as a result – for example, when a person's need for food (a commodity) is met, they enjoy the functioning of being well-nourished. Capabilities are 'the alternative combination of functionings that are feasible for [a person] to achieve'; they are 'the substantive freedom' a person has 'to lead the kind of life he or she has reason to value' (Sen, 1999: 87).

It is important to understand that capabilities do not mean skills or internal capacities. This shifts the focus to individual success or failure, whereas the capability approach points to the social arrangements, for example pedagogical conditions or normative education purposes of schools that enable or diminish capability formation. To emphasize, capabilities comprise the real and actual freedoms people have to do and to be what they value being and doing. The capability approach shifts the space for evaluating equality in education from examination results or relying on what people say they want from schools and colleges to whether each person has the substantive freedom to be and do in ways that they value being and doing.

Sen's distinction between capability and functioning is important because it asks us to evaluate the connections between capability and functioning and to look beneath outcomes to consider what freedom a person had to choose and achieve valued functioning. A focus on capabilities would require us not just to evaluate satisfaction with individual learning outcomes, but to question the range of real educational choices that have been available to people; whether they had the genuine capability to achieve a valued educational functioning. We would need to ask whether people's educational aspirations (what they hoped for now and in the future, see Appadurai, 2004) had become adapted to their circumstances, and whether all children and students had a range of valued learning opportunities to choose from. We cannot overlook that people adapt their (subjective) preferences, according to what they think is possible for them; choices are deeply shaped by the structure of opportunities available to us. We might then ask how, for example, does a marginalized individual or group participate in selecting capabilities as outcomes for education when they have been conditioned to believe that others are superior to them, or when they might question such ideas but educational (external) conditions do not enable their voices?

The capability approach therefore invites a range of more searching questions with regard to equality and the social arrangements that support or constrain it, than just a focus on expressed desire satisfaction. For example, expressed satisfaction would take at face value the working-class girl who rejects going on to college or university. This might appear on the surface to be a choice freely made – she chooses not to go to university in order to study hairdressing. But if we look at her substantive freedom (her capability) to make a genuine choice from equally valuable alternatives, her choice looks more complicated. We need to ask if she could have gone to university if she had wished to – did she have the school and family encouragement, are her parents college graduates, has she the financial means, the school grades, confidence, and the offer of place? In the end it may be that she had genuine alternatives and chose hairdressing as the most valuable; but what the capability approach requires us to do is to ask questions about apparently straightforward individual preferences and choices. It is concerned with identifying and understanding inequalities in and through education and would question the belief that children's accomplishments rest solely on their own individual efforts rather than social and educational arrangements. While we cannot totally eliminate what Nussbaum (1986) describes as the 'fragility of goodness', that is the part luck plays in human lives, we ought to be able 'to end oppression, which by definition is socially imposed' (Anderson, 1999: 288). Oppressions and social disadvantage might include gender, race, social class and disability. Through action research we could begin to change education in the direction of greater fairness and more equality, step by step.

It would still be necessary to respect a plurality of view on what constitutes a good life, anchored in a political philosophy of egalitarianism and equality. Moreover, outcomes (functioning) as much as capability would be important in education, especially the education of children and young people if they are to develop mature capabilities in later life (Nussbaum, 2000). Education would involve expanding their real freedoms through 'the removal of various types of unfreedoms that leave people with little choice and little opportunity of exercising their reasoned agency' (Sen, 1999: xii). If we adopt capabilities as our normative framework for evaluating how well education is going, an education policy which constructed education as primarily or only for economic growth and productivity ought to be challenged for its effects in compromising student learning and narrowing identity and well-being possibilities. Progress and achievement in education would instead be evaluated in terms of whether the freedoms that people have are enhanced. Moreover, life decisions are reached through reasoned reflection; to be actively involved in shaping one's own life and having opportunities to reflect on this is critical for positive social change because we exercise our agency individually and in co-operation with others, and through education we might learn to do both. Moreover, there are close connections between adequate social opportunities and how individuals can shape their own lives and help each other (Sen, 1999). Sen (1999) is clear that individual freedom is always a social product, so that there is a dialectical relationship between social arrangements to expand individual freedom, and how we use our individual freedom to improve the lives of others and instrumentally make social arrangements more effective.

CHOOSING VALUABLE EDUCATION CAPABILITIES

While Sen is a vigorous advocate of participatory public reasoning, in education, we might nonetheless need to qualify a 'pure' participatory approach, given that students arrive in education with unequal amounts of cultural capital, and with uneven advantages regarding their valued social capital. We need to be careful in advocating an entirely open-ended approach in which democratic debate will theoretically allow the best argument to prevail. In practice, the more powerful will be heard and the less advantaged might agree to things that are not necessarily in their best interests.

Sen (2004) is right to argue that there is a real social justice need for people to be able to take part in social decisions and practices of public reasoning; but for education we also need to argue that not everything counts as education or learning. Capabilities in education would not be random but shaped by what it means to be human and to flourish, and to have a right to such flourishing. Moreover Sen, notwithstanding his concern for public participation, does not hold a relativist position that any kind of education agreed by a family or a community will do. For example, he has recently argued that faith schools constrain reasoned identity choices and their agency because 'young children are placed in the domain of singular affiliations well before they have the ability to reason about different systems of identification that may compete for their attention' (2006: 9). Sen (1999) has argued that the identity we are born into need not be the identity we choose. But to have other choices we need to know about other ways of life, and education ought to make this possible.

For example, if we take equality as a central criterion for education we would have to work to secure to all students a level of capability in a number of interlocking valuable dimensions, especially as contemporary education is implicated in reproducing the inequalities of origins and destinies with regard to social class, race, gender, and so on. If we value democratic political deliberation in our society, then schools and universities have a responsibility to foster the values and capabilities that support democratic life. One way or another, in education we do need to take a stand on the capabilities that really matter and through public reasoning contribute to and scrutinize these.

ACTION RESEARCH PROJECTS AND FLOURISHING

The implications for our action research projects would be that we would need to pay attention to how education realized in and through our own practices – whether as teachers, lecturers, health practitioners, community educators or activist-consultants – enhances the freedoms that allow children or students or parents or patients to form a wide capability set from which they might choose valuable functionings to enable their quality of life and well-being. This would always be our 'big' question. Henry Richardson (2007: 411) suggests that when it comes to individual capabilities, 'perhaps the most important thing is for each of us to be capable of treating others with respect; that is something that is up to each of us but which takes proper training'. This then might be a good place to begin our action research.

Our projects might be concerned with human rights and how education develops the capabilities that secure those rights to people. It would not be enough to have a policy in place on race or gender equality rights if we did not also ensure that each person was in a position where they can really be or do in ways that they have reason to choose (Nussbaum, 2000). Through action research we might wish to focus on pedagogic rights such as those advocated by Bernstein (2000) – the rights to enhancement, inclusion participation – and collect and analyze evidence to understand how well we are doing in fostering the capabilities that secure these pedagogic rights to each child or student.

Or we might choose to design a project which considers democracy and public education, drawing on the three core capabilities in education that Nussbaum (2006) advocates – of critical thinking, imaginative understanding and world citizenship – and consider how well we are doing in developing these in our students. Nussbaum states emphatically that:

> Nothing could be more crucial to democracy than the education of its citizens. Through primary and secondary education, young citizens form, at a crucial age, habits of mind that will be with them all through their lives. They learn to ask questions or not to ask them; to take what they hear at face value or to probe more deeply; to imagine the situation of a person different from themselves or to see a new person as a mere threat to the success of their own projects; to think of themselves as members of a homogenous group or as members of a nation, and a world, made up of many people and groups, all of whom derive respect and understanding. (2006: 387)

Action research offers us a robust methodology to find out how and if this is happening in our own schools, and colleges, and where it is not: to ask how and if we are teaching each child to be a critical agent in her life; to form her own conception of the good; and to have equal, democratic citizenship (Anderson, 1999). Or we might prefer Sen's (2004) more open-ended approach of a process of participatory public reasoning to develop a list of valuable capabilities for our own community or educational institution, supported by action research in developing and then implementing and evaluating capability achievements through education.

CONCLUDING THOUGHTS: ACTION RESEARCH AND CAPABILITY FORMATION

Action research ought to enable not just better lives in education for students but also foster the practical wisdom of us as educators as we reflect on own professional work. It suggests a professional ethics in which we take responsibility as professionals for the impact of schooling or college education on our students. Elsewhere (1996b) I have suggested that through action research we might develop ourselves as 'subaltern professionals',[2] by which I mean as professionals committing ourselves to using our expertise and knowledge not to support dominant groups, or sustain inequalities, or perpetuate cultural exclusions in our society, but rather working alongside and with others (including 'subalterns') in the interests of social justice.

Important as our actions are in action research, without some kind of adjudicating theory about equality and which equalities matter, we can be well educated and still not see; we can engage in reflective action as individuals and collaboratively and still have blindspots. For example, Jennifer Esposito and Venus Evans-Winters (2007) comment on their attempts to develop critical action research that is more applicable to work in urban [inner-city] communities in the USA. They remark that on the basis of observing teachers on their own action research courses they came to understand what they were not willing to examine or were not allowed to examine. Noffke (1994) has also suggested that if we do not critique current epistemologies (which may be race, gender and class blind) we may end up with action research which entrenches privileged standpoints. In other words, action research, outside of an egalitarian framework of equality and justice, has no inherent critical direction or purpose. We might, as racially privileged or gender privileged individuals, fail to notice gender or racial unfairness in society, and even in our own actions, however much action research we undertake. Consistent with Sen's emphasis on social arrangements and freedom, Esposito and Evans-Winters (2007: 236) underline the importance of context which extends beyond classrooms 'into the very political and social spaces that (re)produce and (re)structure teachers and student identities'. If we have a guiding theory from capabilities we stand a better chance of addressing this concern and *doing* equality and justice in education

While capability is strong on evaluating opportunities it is less useful for investigating what Sen (2002) calls process freedoms, and here we would need to draw on other theories and ideas about pedagogy and curriculum and learning. But the point would still hold that the lens of capability in an action research study would be directed at the space of capabilities and hence on the formation of substantive freedoms to be and to do. This practical evaluative focus, and the concerns with public reasoning and participation, suggest deep compatibilities with action research, while action research's focus on practices and improvement make it in turn complementary as a research methodology for investigating and implementing capability formation. The capability approach asks us to investigate what it is that participants in education have reason to value and to develop education accordingly. Fostering capability formation in and through education is practical work. Action research is a methodology for development and change. Capability is normatively important for action research; action research is important for finding out how well lives are going in education. Capability asks us as educators how we ought to and can foster our students' flourishing and well-being, and to recognize that social and educational arrangements might diminish our students' capabilities to choose and have good lives.

ACKNOWLEDGEMENTS

My thanks to the editors for their helpful comments on improving my draft chapter, and to colleagues in the Education thematic network of the Human Development and Capability Association for ongoing conversations.

NOTES

1 This chapter cannot flesh out the capability approach and capabilities in great detail. To find out more about this framework of justice see http://www.hd-ca.org and for applications of the capability approach in education see Walker (2006) and Walker and Unterhalter (2007).

2 The term subaltern is originally from the Italian communist activist, Antonio Gramsci, who used it to mean the economically dispossessed. It was famously taken up by Spivak (1988) in her

seminal essay for post-colonial studies, in which she critically explored the notion of whether the subaltern could indeed speak without simply reinscribing their subordinate position in society. Her warning is important for us to bear in mind as action research practitioners committed to social justice in education.

REFERENCES

Anderson, E. (1999) 'What is the point of equality?' *Ethics*, 109: 287–337.

Appadurai, A. (2004) 'The capacity to aspire: Culture and the terms of recognition', in V. Rao and M. Walton (eds), *Culture and Public Action*. Stanford: Stanford University Press.

Bernstein, B. (2000) *Pedagogy, Symbolic Control and Identity*. Lanham: Rowman and Littlefield.

Elliott, J. (2007) *Reflecting Where the Action is. The Selected Works of John Elliott*. Abingdon: Routledge.

Esposito, J. and Evans-Winters, V. (2007) 'Contextualising critical action research', *Educational Action Research*, 15 (2): 221–37.

Fukudo-Parr, S. and Kumar, A.K.S. (eds) (2003) *Readings in Human Development*. New Delhi, Oxford and New York: Oxford University Press.

Gaspar, D. (2004) 'Subjective and objective well being in relation to economic inputs: puzzles and responses'. Paper presented at workshop on Capability and Happiness, St Edmunds College, Cambridge March 2004.

Greene, Maxine (1992) 'Educational visions', in Joe Kincheloe and Shirley Steinberg (eds), *Thirteen Questions: Reframing Education's Conversation*. New York: Peter Lang.

Greene, M. (2001) *Variations on a Blue Guitar: the Lincoln Center Institute Lectures on Aesthetic Education*. New York: Teachers College Press.

Grundy, S. (1987) *Curriculum: Product or Praxis*. Lewes: Falmer Press.

Harvey, D. (2005) *A Brief History of Neoliberalism*. Oxford, Oxford University Press.

Liebenberg, S. (2005) 'The value of human dignity in interpreting socio-economic Rights', *SAJHR* 1: 173–98.

Little, A. (2003) 'Motivating learning and the development of human capital', *Compare*, 33 (4): 437–52.

McGregor, A. (2007) 'Methodology for empirical research on well being', *Maitreyee*, 9: 11–15.

Noddings, N. (2003) *Happiness and Education*. Cambridge: Cambridge University Press.

Noffke, S. (1994) 'Action research: towards the next generation', *Educational Action Research*, 2 (1): 9–21.

Nussbaum, N. (1986) *The Fragility of Goodness,* revised edn. Cambridge: Cambridge University Press.

Nussbaum, M. (1997) *Cultivating Humanity. A Classical Defence of Reform in Liberal Education*. Cambridge, MA: Harvard University Press.

Nussbaum, M. (2000) *Women and Human Development*. Cambridge: Cambridge University Press.

Nussbaum, M. (2006) 'Education and democratic citizenship: Capabilities and quality education', *Journal of Human Development*, 7 (3): 385–98.

Richardson, H. (2007) 'The social background of capabilities for freedom', *Journal of Human Development*, 8 (3): 389–414.

Richardson, L. (1994) *Fields of Play*, New Brunswick: Rutgers University Press.

Robeyns, Ingrid (2006) 'Three models of education: rights, capabilities and human capital', *Theory and Research in Education*, 4 (1): 69–84.

Sen, A. (1992) *Inequality Re-examined*. Oxford: Oxford University Press.

Sen, A. (1999) *Development as Freedom*. New York: Alfred Knopf.

Sen, A. (2002) *Rationality and Freedom*. Cambridge, MA: Harvard University Press.

Sen, A. (2004) 'Capabilities, lists and public reason: Continuing the conversation', *Feminist Economics*, 10 (3): 77–80.

Sen, A. (2006) 'What clash of civilizations? Why religious identity isn't destiny', *Slate Magazine*, 29/03/06 http://www.slate.com/id/2138731/?nav=ais (Accessed 20 September 2006).

Spivak, G. (1998) 'Can the subaltern speak?' in Cary Nelson and Lawrence Grossberg (eds), *Marxism and the Interpretation of Culture*, Champaign: University of Illinois Press.

Walker, M. (1996a) *Images of Professional Development*. Pretoria: Human Sciences Research Council Press.

Walker, M. (1996b) Subaltern professionals: Acting in pursuit of social justice, *Educational Action Research – an International Journal*, 4 (3): 407–25.

Walker, M. (2001) (ed.) *Reconstructing Professio-nalism in University Teaching: Teachers and Learners in Action*. Buckingham: SRHE/Open University Press.

Walker, M. (2006) *Higher Education Pedagogies: A Capabilities Approach*. Maidenhead: SRHE/Open University Press and McGraw-Hill.

Walker, M. and Unterhalter, E. (eds) (2007) *Sen's Capability Approach and Social Justice, in Education*. New York: Palgrave.

25

Demonstrating Quality in Educational Research for Social Accountability

Jean McNiff and Jack Whitehead

This chapter is an account of our (Jean's and Jack's) ongoing educational researches as we try to understand the origin and nature of inclusional practices, so that we can use this knowledge to encourage and support their development by others and ourselves. We aim to do this through the exercise of our educational influence in learning as we encourage others to exercise theirs, initially in our own institutions, and also on a worldwide scale. Because this is an account of our action enquiries, as we express and clarify our meanings of quality in educational research for social accountability, we frame it in relation to the same questions that guide the processes of those enquiries, as follows:

- What is our concern? (We identify our research issue.)
- Why are we concerned? (We explain our concerns in relation to how our values are being denied in our practices.)
- What kind of experiences can we describe to show the situation as it is and as it unfolds? (We offer descriptions of what is happening in our contexts, and gather data as an ongoing process.)
- What do we do about it? (We imagine possible improvements.)
- How do we ensure that any conclusions we come to are reasonably fair and accurate? (We generate evidence from our data, and submit our explanations of educational influences in learning to rigorous validation processes.)
- How do we modify our ideas and practices in light of the evaluation? (We evaluate the influence of our practices in terms of the potential significance of our research, and transform them into new practices on the basis of critical feedback.) (see Whitehead, 1989)

We see this form of critically engaged questioning as enabling us also to demonstrate the methodological quality of our research. This quality is shown through the procedures we use to establish rigour and validity. It is also shown through the moral commitments of the social practices that our research aims to appreciate and influence. The form of our enquiries is significant in enabling us to clarify how we understand quality in educational research for social accountability. We clarify our meanings as they emerge through our practice of enquiry and knowledge-creation as living standards of judgement.

The aim of this chapter therefore is to show how we are seeking, through our educational action research, to make a contribution to existing understandings and practices in the form of new kinds of logics and standards of judgement, by which quality may be judged. This includes our work in developing curricula for masters and doctoral programmes in higher education concerned with life-long education and professional development in a range of cultural contexts.

So we now address our identified concern as the first step in our action enquiry.

WHAT IS OUR CONCERN?

Our main concern is to do with the forms of logic that underpin many cultural and institutional practices. If we appreciate that how we think influences what we do, then it seems reasonable to assume that the deep-level logics we use inevitably influence the surface-level practices we engage in. Our research aim is to offer a dynamically relational form of logic that enables the thinker to appreciate the ecological nature of the transformational relationships between what goes on in the individual mind and what goes on in the social world. We aim to offer an appreciation of the significance of the self-studies of action researchers as they explain their transformational influences in learning, and how their embodied knowledge may be brought into and publicly legitimated by the academy. To reach this level of explanatory adequacy involves engaging with the new living form of logic we are proposing, an inclusional and relational form, that assumes 'an awareness of space and the variably permeable boundaries … that inseparably line it, as connective, reflective and co-creative, rather than divisive' (Rayner, 2005: 1). Our research therefore is about how we can support the legitimization of living logics in the academy. We are also concerned to show the academic validity of the embodied knowledge of practitioners, and the practical realities of living logics for social transformation. We take care to show the validation processes involved in demonstrating the explanatory adequacy of practitioners' enquiries that enable them to claim that they are improving their learning in order to improve their social situations.

Our concerns therefore are about the forms of logic used to make sense of and inform personal and social practices. We are seeking to contribute to transforming the current situation in educational research, in which the two dominant forms of logic, the propositional and the dialectical, useful though they are, are shown to be too limited in terms of their explanatory adequacy. We propose rather an inclusional form of logic that can include propositional and dialectical forms of thought, without denying their rationality. We shall shortly point to the evidence that shows that the validity of claims to educational knowledge grounded in this approach has already been legitimated in the academy. So we make the link that the development of living inclusional practices is grounded in a commitment to the development of living inclusional forms of logic, which include practices of a theoretical and practical nature. First, however, we give the reasons for our concerns, to ground our enquiries.

WHY ARE WE CONCERNED?

We believe that each person is unique, and able to make their contribution to human living in their own way. We question the legitimacy of many social practices, especially forms that exclude, and the kind of logics that embed them, for example, the practice of understanding individuals in terms of socio-historically constituted norms. We support the views of Judith Butler (1999), who says that socially constructed stereotypes of, for example, race and gender, are grounded in a view of an imaginary original norm against which the quality of others' lives may be judged and used to categorize them, a colonizing practice underpinned by the exercise of symbolic power for social control (Bernstein, 2000; Bourdieu, 1991). Derrida (1998) and Kristeva (2002) also maintain that each person should be understood in terms of their own identity formation, in relation with others.

This idea of deconstructing socially constructed 'norms' travels to a range of human practices, including educational research, which is our main context. We question the validity of the idea of original 'norms' that can be applied to practices and used to explain the lives and learning of individuals. This assumption can be seen in explanations for human practices that prescribe the norms and standards of human enquiry for the reproduction of existing human practices. In our view of education, individuals are capable of making their own creative responses, in forming their lives, that are resistant to explanations from such normative perspectives. In our explanations, however, we always seek to take account of the historically and politically constituted nature of what Bourdieu (1991) names 'the habitus', that is, the customary norms of acting and thinking specific to a particular social formation.

A good example of the influence of this idea of the habitus was in Jack's permitting the colonization of his mind by the disciplines approach to educational theory in the late 1960s and early 1970s. In this approach (Hirst, 1983: 18) the practical principles used by individuals to explain their own educational practices and influences were to be *replaced* by principles with more rational justification drawn from the disciplines of education. It was only through experiencing himself as a living contradiction while viewing videotapes of his own practice that led Jack to reject this replacement and to insist on understanding the world from his own point of view as a person claiming originality and exercising his judgement responsibly, with universal intent (Polanyi, 1958: 327).

The importance of taking account of the historically and politically constituted nature of the habitus has been well described by Berlin (2006) who maintains that traditional research practices are underpinned by the tripartite assumptions that (a) there is an answer for everything; (b) the answer can be found; (c) there will be a general consensus about the answer. We do however endorse the idea of seeking 'the whole truth', which is an inclusional stance and would include all truths (rather than 'nothing but the truth', a concept which tends to be more exclusionary and often filters out inconvenient truths – see Fuller, 2005). Our view of 'the whole truth' is that, while each person's truth may exist in relation to the meaning that they give to their own lives, when they share their truth claims as the basis of the justification of their form of living with others, then norms and standards need to be negotiated. In relation to educational research, what each person claims as their truth needs to be tested against other people's truths, and negotiated for public legitimacy and adoption. This has been done in each of the validated and legitimated theses in the database referred to below.

A difficulty arises, however, about what kinds of norms and standards are used, which returns us to the question of which form of logic. In appreciating that people are different, in terms of their own inclinations, giftedness, histories, current circumstances, life goals, and so on, we question the validity of setting normative standards by which all persons should account for themselves. In our view this is a major fault in the standards set by the Teacher Development Agency. These standards, expressed in propositional form, are infused with hier-archical and colonizing power relations. There is insufficient recognition of the unique constellations of values and understandings that constitute the living standards of each individual.

Also, while we agree with Raz (1991) that humans may understand their iden-tities in terms of their attachments, the quality of the social relationships within those attachments is always and inevitably contested (Mouffe, 2001). Similarly, the notion of 'the social' is itself contested (Adorno, 2000), which leads us to state clearly that the meaning we are giving here to the 'social' in a social action is drawn from Schutz's description of the meaning of Weber's concept of social action, which,

> ... by virtue of the subjective meaning attached to it by the acting individual (or individuals), takes account of the behaviour of others, and is thereby orientated in its course ... (Schutz, 1972: 15)

In other words, we understand that the 'social' is constituted by how acting indi-viduals interact with others in relation to the meaning that those interactions have for the individual. Our understanding of the contested nature of social living, and the need to develop inclusional forms of logic to grasp its complexities, travels to our understanding of the nature of scientific and educational enquiry, and the need to develop new critical standards of judgement that can move the field forward and through which individuals give meaning and purpose to their own lives.

Drawing on the ideas of Bohm (1983), Feyerabend (1975), Medawar (1969), Popper (1963) and others, we promote a view of scientific enquiry that informs educational enquiry, as premised on our understanding of the natural order, as an ongoing process of generative transformational self-realization. Every aspect of the natural order is in a process of unfolding what is already enfolded within itself as a possibility, not working towards a given evolutionary end, but engaged purposefully in its own present growth, and in dynamic relation with every other aspect of creation. Our concern, however, is that this capacity is often suppressed through the imposition of the logics, languages and standards of traditional knowledge-creation with their emphasis on the generation of propositional theory. These logics, languages and standards aim to explain the lives of individuals and social formations through abstract general concepts. The result of this is that the embodied knowledge of people is systematically distorted to fit into existing norms and standards and consequently de-legitimized in the social world. We see this happening to other people, and we experience it ourselves, in a range of institutional and social contexts. Such practices deny our values of inclusion, grounded as they are in a deep respect for the other. We try to find ways of transforming the experience of exclusion into the possibilities of inclusion through the articulation of what counts as valid and legitimate academic knowledge.

So, given this range of concerns, we want to offer our understandings of the qualities of educational research that enable us to evaluate our social accountability in contributing to a world of educational quality in which such distortions are minimized as we learn to live our values more fully in what we are doing.

WHAT DO WE DO? IMAGINING POSSIBLE IMPROVEMENTS

We ground our understandings of improvement and our research practices in our values. Our research aim is to show how we live in the direction of those values in our practices, both as explanatory principles and frameworks for how we live our lives, and also for how we judge the quality of those lives. We transform these values into our critical living standards of judgement in relation to the methodological quality of our research (Whitehead, 2004) and in terms of the moral quality of the life lived (McNiff, 2007). However, by adopting this stance, we have to engage with the experience of ourselves as living contradictions (Whitehead, 1989), in that we need to recognize that the values we aim to realize are often not realized in practice, and frequently cannot be so realized, given the often politically constituted nature of institutional and economic contexts. Over the 25 years of our collaboration we have imagined many possibilities for improving our practices and our contributions to educational knowledge. Our publications serve as documentation and evaluation of the imagined possibilities we have acted on through our research (see for example McNiff, 2002; McNiff and Whitehead, 2006; Whitehead, 1993; Whitehead and McNiff, 2006). Throughout, we have focused especially on the nature of the standards of judgement and logics in claims to educational knowledge. These imagined possibilities have been shared in doctoral supervisions with acknowledged influence in successfully completed living theory theses. In our supervisions we stress the importance of Noffke's (1997: 329) view about connecting living theories to power and privilege in society.

The ideas expressed here have highlighted the importance of engaging with issues of social justice and power in living theory enquiries. You can see some of this influence in two of the latest living theory theses to be legitimated in the academy. The first, supervised by Jack, is Eden Charles' Ph.D. (2007). The second, supervised by Jean, is Mary Roche's Ph.D. (2007) (see below for details).

In the same way as we resist the idea of unified discourses about the supposedly potentially unified nature of human practices (since unification is idealized and therefore unrealizable, not to mention undesirable since it can factor out difference and critique that aims to test truth claims); and in the same way that we resist the idea that all human practices are working towards a pre-defined and given end; so we resist the idea that values have to be realized in practice for that practice to be understood as 'good'. We understand the 'good' in terms of human striving, not so much in terms of human 'arriving'. We resist the idea of normative 'best practice' as an idealized or prescriptive norm, other than what is achieved on a moment-to-moment basis as part of an ongoing transformational focus on 'improving practice'. Our work is grounded in a commitment to formative learning, as well as summative achievements in transformational processes. Our entire theoretical framework for the development of inclusional practices is therefore informed by the metaphors of the infinite unfoldingness of dynamic critically self-aware relationships. Practical examples of this framework can be found in the database presented below.

We bring these metaphors to our pedagogical and social practices and use them in explanations and justifications for our practices in which we generate our own living theories. We test the validity of these theories through the rational controls of critical discussions in the public domain. Hence an imagined possibility we believe will improve our practice is to make public the living form of logics and standards of judgement that inform our living theories as we continue to enquire into our practices of inclusionality.

OUR ACTIONS AND DATA GATHERING

We regard our research as a transformational process of action enquiry, where the answer to one aspect reveals new aspects to be addressed. In stressing the importance of generating living theory through action research we see our work as complementary to Somekh's (2005) work on action research as a methodology. We adopt a Foucauldian strategy (Foucault, 1980), of digging beneath the surfaces of sacred grand theories to reveal and present for public scrutiny the stories of practitioners in daily interactions with one another. We particularly identify with Foucault's points about universal and specific intellectuals with a focus on exploring the specific contexts in which the intellectual works. We explain how our action research methodologies are commensurable with our methodologies for social transformation. We express our awareness of the need for methodological inventiveness (Dadds and Hart, 2001: 166 and 169), and we show how we incorporate insights from traditional social theories into the process of generating our own inclusional living theories of practice. We aim to communicate our findings through a range of linguistic and multimedia texts, bearing in mind that a text itself needs to be self-conscious of its own quality, and explain how it should be understood as a quality text (McNiff and Whitehead, 2009). We explain how we formulate our research questions in negotiation with others, how we test the validity of our truth claims as a form of formative assessment, and how we are prepared to modify our practices in light of others' critical evaluation.

OUR VALIDATED AND LEGITIMATED DATABASE

We ground our knowledge claims in a database of masters and doctoral degrees that have been validated and legitimated in UK and Irish Universities (see www.actionresearch.net and www.jeanmcniff.com). From this database we draw evidence to demonstrate quality in educational research for social accountability. The evidence includes the accounts of ourselves and those whose studies and practices we support.

In our supervisions of educational researchers we stress the importance of validation and draw on the four criteria of social validity developed by Habermas (1976). These emphasize the importance of the following factors in establishing the validity of knowledge claims: comprehensibility; truth in the sense of providing sufficient evidence to justify the claims being made; rightness in the sense of justifying the normative assumptions in the research; and authenticity in the sense that the researcher shows over time and in interaction that they are genuinely committed to what they claim to believe in.

These accounts have gained academic legitimacy through the awards of masters and doctoral degrees for the living theories of individuals in which they explain their educational influences in their learning with explicit, values-based standards of judgement. These living standards constitute quality in educational research for social accountability.

The most recent examples we have in mind, with their qualities of social accountability are, in order of graduation: Naidoo (2005); Lohr (2006); Farren (2005); Sullivan (2006); Glenn (2006); Rawal (2006); McDonagh (2007);

Charles (2007); Follows (2007); Hymer (2007); Roche (2007) and Cahill (2007). (The living theory theses of Rawal and Hymer were completed under supervision from tutors at the University of Worcester and the University of Newcastle.)

Eden Charles' thesis on 'How can I bring Ubuntu as a living standard of judgment into the Academy? Moving beyond decolonisation through societal reidentification and guiltless recognition', demonstrates the quality of social accountability we are seeking to support. It also includes a visual narrative with video-clips. This narrative demonstrates how the meanings of the expression of embodied values, such as the African way of being, enquiring and knowing of Ubuntu, has been legitimated in the academy. Charles's thesis also includes original ideas from his responses to being a Black father, international consultant and educator living within a society with a colonial and racist history. These responses are transformatory in the sense of showing how the ideas of 'guiltless recognition' and societal re-identification can help to move beyond the anti-racist and postcolonial critical into the transformatory practices of societal re-identification.

Mary Roche's thesis on 'Towards a living theory of a caring pedagogy: Interrogating my practice to nurture a critical, emancipatory and just community of enquiry' shows the processes involved in developing a critical awareness of one's own social accountability within a normative habitus, including the habitus of one's epistemological stance. It also includes a visual narrative with video-clips. Of special importance are original ideas about how very young children may be encouraged also to interrogate and transform their emerging epistemologies, within a recognition of an existing habitus, in relation to their understandings of what constitutes an emancipatory and just society.

Using such narratives we can show how the values of practitioners are being legitimated in the academy as living standards of judgement. You can immediately access these living theories and others at http://people.bath.ac.uk/edsajw/living.shtml and http://www.jeanmcniff.com/reports.html.

While we draw insights from the theories of traditional academic philosophers, sociologists, social scientists and theologians we believe that much more needs to be done in relation to the kinds of practices and theory generation that nurture personal, social and ecological well-being. We are thinking particularly about the production of research accounts that show how many of us are embedding existing propositional and dialectical theories within our action-oriented living theories and to show how we hold ourselves accountable for our academic and intellectual practices. We see ourselves doing this because we believe that each and every individual needs to account for themselves in terms of the values and understandings that give meaning and purpose to their lives. This applies especially to those in higher education (Moustakim, 2007), who exercise institutional power in what is still recognized as the highest legitimating body for what counts as worthwhile knowledge and who should be seen as a worthwhile knower.

EVALUATING THE INFLUENCE OF OUR ACTIONS IN TERMS OF THE SIGNIFICANCE OF OUR RESEARCH INTO DEMONSTRATING QUALITY IN EDUCATIONAL RESEARCH FOR SOCIAL ACCOUNTABILITY

We believe that the significance of our research lies in the creation of a new epistemology for educational knowledge. In saying this we are taking up the challenge described by Schön:

> If we intend to pursue the 'new forms of scholarship' that Ernest Boyer presents in his *Scholarship Reconsidered*, we cannot avoid questions of epistemology, since the new forms of scholarship he describes challenge the epistemology built into the modern research university (Schön, 1995: 27).

We do not propose a new epistemology lightly (Whitehead, 1993). We believe that the significance of the new epistemology requires the kind of imagination referred to by A.N. Whitehead (1929) in discussing the purpose of the university. The significance of our research lies in comprehending and communicating the living logics of inclusionality and the living standards of judgement that can be used to validate and legitimate the explanations that individuals give for their own lives and learning in accounting to themselves and others for the lives they are living.

It is to such commitments that we give our energies. In evaluating our actions in terms of the significance of our research, we tend to focus on the evidence that our ideas are recognized, acknowledged and affirmed in the living theories of others. We have also learnt much from those we have worked with, including each other, and reciprocate the recognition, acknowledgement and affirmation in the explanations of our educational influence.

As universities respond to the newer digital technologies with regulations that permit the submission of e-media, we anticipate an extension of the influence of visual narratives (Hartog, 2004; Glenn, 2006; Naidoo, 2005; Charles, 2007; Roche, 2007). These visual narratives, with their inclusion of video evidence, enable the meanings of embodied values to be clarified in the course of their emergence through practice. They can support the expression of the meanings of living logics that can communicate relationally dynamic explanations of educational influence (Whitehead, 2006).

We relate our lives as researchers to the quest for how it is possible to improve the social order, not through the imposition of abstract theory that can be applied to practice, but through the generation of our own living theories (McNiff, 2007; Whitehead, 2007), emerging from within the practice and in relation to the ideas of others, that show how we are striving to fulfil our own values and obligations to others.

REFERENCES

Adorno, T.W. (2000) *Introduction to Sociology*. Cambridge: Polity.
Berlin (2006) *Political Ideas in the Romantic Age* (ed. H. Hardy). London: Chatto & Windus.

Bernstein, B. (2000) *Pedagogy, Symbolic Control and Identity: Theory, Research and Critique.* Lanham: Rowman & Littlefield.

Bohm, D. (1983) *Wholeness and the Implicate Order.* London: Ark Paperbacks.

Bourdieu, P. (1991) *Language and Symbolic Power.* Oxford: Polity.

Butler, J. (1999) *Gender Trouble: Feminism and the Subversion of Identity.* New York: Routledge.

Cahill, M. (2007) '*My living educational theory of inclusional practice*'. Ph.D. thesis, University of Limerick.

Charles, E. (2007) '*How can I bring Ubuntu as a living standard of judgment into the Academy? Moving beyond decolonisation through societal reidentification and guiltless recognition*'. Ph.D. thesis, University of Bath.

Dadds, M. and Hart, S. (2001) *Doing Practitioner Research Differently.* London: Routledge.

Derrida, J. (1998) 'Hospitality, justice and responsibility: A dialogue with Jacques Derrida', in R. Kearney and M. Dooley, *Questioning Ethics: Contemporary Debates in Philosophy.* London: Routledge.

Farren, M. (2005) '*How can I create a pedagogy of the unique through a web of betweenness?*' Ph.D. thesis, University of Bath.

Feyerabend, P. (1975) *Against Method.* London: New Left.

Follows, M. (2007) '*Looking for a fairer assessment of children's learning, development and attainment in the infant years: An educational action research case study*'. Ph.D. thesis, University of Plymouth.

Foucault, M. (1980) 'Truth and power', in C. Gordon (ed.) *Power/Knowledge: Selected Interviews and Other Writings, 1972–1977.* Brighton: Harvester.

Fuller, S. (2005) *The Intellectual.* Cambridge: Icon Books.

Glenn, M. (2006) '*Working with collaborative projects: My living theory of a holistic educational practice*'. Ph.D. thesis, University of Limerick.

Habermas, J. (1976) *Communication and the Evolution of Society.* London: Heinemann.

Hartog, M. (2004) '*A self-study of a higher education tutor: How can I improve my practice?*' Ph.D. thesis, University of Bath.

Hirst, P. (ed.) (1983) *Educational Theory and its Foundation Disciplines.* London: Routledge & Kegan Paul.

Hymer, B. (2007) '*How do I understand and communicate my values and beliefs in my work as an educator in the field of giftedness?*' D.Ed.Psy. thesis, University of Newcastle.

Kristeva, J. (2002) 'Interview', reproduced in J. Lechte and M. Margaroni (eds) *Julia Kristeva: Live Theory.* London: Continuum.

Lohr, E. (2006) '*Love at work: What is my lived experience of love and how might I become an instrument of love's purpose?*' Ph.D. thesis, University of Bath.

McDonagh, C. (2007) '*My living theory of learning to teach for social justice: How do I enable primary school children with specific learning disability (dyslexia) and myself as their teacher to realize our learning potentials?*' Ph.D. thesis, University of Limerick.

McNiff, J. (with J. Whitehead) (2002) *Action Research: Principles and Practice* (2nd edn). London: Routledge.

McNiff, J. (2007) 'My story is my living educational theory', in D.J. Clandinin (ed.) *Handbook of Narrative Inquiry: Mapping a Methodology.* Thousand Oaks,CA: Sage, pp. 308–29.

McNiff, J. and Whitehead, J. (2006) *All You Need to Know about Action Research.* London: Sage.

McNiff, J. and Whitehead, J. (2009) *Doing and Writing Up Your Action Research.* London, Sage.

Medawar, P.B. (1969) *Induction and Intuition in Scientific Thought.* London: Methuen.

Mouffe (2001) 'For an agonistic model of democracy', in N. O'Sullivan (ed.) *Political Theory in Transition.* London: Routledge.

Moustakim, M. (2007) 'From transmission to dialogue: promoting critical engagement in higher education teaching and learning', in *Educational Action Research*, 15 (2): 209–20.

Naidoo, M. (2005) '*I am because we are. (My never-ending story.) The emergence of a living theory of inclusional and responsive practice.* Ph.D. thesis, University of Bath.

Noffke, S. (1997) 'Professional, personal, and political dimensions of action research' in M. Apple (ed.) (1997) *Review of Research in* Education. Vol. 22, Washington: AERA.

Polanyi, M. (1958) *Personal Knowledge*. London: Routledge & Kegan Paul.

Popper, K. (1963) *Conjectures and Refutations*. Oxford: Oxford University Press.

Rawal, S. (2006) '*The role of drama in enhancing life skills in children with specific learning difficulties in a Mumbai school: My reflective account*'. Ph.D. thesis, Coventry University in collaboration with the University of Worcester.

Rayner, A. (2005) 'Space, dust and the co-evolutionary context of "His Dark Materials".' Retrieved 27 May 2007 from http://people.bath.ac.uk/bssadmr/inclusionality/HisDarkMaterials.htm

Raz, J. (2001) *Value, Respect and Attachment*. Cambridge, UK: Cambridge University Press.

Roche, M. (2007) '*Towards a living theory of a caring pedagogy: Interrogating my practice to nurture a critical, emancipatory and just community of enquiry.*' Ph.D. thesis, University of Limerick.

Schön, D. (1995) 'The new scholarship requires a new epistemology', in *Change*, November/December, 27 (6): 27–34.

Schutz, A. (1972) *The Phenomenology of the Social World*. London: Heinemann.

Somekh, B. (2005) *Action Research: A Methodology for Change and Development*. Maidenhead: Open University Press.

Sullivan, B. (2006) '*A living theory of a practice of social justice: Realising the right of traveller children to educational equality*'. Ph.D. thesis, University of Limerick.

Whitehead, A.N. (1929) *The Aims of Education and Other Essays*. New York: Macmillan.

Whitehead, J. (1989) 'Creating a living educational theory from questions of the kind, "How Do I Improve my Practice?"', in *Cambridge Journal of Education*, 19 (1): 34–57.

Whitehead, J. (1993) *The Growth of Educational Knowledge*. Bournemouth: Hyde.

Whitehead, J. (2004) 'What counts as evidence in the self-studies of teacher education practices?', in J.J. Loughran, M.L. Hamilton, V.K. LaBoskey and T. Russell (eds), *International Handbook of Self-Study of Teaching and Teacher Education Practices*. Dordrecht; Kluwer Academic Publishers, pp. 871–903.

Whitehead, J. (2006) 'Living inclusional values in educational standards of practice and judgement', in *Ontario Action Researcher*, Vol. 8.2.1. Retrieved 27 May 2007 from http://www.nipissingu.ca/oar/new_issue-V821E.htm

Whitehead, J. (2007) 'Creating a world of educational quality through living educational theories'. Paper presented at AERA 2007 in Chicago, 13 April, 2007. Retrieved 25 May 2007 from http://www.jackwhitehead.com/aera07/jwaera07.htm

Whitehead, J. and McNiff, J. (2006) *Action Research: Living Theory*. London: Sage.

26

Action Research and Pedagogy as Science of the Child's Upbringing[1]

Petra Ponte and Jan Ax

In this chapter we will contend that pedagogical theories could inform the conduct of action research based on social theories. We are referring here not to 'pedagogy as method' which has been dominant in the Anglo-American literature, but to *Pedagogiek*, which we term 'pedagogy as human science', or more precisely, the science of the child's upbringing. This science seeks answers to questions about what kind of human beings children should become and how they can be raised toward becoming such human beings, taking into account the context in which this process of upbringing takes place.

Frameworks are used in which knowledge from different disciplines (psychology, sociology, philosophy, economics, law) are integrated. Pedagogy as human science was more dominant in the Netherlands, Germany and other continental European countries until recently but this dominance is increasingly being replaced by a strong focus toward pragmatic Anglo-American pedagogic literature with a strong psychological focus on the individual learner (see Van Manen, 1994; Westbury, 2000). We start with the underpinning principles that legitimize action research and argue that in addition to principles of justice and critique, principles of pedagogy (*pedagogiek*) are also needed (see Ponte, 2007). We then go on to explore the historical background of pedagogy as human science, constantly exploring questions that teachers doing action research will ask themselves. The chapter concludes by making a link to Anglo-American literature on pedagogy and some closing remarks.

ARGUMENTS FOR ACTION RESEARCH

The general argument made for action research is often as follows. The reality of professional practice is complex, changeable and cannot be accurately predicted in advance by general academic knowledge. As a consequence, practitioners constantly have to face the question: What in the given circumstances is the best way to act, in order to achieve what is important at this moment? In action research this argument is mainly bound up with an agenda for democracy and social justice. Although there seems to be a consensus on this agenda, different orientations can be found. We summarize these as the principles of justice and critique, each in a different way related to the principles of professional development (inspired by the 'ethics' of Poliner Shapiro and Stefkovich, 2001: 1).

The **principles of justice** are grounded in the theories which are part of a liberal democratic tradition. Action research in this tradition is legitimized by a commitment to human freedom, equality of educational opportunity and freedom of belief (Stenhouse, 1975). The **principles of critique** are grounded in critical theories. Action research with a focus on these principles is legitimized by a commitment to demystify claims of truth for the purpose of transforming society and emancipating individuals from false consciousness (Carr and Kemmis, 1986). The **principles of professionalism** refer here to action research as a strategy for professional development. From the *principles of justice* perspective, action researchers should address the question of how to achieve consensus in interaction with children or youths and other stakeholders about what the aims are in given circumstances and the best way to achieve them. From the *principles of critique* perspective, action researchers should address the question of how they can contribute to social equality and justice in a democratic society.

AN ADDITION: PRINCIPLES OF PEDAGOGY

From our argument so far, the agenda of action research would seem to be mainly inspired by the questions 'What benefits human freedom and social equity? or 'What benefits the transformation of the society and the emancipation of its members?' and – based on that – 'What is a good professional?' These questions are certainly inspired by commitment to the people that education is ultimately about, namely the pupils. Elliott (1991), for example, argued that:

> The ultimate criterion for action research is the extent to which those engaging in it experience their teaching as something that enables or constrains the development of their own power in relation to things that matter. (p. 11)

This kind of commitment is certainly important, but it still does not provide answers to questions like: What is our understanding of the children or youngsters we want to teach? What does our understanding mean for the relationship between me as the teacher and the child as the pupil? What do we expect teachers to do on a day-to-day basis in the name of social goals? What do we expect students to learn and why?

Teachers do not usually legitimize their educational actions in the first place because of notions about a better world, but mainly because they want to do justice to children in their daily practice (Van Manen, 1994). This does not mean that they have no political or social motives beyond their classrooms, but they will express these motives mainly through their work and relationships with their pupils (Pratt and Associates, 1998). At the secondary level, love of the subject and wanting to inspire pupils is an additional motive. Teacher professional identity, according to Van Manen (1994: 140), 'is therefore to be found in the educative relationship with the students', so they will also explore the questions in their action research from that perspective. For example, they ask questions such as: How can we get the issue of dropout among immigrant pupils on the agenda of our school? How can we support mentors in counselling difficult pupils? How can I teach ethics to students in the Department of Social Services in a vocational education college? Action research, in other words, will for them be mainly a systematic and empirically based way to identify practical educational problems and to find well-considered practical solutions. Any argument made for action research as a strategy for the professional development of teachers could benefit therefore, in our view, from principles of pedagogy, based on pedagogy as human science. These principles could help to reflect on and transform principles of justice and critique into consequences for the educational practice of teachers or principles of professionalism (see Figure 26.1).

Before examining the various pedagogical (*pedagogische*) schools in relation to questions that action researchers might ask themselves, we will first describe general characteristics of pedagogy as human science.

PEDAGOGY AS HUMAN SCIENCE

The enlightenment and humanist philosophers in the 16th and 17th centuries 'discovered' human beings as individuals who are able to influence their own lives and the context in which they live. With the discovery of the human being as an individual, came the 'discovery' of the possibility and need to raise children in certain ways. It was from this discovery that pedagogy as human science

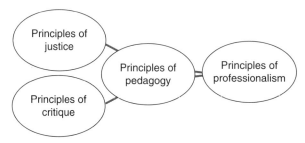

Figure 26.1   Principles that inform the conduct of action research.

developed (Noordam, 1978). The word 'pedagogy' comes from the Latin words 'paidos' which means 'child' and 'agogos' which means 'bringer' or 'guide'.

Pedagogy as human science aims at the formulation of theories, as well as at the transformation of what is called pedagogical (*pedagogische*) praxis. Pedagogical praxis here is seen as the real, existing practice of upbringing and as a natural condition of human beings. Praxis as the process of upbringing always exists, regardless of its quality or implications. Indoctrination, for instance, is highly undesirable, but it is still a form of upbringing. Every upbringing, every praxis therefore, implies a social environment. We become people in and through the social environment and morality is the essence of this. After all, every pedagogical relationship has mores and they are culturally, socially and materially determined. In other words: pedagogical praxis is a culturally and socially embedded situation in which the upbringer purposefully tries to help the child to become an adult. Because of their social-cultural roots, aims and methods are strongly connected and historically determined. Pedagogical aims refer to ideas about what kind of human beings children should become, and pedagogical methods refer to ideas about how to achieve these aims. In line with this, Benner (1973) describes the nature of pedagogy as human science as:

> both practical and theoretical, for it supports, for one thing, the gradual problematisation of pedagogical practice ... the problematisation of pedagogical practice always proceeds from a situation in which accepted norms and conversations of human coexistence become questionable'. (pp. 11–12, translation by the author)

Benner is pointing here to the problematization of the relationship between the child ('upbringee'), the upbringer (teacher) and the social context as the object of pedagogy as human science, which is often summed up in the pedagogical triangle (*pedagogische driehoek*) (see Figure 26.2).

The philosophical and theoretical debate about pedagogical praxis has from the start been fundamental to continental European pedagogy as human science, in contrast with the Anglo-American tradition of pedagogy as method. Boyd (1964), for example, claimed that in the 19th and 20th centuries in the English-speaking world:

> Theories were more or less consigned to 'plan two' in favour of a concentration on mechanical aspects of teaching; in contrast with the countries on the European continent where theory has always been the mainspring of pedagogical debates. (p. 438)

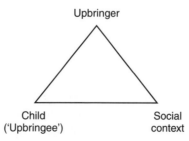

Figure 26.2 The pedagogical triangle.

Because of its autonomous theoretical foundations, pedagogy as human science was able to develop into a separate discipline, often located in separate faculties within universities, where students studied 'pedagogy' (science of the child's upbringing) to become a 'pedagogue', just as others studied psychology to become a psychologist. The discipline of pedagogy was characterized by the integral approach of the research domain, summarized above as the pedagogical triangle. The approach can be described as integral, firstly because the child's upbringing is studied:

- in different domains, such as education, social work, health, child welfare, law and policing;
- from different specialisms, such as theoretical pedagogy, historical pedagogy, educational pedagogy, special education, family pedagogy and social pedagogy;
- with the aid of different disciplines, such as philosophy, psychology, sociology, psychiatry, law and economics.

Secondly, pedagogy as human science includes consistent approaches to:

- the aims, methods and justification of the upbringing process;
- the scientific aims;
- the research strategy to reach those aims.

In contrast with some English-speaking countries, 'science' (*wetenschap*) in continental Europe is used as a general term for academic work in different fields, paradigms and traditions. Various scientific 'schools' have grown up in pedagogy as human science over the course of history, which to some extent still co-exist. They all have their own outlooks on the relationship between the aims, methods and justification of the upbringing process; the scientific aim of pedagogy and the research strategy to reach that aim (Miedema, 1997). Consequently, although there is general consensus about the need to raise children towards adulthood, there is no consensus about what 'raising children' should be, or lead to, and how this process can be studied. There is no consensus because the definitions of 'raising into adulthood' are based on assumptions about what it is to be a civilized human being and how children can be helped to become such human beings (Noordam, 1978).

Teachers also will have different views on human development and it can be assumed that these different views will have a strong influence on the questions they ask themselves in their action research. It also can be assumed that understanding these different views on human development will help them in critically questioning their pedagogical praxis. That praxis is concerned with their actions in the real world as they experience it. Understanding that real world does not allow them to sub-divide problems into questions within separate disciplines (psychological, sociological or philosophical questions), but requires an integrating framework within which educational issues can be examined. Pedagogy as human science offers under-pinning principles for such a framework. The next section explores the significance of these principles for the questions asked by educationalists in general and action researchers in particular, based on the approaches of the most significant pedagogical schools. This section is based on important reviews by, among others, Boyd (1964), Benner (1993), Wulf (1974) and Miedema (1997).

PEDAGOGICAL SCHOOLS AND QUESTIONS IN ACTION RESEARCH

Normative/Dogmatic Pedagogy

Pedagogy as human science grew up in the 16th and 17th centuries as a philosophical discipline. This approach is designated in Table 26.1 as the normative/dogmatic school, because its aims for the upbringing process are derived in a direct line from philosophical, religious or anthropological notions about humankind. There is also a linear link between aims and methods, for instance: if the aim is devotion and absolute obedience to God and church the child must be 'drilled' or disciplined in order to become such a person. The scientific aim is the formulation of philosophical, religious or anthropological principles about humankind and how to become such a human being. The research strategy can be described as 'intuitive deduction' of dogmas from certain views on human beings. It is seen as pre-scientific, because of the absence of empirical research and therefore not relevant for teachers doing action research.

The bases for modern pedagogy as human science were laid down by Locke (1632–1704) and Rousseau (1712–1778) in the 17th and 18th centuries. Locke saw the newborn human child as a sheet of blank slate (tabula rasa) on which things – learned through the child's upbringing – would be written. Rousseau, adopting a rather different point of view, pleaded for the child, who was good by nature, to be given a natural upbringing. His view was that the child's development should be protected from harmful and stunting influences in the culture.

Table 26.1 Main Pedagogical 'Schools' in the Netherlands, Germany and Other Continental European Countries

'Schools'	Aims, Method, Justification of Upbringing	Scientific Aim	Research Strategy	Key Scholars
Normative/ dogmatic Pedagogy	Linear link between aims and methods	Formulation of principles	Intuitive deduction	Locke, Rousseau
Geistes Wissenschaft-licher pedagogy	The child as child – as a specific expression of human existence	Understanding or *verstehen*	Hermeneutics, phenomenology	Dilthey Gadamar Langeveld
Empirical-analytic pedagogy	Interventions of upbringer as causes of changes in child	Explanation and control	Deductive, nomological approach	Brezinka
Critical pedagogy	Emancipation of child from social constraints through communication	Transformation of person and society	Ideology-critique, action research	Blankertz Freire Mollenhouwer

According to Locke, discipline has to be used to raise children in the norms and values of the culture they live in. Teachers with this perspective who carry out action research will ask themselves questions such as: What rules should we get the pupils to follow in order to make them into intellectual people, religious people, servants of the state or critical citizens? How can we reward or punish pupils so that they follow the rules? These teachers can give scope to children's voices by, for instance, asking how pupils interpret the rules. They will use this information to formulate the rules more clearly, in order to write on the 'blank slate' that children are, in their view, in order to direct them on the right path more effectively. A school could, for example, use an argument like this: 'It is in the interests of society that pupils develop their intellectual capacities and that justifies our calling one pupil "top of the school" every year. We want to explore the best way to organize pupils' learning.' A modern day re-emergence of Locke's views can be seen, for instance, in the effective schools movement (Mortimore, 1997).

By contrast, in line with Rousseau's natural education, children should be allowed the freedom to develop into rational, religious or critical people. Teachers with this perspective who carry out action research will ask themselves questions such as: How can we organize the school environment so that children become aware of the natural good that they have within them? How can we let them experience that lying leads not to punishment, but to discomfort; that effort leads not to 'top of the class', but to 'intrinsic satisfaction'? (De Jager, 1975). These teachers will see enabling children's voices in action research not only as a way to realize their own teaching objectives more effectively, but also as a way to give pupils more control over their own learning process. A school could, for example, use an argument like this: 'It is in the interests of society that pupils develop into rational and independent people. That justifies our allowing pupils to work together, on tasks they have chosen themselves, at their own tempo and we want to research the best way to stimulate that'. A modern day re-emergence of Rousseau's views can be seen, for instance, in schools that base their approaches on *reform pedagogiek*, such as Montessori schools, and Jena plan schools based on the ideas of Peter Petersen (Immelman et al., 1981).

Geisteswissenschafliche (Humanistic) Pedagogy

In the original theories of Locke and Rousseau, being a child was understood from a perspective about 'what the child is not yet, but will soon grow to become' (Miedema, 1997: 31). This understanding was reflected in the idea that methods for raising children could be directly derived from goals and that those goals could be directly derived from theories about humankind. These assumptions changed with the development of *Geisteswissenschafliche* (humanistic) pedagogy in the 20th century. Being a child was now seen as a development process that is always driven from two sides: the environment, especially the parents and teachers, and the drive coming from the child him or herself to become someone. In this outlook, being a child is a distinct form of human existence with specific qualities and characteristics which distinguish this stage from other stages of life (Langeveld, 1967). This stage is called the 'pedagogical province' (*pedagogische provincie*), implying that the child is entitled to a protected childhood, separated from the life of adults. This means that methods cannot be derived in a direct line from the aims. This led as far back as 1801 to the formulation of the 'Pedagogical paradox' (*pedagogische paradox*) by Kant (in 'Über Pedagogik'), that is the paradox between freedom and determination in the upbringing of children. Teachers may, for instance, ask themselves in their action research: Saying that the child must grow into a free human being does not mean that the child should grow up in total freedom. What boundaries should I then set as a teacher and how can I do that? Should I protect the pupils in my class from aggressive behaviour or should I help them to learn to defend themselves by allowing them to experience this kind of behaviour?

Geisteswissenschafliche pedagogy became more focused on pedagogical praxis as a field of empirical study. It is understood to be formed by the past, present and future; statements about the upbringing process are always normative and therefore the scientific aim is to understand (*verstehen*) with the help of hermeneutics and phenomenological research strategies as formulated by, for instance, Dilthey (1988) and Gadamar (1976).

Empirical-Analytical Pedagogy

Just like *Geisteswissenschaftliche* pedagogy, empirical-analytical pedagogy criticized the pre-scientific character of the normative/dogmatic school. The empirical-analytic school focused mainly on establishing effective education methods through sound science. The interventions of the upbringer are seen as the cause of changes in the child. The moral justifications for those interventions and the aims of those interventions are not seen as belonging to pedagogy as human science (Brezinka, 1971). The scientific aim is to deliver explanations of upbringing and this is done via deductive-nomological research strategies. Evidence-based practice can be classified under this approach (Hargreaves, 1996). Questions that action researchers using this approach might ask are: What methods do I have at my disposal to reduce aggressive behaviour and how can I use these methods effectively?

Critical Pedagogy

The fourth school in Table 26.1 is the school of critical pedagogy, mainly based on the philosophy of the *Frankfurter Schule*. This school developed firstly in response to *Geisteswissenschaftliche* pedagogy, where concepts such as independence, freedom and self-determination were conceived as relating solely to the relationship between teacher/upbringer and the child being taught or raised, with no regard for the social context of that relationship. Secondly, it developed in response to empirical-analytic pedagogy, which saw no place for normative concepts like independence, freedom and self-determination in an objective science; a science which should be geared solely to controlling the physical or social reality through knowledge of general laws in the education process. Critical pedagogy aspires to connect the normative and the empirical into a practice-oriented pedagogy as human science and, in so doing, to build a bridge between the social theories of Habermas (1981) and others of like mind and theories on human development on the one hand, and available empirical knowledge on the other hand. Blankertz (1969) expressed this connection with regard to the theory of teaching as follows:

> My proposition is that the three basic positions ... only appear to compete with each other; that in reality they survive or, in any case, would have a much better chance of surviving through extensive critique and continual awareness of problems. (p. 7, translation by the author)

Critical pedagogy has been reproached for being another approach where methods are directly derived from aims about what the child is intended to become and for having aims that are directly derived from social critical theories (for instance: If the aim is bringing up liberated citizens, the child must grow up in a totally anti-authoritarian environment). Mollenhauwer (1964/1979) and Freire (1970) tried to avoid this criticism by translating critical social theories into critical theories about the child's upbringing. Their aim is to emancipate young people from social constraints through methods like developing opportunities for communication. The scientific aim is to develop emancipatory knowledge and insight into knowledge interests as a base for social transformation. This knowledge is constructed via a critique of ideology and action research as an addition to the hermeneutics and deductive-nomological research strategies.

Teachers who are doing action research from a critical perspective will base their question on the idea that different children need different approaches in order to realize equal social opportunities for them. They will examine the conduct of their action research and its consequences for social justice and emancipation.

CONCLUSION AND CLOSING REMARKS

These in a nutshell are the fundamentals of pedagogy as human science in the Netherlands, Germany and other continental European countries and the possible consequences of these approaches for questions that teachers doing action research ask themselves. This is not a complete overview and nowadays we can observe a diversification (Miedema, 1997), where alongside *Geisteswissenschaftliche* pedagogy, empirical-analytical pedagogy and critical pedagogy, other approaches have also been influential, such as cultural historical pedagogy (Vygotsky, Russia); pragmatism (Dewey, US), structuralism and post-structuralism (France) and linguistic analytical pedagogy (UK).

Although the descriptions above originate in pedagogy as human science, they should also be easy to reconcile with ideas in the Anglo-American literature on education as moral endeavour (see for instance Goodlad et al., 1990; Noddings, 2002). The important point here though is that these theories are not seen as pedagogy as human science, and are not seen as a separate discipline. In the English-language literature, pedagogy is usually conceived in a narrow sense as method, addressing therefore the question of what instrumental resources are available with which to shape teaching. Pedagogy as method is also, according to some scholars in the Anglo-American world itself, dominated by means-to-an-end thinking and often based on a naive child-centred ethos. This ethos proceeds from the assumption that the teacher can allow him or herself to be guided by the children's needs, dissociated from anthropological views of mankind and educational objectives derived from them (Boyd, 1964). Such pedagogy does not, according to these authors, offer a scientific basis to the theory and practice of education, because it does not challenge our views on how life is to be lived and in what direction we should be guiding children. Simon (1999), for example, claimed that:

> For a combination of social, political and ideological reasons pedagogy – a scientific basis to the theory and practice of education – has never taken root and flourished in Britain (...) Each [educational; addition from the author] 'system', largely self-contained, developed its own specific educational approach, each within its narrowly defined field, and each 'appropriate' to its specific social function. In these circumstances the conditions did not and could not exist for the development of an all embracing, universalized, scientific theory of education relating to practice of teaching. (p. 38)

Simon pleads for a pedagogy which recognizes both the power of education to affect human development and the need for the systematization and structuring of the child's experiences in the educational process. Simon (1999) concurs with Van Manen (1994) and Olson (2003) that instead of a pragmatic 'child-centred' ethos – starting from the standpoint of individual differences – a pedagogy as human science is needed that starts from what children have in common as members of the human race and human society, to establish the general principles of teaching and in the light of these to determine what modifications of practice are necessary to meet specific individual needs. Pedagogy according to Olson (2003) should:

> not offer methodology; rather it should offer a scientific basis for timely, informed decisions by professionals about balancing the welfare of the individual with the demands of society. (p. 210)

The discussion above allows us to assume that teachers shape their relationships with pupils from different perspectives, and that these different perspectives are connected with their explicit or implicit outlook on what kind of human beings children should become and how they can be raised toward becoming such human beings. It can also be assumed that it is precisely these different perspectives that will determine what problems they identify in their action research and what solutions they find. What this involves is in fact problematizing the question, mentioned in the first section of this chapter, which teachers constantly have to face: What in the given circumstances is the best way to act, in order to achieve what is important at this moment? This question cannot be answered by a pragmatic 'child-centred' ethos – starting from the standpoint of individual differences, but by a pedagogic ethos that starts from a theory about what children have in common as members of the human race and human society, a theory about what the educational needs are in the society, what the influences on these needs are, how to determine special needs for specific pupils – and so on.

We have argued that action research as a strategy for the professional development of teachers requires principles of pedagogy in order to transform principles of justice and critique into consequences for their educational practice. We believe that this transformation is necessary to prevent action research from degenerating either into a handy, instrumental method for solving immediate problems or learning from practice, or a handy way to apply academic knowledge in practice; a method that leaves existing inadequate practices as they are. When doing action research, teachers do need to understand conceptual frameworks for questioning, analyzing and acting in the pedagogical praxis. That praxis is concerned with actions in their real world and understanding that reality does not allow them to subdivide problems into questions within separate disciplines (psychological, sociological or philosophical questions). It requires an integrating framework within which educational issues can be examined. Pedagogy as human science offers several perspectives for such a framework and teachers might use these to inform the conduct of their action research.

NOTE

1 This chapter is based on Ponte, P. *Action Research and Pedagogy as Human Science*. Keynote Speech at the Symposium on Pedagogy, Education and Praxis Development, organized by the Ripple-Research Centre, Charles Sturt University, Wagga Wagga, Australia, on March 2 2007.

REFERENCES

Benner, D. (1973) *Hauptströmungen der Erziehungs-wissenshaft. Eine Systematik traditioneller und moderner Theorien.* (In German: Main schools in Pedagogy as Human Science. A system of traditional and modern theories). München: List Verlag.

Blankertz, H. (1969) *Theorien und Modelle der Didaktik* (In German: Theories and models of teaching). München: Juventa Verlag.

Boyd, M. (1964) *The History of Western Education.* London: Adam and Charles Black. (Dutch translation: (1969) Geschiedenis van onderwijs en opvoeding. Utrecht: Aula-boeken).

Brezinka, W. (1971) *Von der Pädagogik zur Erziehungswissenschaft.* (In German: From up bringing to Pedagogy as Human Science). Basel: Belz Verlag.

Carr, W. and Kemmis, S. (1986) *Becoming Critical.* London: The Falmer Press.

De Jager, H. (1975) *Human Development and Theories about Society.* (In Dutch: *Mensbeelden en maatschappijmodellen*). Leiden: Stenfert Kroese.

Dilthey, W. (1988) *Introduction to the Human Sciences*, Ramon J. Betanzos (translation). Detroit: Wayne State University Press.

Elliott, J. (1991) *Action Research for Educational Change.* Buckingham: Open University Press.

Freire, P. (1970) *Pedagogy of the Oppressed*, translated by Myra Bergman Ramos. New York: Continuum.

Gadamar (1976) *Vernunft im Zeitalter der Wissenshaft: Aussätze.* (In German: *Rationality in Century of Science).* Frankfurt: Suhrkamp.

Goodlad J.I., Soder, R. and Sirotnik, K.A. (eds) (1990) *The Moral Dimensions of Teaching.* San Francisco: Jossey-Bass.

Habermas, J. (1981) *Theorie des Kommunikativen Handelns* (In German: T*heory of Communicative Action*). Frankfurt am Main: Suhrkamp Verlag.

Hargreaves, D. (1996) *Teaching as Research-based Profession: Possibilities and Prospects.* London: Teacher Training Agency.

Imelman. J.D., Jeunhomme, J.M.P. and Meijer, W.A.J. (1981) *Jenaplan. Wel en wee van een schoolped-agogiek* (In Dutch: *Ups and Downs of a School Pedagogy)* Nijkerk: Callenbach bv.

Langeveld, M.J. (1967) *Concise Theoretical Pedagogy* (In Dutch: Beknopte theoretische pedagogiek). Groningen: Wolters-Noordhoff NV.

Miedema, S. (1997) *Pedagogy in Plural* (In Dutch: Pedagogiek in meervoud). (5th edn). Houten/Diegem: Bohn Stafleu Van Loghum.

Mollenhauwer, K. (1964/1979) *Introduction to Social Pedagogy* (In German: Einfürung in die Socialp ädagogik). Basel: Belz Verlag.

Mortimore, P. (1997) 'Can effective schools compensate for society?' in A.H. Halsey, H. Lauder, P. Brown and A.S. Wells (eds), Education. *Culture, Economy, and Society.* Oxford-New York: Oxford University Press, pp. 476–87.

Noddings, Nel (2002) *Educating Moral People: A Caring Alternative to Character Education.* New York: Teachers College Press.

Noordam, N.F. (1978) *Het mensbeeld in de opvoeding.* (In Dutch: *Anthropology in Pedagogy as Human Science).* Groningen: Wolters Noordhoff.

Olson, R. (2003) *Psychological Theory and Educational Reform. How School Remakes Mind and Society.* Cambridge: Cambridge University Press.

Poliner Shapiro, J. and Stefkovich, J.A. (2001) *Ethical Leadership and Decision Making in Education: Applying Theoretical Perspectives to Complex Dilemmas.* Mahwah, NJ: Lawrence Erlbaum.

Ponte, P. (2007) 'Behind the vision – action research, pedagogy and human development', in A. Cambell and S. Groundwater-Smith (eds) *An Ethical Approach to Practitioner Research: Dealing with Issues and Dilemmas in Action Research.* London: Routledge, pp. 144–61.

Pratt, D.D. and Associates. (1998) *Five Perspectives on Teaching in Adult and Higher Education.* Melbourne FL: Krieger Publishing.

Simon, S. (1999) 'Why not pedagogy in England?' in J. Leach and B. Moon, *Learners and Pedagogy.* London: Paul Chapman, pp. 34–46.

Stenhouse, L. (1975) *An Introduction to Curriculum Research and Development.* London: Heinemann Educational Books.

Van Manen, M. (1994) 'Pedagogy, virtue and narrative identity in teaching, *Curriculum Inquiry*, 24 (2): 135–70.

Westbury, I. (2000) 'Teaching as a reflective practice: What might didaktik teach curriculum?' in I. Westbury, S. Hopmann and K. Riquarts (eds), *Teaching as a Reflective Practice: The German Didaktik Tradition.* Mahwah, NJ: Lawrence Erlbaum, pp. 15–40.

Wulf, C. (1974) *Worterbuch der Erziehung* (In German: *Dictionary of the Upbringing*). München: R. Piper & Co. Verlag.

Developing Relationships, Developing the Self: Buddhism and Action Research*

Richard Winter

Action research has frequently been interpreted as an attempt to overcome the alienation of work-based relationships in hierarchical, bureaucratized organizations. Rationales for this perspective on action research have drawn on a variety of Western intellectual traditions, such as marxism (Fals-Borda and Rahman, 1991), critical social theory (Carr and Kemmis, 1986; Winter, 1989; Winter and Munn-Giddings, 2001), postmodernism (Stringer, 1996), organizational relations theory (Whyte, 1991), and the literature on 'reflective practice' (Schon, 1983, Elliott, 1991). The purpose of the following argument is to argue that the transformation of relationships also requires a transformation of the self and to suggest how our understanding of this aspect of action research can helpfully be illuminated and informed by analogies and parallels with the complex synthesis of epistemology, psychology, ethics and moral practice represented by Buddhism. Each section of the chapter starts out from a key concept in the methodology of action research and attempts to add both precision and depth through a comparison with some Buddhist themes and doctrines.

* This is a revised version of 'Buddhism and action research towards an appropriate model of inquiry for the caring professions' Winter, R., *Educational Action Research Vol.* 11:1 (2003) pp. 141–60. Reprinted by permission of the publisher (Taylor & Francis Ltd, http://www.informaworld.com).

THE IMPORTANCE OF VALUES: CARE, COLLABORATION

The defining characteristic of action research is that it involves an attempt to create new understanding through negotiating and implementing improvements in the quality of social practices. This has important consequences. Firstly, it means that every phase of the work is in itself intended to enhance professional values (justice, rationality, care, autonomy, etc.). 'Good action research is informed by the values practitioners want to realize in their practice' (Elliott, 1995: 10). In other words, the relationships of the inquiry process must enact and model the values of the organization where the inquiry is taking place. More particularly, it means that the inquiry process must model human values such as 'co-operation' (Heron, 1996; 1998), 'participation' (Reason, 1994) and 'collaboration' (Carr and Kemmis, 1986: 199–200; Winter, 1989, Chapter 4).

Action research requires this form of relationship for a very practical reason: the inquiry process is going to require participants to take part in a change process, and this is unlikely to occur unless everyone feels that the process is one to which they have fully and autonomously committed themselves, rather than one which has been imposed upon them. But action research also insists on 'empowering' 'democratic', collaborative/co-operative relationships for moral and political reasons, i.e. to overcome a widespread sense of alienation, fragmentation and powerlessness (Reason, 1994, Chapter 1). Only within a set of relationships which are experienced as 'empowering', where there is a genuine sense of trust, mutual respect, equality and autonomy, will the inquiry be able to draw on all individuals' inherent creative potential (Heron, 1996). And it is in this universal human capacity for emotional transformation (Dadds, 1995: 121–2), for 'critical subjectivity' (Heron, 1998) and for 'innovative thinking' (Hart, 1996) that action research locates the possibility for developing new and valuable knowledge. Indeed, both Reason and Heron go further and identify this person-centred, experiential, creatively co-operative aspect of action research as having an inherently spiritual dimension, i.e. an essential link with those aspects of human consciousness which transcend ego-awareness and instrumental rationality (Reason, 1994: 50, 53; Heron, 1998: 1–3).

These arguments from within the action research tradition can be related to Buddhist ideas at a number of points.[1] To begin with, one of the most immediately distinctive features of Buddhism was that it rejected the caste divisions of Brahmin culture. Whereas Brahminism emphasized that wisdom and understanding were restricted to the Brahmin caste, and that the lower caste *suddas* were *forbidden* to hear the Vedic scriptures, the Buddhist teaching was intended for *all* people, since all (regardless of status, gender and experience) have the 'ability' to understand (Payutto, 1995: 38–43). Thus, for example, there is the story of the Sakyan princes, who presented themselves to the Buddha in order to be ordained as his followers along with their barber of long standing, Upali, requesting that in order to humble their pride, Upali should be ordained first – a request to which the Buddha readily assented (Nanamoli, 1992: 83). Returning to a research context, one might deduce from this that it is dangerously prideful to assume in advance that we know who will contribute wisdom to our work, i.e. that we can rigidly divide participants into lower caste 'research subjects' (who can only contribute the data of their mundane opinions or experiences) and the 'Brahmin researchers' (who decide on theoretical meanings).

One of the key dimensions of action research is the attempt to establish collaborative, co-operative patterns of communication, in order to heal the distorted or inadequate communication processes that so often limit the effectiveness of professional situations and roles. And on this topic the principle of 'harmonious speech' (a sub-section of the Buddhist 'Eight-fold Path') is instructive:

> At the fourth and the deepest level … right speech promotes concord or harmony. 'Concord' in this context does not mean just intellectual agreement: it is not just sharing the same ideas … It really means what we may describe as mutual helpfulness leading to mutual self-transcendence. (Sangarakshita, 1996: 140)

And indeed, writers on action research regularly invoke, as the basis for collaborative relationships, Habermas's 'ideal speech situation', in which all conflictual, power-based roles are suspended and only the power of the better argument prevails (see Carr and Kemmis, 1986: 142–4). Nevertheless one might respond to all this by saying, 'This is all very fine as an ideal, but how do we put it into practice? How do we learn to converse "harmoniously" and in a climate of "mutual helpfulness" when we live so much of our lives in settings where self-interest, competition and conflict are considered quite normal?'

Buddhism can offer practical answers here, since its basis is not just a system of theoretical principles but also a system of value-based practices in which the aim is quite directly to change one's behaviour. One of the central Buddhist practices is, of course, meditation, and one of the most important meditation practices is based on the principle of *metta*, usually translated as 'loving-kindness' but having much in common with the idea of generosity and the Christian usage of 'love'. In the meditation to develop *metta* the aim is to develop positive feelings, of 'wishing well' first towards ourselves, then towards a close friend, then towards someone we are aware of but do not know well, and then towards someone for whom we have some sense of hostility. The next step is to focus these positive feelings simultaneously and *equally* towards ourselves and the three people we have identified, and finally towards all people in general. (The practice is described in, for example, Proto, 1991: 89–91; Sumedho, et al., 1990: 61–3; Kamalashila, 1996: 25–32.)

The value and effectiveness of meditation practice is widely attested (Dadds, Chapter 22 in this volume). So there are good reasons for thinking that it would also be worthwhile exploring how it might be included within an inquiry process, to guide participants towards 'harmonious speech'. Even from the brief outline above, it is clear that a lot of practical wisdom is implicit in the sequence of stages, e.g. the idea that you can't feel positive towards others unless you are feeling positive about yourself, and the importance of practising one's ability for imaginative empathy on a stranger before tackling the problem of explicitly hostile feelings. But there are further useful details to be noted. *Metta* is the first of a set of four so-called 'sublime states of mind' (see Nyanatiloka, 1970: 37) and in some ways the other three can be seen as an analysis of its key elements.

The first is *karuna* – a sense of compassion for the general suffering and pain that inevitably underlie human beings' words and actions, our own and others. This reminds us that we can avoid responding harshly to others' insensitive or abrasive behaviour, but can instead interpret it as merely careless or, as Buddhists would say, 'unskilful', and thus choose to 'overlook' it. The second is *mudita* – an empathetic joyful pleasure in others' achievements, which reminds us how easy it is to resent others' success ("Why did everyone agree with X's interpretation of the data and ignore my suggestions?") and respond competitively, which prevents the discussion building constructively on everyone's contribution. Finally there is *uppekha* – a state of 'equanimity' in which joy and compassion are combined and transcended in a generalized understanding of both the difficulties and the potentialities of the human condition (see Kamalashila, 1996: 201–4).

Another helpful set of ideas concerning how one might seek a skilful approach to co-operative working may be derived from Vajradaka's suggestions as to the sequence of attitudes one should try to cultivate in preparation for meditation (Vajradaka, 1997). His sequence is as follows: (1) curiosity, (2) contentment, (3) confidence, (4) enthusiasm, (5) kindliness. Like many Buddhist lists this seems to encapsulate neatly a lot of practical wisdom. The first two (combined) suggest that we need to start by cultivating a balance between alertness to new possibilities and an absence of egotistical assertiveness. The implication is that it is this rather complex state of mind that is needed to form a secure basis for confidence, perhaps because an awareness of a desire for egotistical assertion can make us feel nervous about possible disappointment or failure. Our sense of confidence then enables us to feel enthusiasm about the value and probable success of our inquiry. This in turn leads to feelings of kindliness towards the others with whom we are working, as part of our confidence in their capacities, which brings us back to the previous discussion on *metta*.

DIALECTICS: DIFFERENCE, CHANGE, CREATIVITY

The source of the potential creativity of collaborative inquiry lies in the differences between individuals. This is why the need for skilful communication is so crucial, as indicated in the previous section and why action research is frequently said to be founded on a 'dialectical' process – the reflective, developmental dialogue between participants with different experiences, interests and perspectives (Carr and Kemmis, 1986: 33–4, 179; Reason, 1994: 30–1; Winter, 1989: Chapter 4). However, dialectics is not just a matter of learning through dialogue: it is a general theory (with a long tradition going back through Hegel and Marx to Heraclitus) about the nature of the social world and how we understand it. Its relevance for the conduct of action research may be summarized as three basic propositions (see Israel, 1979; Fisk, 1979; Winter and Munn-Giddings, 2001: 213–15, 248). First, all phenomena are changing; so unless we understand the way in which they are changing, we won't understand them in a way which reveals the possibilities for the changes in practice with which action research is concerned. Second, all phenomena (people, situations, ideas, feelings, organizations, etc.) are connected with one another in a dynamic (change-generating) network of mutual influences; so it is always important to consider the broader context of the specific situation on which we are focusing. Third, all phenomena are changing because they are complex, made up of contradictory elements, and therefore cannot be understood as unities; so we must analyze our data in a way that reveals its contradictions and thus enables us to construct new interpretations and to formulate new practical strategies. (In order to clarify the link with Buddhist concepts, this last point will be discussed in the next section, under 'Reflexivity'.)

Action research, therefore, by definition, actively seeks change as its main resource for learning. In this respect it follows Buddhism, within which 'impermanence' (*anicca*) is the first and most fundamental characteristic of existence:

> Impermanence is a basic feature of all conditioned phenomena, be they material or mental, coarse or subtle, one's own or external: 'All formations are impermanent' ... 'Things never persist in the same way, but ... are vanishing and dissolving from moment to moment'. (Nyanatiloka, 1970: 14)

Although at some level we all know perfectly well that our physical bodies, our states of mind, our social relationships, etc., are subject to change, in everyday life we focus on the permanence and fixity of things (e.g. we experience people as individual 'personalities' who have 'beliefs' and hold 'opinions'). Social science follows this familiar perception in identifying, for example, structures, concepts, and specific cause-effect relationships. From both perspectives a radical emphasis on impermanence would seem an unreal abstraction, an unhelpful distraction from what is important. For Buddhism, in contrast, to forget impermanence is to be in a state of delusion, and to focus rigorously upon it is to regain insight into reality (Kamalashila, 1996: 92–3); it is 'a natural law that gives human beings hope', reminding us that 'It is possible ... for people to alter their circumstances, to bring about improvements in the world' (Payutto, 1995: 66).

The principle of *anicca* thus suggests that action research is quite right to embrace change as a source of understanding, and it also implies some quite helpful practical suggestions. As we engage in inquiry we can expect to feel a strong desire to keep certain things fixed (the focus of the topic, our theories, or our initial interpretative framework), and we can feel confident that letting go of these fixed points is a step in the right direction (improving our understanding) rather than in the wrong direction (losing focus, 'getting in a mess'). One might add that it is obviously easier to be aware that other people need to embrace the principle of impermanence and let go of their favourite ideas as the inquiry progresses than to remember that we ourselves need to do so! The quotation from Nyanatiloka also reminds us that change is occurring at every moment (in a discussion, in our thinking, in our actions), so that every moment is an opportunity for innovation, development and learning. In general terms, the implication is that 'reflection' needs to be a process of 'deconstructing' the 'fixed formations' of our spontaneous experience.

Buddhism also provides direct support for the second dialectical principle – the interconnectedness of phenomena – in the law of 'conditioned co-production' or 'dependent origination' (*paticcasammuppada*):

> All things are inter-related and inter-dependent; all things exist in relation to each other; all things exist dependent on determinants.... The fact that all things appear in their diverse forms of growth and decline shows their true nature to be one of a continuum or process .... The form of a continuum arises because the various determinants are inter-related. (Payutto, 1994: 14)

The underlying pattern of the whole of existence, therefore, is one which links together physical events, social events, sensations, feelings, psychological and spiritual states of mind and ethical requirements. This means that explanation must consist in explicating patterns of interrelatedness between a multiplicity of phenomena, rather than seeking a single cause for a single phenomenon, since that would be to return once more to the assumption of fixed and permanent formations (Payutto, 1995: 91). But the inclusion of the spiritual and ethical dimension is of particular importance, since it reminds us that for Buddhism understanding is inseparable from spiritual evolution and ethical action, that *paticcasammuppada* is a process of freeing ourselves from the burden of determinism that is created when we see the world in terms of fixed identities and single causes (Cooper, 1996: 156–7). This poses an interesting methodological challenge, since it suggests that effective inquiry must involve tracing the links between physical events, social relations, organizational structures, psychological states of mind and moral values in order to formulate wise and compassionate action.

This may sound rather like a tall order, but it is clear that the practical points discussed in the earlier section on *metta* are relevant here, and the doctrine of *paticcasammuppada* itself also provides us with further practical guidance, in the form of the law of *kamma*. This states that every action has causes which could be traced backwards (in time) and outwards, to an infinity of personal, social and environmental influences. Similarly, every action has effects which are never ending:

> Whatever we do, with our body, speech, or mind, will have a corresponding result. Each action, even the smallest, is pregnant with its consequences.... As the Buddha said, "do not overlook negative actions merely because they are small; however small a spark may be, it can burn down a haystack.... Do not overlook tiny good actions, thinking they are of no benefit; even tiny drops of water in the end will fill a huge vessel." Karma does not decay or ever become inoperative. (Sogyal Rinpoche, 1992: 92)

Moral actions thus make up a universal system of causes and effects. This has two important consequences. Firstly, since every action is the outcome of a multitude of past influences, individuals are never entirely responsible for the situations in which they find themselves. (This places a limit on the extent to which we need to accept feelings of guilt when we find ourselves involved in painful situations.) Secondly, since every action will create a multitude of future effects, individuals must always take responsibility for trying to make those effects as beneficial as possible. This means that we can never simply hide behind the alibi "There is nothing I can do: I am constrained by forces, events or social structures beyond my control" (Payutto, 1995: 46). Thus, at the heart of action must always be an acceptance of an ethical responsibility for consequences. What we do will always, in the end, 'make a difference'. It will, even if only in a small way, make a situation better or worse, and even if its immediate impact is merely on how people *feel* about what is taking place, that also will eventually have an impact on future events.

As a way of thinking about an inquiry process, then, the law of *kamma* may be seen as insisting that we need to analyze the processes of research (e.g. collecting and analyzing data, discussing development strategies) in a way that helps us to anticipate the effects of our behaviour, to understand the significance of our feelings and to appreciate our moral responsibilities. It also focuses on the creative potential within each moment of the work, and in this respect supports and extends the emphasis within action research on interpreting the dialectical structure of human action as both reflexive and creative.

REFLEXIVITY: DECONSTRUCTING THE SELF, MINDFULNESS

There is a long-standing emphasis in action research on 'critical reflection', which raises the crucial question: how do we try to ensure that 'reflection' is indeed 'critical' and creative, rather than merely an elaboration of the familiar.

One answer to this has already been mentioned: the dialectical principle that phenomena are made up of contradictory elements, even though they present themselves as apparently unified. Thus we can reflect on data by seeking the contradictions it conceals. For example, an interaction within an 'educational' process may contain 'controlling' elements which conflict with the principle of 'learner autonomy'. Another approach to the problem of reflection is provided by the principle of 'reflexivity'. Reflexivity is that aspect of the process of making a judgement about reality (interpreting an event, a piece of data, someone's state of mind, etc.) that is dependent on ('bent-back-into') our previous thoughts and experiences. A judgement such as, 'Martin knows the rules for multiplication' may look at first sight as though it is a simple statement about an objective state of affairs; but when we remind ourselves that it is 'reflexive', we remember that it is constructed by means of our own prior assumptions and experiences about what it means to 'know a rule'. The significance of the principle of reflexivity is that although most of our statements have a reflexive quality, we ignore this most of the time and treat our statements as being about external facts (see Winter, 1989: 41, 1996: 18–21). During an inquiry process it is particularly important that we engage in reflection that entails noticing the reflexivity of our judgements, because it enables a discussion involving differing points of view to move forward in a more creative way than if people are all defending their own view as being 'the fact of the matter'.

Buddhist concepts can throw further light on the nature of reflection and on the need for and the possibility of 'reflexivity', both in terms of theory and practical method. First, there is the doctrine of 'not-self' (*anatta*), which may be thought of as a direct consequence of the principle of impermanence noted above. 'There is no separate Ego-identity... In reality there exists only [the] continually self-consuming process of arriving and passing bodily and mental phenomena' (Nyanatiloka, 1970: 13). Payutto elaborates:

> Human life consists of a current of numerous corporeal and mental phenomena that exist in accordance with interdependent causes and conditions. When people are unaware of this truth they cling to the feelings, thoughts, desires, habits, views, beliefs, and impressions that arise at each moment and take this to be the self, even though this self is continuously changing. (Payutto, 1995: 268)

In other words, the self of which we are conscious in each moment is but another impermanent phenomenon which is always changing in response to the ceaseless flow of events. Whereas our spontaneous tendency will be to 'cling' (*tanha*) to our idea of our fixed self and to the responses and opinions of which our self seems to consist, the doctrine of *anatta* is that in order to understand the nature of reality we must 'let go of' this fixed self. To grasp the importance of *anatta* helps inquiry to be developmental, because it reminds us that our work must be a change process in which we ourselves change. We will always feel tempted to hold on to opinions and ideas that are part of our current sense of ourselves and attempt to focus our work so that it reinforces our sense of 'expertise'. But we can see that the process of inquiry, if it is to result in creative insight or innovative development, requires us to let go of who we were and what we knew when we started. Again, this is where a practical contribution might be sought through the practice of meditation, as a process of stopping the flow of familiar thoughts and feelings in order to create a state of 'concentration' (*samadhi*), which allows unexpected thoughts and feelings to arise.

In order to 'reflect' creatively, then, we need a general shift in our consciousness (of ourselves, of others, of the nature of thoughts, feelings, professional practices, etc.) through developing 'mindfulness' (*sati*). In the context of *anatta* this means developing an intense and continuous awareness of the illusory quality of all fixed identities, of how all the ideas, perceptions and feelings in our consciousness are in a continuous flux of arising and dissolving in response to a multitude of influences, some momentary, some long-term (Nyanatiloka, 1970: 165–7). In this way those taking part in an inquiry (exchanging interpretations of data, for example) may avoid arid personal confrontation and achieve the 'mutual transcendence' which we might take as the ultimate aim of all inquiry (see earlier quotation from Sangharakshita on 'harmonious speech').

CONCLUSION: EMANCIPATORY CRITIQUE, ENLIGHTENMENT

Many writers on action research would hope that action research can (and should) be thought of as having an 'emancipatory' aim – liberating us, through the process of 'critique', from the structures of our existing assumptions and habitual practices ('ideology'), insofar as these are perpetuating 'irrationality, injustice, alienation and unfulfilment' (Carr and Kemmis, 1986: 204). However, in the social sciences even basic concepts are the focus of differing cultural, political and ethical values. So, returning to Carr and Kemmis's list, different individuals will have alternative interpretations of 'rationality', 'justice' and 'fulfilment'. From this perspective, 'emancipation' is itself, within action research, a 'contested concept'. The agreements negotiated within the collaborative process may be seen by some as merely temporary political or interpersonal compromises, and the nature of their validity is therefore always open to question.

Let us, then, see how Buddhism might throw light on the issue of validity in social inquiry. We have already seen that Buddhism offers a powerful intellectual framework for describing the process of 'critique', within which all fixed, separate and permanent entities, including our own 'self' with its thoughts and feelings, are treated as unreal, as constructed 'illusions'. In this way, Buddhism may seem to be, apart from anything else, reminding us of the practical significance of modern theories in biology, radical ecology and sub-molecular physics in conceptualizing the nature of mental events and of observable phenomena (see Capra, 1996; Cooper, 1996).

However, Buddhism is not just a descriptive theory of reality but also a system of practical guidance, in which intellectual insight is inseparable from emotional and spiritual progress. The purpose of Buddhist thinking and practice is to seek 'Enlightenment', usually analyzed into ten 'Perfections': liberality, morality, renunciation, wisdom, energy, patience\ forbearance, truthfulness, resolution, 'loving kindness' and equanimity. A further list of 7 'Factors' of Enlightenment' overlaps somewhat with the 10 Perfections, but adds, importantly: mindfulness, investigation of mental events and concentration (Nyanatiloka, 1970: 125, 35). It is clear, then, that within Buddhism rigorous intellectual analysis also involves rigorous self-awareness, emotional self-discipline and an ethic of generosity towards others. So, whereas Western social science is basically a matter of generalizing from empirical observation, Buddhism is concerned with a much more complex process. It emphasizes that *understanding* other people can only begin from a state of mind in which, having recognized that we are not 'separate' from them, we must necessarily feel compassion towards them. Above all, it entails moving from a state of unwitting 'delusion' (in which our minds and feelings are determined by factors beyond our understanding) to a state of 'freedom', in which we are mentally and emotionally in tune with the real nature of phenomena, including ourselves.

But, we may ask, what is this 'real nature of things'? Are these various Buddhist propositions part of an authoritarian body of 'religious' doctrine, which we are simply asked to accept? Because if so, this is clearly not compatible with what we would take to be the essentially open and critical spirit of inquiry. There are two ways of providing a reassuring answer to this question. First there is the emphasis within Buddhism that doctrines should never be accepted merely because they have been delivered by an authority, but only when one has ascertained for oneself their practical effectiveness in contributing to the qualities comprising enlightenment (see *The Kalama Sutta:* Woodward, 1932). Similarly, Payutto emphasizes the importance of each person making up their own mind through a process that he specifically describes as 'critical reflection', i.e. on how principles are to be applied on different occasions (Payutto, 1995: 227). Second, although Buddhism, unlike most recent Western philosophy, does indeed suggest that human beings can gain access to an 'ultimate' reality, this is not the realm of a separate Divine Creator Being, but a level of awareness within each of us as individuals:

> In Buddhism it is always, clearly, even categorically stated that ... archetypal forms [i.e. The Buddha and other Fully Enlightened Beings] are ultimately phenomena of one's own True Mind, or projections from one's own unconscious, and that they are to be integrated. (Sangharakshita, 1996: 43)

In Tibetan Buddhism this is referred to as our 'Buddha nature' (*rigpa*) – 'the innermost essence of mind, [usually] enveloped and obscured by the mental scurry of our thoughts and emotions [but capable of offering us occasional glimpses of] a primordial, pure pristine awareness ... the knowledge of knowledge itself' (Sogyal Rinpoche, 1992: 47).

In other words, the validity of Insight and Enlightenment within Buddhism is not externally derived, but rests on *human* capacity for recognizing courage, wisdom compassion and other forms of fine ethical and spiritual action, based on our own conscience or 'self-respect' (*hri*) and our awareness of the 'wise opinion of others' (*apatrapya*) (Sangharakshita, 1998: 119, 125–7). At this level Buddhism can support and enhance the humanistic optimism underlying action research, creating a model of inquiry that is clearly based on our deepest and most comprehensive awareness of human nature and human understanding (see Dadds' portrayal of 'objective subjectivity' Chapter 22 in this volume). At its best, the process of action research generates a sense of the developmental creativity and imaginative compassion inherent in relationships of inquiry and professional 'care'. To this, Buddhism adds, firstly, an ideal – a recognition 'that the transcendental is there beyond one's mundane experience of the world, and that one is trying to work towards that' (Sangharakshita, 1998: 137). And, secondly, Buddhism offers a methodology – an account of the possibility of (and practical methods for) self-transcendence on the part of the individual and mutual transcendence in human interaction. In this way, Buddhism simultaneously re-defines the scope of social practices and offers practical guidance for re-defining the processes and relationships of inquiry.

NOTE

1 Among the first to do so was Arphorn Chuaprapaisilp, whose article on Thai Buddhism and Action Research was published in *Educational Action Research,*, 5 (2), 1997: 331–6.

REFERENCES

Capra, F. (1996) *The Web of Life: A New Synthesis of Mind and Matter,* London: Harper Collins.
Carr, W. and Kemmis, S. (1986) *Becoming Critical: Education, Knowledge and Action Research,* Lewes: Falmer.
Cooper, R. (1996) *The Evolving Mind: Buddhism, Biology & Consciousness,* Birmingham: Windhorse.
Dadds, M. (1995) *Passionate Inquiry and School Development: A Story about Teacher Action Research,* London: Falmer.
Elliott, J. (1991) *Action Research for Educational Change,* Buckingham: Open University Press.
Elliott, J. (1995) 'What is good action research? – Some criteria', *Action Researcher,* 2.
Fals-Borda, O. and Rahman, M. (eds) (1991) *Action and Knowledge: Breaking the Monopoly with Participatory Action-Research,* New York: Apex.
Fisk, M. (1979) 'Dialectic and ontology', in J. Mepham and D. Ruben (eds), *Issues in Marxist Philosophy, Vol 1: Dialectics and Method,* Brighton: Harvester Press, pp. 117–44.
Hart, S. (1996) *Beyond Special Needs: Enhancing Children's Learning through Innovative Thinking,* London: Paul Chapman.
Heron, J. (1996) *Co-operative Inquiry: Research into the Human Condition:* London: Sage.
Heron, J. (1998) *Sacred Science,* Ross-on-Wye: PCCS Books.
Israel, J. (1979) *The Language of Dialectics and the Dialectics of Language.* Brighton: Harvester Press.
Kamalashila (1996) Meditation: The Buddhist Way of Tranquillity and Insight, Birmingham, Windhorse.
Nanamoli (1992) The Life of the Buddha According to the Pali Canon, 2nd edn. Kandy: Buddhist Publication Society.
Nyanatiloka (1970) Buddhist Dictionary: Manual of Buddhist Terms and Doctrines, 3rd edn, revised by Nyanaponika, Taipei, Buddha Educational Foundation.
Payutto, P. (1994) *Dependent Origination: The Buddhist Law of Conditionality.* Translated by B. Evans, Bangkok, Buddhadhamma Foundation.
Payutto, P. (1995) *Buddhadhamma.* Translated by G. Olson, Albany, State University of New York Press.
Proto, L. (1991) *Meditation for Everybody,* London: Penguin.
Reason, P. (1994) *Participation in Human Inquiry,* London: Sage.
Sangharakshita (1996) *A Guide to the Buddhist Path,* 2nd edn. Birmingham: Windhorse.
Sangharakshita (1998) *Know Your Mind: The Psychological Dimension of Ethics in Buddhism,* Birmingham: Windhorse.
Schon, D. (1983) *The Reflective Practitioner.* New York: Basic Books.
Sogyal Rinpoche (1992) *The Tibetan Book of Living and Dying,* London: Rider (Random House).
Stringer, E. (1996) *Action Research: A Handbook for Practitioners,* London: Sage.
Sumedho, Santacitto, Anando and Sucitto (1990) *Peace and Kindness,* Hemel Hempstead: Amaravati.
Vajradaka (1997) 'Quality control', in Dharmalife – Buddhism for Today, No 6: 49 Published by Windhorse, Birmingham.
Whyte, W.F. (1991) *Participatory Action Research.* Newbury Park: Sage.
Winter, R. (1989) *Learning from Experience: Principles and Practice in Action Research.* Lewes: Falmer.
Winter, R. (1996) 'Some principles and proce-dures for the conduct of action research', in R. Zuber-Skerritt (ed.) *New Directions in Action Research,* London: Falmer, pp. 13–27.
Winter, R. and Munn-Giddings, C. (2001) *A Hand-book for Action Research in Health and Social Care,* London: Routledge.
Woodward, F.L. (1932) *The Kalama Sutta,* in *The Book of the Gradual Sayings,* Oxford: Pali Text Society. Oxford University Press, Vol. 1, pp. 171–5.

28

Teaching and Cultural Difference: Exploring the Potential for a Psychoanalytically Informed Action Research

Terrance Carson

Action research is rooted in a belief in the transformative possibilities of personal and collective action. The process is triggered by willingness on the part of participants to take action on a question of interest, with a commitment to systematically and continuously observe, reflect and act on what happens as a result of this engagement. In contrast to other forms of research, action research does not depend upon extensive data gathering, or specialized expertise before beginning work. Rather, as Richard Winter has suggested 'what is specific to action research as a form of inquiry is that it uses the experience of being committed to trying to improve some practical aspect of a practical situation as a means for developing our understanding of it' (2002: 27).

The experience of being committed to trying to improve a practical situation immediately implicates the subjectivities of those undertaking the action research. The choices of the questions needing attention, and the subsequent paths that the action and reflection take are all immanently related to the identities of the people involved, and their interpretations of the history, context, and social relations of the practical situation. Given the significance of identity in action research it is curious that more attention is not given to what action research does to the subjectivities of the practitioners. Action research seems to have had an overwhelmingly outward focus, concerned with improvement and changes in relationships, understandings and practices that have been wrought by the project in question.

That this outward focus of attention should dominate action research writing is also somewhat surprising in light of the requirements for a reflexive methodology, which ought to foreground critical self-reflection. However, the empirical analytic, interpretive and critical theoretic discourses that inform understandings of reflectivity in action research tend to restrict reflection merely to what is consciously intended. This is a limited form of self-reflection – the kind that is willed into existence and mobilized entirely by a conscious decision to critically reflect. Left out of such reflections are the passions, the investments, the hopes and the fears that can be the real sources for driving action, for resisting reflection, and which very well may have been instrumental in creating the situation needing change in the first place. Passions, drives and resistances are, at best, only partially available to intentional reflection.

This chapter explores the potential of psychoanalytic theory to broaden understandings of the self and to extend the meaning of critical self-reflection in action research. Because psychoanalysis attends to the unconscious, it opens up possibilities for greater insight into the self and to why certain questions are taken up and how these unfold through action research. This contribution is especially important as many of the questions we now face implicate identities, such as is the case with the action research project described in this paper that concerns the preparation of teachers for the increasingly diverse public schools in Canada.

Psychoanalysis can help action research, in its recognition that learning is 'a dynamic psychical event' (Britzman, 1998: 5), that is not entirely under the control of the ego. In this way, psychoanalysis supplements the educative value of action research by helping to better understand what is at work both in learning from knowledge and from resistances to knowledge. Psychoanalysis accomplishes this by explaining how knowledge is experienced as interference that unsettles the ego's integrity and mobilizes its defences. Defence mechanisms can take many forms, including denial, ignoring, rationalizations, and forgetting – any of which might be mobilized as resistances to learning. Psychoanalysis understands that it is by working through resistance, as opposed to trying to overcome it, that genuine learning, and real change take place.

A BRIEF HISTORY OF THE SELF IN ACTION RESEARCH

We might begin a discussion of the contributions of psychoanalytic theory to action research with a review of how the self has been previously constructed in action research theory and practice. Action that is launched by practitioners' interpretations of their situations has been a common theme of action research since the beginning with Kurt Lewin's early experiments in community action and development in the 1930s and 1940s and the teacher as researcher movement in the United States in the 1950s (Corey, 1949) and in the UK in the 1960s and 1970s (Elliott and Adelman, 1973; Stenhouse, 1975). Critical reflection by participants was integral to identifying the question, deciding the course of ongoing action, and fashioning meaning from the results.

The critically self-conscious acting, autonomous subject occupied the centre of action research, but who this self 'was', seldom was open to inquiry. On the contrary, the practitioners' attention was directed outwards towards learning and the changes resulting from taking action on a problem of practice. The declared intention of action research was for the empowerment and the enlightenment of the participants. In the Ford Teaching Project, for example, teachers became active developers of new curricula; in so doing teachers participated in changing the professional culture of their schools as they exercised more active control over their educational work. As Elliott (1991) noted, through action research a new possibility of the teachers as researcher was realized with a consequent change in professional identity. But in this, and other action research projects, the figure of the rationally acting empowered self remained the central idea of the subject in action research. In fact, the integrity and agency of the self was affirmed and strengthened.

Abraham Shumsky (1958) was a notable exception among the early action research writers in his foregrounding of the complicated effects of action research on the identities of practitioners. Shumsky warned that regarding 'the methodology of research [purely] as a logical subject matter, without exploring the aspects of behavior and feelings will result in a meager harvest, p. 2'. His concerns for identity conflict in teachers becoming researchers proved to be well founded, as this was a contributing factor in the subsequent decline of action research in America in the following two decades.

A renaissance of action research that took place in the 1980s owed much to Carr and Kemmis's (1986) development of a critical emancipatory action research. Their move to incorporate critical theory resituated reflection in action research within a wider political and social critical context. Leaning heavily on the critical theory of Jürgen Habermas, Carr and Kemmis argued that the participants' interpretations and commitment to change were not a sufficient basis for analysis and action, because power relations that produce a false consciousness act to distort these interpretations. Only by laying bare already existing inequities, which are embedded in historically rooted patterns of distorted communications, social relations, and practices will a critical consciousness be achieved. A critically informed action research imagines a figure of the ideal enlightened and rational self who emerges through critical social reflection. This is a self, who, by working with others creates an ideal speech community in which decisions are made on the basis of rationality and justice rather than hierarchically through relations of power.

Critical action research understands identity to be, in principle, transparent and fully accessible to the rational subject who is dedicated to achieving understanding and social justice through a critically informed praxis. To be sure, critical theory acknowledges that identities are constructed and that identifications with social class, gender, and race historically structure identity. But while a critically informed action research might be open to more complex understandings of sub-jectivity, the identity of the reflective practitioner is once more affirmed as the intact and fully rational self.

The conscious image of the self that is promulgated in the history of action research is that of the autonomous, reflective practitioner empowered to effect change. The fact that this image of the empowerment continues to persist in the face of the fact that many action research projects actually yield rather modest and ambiguous results probably says as much about how the promise of action research connects with the desire for affirmation of identity as it does about actu-ally effecting any real change in objective situations. Mark Bracher points out that identity – 'the sense of oneself as a force that matters in the world' (2006: 6) – is a basic desire. Arguably, action research remains popular because it taps into a deep wellspring of desire for meaning and agency that is found lacking in modern community and corporate life where so much of modern work life takes place in impersonal, complex organizations.

RE-IMAGINING THE SELF IN ACTION RESEARCH: ENGAGING DIVERSITY IN TEACHER EDUCATION

In the present context of the global migration of peoples and cultures, demands for recognition, and hybrid identities, the figure of the unitary self as the acting subject of change now becomes increasingly complex and open to question. Identities and terrains of practice have become more complicated and contested. At the same time, new issues for action research inquiry emerge from the effects of these very same phenomena. For example, in education, complex questions of identity increasingly shape debate over public education and the preparation of teachers. Public schools reflect the changing face of the communities they serve while they are also participating in the creation of new understandings of citizen-ship that are being forged from diversity.

This chapter takes up the question of the self in action research through the lens of the Teaching and Culture Project (TCP) at the University of Alberta. With an undergraduate enrollment of over 3,000 students in the Faculty of Education, the university houses the largest teacher education program in Canada. Like many teacher education programs in the country, preparing teachers includes the question of learning to teach across cultural difference. The issue is largely driven by demography; most teacher education candidates continue to come from overwhelmingly middle class, non-immigrant, and non-Aboriginal family backgrounds. A disproportionate number of these candidates have themselves gone to school in rural or suburban communities, which tend to be much more ethno-culturally homogeneous than the cities. By contrast, the urban schools have become ever more cosmopolitan. Canada's urban population, which now constitutes over 80 percent of the nation's total population, has been increasing rapidly, mainly through immigration as well as through higher birth rates among a growing urban Aboriginal population. Canadian cities are magnets for new settlers seeking employment, housing, and better educational opportunities.

While addressing demographic change, the Teaching and Culture Project has developed within the context of a revised teacher education curriculum that is based on teacher identity formation. The thinking around teacher identity formation has been influenced by Deborah Britzman's observations that learning to teach 'is a time that is taken up with negotiating, constructing, and consenting to their identity as a teacher' (2003: 221). According to Britzman, the problem with traditional teacher education is that those involved in the programs 'have already taken up particular orientations to autonomy, authority, certainty, and order … [which work] to dismantle this negotiatory stance and threaten to make *student teacher* an oxymoron' (p. 221).

Taking this threat seriously, the revised program at the University of Alberta is attempting to open up spaces for students to negotiate teaching identities. The conceptual framework for the program draws on Mikhail Bakhtin's (1981) insights that identities are negotiated through a complex process of consenting to and refusing an array of 'authoritative and internally persuasive discourses' (Britzman, 2003: 220). While the university coursework that constitutes the formal curriculum of the teacher education program is important, it is only one of several authoritative discourses student teachers are negotiating. Other authoritative discourses will include discourses of the subject area disciplines, the professional teaching standards, and most significantly, the discourses of veteran teachers. It is commonplace to find student teachers trying to negotiate these authoritative discourses of 'practice' with the discourses of educational 'theory' during their teacher education program.

While authoritative discourses originate from external sources, internally persuasive discourses are autobiographically located in family histories, school experiences, gender identities, faith traditions, cultural backgrounds, and political commitments. Internally persuasive discourses can take the form of explicit investments that are held by student teachers entering the teacher education program. More usually, however, internally persuasive discourses are not explicit, but are provoked into consciousness through encounters with authoritative discourses that circulate in the program. Much of learning to teach becomes a struggle for personal voice in which student teachers are trying to sort out where their own experiences and deeply held personal investments fit in relation to the authoritative discourses they encounter.

THE INTERVENTION OF THE TEACHING AND CULTURE ACTION RESEARCH PROJECT

The Teaching and Culture Project is concerned with responding to the growing diversity of public schools by introducing greater attention to this diversity in the teacher education program, within this framework of teacher identity formation. The TCP received seed grant funding in 2005 from a 'Multiculturalism in Canada Strategic Grant Program' sponsored by the Social Sciences and Humanities Research Council of Canada. From 2005 to 2008 an ongoing series of 'Diversity Institutes' have been developed and made available to student teachers on a voluntary basis. The planning of these workshops over the three years has followed a spiral process of collaborative action research. Each year the Diversity Institute prepares a series of workshops, which are offered to teacher education candidates during a professional term in the teacher education program. In keeping with an action research framework the results of the workshops are observed and reflections lead to the plan for the series of workshops in the subsequent year. In this fashion ongoing reflections about how diversity should be included in teacher education have allowed us to better understand how subjectivity, identity and otherness are implicated in the preparation of teachers for engaging with diversity.

The first step of the project was to conduct a needs assessment and collect demographic data on the backgrounds of the students in the teacher education program. With few exceptions, the student teachers surveyed claimed that diversity was not presently sufficiently addressed in the teacher education program, and strongly supported that more attention was needed. Demographic data also bore out the fact that the vast majority (94 percent) of the respondents were Canadian born, with only 1 percent being of Aboriginal heritage. For 90 percent of the students their first language was English, and a substantial number (70 percent) had Canadian born parents. Unsurprisingly, the results indicated that student teachers were well aware of the importance of attending to diversity in teacher education, but felt that they lacked the necessary knowledge and the personal experience for teaching in culturally diverse contexts. One of the student teachers expressed the lack as follows:

> Okay I am not a minority ... I just remember feeling like I don't have a background that some other people will have ... Part of me felt kind of bad – less cultured.

We interpreted the survey results in the light of students negotiating teaching identities. Diversity Institute planning pondered over what kinds of authoritative discourses might be introduced, and how students might engage with these autobiographically. A major issue was trying to mediate conflicting demands to represent a range of diversities, appropriately, and in some depth, in a way that student teachers might enter into relationship with them. Having this in mind we planned the 2005 Diversity Institute around the model of a 'bridge of cultures' suggested by Dee and Henkin (2002). The bridge metaphor represented a crossing over from an awareness of difference to a becoming different in oneself through discovering new modes of understanding the world. In the spirit of crossing over from awareness of difference to becoming different, workshops were offered covering a diversity of diversities that included race, culture, ethnicity, sexual orientation, disabilities, language, and religion. These were planned as interactive sessions through drama performances, role-play, artifacts, case studies and personal narratives, which offered the participants insights into a variety of cultural perspectives and meanings of diversity.

While participants found the Diversity Institute personally helpful, it fell short of our hopes that teacher identities would change to include diversity. Most student teachers left the Institute with their self-regard not only intact, but also reinforced as being empathetic, open-minded, people committed to accepting diversity. In our analysis of this result we appreciated that this openness to the other was a good beginning, but worried that along with this spirit of self-congratulation there was also a distancing from the other. Student teachers seemed to regard culture to be something possessed by others. As members of the majority they did not see themselves as participants, but only as spectators or samplers who were open to the unique cultural experiences of others.

Critical reflection extended not only to students' responses, but also to our own relationship with diversity as expressed in the workshop plan. By employing the metaphor of the bridge we realized that we had been attempting to predict and control the desired path for teacher identity change. We had to acknowledge that our attempts to interfere in teacher identity formation – by trying to anticipate a path of learning that would lead student teachers from awareness of difference to a reflective discovery of personal responses, and ending up with 'becoming' someone having a different relationship with diversity – was not only a failure, but betrayed a naive understanding of what is at work in teacher identity formation.

DEPLOYING PSYCHOANALYTIC THEORY TO INFORM THE ACTION RESEARCH

Peter Taubman (2006) has argued that psychoanalytic theories expand critical self-reflection by offering a dynamic sense of the self that is 'unconsciously complicit in the creation of our own realities' (p. 4). Taubman goes on to suggest that by entering into a relationship with the contents of the unconscious that includes drives, projections, repressions and so forth, teacher education will have a much fuller understanding of the deeper personal and emotional investments that are so much a part of teacher identity formation. In so doing, psychoanalytic theory supports and provides insight necessary to appreciate the complexities of negotiating teaching identities.

Psychoanalytically informed critical reflection helps understand the impossibility of satisfying the desire for certainty in mapping paths of teacher identity. Mere knowledge and more experience – especially the knowledge and experience of those who are, by definition, strangers to the self – cannot be provided as pre-given sets of truths to be taken up sometime in the future as necessarily effective responses to diversity in one's own teaching practice. Taubman cautions that psychoanalysis provides us with insight rather than certainty of prediction. He avers 'psychoanalytic understanding urges us to take responsibility for the meanings we give, as opposed to those pre-given ones from which we choose … [These are meanings] that can only arise from our own unique experiences' (2006: 9). The implication of this insight lent further support to the teacher identity framework of the teacher education program, concluding that teacher education for diversity would also entail opening up spaces for student teachers to engage experientially and relationally with difference.

This insight created some difficulties in planning the next Diversity Institute, in letting go of fixed representations of diversity along with maps of teacher identity formation. We sensed that we had come to the limits of curriculum planning, and now needed to prepare differently. We found the distinction that psychoanalysis makes between education and learning intriguing as we began planning for pedagogical encounters with diversity with student teachers, rather than constructing a plan for development. In this respect Deborah Britzman's (1998) description of the complicated history of education and psychoanalysis was helpful. Britzman contrasts a psychoanalytic theory of learning with education's preoccupation with incremental knowledge, 'as if the time of education could set precisely the time of learning, p. 4'. By contrast, psychoanalysis concerns itself with what is awakened in the learner by knowledge. A good example of this is the way in which much of the history of aboriginal relations with Canada, such as the Indian residential schools, constitutes difficult knowledge for non-aboriginal teachers. Difficult knowledge will be resisted, as Britzman explains, because such 'learning is a relearning of one's history of learning – new editions of old conflicts – and that it is precisely this unconscious force that renders the work of learning so difficult in intimacy and in public' (1998: 5).

The plan developed for the 2007 Diversity Institute was guided by attempts to seek out spaces for student teachers' autobiographical engagements between 'personal, practical and professional knowledge' (Connelly and Clandinin, 1990), and understanding the lived experiences and histories of others who were different from them. In the effort to deepen autobiographical engagement, we had student teachers join one of four working groups representing dominant themes of diversity: Aboriginal Experience, Sexuality and Gender Identities; Faith and Spirituality; or Race and Culture. Within these working groups there would be opportunities to reflect on one's own identity in relation to the complexities and ambiguity of diversity in contemporary schools, as well as appreciating the diversity of expressions, articulations and understandings that diversity takes. The Institute attempted to create dialogical spaces within these working groups, while also encouraging dialogue between the groups in the form of cooperative learning activities.

CRITICAL REFLECTIONS ON DIVERSITY AND DIFFICULT KNOWLEDGE

Despite our best efforts to foster autobiographical engagements with diversity in the 2007 Diversity Institute, we noticed that many of the student teachers responded in much the same way as they had to previous Institutes. While continuing to claim an openness and acceptance of difference, a lack of personal relationship with diversity continued. To be sure, many did go away from the Institute with a deeper sense of how history plays out in present educational experiences of Aboriginal youth, or gay and lesbian youth for example. As open and accepting individuals they felt implicated in this history and with the need to develop safe and caring school environments for marginalized youth. At the same time they felt vulnerable as new teachers, fearing to upset parents and communities by giving undue attention to diversity. Most of all they continued to worry about their own lack of experience and sought answers in more skills and knowledge about diversity.

Critical reflections on student teachers' dialogue with diversity in the 2007 Institute was helped by psychoanalytic insights on learning from difficult knowledge. The continuing desire to know more before acting can be read psychoanalytically as a form of unconscious resistance against having a personal relationship with diversity. Defence mechanisms are unconsciously mobilized to protect the integrity of the ego. Complicating this further, we can understand that this desire for more information is closely bound up with the unconscious drive in teacher identity, that Deborah Britzman (2003) describes as the 'cultural myths of teaching'. These function to disorganize teacher education as they structure a particular discourse about power, authority and knowledge in the formation of teacher identity disrupting possibilities for student teachers to negotiate other authoritative and internally persuasive discourses. Britzman names the three cultural myths as 'everything depending upon the teacher, the teacher is knowledgeable, and that teachers are self made' (p. 223). Cultural myths disorganize the negotiation of teacher identities, because they remain largely hidden while being powerful arbiters of the kinds of learning that beginning teachers fashion from knowledge. In the case of teaching for diversity, those 'others' who represent diversity in the schools are potential threats to teachers' control. They are strangers, having different backgrounds and experiences from oneself. The insistence on finding out more about diversity, while continuing to profess a stance of unbounded openness, betrays identification with the cultural myth of the knowledgeable teacher who is in charge while, at the same time, unintentionally inhibiting the development of a deeper relationship with those who have been positioned as 'diverse'.

The planners' relationship with diversity is equally fraught with the difficult knowledge of a shifting and seemingly uncontainable diversity of students in the urban public schools of Canada. The reality of diversity is easily supported with reference to the 2006 Canadian census numbers; for example 40 percent of the population of Toronto do not speak either English or French as their first language, there are high birth rates among an increasingly urban Aboriginal population, one-third of Edmonton public schools requiring programs for English language learning. Statistical data is bolstered by many individual accounts of settlement problems experienced by newcomers as further evidence that diversity needs addressing. While there is ample evidence that the community is changing rapidly and public schools must respond, the failure of the Teaching and Culture action research project to engage more deeply with student teachers' identity might be traced to the way the term 'diversity' has been constructed as the master signifier upon which to focus our educational activities. In this way the term functions as an unexamined and unelaborated objectifying move that takes the place of having to engage more deeply with an array of complex questions of coming to terms with difference, of balancing recognition with social cohesion, of meeting the local challenges of globalization, and understanding respect for human rights and social justice that now face teachers in the public education system.

Psychoanalytic theory provides critical insights concerning language, suggesting how we are complicit in the constructing diversity as a fantasy structure. Drawing on the work of the French theorist, Jacques Lacan, Taubman explains that 'fantasies serve as a defences against the horror of the Real ... [an] escape from the truth of our being' (2006: 10). Taubman offers the experience of hurricane Katrina as an example of an encounter with the real. As an event, Katrina constituted a momentary shock of coming face-to-face with racism and classism in the United States. in the midst of the uncontrollability of nature. Taubman explains that in confronting the real 'we are rendered speechless and flee into soothing fantasies of quick remedies, blame, and the next news story' (Taubman, 2006: 11). The significance of Lacan's contribution for our action research project is to say that the real does not lie underneath the fantasy, waiting to erupt. Rather fantasies are constructed as explanations to escape the real by creating what we can now take to be reality.

ASSESSING THE CONTRIBUTION OF PSYCHOANALYTIC THEORY TO ACTION RESEARCH

We have come to regard psychoanalysis to be a necessary informing discourse for the teaching and culture project, because the work of the project is directly concerned with two interrelated aspects of identity – re-thinking the framework of learning to teach around the negotiation of teacher identities, and teasing out a new understanding of identity in relation to engagements with 'diversity' in the preparation of teachers. While the focus of the project was particularly on identity, there has been a companion focus: the question of the self in action research more generally. This was most apparent in the psychoanalytically informed insight that in constructing the problem as one of preparing teachers *for diversity* we were also unconsciously complicit in creating the problem itself. This became apparent as we grappled with trying to understand the continuing tendency of student teachers to objectify diversity as the possession of others. Taubman's (2006) explanation of Lacan's fantasy structure has helped us to reposition our connection with the question, and to go forward with a more relational approach to diversity with student teachers. This insight not only influenced our pedagogical approaches in the Diversity Institute, it has also helped us to better appreciate what is at stake in teacher identity formation.

In the end, one of the most important contributions of psychoanalytic theory to action research is the attention to relationships. Reflection and action through collaborative relationships is a central feature of action research practice. Psychoanalysis informs insight into relationships through its concern with the role of the unconscious as it affects both inter-psychic and intra-psychic relationships. As such, psychoanalysis can open up participants in action research to a more broadly informed perspective on how they are engaging together with a question. At the same time, an appreciation of learning from an intra-psychic perspective can teach us to be patient with others, and with ourselves, by helping us to tolerate difference and to value the importance of resistance in bringing about real change.

REFERENCES

Bakhtin, M. (1981) *The Dialogical Imagination*. Michael Holquist (ed.). Austin: University of Texas Press.

Bracher, M. (2006) *Radical Pedagogy: Identity, Generativity, and Social Transformation*. New York: Palgrave Macmillan.

Britzman, D. (1998) *Lost Subjects, Contested Objects: Toward a Psychoanalytic Inquiry of Learning*. Albany: SUNY Press.

Britzman, D. (2003) *Practice makes Practice: A Critical Study of Learning to Teach* (revised edition). Albany: SUNY Press.

Carr, W. and Kemmis, S. (1986) *Becoming Critical: Education, Knowledge, and Action Research*. London: Falmer Press.

Chambers, C. (2003) 'As Canadian as possible under the circumstances: a view of contemporary curriculum discourses in Canada', in William Pinar (ed.), *International Handbook of Curriculum Research*. Mahwah, NJ: Lawrence Erlbaum.

Connelly, M. and Clandinin, J. (1990) 'Stories of experience and narrative inquiry', *Educational Researcher*, 19 (4): 2–14.

Corey, S. (1949) 'Action research, fundamental research, and educational practices', *Teachers College Record*, 50: 509–14.

Dee, J. and Henkin, A. (2002) 'Assessing dispositions towards cultural diversity among pre-service teachers', *Urban Education*, 37 (1): 32–40.

Elliott, J. (1991) *Action Research for Educational Change*. Buckingham: Open University.

Elliott, J. and Adelman, C. (1973) 'Reflecting where the action is: the design of the Ford Teaching Project', *Education for Teaching*, 92: 8–20.

Shumsky, A. (1958) *The Action Research Way of Learning: An Approach to in-service Education*. New York: Horace Mann-Lincoln Institute Teachers College Press.

Stenhouse, L. (1975) *An Introduction to Curri-culum Research and Development*. London: Heinemann.

Taubman, P. (2006) 'The beautiful soul of teaching: the contribution of psychoanalytic thought to critical reflection and reflective practice', In Mordecai Gordon and Thomas O'Brien (eds.) *Bridging Theory and Practice in Teacher Education*. Rotterdam: Sense Publishers.

Winter, R. (2002) 'Managers, spectators, and citizens: where does theory come from in action research?', in Christopher Day et al. (eds). *Theory and Practice in Action Research: Some International Perspectives*. Oxford: Symposium Books.

29

Complexity Theory and Action Research

Dennis Sumara and Brent Davis

'Complexity theory' (more recently, 'complexity science', 'complexity thinking', or simply 'complexity') is the title chosen by a group of researchers from many different disciplines who first came together in the 1970s around the realization that the assumptions, methods, and metaphors of classical analytic science were inadequate for the study of certain phenomena. Specifically, it was noted that some 'things' – including economies, brains, anthills, and social movements – manifest possibilities and attributes that are not present in any of their parts.

As researchers, we came across complexity theory at about the same time that we began to learn about action research – late in the 1980s. We were impressed by the deep complementarities of the two movements and felt that complexity might make an important contribution to the theory and practice of action research. The intention of this chapter is to explore this hunch, speaking from our own research experience to develop the suggestion that complexity might provide a framework to assist action researchers in their efforts to improve the learning and work experiences of teachers, students, and communities.

We begin with a brief description of complexity theory, highlighting how it complements and clashes with traditional attitudes toward research and theory. We then highlight three aspects of complexity-informed action research – namely the transphenomenal character of educational concerns, the complicitous nature of educational action, and the pragmatic orientation of educational projects. The discussion is illustrated with specific reference to a project involving the two of us, the staff of an elementary school, and the surrounding community that was organized around a group's desire to work in a more collective, mutually supportive manner.

WHAT IS *COMPLEXITY THEORY?*

Complexity

Complexity refers to an emergent recognition that some phenomena cannot be described or understood in terms of mechanical metaphors, cause–effect logics, or linear images – a statement that should not be read as a rejection of the classical scientific method. Complexity does not discard an analytic attitude. Rather, it highlights the limitations of and seeks to elaborate that attitude toward research that frames phenomena in terms of predictable sums of their parts.

And so the point is not that modern science is in any way misguided; it is that its tools can only take us so far in studies of, for example, large-scale economies, ecosystems, and brains. These sorts of phenomena are *complex*. By way of preliminary (but inadequate) description, a complex unity is one that arises in the interactions of other systems as their collective actions give rise to actions and traits that are not possible independently. In this sense, economies cannot be reduced to consumers, ecosystems are more than collections of species, and brains transcend neurons. Such phenomena are better characterized in terms of adequacy rather than efficiency, and growth rather than progress. They call for holistic, contingent, and exploratory approaches to inquiry.

In fact, in a strong sense, a complex phenomenon 'dictates' how it must be studied. In other words, there are no generalized, universal methods within complexity. This point helps to explain why complexity resists precise and concise definition. Complexity theory is conceived more in terms of *what* one investigates than *how* one investigates. Hence, biologists tend to talk about complexity in terms of living systems, physicists in terms of non-linear dynamics, and economists in terms of micro- and macro-economies. Perhaps not surprisingly, then, as educators and educational researchers we find ourselves gravitating toward a particular interpretation: complex systems are systems that learn.

Theory

The word *theory* means something different in the phrase *complexity theory* than it means in more familiar uses, such as 'critical theory', 'feminist theory', and 'poststructuralist theory'. Each of these arose in particular historical circumstances, can trace its lineage to particular philosophical traditions, is identified with particular cultural circumstances, and can be articulated in terms of particular ends or desires. Although none is fully unified, each has a coherence that makes it possible for participants and commentators to observe, embrace, reject, or otherwise engage.

Complexity theory does not have quite the same status. It is more an *intertheory* than a theory. As a movement, it arose in an explicit attempt by researchers across disciplines to speak to one another in the hopes of, for example, learning how studies of anthills might inform studies of brains or how insights into the dynamics of ecosystems might inform designs of buildings. In this sense, complexity theory is an instance of what it seeks to study: an emergent phenomenon that exceeds its interacting parts.

We in no way mean to suggest that complexity theory is a metatheory, nor that the movement is somehow conceptually neutral or above politics. Quite the contrary, complexity theory invites researchers to be attentive to their own agency, the consequences (intended and otherwise) of their actions, and the ethical implications of their participations in events and systems (social, political, cultural, ecological, etc.). Such transphenomenal attentiveness is a good starting place for articulating the deep complementarities between educational action research and a complexivist attitude.

TRANSPHENOMENALITY

We have participated in many action research projects over the past few decades. Through the course of such participations, a favorite 'research' activity has come to be ongoing interrogations of usages of the word *they* in transcripts and recordings. Typically, the term is used to refer to individuals, to classroom collectives, to social groupings (e.g., adolescents), to political factions, to society, to clusters of neurons – in brief, to almost any coherent collective that is relevant to the educational project. Educators, it seems are adept level-jumpers, able to move fluidly among and across levels of coherence.

In complexity terms, this capacity might be described as an at least tacit awareness of the transphenomenal character of complex events. We first began giving serious attention to this capacity during an action research project involving the teaching staff of an inner city school (Valleyview Elementary) and ourselves that was undertaken in the mid-1990s (see Davis and Sumara, 1997; Sumara and Davis, 1997).

This collaboration was prompted by a major upheaval in the school. Although the school building itself was a fixture in the community, all but one member of its staff was new in the first year of that project. There had been a series of tensions between the community and the previous staff, and the school board's response was to replace everyone but the vice principal. That meant that the new principal had opportunity to hand-pick most of the teachers, and the resulting cohort was made up of mainly established and very successful practitioners – who, for the most part, barely knew one another and had few or no connections to the community. Not surprisingly, then, the research group at Valleyview began clumsily and uncomfortably with self-introductions and admissions that the shared trait of group members was that every participant was, in a sense, 'orphaned'.

Oriented by the conviction that a sense of collectivity was an emergent phenomenon, we suggested that the group engage in in-service-like sessions around recent developments in the learning and teaching of English language arts. The group readily agreed and soon settled on the book *The Giver*, by Lois Lowry (1993).

The Giver is an award-winning futuristic novel, written around the character of Jonas who is born into a community that is safe, orderly, and predictable. Rules are strictly obeyed and the community oversees almost every aspect of one's life, including decisions on career, marriage, and adopted children. Citizens strive for sameness and avoid doing or saying anything that might offend. Social order is maintained in large part by assigning one person, the Receiver of Memories, full responsibility for knowledge of the past. Only the Receiver knows the history of the community, and so only the Receiver bears the burden of sorrow and pain that memories bring. On his twelfth birthday Jonas is named to succeed an aging Receiver (who becomes the *Giver* of Memories). Gradually, through the memories Jonas receives from the Giver, he comes to realize various truths, including the unfairness of depriving people of opportunities to make choices for themselves. He also learns that there are different ways to live, and these memories prompt his conclusion that the community must change.

In the context of the research group, an interesting shift occurred at the point of selecting the novel, as reflected in the transcripts of the meetings. Whereas most of the articulations prior to the suggestion of a shared reading were 'I' statements (i.e., comments about personal interests, backgrounds, responsibilities, expectations, professional anxieties, and so on), the bulk of the subsequent remarks were 'we' statements that began to reflect senses of shared projects and shared purposes. This observation was in part prompted by our advance reading of *The Giver*. As noted in the synopsis, one of the themes explored in the book is the relationship between group identification and group memory/history.

At the same time that we noticed this shift, we began paying attention to uses of other pronouns – especially *they*. In these early stages of the collaboration, *they* was used most often to refer to students, their parents, and the surrounding community. In brief, the identifications of particular *they*'s were being used to define a particular *we*, thus highlighting how identifications are two-way processes. Identifications define the identifier at the same time as they define an identified. On this count, the most potent *they* during our early discussions seemed to be parents in the community. As we delved into *The Giver* and its not-uncontroversial treatments of such topics as eugenics, euthanasia, and burgeoning sexuality, it became clearer and clearer how the collective was cohering around an imagined other – specifically the *they* comprising the community served by the school.

We develop this matter further in subsequent sections. For our present intentions, it serves to illustrate how complexity thinking might be useful for making sense of a fundamental unity of action, identity, and perception that is implied in the phrase 'action research'. Such happenings are inherently transphenomenal, and we have come to regard them as opportunities to attend simultaneously to the professional, personal, and political dimensions of individual and collective activity within action research settings.

In terms of practical action, we have found that an explicit attentiveness to transphenomenality within action research collaborations has helped us to be aware of how we define ourselves and, at the same time, the ranges of intention and influence. In the Valleyview project, for example, the project began with a very constrained sense of *we*, one that felt itself at odds with (rather than embedded in or part of) a surrounding community. It was our conviction that this manner of positioning was not only flagged by the use of pronouns *we* and *they*, it was in fact held in place by such usages.

For that reason, we made a deliberate effort to interrupt usages by seeking to expand the *we*. That is, and in a complexity-informed move that we have attempted to incorporate into all subsequent action research projects, we did something that we hoped might help to shift the boundaries that defined the us/not-us: we suggested that parents from the community be invited to participate in a reading group similar to the one in which the group's own sense of collectivity had begun to emerge.

COMPLICITY

In response to this suggestion, copies of *The Giver* were distributed to parents on the school's advisory board, who passed along other copies to some of their friends. Other parents were invited to take part through the school newsletter. A few weeks later, a discussion group convened, bring together most of the teachers, the researchers, and about a dozen parents.

This new situation, of course, was the source of tremendous worry and anxiety for all who attended. For our part, we assumed that concerns were prompted by the novel's treatments of various issues – which, in fact, have contributed to its status of one of the most frequently banned books in the United States. However, it was later revealed that the primary concern was one of identity: different factions represented in the gathering wondered about the others' intentions, interpretations, and motivations.

In an effort to ease the situation, Dennis explained his interest in joint reading, which seemed to be sufficient to allow most of the parents to relax. As the focus of discussion shifted to the actual reading of the book, a lively discussion began to unfold. Soon the boundaries separating such identity categories as 'university researcher', 'classroom teacher', and 'parent' began to dissolve, allowing a community dedicated to collective sense-making to emerge. Significantly, what is well known about acts of reading became apparent to everyone in the group: no two readings or interpretations of a given text are alike. In particular, when the text is a literary one that asks readers to develop identificatory relations with characters and situations, the interpreted responses can say more about the reader than the reader can say about the text. Even though the meeting had begun as a collection of suspicious and worried strangers, the shared interpretive discussions quickly created an event that became deeply interesting to all present.

Curiously, without revealing many personal details, members became known to one another in ways that are not typical of teacher/parent interactions. Fictive identities dissolved within the interpretive moment, replaced by identities that were surprising to many. As one parent commented, 'I didn't really expect to enjoy this discussion. That hasn't been my experience in school before this'.

Teachers in the group were also surprised, mostly at the parents' insistence near the end of the meeting that the *Giver* ought to be taught in some of the grades 5 and 6 classes. This insistence was tellingly phrased in the language of collectivity: '*Our* kids should read this. *We* should teach it'.

This particular moment foregrounds for us another critical element of complexity-informed action research. The shifting *we* flags not only the transphenomenal character of educational phenomena, it signals the complicitous nature of researchers' involvements. On this matter, one of the distinguishing features of complex systems is that they are open. They constantly exchange energy, matter, and information with their contexts. In the process, they affect the structures of both themselves and their contexts.

The term *context* must be used carefully. In complexity terms, it is not meant to imply the presence of a clear, unambiguous physical boundary between an agent and its environment. For complex systems, agents are necessarily parts of their contexts. It is not always possible (or useful) to determine with certainty which components are parts of the system (i.e., 'inside') and which belong to the environment (i.e., 'outside'). In fact, the closer one looks at the boundary of a complex/open system, the more troublesome the issue becomes. For example, at the cellular level, it is usually not clear which molecules belong to the system and which to the setting when one zooms in on a cell membrane. The same is true when attempting to distinguish between *person* and *not-person* at the level of the skin, or when attempting unravel a *we* and a *they*. One cannot specify simply – or, perhaps more appropriately, simply cannot specify – the locations of such boundaries in objective terms. Thus, for the purposes of studying a complex form, the physical or conceptual boundaries of a complex/open system are always dependent on the criteria that are used to define or distinguish the system from its backdrop.

The critical point here is not that researchers must define boundaries of the phenomena that they study (although this is a vital point). Rather, the main issue here is that complexity thinking compels researchers to consider how they are implicated in the phenomena that they study – and, more broadly, to acknowledge that their descriptions of the world exist in complex (i.e., nested, co-implicated, ambiguously bounded, dynamic, etc.) relationship with the world.

Complexivists Cohen and Stewart (1994) make the point through a play on words. They recombine the roots of the common words *simplicity* and *complexity* to generate *simplexity* and *complicity*. For them, *simplexity* refers to 'the process whereby a system of rules can engender simple features. Simplexity is the emergence of large-scale simplicities as direct consequences of rules' (p. 414). Examples of simplexities include Newtonian mechanics and formal mathematics, whose 'properties are the direct and inescapable consequences of the rules' (p. 412). With their development of the word *complicity*, they powerfully foreground the fact that the researcher is always already entangled in the phenomenon researched. Researchers are aspects of even grander systems, shaped by and contributing to the shapes of the phenomena in ways and to extents that they simply cannot know. Such realizations render research a profoundly ethical undertaking.

Notably, *implication*, *complicity*, and *complexity* are all derived from the Indo-European *plek-*, 'to weave, plait, fold, entwine'. Such, then, is an important lesson of complexity thinking. As researchers interested in issues swirling about human knowledge – what it is, how it is developed and sustained, what it means to know, and so on – we are woven into what we research, just as it is woven into us.

PRAGMATICS

Returning to the account of the action research project at Valleyview School, at the end of the reading group meeting with teachers and parents, it was agreed that some of the children in the school should have an opportunity to read *The Giver*. It was soon decided that Dennis would co-teach a unit in a class of students from Grades 5 and 6 (see Sumara et al., 1998).

Because Dennis and the teacher felt that the novel was somewhat complex and difficult for some readers in the class – and because they wanted to actively participate with readers as they moved through unfamiliar in-text marking practices – they took turns reading the novel aloud in class over the period of one week. Following each chapter, the students were invited to talk about what they had noticed. For example, after reading the first chapter, the children were asked to identify phrases or sentences that had caught their attention. This query sponsored an interesting discussion of the associations and interpretations that readers were making with the text and, as well, provided evidence of how readers never really read the same text. What one reader found significant, others often did not even notice.

In the exercise of 'pointing' to what had been noticed, a collective site of inter-personal/intertextual recognition and identification was emerging. The usually private act of reading was becoming more publicly constituted. As well, working from the premise that identity emerges from relational identifications, these acts of pointing and discussing broadened the horizons of identification practices for all readers. Near the completion of the unit of study, Dennis asked the students if they felt that books could change: Was *The Giver* different for having been read? The consensus of class members was that, yes, novels are not static objects. Rather, what a novel *is* only makes sense in the context of bringing it to life through reading and discussion – that is, by weaving it into an ever-evolving fabric of relationships. In other words, prompted by in-text marking practices and discussions of the shifting meanings of the stories they read, these readers came to regard literature not as a fixed backdrop of their in-school activities, but as part of a complex and shifting cultural landscape of which schooling was part.

Correspondingly, for these students, the curriculum around *The Giver* was not a set of mandated facts or skills to be mastered, but an occasion for engagement. It, too, was a shifting, negotiated form. Similar dynamics were clearly at work on the classroom level, with the establishment of collective truths (e.g., a collective assumption arose that a dome covered Jonas's community, even though there is no mention whatsoever of such a possibility) that were valid insofar as they were viable and useful. And, of course, the dynamics of this emergent common sense were also similar to the dynamics of individual sense, records of which were included in every student's copy of the novel.

This event, and others like it, remind us of an important distinction that separates much of research in education from research in other domains – namely a deep concern for pragmatic action. This emphasis is, of course, shared by both action research and complexity theory.

EDUCATIONAL (AND) ACTION RESEARCH

This claim should perhaps be contextualized. As with any research domain or attitude, complexity theory is subject to ongoing evolutions. For example, one device that we have found to be useful to interpret the history of the movement is the identification of three '(em)phases' – namely (1) observational and descriptive studies, (2) efforts to offer generalized characterizations of complex phenomena, and most recently (3) pragmatic efforts to effect transformations of complex phenomena.

Most accounts of the emergence of complexity theory suggest that it cohered in the late 1970s or early 1980s, at which time the name was invented and applied to the movement. Prior to the coining of the phrases 'complexity theory', 'complexity science', and 'complexity thinking', what has come to be described as research into complex phenomena consisted of disparate and largely unconnected investigations of specific phenomena. Examples include Jane Jacobs' (1961) examinations of the rise and decline of cities, Deborah Gordon's (1999) multi-year observations of the life cycle of anthills, Friedrich Engels' (1987) studies of the emergence of social structures in the free-market world, Rachel Carson's (1962) examinations of the ecological implications of industrialized societies, and Humberto Maturana's (1981) research into self-producing and self-maintaining biological unities. Such studies were principally *observational and descriptive* in nature. The theme that unites these diverse projects is the desire to generate rich accounts of specific phenomena, oriented by a suspicion that anthills, cities, biological unities, cultures, and so on must be studied at the levels of their emergence, not in terms of their sub-components – and certainly not in terms of fundamental particles and universal laws.

As more and more such studies were published, a handful of researchers undertook to identify some of the qualities and conditions that seemed to be common across the range of phenomena studied. For instance, there seems to be tremendous redundancy among the agents that come together within most complex systems. Phrased differently, the emphasis in complexity studies moved beyond a focus on *case-specific descriptions* of specific instances toward efforts to articulate more *generalized characterizations.*

By the 1990s, complexity research was a clearly discernible domain, evidenced by the appearance of institutes and conferences designed to bring together researchers who previously had little occasion to interact, along with the publication of several popular histories of the nascent field. By then, prompted by the accumulation of inter-case comparisons, the focus of complexity research had begun to shift toward what might be called a *pragmatics of transformation.* Investigators had begun to turn their attentions to the prompting and manipulation of complex systems. Could one occasion the emergence of a complex unity? If so, how? Once emergent, could a complex phenomenon be deliberately manipulated? If so, how and to what extent? And what are the moral and ethical implications of such efforts?

As we have elaborated elsewhere (Davis and Sumara, 2006), educational research has a long history of adopting and adapting theoretical frames from other domains – particularly psychology, sociology, and literary criticism. Unfortunately, such frames are not always well fitted to the particular, pragmatic concerns of educationists. For the most part, those theories tend to be strictly descriptive (i.e., aligned with the earlier emphases of complexity research). They are focused much more on the characterization of specific phenomena than on how one might go about affecting those phenomena. Action research is an exception to this trend – as is, we would argue, complexity theory. The reasons for this claim are instructive.

First, both action research and complexity theory (as just noted) are oriented by an intention toward pragmatic action. They are about (or have come to be about) making a meaningful difference in the world. To this end, complexivists have paid particular attention to the sorts of conditions that must be in place for complex unities to arise, and to the manners in which those conditions might be manipulated to affect the actions and identities of complex phenomena. These conditions include redundancy among agents, diversity within the system, decentralized control, and, positive and negative feedback loops, networked interactions among agents (cf. Davis and Sumara, 2006). Such matters have immediate and obvious relevance for those interested in action research, given emphases on collective action and mindful engagement with other overlapping, interlacing, and intersecting phenomena.

Second, unlike many of the theoretical frames borrowed by educationists from other domains, neither action research nor complexity theory arrive 'complete'. Rather, both are understood as plastic and open to elaboration. In terms of an idea already developed, both are oriented toward and by the complicity of the researcher. One does not *take up* a complexity frame; one *takes part in* and inevitably contributes to understandings of complex happenings. The distinction is an important one, not in the least because of the manner in which it positions educational research as a full partner in the project of knowledge production – not merely an area to apply ideas developed elsewhere.

Third, as already noted, educational research is concerned with transphenomena. Or, in slightly different terms, education is necessarily transdisciplinary. As a domain of inquiry, it sits at the intersections of many other areas of inquiry – including various subject matter disciplines (e.g., mathematics, English literature, etc.), psychology, philosophy, sociology, and history. This point is, of course, reflected in the ranges of subdisciplines that are represented at major conferences, where the qualifiers *education* or *educational* are attached to psychology, history, sociology, leadership, physics, art, and many other conventionally recognized fields. A trans-disciplinary attitude is well represented in action research and complexity theory. However, it tends not to be represented in the focused theories that educationists have taken up from specific domains (e.g., behaviorism from psychology).

CLOSING REMARKS

As the parent/teacher/researcher group's experience of shared reading and thinking shows, many of the beliefs about identity and inquiry that infuse school practice serve to reduce complexity and thereby limit possibility. For example, although researchers working from psycho- and sociolinguistic perspectives have convincingly demonstrated that all language-learning and language-using experiences are inescapably communal, a widespread belief in the autonomy of the learner and the corresponding privilege assigned to the 'individual' serves to undermine the potential for these understandings within the context of the public school. And so, although greater numbers of elementary school teachers are subscribing to models of learning that encourage students to develop their thinking within highly social and collaborative environments, the competing desire for children to demonstrate individual mastery persists.

In spite of dramatic developments in understandings of such matters, identity and research continue to be conceived in rigidly dichotomous rather than ambiguously bounded terms. The emergence of personal identity, for example, is popularly thought of as a process of unfolding that occurs apart from the emergence of collective identity. Although theorists and researchers from virtually every domain of inquiry have demonstrated one's 'identity' is a dynamic and complex mix of the biological and the experiential, an assumption of individualized and essentialized 'selves' continues to infuse schooling practices. The 'personal response journal', for example, often functions as a place to record the idiosyncratic experiences and interpretations of particular readers rather than as a location to examine the complex ways in which reading is *always* an act of collective cognition emerging from readers' past, current, and anticipated social relations. This insight was made evident in the collective readings and rereadings of *The Giver* within the teacher and the teacher/parent reading groups. There it became clear that 'individual' responses to passages were entangled in readers' conversations with one another, with their previous experiences in different settings, and with their students or children. Collected within the responses, then, were not only the markers of reading, but the traces of co-evolving identities and representations of complex, co-emergent patterns of thinking and responding.

Recognizing these emergent patterns meant that the shared reading of *The Giver* became an opportunity for adults and children to become curious about the making of identity and the complex ways in which language and cultural practices contributed to the ongoing, nested, and self-similar evolutions of individual and collective identities. Most importantly, reading the novel helped readers to understand the relationship among the phenomena of learning to perceive, learning to think, and learning to inhabit a particular social identity. Through the shared reading, participants came to wonder whether society was, in fact, more like than unlike the tightly regulated one described in the novel. At the same time, teachers, by interacting with parents in this shared reading location, began to dissolve the well-developed fictionalized identities of 'these parents' and 'this community'. Correspondingly, parents began to express similar re-perceptions and re-interpretations of what they understood as teacher identity and the experience of schooling.

In other words, and in sum, educational action research suggests that research is always and already a site for learning, and it is thus that educational action research can be wedded to the complexivist interest in the study of 'learning systems'. Many complexivists within education have been working to do precisely this: to tease out how particular complex learning systems cohere and unfold. How do classroom collectives emerge? What is the structure of a body of knowledge? How are individual knowers implicated in collective knowledge? The resultant literatures have placed a significant emphasis on the sorts of conditions that are necessary for the creation, maintenance, and development of complex unities. When considering educational action research from a complexity theory perspective, then, it is important to consider not just the original concerns and the desired ends, but the immediate conditions for collective action. There is never any guarantee that complex collectivity will emerge, but failing to attend to the necessary conditions for complex co-action will almost certainly ensure that it will not arise.

REFERENCES

Carson, R. (1962) *Silent Spring.* New York: Houghton Mifflin.
Cohen, J. and Stewart, I. (1994) *The Collapse of Chaos: Discovering Simplicity in a Complex World,* New York: Penguin.

Davis, B. and Sumara, B. (1997) 'Cognition, complexity, and teacher education', *Harvard Educational Review*, 67 (1): 105–25.

Davis, B. and Sumara, D. (2006) *Complexity and Education: Inquiries into Learning, Teaching, and Research*. Mahwah, NJ: Lawrence Erlbaum.

Engels, F. (1987) *The Condition of the Working Class in England*, New York: Penguin.

Gordon, D. (1999) *Ants at Work: How an Insect Society is Organized*. New York: Free Press.

Jacobs, J. (1961) *The Death and Life of Great American Cities*, New York: Vintage.

Lowry, L. (1993) *The Giver*. New York: Bantam Doubleday.

Maturana, H. (1981) 'Autopoiesis: reproduction, heredity and evolution', in M. Zeleny (ed.), *Autopoiesis, Dissipative Structures, and Spontan-eous Social Orders*. Boulder, CO: Westview, pp. 48–80.

Sumara, D. and Davis, B. (1997) 'Enactivist theory and community learning: toward a complexified understanding of action research', *International Journal of Educational Action Research*, 5 (3): 403–22.

Sumara, D., Davis, B. and van der Wey, D. (1998) 'The pleasure of thinking', *Language Arts*, 76 (2): 135–43.

30

Agency through Action Research: Constructing Active Identities from Theoretical Models and Metaphors

Bridget Somekh

Since I first became a teacher action researcher in the late 1970s, my key question has been 'Can action research enable teachers and school leaders to make a difference for the better to children's education?' Asking this question immediately raises issues of agency and power. In what sense can humans be said to be in control in their workplace and able to bring about change in their own practice? Can they do this by their own efforts alone, or are they dependent on colleagues and constrained by institutional and ideological structures? Behind what appears to be a simple aspiration, lie the well-rehearsed arguments of the structure vs. agency debate (Giddens, 1984). What seemed a modest aim in the 1970s, when education policies in England, such as the introduction of comprehensive schools to replace selection by ability, were consciously directed towards greater social justice for all, now seems more radical and more ambitious in times dominated by an audit culture that measures schools' success in terms of their students' test scores. The values and ideology that underpin the development of policy create structures and systems that the teacher action researcher is forced to work within. It is not that our current Labour Government is opposed to the aspiration of improving children's education; it is rather that policies are grounded in a different understanding of what making education 'better' for children might mean. Perhaps developing agency through action research means seeking spaces and leverage points where there are opportunities to create improvements consonant with our own values.

When I was still a teacher the focus of my action research was on my own classroom and school; later, when I became a researcher in a university, my focus moved to collaborative project work. Although I have worked almost continuously with teachers, students and managers/leaders in schools and universities, this has been as an action research partner and facilitator, not a teacher educator. By involving teachers in externally funded research I have offered them a 'participation-in-research' approach to professional development as well as the opportunity to generate knowledge to inform changes in their practice. This has meant that I have been able to provide them with small amounts of funding to 'buy time' in the form of substitute teachers, and provide refreshments at after-school meetings, but opportunities to gain accreditation for their research have always been an optional extra, often not taken up. So I have never been able to expect *teachers* to devote a large amount of their 'home' time to action research undertaken as part of project work, as is common when action research is part of post-graduate study; although when working with *teacher educators* the requirement for them to carry out research as part of their job has proved a useful incentive.

This chapter is intended both as a marker of the achievements of the teachers and teacher educators I have worked with in generating actionable knowledge, making an impact on their schools and classrooms, and making a difference to their students' educational opportunities; and a reflection on my own role in working with them as a facilitator and co-researcher. Its particular focus is on the models of self and identity that have informed the design of these participatory action research projects and the analysis of data; and how these models provide metaphors for understanding and developing agency.

Elsewhere (Somekh, 2006: 15) I have defined agency as 'the capability of a self to take action that will have an impact on a social situation'. It follows that the conduct of action research and its power to bring about change and improvement depends to a very great extent on the 'self-as-research-instrument' of the researchers. The reflexivity which lies at the heart of the action research process is, therefore, not only a means of deepening self-understanding and raising sensitivity to the nuances of professional experience – a process of self-education – but a crucial means of increasing the power of action research to have developmental impact. This raises several important questions: What model of the self do we assume (in both the mental and active sense) as action researchers – and do we have a choice? Does our performance of the researcher-self change as a result of being *action researchers*? Do we develop agency through the action research process? How does our understanding of our researcher identity affect our ability to generate substantive knowledge and take transformative action?

ASSUMING THE UNIQUE, AUTHENTIC SELF

I am the product of a Christian education, assuming when I started out as an action researcher that I had a unique identity – a soul – that had special meaning in the eyes of God who would not allow even a sparrow to fall unnoticed (Luke, 12: 16–34). When studying for my first degree at the age of 20, I went briefly into psychoanalysis and began to understand that my intentionality was nowhere near as rational as I had thought. Others often did not understand my behaviour in the way I had hoped and expected; and often I found it hard to account for my own actions in retrospect. Freud's three-part model of the ego, the id and the super-ego encouraged me on a journey of self-discovery to better understand my own unique, authentic self. Complex, emotion-torn, and often misguided, but capable of analysis and not to be condemned for 'sins', my self was now reconstructed as borne of the sub-conscious drives from the engine of my libido overlaid with sub-conscious reactions to the vicissitudes of early life in my family. It was a somewhat fanciful, but wholly enticing metaphor that gave me self-reflective tools to begin to handle my own emotions for the first time.

Fifteen years later, in my own classroom, my early action research adopted Lewin's cycles of fact finding, action and evaluation (1946) and my focus was on investigating my interactions with my students, developing 'hypotheses' for how to improve my teaching by bringing my behaviours into line with my intentions, and testing them out in practical actions (Elliott, 2007). Although Lewin's work had focused on 'the scientific study of human behaviour on a group level' (Gold, 1999: 263) my understanding of action research, in the tradition of Elliott, was of myself working alone in my own classroom, facilitated by an 'outsider' who deliberately stood back to enable me to retain power as a researcher in my own right (Elliott, 1988). Through action research I investigated my own practice to uncover the tacit knowledge – both personal and professional – that informed my actions (Polanyi, 1958). For example, I developed a new way of teaching poetry, through individual project work, that would allow my students to develop their own personal, authentic response and soak up the techniques of practical criticism through investigation and representation, using me as a consultant (Somekh, 2006: 62–88). In the Pupil Autonomy in Learning with Microcomputers (PALM) project, the first funding I won as a university-based researcher to carry out action research in partnership with teachers, I carried forward the same assumptions about the nature of self and attempted to work as a facilitator of the participating teachers' action research (Somekh, 2006: 89–111). Using techniques such as 'dilemma analysis' (Winter, 1982) we worked with teachers to identify the conflicts between their values and practices, and decide upon possible courses of action that would bring these into better alignment. From the 35 action research studies by teachers, published in the *Teachers' Voices* series, the cross-case analysis carried out by 50 teachers participating in a PALM weekend conference identified seven key issues related to autonomy in learning. These were all crucial to developing a pedagogy that would maximize the value of new technology and included: the need for teachers to find the right balance between giving students choice over how they used technology and providing structure for their learning; and the need for teachers to develop 'framing tasks' to build computer-based tasks (usually involving pairs or small groups working at the one available computer) into ongoing classroom activity (Somekh and Davies 1991). This knowledge, generated by teachers, is still key 20 years later to integrating technology effectively in pedagogic practice. Pupil autonomy, named in PALM's title, was construed as 'autonomy from the teacher' – students taking greater responsibility for, and control over, their own learning – rather than necessarily working alone. Nevertheless, in retrospect it seems clear that the PALM project's understanding of agency and impact was grounded in a model of a unique self whose authentic 'voice' should be nurtured and privileged.

ASSUMING THE MULTIPLE SELF, CONTEXTUALLY AND SOCIALLY SITUATED

Like most educationalists in the UK, my doctoral study took place after I had moved out of school teaching into the university. It was based on two projects for which I acquired grants from the National Council for Educational Technology (NCET), the PALM project already mentioned and the Initial Teacher Education and New Technology Project (INTENT). Project INTENT came towards the end of my doctoral study. This time my collaborative partners were teacher educators, required by government to incorporate the use of new technologies in their work at four levels: using it to prepare their classes; to teach their classes; to prepare pre-service teachers to use it in their teaching; and to observe them using it, and evaluate its use, in school placements. Five teacher-education colleges/universities opted to work with me to develop models for doing this well. My reading for doctoral study and my leadership role in a group of 12 teacher educators, who included highly experienced and respected scholars as well as young enthusiasts, moved my understanding of agency forward both theoretically and experientially (Somekh, 2006: 112–29). I discovered theories of organizational management and leadership that were powerful in enabling or constraining agency by giving their members ownership (Fullan, 1982) or customizing organizational structures and cultures to suit local purposes (Morgan, 1986). These ideas were not entirely new for me because I had carried out research into organizational power in my own school, and been involved in Elliott's Teacher–Pupil Interaction and the Quality of Learning Project (TiQL) in which a Deputy Head Teacher had led a group of teacher-researchers in each school (Ebbutt and Elliott, 1985).

But looking back I can note a significant shift in my own focus away from a concern with individuals towards a focus on group processes. Project INTENT adopted a strategy of two-level action research, led by a partnership of a senior professor/manager and an IT coordinator in each college, working alongside colleagues in their teaching of pre-service school teachers. Both carried out action research at their own level, one into the management of change and the other into the facilitation of change in teaching. Other colleagues were supported in carrying out their own action research studies as a means of professional development and writing articles about their action research for publication. This strategy of functioning at several levels and forming cross-level partnerships proved to be a powerful lever for organizational change. Previously senior managers had thought that technology was expensive and of only peripheral interest in teacher education, and had seen IT coordinators as 'empire builders' who made unreasonable demands on the organization's budget; whereas IT coordinators had found senior managers unreasonable and oppositional. Through establishing this new alliance each came to understand the other's purposes and able to provide mutual support for each other's action research activities and for other colleagues.

The shift in the focus of my work to ways in which action research could support the agency of the individual within the organization was informed by theories from my reading. These included Pirsig's (1974) exploration of the relationship between human beings and the physical world; Mead's (1934) model of the self and social interaction; and Giddens' structuration theory (1984). INTENT and the other projects I was involved in during the years 1990–96 provided an exploratory canvas to investigate the practical power of these theories. All three presented models of the self which provided me then (and now) with clarifying metaphors.

Pirsig rejected the dichotomies of 'self' and 'other' that derive from the philosophy of Aristotle, and passionately asserted that through reflection on experience we participate in creating value itself. He provided a concept of human agency in terms of inter-relationship and participation. Humans create the world as they live in the world, and quality can only be judged in terms of human values of participation and reflection:

> The Quality which creates the world emerges as a *relationship* between man [sic] and his experience. He [sic] is a *participant* in the creation of all things. The *measure* of all things ... (Pirsig, 1974: 368)

Mead (1934) saw 'mind' or 'consciousness' as three-fold: the 'I' who is the actor and problem-solver within the environment; the 'me' who is the object of self-scrutiny, continuously linked to the 'I'; and the 'generalized other' which is the discourse/culture of the group. Only through 'engagement' of the 'I' and the 'me' with the 'generalized other' does the individual 'develop a complete self':

> It is in the form of the generalized other that the social process influences the behaviour of the individuals involved in it and carrying it on, i.e., that the community exercises control over the conduct of its individual members; for it is in this form that the social process of community enters as a determining factor in the individual's thinking. (Mead: 55)

This self that is socially created and re-created through the process of interaction with others, is no longer a unique individual with a core identity and a 'voice' waiting to be empowered, but rather a fluid identity, contingent and situated. In one sense its activities are constrained by the continuous 'performance' of routinized interactions with others – easily observable in any social gathering, such as a classroom or formal meeting, where actions of one participant initiate the responses of another. Yet this responsiveness to social interactions provides levers for change that can be used to re-position the action-researcher strategically and politically. In Project INTENT the creation of a partnership between a manager with a powerful role in the organization and an IT coordinator working at grassroots level disrupted the established hierarchy of control. This mechanism alone provided new opportunities for agency, although they differed between the five participating organizations, depending on the nature of the organizational structure and the extent to which each of the partners had the interpersonal skills and vision to capitalize on them (Somekh et al. 1997).

Through Project INTENT I had come to understand that action research can be a powerful means of supporting organizational change; and what I learned from experience fitted with my reading at the time of Giddens' (1984) Structuration Theory. Drawing on the work of Goffman and Mead, Giddens poses a resolution of the structure-agency debate, in which although human agency is constrained by institutional structures, these are themselves constructed and reconstructed by human agents:

> The structural properties of social systems are both medium and outcome of the practices they recursively organize. Structure is not 'external' to individuals: as memory traces, and as instantiated in social practices, it is in a certain sense more 'internal' than exterior to their activities (…) (Giddens: 25)

My question then became whether participatory action research could provide a means for human beings to intervene in the institutional structures in which they worked and through changes in their practice manage a process of development and change. In terms of structuration theory, Giddens conceptualized power as 'the capacity to achieve outcomes' that, rather than being 'an obstacle to freedom or emancipation', could become 'their very medium' (p. 257). For me this was a new and very exciting way of understanding what it might mean for teachers to be empowered and I wanted to explore how action research could assist this process.

The Management for Organizational and Human Development project (MOHD), which I coordinated in 1995–97, was a network of seven research centres in five countries funded by the European Union. The overarching focus of MOHD's action research, in the many local projects in schools, colleges and the research centres themselves, was an exploration of the question, 'In what ways can individuals, regardless of their formal position in the hierarchy, learn to understand their own power and make a conscious contribution to organizational development?' MOHD action research showed that by understanding the self as 'multiple' it became possible for individuals to adapt their roles to suit individuals' needs and develop greater interpersonal sensitivity, thereby increasing their own agency and maximizing the possibilities for change and development (Somekh and Thaler, 1997). To explore the complexity of roles and relationships in which the multiple selves of managers were co-constructed, MOHD used a technique of 'identifying and exploring metaphors to make explicit the implicit images they had of their professional roles' (Thaler et al., 1997: 324). This is an example of how MOHD's action research used methods that supported a more open and flexible analysis of data, consonant with the more fluid model of the multiple self, rather than techniques such as 'pattern analysis' (Ireland and Russell, 1978), used extensively in the PALM project, that focused on the routine performances of social practice and assumed a more straightforward relationship between cause and effect.

ASSUMING THE CULTURALLY MEDIATED SELF, MIND AND ACTIVITY

Between 1998 and 2001 I became involved in another European-funded research project, REPRESENTATION, which explored children's conceptualizations and representations of computer technologies. We developed a paper-based method in which children drew concept maps made up of drawings to 'tell the researchers their ideas about "Computers in My World"'. Through this concept-mapping task children aged 8–11 drew anything between 10 and 100 small drawings of different computer-related artifacts in 20 minutes, showing how they conceptualized and categorized them through how they arranged them on the page and the links they drew between them (Pearson and Somekh, 2003). We were surprised by the complexity of the children's mental models of computer technologies revealed through this method.

My understanding of the self now shifted to a fascination with *the embodied mind*, and the processes of perception and representation that lie at the core of human agency. Here was another metaphor to shape the design of action research. The REPRESENTATION project and my participation over the same period in a series of seminars on sociocultural theories, led to my becoming immersed in reading post-Vygotskian cultural psychology and activity theory and debating its implications for action and research. The self – or identity – shifted in my understanding into what Wertsch calls in the title of his book, 'mind-as-action' (1998). The self is contingent on the culture and history of its embodied experience as a member of a human activity system mediated by numerous cultural tools, the foremost of which is language. The self *is* the mind whose agency is mediated by language, thought *is* intra-mental speech, and perception is a form of action in which the mental models (or secondary artefacts) of conceptual tools and physical artefacts are essential enablers of our behaviours, and essential precursors of envisioning and imagining new practices (or constructing tertiary artefacts) (Wartofsky, 1979). The agent and cultural tool becomes the single unit of analysis in which the tool is, as McLuhan termed it, 'an extension of the self' (1964: 7). In Wertsch's metaphor (op. cit. pp. 27–8), the pole vaulter's object is to make the jump but the jump itself is achieved by means of pole and pole vaulter acting as one. The agent is in no sense a free agent but a participant in an activity system that enables and constrains individual and group actions through its extensive cultural tools, organizing rules and procedures, divisions of labour between participants and established practices (Engeström et al., 1999). Identity is constructed by participation in the group activity or 'community of practice', and by reification of concepts and practices through naming and categorization (Wenger, 1998) to increase the community's cultural capital.

For the subsequent 10 years I have been involved in directing a series of funded projects enquiring into the role computer technologies might play in transforming students' learning. All have involved some form of participatory action research with either teacher-researchers or student-researchers or both. On several occasions we have worked with student researchers to explore how they use the internet, mobile phones and other digital technologies at home; and how their wide-ranging knowledge and skills might be brought into the school and used to transform their learning. Over this period there has been a massive transformation in our society as a result of technology – in how we communicate with others, our access to knowledge and information, and our ability to publish texts and images in the international forum of the internet. Yet, the *affordances* of computer-based tools, that is, their latent possibilities for changing human activity, have been taken up differentially, depending on their contexts of use. The transformation in social practices observable in the wider society has not been matched by changes of the same order of magnitude in social/pedagogic practices in schools. Classrooms are spaces heavily constrained by technologies from the past, and human interactions between students and teachers in schools abide by the ritualized performances of question and answer, task-setting and seat-work, that were developed for previous technologies of pencil and slate before even the text book was ubiquitous. Schools are places where the established discourse of tasks, control, order and discipline mobilizes values of hierarchy and discourages risk-taking: in this sense, discourse is the most powerful of the cultural tools that constrains technology use in schools.

These new understandings of mind-as-action, or what Gee (1992) terms the 'social mind', in which 'meaning and memory, believing and knowing, are social practices that vary as they are embedded within different Discourses within a society' (p. 141), aroused my interest in new ways of designing collaborative action research with teachers and school leaders. In the Developing Pedagogies with E-Learning Resources (PELRS) project (see Saunders and Somekh, Chapter 15 in this volume) we worked in partnership with teachers to explore the possibilities for radical changes in pedagogy. Our aspiration was to change the nature of teacher-student relationships and give students a choice over when and how they used computer-based technologies to help them with learning. PELRS showed that teachers' agency in developing radical pedagogic change with computer-based technologies could be greatly increased by incorporating insights from activity theory into the action research design. The main obstacles to transformative practice proved to be at the policy level rather than being due to teachers resisting change. In follow-up research to PELRS we plan to focus specifically on secondary (high) schools where the barriers in terms of organization of the school day and pressure of assessment are greatest, and seek active involvement in the research from representatives of government departments and agencies directly involved in policy.

The 'mind-as-action' metaphor of the self is important in allowing me to understand why, as Lewin famously said, 'Nothing is as practical as a good theory' (1951: 169). Action is not separate from mental processes, because mental processes are social constructions and action necessarily originates in the mind's perceptions and imaginings.

AGENCY THROUGH ACTION RESEARCH

These ways of understanding the self and identity are interlocking and over-lapping metaphors that I use as an action researcher, both in everyday life and in designing collaborative projects with teachers and school leaders. They are drawn from bodies of literature which have their own constituent communities of practice, and moving into and between them has involved me in border crossings and brokerage between people and ideas. This has not been only in terms of reading different books, but in attending conferences and participating in networks where I meet groups of people who are largely unknown to one another. My habit as an action researcher of engaging with theories as data to be interrogated and tested out in practice, may have been partly shaped by my early training, as a student of literature, in practising the poet Samuel Coleridge's concept of 'willing suspension of disbelief' (Coleridge, 1817) in order to imagine new truths. The definition of agency as 'the capability of the self to take action that will have an impact' does not presuppose that action should consist in endless pursuit of activities and tasks. In an excellent review of the development of the concept of identity in Western thought, Smith (1997) ends by recommending we spend more time in schools on reflection and less on acting and doing:

> Certainly the most profound disease in Western pedagogy is activism, or action for its own sake. (...) There is so little opportunity to find one's original face, because every space is seen to require some sort of instructional intervention. (p. 277)

'To find one's original face' is of huge importance in learning to use one's 'self-as-research-instrument' powerfully. But 'original' does not mean unique and separate; it does not mean as a mind separated from the body, or vice versa. For me, agency starts with the reflexive construction and reconstruction of an open and enquiring mind, and the aspiration to continuously learn from both reading and experience. Action research has offered me tools to construct myself as powerful rather than powerless, by building strategic alliances and seeking spaces for leverage. One of these tools is the playful intention to use various metaphors of identity to help me engage actively with the interpersonal relationships and social practices, institutional structures and ideologies which co-construct my life and work. Setting aside any notion of a unique unitary self opens up the possibility of 'bracketing' our known identity and experimenting with adopting different identities as a form of strategic action. In this sense we can adapt our self-as-research-instrument. In action and agency, just as in writing, I have found Foucault's (1974) resistance to normative notions of consistency and conformity liberating and empowering.

> I am no doubt not the only one who writes in order to have no face. Do not ask who I am and do not ask me to remain the same: leave it to our bureaucrats and our police to see that our papers are in order. At least spare us their morality when we write. (p. 17)

My current thinking is that we do have a choice over the models of the self that we *assume*, both in basing our search for self-understanding upon them and performing them in our relationships with others. At the very least we have the capability *not* to construct ourselves as victims and invest our power solely in resistance. There are always spaces for strategic action.

Perhaps technology's transformation of social processes, outside the school, has been most anarchic in supporting a post-modern playfulness in inventing new ways of representing the self through fictionalized identities, crossing genders and age gaps, whether as participants in chat rooms, through the construction of avatars, or the presentation of second selves in social networking sites.

I once took part in an exercise in which participants at a meeting were asked to introduce themselves with a metaphor for their researcher identity. Mine was the metaphor of the adventure playground. I think we can choose what research methods to use and even what researcher identities to perform.

REFERENCES

Coleridge, S.T. (1817) *Biographia Literaria – or Biographical Sketches of my Literary Life and Opinions* (1817). Reprinted in Read Books, 2006.

Ebbutt, D. and Elliott, J. (eds) (1985) *Issues in Teaching for Understanding*. London: Longman for the SCDC.

Elliott, J. (1988) 'Educational research and outsider-insider relations', *Qualitative Studies in Education*. 1 (2): 155–66.

Elliott, J. (2007) *Reflecting Where the Action Is: The Selected Works of John Elliott*. London and New York: Routledge.

Engeström, Y., Miettinen, R. and Punamäki, R.-L. (eds) (1999) *Perspectives on Activity Theory*. Cambridge UK, New York and Melbourne: Cambridge University Press.

Foucault, M. (1974) *The History of Sexuality*, vol. 1 English translation by Robert Hurley. London: Penguin.

Fullan, M.G. (1982) *The Meaning of Educational Change*. Toronto: OISE Press, The Ontario Institute for Studies in Education.

Giddens, A. (1984) *The Constitution of Society: Outline of the Theory of Structuration*. Cambridge: Polity Press.

Gee, J.P. (1992) *The Social Mind: Language, Ideology, and Social Practice*. New York and London: Beingin & Garvey.

Gold, M. (ed.) (1999) *The Complete Social Scientist: a Kurt Lewin Reader*. Washington, DC: American Psychological Association.

Ireland, D. and Russell, T. (1978) 'Pattern analysis', *CARN Bulletin 2, Cambridge Institute of Education,* 2: 21–5.

Lewin, K. (1946) 'Action research and minority problems', *Journal of Social Issues,* 2 (1): 34–46.

Lewin, K. (1951) *Field Theory in Social Science: Selected Theoretical Papers.* New York: Harper Row.

Mead, G.H. (1934) *Mind, Self and Society* (Vol. 1). Chicago: University of Chicago Press.

McLuhan, M. (1964) *Understanding Media.* London and New York: Routledge & Kegan Paul.

Morgan, G. (1986) *Images of Organization.* Beverly Hills and London: Sage.

Pearson, M. and Somekh, B. (2003) 'Concept-mapping as a research tool: a study of primary children's representations of information and communication technologies (ICT)', *Education and Information Technologies,* 8 (1): 5–22.

Pirsig, R. (1974) *Zen and the Art of Motorcycle Maintenance.* London: Bodley Head. Reprinted Corgi/Transworld, London.

Polanyi, M. (1958) *Personal Knowledge: Towards a Post-critical Philosophy.* London: Routledge & Kegan Paul.

Smith, D.G. (1997) 'Identity, self, and other in the conduct of pedagogical action: An east/west inquiry', in T. Carson, A. and D. Sumara (eds), *Action Research as a Living Practice.* New York: Peter Lang.

Somekh, B. (2006) *Action Research: A Methodology for Change and Development.* Maidenhead, UK and New York, US: Open University Press.

Somekh, B. and Davies, R. (1991) 'Towards a pedagogy for information technology', *The Curriculum Journal,* 2 (2): 153–70.

Somekh, B. and Thaler, M. (1997) 'Contradictions of management theory, organisational cultures and the self', *Educational Action Research,* 5 (1): 339–55.

Somekh, B., Whitty, G., and Coveney, R. (1997). 'IT and the politics of institutional change'. in B. Somekh and N. Davis (eds.), *Using IT effectively in teaching and learning.* London and New York: Routledge.

Thaler, M., Somekh, B., Draper, S. and Doughty, G. (1997) 'Agency in organisational change', in T. Carson and D. Sumara (eds), *Action Research as a Living Practice.* New York: Peter Lang.

Wartofsky, M. (1979) *Models: Representation and Scientific Understanding.* Dordrecht: Reidel.

Wenger, E. (1998) *Communities of Practice: Learning, Meaning and Identity.* Cambridge, UK, New York and Melbourne: Cambridge University Press.

Wertsch, J.V. (1998) *Mind as Action.* New York and Oxford: Oxford University Press.

Winter, R. (1982) 'Dilemma analysis: a contribution to the methodology of action research', *Cambridge Journal of Education,* 12 (3): 161–74.

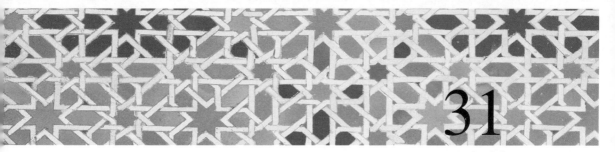

31

Existentialism and Action Research

Allan Feldman

Existentialism is one way, of many possible ways, of looking at the world.[1] It serves as a theoretical framework for a methodology that makes problematic *existence*. To philosophers this has led to questions like, 'What is existence?' 'What does it mean to be?' 'What is it to human beings that we are beings who are aware of our own being?' And, 'What does it mean that we are aware that we will eventually cease to exist?' When existentialism becomes the theoretical framework for a research methodology in education, it leads to other questions, including the one that has framed my scholarly work: 'What does it mean to teach and to be a teacher?' This question is important because it distinguishes the act of teaching from *being* a teacher. Any person can teach, if we define teaching to mean helping someone else to learn. But not all people who teach *are* teachers. That is because ontologically there is significance to saying, 'I am a teacher'. The existential lens also allows us to ask ourselves questions like, 'Who am I as a teacher?' 'How does the way I am a teacher affect how I teach?' And, 'How do I change who I am as a teacher to improve my educational situation for myself and my students?' When existentialism becomes a theoretical framework for action research, it allows for teachers and other practitioners to inquire systematically into these questions.

EXISTENTIAL CHARACTERISTICS OF PERSONHOOD

From my experience with action research and my reading of the existential literature, especially that of Maxine Greene (e.g., Greene 1967, 1973, 1988), I identified three existential characteristics of personhood that have implications for action research. They are: situatedness, the emergence of self, and freedom. I explain each of these briefly below.[2]

Situatedness

People always find themselves situated. Situation goes beyond the human interaction with a single object, event, or set of objects or events, and is instead a web of relationships that spread through time and space (Greene, 1973) and are constituted by the milieu of 'traditions, institutions, and customs, and the purposes and beliefs they carry and inspire'(Dewey, 1938: 43). The interactions between teachers and pupils are among humans immersed in situations, and almost everything that occurs in an educational situation is affected by the teacher's past and present, presence, moods and gestures, expectations, intentions, and the pupils with whom he or she is continually engaged.

The Emergence of Self

Existence precedes essence (Sartre, 1956, 1982). As we go about living our lives we construct who we are and our selves emerge through our experiences (Greene, 1973). Often we are not aware of our self-construction or we suppress this knowledge because if we acknowledge it, then we also acknowledge that we are the ones responsible for who we are, and that it is to ourselves that we are accountable.

Freedom

Maxine Greene has told us that human freedom 'is the capacity to surpass the given and look at things as if they could be otherwise'(Greene, 1988: 3) and to be able 'to name alternatives, imagine a better state of things, [and] share with others a project of change'(Greene, 1988: 9). To be free, therefore, requires that we be aware of the possibilities for action. It also requires that we interrogate the constraints to our actions because while there are constraints that limit what we can, they do not necessarily limit our freedom to choose what we ought to do if we could, and what we can do given the limitations. However, we also find ourselves constrained by beliefs that are mythic in their power but not real (Britzman, 1986; Tobin and McRobbie, 1996). Unless we can distinguish the real and the mythic, even though freedom to choose is an essential part of being human (Sartre, 1956), we act as if we have very limited choices or none at all.

EXISTENTIALISM IN EDUCATION

Existentialism is fundamentally an educational philosophy because it is a theory of human *becoming*. It describes the way we find ourselves immersed in situations in which we take actions that change ourselves and our situations (Heidegger, 1962). This said, other than during a span of about 25 years during the post-war period (e.g., Denton, 1974; Kneller, 1958; Morris, 1966; Smith, 1977),[3] little has been written about the ways in which existentialism can help us to understand and improve education.

Fifty years ago, George Kneller wrote that an existential approach to education is concerned with the

> unfolding of the individual as a whole in the particular situation in which he finds himself, within a definite time and space into which the individual has been born through no fault of his own, but which nonetheless defines him. (Kneller, 1958: 118–19)

Because existentialism helps us to understand how we construct ourselves through the choices we make and the actions that we take (or don't make and don't take), it also helps us to understand how we learn (Jarvis, 2005). This suggests that learning happens as a result of being in and experiencing the world. Clearly you do not need to embrace an existential worldview to agree with this. What are missing are the intentions of the individuals that relate to their interests, or as Sartre and Greene refer to it, their projects. An existential philosophy of education has to be more than a philosophy of learning – it must embrace the full situatedness of the individuals and their acknowledgement of their projects. That is, for being in the world to lead to educational change, people need to be aware of their situatedness, their creation of their selves, and their freedom to choose how to act. This awareness is not easy to achieve. In fact, it is often something that we flee, because to be aware that we create ourselves and are therefore responsible for who we are and for how our choices and actions affect others is, as Van Cleve Morris put it, a 'mountainous' responsibility (Morris, 1966). The role of the teacher, therefore, is to help students gain this awareness and not to flee from it.

Another major aspect of existential thought is that of the relation between self and other. An existential approach to education makes clear that it is not enough to be aware of and acknowledge one's own becoming – it is also imperative to be aware and acknowledge the humanness of other people. The recognition of both teacher and student (and administrators, parents, and policy makers) that each is an individual human being who is situated, whose self emerges through experience, and who has freedom to choose is the basis for an existential approach to education. Unfortunately, this occurs infrequently. Teachers, like all human beings, are prone to objectify others, such as students, and the students often cannot imagine teachers having lives outside of schools. The result is that teachers engage in an 'I-It' relationship with their students rather than an 'I-Thou' relationship (Buber, 1937), which leads to the objectification of students, making them into objects that can be manipulated through technical means. It allows teachers to look at these 'objects' and remove their responsibility for them by shifting the blame for failure to defects in the 'raw materials', and eliminates the possibility of joy that comes from acknowledging the responsibility that they would have for their students' success. The I-It relationship also deprives students of their rights as human beings: 'to have a voice and be heard, to search for one's own meanings, and to be a potent person in the world (Smith, 1977)'. And, it leads teachers to abandon moral, social, cultural and political objectives and instead focus on the subject matter rather than the person who is a student.

An I-Thou relationship between teachers and students begins to emerge when they acknowledge and become involved with each other as individuals. To be involved means to take on the responsibility that they have for others. To become involved,

> is thus to make contact with that for which there is no precedent. Each encounter between teacher and learner therefore inevitably starts from scratch. It begins anew with a fresh creation still in the act of creating itself. The teacher's task is to see to it that this subjective selfhood, *de novo*, quickens its awareness of itself, of its freedom, and eventually to its responsibility for its own way of living a single human life. (Morris, 1966: 152)

So to be an existentialist teacher means to be aware of the dialectic between oneself as a teacher and who your students are as human beings.

EXISTENTIAL CONCEPTS OF ACTION RESEARCH

In some ways action research has always had a connection with existentialism, but this is not at all evident from the literature. Although references to existentialism and action research can be found as early as 1955 (Blum, 1955) and again 20 years later (Sussman and Evered, 1978), there is little contemporary work (Feldman, 2002, 2007; Lambert, 2005) that discusses the existential basis of action research. Because of the paucity of literature that connects existentialism explicitly to action research, I examine instead three similar but different methods and show how they relate to existentialism and action research. These methods are: T-groups, existential psychology, and self-study.

T-Groups

While Kurt Lewin's influence on action research is well known and documented in education (see other chapters in this volume), his work in social psychology is often overlooked. As a social psychologist, Lewin helped to develop sensitivity training and what became known as T-groups. T-groups bring together a small group of people to study their own behavior. They provide participants with the opportunity to learn about themselves, their impact on others and how to function more effectively in interpersonal situations. T-groups have the following four elements: participant observation, cognitive aids, feedback and unfreezing (Yalom, 1995).

Each of these four elements has its counterpart in action research. The focus of the T-group is on the participants, and like people researching their practice, they pay close attention to their actions and beliefs. Cognitive aids, such as models for organizing ideas and references to the research literature, help participants to make sense of their observations in the same way that they help action researchers to analyze their data. Feedback is equivalent to the part of the action research cycle in which data is used to inform and modify practice and research. T-groups help to unfreeze participants' belief system by creating environments in which it is safe to challenge one's own values and beliefs, similarly to what can happen in collaborative action research groups.

Lewin's work with T-groups is also related to his earlier development of field theory. Lewin sought to understand how and why people behave as they do in social situations. He posited that a person's behavior is affected by the totality of his or her situation, a field, which is 'the totality of coexisting facts which are conceived of as mutually interdependent' (Lewin, 1951: 240). People behave as they do as a result of the way in which various forces in their field interact, and because of the tensions between their self-perceptions and their situations (Lewin, 1951).

Field theory and T-groups have existential implications as well as action research ones. Lewin was concerned with the self in the world and his field theory provides a social psychological model for being and becoming. T-groups use methods similar to action research to help people uncover the forces that shape their values and beliefs and cause them to behave in certain ways. This is reminiscent of existential education, in which the goal is to help people become aware of their humanness and to acknowledge their responsibility for themselves and for others.

Existential Psychotherapy

Existential therapy is another method that has as its goal personal change, and, as its name implies, it is tightly connected to existential philosophy. Irvin Yalom defines existential therapy as 'a dynamic approach to therapy which focuses on concerns that are rooted in the individual's existence' (Yalom, 1998a: 169–70). Existential psychotherapy builds upon this by focusing on specific conflicts – those that relate to existential concerns like mortality, freedom, isolation, and meaninglessness, which constitute 'the individual's confrontation with the givens of existence' (Yalom, 1998a: 172).

It should be clear that existential therapy is not action research. However, there is a similarity that allows it to be a useful model for conceptualizing an existential form of action research. This can be seen by looking at John Elliott's characterization of action research:

> Action research might be defined as 'the study of a social situation with a view to improving the quality of action within it' (Elliott, 1991: 69).
> Action research improves practice by developing the practitioner's capacity for discrimination and judgment in particular, complex, human situations. (Elliott, 1991: 52)

In existential psychotherapy, the focus of the 'study' is the patient's mental health. From an existential perspective, mental health is a way of being in the world, which is improved as the patients improve their capacity to discriminate the authenticity of their existence and become able to uncover their freedom. This then enables them to choose responsibly and project themselves toward their potentialities. Because of the similarity between this and Elliott's definitions of action research, the idea that there can be existential forms of psychotherapy and casework that lead to personal change, opens the possibility of existential forms of action research that lead to changes in one's way of being a practitioner.

Self-Study of Teacher Education Practices

While T-groups and existential therapy and casework may be thought of as distant cousins of an existential form of action research, self-study research has a much closer familial resemblance. Self-study, which has been developed over the past 10 years by teacher educators, is akin to action research in its focus on practice:

> the term self-study is used in relation to teaching and researching practice in order to better understand: oneself; teaching; learning; and the development of knowledge about these. (Loughran, 2004: 9)

Ken Zeichner and Susan Noffke, in their review of practitioner research (2001), distinguish self-study from other varieties of practitioner research in two ways. First, it originally developed as self-study of *teacher education practices*. Second, they found that there is a preference among its practitioners to use narrative and life history forms of inquiry. While these characteristics give self-study a particular niche in the world of practitioner research, they seem like little reason to distinguish it as a species separate from action research.

As part of the development of the *International Handbook of Self-Study*, Frederick Lighthall (2004) analyzed a sample of 125 self-studies to identify common features of self-study research. Lighthall found little that distinguishes self-study research from other forms of practitioner research. However, he did suggest the self 'is inescapably implicated in all [self-study] inquiries to some degree' (Lighthall, 2004: 226). This is also what Feldman et al. (2004) claim is the salient feature of self-study research – the problematization of the self in practice as the focus of self-study research.

The problematic nature of the self in practice is made explicit by Robert Bullough and Stefanee Pinnegar (2004). They identify four problems for self-study: definition, form, scholarship, and ontology. As I have already demonstrated, self-study is ill defined. Bullough and Pinnegar also note the dilemmas faced in deciding who the self-study is for and how the research should be represented. They suggest that the privileging of personal experience can raise questions about warrants and validity of self-studies. Finally, they raise the problem of the self in self-study.

> ... the self is never merely psychological and individual but is formed and maintained in a relationship to others. As a result, at its core, self-study embraces a moral imperative. Our being as teachers and teacher educators is wrapped up in the exploration of the point where, in practice, we meet and souls and selves touch. (Bullough and Pinnegar, 2004: 340)

The problematization of the self in practice is why existentialism can serve as a theoretical basis for self-study (Feldman, 2003; Feldman, et al., 2004) for several reasons. First, existentialism puts the self as a being becoming at the center of its focus. Second, existentialism connects explicitly the experiences that we have with who we are immersed in our situations. Clearly it would be impossible to study one's self in practice without using personal and professional experiences as resources for research. Finally, the role of responsibility in existentialism requires a self-critical stance to one's being in the world, and therefore one's way of being a research and a teacher educator. Because existential responsibility is toward oneself and to others, it is necessary to also pay close attention to how one interacts with others, especially those for whom we care (Feldman et al., 2004).

I end this section by noting that one significant difference between self-study and action research is that the former does not connect itself explicitly to the taking of action. While there is much in the literature that states that the purpose of self-study is the improvement of practice, that this improvement comes about through taking actions that are part of the self-study process is infrequently made explicit.

EXISTENTIAL ACTION RESEARCH

I now turn to what it would mean for there to be an existential form of action research. To do so I begin with a definition of action research. The one that I use when working with teachers and other practitioners draws upon the work of Lawrence Stenhouse (1981, 1983):

> Action research happens when people are involved in researching their own practice in order to improve it and to come to a better understanding of their practice situations. It is action because they act within the systems that they are trying to improve and understand. It is research because it is systematic, critical inquiry made public. (Feldman, 2002: 242)

This definition must be modified in several ways if it is to describe an existential form of action research. First, it must respond to the notion that human beings are immersed in situations that they both find themselves thrown into and create. The idea of focusing on one's practice is antithetical to existential situatedness. That is because to speak of one's practice is to suggest that what we do is somehow different from who we are and how we live our lives. This can lead to the feelings of alienation and inauthenticity (Pedevillano, 2004). It can also lead to feeling defined and constrained by structural and political pressures (Greene, 1978), and result in teachers and other professionals coping 'by becoming merely efficient, by functioning compliantly – like Kafkaesque clerks' (Greene, 1978: 28).

Because existential action research is an activity that involves working and interacting with other human beings, it is important for those who engage in it to examine their own being in their social and historical situations, rather than a practice situation that is separate from themselves. This reduces the likelihood of relationships becoming polarized into 'we-they' or the objectification of the I-It relationship (Buber, 1937). Therefore, instead of focusing on *practice*, an existential form of action research focuses on *being*, and in particular, one's own being.

The shift of focus from practice to being raises the question of what is improved in existential action research? It is not enough to say that it is *being* that is improved – it is also important to say what aspect of being and in what direction the improvement is in. When one improves one's own being by engaging in action research, what is improved is 'the capacity to surpass the given and look at things as if they could be otherwise'(Greene, 1978: 3). This is evidenced in a feeling and awareness of the incompleteness, disquietude, contradictions, dissonances and dilemmas that become a part of one's being, which leads to the recognition of the existential freedom to choose.

The improvement of being has a direction because we create ourselves through our freedom to choose and our experiences. Because we make ourselves, we are responsible for whom we are and for whom we are becoming. Existential forms of action research can lead to an awareness of this responsibility, and then to the acknowledgement that the responsibility goes beyond the individual because of our immersion in situations that are dispersed through time and are part of webs of human relations. To be responsible in an existential sense means to be 'responsible in relation to the historical, biographical, social, political and moral milieu that constitutes one's way of being in the world' (Feldman, 2007: 244). This sense of responsibility sets the direction for the improvement of one's being.

There is one more aspect of action research that must be examined relative to existentialism: the taking of action. When one engages in action research, one not only learns about the system under investigation – one also takes actions to improve it. An existential form of action research should lead to actions that improve one's capacity to surpass the given and to behave in ways that are more responsible for oneself and others. But one of the important distinctions that existential thought makes is the difference between freedom to choose and freedom to act. An existential form of action research should lead to one being able to identify and illuminate all the possibilities that one has, whether they are constrained or not. It is also important to be able to distinguish those choices that are truly constrained from those that only appear to be (Britzman, 1986; Tobin and McRobbie, 1996). One way to do this is to engage in fully democratic conversations with others engaged in the same or similar enterprises.

> ... freedom shows itself or comes into being when individuals come together in a particular way, when they are authentically present to one another (without masks, pretenses, badges of office), when they have a project they can mutually pursue. (Greene, 1988: 16–17).

All this leads to the following definition of existential action research:

> Existential action research happens when people work together to research their own ways of being a teacher to increase their capacity to choose freely and to act responsibly for themselves and those they care for. (Feldman, 2002: 244)

EXISTENTIAL AWARENESS OF OTHERS: AN EXAMPLE
OF EXISTENTIAL ACTION RESEARCH

An existential approach to action research can help teachers become aware of the ways they objectify students. For example, JoAnne Devine, a middle school teacher in an urban district, learned the importance of focusing on her students as people. Devine's starting point for research was that she felt uncomfortable about the tracking that was occurring in her school and the effects that it had on her, her students, and their interactions. She was particularly concerned about the class she met at the end of each day in which 'all of the low students and behavior problems' were 'lumped together' (Devine, 1994). This tracking caused management problems for Devine, but she was also concerned about the way tracking led to her low expectations for these children.

In response to an assignment in the action research course and after discussions with her peers in a collaborative action research group, she decided to do a pattern analysis in her last period class. To do this she arranged the classroom into five learning centers rather than her usual rows of seats facing the blackboard. While the students worked at the centers in small groups, Devine went from group to group asking and answering questions. As a result of observing the patterns of interaction in her class, she decided, 'it was necessary to talk to the kids'. She did this informally during lunch, recess, or when they were working on in-class assignments.

> I learned many things about these children's personal lives as well as what they thought about school. I was amazed at how they continue to want to talk with me. I'm finding that by learning more about these kids and telling them things about me that some walls are breaking down. Stephen has begun to act 'less tough' in my presence. He still acts out but when I talk to him about it he acknowledges me and will say things like, 'I forgot' or 'okay'. Our battles have become manageable and become less frequent. (Devine, 1994)

As she continued with her action research, Devine talked with the students individually and shifted her instruction so that the students took more responsibility for their learning. She also instituted time for students to meet with her before and after school for homework help. The conversations continued, she provided opportunities for students to take on more responsibility, and she accepted the responsibility of providing them with a safe, supportive place in which to learn. As a result, her students found her classroom to be a safe harbor in the storm of their lives, where they could attend to themselves and begin to accept the responsibility of who they are.

CONCLUSION

I end this chapter by noting that many people associate existentialism with a sense of gloominess and negativity. That is because within the existentialist literature a specialized language has emerged that helps us to talk about characteristics such as situatedness, the construction of the self, and freedom. As we have seen, existentialism is concerned with the primacy of experience. For example, when we become aware of how we are situated, and of existence we acknowledge that because we *are*, we will *cease to be*. This leads us to ask, for example, 'How do we live knowing that we will die?' Existentialists answer by pointing to our feelings such as angst, anxiety, dread, meaninglessness, self-estrangement, and even nausea (Yalom, 1998b). It is important to note that these feelings are signs of awareness of our situatedness and can serve as starting points for action research from which actions can be decided upon freely to create oneself anew. It is when these feelings are seen as harbingers of the need to change rather than states from which there is no escape, that these words lose their gloominess, and instead open spaces for a standpoint that includes personal insight and artistry, as well as issues of our existence and the human condition. The deeper and more complete examination of one's way of being can help teachers and other practitioners construct hopeful paths to meaningfulness, choice, and freedom, which comprise a more complete and embracing understanding of these existential concepts.

NOTES

1 It is important for me to make it clear that I do not claim to be a philosopher, and I am certainly no expert in existentialism. What follows is my interpretation of existential literature and how it relates to educational action research.

2 For a more detailed explanation see Feldman (2002; 2007).

3 For an extensive list of postwar writings on existential and education, see the bibliography compiled by Albert Miller (1969).

REFERENCES

Blum, F.H. (1955) 'Action research – A scientific approach?' *Philosophy of Science*, 22 (1): 1–7.

Britzman, D. (1986) 'Cultural myths in the making of a teacher: Biography and social structure in teacher education', *Harvard Educational Review*, 56 (4): 442–56.

Buber, M. (1937) *I and Thou* (R.G. Smith, Trans.). Edinburgh: T. & T. Clark.

Bullough, R.V. and Pinnegar, S.E. (2004) 'Thinking about the thinking about self-study: An analysis of eight chapters', in J.J. Loughran, M.L. Hamilton, V.K. LaBoskey and T. Russell (eds), *International Handbook of Self-Study of Teaching and Teacher Education Practices*. Boston: Kluwer Academic Publishers, pp. 313–42.

Denton, D. (1974) 'That mode of being called Teaching', in D. Denton (ed.), *Existentialism and Phenomenology in Education*. New York: Teachers College Press, pp. 99–115.

Devine, J. (1994) *Action Research Report*. Amherst, MA: University of Massachusetts.

Dewey, J. (1938) *Logic: The Theory of Inquiry*. New York: Henry Holt and Company.

Elliott, J. (1991) *Action Research for Educational Change*. Philadelphia, PA: Open University Press.

Feldman, A. (2002) 'Existential approaches to action research', *Educational Action Research*, 10 (2): 233–52.

Feldman, A. (2003) 'Validity and quality in self-study', *Educational Researcher*, 32 (3): 26–8.

Feldman, A. (2007) 'Teachers, responsibility and action research', *Educational Action Research*, 15 (2): 239–52.

Feldman, A., Paugh, P. and Mills, G. (2004) 'Self-study through action research', in J. Loughran, M.L. Hamilton, V. Laboskey and T. Russell (eds), *International Handbook of Self-Study of Teaching and Teacher Education Practices*. Dordrecht, The Netherlands: Kluwer Academic Publishers.

Greene, M. (ed.) (1967) *Existential Encounters for Teachers*. New York: Random House.

Greene, M. (1973) *Teacher as Stranger: Educational Philosophy for the Modern Age*. Belmont, CA: Wadsworth Publishing Company.

Greene, M. (1978) 'Teaching: The question of personal reality', *Teachers College Record*, 80 (1): 23–35.

Greene, M. (1988) *The Dialectic of Freedom*. New York: Teachers College Press.

Heidegger, M. (1962) *Being and Time* (J.M.E. Robinson, Trans.). San Francisco: Harper.

Jarvis, P. (2005) 'Towards a philosophy of human learning: An existential perspective', in P. Jarvis and S. Parker (eds), *Human Learning: An Holistic Approach*. New York: Routledge, pp. 1–15.

Kneller, G. (1958) *Existentialism and Education*. New York: John Wiley & Sons.

Lambert, E.A. (2005) 'Action research and the study of human being', *International journal of Action Research*, 1 (3): 290–310.

Lewin, K. (1951) *Field Theory in Social Science; Selected Theoretical Papers*. New York: Harper & Row.

Lighthall, F. (2004) 'Fundamental features and approaches of the s-step enterprise', in J.J. Loughran, M.L. Hamilton, V.K. LaBoskey and T. Russell (eds), *International Handbook of Self-Study of Teaching and Teacher Education Practices*. Boston: Kluwer Academic Publishers, pp. 193–246.

Loughran, J.J. (2004) 'A history and context of self-study of teaching and teacher education practices', in J.J. Loughran, M.L. Hamilton, V.K. LaBoskey and T. Russell (eds), *International Handbook of Self-Study of Teaching and Teacher Education Practices*. Boston: Kluwer Academic Publishers, pp. 7–40.

Morris, V.C. (1966) *Existentialism in Education: What it Means*. Prospect Heights, IL: Waveland Press.

Pedevillano, E.D. (2004) 'Teachers' interpretations of a reflective practice school reform initiative: an existential analysis'. Unpublished dissertation, University of Massachusetts, Amherst.

Sartre, J.-P. (1956) *Being and Nothingness* (H. Barnes, Trans.). New York: Philosophical Library.

Sartre, J.-P. (1982) *Existentialism and Humanism*. London: Methuen.

Smith, J. (1977) 'Toward an existential model of teaching and learning', *Viewpoints*, 53 (3): 71–80.

Stenhouse, L. (1981) 'What counts as research?' *British Journal of Educational Studies*, 29 (2): 103–114.

Stenhouse, L. (1983) *Authority, Education and Emancipation*. New York: Heinemann Books.

Sussman, G.I. and Evered, R.D. (1978) 'An assessment of the scientific merits of action research', *Administrative Science Quarterly*, 23 (4): 582–603.

Tobin, K. and McRobbie, C. (1996) 'Cultural myths as constraints to the enacted science curriculum', *Science Education*, 80(2): 223–41.

Yalom, I.D. (1995) *The Theory and Practice of Group Psychology*, 4th edn. New York: Basic Books.

Yalom, I.D. (1998a) *The Yalom Reader*. New York: Basic Books.

Yalom, I.D. (1998b) *The Yalom Reader: Selections from the Work of a Master Therapist and Storyteller*. New York: Basic Books.

Zeichner, K.M. and Noffke, S.E. (2001) 'Practitioner research', in V. Richardson (ed.), *Handbook of Research on Teaching* Washington, DC: American Educational Research Association, pp. 298–332.

PART IV

Political: Popular Knowledge, Difference, and Frameworks for Change

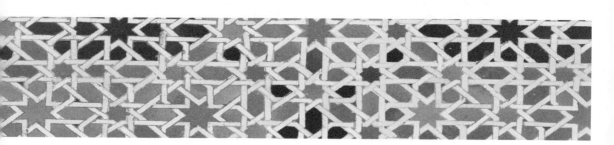

Introduction to Part IV

The ten chapters in Part IV present the work of those who engage in action research that aims to challenge and transform oppressive structures and ideologies. In this sense they are primarily *political* in their orientation. They encompass action research that promotes social justice in relation to class, gender and race. Some of the chapters present and analyze the role that action research has played in furthering educational transformation in countries where totalitarian regimes have been replaced by more democratic political structures. Taken together, they show the ways in which action research both emerges from and is employed by social movements, which work explicitly to dismantle existing power relations and to create new forms of social structures. While action researchers in the political dimension engage with activist agendas, they also enhance new forms of personal and social relations and build a new form of professional knowledge.

The first three chapters focus on *working with and for students and schools* using action research as a means of confronting taken-for-granted oppressive practices. All three chapters are written from a standpoint committed to promoting social justice for young people. The first, by Maguire and Berge, presents action research projects from Sweden and New Mexico that worked with theories from feminisms and gender studies. In New Mexico, the 'feminist-informed' action research was carried out by teachers on a masters' programme and encompassed work to overcome disadvantage engendered by race and social class as well as gender. In Sweden the focus was on teacher groups who worked with the university researchers with a more specific gender-equity agenda. This chapter is of particular interest in illustrating how action research is strongly shaped by different cultures and local contexts. Yet, there are clear knowledge outcomes from an analysis of the differences and similarities across the studies in both countries: for example, the importance of 'intentional dialogue' that reveals the strong, but typically unnoticed, effects of normalizing assumptions; and the power of grounding teachers' action research in knowledge of theories that explain how wider societal processes impact on social formations in the school.

The second chapter, by Thomson and Gunter, focuses on issues of student participation and student voice, drawing on the authors' experience of working in both Australia and the UK. They ground their argument in a succinct review of the research literature, drawing attention to the tendency for such work to be little more than cosmetic. They then go on to clarify their own standpoint: supporting the rights of young people to be actively involved in all aspects of their school's work; and seeing it as the duty of schools as public institutions to create the conditions that make this possible. The chapter contains a case study of a student research project which they facilitated over three years, drawing out the problematic issues that arose as well as acknowledging its achievements. The final chapter in the group, by Murrell, focuses on work with young people within their communities, within a broader concern for closing the 'achievement gap' whereby African-American and Latino students show a consistent pattern of underachieving at school by comparison with their European-American counterparts. The chapter starts with a wide-ranging critique of the existing literature on youth development. Murrell then draws on new theorizations of youth development that place emphasis on understanding the cultural impact of young people's out-of-school lives on their identity formation and respecting and building upon their 'non-dominant cultural capital'. Hip-hop and technology are two elements of youth culture that are subversively crossing the boundaries between young people's identities in school and community. The theoretical arguments in the chapter are illustrated by an account of a participatory action research project in Boston in which African-American and Latino young people have the opportunity to participate in 'authentic civic engagement' and to become 'activists on the conditions affecting their lives'.

The next group of chapters carry forward the emphasis on theorizing action research observable in the first group, but focus on *professional development, teacher voice* and *knowledge production*. The opening chapter by Brennan and Noffke argues strongly for the importance of action researchers drawing on social theory to understand how data are interpreted and how the purposes for which they are collected change over time. For example, critical race theory was used with teachers analyzing data in relation to students' underachievement in their school. Some teachers found that their understanding of the data shifted, leading them to a new understanding of their students' social skills which had previously gone unnoticed because of their taken-for-granted assumptions. Brennan and Noffke argue that concepts from social theories can help practitioners to see the political implications of their data, but a range of theories needs to be employed. They argue that, used generatively as part of the investigatory process of action research, social theory can 'articulate the links' in data and 'help to make sense of local practice'. The next chapter, by Gitlin, introduces the theory of 'educational poetics' which makes 'commonsense' the object of inquiry, and seeks 'relations of freedom' as an expected outcome. This approach is illustrated through a case study of a teacher's educational poetics text reporting on research through which she transformed the practices in her own classroom by changing her relationships with her students. Educational poetics work is akin to action research in its focus on envisioning cultural change and working with students in new ways.

The third chapter in this group, by Flores-Kastanis et al., introduces the tradition of educational participatory action research (EPAR) in Latin America. It starts by mapping the development of PAR in three countries, showing how it has been shaped by the operation of power and ideology during years of political instability. The chapter offers a wide-ranging discussion of the influence of the work of Freire on the developing tradition of action research in Latin-America, and the political meaning invested in the word 'participatory' in the PAR developed by Fals-Borda and colleagues. The chapter concludes with an 'action plan' for EPAR, including work to generate a new understanding of epistemology, a new language that crosses boundaries between social actors and academics, and a role for the state as a broker of scientific and political legitimacy: participation needs to be 'reconceptualized' with a greater emphasis on dialogue and acceptance of a wider range of kinds of EPAR.

The final four chapters, the group around *policy and change,* are strongly oriented towards transformation of educational systems and communities. The first, by Robinson and Soudien, reflects on the role of action research in teacher development and political transformation in South Africa. They turn their attention first to teacher development and the importance of establishing 'a dialogic relationship between self and context or self and the social'. They note that many accounts of action research in other countries do not identify clearly with political imperatives, and in the following section point out that this is not the case in South Africa. Education in a South African context is politically engaged, and the tradition of action research derives from the strong culture of resistance under the former apartheid regime. The chapter ends with suggestions for moving forward in a partnership between government and the education community. It calls for establishing 'collective responsibility'. There are some parallels here with the call of Flores et al.' for giving the state a role in legitimizing the role of action research.

The Chapter 39, by Pérez Gómez et al., focuses on the impact of action research in Spanish schools in the post-Franco era, and makes an interesting comparison with the South African case. In Spain, action research grew out of the grass-roots work of teachers' groups, resistance movements and socialist politicians that had begun to emerge under the Franco regime. It drew on the developing body of action research work in England and Australia, through the influence of Stenhouse, Elliott and Kemmis. The emphasis was on teachers as researchers transforming their own practice, with a strongly political orientation grounded in critical theory. Action research has played an important role in building new traditions of education in Spain, albeit in pockets of activity rather than across the whole system. The chapter ends by describing current initiatives including the establishment of a Spanish-Latin-American group within CARN (the Collaborative Action Research Network).

The paper by Brydon-Miller et al., on popular education and action research, widens the focus even further, with a combined authorship spanning five organizations in four countries: India, South Africa, Guatemala and the USA. It combines personal narratives and histories of the community-based development work carried out by each group with collaborative reflection across groups on how projects with a similar focus are played out in different contexts. The chapter embodies a wealth of knowledge generated through praxis, including most importantly knowledge about sustainability. Each organization has manifested the 'ability to move beyond the issues that first inspired the founders' to establish it. Sustainability depends on being engaged with local communities and able 'to address critical social and economic issues'. Modern technology is among the resources used to support active engagement and an orientation to build partnerships rather than looking inwards. The final chapter, by Zipin and Hattam, presents a collaborative project in Australia, in which university researchers worked in partnership with schools, the professional body for Secondary School Principals, and a department of regional government. This was an ambitious project, seeking to improve schooling for children in an area of high poverty through a programme of collaborative action research. This chapter is particularly interesting for its detailed and sensitive analysis of the relationships between the partners, particularly with regard to their differences in purposes and the operation of power.

The chapters in this Part IV focus on contexts in which educational practice forefronts issues of oppression and injustice. Yet, what is also evident in the chapters is the sense in which individual identity issues intersect with the development of a professional knowledge base for teaching and learning. What we (as educators) *know* as our *knowledge base* is integrally connected to our understandings of 'professional' and is deeply intertwined with how individuals learn thought action research. This section shows how political agendas match with individual commitments.

32

Elbows Out, Arms Linked: Claiming Spaces for Feminisms and Gender Equity in Educational Action Research

Patricia Maguire and Britt-Marie Berge

Educational action researchers are working in a time of contradictory forces. While educational action research (EAR) has enjoyed a period of rapid expansion and increased legitimacy, 'scientifically based research' seeks to reassert its monopoly in educational reform. Although education has been promoted worldwide as a human right, particularly for girls, it has not yet fulfilled its promise to unsettle structures, practices, and socialization that limit opportunities for girls and boys (Knoppers, 1997). Girls' advancements and feminists are blamed for the so-called boy crisis in education. Feminisms continue to be marginalized in the discourse and practice of EAR (Griffiths, 2003; Maguire, 2001; Weiner, 2004). Feminism is not a homogeneous monolith theory or world view. We use the plural feminisms to denote recognition of the wide range of feminist theories and positions, the details of which are beyond the scope of this chapter. Despite many instances of reform and resistance, schools and the universities that educate teachers remain sites for 'doing gender' in ways that reproduce inequitable relationships and support prevailing power arrangements (Weiler et al., 2000). Indeed, schools are gendered, raced, and classed sites. Our work is positioned at these intersections.

The chapter begins with describing the broader context for EAR and feminisms, specifically in Sweden and the U.S. We draw from our work in gender equity and feminist-informed teacher action research projects. There is a growing body of after-school youth action research projects with a gender or feminist focus (Institute for Community Research, 2007). Examples of feminist school-based EAR, however, are rare or difficult to locate (Catelli, 2000; Forsberg, 1998; McIntyre et al., 2007). While attention has been given to equity issues in recent teacher research (e.g. Caro-Bruce et al., 2007; National Writing Project, 2005), more focus is given to race and class than gender. This chapter focuses on teacher action research projects in classrooms because this is where our work is situated.

After brief descriptions of our projects and a sampling of teacher insights and changed practices gained through feminist-informed EAR, we identify lessons we are learning with teachers using EAR to unsettle the gender regime. We intend to claim space for feminisms in EAR, moving it from after-thought to center-thought.

BACKGROUND CONTEXT

Despite the growing inclusion of AR (and related approaches, such as teacher inquiry, teacher action research, critical practitioner inquiry) in teacher education programs and in-service teacher professional development, there is still too little focus on gender and other power inequities which shape children's school experiences. Few teacher educators or teachers have exposure to the multiplicity of feminisms that would enable them to see beyond the stereotypical and mass media images of feminism (Blackwell, 2000; Maguire, 2004). Even if teacher educators and teachers do not claim feminist alliances, they should examine how their daily practices and choices, and the larger choices of curriculum, pedagogical methods, assessment, and resource allocation may impact girls and boys, and may differently impact those boys and girls based on the intersections of race, class, ethnicity, and other positionalities. It is taking greater energy to hold open spaces for feminist work of all kinds, including the work for gender justice in and through schools and universities, whether in the Swedish context of jämställdhet, which promotes gender equity, or the U.S. context of No Child Left Behind, which essentially ignores gender (Sadker and Zittleman, 2005). Claiming space for feminist work in EAR requires elbows out and arms linked.

Generally, teachers have little control over most areas of school life. Yet rhetorically, the responsibility to improve education is being outsourced to individual teachers as if there are no broader social conditions critical to school improvement. Meaningful teacher participation in educational reform is constrained by national evaluations, assessment mandates and prefabricated 'teacher proof' curricula intended to raise scores on high stakes standardized exams (Nichols and Berliner, 2007).

Sweden is internationally recognized as an example of state feminism. Feminists in high-level positions were able to put gender as a priority on the state agenda (Florin and Nilsson, 1999). In the 1970s, *jämställdhet* was introduced by the central government into most areas of Swedish society, including the national education curricula. As a policy, *jämställdhet* stresses equality between the sexes as well as equally valuing differences between the sexes. But recently neo-liberalism has affected Swedish education policy. From being a strong, highly centralized welfare state, 'deregulation', 'decentralization', and 'the wasteful public sector' have become terms in the political rhetoric. The national curriculum is now less regulated and schools can differ more than was previously allowed. This opens up opportunities for school EAR projects which are supposed to be anchored in the needs of the local contexts. Ironically, because of *jämställdhet*, through which a lot has been accomplished in terms of national gender equity policies, lingering and nuanced inequitable gender practices in classrooms may remain invisible at the local level, because teachers don't expect such inequities to exist. The state, more than grassroots feminist teachers, has been responsible for gender equity advocacy. Because of a long tradition of central government control of schooling, activism for gender equity is not always viewed as a responsibility of individual teachers. Sometimes then there is a gap in Sweden between the central government's top-down emphasis on *jämställdhet* and teachers' activism at the school level.

In Sweden and the U.S., a normalizing process, i.e. a backlash to gender equity in education, has become visible. As the gap on some educational achievement measures closes in favor of girls (Arnot et al., 1999), some argue that girls' advancements come at boys' expense. When the Swedish National Agency for Education suggested support for gender equality in schools, the mission became 'to take actions in support of boys' achievements and successful developmental processes' (Myndigheten för Skolutveckling, 2006: 11). Analyzing National Assessment of Educational Progress (NAEP) results since 1971, Mead (2006) demonstrated that in the U.S. the boy crisis argument distorts data. Mead wrote:

> The real story is not bad news about boys doing worse; it's good news about girls doing better ... with a few exceptions, American boys are scoring higher and achieving more than they ever have before. But girls have just improved their performance on some measures even faster. (p. 3)

Mead redefines the boy crisis as a 'some boys' crisis', arguing that the defining issues of American achievement gaps are race and class, not gender. We argue that how gender is experienced or performed by boys and girls is always mediated by the intersections of race, class, culture, sexuality, and other positionalities (Mohanty, 2004). The shift of feminist analyses from women to gender (Kemp and Squires, 1997); *jämställdhet* as gender equity policy, and the expansion of feminisms to include the intersections of gender, race, class, and other identities have all opened the door for attention to boys as boys. Feminisms examine and unsettle schools as gendered, raced, and classed sites which can be limiting or expanding for girls and boys.

GENDER – EQUITY AND FEMINIST-INFORMED TEACHER ACTION RESEARCH PROJECTS

In this section, we describe our gender equity or feminist-informed EAR projects, two in northern Sweden and one in the rural southwest U.S.A. The teachers involved in the two fairly homogeneous Swedish contexts were aware of how social and cultural backgrounds can affect school dynamics, but on their own initiative wanted to explore teaching strategies to reach the national curriculum aim of *jämställdhet*. The teachers involved in the U.S. project did not begin with an expressed interest in gender, indeed, one project purpose was to develop such interest. Given the multiracial, multilingual, economic context of the U.S. project, a focus on gender alone was insufficient to the task of using AR as a tool to understand and unsettle classroom power inequities. The projects differed in rhetoric based on national and local conditions. While using different terms (gender equity AR or feminist-informed AR) the Swedish and U.S. projects were both grounded in feminisms, and introduced teachers to a range of feminist concepts, including gender; multiple positionalities or the intersections of gender, race, class, ethnicity, sexuality, and other identities in shaping daily experiences and relationships of power; voice and silence; everyday experience as a source of knowledge; and reflexivity (Maguire, 2001; Reid and Frisby, 2007).

Both projects in northern Sweden were fairly homogeneous racially. The children in project classrooms were almost all white Swedes, as were the teachers. One project was set in a coastal region with a slowly growing population and a university. The context was a primarily white, middle-class, well-educated area with nuclear families. The project was initiated by a group of nine teachers, five female and four male. It included 120 pupils, 7–12 years old from one compulsory school (Berge with Ve, 2000). The other project was set in an inland region where many young people emigrated out of the area for education; and young women in particular did not return. The rate of unemployment was higher among women as was the rate of illness. Reported crimes of violence and sexual harassment within families had increased. These patterns supported more traditional gender patterns in children's families. The inland project was inspired by the coastal project and 13 women and one man from three pre-schools and two compulsory schools took part (Berge, 2001b). Both projects got funds for some reduction in teaching duties.

In both projects the teacher groups met approximately once a week for critical reflection and planning. Both AR processes started with contextual analysis of the pupils' home districts. The next step was to collect data (videotaped classroom observations; interviews, written essays, and drawings from students; and teachers' voices through diaries) in order to analyze classroom gender choreography, i.e. how gender is performed or experienced, by scrutinizing power relations, power dynamics, and the intersections of identities. When teachers planned their actions for change they started from their analysis of the gender choreography: How could lack of equity be challenged and changed?

Who should have the preferential right of interpretation? The group tried to look at the data from as many positions as possible. Teachers gave their opinions based on learning from prior experiences in everyday practice and from knowledge about children's backgrounds. The university teachers brought different feminist theories for use as interpreting lenses. Before final interpretations were made every team member was supposed to make analyses from all angles with the help of all lenses that had been presented. The idea was that perspective shifts would function as deconstructive processes and make the second interpretation more nuanced than the first. (Berge with Ve, 2000; Berge, 2001a, 2001b).

The project in the southwestern U.S.A started in 2000 within a university-based teacher education master degree program in rural New Mexico by including a feminisms component in a new two-semester EAR course. The course was developed by one of the authors and in two of seven years was co-taught with a male faculty member. Between 2002 and 2007, 106 teachers conducted classroom teacher research projects as part of the course. There were 56 female and 48 male teachers, of whom 72 percent were white and 28 percent were people of color. All taught full time in K-12 schools with high percentages of Native American and Hispanic students. New Mexico is the third poorest state in the U.S., and the local area is one of the poorest in New Mexico. Many of the teachers differed from their students in terms of race, class, and cultural heritage. Teaching in their own classrooms during the day, teachers took graduate classes at night or weekends. Most were in their third year of teaching. Very few had any undergraduate teacher education preparation; they were hired to teach on alternative licenses. Of the 106 teacher research projects, only three started out with specific gender related topics; by the end, about 60 percent applied some feminist concepts to their projects, even if only in the final analysis phase. None of these teachers had release time to conduct AR. The teacher-researchers used a wide range of quantitative and qualitative data collection methods, including student and teacher journaling. The university faculty also engaged in self study to better understand how to help teachers' develop an understanding of feminist-informed AR.

The course presumed that a feminist-framework could inform any EAR, since schools are populated by girls, boys, men, and women, all of whom are gendered beings. How gender is performed is always mediated by one's experiences of race, class, sexuality, physical ability, nationality, and so forth. Most teachers entered the masters program with little prior exposure to feminist scholarship or information about women's movements (Maguire, 2004). In the AR course, teachers are introduced to a range of feminist concepts that have historically informed some action research (Maguire, 1987; Maguire, 2001; Reid and Frisby, 2007). They are asked to explore how concepts, such as gender, multiple positionalities (e.g. the intersections of gender, race, class, ethnicity, sexuality, and so forth), power dynamics, voice and silence, everyday experience as a source of knowledge, reflexivity, and relationship might inform and help them make sense of their classroom practices and developing EAR. Their own experiences and theories served as lens to critique and revise an always tentative framework for feminist-informed EAR.

Through readings on feminisms, class and web-based discussions, writing activities, and work with their students, teachers were invited to explore the implications of feminist AR concepts, personally and structurally, for their teacher research and daily teaching practices. Discussion, disagreement, critique, and possible application took place over six months. For many, it was their first sustained reflection and analysis of their beliefs and practices using feminisms' lens (Maguire, 2004). Course instructors were not promoting unquestioned consensus, but time, activities, and space for teachers to move beyond their initial understandings of feminisms to explore how feminist concepts might inform their practices and vice versa.

NEW INSIGHTS AND PRACTICES

In this section, we give several examples of insights and changed practices that teachers and their students experienced as a result of the gender equity or feminist-informed AR projects. Although project frameworks differed somewhat between contexts, and used different terms, the Swedish and U.S. projects were grounded in feminist theories and concepts. In the Swedish contexts, insights and changed practices built on gender choreography analyses through which teachers and students shifted their perspectives after paying closer attention to how they perform gender in the classroom. In the New Mexican context, insights and changed practices build on examination of the intersections of gender, race, class, culture, and other identities in daily classroom practices and relationships.

In the Swedish projects, every teacher made the final decision of how to interpret the gender choreography in her or his classroom and what to do next. There were occasions when high rates of agreement on how to interpret gender choreography made it difficult to create deconstructive processes through perspective shifts. Teachers were then asked to experiment by thinking of a girl in a boy's position and vice versa. Deconstructive processes and subsequent actions appeared in moments of equity when power relations were challenged, equalized, reversed, or hybridized. Since these negotiations took place in larger contexts where power operates through economic distribution, politics, and symbols, they could also appear in moments of normalization where hegemonic institutional, cultural, and gendered superior and subordinated positions become reproduced. Thus, there were simultaneously moments of both advances and backlashes; in other words 'in-between' processes. Examples of negotiations in-between moments of normalization and moments of equity are presented.

The norms for teachers' teaching appeared gendered, even when they attempted to act more gender conscious. For example, one teacher group reacted differently to the same problem based on students' gender. In one classroom the 'smart' girls set the tone and in another the opposite was true. The male teacher of one of the classes suggested having the talented girls help the teachers improve the boys' reading abilities, as a kind of leadership training for girls. A colleague asked whether this might put girls at risk of falling into a subordinate nurturance trap. The teacher's immediate reaction was to deny the risk. Regarding the classroom where talented boys set the tone, the discussion revolved around how challenging assignments would divert the boys' energy from harassing others. The strategy of boys as teacher-helpers was not broached. For both cases, the teachers focused on boys' needs, presupposing girls' compliance. Reflections on these *in-between* situations resulted in new processes where the teachers tried other actions with both girls' and boys' needs in mind (Berge with Ve 2000: 38ff.).

In the New Mexican projects, teachers' analyses of students' gendered behavior led to insights of how teachers and students 'did gender' in cultural contexts which influenced their perceptions and classroom practices. In one case, high school students, who were primarily Native American, were analyzing photographs of their work in an agricultural AR project. The teacher had noticed a gendered work division early in the project, but had been unsure how to discuss it with students, as she differed from them culturally and wondered how culture contributed to different gender roles. A male student pointed out the gendered work division during photograph analysis. Several girls admitted they had wanted to join the construction group but worried about feeling out of place. The teacher realized that after she noticed the male-dominant voices in the project, she brainstormed ways to help the females speak up, rather than help the males become better listeners. Despite considering herself a feminist, her first impulse was to 'fix the girls'(Personal communication, 2007). She had also been concerned about imposing her own cultural lens on the photo voice analyses.

In some cases the Swedish teachers tried teaching in temporary single-sex groups. In interviews and essays, children in these groups expressed greater awareness of what gender equity could mean. In spite of these moments of gender awareness a kind of 'gender war' periodically appeared during co-ed situations. After these insights from gender choreography analyses, the pedagogy changed to include drama exercises followed by reflections in co-ed groups. These dramas enabled children to experience different positions of power and powerlessness. The girls became more inclined 'to put their feet down', and one of the boys declared '… I have learnt that it is also possible to talk and negotiate' (Ekesrydh, 1997: 23ff.).

In the New Mexican teacher EAR, some male teachers had new realizations about how they 'did masculinity' and how their masculinity was mediated by their race and class identities. For instance, a secondary math teacher wrote, 'I suppose it is my core belief, subconsciously what a male is supposed to be … puff their chest out, use their bigger frame and loud voice to get what they want … I do that sometimes. It works … I am ashamed that I didn't recognize this before' (Personal communication, 2001). Another teacher realized he was scared of some of the older, bigger teen boys. Several teachers noticed that their ideas of what it meant to 'be a man' resulted in their escalating conflicts with boys, particularly when their students came from economic and racial backgrounds different from their own. This acknowledgment led to changes in teacher behavior, and additional exploration of how their own identities played out in power struggles for classroom authority.

There were also examples when 'in-between situations' of both progress (equity) and backlash (normalization) occurred in the same arguments. In one Swedish pre-school, teachers used pictures to analyze how symbols of femininity and masculinity permeated the youngest children's gender awareness. When the teachers placed a man into a picture of a kitchen, some children rejected it, noting that it was their mothers who usually cooked. But there were also agreements. 'In our house my daddy is the one who cooks…'. However, this pre-schooler seemed well aware of the 'normal'when the child said, '… but that is *just* because our mother works so late; because in real life it is the mothers' duty'. Subsequently, the teachers taught both boys and girls how to cook in a kitchen with adults of both sexes. After one such lesson, one boy commented: 'Girls cannot do their own pancakes. But I can!' He had transferred gender positions, but not without degrading girls. This became the starting point for new actions. (Forsström et al., 2001: 50ff.).

In the New Mexican EAR projects, some teachers decided to examine curriculum choices, considering gender, race, culture, and increased students' voice. For example, a middle school teacher was working to develop more racially and culturally inclusive and less sexist literature curriculum. After one reading in which it wasn't clear whether a book author was male or female, he asked his students to draw a picture of the author. With few exceptions they drew white men. He noted, 'The most unsettling answer of all was they very innocently stated the author had to be a white male because almost all authors are' (Personal communication, 2003). He worked to include more women and minority authors and characters in the class literature. Another teacher had assumed that her students' low reading scores were linked to their dislike of reading. Through discussions and journaling, students revealed that they actually like to read but had little access to print materials at home. Most of these students came from low-income families. As she paid attention to gender, class, and her students' voices, she learned that her classroom library didn't have sufficient variation in genres to cover the diverse and sometimes differing reading interests of the boys and girls. She also allowed students to take classroom books home.

While these are just a few examples of what happens for teachers and students who intentionally engage in gender choreography analyses and feminist-informed EAR; they demonstrate some of the possibilities of these approaches.

LESSONS LEARNED WITH/BY TEACHERS AND STUDENTS

The most obvious lesson is that teachers and students need structured and intentional spaces and resources to tackle contextually bound equity issues on an individual and collective basis. Intentional dialogue, encouragement, challenge, and concrete resources were essential to these efforts. Individual interpretations of classroom and school gender choreography and exploring the intersections of identities benefited from group discussion. And group discussion benefited from explicit exposure to a range of feminist theories, scholarship, and concepts. The group discussions and activities helped teachers make connections and applications to their daily practices – to see anew gendered, raced, and classed arrangements in their teaching practices, expectations, interactions, and curriculum. Without intentional and explicit attention and supportive resources, how gender and other power dynamics played out in the classroom easily remained below the radar, whether teachers were self-identified feminists or otherwise.

This work builds on underpinning philosophies and premises. For example, it is based on a belief that good educators must be willing to dive into the messy and threatening business of better understanding and improving their practices for the sake of all students. Teachers are required to embrace the discomforts of examining their assumptions and positionalities and impact on their practices. A belief that teachers and students can build spaces of possibility, in part through AR processes, is central.

As teachers saw how their 'normal' practices might be excluding, hurting, or limiting some students, most were willing to push through their own discomforts to try new classroom strategies, materials, and practices in AR cycles. Along with teachers we learned that left alone, normalizing forces are very strong. Gender and other power arrangements are deeply anchored in teachers' and students' everyday routines. Routines easily become experienced as 'normal' and hence difficult to see. One way of making routines visible is to make changes in teachers' and students' everyday practices through EAR. Without this intentional work, schools will remain gendered, classed, and raced places that normalize and render invisible inequitable practices and relationships of power that are damaging and limiting to both girls and boys, women and men.

Examining the connections between classroom micro contexts and the socio-economic-political macro contexts is necessary. Gender and other power relations are always contextualized. This in turn generates a wide range of possible local strategies for action. We argue that moments of normalization simultaneously show those starting points from where moments of equity or transformation can be reached, which is another reason that gender choreography analysis and other feminist components are essential to the counter-hegemonic tradition of EAR. We cannot begin to change what we are unable to see.

These projects demonstrate that through feminist-informed AR, teachers can continue to build more equitable classrooms and relationships. EAR can be a powerful tool to challenge and transform unjust beliefs, policies, structures, materials, and daily practices while supporting educators to make personal and professional changes toward those ends. If EAR is going to be such a tool, however, action researchers must purposefully and proactively understand and consider the many ways that feminist theories, analyses, and practices can inform our work to help make schools more equitable, democratic, and transformative places. If not, what are schools and classrooms, and teacher-student practices and relationships within them, being transformed out of and into through AR? This requires teachers, and those who educate them and learn with them in schools, universities, education departments, and donor agencies to understand schools as sites for reproducing, maintaining, or unsettling inequitable relationships of power. This is a tall order. But action research and feminisms, regardless of scale or site, are deeply political acts. To counter the neo-liberal attack on education, teacher education, and action research, action researchers need feminisms and intentionally built alliances with other social justice movements and discourses. We need to put our elbows out and link arms.

REFERENCES

Arnot, M., David, M. and Weiner, G. (1999) *Closing the Gender Gap: Postwar Education and Social Change*. Cambridge: Polity.

Berge, B-M. (2001a) 'Action research for gender equity in a late modern society', *International Journal of Inclusive Education*, 5 (2/3): 281–92.

Berge, B-M. (2001b) *Kunskap bryter könsmönster – aktionsforskning är verktyget*. [Knowledge breaks gender patterns – action research is the tool]. Rapport från projektet Vidgade Vyer i Jämtlands län. Östersund: Länsstyrelsen i Jämtlands län.

Berge, B-M. and with Ve, H. (2000) *Action Research for Gender Equity*. Buckingham: Open University Press.

Blackwell, P. (2000) *Education Reform and Teacher Education: The Missing Discourse of Gender*. Washington, DC: American Association of Colleges for Teacher Education.

Caro-Bruce, C., Flessner, R., Klehr, M. and Zeichner, K. (eds) (2007) *Creating Equitable Classrooms through Action Research*. Thousand Oaks, CA: Corwin Press.

Catelli, L.A. (2000) 'Action research to effect change for adolescent girls at an urban middle school: A matter of life and death', *Research in Middle Level Education Annual*, 23: 133–48.

Ekesrydh, M. (1997) Att få alla att synas – undervising med könsperspektiv [To make every child visible – teaching for gender equity], in B-M. Berge (ed.), *Jämställdhetspedagogik på Storsjöskolan i Holmsund – ett aktionsforskningsprojekt*. [Gender Equity Pedagogy at Storsjöskolan in Holmsund – an action research project]. Arbetsrapporter från Pedagogiska institutionen, Umeå universitet. Nr 115, 20–32.

Florin, C. and Nilsson, B. (1999) 'Something in the nature of a bloodless revolution', in R. Torstendahl (ed.), *State Policy and Gender System in the Two German States and Sweden 1945–1989*. Uppsala: Uppsala University, Department of History, pp. 11–78.

Forsberg, U. (1998) Jämställdhetspedagogik – en sammanställning av aktionsforskningsprojekt. [Gender Equity Pedagogy – a survey of action research projects]. *Pedagogiska rapporter från pedagogiska institutionen*, Umeå universitet. Nr 55.

Forsström, A., Johansson, M. and Leandersson, M. (2001) Aktionsforskning på avdelningen Vargen [Action research in the pre-school group 'the Wolf'], in B-M Berge (ed.), *Kunskap bryter könsmönster– aktionsforskning är verktyget*. [Knowledge breaks gender patterns – action research is the tool]. Rapport från projektet Vidgade Vyer i Jämtlands län. Östersund: Länsstyrelsen i Jämtlands län, pp. 46–53.

Griffiths, M. (2003) *Action for Social Justice in Education: Fairly Different*. Maidenhead: Open University Press.

Institute for Community Research (2007) *Empowered Voices: A Participatory Action Research Curriculum for Girls*. Retrieved http://www.incommunityresearch.org/publications/empoweredvoices.htm

Kemp, S. and Squires, J. (eds) (1997) *Feminisms*. Oxford: Oxford University Press.

Knoppers, A. (1997) 'The construction of gender in physical education', in M. Anderson, L. Fine, K. Geissler and J. Ladenson, J. (eds), *Doing Feminism: Teaching and Research in the Academy*. East Lansing, Michigan: Women's Studies Program, Michigan State University, pp. 119–34.

Maguire, P. (1987) *Doing Participatory Research: A Feminist Approach*. Amherst, MA: Center for International Education, University of Massachusetts, Amherst.

Maguire, P. (2001) 'Uneven ground: feminisms and action research', in P. Reason and H. Bradbury (eds), *Handbook of Action Research*. London: SAGE, pp. 59–69.

Maguire, P. (2004) 'Reclaiming the F word: Emerging lessons from teaching about feminist-informed action research', in M. Brydon-Miller, P. Maguire and A. McIntyre (eds), *Traveling Companions*. Westport, CT: Praeger, pp. 117–36.

McIntyre, A., Chatzopolous, N., Politi, A. and Roz, J. (2007) 'Pre-service teachers and participatory action research: Reflections on gender, culture, and language', *Teaching and Teacher Education: An International Journal of Research and Studies*, 23 (5): 748–56.

Mead, S. (2006) *The Evidence Suggests Otherwise: The Truth about Boys and Girls*. The Education Section. http://www.educationsector.org/usr_doc/ESO_BoysAndGirls.pdf

Mohanty, C.T. (2004) *Feminism without Borders: Decolonizing Theory, Practicing Solidarity*. Durham, North Carolina: Duke University Press.

Myndigheten för Skolutvecklings (2006) 'Minskade könsskillnader i utbildningsresultat. Myndigheten för kolutvecklings förslag på insatser för en satsning påjämställdhet i grundskolan under 2007–2010'. [Reduction of gender differences in educational achievements. The Swedish National Agency of Education suggests supportive contributions to gender equality in compulsory schools during 2007–2010] Dnr 2006: 623.

National Writing Project (2005) *Working toward Equity: Writings and Resources from the Teacher Research Collaborative*. Berkeley, CA: National Writing Project.

Nichols, S. and Berliner, D. (2007) *Collateral Damage: How High Stakes Testing Corrupts America's Schools*. Cambridge, MA: Harvard Education Press.

Reid, C. and Frisby, W. (2007) 'Continuing the journey: Linking feminisms and action research', in P. Reason and H. Bradbury (eds), *Handbook of Action Research* (2nd edn). London: Sage.

Sadker, D. and Zittleman, K. (2005) 'Again! Just when educators thought it was no longer an issue, gender bias is back', *Principal*: 19–22.

Weiler, K., Weiner, G. and Yates, L. (2000) 'Series editor's preface', in B-M. Berge with H. Ve (ed.), *Action Research for Gender Equity*. Buckingham: Open University Press.

Weiner, G. (2004) 'Critical action research and third wave feminism: A meeting of paradigms', *Educational Action Research*, 12 (4): 631–43.

33

Students' Participation in School Change: Action Research on the Ground

Pat Thomson and Helen Gunter

SCHOOL REFORM AND AN EMERGING ROLE FOR STUDENTS

School reform is a contentious business. In recent years, governments across the world have busied themselves with educational agendas designed to raise educational achievement. This agenda has significant variations from place to place.

In many English-speaking and European nations, children and young people have emerged not simply as objects of school change, but also as participants in its production. In Australia student participation (Holdsworth, 2000), and in the UK 'pupil consultation' and 'pupil voice' (Macbeath et al., 2003; Rudduck and Flutter, 2004), have had official policy endorsement, whereas in the US, interest in the active role of students in change has largely emerged from reform movements and through opposition to top-down reforms (Cook-Sather, 2002; Wasley et al., 1997; Wilson and Corbett, 2001). But while there are important regional inflections to participation and voice, there is sufficient commonality across the UK, Australia and the US to venture an analysis which works across localities. The focus of this chapter is to discuss dominant and more subversive versions of students' participation in school change, and it features a case study from England – it is, however, one which has resonance in other parts of the UK, Australia and North America.

The chapter gives a brief summary for the rationales given for students' involvement in school reform and the various roles they can have. It highlights the notion of students as researchers and considers the notion of 'student standpoint' research and its connections with traditions of action research. A case study of student research in one high school in England is presented in order to highlight some of the possibilities, pitfalls and dilemmas in such work. We begin with some brief comments on nomenclature.

A Caveat on Participation – What's in a Name?

Australian researchers and activists have long used the term student participation – a notion which has multiple interpretations (Anderson, 1998; Thomson and Holdsworth, 2003), but which has important links with democracy, agency and action (Thomson, 2007). Student participation is generally taken to mean either or all of:

- involvement in formal school decision making: this can range from being consulted occasionally by staff, to formalized student councils and forums, to representative places on school committees (e.g. Lyons, 2003);
- initiating, deciding and acting in the school, and beyond the school boundaries, in school reform, curriculum change (purposes, practices and directions), community projects and neighbourhood capacity building (Apple and Beane, 1995);
- community or social activism and 'organizing' through projects concerned with human rights and social justice (e.g. Fine et al., 2004), the environment (e.g. Thomson et al., 2005) and local, state or national issues (e.g. Edwards and Percy-Smith, 2004).

The term 'participation' is not quite the same as the notion of 'voice'. There are debates about the notion of voice (Fielding, 2001; Hargreaves, 1996; Kenway et al., 1996), but for the purposes of this chapter, we take there to be some consensus among critical scholars on two counts. First, students do not speak with one voice, but many. Unfortunately, when schools work with representative structures or select students for consultative projects, they are more likely to select students whose voices are compatible with school goals, effectively excluding children and young people whose language and view may be oppositional or aberrant (Morrow, 2002). Second, the area where young people are least likely to be asked for their views, or invited to assist in change, is in the classroom (Arnot et al., 2003). Certainly, in England and in many states of the US where curriculum, pedagogy and assessment are highly centralized and there is regulation of teacher adherence to external prescriptions, doing this is not easy. However, researchers argue that there is room for movement and that there is a radical potential in practices where students create knowledge (Steinberg and Kincheloe, 1998).

We bring these understandings of both voice and participation to our discussion of action research and reform.

Why Involve Students in School Reform?

Across the growing corpus of professional and research literatures that discuss students' participation/voice in changing schools, a number of arguments emerge. One line of reasoning is to do with the rights of young people:

- It is the moral right of young people to have a say in all decisions that are of concern to them.
- The rights of young people are enshrined in the UN Convention on the Rights of the Child and this places a legal obligation on schools.

Another thread of argument concerns the educational needs of the children and young people themselves:

- Young people must learn how to become and be citizens of liberal democracies and this does not happen through book learning alone, but also through practice.
- Through participation in a range of participatory activities young people learn skills which are important to them in their futures – leadership, team work, negotiation, decision making.
- Participation in school change provides an avenue for social education and teaches the practices of empathy and conflict resolution, and understandings of diversity and equity.

A further set of reasons focuses on the benefits to the school:

- Students have important insights into what needs to change in their schools: these perspectives are important because school reform will be better if the views of all of those who are involved are taken into account.
- If students have ownership of reforms, then they are likely to support them, rather than resist. They can also assist their families to understand the needs for and directions of change.

A final rationale refers to the purposes of schooling:

- Schools do not simply teach about democracy, they have an obligation to contribute to it through their everyday practice: this means involving teachers, students and parents in decisions.

In practice many of these reasons are combined, yet there are often important differences in emphasis. For example, those who focus on teaching about citizenship and also believe that school reform can be improved by the input of young people may well opt for a civics curriculum, the development of student representation on school councils, and the involvement of young people in consultation about priorities for improvement. In England, official policy rhetoric puts together the legal requirements of the UN Convention, the need to teach civics and vocational skills, and the pragmatic benefits of fully informed reform to support students' involvement in school councils, school development planning and school and teacher evaluations. In contrast, a commitment to the rights of young people, the democratic mission of schooling and the social purposes of participation may lead to student-initiated reform projects and a push for nego-tiated curriculum. There are of course multiple other variations, but the point here is simply to suggest that purposes are manifest in material practices.

The implication of such differences is that schools need to debate *why* they wish to facilitate greater student involvement in change, as well as how. Our view is broadly moral and educational, in that: we support the right of young people to have a say in all aspects of their schooling, including curriculum, assessment and pedagogy; we recognize the important social, civic and vocational learning that occurs through such involvement; and we regard schools as morally obliged to move in such directions by virtue of their being public institutions with a duty to act for the greater public good. This chapter should be read in this light.

'Official Student Voice': A Brief Note

Involving students in school improvement takes many forms. But some approaches appropriate and/or sideline students' opinions and contributions. Four examples suffice to demonstrate the point:

1 The student council which is only able to run socials, raise funds for charity and discuss the colour of the school uniform offers a limited number of young people restricted experi-ences of leadership.
2 Student consultations which begin by asking students what they like and dislike about school more often than not produce complaints about toilets, break times and food. These are important issues for young people whose rights to comfort and privacy are often not taken seriously. However, consultation ought not to stop at these points.
3 Students are often asked about their levels of satisfaction with their schooling. The results are more often than not used for audit purposes to demonstrate school efficacy, rather than to initiate holistic school self-appraisal.
4 School self-evaluation processes frequently ask students for their views on teaching and learning – how do you learn best? They are generally *neither* asked about the nature of the curriculum, offered the opportunity to analyze the collated data, nor allowed to be involved in the development of alternatives. Students are simply data for questions others have decided are important, and the objects of reforms they have no part in designing.

These kinds of activities neither allow young people to have a meaningful and ongoing say in their own education, nor do they allow schools to hear and ben-efit from the experiences and ideas of those who they are meant to serve. They are not the kind of activities we have in mind when we talk about student(s) voice(s) and participation.

A Move to Students as Researchers

There is in some states in Australia and in England a growing tradition of stu-dents as researchers – this is a subset of the range of activities which come under the general label of student participation/voice.

Those who advocate a students-as-researchers approach argue that school change does not occur simply by discussing a problem in order to arrive at an answer, as is assumed when there are consultations with a student council or the whole student body about priorities for change. Nor is it simply about the use of existing data, as might be the case, for example, if a student council decided to use pupil attendance data to provide an evidence base for a discussion about student engagement. Rather, a students-as-researchers approach means that children and young people conduct a specifically designed inquiry to provide data to inform recommendations for change (Fielding and Bragg, 2003). Students might survey their peers or conduct a range of focus groups across year levels or interview a representative sample of the school. Such an investigation takes them beyond a role as representatives, and allows them to speak about the views of all students, rather than simply giving their own opinions.

We have argued (Thomson and Gunter, 2007: 331) that student research can be considered to come from the student(s) 'standpoint' if it:

- addresses issues of importance to students and is thus in their collective interests;
- works with students' subjugated knowledges about the ways in which the school works;
- allows marginalized perspectives and voice to come centre stage;
- uses students' subjectivities and experiences to develop approaches, tools, representations and validities;
- interrupts the power relations in schools including, but not confined to those which are age related; and
- is geared to making a difference.

Some – but not all – students-as-researchers projects take an action research turn. That is, they not only adopt a process which begins with interrogating a problem, issue, need or desire, and exploring its dimensions (reconnaissance), but they also build in opportunities for reflection in order to modify their activities (Day et al., 2002). These students-as-researchers projects take the view that the research must itself be a process of change. That is, change is not the end result of the research, but rather happens in and throughout it – even if there are decisive points at which new activities and practices are initiated. The direction of this kind of research is relatively open-ended and invites change, as cycles of inquiry and reflection produce deeper knowledge and simultaneously alter the context within which researchers are working. It thus stands in opposition to the 'what works' and 'how could this be improved' kinds of inquiries, and opts instead for a 'what is going on here and how might it be different?' approach.

Action-oriented student research projects also take the participatory nature of the research seriously (cf. Kemmis and McTaggart, 1988), and foreground both the relations between the students and the adults who support young people in this work and their collective relationship with the wider school. Questions about power relations: Who is participating? Who speaks? Who listens? Who is dominating conversation? Who decides what should and can be done? What happens, and in whose interest is this? – are central to the conversations between adults and the young people involved as researchers (Zeni, 1998), and also to the ways in which students work with research informants who are often, but not always, their peers. These kinds of projects also often pose challenges to teachers and school leaders: their open-endedness may challenge taken-for-granted practices and unexamined beliefs.

We provide a short case study to exemplify some of the possibilities, issues and dilemmas that are intimately entwined in action-oriented student research projects. As Elliott (2007: 125) notes, case studies of action research projects do not offer generalizable findings but rather the unstructured and reflexive identification of common problems. Our account is therefore not a detailed report of the research *per se*, but rather a narrative with specific 'points' to make (Polanyi, 1979).

STUDENT RESEARCH AT KINGSWOOD HIGH SCHOOL

Kingswood is a specialist humanities school with some 1,600 students situated in a relatively comfortable small town in the north of England. With a history as a successful comprehensive school, the enrolment is predominantly middle class, but with significant enrolment from nearby council estates.

Our work with Kingswood did not begin with student research. We were both invited into school to undertake a formal evaluation of significant reforms the school had made to curriculum structure and organization. We began the planning by working with a group of eight students, selected by the school, as consultants in the design and piloting of a questionnaire. The head had commissioned us to focus on teaching and learning, but the students advised us to include a range of questions related to school climate and amenities. We analyzed the student questionnaire data, which was administered to the whole school, alongside class observations, student focus groups and interviews with adults (workforce, parents, governors). Having formally reported back to the school (see Hollins et al., 2006) we returned to share the questionnaire data with the student group. We discussed the trends in the data, and they identified safety and bullying as the top priority for further investigation. They voted on an action research project, and we conducted the negotiations with the headteacher who agreed to the project outline we suggested.

We did consider at that point whether we ought to ask for a more representative group of young people since the group were white, middle class and academically successful. We decided against this on the grounds that any newcomers would be involved in a project that they had not initiated, and that ownership of the project was more important. However, the elite nature of the group continued to bother us throughout the project and there is little doubt that, while the group did learn to empathize with, and speak about and for, the diverse student body, the learning about research that occurred through the project added to the educational advantages the group already enjoyed.

Action Research into Bullying

The decision to focus on safety and bullying led to two 'cycles' of research.

Cycle 1: the students wanted to know more about peers' experiences. They realized that asking their fellow students directly about whether they had been bullied and what happened as a result might not produce a lot of data. Together, we decided that the best way to stimulate students to talk about these matters safely was to combine focus group interviews with trigger photographs (photo-elicitation). Student researchers used their own experiences to design and produce:

(a) some pictures of realistic and ambiguous but fictionalized events that would stimulate conversation about safety, scope and scale of bullying and actual and preferred interventions;
(b) some pictures of student dress (bags, footwear) that would stimulate conversation about the various subcultural groups within the school and their connections with bullying;
(c) a list of abusive phrases that would be used to produce information about how prevalent was their use and in what circumstances.

The group eventually decided not to use the list of phrases because they thought it would be unethical to present offensive words to younger children. After a pilot interview, they conducted 14 focus groups of students from across the school, analyzed the data and produced a powerpoint report which they presented to the headteacher, the whole school staff and at an international seminar of researchers and policy makers. They identified a form of what the group came to describe as 'low-level bullying' – ongoing name calling (some of it sexual in nature), pushing and teasing – where there was no single perpetrator. This was more an everyday culture, the way things were done in the school, including in classrooms in front of teachers. The research found that a majority of students believed that staff did not always take such incidents seriously although they did deal with obvious cases of serious bullying.

During this cycle, (reported in Thomson and Gunter, 2006) the students struggled with taking on a researcher stance: they did not find it easy to move from focusing on anecdotes of their own experiences and beliefs to reporting the range of views of their peers. They also had to ensure that their peers did not name names and that they anonymized their data. This was a challenge to their usual way of being and behaving in the school. During this stage, we sometimes had to confront students and challenge not only their lapses into 'student' rather than 'researcher', but also their individualist views of education. We see this as a pedagogical response, and suggest that the 'critical friend' role we played in this student research project did require us to exercise our teacherly dispositions in order to manage the group, and ensure that it acted equitably.

Cycle 2: the students wanted to get staff perspectives on incidents identified as low-level bullying. They realized that they could not ask staff directly to talk about incidents that they had been involved in, or how and why they had or had not dealt with specific incidents in particular ways. They decided that the best way was to present staff with dramatic, realistic but fictionalized written scenarios of incidents drawn both from Cycle 1 data and their own observations. They piloted the scenarios, and following this, 11 volunteer staff were made to read the scenarios and asked to talk about the incidents and how they might handle the situations. In addition, the staff were asked for their views on possible interventions, from a quiet chat with a student through to involving parents and/or the police. Students analyzed the data, finding that staff agreed on what constituted very serious issues and what should be done. This matched the data they had from their peers. However, there appeared to be a range of views and practices related to the low-level bullying about which the student informants and the student researchers were most concerned. The researchers also learnt about professional decision making: for example, a teacher may play down a situation in a lesson in order to maintain a working consensus – but the students interpreted this as inaction. They produced a powerpoint report which they then presented to the headteacher and the school development team

During this cycle (reported in Thomson and Gunter, 2007), we were keen to have the students consider what might be done within the school to intervene in the culture of low-level bullying. We were certain that the root causes of low-level bullying lay in a tangle of setting and testing, classed and gendered divisions among the students and subcultural 'taste' groups. We introduced notions of peer mediation and through extending the student researchers analyses of 'stereotypes' in their data, suggested the need for the various student subcultures to mix together. But we were in no position to ensure that this happened and had now to hand over the project to the school.

However, by the end of this cycle a significant shift had occurred in the school to which this research project had somehow contributed. When we began the project with the students there was little support for student participation through formal processes. By the time we had completed the second cycle, the school had introduced an elected student parliament which was to be consulted on school policy, and which would conduct, each year, a major student-initiated research project. One of the student research team was a key member of the new student parliament. We have pursued with the headteacher what influence the bullying research project might have had on this development, and what seems to have been key were the thoughtful and mature presentations made by the students to him and to staff. He remains somewhat skeptical about action research and of the benefits of critical external support for its conduct.

Further action: the students wanted to work with a group of staff on developing school policy and interventions. The student researchers led a whole staff in service session using the scenarios from Phase 2. The staff discussed the scenarios and how they would handle them, and the students talked to them about the importance of addressing low-level name calling and pushing. Student researchers also challenged some taken-for-granted practices such as attempting reconciliation meetings between apparent bullies and victims, something the student body had generally agreed was highly ineffective. The student researchers also formed a working group with staff to revise the school bullying policy. The staff-student group are now working on implementation strategies.

We had little to do with this phase of the project, although one of us helped prepare for and attended the staff meeting run by the student researchers. We were emailed a copy of the revised bullying policy, and were disappointed to see so little written into it about low-level bullying. The school also appeared to have not taken up the idea of peer mediation or the more general issue of student culture(s). The student researchers were more sanguine about this than we were. In a debriefing conversation about the whole project, they stated that they thought their most important activity had been the staff in service, where they had been able to put the findings of the project to the staff. One of the student researchers emphatically reported she was confident that staff would not forget that 12- and 13-year-olds can feel very wounded by what may appear to an adult to be harmless teasing, and that this cannot be ignored.

Reflections on the Project

We have written, and encouraged the students do so through the use of powerpoint reports, after each cycle in order to reflect on the processes, purposes and content of the project. This has been important for the students, but as important for us as we worked on and worked out which dilemmas we could address and which we just had to live with.

In addition to the questions of selection of participants and the capacity of external researchers to advocate on behalf of student researchers with their schools, we have identified the issues of time and accreditation as major issues that we might wish to attend to next time. The project was unfunded, and we went to the school when we could find time over three school years. We worked in full- and half-day blocks of time which students had out of their normal timetables. We had to make sure that the students did not miss too many of the same lessons, and indeed the parent of one of the students withdrew him from the project half way through because of a concern about his general progress. The long breaks between visits meant that we had to spend time each session reminding ourselves where we were up to, and we had no means of ensuring that students received any credit in their formal courses for the work they had done. If we had been staff within the school, rather than external university-based researchers, some of these issues and challenges might have been easier to manage. But if that was the case, we are not sure that the school would have had the research expertise to tailor-make research tools such as the trigger photographs and the scenarios.

On a positive note, and reinforcing our view that student action research is worth pursuing, the student researchers reported a variety of benefits from their involvement, from working with others with whom they wouldn't normally mix, to understanding how the school worked and having a role in changing it. Perhaps the most telling comment was from the oldest researcher: he had been in Year 10 when the project started and at our last meeting had just done his final exams and was looking forward to university. He told us that this was the only time he could remember at school where he got to decide what to do and how to do it.

His comment takes us back to the questions of who is selected for such projects and why the benefits of involvement in research projects cannot be spread more inclusively across school populations. Surely all young people deserve this kind of experience – and more than once! The most fundamental reason for student participation is to redress a power inequity. Young people are generally disenfranchised in their schooling, and student participation projects are one way of beginning to disrupt the intergenerational power relations embedded and embodied in every aspect of schools. They are also, as this action research project suggests, a way of finding out about and changing some of the practices that prevent young people from getting the most out of their education. In this endeavour, the importance of finding an open-minded headteacher and a staff prepared to be challenged, as was the case at Kingswood, cannot be underestimated. Neither, however, can the difficulties.

REFERENCES

Anderson, G. (1998) 'Towards authentic participation: deconstructing the discourses of participatory reforms in education', *American Educational Research Journal*, 35 (4): 571–603.

Apple, M. and Beane, J. (1995) *Democratic Schools*. Alexandria, VA: Association for Supervision and Curriculum Development.

Arnot, M., McIntyre, D., Pedder, D. and Reay, D. (2003) *Consultation in the Classroom: Pupil Perspectives on Teaching and Learning*. Cambridge: Pearson Publishing.

Cook-Sather, A. (2002) 'Authorising students' perspectives: toward trust, dialogue, and change in education', *Educational Researcher*, 31 (4): 3–14.

Day, C., Elliott, J., Somekh, B. and Winter, R. (2002) *Theory and Practice in Action Research*. Oxford: Symposium Books.

Edwards, R. and Percy-Smith, B. (2004) 'The young people's taskforce: creating new forms of practice and policy in response to youth homelessness and social exclusion', *Youth and Policy*, 84 (21–37).

Elliott, J. (2007) *Reflecting Where the Action Is. The Collected Works of John Elliott*. Abingdon: Routledge.

Fielding, M. (2001) 'Beyond the rhetoric of student voice: new departures or new constraints in twenty first century schooling?', *Forum*, 43 (2): 100–10.

Fielding, M. and Bragg, S. (2003) *Students as Researchers: Making a Difference*. Cambridge: Pearson.

Fine, M., Roberts, R.A., Torre, M.E., Bloom, J., Burns, A., Chajet, L. et al. (2004) *Echoes of Brown: Youth Documenting and Performing the Legacy of Brown v Board of Education*. New York: Teachers College Press.

Hargreaves, A. (1996) 'Revisiting voice', *Educational Researcher*, 25 (1): 12–19.

Holdsworth, R. (2000) 'What is this about a "whole-school approach"?', in R. Holdsworth (ed.), *Discovering Democracy in Action: Learning from School Practice*. Melbourne: Australian Youth Research Centre & Commonwealth of Australia.

Hollins, K., Gunter, H. and Thomson, P. (2006) 'Living improvement: a case study of a school in England', *Improving Schools*, 9 (2): 141–52.

Kemmis, S. and McTaggart, R. (eds) (1988) *The Action Research Planner* (3rd edn). Geelong: Deakin University.

Kenway, J., Blackmore, J. and Willis, S. (1996) 'Beyond feminist authoritarianism and therapy in the classroom?', *Curriculum Perspectives*, 16 (1): 1–12.

Lyons, G. (2003) *Secondary School Councils Student Handbook*. London: SCUK.

Macbeath, J., Demetriou, H., Rudduck, J. and Myers, K. (2003) *Consulting Pupils: A Toolkit*. Cambridge: Pearson Publishing.

Morrow, G. (2002) '"We get played like fools": young people's accounts of community and institutional participation', in H. Ryan and J. Bull (eds), *Changing Families, Changing Communities*. London: Health Development Agency, pp. 143–157.

Polanyi, L. (1979) 'So what's the point?', *Semiotica*, 25: 207–42.

Rudduck, J. and Flutter, J. (2004) *How to Improve Your School*. London: Continuum.

Steinberg, S.R. and Kincheloe, J. (eds) (1998) *Students as Researchers: Creating Classrooms that Matter*. Bristol: Falmer.

Thomson, P. (2007) 'Making it real: engaging students in active citizenship projects', in D. Thiessen and A. Cook-Sather (eds), *International Handbook of Student Experience in Elementary and Secondary School*. Dordrecht: Springer, pp.775–804.

Thomson, P. and Gunter, H. (2006) 'From "consulting pupils" to "pupils as researchers" a situated case narrative', *British Journal of Educational Research*, 32 (6): 839–56.

Thomson, P. and Gunter, H. (2007) 'The methodology of students-as-researchers: valuing and using experience and expertise to develop method', *Discourse*, 28 (3): 327–42.

Thomson, P. and Holdsworth, R. (2003) 'Democratising schools through "student participation": an emerging analysis of the educational field informed by Bourdie', *International Journal of Leadership in Education*, 6 (4): 371–91.

Thomson, P., McQuade, V. and Rochford, K. (2005) 'My little special house: re-forming the risky geographies of middle school girls at Clifftop College', in G. Lloyd (ed.), *Problem Girls. Understanding and Supporting Troubled and Troublesome Girls and Young Women*. London: RoutledgeFalmer, pp. 172–89.

Wasley, P., Hampel, R. and Clark, R. (1997) *Kids and School Reform*. San Francisco: Jossey-Bass.

Wilson, B. and Corbett, H.D. (2001) *Listening to Urban Kids. School Reform and the Teachers They Want*. New York: State University of New York Press.

Zeni, J. (1998) 'A guide to ethical issues and action research', *Educational Action Research*, 6 (1): 9–19.

34

Community Action and Agency in the Education of Urban Youth

Peter C. Murrell, Jr.

It is a lamentable fact that public schools, particularly those in large metropolitan school districts, are dramatically less successful in educating working class, urban African-American and Latino learners than their white, middle-class European-American counterparts. Despite decades of educational reform initiatives in our nation's public school systems, African-American, Latino, Native American and immigrants for whom English is not their first language fall far behind English-speaking, European-Americans on virtually all measures of school achievement. Even when parents' wealth and income are comparable, African-American learners fall far behind their European-American counterparts on virtually every measure of school achievement (Ogbu, 2003). These disparities in educational attainment are patterned according to race, ethnicity, social class and economic opportunity (Anyon, 2005; Bourdieu and Passeron, 1977; Bowles and Gintis, 1976; Lee and Byrk, 1988). Despite the wide recognition of this educational disparity – the so-called *achievement gap* – as the principal challenge in education (cf. Ladson-Billings, 2006), effective change remains elusive.

What is it that the least well-served populations of ethnic-racial minority learners are not getting educationally that their more advantaged European-American counterparts are? This chapter takes up the challenge of determining what is missing in the education of ethnic-racial minority youth, by drawing on an important recent multidisciplinary theoretical turn in the scholarly work on youth development at the intersections of identity, race, culture and achievement.

There is an emerging research literature regarding identity and academic development for African-American youth (e.g., O'Conner, 1997, 2001; Carter, 2005; Spencer, 1999, 2001), Latino youth (e.g., Flores-Gonzáles, 2002; Stanton-Salazar and Dornbusch, 1995) and other young people of diverse racial-ethnic backgrounds (e.g., Roth, 2004). Drawing on this new interdisciplinary theoretical turn in youth development that draws on critical theory, cultural studies, cultural psychology, sociolinguistics, semiotics and other disciplines, this chapter articulates a conceptual system for cultivating the development of academic proficiency and adult agency of urban youth in diverse communities.

This chapter will first identify key shortcomings in contemporary theory on youth development, as it is applied to questions of underachievement among racial-ethnic minority populations and then describe the new turn in formal inquiry into youth development – a turn characterized by a multidisciplinary, phenomenological and culturally contextualized account of how young people acquire and develop academic proficiencies and other abilities for coping with adult life. The discussion then offers a conceptual framework for grappling with the trenchant underachievement and disengagement of young people of color and concludes with an illustrative example of the framework for educating urban youth in school and out of school based on community action research.

TOO MUCH SCHOOLING, TOO LITTLE EDUCATION

The principal shortcoming of contemporary theory in human development and academic achievement is its lack of contextualization in the cultural lives and socialization experiences of young people. Understanding academic achievement requires an understanding of education as the *socialization of academic potential* in racially, linguistically and culturally diverse city communities – and not just the schooling experience. In this view all human development, especially the acquisition of the proficiencies needed for educational success and academic life, is culturally embedded and the development of those abilities needed for academic success and adult life takes place through a continuous, ongoing interchange among people engaged in purposeful and meaningful activity in socially framed contexts over time (Rogoff, 2003). The socialization or *enculturation of academic ability* is a dynamic sharing of meaning systems through shared activity, and the learning is best understood as the continuous exchange between younger and older generations, between novice and expert, and between learner and teacher. Development, especially the acquisition of social and scholastic proficiencies, is based on interaction, communication and exchange in a shared cultural space.

Trends in American society reveal an increasing disconnectedness of social relationships and shared public spaces, resulting in a decline in social capital (Putnam, 2000) and shared public space within which the socialization of young people can acquire this capital. Both trends contribute to a myopia regarding the social and cultural lives of young people, and how they develop that out to be applied in education. As a result, our understanding of youth development and scholastic achievement is informed primarily by schooling, and excludes other participatory contexts that shape the development of young people. Out-of-school participatory cultural spaces young people create for themselves are often much more vibrant, imaginative, innovative and dynamic than those extant in-school settings.

For example, young people's interpretation and consumption of hip-hop culture can be a defining force in their life choices and successful negotiation of schooling (Dyson, 1996; Dimiatridis, 2003, 2005; Flores-Gonzáles, 2002; Lopez, 2002; Mahiri, 1998; Perry, 2002; Stevenson, 2003). The discourse styles emanating from hip-hop, are an important part of social identity and identity formation (e.g., Alim, 2003). The material face-to-face social spaces are augmented and extended with the uses of technology and the creation of multimodal digital tools (e.g., instant messaging, online journaling, chat spaces, wikis, blogging and so on). With the advent of handheld telecommunication devices and the Internet, the shared social spaces of many adolescents are now fluid, globally distributed, overlapping and continuous (Jenkins et al., 2008; Lam, 2006; Leander and McKim, 2003; Leander and Sheehy, 2004; Roswell and Pahl, 2007; Stein, 2007). Thus, there is a dynamic, rapidly changing, vibrant and diverse youth culture that people participate in that is little known by adults or the research community.

Given these subaltern cultural participatory spaces, one limitation of contemporary educational theory is in undertheorizing *interpersonal life* by not fully accounting for all of the rich and varied cultural fields in which young people develop, interact and form an intellectual identity. The meaning that young people make of themselves is not limited to what they do in school. The other limitation concerns undertheorizing the *intrapersonal life* of young people, particularly the static formulations of identity disconnected from the social and cultural contexts that animate young people's agency and self-improvization. Undertheorized is the formation of *social identity* (Jenkins, 2004) and the proposition that peer group affiliations are far more important referential anchors to adolescents' 'identity work' than academic status. The group affiliations and informal shared space of the group is an important canvass for their social identity portraitures. The group creates a micro-society, a micro-culture to which adults are not privy. These shared social spaces, young people cocreate away from the gaze of adults, constitute a significant site of their socialization (Anderson, 1990, 1999). Yet, these contexts of experience are largely invisible to school personnel and other adults working with children and youth outside of school settings.

Youth activity outside of school settings is already an invisible space with respect to adult participation and oversight. The advent of technology allows young people to bring their *subaltern cultural space* from outside school *into* school under the very noses of teachers and administrators – such as the almost constant communication of text messaging. The emergence of digital participatory

youth cultures has led to a need to dramatically reconsider what constitutes education in a global, diverse and technological society. For example, schools are no
longer the only sites of literacy and learning (Jenkins et al., 2008; Kellner, 1995),
and, indeed, our traditional conceptions of what constitutes literacy are being
transformed (Lam, 2006; New London Group, 1996; Sperling and DiPardo, 2008).

The emergence of multimodal forms of communication, expression and creative language outside of school curriculum and school settings buttresses the
critical distinction Dewey made between *education* and *schooling* (Dewey,
1998). For African-American young people in particular, there is indeed 'too
much schooling, and too little education'– referring to the idea that throughout
American history the social institution of formal schooling has been as much a
tool of oppression as it has a vehicle to education (Anderson, 1988, 1995;
Shujaa, 1994). Technologically mediated shared spaces and hip-hop culture are
the ingredients for a shared cultural space that opposes racism and all forms of
oppression. These meanings are both received and created in these *subaltern cultural spaces*. To develop a comprehensive approach to improving the educational
development of young people, the subaltern spaces, young people create and
participate in out of school, must be incorporated into educational systems and
theoretical work..

Theorizing about youth and youth development is supported by new thinking
about adolescence that more carefully reinterprets Erikson's theory with regard to
issues of agency and cultural context (e.g., Côté and Levine, 2002; Jenkins, 2004;
Murrell, 2007). The new turn in youth development urges a contextualized view of
social identification – and the dimensions of situated experience that shape this
developmental process. This implies that the development of an *achievement identity* – a social identity as an intelligent person capable of knowing and negotiating
the complexities of a world of ideas – cannot be fully understood only in reference
to schooling experience. Another recent theoretical turn as important is the appropri-
ation of the notion of *cultural capital* (Bourdieu, 1986; Bourdieu and Passeron,
1977). Carter (2005) makes an important distinction between *dominant* and *nondominant* cultural capital. *Dominant* cultural capital corresponds to the Bourdieu conception – that of symbolic and actual resources that eventually yield economic social
returns in the dominant culture. *Nondominant* cultural capital, on the other hand,
connotes those cultural elements – tastes, appreciations, meaning systems, understandings and affinities – emblematic of lower-status groups. The caché of *nondominant* cultural capital is that it allows members to gain 'authentic' cultural status
positions within the subaltern cultural communities outside of the mainstream.

A NEW CONCEPTUAL FRAMEWORK – SOCIAL
IDENTIFICATION AND INTELLECTUAL AGENCY

To properly address the issue of underachievement of children and youth representing the variety of racial-ethnic populations in urban school systems, we need

to view schooling as one of several sites of socialization. Moreover, we need to recognize the challenge in all of the socialization experiences of young people – so that we can help them work successfully through the parallel and intermingled developmental tasks of *achieving academically* and *identity realization*. We need to look at the developmental supports for young people more critically by asking different questions. Instead of asking 'what's wrong with them?' or 'what are they missing?' we need to ask: 'what aren't they finding in schools that they need to identify with in order to learn, achieve and develop?' In short, we need to examine not just the young person, not just the school environment, but also the person in context as the unit of analysis to understand how both mutually constitute each other in the social and cultural practices of schooling.

Understanding how young people manage the shifting and changing social identities, they express in different social settings, is critical to supporting their academic and personal development. To develop this foundational knowledge a whole new approach will be required of researchers, educators and practitioners – one that views cultural competency as the capacity to successfully address the social, mental health and educational needs of African-American youth. This approach is predicated on understanding the major way that social identity formation in young people mediates the acquisition of intellectual and social tools, and much of this occurs during unstructured time.

The major and critical role that social identity development plays in young people's capacity for growth, adjustment and the acquisition of intellectual and social skills, is not very well addressed in contemporary thinking on youth development. The cultural and social worlds of young people are so fluid and dynamic that they defy the simple descriptive characterization one finds in case literature and research literature. Even if it were possible to describe in a research paper or report the fluid and dynamic social worlds adolescents experience on a day-to-day basis, that knowledge would be obsolete before such a publication hit the press.

To handle this fluidity, the conceptual model used to interpret youth development in out-of-school settings is *situated-mediated identity theory* (Murrell, 2007). It is also informed by an emergent, vibrant literature on the situated and socially mediated nature of racial and cultural identity development among youth (cf., Flores-Gonzáles, 2002; Perry, 2002; Sadowski, 2003; Weiler, 2000; Yon, 2000). This is the conceptual framework used to interpret the relationships between in- and out-of-school experiences on the one hand and the psycho- and socio-cultural processes experienced by youth growing up in ethnically, racially and linguistically diverse urban communities on the other hand. The long-term aim is to develop a system of practice that educators and other committed adults can apply to promoting healthy social and emotional development of children and youth in association with their school achievement.

Briefly, situated-mediated identity theory is an applied cultural psychology of school achievement based upon a relatively new conception of identity called *situated identity* as the critical dimension of school experience that mediates achievement and scholastic success. The theory is based on six premises: (1) Self and realizations of self (identity) are socially constructed through various forms of relational activity in human interaction, especially communication; (2) Identity is best understood as situated and fluid, not static and fixed, and is seen in the representations of self that individuals put forth to the wider social world; (3) the situated representations of self taken on by an individual (role or positionality) are situated roles that individuals assume and express (consciously or unconsciously) in any given setting or social environment; (4) the positionality or set of roles assumed in-school settings profoundly shapes achievement and ultimately determines school success; (5) shared *situated identities* created and mediated by common experiences in-school settings (which some theorists have referred to as *academic identities*) form a *local culture* that shapes school performance and sense of self; and (6) finally, this local culture – the structure of the immediate cultural-social context of instructional activity settings together with the situatedness of a learners performance – can be shaped so as to mediate positive and productive academic identities in ways that ultimately lead to school success (Murrell, 2007).

The ongoing action research project described in the next section uses social identity theory as the lens to understand achievement performance and development in the shifting social milieu of young people's out-of-school experience. It is predicated on the critical role that social identity development plays in young people's capacity from growth, adjustment and the acquisition of intellectual and social skills. It is also predicated on the proposition that young people are fully capable of developing *intellectual agency* outside of school when engaged in a collective, mutually supportive and purposeful political activity (Freire, 1970). Finally, the on-the-ground work is predicated on a disposition of openness to youth culture.

Many forms of popular youth culture change on a daily basis. Therefore, it is not possible to gain a sufficiently contextualized understanding of the social and cultural ecology of youth development from literature alone. This kind of knowledge can only be developed through rich interaction with young people as they grapple with developmental tasks of adolescence made more challenging by the demands and stresses of their experience in complex urban settings. The research must have the cultural currency to recognize the complex terrain presented to children and youth in underresourced urban neighborhoods.

Young people are fully capable of critically interrogating the conditions of their experience – both in school and out. They do this on a regular basis in the subaltern cultural spaces they create out of school. Providing legitimate and authentic opportunities to do this automatically expands the richness of context for their intellectual development. One theme that frequently resonates with young people is a contextualized critical analysis of those initiatives designed to 'help' them. They easily recognize the unavoidable contradictions of positionality. Efforts designed to help urban elementary children in the 'safe' public spaces in school may serve to demonize the contexts of their lived experience outside of school as 'unsafe' public spaces. So the very arrangements of help and assistance to children in their families also communicate to them their marginality and a subaltern identity – an identity of one who lives somewhere unsafe seeking somewhere safe in order to have any hope of educational opportunity.

As an example, consider the innovative and powerful Harlem Children's Zone led by Geoffrey Canada. The Harlem Children's Zone is an area that covers less than one square mile and is home to some 10,000 children, nearly all of whom live in poverty, and two-thirds of them score below grade level on standardized tests. This is the area where Canada has focused on saving 'block by block, child by child' (Canada, 2007). While creating the project as a safe-haven school for a limited number of children in the zone, it positions the public spaces that children and youth occupy going to and from the school as unsafe and desolate. The school is the favored space, the location where:

> They get what middle-class and upper middle-class kids get, Canada explains. They get safety. They get structure. They get academic enrichment. They get cultural activity. They get adults who love them are prepared to do anything. And I mean, I'm prepared to do anything to keep these kids on the right track.

Now consider a more different way to position young people with respect to their educational experience than that described above, where adults provide all the answers, all the services and all the initiative. Consider an enterprise that attempts to mobilize the intellectual agency and development of young people where they are – namely, on the street and typically *not* in the school. From the very beginning, it engenders a different *positionality* among young people. Despite the value of programs offering a safe-haven as the shared space, coming to a safe-haven location still positions children and youth as marginal and as individuals in need. Where they live and where their families dwell become subaltern spaces.

COMMUNITY ACTION RESEARCH – EMBRACING AND ANIMATING THE SUBALTERN CULTURAL SPACE

Successful youth work in Boston is characterized by three principles: (1) that social identity formation in young people mediates the acquisition of intellectual and social tools, and much of this occurs during unstructured time; (2) understanding how young people manage the shifting and changing social identities they express in these subaltern spaces is critical to developing their intellectual potential and agency; and (3) the actions and activities of discovery, critique, investigative inquiry and authorship develop real academic proficiencies. The community action research initiative described below is an example of people as members of the subaltern cultural space.

Our Boston Project for the out-of-school context is *Social Justice Education* (2000). This is a youth leadership program operating after school each afternoon offered to youth between the ages of 11 and 25 in the communities of Roxbury,

Dorchester, Mattapan and Jamaica Plain. The community-based agency, *Social Justice Education*, runs this program for youth free of charge. The work is centered in one of the longest standing youth development projects in Boston, *Education for Liberation*. This is a project serving Boston youth who are not in school but are struggling to become educated individuals.

Education for Liberation develops youth leaders by focusing on issues and building skills relevant to their lives, including: Political Consciousness and Community Organizing; Literacy Development and Journalism; Youth Culture, and Physical, Emotional and Spiritual Health. Education for Liberation is based on the principles and strategies of Liberation Pedagogy and the Recovery Movement, and emphasizes the development of trusting relationships that 'go the extra mile' in recognizing and building on the initiatives and assets of each youth leader. It operates principally as an after-school program but is open to individuals not currently in school. *Education for Liberation* addresses the issue of the disenfranchisement of youth from Boston's communities of color and working class communities, and seeks to equip and empower them to be impactful agents in the healing and transformation of their personal lives, families, communities and society. Approximately 500 youth participate annually in this program, many of whom are participants in a variety of allied youth initiatives.

Education for Liberation expects out-of-school participants to enroll in school as a requirement for remaining in the program. The program is facilitated by community counselors and former graduates, who engage participants in a method of research called 'Participatory Action Research' that provides a platform for gaining the necessary knowledge to collectively change their living conditions and power relations. Topics of research typically are human rights, economic, educational and other current issues that may be analyzed from the local, national and/or international perspective, and are explored to discover connections to young people's lives and futures. Participants write articles, poetry, and research reports about these topics for inclusion in the youth newspaper, *Love in Action*, that is published by Social Justice Education and distributed freely in Roxbury, Dorchester, Mattapan, Jamaica Plain and other Boston neighborhoods.

Concurrent with Participatory Action Research, the Education for Liberation program organizes Youth in Recovery Meetings where participants gather in men's and women's groups weekly to address family issues, racism and colorism, sexuality and relationships, violence and other abuse, and issues of drugs, alcohol and compulsive eating. Through this powerful and empowered healing process, young people begin to reclaim their physical, emotional and spiritual well-being and strength.

COMMUNITY-BASED ACTION
RESEARCH – WHAT WE LEARNED

What manner of structuring out-of-school activity can meet the developmental and educational needs of urban youth of color? The structure should be one that animates and encourages the improvization of self, individual agency, collective agency. There are a number of features of contexts that mobilize the interest, participation, engagement and development of young people. One is that whatever the context or activity setting, there is an authentic civic engagement – an activism on the conditions affecting their lives. Many of the participants in *Education for Liberation* are members of the youth leadership front that animated a movement for gang peace within the city of Boston. It is an issue that is persistently addressed in the activism of virtually all of the youth groups. Members of the newspaper staff express this value:

> Although we are still teenagers, almost everyone we know has been personally affected by violence in some way. Why do so many of us continue to walk around ready to fight, to kill, to hurt others, when we ourselves have felt the pain of losing someone precious. And, how can we stop this madness? (Dunham et al., 2007: 4)

In addition to the cultural value of civic engagement and activism is the value of personal and collective development. The critical optic that older, more experience youth inculcate in the younger members is the proposition that, for people who have had hard lives, not all development is forward moving, but rather recovery. In the words of one youth:

> It is said that if you're not in recovery you're in relapse. Recovery does not mean doing the same thing time and again, expecting different results. How can we expect different results in recovering ourselves, our communities, our children, if we continue doing the same old things that end in the same results … . How can the courts, programs, people in power expect different results doing the same things, over and over? This model that is currently being used in our communities is broke. It's a revolving door that needs grass roots re-organization to begin a real recovery process. (p. 12)

Both of these values are embodied in a 'New Code of the Streets' written by members of the *Love in Action* staff to be unveiled at an upcoming youth leadership summit. The code reads as follows:

Man Up
Take Responsibility
Each One Teach One
Find a New Hustle
Think outside the Block
Be Real with Yourself
Be an Individual
See as One Community
Set Goals
Use Your Intelligence
Always Progress
Live above the Influence
Get Educated
Learn from Your Elders' Mistakes
Seize Opportunity

Support Others' Positive Choices
Use Political Power
Stay Informed and Inform Others
Work for Better Government
Stand Up for Change
(Dunham et al., 2007: 4)

These are individuals working on their individual agency through collective identity and action. The manifest product is the newspaper, *Love in Action*. They are not asked to give up their subaltern cultural space in order to develop the capacities to write critically, think incisively and mobilize effectively. Each is adopting a positionality as a change agent operating on those conditions that simultaneously impact on their lives in their personal relationships, their neighborhoods, locally, nationally and internationally. Each is developing skills in recovery counseling, political analysis and community organizing. Each is engaged in action that has formative value in the development of intellectual and scholastic proficiencies, and is situated in a political awareness and collective engagement.

REFERENCES

Alim, H.S. (2003) '"We are the streets": African American language and the strategic construction of a street conscious identity', in S. Makoni, G. Smitherman, A.F. Ball and A.K. Spears (eds), *Black Linguistics: Language, Society, and Politics in Africa and the Americas*. New York: Routledge.

Anderson, E. (1990) *Streetwise: Race, Class, and Change in an Urban Community*. Chicago: University of Chicago Press.

Anderson, E. (1999) *Code of the Street: Decency, Violence, and the Moral Life of the Inner City*. New York: W.W. Norton & Company.

Anderson, J. (1988) *The Education of Blacks in the South, 1860–1935*. Chapel Hill: University of North Carolina Press.

Anderson, J. (1995) 'Literacy and education in the African-American experience', in V.L. Gadsen and D.A. Wagner (eds), *Literacy among African-American Youth: Issues in Learning, Teaching, and Schooling*. Cresskill, NJ: Hampton Press, pp. 19–37.

Anyon, J. (2005) *Radical Possibilities: Public Policy, Urban Education and a New Social Movement*. New York: Routledge.

Bourdieu, P. (1986) 'Forms of capital', in J.G. Richardson (ed.), *Handbook of Theory and Research for the Sociology of Education*. New York: Greenwood Press.

Bourdieu, P. and Passeron, C. (1977) *Reproduction in Education, Society, and Culture*. Beverly Hills, CA: Sage Publications.

Bowles, H. and Gintis, S. (1976) *Schooling in Capitalist America: Educational Reform and the Contradictions of American Life*. New York: Basic Books.

Canada, G. (2007) http://www.cbsnews.com/stories/2006/05/11/60minutes/main1611936.shtml, retrieval date 9.27.07.

Carter, P.L. (2005) *Keepin' It Real: School Success beyond Black and White*. New York: Oxford University Press.

Côté, J.E. and Levine, C.G. (2002) *Identity Formation, Agency and Culture*. Mahwah, NJ: Lawrence Erlbaum Press.

Dewey, J. (1998) *Experience and Education*. New York: Kappa Delta Pi Publications.

Dimitriadis, G. (2003) *Friendship, Cliques, and Gangs: Young Black Men Coming of Age in Urban America*. New York: Teachers College Press.

Dimitriadis, G. (2005) *Performing Identity/Performing Culture: Hip Hop as Text, Pedagogy, and Lived Experience*. New York: Peter Lang.

Dunham, D., Rodriguez, A. and Jean Baptiste, A. (2007) *Love in Action*, p. 4.

Dyson, M. (1996) *Race Rules. Navigating the Color Line*. Reading, MA: Addison-Wesley.

Freire, P. (1970) *Pedagogy of the Oppressed*. New York: Continuum.

Flores-Gonzáles, N. (2002) *School Kids/Street Kids: Identity Development in Latino Students*. New York: Teachers College Press.

Jenkins, R. (2004) *Social Identity*, 2nd end. New York: Routledge.

Jenkins, H., Clinton, K., Purushotma, R., Robison, A.J. and Weigel, M. (2008) 'Confronting the challenges of participatory culture: Media education for the 21st century', Occasional paper, Comparative Media Studies Program at the Massachusetts Institute of Technology. Retrieved January 1, 2008. http://www.digitallearning.macfound.org/atf/cf/%7B7E45C7E0-A3E0-4B89-AC9C-E807E1B0AE4E%7D/JENKINS_WHITE_PAPER.PDF

Kellner, D. (1995) *Media Culture: Cultural Studies, Identity and Politics between the Modern and the Postmodern*. New York: Routledge.

Ladson-Billings, G. (2006) 'From the achievement gap to the education debt: Understanding achievement in U.S. schools', *Educational Researcher*, 35 (7): 3–12.

Lam, W.S.E. (2006) 'Culture and learning in the context of globalization: Research directions', *Review of Research in Education*, 30: 213–37.

Leander, K. and McKim, K.K. (2003) 'Tracing the everyday "sitings" of adolescents on the Internet: A strategic adaptation of ethnography across online and offline spaces', *Education, Communication and Information*, 3: 21–40.

Leander, K. and Sheehy, M. (eds) (2004) *Spatializing Literacy Research and Practice*. New York: Peter Lang.

Lee, V. and Byrk, A. (1988) 'Curriculum tracking as mediating the social distribution of high school achievement', *Sociology of Education*, 61: 78–94.

Lopez, N. (2002) *Hopeful Girls, Troubled Boys: Race and Gender Disparity in Urban Education*. New York: Routledge.

Mahiri, J. (1998) *Shooting for Excellence: African American Youth Culture in New Century Schools*. Urbana, IL: National Council of Teachers of English.

Murrell, P.C., Jr. (2007) *Race, Culture, and Schooling: Identities of Achievement in Multicultural Urban Schools*. Mahwah, NJ: Lawrence Erlbaum Associates.

New London Group (1996) 'A pedagogy of multiliteracies: Designing social futures', *Harvard Educational Review*, 66: 60–92.

O'Conner, C. (1997) 'Dispositions toward (collective) struggle and educational resilience in the inner city: A case study of six African American high school students', *American Educational Research Journal*, 34 (4): 593–629.

O'Conner, C. (2001) 'Making sense of the complexity of social identity in relation to achievement: A sociological challenge in the new millennium', *Sociology of Education, 74* (extra issue). Current of thought: Sociology of education at the dawn of the 21st century: 159–168.

Ogbu, J. (2003) *Black American Students in an Affluent Suburb: A Study of Academic Disengagement*. Mahwah, NJ: Lawrence Erlbaum Associates.

Perry, P. (2002) *Shades of White: White Kids and Racial Identities in High Schools*. Durham, NC: Duke University Press.

Putnam, R.D. (2000) *Bowling Alone: The Collapse and Revival of American Community*. New York: Simon & Schuste.

Rogoff, B. (2003) *The Cultural Nature of Human Development*. New York: Oxford University Press.

Roth, W.M. (2004) 'Identity as dialectic: Re/making self in urban school', *Mind, Culture, and Activity*, 11 (1): 48–69.

Roswell, J. and Pahl, K. (2007) 'Sedimented identities in texts: Instances of practice', *Reading Research Quarterly*, 42: 388–404.

Sadowski, M. (2003) 'Introduction: Why identity matters in school', in M. Sadowski (ed.), *Adolescents at School: Perspectives on Youth, Identity and Education*. Cambridge, MA: Harvard Education Process.

Shujaa, M. (1994) *Too Much Schooling, Too Little Education: A Paradox of Black Life in White Societies*. Trenton, NJ: African World Press.

Social Justice Education (2008) http://socialjusticeeducation.org/

Spencer, M.B. (1999) 'Social and cultural influences on school adjustment: The application of an identity-focused cultural ecological perspective', *Educational Psychologist*, 34 (1): 43–57.

Spencer, M.B. (2001) 'Identity and school adjustment: Revisiting the "acting white" theory', *Educational Psychologist*, 36 (1) : 21–31

Sperling, M. and DiPardo, A. (2008) 'English education research and classroom practice: New directions for new times', *Review of Research in Education*, 32: 62–108.

Stanton-Salazar, R. (2001) *Manufacturing Hope and Despair: The School and Kin Support Networks of U.S. Mexican Youth*. New York: Teachers College Press.

Stanton-Salazar, R. and Dornbusch, S.M. (1995) 'Social capital and the social reproduction of inequality: The formation of information networks among Mexican-origin high school students', *Sociology of Education*, 68 (2): 116–35.

Stein, P. (2007) *Multidimensional Pedagogies in Diverse Classrooms: Representation, Rights and Resources*. New York: Routlege.

Stevenson, H.C. Jr. (2003) *Playing with Anger: Teaching Coping Skills to African American Boys through Athletics and Culture*. Westport, CT.: Greenwood Publishing, Praeger.

Weiler, J.D. (2000) *Codes and Contradictions: Race, Gender Identity and Schooling*. Albany, NY: State University of New York Press.

Yon, D. (2000) *Elusive Culture: Schooling, Race, and Identity in Global Times*. Albany, NY: State University of New York Press.

35

Social-Political Theory in Working with Teachers for Social Justice Schooling

Marie Brennan and Susan E. Noffke

Social theory and political theory, in particular, has not surprisingly been in ferment in past decades, as the changing 'flows' (Appadurai, 1990) of people, finance, media, information, cultural forms and information are felt in even remote parts of this globe we call 'earth'. Various explanations of changed lived experience pay attention to inter-dependence of various 'locals' and to the power at work there (Appadurai, 1996; Bauman, 1998; Popkewitz and Brennan, 1997), including in government operations and other forms of 'governmentality' (Foucault, 1991). New institutional forms and practices emerge and participants in them need resources with which to think and to explain to themselves and one another how social relations work, how institutional practices themselves call forth different kinds of people and practice in coming to terms with both continuing histories of power relations and emergent forms.

Changes in the global contexts and theorizing about it have particular salience for action research in its various forms, concerned with local scope, particular practices and a range of collaborative processes. Given that many forms of action research are explicitly about work toward redressing social injustice (see Griffiths, Chapter 7 this volume), we need to understand how local settings, forms of practice and inter-relationships are altering, and the effects in terms of justice. There is urgency in seeking explanations and conceptual tools relevant to the particular circumstances and to their relationships to other sites. This is particularly so when it comes to the 'research' aspects of the action research work: when trying to work up/through/in data. The spaces provided by the need to reflect, called forth by the production of 'data', are an important means of understanding the constitution of the local in relation to other locals, and the constitution of issues in practice.

This chapter draws together issues of both the personal and political as we work through the issue of 'data' in action research. In this exploration, our personal excursions into social theory play a role as we use our 'readings' to help us understand and further advance our understandings of socially just education through work with colleagues in schools. However, we also wish to highlight the ways in which we work with our colleagues to 'analyze' data, asking questions explicitly and indirectly from forms of socio-political theories germane to the problematic of the action research project. Socio-political theory is part of the work of action research and occurs in two directions: (1) bringing existing social theory into more explicit connection to the practice and setting under investigation because it is relevant to the problematic being investigated; and (2) making problematic some aspects of social theory as the practice, or emerging practice, challenges conceptions developed elsewhere in different times and places. All theory in this sense is provisional and in need of local specification, modification and addition. Theory can shed light on practice, if called upon to make those connections, and practice sheds light on theoretical explanations and their adequacy for the new setting.

'Data' in most forms of research follow design plans and are tailored to preset research questions. Our experiences with action research have led us to a different way of thinking about data in the process of researching because data are part of the lived experience of the research context, rather than abstracted away from the setting. We look at data as a means of constructing groups (Brennan and Noffke, 1997) and of providing 'testimony' for their social actions – data provide a means for identifying potential interventions in the setting; they are representations made from the local about the local, and also provide insights into their connections to other settings and people. Examining 'data' allows for slowing down the movement between doing and the next action, long enough to 'see' the practice rather than being immersed in it as an actor. Data are constructed representations of the practice, which can thus provide both a connection to the site of practice and a 'distance' to seeing it also from the 'outside'.

We also use data to examine and extend the lenses we use as part of data analysis: data analysis always occurs through the use of our personal lenses; through our identities as 'white' in racialized societies, through our positions in universities and/or as people who have been activists in education. Data and data analysis thus provide an opportunity to be reflexive about what is at stake in changing interpretations, knowledge and action as they intersect in action research projects.

In all of our efforts over the past three decades, we have sought to improve the educational experiences of school children by working as teachers and with teachers engaging in action research. And also through these experiences, we have sought out new interpretations of our work and that of those with whom we work through readings of social theory. In this chapter we begin by looking at the current context for 'data' in teachers' lives. Then, through a description of a school-based action research project organized around issues of racial equity in schooling and another with student teachers' working on physical education projects, we outline how issues of social theory come into play in work with teachers. The data teachers gather through their experiences become ways to unpack their understandings (as well as our own) and also serve to create and sustain working groups. But these workings also reveal ways in which the personal intersects with the political – our data, coming from ourselves and our practices, become the boundaries of our understanding of the political contexts in which we work.

The final part of the chapter reflects on the efficacy of using different forms of social theory in relation to local projects, and offers some cautions drawn from Edward Said about how theory might 'travel', relevant to our concerns in working with teachers for social justice through action research. What we hope to achieve in this chapter is an exploration of how social theory can play a role in working with teachers for social justice schooling, in particular how theoretically informed/ infused 'data' might be used in the action research process.

DATA IN TEACHERS' LIVES IN THE PAST DECADES

Data are always 'local' at some point in their production. In the 1980s, when we started teaching action research at universities, teachers had a different set of issues about 'data' from today. Often engagement in action research involved the process of starting to take themselves seriously as producers of knowledge. They tended to see experiential knowledge as in opposition to research-based knowledge and often reified experiential knowledge, rejecting research-based knowledge ('theory') as too disconnected from experiential knowledge. The pedagogy of action research projects was to get them to see their work, their context, as 'data' that could be used as a 'conversation' with a range of 'knowledges'. The status of the teaching profession and women workers of the profession could be celebrated through action research, building the profession as communities.

Changes in the context remind us that data do not exist 'out there', ready to be interrogated, but rather emerge from the processes of questioning and action in specific projects. Over the past 20 years of the US presidents, there has been a progression toward a federal educational policy that has a strongly punitive approach in which 'data', specifically those resulting from high-stakes testing, are used to 'measure' the performance of teachers and students. In this climate, teachers are surrounded by and measured against large sets of data. The movement generally goes by the name of 'evidence-based practice' and it is not restricted to the USA. Indeed, the movement to 'standards' is part of globalization: the movement to forms of supra-national organization seems to have spawned large-scale projects at the national level for the purposes of international comparison. The focus on large-scale quantitative studies is valorized at the expense of other forms of data. This approach positions teachers' own judgments as not to be trusted: teachers are positioned to implement decisions made elsewhere, and decontextualized data are used to 'beat teachers over the head' to alter their behavior and that of their students.

Ironically, the teaching profession since the 1980s has won a contradictory victory. Teaching is more professionalized (Labaree, 1992): there are licensing, standards and certification, but at the same time there is far more external control through a wider range of mechanisms which are largely focused on production of, and reaction to, data. Individual teachers are, in this version of 'professional', responsible for having their practice controlled by data produced elsewhere, and data are used to control their work. There is thus a different relationship for 'data' and teachers' work to be forged today than in previous eras.

Given this new context for the use of data, there is a danger for many teachers that producing local or classroom data for even small groups means it may be taken over and used for further surveillance of themselves or their students. The problem now is how data might be shown to have potential for serving a resistance agenda. By bringing new resources to 'see' and 'work with' their world, through social theories or concepts drawn from social theory relevant to the issues, teachers can understand the lines of flight and dirty operations of power. Data can avoid contributing to surveillance (as is the case with testing), as well as build communities to support divergent interpretations among their profession. Our point is that theoretical resources serve this end.

FROM NEW REPRESENTATIONS TO NEW SPACES FOR ACTION

In the examples from projects we describe below, we try to show some of the multiple dimensions of using social theory-informed data analysis to construct representations of local practice in such a way that teachers and student teachers find different insights, linked to the social movements which gave birth to social theory, thus opening up new spaces for action in their projects, and generative for further explorations of new data in their work.

Learning 'Social Skills'

In an elementary school with a predominantly African-American and low-income school population, a series of projects emerged around improving African-American students' achievement and quality of their schooling.

The school district was under court mandate to address the differences in achievement between African-American and white students' achievement levels, and to devise ways to 'close the gap'. In one project, an action research group looked at the issue of student behavior, and concluded that students needed work at improving their 'social skills', as a means to improving their achievement, and also to improve the overall social climate of the school. A series of whole class lessons were constructed to teach students directly how to react 'better' to common situations in school. Around the same time as these lessons were being implemented, a local branch of the Urban League held a 'Celebration of Excellence' in which the achievements of local African-American students could be highlighted. Some of the members of the action research group, including the university participant (Susan), attended that event.

What we saw at that event was quite enlightening and became 'data' for our group discussions. Some of the same students who were seen as lacking in 'social skills' at the school, in this context assumed roles which required a wide range of social competencies. They were responsible, without adult supervision, for organizing performances (e.g. step dancing routines), and also looked after younger children on the nearby playground, again without adult supervision. They clearly had a lot of 'social skills' which were not being seen in the school situation. The action research group used this experience as a form of data, which allowed some members (not all) of the group to reframe the 'teaching social skills' question to be reframed as 'What are we doing in the school that isn't communicating the same expectations that are evident in other settings?'

So what role did theory play in this event, and how was this 'data analysis'? What we can see in this example are the various uses of data. The data from the project first led to naming the project focus as 'behavior management problems' of African-American young people. For several teachers, this changed when they found a new lens for looking at their students. Many teachers could see a range of other interpretations of data based on the school as a result of seeing data from elsewhere, which led to different 'stories' of the 'problem'. Concepts from Critical Race Theory (CRT) were useful in interpreting/analyzing the 'data' generated by visiting the Urban League event.

A key concept from CRT, that of 'counter-narrative' (Ladson-Billings and Tate, 1995; Ladson-Billings, 1998) could be developed in action: the new story the teachers constructed from the event experience – of African-American young people as responsible, caring, competent and 'well behaved' – meant that a new resource was added to the school site for teachers to include in their relationship with students. Some teachers could see their previous interpretation as an example of 'endemic racism' (also a key element to CRT), and in altering their naming of the problem and seeing the responsibilities students performed in their community, could re-interpret the school's role in building and sustaining a deficit view of students.

Group singular CRT was not infused in the groups as an academic literature. Rather, the key concepts of 'counter-narrative' and 'racism as endemic to US American society' were introduced partly by the 'outsider' and partly from the action research group members. Although not all members of the group saw the issues in the same way, there was enough of a 'critical mass' of teachers who could then devise alternative actions in that social setting. And whereas a small group did continue their lessons on 'social skills', another moved more toward trying to identify ways in which teachers could connect with the social skills the students clearly had outside of schools. This small-scale sharing of a new way of seeing created a new space for actions, ones that built from student and community strengths.

The stakes in this project seem really small; however, given the huge percentage of African-American young men who enter the 'school to prison' pipeline, the stakes are enormous. Finding a language system which could give teachers a new way to 'process' their experiences with children in new ways (i.e. to see that racism plays a role in schooling and that counter-narratives are important), indicates that social theory can give teachers a language to interpret their 'lived experiences' in new ways.

It is crucial to see this event of 'data analysis' clearly. The 'outside' researcher inserted the concepts from CRT, but many of the teachers were looking for a new way to 'name' their experiences. The concepts from theory fit the social agenda of the teachers. It was 'imported' partly via the outsider, but merely 'named' a situation some of the teachers already felt. The theory was useful in identifying new actions, ones that could then be seen as part of a larger social movement.

Physical Education for All?

In an Australian research class for pre-service teachers, a large group of Physical Education students often posed a challenge to peers from other specializations. The PE students were often seen as 'snobbish' by other students, because in Australia the science background and high-level school completion scores of PE students outranks those of other student teachers, particularly those in primary school programs. Many academics in the program reported group resistance by the PE students to work they did not enjoy, especially work informed by equity concerns or other analyses from the social sciences. In the research class, which relied on small group action research projects in long-term placement settings as the main assessment item, the PE students were often not interested in doing action research for their final year teacher education project, and were mainly planning projects based on replication of larger-scale empirical-analytic studies, without an action component on their own part (e.g. tallying the numbers of students participating in different sports training, or weighing students and measuring fitness levels).

In endeavoring to break down the stereotypes of research and of PE as a teaching specialization, the university teacher provided a range of other data from a variety of research genres – on the history of body size and shape, the links between previous generations of eating/starvation and current bodily states, and different metabolic rates for different kinds of bodies. This set of data, still from inside their largely scientific paradigm, intrigued a pair of students who then changed their project focus and data gathering to see which students they were actually teaching – only those like themselves or able to imagine like themselves or students with diverse body types, backgrounds and interests in sports and other activities. They began to see that demanding participation in competitive team sports might not encourage those who did not normally participate to do so, to seek other ways of organizing fitness and to examine the potentials of cooperative sports. They also began to see ways to explore in practice – action research – issues which were not covered in the PE curriculum literature.

In reflecting on their project toward the end of their placement, two PE students became quite articulate about the 'jolt' provided by the initial data about body image, the histories of different bodies and male–female differences. By then, turning their project into a cooperative one with their high school students, investigating opportunities for fitness in diverse lives and among those with investments in the 'body', they found new relationships emerging with their students. Instead of a tussle of wills about participation in a cross-country run or basketball/football/hockey team, there was negotiation around building skills, the range of activities and targets set in conjunction with students. This also reduced the 'reporting' of non-compliance around participation, which had dominated their relationship with students to that time. They introduced a series of cooperative activities and noted that levels of participation increased very significantly, especially among those who had previously been most resistant to PE. Their own data, discussed as feedback with groups of students, they reported as having taught them about their students, their own teaching and about different ways to achieve physicality with different groups of students. Perhaps more importantly, these student teachers convinced both their peers and their supervising teachers to take an approach to PE that acknowledged the diversity in the student group not by treating everyone 'the same' but through thinking about classed, raced and gendered bodies. The women student teachers teased the male students about becoming feminists, and were quite impressed by their response about learning to listen differently to girl students in their data on participation.

They were invited to run an in-service meeting for PE staff with their own data, and set the readings provided for them, as well as further materials they identified themselves, for staff preparation for the professional development activity. This was by no means a 'success story' in changing the whole PE cohort, but enough were convinced by the projects undertaken to consider advising the following year students to 'do' action research projects in their placements.

Provision of data from outside the expectations – the usual lenses brought by immersion in the subject – required new questions to be asked, if they were taken seriously. In this instance, the student teachers were surprised at the 'knowledge' they didn't have and the challenge to their deficit view of high school students who were not enthralled by competitive sport, and not motivated to develop a 'good' body. The provision of data from feminist and class-based analyses elicited quite different ways of engaging with the task of teaching ALL students. It helped to change the student teachers' relations to their own practice, and to their usual ways of being in that practice. New questions emerged for two key students, who designed projects which directly addressed health and fitness and the range of ways which students could engage. With these new projects, new data emerged which both confirmed the earlier data and challenged the students' more medical/anatomical science understanding as the main explanation for PE curriculum. Further, the recognition of their peers and supervising teachers enhanced the image of teacher research on practice and introduced new elements into discussion.

WHICH THEORIES COME INTO PLAY?

What kinds of theories seem to make sense/help teachers to make sense of their lives and practices? Discussions of concepts – whatever they are – will only make sense when there is an authentic connection to the issue under investigation. Sometimes the concept can be brought in quite explicitly, e.g. 'this is related to issues of the movement of global capital away from the public sector', or 'it may not be fashionable to talk of feminism but this is an example of sexism at work'. At other times, someone in the group (the facilitator or a member of the group) can bring in a particular concept because it helps to understand a particular problematic. Usually this is not accompanied by explicit definitions or reading around the issue. To say 'Racism is endemic' actually does communicate the core idea. What makes the concept 'useful' is its explanatory power about the issue in its setting to those involved. If the concept doesn't 'work', then other theories and concepts have to be tried. Concepts from social theory – neo-liberalism, performativity, gendered/classed understanding of bodies, community funds of knowledge, for example – can help teachers to understand the multiple connections of their practice to other sites and movements that promote or resist particular assumptions and effects.

Theories are related to the politics of the contexts in which the action/actors are currently operating. How to make the issue and the way of seeing and therefore acting upon/within problematic is a move that facilitators and teacher action researchers work on together in dialogue. The practice – of administrators, policy workers or one's own – is in turn no longer seen as 'normal' or even desirable/required.

What we see as important in bringing a range of theoretical resources to teacher action research includes, first, acknowledging teachers as intellectuals and cultural workers, a status not often recognized, even among teachers themselves. Second, the problematics that underpin teachers' projects are already connected into wider social worlds and movements which social theory could help to be articulated. Third, the teachers find the theory helps them to see their own issue, embedded in practice, somewhat from the outside. Lastly, we generally need to 'over-resource' with theoretical resources in order for teachers to find different connections into and out of their work in relation to other sites.

MOVING THEORY

Edward Said, a great theorist who engaged in specific and global political work, expressed significant concern that ideas can lose their force when moved from the 'messy', lived situations which gave rise to their explication, their connections to practice and place. But he also notes that movement of theory is 'normal'. In his 1983 essay 'Travelling theory', Said argued that:

> [c]ultural and intellectual life are usually nourished and often sustained by … circulation of ideas, and whether it takes the form of acknowledged or unconscious influence, creative borrowing, or wholesale appropriation, the movement of ideas and theories from one place to another is both a fact of life and a usefully enabling condition of intellectual activity. (1983: 226)

In a later essay, 'Travelling theory reconsidered' (2003), he reiterated his concern that theory, when it travels, can be 'tamed' or 'domesticated' such that it loses its fire and political edge. However, he also noted that sometimes, theory can take new fire when it moves. This is not just 'borrowing' or 'adaptation' but:

> [t]here is in particular an intellectual, and perhaps moral, community of a remarkable kind, *affiliation* in the deepest and most interesting sense of the word. As a way of getting seriously past the weightlessness of one theory after another, the remorseless indignations of orthodoxy, and the expressions of tired advocacy to which we are often submitted, the exercise involved in figuring out where the theory went and how in getting there its fiery core was reignited is invigorating … (p. 452)

In the current era, when teachers working together is not only made more difficult in a judgmental and punitive context, any potential for seeing connections to others, and to new spaces of action is welcomed. As one of the strategies for making such connections, using social theory to articulate the links has not been much discussed in the action research literature, yet is emerging in our practice as part of making sense of local practice. Such a move also reminds us that any local is multiply connected to other spaces, people and times.

REFERENCES

Appadurai, A. (1990) 'Disjuncture and difference in the global culture economy', *Theory, Culture, and Society*, 7: 295–310.

Appadurai, A. (1996) *Modernity at Large: Cultural Dimensions of Globalization*. Minneapolis: University of Minnesota Press.

Bauman, Z. (1998) *Globalization: The Human Consequences*. New York: Columbia University.

Brennan, M. and Noffke, S.E. (1997) 'Uses of data in action research', in T.R. Carson and D. Sumara (eds), *Action Research as a Living Practice*. New York: Peter Lang, pp. 23–43.

Foucault, M. (1991) 'Governmentality', in G. Burchell, C. Gordon and P. Miller (eds), *The Foucault Effect: Studies in Governmentality*. Chicago: University of Chicago Press.

Labaree, D.F. (1992) 'Power, knowledge, and the rationalization of teaching: a genealogy of the movment to professionalize teaching', *Harvard Educational Review*, 62: 123–54.

Ladson-Billings, G. (1998) 'Just what is critical race theory and what's it doing in a nice field like education?', *Qualitative Studies in Education*, 11 (1): 7–24.

Ladson-Billings, G. and Tate, W.F. IV (1995) 'Towards a critical race theory for education', *Teachers College Record*, 97 (1): 47–68.

Popkewitz, T. and Brennan, M. (eds) (1997) *Foucault's Challenge: Discourse, Power and Knowledge in Education*. New York: Teachers College Press.

Said, E. (1983) 'Travelling theory', *The World, the Text and the Critic*. Cambridge, MA: Harvard University Press.

Said, E. (2003) 'Travelling theory reconsidered', *Reflections on Exile and Other Essays*. Cambridge, MA: Harvard University Press.

36

Rethinking Action Research: Commonsense and Relations of Freedom[1]

Andrew Gitlin

Action research continues to make a significant difference in the lives of teachers, teacher educators, and many others who see the value in knowledge produced from the corridors and classrooms of our schools. Given the success of action research, proposing an alternative approach may seem a bit odd. It should be remembered, however, that action research as a practice asks teachers to reflect consistently on their means and ends (Stenhouse, 1975). To take action research seriously, to do action research on action research, therefore, requires action researchers to consistently reflect on the means and ends of this influential practice. This chapter does so by illustrating an alternative approach to action research, educational poetics. Educational poetics differs from many other approaches to action research because it is based on two fundamental principles: (a) having commonsense (i.e., the normative assumptions of a culture(s) that are viewed many times as necessarily right-minded as opposed to a social construction reflecting dominant relations of power) as an object of inquiry, and (b) suggesting that relations of freedom (i.e., our ability to create, be inventive, and move from the known to the unknown) is an expected outcome of this alternative approach.

The chapter begins with a snippet of an educational poetics text, then uses this text to draw out some of the key conceptual underpinnings of educational poetics.

THE PRACTICE OF EDUCATIONAL POETICS

In our book (Gitlin and Peck, 2005: 83–8) on Educational Poetics, Marcie Peck, a middle school teacher and graduate student at the University of Utah, presented her reflections and insights on her first experience of working with Educational Poetics. What follows is an abbreviated snippet (not the full educational poetics text) of an educational poetics text written by Marcie.

When I was a new English teacher, the department head handed me two items: a textbook and a list of all the topics I must cover that year in 7th-grade English. After reviewing the text and the list, I began planning the curriculum. As the year progressed, I dutifully checked items off the list: parts of speech one, drama experience one, topic sentence one. Over the course of the first few years, I became very proficient in covering the list, and I felt a great deal of satisfaction when, at the end of the year, every topic listed had a check next to it. I defined myself as a successful teacher because I was able to cover 'the list'. In fact, the list took precedence over questions about what students should learn and even how that learning should occur.

As the years progressed, though, I became unhappy with what was happening in my classroom. My emphasis on efficiency, on getting through the required curriculum, no longer engendered much enthusiasm. As I looked out at the students in my class, they mostly looked bored and disinterested. Blaming their passivity on laziness and lack of commitment only worked for so long, as I noticed that even the 'good' students were quite often lacking in any passion for the classroom curriculum or pedagogy. For the most part, students did their work, but only because they wanted good grades, not because they were engaged in what they were doing. I was bored myself, and had to agree reluctantly with Gatto (2003) that boredom is the common condition of school teachers (p. 33).

Returning to graduate school seemed a way to address some of these questions, although to be candid, the pay increase tied to further credentials probably was the biggest influence on my decision to obtain a graduate degree. I now found myself on the other side of the desk and began to see the classroom from a more student-oriented perspective. I noticed that I too was quite often bored in class and resorted to talking to my neighbor, drawing pictures, and even passing notes to keep myself awake. I wanted a good grade, so I pretended to be interested as often as I could and completed my assignments in a timely manner.

The two years it would take to get a Master's degree loomed before me as I sat passively in class for six hours each week. As I began each new term in my Master's program and reflected on past terms, I was appalled by the fact that I had spent 15–20 hours a week studying a subject and yet could remember so little of it. Linked to this dismay was my recollection of the typical English department meeting we always held after the first month of school, where the 8th-grade teachers complained that the 7th-grade teachers hadn't taught the 7th graders anything the previous year. The 7th-grade teachers would profess innocence, declaring that they had spent six weeks on parts of speech and three on comma usage. Then the 9th-grade teachers would accuse the 8th-grade teachers of similar shenanigans, and eventually everyone would leave in a bad mood. Clearly, the commonsense notion of efficiency was stalling between grades and was directing our teachers' notions of success or lack of success as an educational community of some sort.

Efficiency and fragmentation, aspects of school commonsense, became so ingrained in institutional policy that instead of being viewed as just one way of conducting school, this approach has become the unquestioned standard type of schooling commonsense that shapes what happens in the corridors of our educational institutions. I observed this school commonsense play out in my classroom and in the graduate classes I was taking with trepidation. The most troubling aspect of this form of school commonsense was that it appeared to teach both students and teachers to depend on outside authorities, such as other teachers, texts, and the dominant societal culture, for answers, rather than to rely on their own critical judgment. Without a critical engagement with authority, another aspect of school commonsense, the traditional school approach continues to go unchallenged, leaving both teacher and student disconnected, passionless, and bored followers of the dictates of commonsense, regardless of the rightness of this traditional approach.

These initial observations about some of the implications of schooling commonsense became the catalyst for my inquiry project As I recognized the unquestioned nature of this school commonsense, my inquiry project moved toward ways to confront it and the related implications for my teacher role and relations. However, my initial inquiry work was not an example of foreseeing. Instead, I was working on my questions while at the same time being influenced by what authorities said might be a solution. For example, one solution that I found compelling was cooperative learning (Kagan, 1994), in which students work together developing academic and social skills.

I restructured many lessons and involved my students in cooperative groups as much as possible. I was very pleased with the results. Most students no longer appeared bored but were instead quite involved in what they were doing in the group. No one fell asleep in class and there was a lot of interaction. Students who in the past seldom worked were completing some if not all of their work. My classroom was definitely a changed place, and I felt I had solved the problem of boredom found in traditional schooling, a form of school commonsense.

This satisfaction didn't last long, though. As time progressed, I began to see that perhaps nothing had really changed in my classroom after all. Yes, I had altered the method of knowledge delivery through cooperative education, but I hadn't addressed the underlying commonsense that I was operating from. I was still the authority and students were still treated as empty vessels with interests that had little import in terms of my curriculum-making. I realized that just because the students were interacting with each other didn't necessarily mean that they were engaged in learning as opposed to being bored. Although it appeared on the surface that my classroom was a much different place, that was true in outward appearance only. It was as much a facade as Jay Gatsby's huge library in *The Great Gatsby* (Fitzgerald, 1995), which contained row upon row of impressive leather-bound books with engraved titles, but when opened, contained no pages.

To begin to break the hold of these cultural aspects of school commonsense, I found I needed to engage my imagination and look beyond the 'is' to the 'ought'.

Attempting to do so reminds me of an exchange between the two attorneys in the play *Inherit the Wind* (Lawrence and Lee, 1978). Drummond is interrogating Brady on the witness stand concerning what Brady thinks about certain topics. Irritated that his ready cliches do not satisfy Drummond, Brady finally in frustration declares, 'do not think about things I do not think about!' (p. 86). I too did not think about things that I saw little reason to think about, such as most aspects of the commonsense of school culture. Since I had no point of reference to start the inquiry process, I directed my imagination at the construction of commonsense in my classroom to the traditional classroom culture.

As I continued to use my imagination to envision an alternative school culture, I eventually settled upon a possible direction or intervention. This intervention was based on the possibilities of exploring and addressing forms of school commonsense through an examination of the possibilities and limits of a democratic classroom. Of course, in order to do so, I had to consider what a democratic classroom meant from my perspective as a practicing teacher. My first thought was that a democratic classroom involves a sense of student engagement contrasted with the boredom I felt in graduate studies and my students felt in my classroom. Engagement was important to me, for when students are engaged they are less likely to be passive knowledge consumers and can assume an active role in meaning-making (Apple and Beane, 1995: 16). In becoming knowledge producers, I wanted students and myself to engage in a critical conversation (Fraser, 1997: 49), where we focused on commonsense.

I also wanted a sense of community, but not a community where exclusion went unnoticed. Instead, I wanted a community/non-community where as Barth (1990) states: 'School is not a place for important people who do not need to learn and unimportant people who do' (p. 43). Put another way, we, students and teachers in such a community, would try to act in ways that would allow us to gain inclusion, see the boundaries of our inclusive club, and consistently rethink that club. In part, what this meant was that community was not an 'engineering of consent' toward a pre-determined decision, the known, that too often creates an illusion of democracy, but was instead a 'genuine attempt to honor the right of people to participate in making decisions that affect their lives' (Apple and Beane, 1995: 8). Apple (1990) describes this type of school community as one that enhances democracy at the grassroots, empowering individuals who had heretofore been largely silenced, creating new ways of linking people outside and inside of the schools together so that schooling is not seen as an alien institution, but something that is integrally linked to the political, cultural, and economic experiences of people in their daily lives (p. 40).

Finally, I believed that some shared authority was essential for democracy. While authority may be legitimate for all sorts of reasons, when authority dominates cultural practice and thought, it becomes part of the affirming culture and therefore stands in the way of critical dreaming and other attempts to move beyond the conservative force of commonsense. In addition, sharing authority helps students to move away from what Shor (1987) calls an 'authority-dependent personality' (p. 51), to one that trusts in its ability to construct its own knowledge. I wanted students to be critical readers of their society and to ask questions, such as, who said this and why should I believe this? (Apple and Beane, 1995: 13).

In practice, what this view of democracy meant to me was that students would in large measure determine the curriculum. On the surface, this idea may appear as ludicrous as Postman and Weingartner (1969) suggesting that the kindergarten teacher and the high school biology teacher change places every few years (p. 138). But it is exactly this sort of madness I desired as a participant in educational poetics. I imagined a classroom where students must choose what goals to set for themselves and how to pursue those goals so that the learning task they set for themselves is accomplished (Chanoff and Gray, 1986: 187). Students in the 7th grade would actively participate in choosing what assignments to complete and also engage in self-evaluation of their learning (O'Loughlin, 1995: 111).

Allowing students to take responsibility for their educational decisions may be a difficult step for educators to take, because many educators feel that students either cannot or will not take responsibility for themselves and that without supervision there will be chaos.

But this role and pedagogical alternative is central to democratic education, for as hooks (1994) states:

> The bottom-line assumption has to be that everyone in the classroom is able to act responsibly. It has to be the starting point that we are able to act responsibly together to create a learning environment. All too often we have been trained as professors to assume students are not capable of acting responsibly, that if we don't exert control over them, then there's just going to be mayhem. (p. 152)

As a middle school instructor, 'mayhem' is always a concern. But I wondered! Maybe mayhem is exactly what is needed to shake up and shake off the conservative influence of the affirming school culture, in this case the traditional school approach. I felt strongly that unless I allowed students some level of responsibility in their education, it would never become meaningful to them or to me, and more importantly, wouldn't be challenging school commonsense, which seemed to be creating an alienating situation in which the payoff of grades or money was all that counted, with little if any emphasis on exploiting our human potential to imagine and be free.

COMMONSENSE AND RELATIONS OF FREEDOM

Marcie's first move to participate in educational poetics was to interrogate commonsense, or put simply, to use commonsense as an object for inquiry. She examined the school commonsense by looking at the assumption that getting through material is an educational good, and her own commonsense that students are to blame for their passivity.

A focus on commonsense as an object of inquiry may appear strange because sense is usually associated with what is commonly thought to be right, desirable, and the way to live one's life. Commonsense is all of that. It is also, however, a facade, a constraint that we often drape over ourselves to appear desirable in one way or another. Understood in this way, commonsense stands in the way of madness, when madness is seen as our ability to move beyond the everyday and to see the world anew, unencumbered by the norms of what is supposed to be desirable and right. As opposed to fearing this madness, a focus on commonsense suggests how we might embrace this commonsense to become ourselves. This need to move beyond commonsense has been expressed for almost a century in the field of poetics.

> All who have given any real thought to art or beauty have recognized this essential truth, seeing in the poet's madness not something for the physician to diagnose, but fancy eternal contrast with the commonsense of the practical world. For the madness of poets is nothing more than unhampered freedom of expression of the *real self*, [emphasis added] and not of mere eccentricity or whim (Springard, 1917: 95–6).

In this way, a focus on commonsense is also connected to a type of freedom or relations of freedom where teachers like Marcie make their identities as opposed to having their identities made for them through the taken-for-granted nature of commonsense norms.

This is not to say that within this alternative approach to action research, one should throw out commonsense understandings at every opportunity. Commonsense is not a distorted belief system, it is instead a system of thought found in local and broad-based communities that has become accepted, naturalized, and reified in many instances. In this way, commonsense differs from many conceptions of ideology because commonsense is not something to be challenged in all instances. Furthermore, the confrontation of commonsense is not tied primarily to understanding limiting belief systems, as is the case in ideology, but seeing belief systems anew in imaginative and inventive ways, such as Marcie's moves from democracy to having students take responsibility for learning and the notion of mayhem. It is the tie to imagination that clearly demarcates the confrontation of commonsense from the one of ideologies.

The purpose of having commonsense being the object of inquiry is to create some space between the suffocating aspects of commonsense that limit identity formation and the making of historical futures (i.e., integrating the lessons of history into foreseeing without allowing history to dictate what one sees as true and possible), in order to experiment with understandings and practices that move beyond current normative cultural practices and thought. When this is the case, an inquirer utilizes her/his ability to be free as a basis to engage with and challenge everyday politics and move to a *deep politic* that looks at the foundations that constrain our ability to see, think, act, and imagine a world quite different from the one we participate in currently. In this sense, a deep politic is a politic that (a) goes beyond the commonsense way of thinking about politics (currently that would include a race, class, gender analysis), (b) attempts to move below the surface toward the deep reasons for why things remain the same (the affirmative aspects of culture that tie us to the past. More will be said about affirmative culture shortly), and (c) provides a methodology, a form of inquiry, to move beyond the press of the everyday that exploits our human potential to imagine and ultimately to be free. One way to see the political import of this process more clearly is to utilize *The Awakening*, as an exemplar.

In her 1899 novel, *The Awakening*, Kate Chopin chronicles the journey of the protagonist, Edna, from her beginnings as a wealthy lady of privilege schooled in the traditions of her society, to her arrival at a place of creative self-awareness where she is able and willing to interrogate the societal structures which she feels circumscribe her life to a small, suffocating existence. At one point in the novel, the author talks about Edna's husband and his unease with the changes he finds in his wife; he could see plainly that she was not herself. That is, he could see that she was becoming herself and daily casting aside that fictitious self which we assume like a garment with which to appear before the world (p. 96).

What becomes apparent in looking at this passage is that certain aspects of culture, those that support cultural stability, what Marcuse (1955) refers to as the affirmative aspects of culture, often stand in opposition to the human possibility of moving beyond the 'is' to imagine and create an 'ought' a better world in some sense of the word better. In Edna case, the affirmative aspect of culture was a series of codes and norms, of cultural commonsense tied to the Victorian ethos which narrowly defines women as solely objects of the male gaze. Most women living in Edna's time defined themselves by those cultural codes. For these women to step out of these codes was to risk being highly valued by the dominant cultural power brokers. Nevertheless, Edna's makes a bold move and while there is a price to be paid, she is exploiting her ability to remake herself based on a set of values and practices that are not solely judged on the standard of affirmative culture, the way things are done here. As a result, she is challenging commonsense and participating in relations of freedom, allowing her imagination to move beyond the dictates of the past to imagine a different role for women and herself as an individual. In much the same way, Marcie imagines a different teacher role and relations with students and therefore begins to enter into relations of freedom less beholden to the dictates of school commonsense such as the dependence on outside authorities.

Affirmative Culture and Commonsense

All cultures have traditions and orientations that emerge and continue to evolve over long periods that define or bound what it means to participate, live, and act within a specific cultural community. These traditions and orientations are the essence of what makes cultures powerful and insightful as exemplars of human possibilities. In contrast, however, affirmative culture reflects macro-societal understandings (many times Western and Capitalistic) that seep into local cultural communities and begin to reify cultural traditions thereby stopping or slowing down their evolution. For example, there is a sense in many societies, especially those of a Western persuasion, that reason is the only path toward progress.

Note once again how this differs from ideology. Where affirmative culture is an aspect of commonsense, the point of confronting affirmative culture is to look back at the codes which are forming our identities, orientations, etc., such as reason. In contrast, ideology begins with the acceptance of the dominant code of the time, the Enlightenment code of having reason be the way to move forward and make progress. In this sense, commonsense directs one to look back at their communities while also looking out in imaginative ways. In contrast, those using ideology are less prone to look back at the assumptions emerging from their communities and are less likely to center imagination and a freedom quest as a primary approach to moving forward. This macro understanding can seep into a variety of more local cultural communities and inform how they see themselves, how they move forward, how they behave, and how they solve difficult issues, etc. The 'problem', if you will, with reason as the *only* path toward progress is that this orientation is likely to keep many of the traditions anchored to the past because alternative forms of knowing, such as more intuitive or holistic ways of knowing, that might produce unexpected insights and understanding will at best be underutilized, thereby limiting the innovative nature of knowledge to push cultural practices forward.

Much the same case can be made for conflict or resistance to established cultural ways of being. Often at a societal level, conflict or resistance is viewed as a deviance of some sort that needs to be curtailed or punished (e.g.,Willis, 1977). Put differently, it is assumed that conflict and resistance needs to be policed in some fashion. However, where resistance or conflict is curtailed, conformism seeps into local cultural communities and tends to keep cultural understandings and practices from evolving. For example, Marcie relinquishes the role of policewoman teacher by shifting the responsibility to the students for learning – making them producers of knowledge. She knows this ambiguous authority structure will cause behavior issues, but the mayhem is a move toward acknowledging the importance of resistance and conflict as a challenge to affirmative culture and the way a lack of resistance and conflict ties us to the status quo. For when affirmative culture goes unchallenged, the development of culture is in the hands of those that historically have been able to forge the codes, representations, discourses, and structures (like the economy) that currently circulate as naturalized and universalistic approaches to a commonsense view of living. And it is this stagnation that anchors cultural practices and traditions to the past. So what is affirmative culture? It is the aspects of macro-societal understandings that at times seep into local cultural communities making these communities list toward the past as cultural development is slowed and at times stopped.

In this sense, affirmative culture is a specialized form of commonsense. It is a commonsense that moves across local cultural communities and infiltrates their normative structures and traditions – binding things to the past. What educational poetics attempts to do is to challenge the conserving influence of affirmative culture. It does so, by asking the inquirer (e.g., academic researcher, teacher educator, teacher, etc.) to move toward an authentic self, a self that casts aside the aspects of culture that are stable and suffocating – as Edna did with Victorian rules, and Marcie did with the school codes, and normative assumptions.

When inquirers act in this way, they are engaging in a deep politic that has the potential not only to further a human quest to be free, but as importantly enables us to rename the world based on a vision and practice of what is deemed to be right as opposed to what has solely become habit and tradition – a form of commonsense. For Marcie, she does so by looking at community, a learning community as one that is not focused on excluding 'others' to legitimate those within the community confines. Clearly, she is renaming the world based on what she considers to be right and just.

COMMONSENSE AND CONTEXT

One reason that contexts, such as the school context, are such an important part of educational poetics is that, at a deep level, contexts preform a coordinating function that makes commonsense difficult to see and to challenge (Marcuse, 1958: 66). This coordinating function helps produce an unnamed conformism to contextual priorities that becomes the watchword of a secular faith – a faith that suffocates the exploration of cultural needs and interests – and relations which are defined by economics, bureaucracies, and mass media (Reitz, 2003: 162), etc. Now, this unnamed conformism is not guaranteed; rather it is a contextual priority that requires cultural participation. And it is this participation that provides an opening, a space for inquirers using educational poetics, to see and challenge commonsense and the contexts that support commonsense. Educational poetics utilizes this opening to explore the creation of authentic selves that escape the shroud of affirmative culture and commonsense more generally. Marcie is exploding this conformism by suggesting the unthinkable (within educational terms) – mayhem and does so to challenge the context of teaching that has left her and the students in her class bored, passionless, and simply going through the motions.

The importance of context should not make one assume that educational poetics is focused on teachers and their contexts. Academics and the context of research and inquiry also need to be interrogated. One of the specific and foundational ways academics contribute to commonsense involves knowledge production. In the academic culture, for example, there is a general agreement that research, in its many variations, counts as a legitimate form of knowledge production. That is why you very likely have heard someone who's trying to get his or her point of view across say, 'The research says that…'. These speakers don't usually say 'my friend told me', or 'I feel this may be helpful given my conversation with so and so'; instead, they often use the word, and related authority of, 'research'. The challenge that commonsense poses to this authority is not only to see it – to see research, for example, as an attempt to gain authority – but also to (re)imagine it, and challenge aspects of its production which tend to suffocate our human potential, as Edna's and Marcie's potential was suffocated by the cultures of their times. What this means is that academics also need to make a 'double move' when engaging alternative approaches to inquiry like educational poetics. They need to look out at the world to consider their research project and at the same time that they need to interrogate how the codes, the norms of what it means to do research, drive their orientation to knowledge production in a way that turns back the progressive intent of the project toward a reinforcement of the status quo. Marcie, although not an academic, exemplifies this looking out and looking back process when she looks back at commonsense values concerning what counts as engagement, the linkage of 'is' and 'ought' about her boredom as she looks out at her students and the school culture.

Commonsense and the Status Quo

One way that educational poetics tries to deal with this reinforcement of the status quo is to see aesthetics, in this case poetics, as creating some distance from cultural realities (commonsense), as well as provide a way to imagine and see these realities anew (Marcuse, 1977). It is this aesthetic dimension which I see as helping cast aside the cloak of commonsense, the cultural stability that reinforces the alienated self (Fromm, 1961), as part of our quest to free ourselves and our visions from the seduction of our everyday locations and perceptions. I have found that imagination and passion enhance our ability to disengage somewhat from aspects of cultural stability that are suffocating in order to look back at the realities of our cultural worlds. Imagination and passion are not commonly associated with research. And of course that is exactly the point – to consider what knowledge production would mean (inquiry as educational poetics in this case) if inquirers bought passion and imagination to their projects as opposed to detaching themselves from research to achieve an 'objectivist' view of validity.

As Thoreau (1849) states, '[a] true account of the actual is the rarest poetry, for common sense always takes a hasty and superficial view' (p. 477). Like Thoreau, Marcie wants to go beyond the 'hasty and superficial view' of commonsense toward a more poetic or imaginative understanding of reality. When she started to cast off these garments of commonsense, her path became a search for relations of freedom, a freedom embodied in the human potential to use imagination and creativity to see anew, to move to the unknown, to be inventive.

TURNING POINT

The importance of this alternative methodology, educational poetics, is to raise questions, as opposed to becoming a rubric or framework to be followed. In our view, one such question is: what role should (if any) commonsense and relations of freedom play in the development of action research projects that aim explicitly to make our classrooms and our global society more just.

NOTE

1 This chapter includes some material first published in A. Gitlin and M. Peck (2005) *Educational Poetics: Inquiry, Freedom and Innovative Necessity.* New York: Peter Lang.

REFERENCES

Apple, M. (1990) *Ideology and Curriculum,* 2nd edn. New York: Routledge.
Apple, M. and Beane, J. (1995) *Democratic Schools.* Alexandria, VA: Association for Supervision and Curriculum Development.
Barth, R. (1990) *Improving Schools from Within.* San Francisco, CA: Jossey-Bass.
Chanoff, D. and Gray, P. (1986) 'Democratic schooling: What happens to young people who have charge of their own education?', *American Journal of Education,* 94 (2): 182–213.
Chopin, K. (1899) *The Awakening.* New York. Avon Books.
Fitzgerald, F.S. (1995) *The Great Gatsby.* New York: Scribner.
Fraser, J.W. (1997) *Reading, Writing, and Justice: School Reform as if Democracy Matters.* New York: State University of New York Press.
Fromm, E. (1961) *Marx's Concept of Man.* New York: Frederick Ungar Publishing Company.
Gatto, J. (2003) 'Against school: How public education cripples our kids and why', in *Harper's* 307 (1840) : 33–40.
Gitlin, A. and Peck, M. (2005) *Educational Poetics: Inquiry, Freedom and Innovative Necessity.* New York: Peter Lang.
hooks, b. (1994) *Teaching to Transgress: Education as a Practice of Freedom.* London: Routledge.
Kagan, S. (1994) *Cooperative Learning.* San Clemente, CA: Kagan.
Lawrence J. and Lee, R. (1978) *Inherit the Wind.* New York: Bantam Books.
O'Loughlin, M. (1995) 'Daring the imagination: Unlocking voices of dissent and possibility in teaching', *Theory into Practice,* 34 (2): 107–16.
Marcuse, H. (1955) *Eros and Civilization: A Philosophical Inquiry into Freud.* New York: Vintage Books.
Marcuse, H. (1958) *Soviet Marxism: A Critical Analysis.* New York: Columbia University Press.
Marcuse, H. (1977) *The Aesthetic Dimension: Toward a Critique of Marxist Aesthetics.* Boston: Beacon Press.
Postman, N. and Weingarten, C. (1969) *Teaching as a Subversive Activity.* New York: Delacorte Press.
Reitz, C. (2003) *Art, Alienation and the Humanities: A Critical Engagement with Herbert Marcuse.* New York: SUNY Press.
Shor, I. (1987) *Critical Teaching and Everyday Life.* Chicago, IL: University of Chicago Press.
Spingard, J.E. (1917) *Creative Criticism and Other Essays.* New York: Harcourt, Brace & Company.
Stenhouse, L. (1975) *An Introduction to Curriculum Research and Development.* London: Heinemann Books.
Thoreau, H. (1849) *A Week on the Concord and Merrimack Rivers.* From Bartlett's Familiar Quotations (1992). Boston, MA: Little, Brown.
Willis, P. (1977) *Learning to Labour: How Working Class Kids Get Working Class Jobs.* Westmead: Saxon House.

37

Participatory Action Research in Latin American Education: A Road Map to a Different Part of the World

Eduardo Flores-Kastanis,
Juny Montoya-Vargas, and
Daniel H. Suárez

"En Memoria de Orlando Fals-Borda (1925-2008)"

A THEMATIC CONCERN

How has Educational Participatory Action Research (EPAR) presented itself in Latin America (LA)? This is the question we try to address in this chapter. A handful of publications have appeared in Latin American scholarly journals over the past five years (Contreras, 2002; Chavarría and Orozco, 2006; Flores, 2006; Hamel, et al., 2004; Mendoza, 2003; Muñoz, et al., 2002; Salcedo, et al., 2005). This contrasts with the large number of EPAR projects in LA since the early 1980s that have been presented at conferences, discussed in e-mails, blogs and web sites, but never published. Why has EPAR remained out of view in publications, but very present in the field? This is our thematic concern.

Not a total or systemic explanation, our chapter is more like a road map, recording the most visible points of our landscape, leaving most of what is in between blank; gaps to be filled by those who have been there, or those willing to go and see what lies in between. We hope this road map will find its way to our Latin American colleagues at those intermediate points, so together we can chart a more detailed, and much needed, map of EPAR in LA.

MAPPING THE ROAD

We structured this chapter following the logical line of thinking that resulted at the end of our discussions, although we progressed in several cycles similar to action research itself. We used a heuristic called the Foucauldian 'triangle' (Flynn, 1988), which views social issues that matter as responses to ethical, political *and* epistemological needs. This was necessary because we were so immersed in the political aspects of education and EPAR (as Latin Americans we politicize *everything*) that we were missing the larger picture that provides a better explanation of EPAR in LA – specially the paradox of a form of research that is almost invisible in academic publications, but very visible in schools and classrooms.

We begin presenting a very brief historical view of EPAR in our three countries (Argentina, Colombia and Mexico), setting the initial context for our discussion. We focus on the commonalities in these histories that we believe may be present in all Latin American countries: how participation was overtly repressed by the State in the past, and still is to a lesser degree today. Under these conditions, radically different from more democratic countries where much has been written about action research, EPAR in LA moved in another direction, one that had to respond to the ethical requirements of morally authentic, not simulated, participation. On this point the work of Paulo Freire, the Brazilian pedagogue, becomes so important to understand EPAR in LA that it makes him a required landmark in our road map.

Following our triangle, the chapter goes on to explore the political response of EPAR in the work of Colombian sociologist Orlando Fals-Borda, a second landmark in our road map. Just as Freire's work is crucial to understanding the ethical response to EPAR in LA, Fals-Borda's work is seminal to understanding how EPAR faced the political challenges of improving people's lives in a region that strongly dislikes and actively works to neutralize community participation (see Fals-Borda and Rahman, 1991, and Fals-Borda, 1970). If Freire represents our soul as action researchers in Latin America, Fals-Borda is our fist. Neither was part of the educational community in the 1970s, outsiders to an academic establishment they considered aligned with the forms of repression so diligently and creatively developed by Latin American governments. Educated as a lawyer and a sociologist, more concerned with actual participation in communities, much less with presenting their work in academic forums, their influence is why EPAR in the 1970s and 1980s takes on a clandestine form in LA. Much work is done, but hardly any is publicly presented and discussed. Both returned to the establishment 20 years later, once they were *Paulo Freire* and *Orlando Fals-Borda*, not just some Latin Americans with radical ideas. But the absence of public discussion in academic and other forums remained, and accounts for what we see as a *refusal* by those of us who practice action research to work on the epistemological foundations of EPAR, to justify why what is done is based on and contributes to knowledge. Ethical and political matters, responding to a state of affairs that is anything but democratic, were (and still are) more important.

However, epistemological issues cannot be ignored forever, and have slowly begun to appear since 2000 in Latin American publications written by Latin American researchers. A beneficial (albeit unintended) effect of Latin America's move toward neo-liberal, 'globalized' regimes with weak democracies is that repression has adopted other modes, more economic and technocratic in nature, but more open to different forms of participation. Action researchers have taken advantage of this, allowing EPAR to start appearing in Latin American academic and professional forums, responding to epistemological matters not addressed before. Our road map begins to branch out to different regions and interests, less defined, more like rural roads slowly opening up new territories. In this new landscape we present in the last section of the chapter an initial action plan to deal with epistemological issues, in ways that are ethically acceptable and politically feasible in our particular context; inviting Latin American action researchers to participate, starting from what has already been done on EPAR epistemology in other countries, but advancing on our own terms, and openly recognizing Latin America's contribution to the field of action research, which is not a small one.

A VERY BRIEF HISTORY OF EPAR IN ARGENTINA, COLOMBIA AND MEXICO

Our conversation on how EPAR has presented itself since the late 1970s led us to recognize a number of common patterns in our three countries, among the wide array of events and people involved in the history of EPAR in Colombia, Mexico and Argentina.

Colombia has always been a democracy. But one with weak institutions, to the extent that the will of the people is acknowledged *de jure*, but *de facto* ignored. This leads to a democratic impasse, where different groups (the government, the FARC (Revolutionary Armed Forces of Colombia), the paramilitary, the drug cartels, and also many and different groups of the civil society) use different forms (legal and illegal) to make themselves heard. If a group's voice can be heard loud enough and long enough, it will prevail, and to a certain extent it will be able to exercise power. And if a group keeps to itself, other groups will leave it alone. To have power one must be in the public spotlight without crowding others out. Power is not given to anyone. It is determined by visibility. And there is always a danger in this. Who is most visible rarely speaks for the many, but usually for the select few.

Mexico, on the other hand, until 2000, was one of the most successful monarchies in the world, albeit only a six-year monarchy. Governed by the same party for over 70 years, in Mexico the sitting president was like a king, anointed instead of elected, with the entire bureaucratic, legislative and judicial systems at his (not her) beck and call for six years only. In those six years he could do as he pleased. He then chose his successor, and went into exile. Based on co-optation (as all ruling monarchies), power is granted and taken away by the will of the king and his court. If a group seemed to be gaining popular support, it would be offered a place in court. Or would be summarily executed. Most groups preferred (and eventually sought) co-optation. Some say Mexico is still this way, only now we have a new ruling party. Only time will tell.

If one is president of Argentina, the probability that one will be ousted from office (by the military, by civil uprisings, by one's own party or by the opposition) is well over 65 percent. If one also includes natural illness or death, the probability is almost 70 percent. Thus government changes regularly, in a state of constant flux, normally moving from one side of the political spectrum to the other as a wide-arc pendulum, and power is based on the use of force. Not only military force, although Argentina has suffered more than its share of violent repression. In a less obvious but just as violent way, political, financial, corporate, intellectual or popular repression is still repression. Groups that pursue social change deal with these forms of repression, opening and maintaining spaces that allow them to act. The downside is that in most occasions, groups must counter other groups with forms of repression of their own to maintain their space.

Why do we say that EPAR has evolved in similar ways in political contexts that are so different? Our conclusion is that what happens in each of our countries represents one face of a very irregular prism that eventually produces the same result: a systematic and recurring (although not necessarily intentional) program that Latin American states engage in to silence voices that ask and demand and promote social change. Strategies may be different, but the end result is the same. In Mexico EPAR was co-opted by the Mexican Ministry of Education, and adopted in all its public teacher preparation programs as the 'official' form of research so that teachers could obtain their degree. Institutionalizing EPAR is the best way to eliminate its critical stance. The best way to silence a group who wants change is to have the opposing group that wants to maintain the status quo sponsor the change initiative.

In Colombia Orlando Fals-Borda became 'the' voice of PAR, and as such any other group that intended to do PAR has first to establish their position in relation to Fals-Borda. But this also means establishing a position on other issues, not just PAR. Political positions with irreconcilable differences, which make groups that could work together not work together. Or leads to very fragile and uncomfortable alliances. Or to 'reinventing' forms of PAR that look different enough not to be associated with existing voices, like the 'Movimiento Pedagógico' of the 1980s and 1990s (Rodríguez, 2002); and 10 years later, a university-based form of EPAR related to teacher preparation embracing just the methodological aspects of PAR and ignoring its political and ethical commitments (Ávila, 2005). Different voices that rarely speak to each other.

In Argentina EPAR became the way to give voice to 'popular movements', groups of little academic stature: community groups, teacher unions, adult educators working on literacy with disenfranchised groups and agrarian communities. An early attempt in the 1960s by professors and researchers at the

University of Buenos Aires was abruptly ended by one more military coup, leading to massive emigration of academics abroad. After this attempt, EPAR became at worst a 'subversive' activity (with dire consequences under a military regime), and at best an activity that 'lacked academic rigor and could not be considered serious scholarly work'.

Strategies to silence voices demanding social change fit the particular political model of each country, and we believe that analyzing other Latin American countries would lead us to identify different strategies that achieve the same purpose. These strategies are not aimed exclusively at EPAR. Other ways of trying to achieve social change are silenced in similar ways, eliminating them from the political landscape, or making them go underground. This explains why EPAR has remained as a fringe academic movement. It emerged in the 1970s in all our countries, a loose linking pin of several popular education movements, changes in the social sciences (mainly the rise of critical theory), severe economic and political crises which hardened the position held by each regime, followed by open forms of opposition and repression, and a widening gap between the very rich and the very poor. Advocacy by groups associated with leftist tendencies led to co-optation (Mexico), repression (Argentina) or assimilation (Colombia). Although there are examples of successful EPAR projects from the 1970s onward, they are isolated local cases, short-lived for lack of support or government interference. Very few have continued over time, a trickling stream of work known by few and ignored by most. The potential for social change of EPAR, although demonstrated in isolated cases, remains unfulfilled. At least in Latin America, the double promise of EPAR (to transform the social sciences, and to achieve social and political change) is yet to be seen.

In this context, achieving social and political change is much more important than transforming the social sciences, and achieving social change in LA is primarily not a problem of economics or knowledge, but an ethical problem. This is where our road map hits its first major landmark. Paulo Freire. *Our* Paulo Freire.

PAULO FREIRE AND EPAR: THE ETHICS OF PARTICIPATION

Since Freire's first works *Education as the Practice of Freedom* (1981) and *Pedagogy of the Oppressed* (1968) were translated into Spanish in the late 1970s, his ideas on social and educational participatory research between academics and ordinary people as a constitutive part of pedagogical practice of an emancipatory nature have profoundly shaped the social and academic landscape in LA. He is also one of the few Latin American thinkers (Orlando Fals-Borda is another one) whose work has had major diffusion, comments and applications in the United States and most European countries. His work has been translated from Portuguese to more than 20 languages, with many admirers and followers around the world. He has become a 'radical hero' to militants of critical pedagogy and popular adult education and is emblematic for educational experiences aimed at 'emancipation', 'liberation' and 'radical transformation' of society (Coben, 1997). And he is Latin American. He is *our* Paulo Freire, not a European or North American author with relevant ideas for what we do. Thus his intellectual influence also includes an emotional component that needs to be understood traveling the road of EPAR in our part of the world.

Freire's contributions to the international literature come from his first works. Adopting an innovative eclecticism, Freire underscored the importance of articulating education within a wider project of political and cultural liberation, oriented to 'reading the world', and for popular education to become cultural and political action for the transformation of society, promoting cooperation, autonomous decision making, political participation and ethical responsibility. He established the methodological requirement for educators to perform participatory inquiry processes to attune their teaching with the verbal universe and sense making of the people. In *Pedagogy of the Oppressed*, he affirms:

> ... the methodology proposed requires that investigators and the people (who would normally be considered objects of that investigation) should act as *co-investigators*. The more active an attitude men and women take in regard to the exploration of their own themes, the more they deepen their critical awareness of reality and, in spelling out those themes, take possession of that reality (p. 131) ... Thematic investigation thus becomes a common push towards awareness of reality and towards self-awareness, which makes this investigation a starting point for the educational process and for cultural action of a liberating character (pp. 132–133) ... professional investigators and the people, in this sympathetic operation that is the investigation of the generative theme, are both subjects of the process. (p. 134)

Freire's emphasis is on the ethical dimensions of egalitarian participation in political and pedagogical action, not the epistemological one. Disseminated under the premises of 'dialogue' and 'horizontality' in the relationships of power and knowledge, and the ethical requirement of 'authentic' participation, his work informed a great deal of methodological and theoretical concerns in the field, and also called into question forms of intervention oriented toward co-participation in the production of knowledge, sacrificing horizontality and authentic participation (Anderson, 2002; Hernández, 2007).

The Freirian concept of participation is very provocative and fertile, transcending the field of popular education and even PAR. However, it is important to note that many uninformed and dogmatic appropriations of Freire's ideas tend to convert his ethical demands of participation, as well as other theoretical and methodological principles, into normative criteria used to distinguish 'good practices' (real 'Freirian' ones) from those that are not (Coben, 1997). A 'Freirian orthodoxy' delimits the margins of 'legitimate' dialogue and defines who are 'valid' speakers, reducing the field of interaction, clustering it and excluding it from productive exchanges with other traditions of social and pedagogical thought. It is difficult to evaluate how much influence this trend has, but we can affirm that it has contributed to presenting a prophetic and romantic vision of Freire that blurs the ethical and theoretical tenor of his intellectual production and potential contributions to the conceptual revitalization of EPAR in LA. More perniciously, it makes a significant part of Freire's intellectual production invisible.

Beyond the extensively diffused interpretation of Freire's first works, there is another Freire, whose more suggestive and renewed intellectual production comes from his academic, political and governmental experiences, often ignored outside of LA. This work has not been sufficiently read, critiqued and debated in the field of EPAR in LA, much less outside our part of the world. This later production emerges from his critical reflection on the canonized texts from his first phase (especially *Pedagogy of the Oppressed*). His later work revises many of his most radical tenets regarding participation and the possibilities and limits of social revolutionary change. Freire also reflects on his own militancy in the rows of the Party of Brazil and experience at the Office of the Secretary of Education of the Municipality of Sao Paulo (1989–1992), sharing new contributions and suggestive theoretical intuitions for teaching, schooling and educational politics and ethics.

In his last written works, especially in *Pedagogy of Hope* (1992), *Pedagogy of Freedom* (1996) and *Pedagogy of Indignation* (1997), Freire clearly shifts his concerns to the field of public school administration, and a reformulated ethics of participation. Freire expands the conceptual bases and social environments for participation and dialogue, and states the need to generate different conditions and new discursive and practical rules for a respectful and plural conversation, one that recognizes differences and dissidences in a framework of equality for the effective participation of majorities in the making, development and evaluation of public policy. This seems to be the democratic ethical imperative of the last Freire, one we need to acknowledge and enact if we are to respond to the epistemological demands placed now on EPAR.

Freirian orthodoxy, as well as many Latin American academics working with EPAR, still link Freire with extreme emancipatory political positions and a furious and urgent political radicalism, positions Freire abandoned long ago for more democratic ones derived from his social, political and personal experiences throughout the 1990s. His last intuitions and theories still have to be explored and discussed, but can potentially revitalize EPAR, setting conditions for dialogue among diverse and unorthodox communitarian, academic and social experiences that try to develop processes of co-participation for the production of knowledge with explicit intervention objectives and democratic aims. These experiences are found at the margins of educational systems in movements, networks and collectives of educators disseminated across LA, but also at the center of local and national government initiatives looking for legitimacy in the new Latin American social context. Hard to recognize and classify as PAR, they are excluded by the orthodox Freireans arguing that they are not 'Freirian', when in fact they are.

If we don't rise above this mutual distrust, our need to address epistemological concerns is severely thwarted. We need to recognize these different experiences from the margins and the center with their particular logic and contexts, understood in their own languages and modulations, thickly described and respectfully translated to other language-playing fields. A new, less dogmatic, more democratic reading of Freirian ethics will help us in this endeavor. And would make Paulo proud.

FALS-BORDA AND PAR: THE POLITICS OF PARTICIPATION

In terms of the politics of action (Noffke and Brennan, 1997), we can say that for Orlando Fals-Borda, PAR was created to transform not just the personal or the professional but the whole political arena. Working with local groups, PAR's practitioners envisioned large-scale effects such as the development of a 'sociology of liberation' aimed to overthrow the dominant power and class structures, and to ensure actual satisfaction of people's needs. 'Participation' always means political involvement, even when the project is not political itself (Fals-Borda, 1987).

Fals-Borda initiated empirical Sociology in Colombia founding the College of Sociology at the National University in 1961, oriented 'toward the liberation of the most vulnerable population of society by means of collective and organized work, the study of poverty, and toward social modernization, summarized and articulated in different research programs and communal actions that each member in turn studied and prompted' (Segura and Camacho, 1999: 27). However, by the end of the decade, sociological studies were criticized as heirs of Positivism and American Pragmatism, contributing nothing to social change. This perception, along with 'the discomfort that a remote from reality and routine-bound Academy, an incompetent State, and a dogmatic and outdated Left generated me' (Fals-Borda, quoted by Grisales, 2004) led Fals-Borda and other academics to leave the National University and work on their own.

Fals-Borda and his colleagues developed a method to systematize popular knowledge and give it back to the groups they worked with, to motivate collective action toward social and political change against oppressive powers. Doing so was called 'systematic devolution' and followed certain rules: To return local, cultural and historical materials in a systematic way and according to the political and educational level of development of the base-groups providing the information; to express results of the studies in an accessible language; to allow base-groups to control the research and how to disseminate the results of their work. Researchers should not define the tasks for research; this should be done in constant consultation with the people; to recognize general scientific techniques and put them at the service of the people; and, finally, to give intellectuals direct feedback from the bases (Fals-Borda, 1992).

Fals-Borda and other Colombian social scientists initiated the '*Rosca* of research and social action' (Parra, 1983), and developed a methodology called 'Study-Action', which evolved to Participatory Research (PE) and later to Participatory Action Research (PAR) as it is known today. (The word '*Rosca*' possesses a double connotation, one as 'circle' and a second one as a kind of nepotism, that in which people include only their friends or relatives into the circle. To use this word was meant as a political statement because it was the first time that such a negative word was used to name a research group and it was the first time that a group with such a name got legal personality.) 'This new way of looking –and maybe it is more appropriate to say of listening – was what was called PAR. As with great things, it did not have an inventor. Nobody discovered it' (Molano, 1998). This may be the case; however, PAR's introduction to the international community through the World Symposium in Cartagena (1977) led PAR to being applied in many parts of the world, earning worldwide acceptance as a legitimate perspective for knowledge production, and giving Fals-Borda international recognition as a social scientist (Grisales, 2004).

Today, the Cartagena version of PAR conserves most of its central characteristics, such as 'the reinstatement of ethics in the processes of research and social promotion, the demand of democracy as a source of political and intellectual inspiration, and the demand of subject-subject relations in the investigation' (Segura and Camacho, 1999). However, it has also experienced important changes. In its initial stages there was excessive confidence in popular knowledge, and a deeply entrenched distrust of academia. It was also deeply political, intent on achieving radical political change at all costs. Over the years, these positions have changed. 'I do not accept', says Rodríguez (in Fals Borda and Rodríguez, 1987), 'that Participatory Research is a paradigm opposed in absolute terms to academic research (p. 34) … it is not about popularizing social knowledge by means of watering it down but of democratizing the knowledge produced by the university by making it be committed to the popular cause' (p. 38). Over the years, it has opened up to the idea of confrontation and co-existence of alternative paradigms, and therefore greater epistemological and theoretical flexibility: 'Although it did not achieve its political aims, PAR has enriched the national and international perspectives of social investigation' (Segura and Camacho, 1999).

From two different directions, one coming from an ethical concern, another from a political demand, EPAR in LA has moved in 40 years to the point where it is now ethically required, and politically necessary, to address its epistemological needs. Our road map leads to this intersection, with uncharted terrain before us. Where to continue from here is what we present in the last part of this chapter.

KNOWLEDGE FOR EPAR: AN INITIAL ACTION
PLAN FOR LATIN AMERICA

Latin America has not yet made an epistemological contribution that equals the contributions of Freire or Fals-Borda. Yet we don't need another radical hero. This is something that all of us have to do. We need knowledge produced by EPAR to be shared and used in academic and practical fields. As we specified and problematized our historical peculiarities, we also reflected on how critically recognizing our specificity can contribute to revitalize and reconceptualize EPAR in our part of the world. Our action plan responds to this epistemological need, a new direction on our road map to places yet to visit.

We first need to accept the role that the State has played and could play in configuring the scientific field in general, and of EPAR in particular. The State is a fundamental actor in LA, establishing what is 'valid knowledge' in scientific and academic sectors, and a key player to legitimate, validate, support, finance and develop certain modalities of social research at the expense of others. The Latin American State played a central role in the loss of scientific and political legitimacy of EPAR. However, during the last two decades, neo-liberal policies have led the State to relinquish its hold on the support of culture, education and science, leaving the field to academics and researchers, especially in terms of what is to be considered valuable knowledge, and how the main actors and public institutions reposition themselves in the 'knowledge production' market. Under this new logic, some government policies have aimed at promoting social, public health and productive and/or educational initiatives by empowering actors in local communities, favoring isolated EPAR initiatives, via public calls for proposals or financing these initiatives directly. These policies have generated many questions relating to different kinds for EPAR. Two of these questions, which our action plan focuses on, are:

1   How to address the theoretical and methodological imperative of authentic participation of all actors (researchers and community members) in designing, developing and validating research projects?
2   How to produce critical knowledge effectively that leads to real transformation and change?

Definitions of 'participation' are important, to recuperate and critically reconstruct experiences involving 'authentic participation' and differentiate them from those derived from repressive strategies that distort the subject-subject relationship. We now have an ample social diffusion and dispersion of varieties of action research and approaches to knowledge building that require participation of researchers and social actors (teachers, popular educators, community members, social organizations), as well as certain (unclear) orientations to change or transform the realities of these groups. It is important to understand how these groups conceptualize participation theoretically, and how participation really presents itself. This work of reconceptualization, systematization and recovery is critical to identify and reconstruct real EPAR experiences, regardless of the fact that they 'fit' or not what is now delimited as 'EPAR', or use or not 'accepted' EPAR discourse. It can give us clues on how to rethink and generate a more sensible theoretical and methodological language for our region.

One of the peculiarities derived from the historic and political construction of EPAR in LA is that it has found an important space for experimentation and development in the social and community field, especially in initiatives of popular organizations and social movements to produce knowledge collectively about their own interests, problems and struggles, supported or not by the State, with or without the collaboration of researchers. In this context, an action plan to consolidate processes of authentic participation, and to move ahead to engage in 'transformative actions' intentionally makes sense. These concerns have primacy over questions solely focused on epistemological validity, methodological issues, and how 'critical' knowledge derived from EPAR really is. *The first step in achieving this is fundamentally changing the language we use when talking of and about EPAR. We need to speak in less dogmatic and more inclusive terms of what we do and aim to achieve, understanding the tentative nature of knowledge, and the ethical imperative of knowledge in a democratic society.* This is something we Latin Americans have to learn how to do, and we need to start doing *now*.

Our history has caused EPAR to conform itself as a social practice focused on 'contestation' and 'resistance' that seeks drastic change in its extreme manifestations, or seeks to create spaces and positions of influence for certain groups displaced from decision-making processes in its less radical versions. Both practices make these groups more visible and influential, but do little for real social change. These conditions of knowledge production have given EPAR a peculiar form of development in our countries, one significantly different from forms adopted in more democratic countries, where spaces and policies are institutionally framed, and where EPAR is under the patronage of academic and university groups that are protected and provide relative protection for groups outside them that engage in EPAR. In protected space radical language is useful, even expected. In unprotected space, it leads to exclusion and repression.

Our tendency toward 'activism' and radical political intervention has caused a considerable number of EPAR projects to disdain the critical potential of the knowledge they generate, or to acknowledge it in not very rigorous terms. As EPAR favors political practices of 'resistance', much of the knowledge gathered in the field lacks systematic reflection on the conditions and criteria used to generate this knowledge, as well as the epistemological strategies that guarantee its value and impact as social knowledge. This lack of interest to reflect on and publish what is done, or to try to agree on common methods effectively eliminates opportunities to share political and cultural practices that have achieved social change, and turn those experiences into critical social inquiry. The absence of active and public reflection makes the knowledge we produce conceptually weak, more aligned with pamphlets and slogans so extreme that they become meaningless. Knowledge becomes dogmatic, losing the critical value it may have had at some point.

Many social experiences that achieve the collective construction of critical knowledge and include effective practices of transformative community intervention are 'wasted' because of a certain 'indolent rationality' that affects our practice of intellectual production and how we recognize and revisit research problems in our part of the world (Santos, 2006), *because we can't agree on how to talk about our work without carrying a political flag or an epistemic chip on our shoulder*. We cannot engage in conversations that are reciprocally productive with other experiences; and we are not in the position to dispute the 'truth' that institutionalized academic definitions of EPAR generated in Europe or in the English-speaking knowledge producer countries take for granted, but which does not represent Latin America's different political, social and educational experiences. This division in the field of EPAR between 'social experiences' and 'academic experiences', as well as the absence of horizontal conversations and translations between the social and the academic, explain why today EPAR in Latin America is loosely structured and of little social or academic legitimacy to produce knowledge collaboratively with real emancipatory and transformative political power.

This is why it is not convenient to agree on a single and exclusionary definition of EPAR in Latin America, without recognizing the heterogeneous experiences and epistemic and methodological heterodoxy that in many ways represents strategies against an authoritarian State or to maintain a radical language that does not describe what EPAR has actually been able to achieve, much less than we would like, but much more than meets the eye. Following Freire, we need to open and maintain a horizontal dialogic conversation between all actors in the EPAR field, embracing our differences. Following Fals-Borda, we must do so as a measure of political action, not to maintain the status quo but to change it.

Our plan obeys two reasons. On the one hand, because of its degree of social capilarization, not all EPAR experiences that have and are taking place have been systematized and published, making it difficult to identify them. One group resists labeling its work as EPAR because it will not be viewed as legitimate research. Another group that does EPAR from academic or state initiatives has difficulties voicing the authentic participation of social and community actors. On the other hand, in order to be published, what has been done is rephrased to look more 'academic', and this translation makes the basic tenets that have been followed in reality invisible. We need to bring these groups who are really doing EPAR together to start talking about what we do and why we do it without alienating each other. We need to generate a new language for EPAR that allows these groups to talk to each other, recognizing attempts made in academia, even though they sacrifice participation in their quest for knowledge, and recognizing attempts made by social and community groups, even though they sacrifice knowledge in their quest for social change. We need a language that is less dogmatic, less 'critical', less orthodox and less exclusionary, more inclusive, more focused on finding common ground, more accepting of heterodoxy and more Latin American and less Anglo-European. Opposites in traditional linear reasoning clash and attack each other. Opposites in dialectic reasoning are the necessary requirement to achieve new knowledge that synthesizes both. At last in Latin America opposites are visible. It is time to work with both to design a new platform to generate knowledge relevant to all.

This chapter in the Handbook is the first action of our plan. We hope it will not be the only action we undertake. We invite Latin American action researchers to participate, based on Latin America's contribution to the field regarding the ethics and politics of EPAR, a topic that has only begun to be discussed in more epistemologically driven contexts. *Praxis* is, after all, action that is conceptually true and *morally just*. We cannot claim a contribution to EPAR epistemology, but we can speak, and speak loudly, to the ethical and political issues of action that is just, as we face these issues day after day in our societies in Latin America, which are profoundly unjust.

REFERENCES

Anderson, G.L. (2002) 'Hacia una participación auténtica: Deconstruyendo los discursos de las reformas participativas en educación. [Toward authentic participation: Deconstructing discourse from participative reforms in education]', in M. Narodowski, M. Nores and M. Andvada (eds), *Nuevas tendencias en políticas educativas: Estado, mercado y escuela*. Buenos Aires: Temas.

Ávila, R. (2005) 'La producción de conocimiento en la investigación-acción pedagógica (IAPE): Balance de una experimentación. [Knowledge production in Pedagogic Action Research (PAR): Balance of an experiment]', *Revista colombiana de educación*, (49): 15–36.

Chavarría, M.C. and Orozco, C. (2006) 'Ecoanálisis como puerta de entrada a la decodificación de lo cotidiano: Hacia una educación posible. [Ecoanalytical approaches as entry points towards the decoding of everyday life: Envisioning possibilities in education', *Actualidades Investigativas en Educación*, 6 (3): 1–36.

Coben, D. (1997) *Radical Heroes: Gramsci, Freire and the Politics of Adult Education*. New York: Garland.

Contreras, R. (2002) 'La Investigación Acción Participativa (IAP): Revisando sus metodologías y sus potencialidades. [Participatory Action Research (PAR): reviewing its methods and possibilities]', in J. Durston and F. Miranda (eds), *Experiencias y metodología de la investigación participativa*. Santiago de Chile: ECLAC.

Fals-Borda, O. (1970) *Ciencia propia y conocimiento popular*. [Local Science and Popular Knowledge]. México: Editorial Nuestro Tiempo.

Fals-Borda, O. (1987) *Ciencia propia y colonialismo intelectual: Los nuevos rumbos*. [Local Science and Intellectual Colonialism: New directions]. Bogotá: Carlos Valencia Editores.

Fals-Borda, O. (1992) 'La ciencia y el pueblo: Nuevas reflexiones. [Science and the People: New Reflections]', in M.C. Salazar (ed.), *La investigación-acción participativa: Inicios y desarrollos*. Bogotá: Editorial Popular.

Fals-Borda, O. and Rodríguez, C. (1987) *Investigación participativa*. [Participative Research]. Montevideo: Instituto del Hombre-Ediciones de la Banda Oriental.

Fals-Borda, O. and Rahman, M.A. (eds) (1991) *Action and Knowledge: Breaking the Monopoly with Participatory Action-Research*. New York: The Apex Press.

Flores, K.E. (2006) 'Encontrando al profesor "virtual": Resultados de un proyecto de investigación-acción. [Finding the "virtual" professor: Results of an action-research project]', *Revista Mexicana de Investigación Educativa*, 11 (28): 91–128.

Flynn, T. (1988) 'Foucault as Parrhesiast: His last course at the Collège de France', in J. Bernauer and D. Rasmussen (eds), *The Final Foucault*. Cambridge, MA: The MIT Press. pp. 102–18.

Freire, P. (1968) *Pedagogy of the Oppressed*. New York: Seabury.

Freire, P. (1981) *La Educación como práctica de la libertad*. [Education as the Practice of Freedom]. México, DF: Siglo XXI.

Freire, P. (1992) *Pedagogy of Hope: Reliving Pedagogy of the Oppressed*. New York: Continuum.

Freire, P. (1996) *Pedagogy of Freedom: Ethics, Democracy, and Civic Courage*. Lanham, MA: Rowman & Littlefield.

Freire, P. (1997) *Pedagogy of Indignation*. Boulder, CO: Paradigm Publishers.

Grisales, P. (2004) Orlando Fals-Borda. from http://www.universia.net.co

Hamel, R.E., Brumm, M., Carrillo, A., Loncon, E., Nieto, R. and Silva, E. (2004) '¿QUÉ HACEMOS CON LA CASTILLA? La enseñanza del español como segunda lengua en un currículo intercultural bilingüe de educación indígena. [WHAT DO WE DO WITH CASTILE? Teaching Spanish as a second language in an intercultural bilingual curriculum in indigenous education]', *Revista Mexicana de Investigación Educativa*, 9 (20), 83–107.

Hernández, N. (2007) *Participación e incidencia de la sociedad civil en las políticas educativas: El caso colombiano*. [Participation and the incidence of civil society in educational policies: The Case of Colombia]. Buenos Aires: FLAPE.

Mendoza, V.M. (2003) 'Nuevos horizontes de diálogo para el modelo de Investigación-Acción en el campo de la educación. [New horizons for dialogue on the Action-Research model in the field of education]', *Revista del Centro de Investigación: Universidad La Salle*, 5 (20), 27–42.

Molano, A. (1998) 'Cartagena revisited: From the 1977 World Symposium', in O. Fals-Borda (ed.), *Participación popular: Retos del futuro*. Bogotá: ICFES, IEPRI, Colciencias. pp. 3–10.

Muñoz, J.F., Quintero, J. and Munévar, R.A. (2002) 'Experiencias en investigación-acción-reflexión con educadores en proceso de formación. [Experiences with reflective-action-research with student teachers]', *Revista Electrónica de Investigación Educativa*, 4 (1).

Noffke, R.S.S. and Brennan, M. (1997) 'Reconstructing the politics of action in action research', in S. Hollingsworth (ed.), *International Action Research: A Casebook for Educational Research*. New York: Routledge.

Parra, E. (1983) Investigación-acción en la Costa Atlántica: Evaluación de La Rosca, 1972–1974. [Action-Research in the Atlantic Coast: Evaluation of La Rosca, 1972–1974].CA: FUNCOP.

Rodríguez, A. (2002) 'El movimiento pedagógico: Un encuentro de los maestros con la pedagogía. [The 'Movimiento Pedagógico': An encounter of teachers with pedagogy]', in H. Suárez (ed.), *20 años del movimiento pedagógico: Entre mitos y realidades*. Bogotá: Editorial Delfín. pp. 15–60.

Salcedo, L.E., Forero, F., Callejas, M.M., Pardo, A. and Oviedo, P.E. (2005) 'Los estilos pedagógicos y la investigación-acción: Implicaciones en el desarrollo profesional de los docentes universitarios. [Pedagogic styles and action-research: Consequences for university professors' professional development]', *Pedagoga y Saberes*, 23.

Santos, B.D. S. (2006) *Renovar la teoría crítica y reinventar la emancipación social*. [Renovating critical theory and reinventing social emancipation]. Buenos Aires: CLACSO.

Segura, N. and Camacho, Á. (1999) 'En los cuarenta años de la sociología Colombiana. [Forty years of Colombian sociology]', *Revista de Estudios Sociales*, 4(Agosto), 23–35.

Suárez, D.H. (ed.) (2006) *Latinoamericana: Enciclopedia contemporánea de América Latina e do Caribe*. [Latinoamericana: Contemporary encyclopedia of Latin America and the Caribbean]. Río de Janeiro: Laboratorio de Políticas Públicas (UERJ) y Boi Tempo.

38

Teacher Development and Political Transformation: Reflections from the South African Experience

Maureen Robinson and Crain Soudien

Teacher development has been at the heart of recent moves to improve the South African educational system from that inherited by the first democratically elected government in 1994 (Welch, 2002). Against the backdrop of the apartheid government's discriminatory policies in education, which had the effect of eroding the substance of teaching and learning processes in black schools, central to the new policy approach has been the ideal of a capacitated and empowered teaching corps. Many initiatives have emerged in the country in response to this vision. What we do in this chapter is reflected on the work of the new government itself in this arena. In focusing on the link between teacher development and educational change in a context of social and political transformation, we look at how the new authorities conceptualized, structured and carried out a significant teacher development initiative. We make the argument that this initiative was informed by an understanding of the centrality of teacher work in educational change but failed to engage sufficiently with both the legacy which accompanies teachers into their current situation and the impact of ancillary policy development in arenas, such as curriculum reform and teacher employment strategies.

The chapter is structured around four distinct but connected sections. The first part consists of an introductory discussion of inquiry approaches to teacher development, the second moves on to a consideration of the South African context, the third provides a brief description of the national intervention and the

final section works with data generated out of a series of discussions and interviews with key trainers involved with the intervention. Important in the approach
taken in this chapter is an attempt to understand the relationship (and potential
contradiction) between teacher voice and systemic regulation within curriculum
innovation. The concept 'voice' is consistent with an inquiry-based or action
research-oriented model of teacher development, with curriculum innovation
emerging mainly from teachers' own personal and professional aspirations
and actions. 'Regulation' refers to a teacher development and curriculum
innovation strategy that is based on a national agenda, driven by a central political vision.

Cognisant as policy makers in South Africa have been of the importance of stakeholder participation, ironically, the nature of much of the country's reform has been
characterized by a top-down approach. This ambiguity has pervaded much of the
country's policy work and is evident in important legislation such as the school governance regulations (see Soudien and Sayed, 2004). Strong centralist inclinations
are evident in the approach the Department of Education has taken to issues such
as the appointment of teachers. In the case of teacher development, the argument
for this approach has been the urgency of protecting the new national project and of
building social cohesion against the fissiparous possibilities that inhere in leaving
the responsibility for this kind of work to atomized and independent structures.
A second position argues that many teachers in the country do not have the professional expertise or academic background to formulate their own curriculum goals,
and that it is the task of a national government to support a streamlined and coherent approach to educational renewal.

The question motivating this chapter is: how does the community of teachers
participate in a national agenda of teacher development, and at the same time
maintain its own ability to explore professional meaning in education? Is the
exploring of professional meaning (for example, through action research) undermined when the state has already defined the goals and content of education,
however 'democratic' these may be? Behind these questions is a concern about
the dangers of a state-led project which assumes that because the South African
teaching corps has been so enfeebled by their apartheid experience, only a
tightly scripted reform agenda will change and/or improve teacher capacity.
Central to this concern is our argument that it is precisely this experience of
apartheid which needs to be engaged with in a way which acknowledges the
complex history which teachers bring to the present. Our contention is that critical elements of many teachers' experience (not all) over the past 20 years, such as
their participation in reflective exercises about their practice and role in the education process, in organizations such as teacher unions which understand teachers as people with possibility, are fundamentally underplayed. We are under no
illusions about the scale of the difficulties that teachers bring from their past and
we discuss some of these issues below, but we wish to assert the signal importance of working with teachers as agents of possibility who have the capacity to
intervene in their own fates.

In the context of these opening remarks, the central dilemma discussed in this chapter is that of the ways in which teachers' personal and professional learning can work in symbiosis with systemic educational change, so that the political context of policy change engages meaningfully with the professional context of teaching. Our specific area of concern is systemic approaches to educational renewal rather than small cases of classroom-based action research. Such questions are crucial at this juncture in South Africa (and perhaps globally too) as we are simultaneously talking here about the development of society as a whole, the advancement of communities, as well as the learning of individuals. Action research in this view is, therefore, fundamentally about the politics of position. In this politics the location of the self in relation to the self is crucial as a statement of personal ethics, but it is the larger question of the self in relation to the social and the limits and possibilities in that relationship that are important to understand.

AN INQUIRY-ORIENTED APPROACH TO TEACHER DEVELOPMENT

Approaches to educational change have over the years undergone a variety of orientations (Lieberman, 1998). The orientation informing the argument in this chapter is that which places teachers at the center of school change, which focuses on how teachers themselves make meaning of the change, which argues the interlinking of personal and professional learning (Fullan, 1991). Pivotal, however, as suggested above, is the dialogical relationship between self and context or self and the social.

The core principles and values of this approach have been summarized as involving teachers as learners, active participation by teachers, collaboration, collegiality and conversation, cooperation and activism (Sachs, 2000); as containing notions of emancipation and empowerment of teachers, the establishment of self-critical, self-reflecting communities, the ability to forge contracts based on moral responsibility, critical friendship and trust (Day and Hadfield, 2004); as including mutual trust, caring support, constructive critique and collaborative norms (Stevenson, 1995); and as being based on the power of action through inquiry (Burnaford et al., 2001).

Much of this orientation has been developed working with teachers in relatively stable and well-resourced societies, like the United States, Australia or the United Kingdom, where particular assumptions of the context of teaching and learning may well be prevailing. Even in such contexts, however, the difficulties of translating reflection into systematic school-based research have been acknowledged. Peters (2004), for example, writing from Australia, argues that more attention needs to be paid to 'examining the assumptions that underpin any associated expectations [of teacher research], and determining the nature of the conditions that will enable such expectations to be achieved' (p. 553). She identifies a number of conditions that support teacher research, for example, teacher expertise, shared priorities, the existence of an 'inquiry stance', time and integration into normal workload (p. 552).

Different views prevail about the relationship between action research and the broader social context. While in most cases being cognisant of the broader systemic environment, it is interesting to note that specific action research initiatives are often written from the perspective of a relatively low identification with the political imperatives underpinning the change agenda. Day and Hadfield (2004), for example, specifically motivate the need to rediscover the power of teacher choice because of the centralized, standards-driven change agenda in the United Kingdom that has undermined the traditional autonomy of teachers. Teacher development, they argue, has been limited 'to those activities which promote the agenda of 'the system' (p. 577), something which needs to be cautioned against. McNiff (2002) describes the power of action research in the realm of the personal, the relational and the broadly social. Less clear in her account, however, is a sense of how the personal and the relational articulate with systemic or political issues.

The difficulty of linking individual teacher change, school development and broader systemic change is noted by Hargreaves et al. (1998), in their introduction to the *International Handbook of Educational Change*. As they put it: 'While we have learnt a lot about how to improve individual schools or small clusters of schools … we are only just beginning to understand the challenges of scaling reform up from small samples of improving schools, to entire school systems' (p. 6). Termed the 'implementation problem' (Lieberman, 1998: 17), this insight has important implications for countries undergoing fundamental social change and gives rise to important questions about the relationship between policy and practice.

A DIFFERENT SOCIAL AND HISTORICAL CONTEXT

In an attempt to interrogate this theory of how teachers and systems change, this chapter looks at some of the debates on educational change from a different historical and geographical lens, asking how these principles play themselves out in a context that is different from the one in which they were conceptualized. In contrast to the context from which the change literature discussed above emanates, the educational change process in South Africa has, since the advent of democracy in 1994, displayed a high level of engagement with the national political and social goals of nation-building. With this has come a concomitant emphasis on the strong relationship between educational practice and social transformation. Such fundamental social goals are pursued, however, within a much more difficult context for teacher learning than that from which the change literature emanates. In this respect one could say that the context for change in South Africa is more able to rely on the macro or 'big picture' of social transformation, but less able to rely on the micro or 'small picture' of teacher learning, and the questions become, therefore: What can we learn about the conditions that enable personal and organizational, as well as systemic change? What dilemmas, tensions and contradictions exist in this relationship?

The questions raised here do not in any way attempt to contradict the theory of change that has as its starting point a commitment to teacher engagement with the change process. Rather they build on a strong tradition of action research in South Africa and an action research philosophy that pre-dates the end of the apartheid era. This tradition built on the strong culture of resistance that existed among many teachers during the apartheid era and was firmly located within an emancipatory framework, with action research being conceptualized as a powerful strategy for challenging authoritarian forms of educational practice. This tradition of action research assumed – almost without thinking it could be otherwise – that there was a close link between the personal, the professional and the political (Van den Berg and Meerkotter, 1994; Robinson and Meerkotter, 2003). The writings are well captured in a small volume entitled *Emancipatory Education and Action Research* (Davidoff et al., 1993) containing reflections by educators on the deep political role of the teacher and the contribution of action research to wider social change.

One of the central principles of action research is that it is based on the real questions of real teachers, so that by implication teacher development becomes located within the real conditions of teachers' work. The challenging context for teacher development in South Africa has been outlined in a range of studies. Adler and Reed (2002), for example, note a number of difficulties impacting on teacher 'take-up' of a particular in-service programme. These included a lack of educational resources, the multilingual nature of many classrooms, a culture of following 'prescriptions' (p. 122) and, in some cases, a limited subject and pedagogic knowledge base (p. 130). Fleisch (2002) also notes that there are schools that can be described as mediocre or dysfunctional, and that these schools require particular interventions. In a survey on reasons for potential attrition in education (ELRC, 2005), it was found that more than half of the 20,626 teachers surveyed in all regions of South Africa would leave the profession if they had the chance, the main 'push' factors being poor remuneration, challenging working conditions, poor relationships with the education department, a lack of respect for the profession and stress due to transformation in education, such as the implementation of new curricula (p. 25). Hargreaves (1998) has argued that teachers' emotions play a fundamental role in their willingness or otherwise to embrace educational change. The low morale of the teachers in the ELRC study certainly sound a warning cry to those assuming positive teacher engagement with change initiatives.

Noffke and Brennan (2004), looking at the global context of education, argue that it is the very 'conditions that cry out for action research [that] make its realization difficult' (p. 8). Taking this point to a regional, rather than global level, the question becomes – how feasible is an action research approach under these conditions described above? And in a situation where teacher development is seen as a tool for social transformation, one would need to ask if an action research approach *promotes* – or *depends on* – conditions of teacher professionalism, collegial cultures and a well-resourced system of support.

A SPECIFIC CURRICULUM INTERVENTION

In order to locate the discussion about action research and policy change, it is necessary to give some background about the national school curriculum introduced in South Africa in recent years. The Revised National Curriculum Statements (RNCS) were introduced into schools, starting with Foundation Phase (Grades 0–3) in 2004, and moving to Intermediate and Senior Phases (Grades 4–9) in 2005. The RNCS was a second national curriculum renewal intervention after the advent of democracy in 1994. It was a streamlined and revised version of the first new national curriculum, which was introduced in 1997 and subsequently heavily critiqued for its complexity.

The RNCS adopts an outcome-based approach as the form around which teaching and learning is constructed. It is underpinned by seven generic critical outcomes toward which all learning should be directed. These include critical thinking, the ability to organize and manage information, communication, and literacy in science and technology. In addition, each learning area has its own set of discipline-specific outcomes, which are linked to particular assessment standards for each grade of schooling.

This new curriculum is framed within an extensive set of other new policies impacting on schools aiming at the attainment of equality and equity in the system. Underpinning these initiatives is the Manifesto on Values, Education and Democracy (Department of Education, 2001), with its ten core values of democracy, social justice and equity, equality, non-racism and non-sexism, *ubuntu* (human dignity), respect and reconciliation.

The implementation of these policies is aimed at fundamentally overhauling almost every component of education in the former apartheid state and addresses virtually every aspect of teachers' lives, from school admission to quality management, classroom methodology, learning content, broader goals and visions, school organization and so on.

Teachers' orientation to the RNCS was designed as a five-day programme, offered during school holidays as a generic training for all regions in the country. On Day 1 teachers discussed the deeper principles underpinning the new curriculum – the fundamental values of the Constitution, the principles of the revised national curriculum (social justice, human rights, healthy environment, inclusivity) and the eight learning areas of the curriculum (Languages, Mathematics, Life Orientation, Economic and Management Sciences, Technology, Natural Sciences, Social Sciences and Arts and Culture). Day 2 introduced (or reminded) teachers of the range of policies informing their work: policies on religion, HIV/Aids, inclusive education, multi-grade classes, consolidating these all in terms of an agenda for social justice. Day 3 focused on assessment policies, assessment standards and the nature of progression, while Days 4 and 5 concentrated on the development of learning programmes, work schedules and lesson plans. The programme concluded with the identification of monitoring, evaluation and support structures at schools, and teachers in the same geographical areas making arrangements for a common plan of action regarding the implementation of the revised curriculum in their schools.

A CRITICAL ASSESSMENT OF THE INTERVENTION

The impact of this intervention can only be properly assessed through an examination of how teaching and learning is taking place on the classroom floor. These kinds of examinations have not yet been done systematically in the country. There is a great deal of evidence, however, that the schooling system is failing to produce substantial learner achievement. Literacy and numeracy levels in the country have been shown to be poor (see Taylor and Vinjevold, 1999; Taylor, 2006; Soudien, 2007). What is not known is the relationship between the country's policy interventions and these learner outcomes. We cannot, therefore, say with any degree of certainty that curriculum interventions are such as described above account for what is happening in classrooms around the country today. It is possible, however, to suggest the strengths and weaknesses of interventions such as these, particularly in relation to the overall goal of building teacher capacity to deliver quality education. We do this by drawing on the insights of seven curriculum advisers from the Western Cape province, all of whom were key participants involved in the delivery of the intervention. Discussions took place with these key informants in one focus group interview (March 2005) and four individual interviews (March 2007). Their reflections draw attention to key issues in the process. These, we suggest, raise some interesting debates about this intervention.

In assessing the initiative in which they were involved, all of the respondents, without exception, were critical of how it engaged with the realities that teachers brought with them from their pasts, citing difficult conditions, demoralization, inadequate and unequal resourcing, and poor management and leadership. In assessing this initiative this is an important point of departure for our discussion because it highlights the centrality of the question of the politics of location. How does an initiative which is about teacher improvement understand its own environment? How much, in other words, does it model for the teachers the deep attribute of self-reflection that is the sub-text of the competencies it is expecting them to demonstrate in their own work?

Critical in what the initiative expected of teachers was the development of a classic action-research disposition. As one respondent said, '(t)his involves coming up with an issue, thinking out a problem, planning for it, collecting data and reflecting on it ...'. While action research itself never explicitly premised or preceded the training that was provided, in the broad constructivist orientation of the Department of Education it certainly presumed that the qualities of the reflective teacher, one who was able to recognize and act upon challenges, would rise to the fore.

Valuable as this positive orientation to teacher development was, it was hedged in by ambiguity, including the ambiguities and contradictions of centralization and devolution of responsibility to the individual teacher herself discussed above. There remained a pervasive anxiety in the process about what could be expected of teachers. As a consequence of this anxiety, the initiative was framed and delivered in a homogenized and undifferentiated way. One of the respondents explained, for example, that 'cultural' factors (such as the working conditions of teachers, teacher qualifications and competencies, school cultures and human resources) had played, in his view, a lesser role in devising the strategy for the teacher development initiative.

The core of the difficulties confronting teacher development in South Africa are evident in the responses of the group of state-employed curriculum advisers we worked with in this exercise. Audible in their responses was the necessity for a centrally steered programme of teacher development. At the same time, as the data we adduce shows, they were, so to speak, critiquing this very approach.

There was a powerful argument being made by many of the respondents that a strongly state-steered initiative was necessary for the country. The reason for this, as they saw it, was that the national department had to offer one generic training model to teachers all over the country. This was important because 'you would make sure that everybody got the same message and so then you can't say that you didn't know what you were doing. You had one voice coming through and that voice was the voice of the national policy'. Probed about the potential negative consequences of offering teachers 'one message', their answer was simply: 'I think that's the correct thing to have done. Given our history, it was the correct thing to do', Anticipating the critique that this implied a silencing of teachers' voices, the response was that the curriculum on which the intervention had been based was revised precisely because of the heavy criticism of the earlier curriculum, thereby showing that the Department of Education had 'listened'. These respondents were confident that sufficient opportunities had been built into the generic training model for teachers to engage and make meaning of what was being presented.

They conceded, however, that a number of assumptions had been made about the conditions that existed in teachers' working lives to support engagement with fundamental curriculum change. As they put it: 'The biggest assumption we made was to say that teachers would be more than willing and excited by the possibility of developing their own curriculum within a national framework'. In addition, assumptions had been made that 'teachers would grab this opportunity for a change in curriculum … that [they] wanted to bring about political change … [or] whether people were prepared to deal with the consequences of change'. In concrete terms, it had become clear that many teachers did not want to share their work, resisted team teaching, had a dearth of content knowledge, did not want colleagues and peers in their classrooms, did not have 'nice small classes', and that many lacked the most basic resources.

The theory of teacher development underpinning this paper argues that sustainable and meaningful change depends on teachers being able to identify with the principles and procedures of the change, and to see its purpose in their own environment. For the departmental advisers, who shared a deep commitment to social justice in the country, it seemed an obvious move to spend the first two days of the orientation programme discussing the underlying values and policies of the Constitution, and the next three days linking these to classroom methodologies. To their surprise, they found that the majority of teachers evaluated this sequence of activities negatively, indicating their preference to start with looking at learning programmes. As one adviser commented: 'Maybe we in our minds had it clear how these things were going to interface with one another but maybe teachers don't see it that way, they are concerned with what's happening in the classroom'.

Interestingly, when the individual respondents were interviewed two years later the *sotto voce* critique which surfaced on the edges of the earlier descriptions of what had happened became much more strident. A respondent, in reflecting on what they had done, suggested that '(w)e did not have a full grasp of the issues involved'. While this retrospective look repeated much of the commentary heard the first time, namely, that resourcing and so on were important, significantly, the context evoked in the more critical discussion had a great deal more to do with the politics of position.

Acknowledgment of the demoralized state of the profession was made repeatedly by a number of the interviewees. Teachers were looked at in a much deeper way. The legacy of the country, and the way it not only divided the country but systematically positioned black teachers as inferior, the lasting impact of underresourcing on teachers' sense of their professional selves, featured strongly in the analysis that they made of the intervention. Critical, for example, in the way the interviewees described the process was the failure of the programme to understand how *really* to involve teachers in relation to and with a consideration of their actual teaching conditions.

> There was little teacher participation in the whole process, e.g., the development of the curriculum. This alienates the teacher. The expectations on the teacher are too high. Teachers are being made to for go their holidays in order to attend training workshops. As a result, teachers do not do this willingly or wholeheartedly (interview).

What was needed, it was suggested by the same respondent, was 'a need to interrogate our theories and come up with what works in our local context'. As a consequence, many felt that the intervention was essentially a once-off initiative that failed to deal with the demands of sustainability. Its emphasis, it was felt, echoing the criticism that Jansen (1999) has made about the symbolic significance of policy, was on form. She argued, '(h)onestly, at this stage I do not think the national strategy for teacher development is comprehensive enough.

I think (it) … has failed completely. I have been involved in the training, and the training emphasizes policy rather than strategy …. What you find is that teachers are working within the policy, but they are still using the old transmission strategies'. Another commented that the approach had been 'hasty … too intermittent, too thin in strategy, too rich in policy …'.

Coming out of these observations is a sense that the training succeeded in imparting to teachers a sense of the new policy vocabulary, but little sense of how they could engage strategically with the conditions of their context. A respondent observed that '… teachers have mistakenly interpreted this to mean that if they involve learners in group-work, then they have transformed classroom practice …. Teachers have kept themselves very busy, but very little learning is actually taking place'. The importance of a strategic sense being imbued in teachers was never made a central element of the training process. They were not brought to a point where the challenge of context was made clear to them.

Ironically, as one respondent suggested (bearing out the point we are making) teachers, as human beings, have the capacity to change and adapt and are not simply deficit figures to whom things are done,

> many teachers are making the effort to train themselves. They are getting the message that, unless they make the effort, no one else will do it for them. I am surprised at how the teachers are finding ways of coping. Teachers are beginning to spend their own money on buying books to study and develop themselves …. These developments show that teachers do not feel that they own the official programme of change, and have to claim ownership through their own unofficial efforts.

As cognisant as the programme was of the importance of the teacher, it seemed to come at the question of the teacher in an extremely individualized way. Teachers were asked to reflect in their daily work, but were largely expected to do this by themselves. The intention of the initiative was 'help structure the work of teachers more … however, experience on the ground is indicating that the strategy has increased the workload on the teacher in unsustainable ways'.

An important opportunity that the programme therefore lost was localizing the philosophy of action research around the real challenges that teachers work with. 'Critical thinking', said one respondent, 'is context based'. Key in this context, as another said, 'was the need for understanding by teachers, who have largely been left to struggle with the new demands on their own'.

EMERGING DILEMMAS

This limited foray into trying to understand the principles informing the introduction of a national curriculum based on emancipatory social goals, begins to raise some interesting dilemmas for those supporting an action research approach to teacher development. These dilemmas revolve around the central question of how to balance regulation and voice, and how to ensure a coherent, far-reaching new system of education, that builds directly on the immediacy of teachers' concerns and questions. They respond to the caution expressed by Noffke and Brennan (2004), that many of the definitions of action research are produced 'in an almost timeless, ahistorical manner. ... For the most part, there has been far greater attention to theorizing theory, than there has been to understanding how that relates to context ... the urgency for action creates a strong theory of action, and an important balance to the action-research connection' (Noffke and Brennan, 2004: 8).

Hargreaves (1998) has identified many of these challenges in an international context, but the final section of this chapter articulates the specific dilemmas as emerging from the South African context. These are framed as a set of dilemmas precisely because of their obvious complexity and as an intended aid for further reflection and strategic action in context. In an attempt to order thinking, the dilemmas have been clustered into three central headings.

The Policy Should Be the Driver, but the Practice Must Be the Co-driver

The design of the orientation programme to the revised curriculum began with the 'big picture', the vision of the new South Africa, in the belief that teachers needed first to understand where they were going, and why they were being expected to teach in a particular way. This 'outside-in' approach to reform runs the risk, however, of promoting an externally driven vision of reform [and] ... the predominance of discourses external to the logic of education'. (Fataar, 2005: 2). In so doing, it could well contribute to the undermining of teacher professionalism, and draw attention away from understanding teaching and learning within the real conditions of school classrooms (Fataar, 2005).

These, then, are some dilemmas identified in this category:

- How do we move from policy to practice *and* from practice to policy?
- How do we organize policy centrally *and* ensure decentralized involvement?
- How do we install clear policy drivers to steer change in particular directions *and* support teacher engagement with their own professional questions?

The Teachers Must Have a Voice, but Should It Be the Loudest Voice?

This set of dilemmas recognizes the importance of teacher engagement in change if it is to be lasting and meaningful. Its concern, however, is with who sets the agenda for change, and to what extent fundamental change is likely to be driven by the questions and concerns of individual teachers, or even professional communities. What, it asks, do we gain and what do we lose, when there is a centralized set of policies that define educational practice?

These, then, are the dilemmas identified in this category:

- How do we maintain a slow pace of change preferred by teachers *and* respond to the fast need for change in a country which is seeking fundamental transformation?

- What enables a common vision of educational renewal *and* avoids a culture of compliance?
- How do we acknowledge the negative context for teacher learning *and* maintain high levels of morale and agency among teachers?

Working Small Is the Best Way to Think Big

South Africa's education policies reflect a strong commitment to social transformation. The data has, however, shown that the sum total of the new policies may well be overambitious in terms of the daily demands on teachers, thereby undermining their full potential to effect sustainable change. This suggests that it may well be wiser in the long run not to try to overhaul the whole education system, but to do less, and to learn from examples of good practice, particularly as these relate to student learning. The central question to be asked here is, therefore: Can a comprehensive set of new policies be developed *and* a policy overload and innovation exhaustion be avoided?

MOVING FORWARD

Having outlined the sets of dilemmas, this paper attempts to offer a way forward for sustainable teacher development within a broad social development agenda. The following central factors are offered as a basis to support an integration of professional, organizational and systemic learning, at least in a South African context:

- shared vision and values;
- simple policy frameworks;
- supportive conditions for teaching and learning;
- inspired teachers.

While acknowledging the complexity of attaining these factors, an honest mapping of the terrain would identify points of incoherence, where the dilemmas identified earlier do not live in healthy tension, but in fact actively contradict one another, thereby creating confusion and resistance at local level. This terrain mapping would bring together research, policy and practice in a symbiotic relationship, with each informing the other. In so doing, policy would be working *with* teachers, seeing them as 'agents of knowing and constructors of knowledge' (Grimmet, 1995: 124) in their own immediate contexts and within the parameters and value systems of national policy.

Two examples of strategies to do the above are suggested here, both drawing from the South African policy and practice environment. As the one adviser interviewed commented: 'If we would have been covering the critical outcomes, then we would have been covering everything and anything that we need to have'. The critical outcomes of the revised curriculum provide an excellent base for a shared sense of vision, and a good starting point for educators to reflect – alone, or in professional communities – on the way in which they, in their daily practice, could contribute to the attainment of these outcomes in their own teaching.

A second suggested strategy builds on what one respondent called . . . 'the sense of purpose and personal and group responsibility.. of the struggle culture of the 1970s and 1980s' and seeks to establish collective responsibility for the fact that many learners continue to attain extremely low standards of achievement. This strategy takes the view that if teachers, researchers and policy makers were to work together to try to answer why this is so, a conversation on the relationship between teaching strategies, social aspirations and classroom conditions would immediately ensue. Such conversations would simultaneously, and powerfully, show respect to the learners in the country, acknowledge teachers' professional abilities to engage with appropriate teaching strategies and, perhaps most importantly, engage policy makers in the detail of what good teaching and learning could look like.

REFERENCES

Adler, J. and Reed, Y. (2002) (eds) *Challenges of Teacher Development: An Investigation of Take-up in South Africa.* Van Schaik: Pretoria.

Burnaford, G., Fischer, J. and Hobson, D. (2001) (eds) *Teachers Doing Research: The Power of Action through Inquiry.* New Jersey: Lawrence Erlbaum.

Davidoff, S., Julie, C., Meerkotter, D. and Robinson, M. (1993) (eds) *Emancipatory Education and Action Research.* Pretoria: Human Sciences Research Council.

Day, C. and Hadfield, M. (2004) 'Learning through networks: Trust, partnerships and the power of action research', *Educational Action Research,* 12 (4): 575–86.

Department of Education (2001) *Manifesto on Values, Education and Democracy.* Pretoria: Government Printers.

Education Labour Relations Council (ELRC) (2005) *Potential Attrition in Education: The Impact of Job Satisfaction, Morale, Workload and HIV/ AIDS.* Cape Town: HSRC Press.

Fataar, A. (2005) 'Response to the Western Cape Education Department's Human Capital Strategy document'. Unpublished paper.

Fleisch, B. (2002) *Managing Educational Change: The State and School Reform in South Africa.* Kenwyn: Juta.

Fullan M. (1991) *The New Meaning of Educational Change.* London: Cassell.

Grimmet, P. (1995) 'Developing voice through teacher research: Implications for educational policy', in J. Smyth (ed), *Critical Discourses on Teacher Development.* London and New York: Cassell.

Hargreaves, A. (1998) 'The emotions of teaching and educational change', in A. Hargreaves, A. Lieberman, M. Fullan and D. Hopkins (eds), *International Handbook of Educational Change.* Dordrecht: Kluwer.

Hargreaves, A., Lieberman, A., Fullan, M. and Hopkins, D. (1998) (eds) *International Handbook of Educational Change.* Dordrecht: Kluwer.

Jansen, J. (1999) 'Why outcomes-based education will fail: An elaboration', in J. Jansen and P. Christie (eds), *Changing Curriculum: Studies on Outcomes-based Education in South Africa.* Kenwyn: Juta and Co. Ltd.

Lieberman, A. (1998) 'The growth of educational change as a field of study: Understanding its roots and branches', in A. Hargreaves, A. Lieberman, M. Fullan and D. Hopkins (eds), *International Handbook of Educational Change.* Dordrecht: Kluwer.

McNiff, J. (2002) *Action Research: Principles and Practices*. London: Routledge Falmer.

Noffke, S. and Brennan, M. (2004) 'Action research in the US and Australia: Riding the waves or keeping the dream alive?' Paper prepared for the annual meeting of the American Educational Research Association, San Diego.

Peters, J. (2004) 'Teachers engaging in action research: Challenging some assumptions', *Educational Action Research*, 12 (4): 535–55.

Robinson, M. and Meerkotter, D. (2003) 'Fifteen years of action research for political and educational emancipation at a South African university', *Educational Action Research*, 11 (3): 447–66.

Sachs, J. (2000) 'Rethinking the practice of teacher professionalism', in C. Day, A. Fernandez, T. Hauge and J. Moller (eds), *The Life and Work of Teachers: International Perspectives in Changing Times*. London and New York: Falmer Press.

Soudien, C. (2007) 'The "A" Factor: Coming to terms with the question of legacy in South African education', *International Journal of Educational Development*, 27 (2): 182–93.

Soudien, C. and Sayed, Y. (2004) 'A new racial state? Exclusion and inclusion in education policy and practice in South Africa', *Perspectives in Education*, 22 (4): 101–16.

Stevenson, R.B. (1995) 'Action research and supportive school contexts: Exploring the possibilities for transformation', in S. Noffke and R. Stevenson (eds), *Educational Action Research: Becoming Practically Critical*. New York and London: Teachers College Press.

Taylor, N. (2006) 'School reform and skills development', in S. Brown (ed.), *Money and Morality*. Cape Town: Institute for Justice and Reconciliation.

Taylor, N. and Vinjevold, P. (1999) *Getting Learning Right: Report of the President's Education Initiative Research Project*. Johannesburg: Joint Education Trust.

Van den Berg O. and Meerkotter D. (1994) 'Action research in South Africa: Classroom transformation in a political cauldron', in Y. da Costa, C. Julie and D. Meerkotter (eds), *Let the Voices Be Heard: Process and Practice in Education*. Cape Town: Wyvern Publications.

Welch, T. (2002) 'Teacher education in South Africa before, during and after apartheid', in J. Adler and Y. Reed (eds), *Challenges of Teacher Development: An Investigation of Take-up in South Africa*. Pretoria: van Schaik.

Western Cape Education Department (2004) WCED Intermediate Phase: Orientation Courses. Participants' Manual.

39

The Impact of Action Research in Spanish Schools in the Post-Franco Era

Àngel I. Pérez Gómez,
Miguel Sola Fernández,
Encarnación Soto Gómez and
José Francisco Murillo Mas

OVERVIEW

In this chapter we describe how and to what extent ideas on Action Research (AR) have helped shape current schools in Spain. To this end we first provide some historical background, essential in order to understand the evolution of schools as institutions, particularly since the end of the Franco dictatorship. Next we examine the impact of AR on the ideas and discourses assimilated and disseminated to schools mainly by agents of the universities. This is followed by a brief analysis of how AR really impregnates educational policy and practice in the Spanish State. Finally, we briefly describe the current state of penetration of AR in school practice and some initiatives which promise greater development in the near future.

HISTORICAL MILESTONES: THE EMERGENCE OF ACTION RESEARCH IN SPAIN

Experiences of participatory research in education have been developed in Spain since the 19th century, promoted by socialist and anarchist currents, although popular movements were aborted during the Civil War and quelled throughout the

Franco dictatorship. The Spanish Civil War began on 18th July 1936 with an uprising by troops loyal to Franco, ending with the military victory of the rebels on 1st April 1939. The Franco dictatorship lasted up to the death of the dictator in 1975, when the process of transition to the current parliamentary monarchy began. It should not be forgotten that amongst the interesting events which took place during the Second Republic (1931–1939), we find the creation of Collaboration Centres and the first Summer Schools. These were meetings organized by and for teachers, through pedagogical innovation groups, held during the summer break in order to share experiences and learn about new methodologies, ideas and experiences. The Summer Schools, which were very well attended by members of the teaching profession, would become the ideal instrument for the dissemination of a new pedagogical culture, different from the official line, and often in direct opposition to it. From the mid-1960s we could say that the Pedagogic Renovation Movements (MRPs) offered the only true possibility for teacher training until the Teacher Centres ('CEPs') appeared in the mid-1980s.

The MRPs in fact comprise diverse collective groups, each of which is autonomous and independent, brought together in a confederation. They are characterized by being social movements, which defend a high level of commitment to quality education in state schools, in order to achieve a democratic society, with the goal of influencing the educational sphere from outside the officialdom of the Administration. The first common declaration in defence of quality state schools was made at an MRP meeting held in Seville in 1981. 'An MRP is a social movement of teachers which, from a historical perspective, tries to converge with other social movements in the liberating transformation of schools and society' (Martínez Bonafé, 1993: 104).

The activities of the MRPs passed through different stages over time, in keeping with political events which would ultimately lead to the change of regime and the consolidation of democracy. The different authors who have studied the period concur to a large extent in identifying the first era (up to the mid-1980s) as the most dynamic, not only in terms of activity but also with regards to political significance.

With the advent of democracy, and in particular during the first term of government of the Spanish Socialist Party (PSOE), many leaders of these educational renovation movements, who had opposed the Franco regime and built up significant recognition, were promoted to posts in the educational administration or in Teacher Centres ('CEPs'), or took up positions in universities. There were two significant consequences: first, they brought about substantial changes in educational policy, incorporating the ideas of renovation into future laws, whilst impregnating the principles and strategies of school reform and in-service teacher education. Moreover, many schools and teacher groups were left bereft of innovative staff and, in particular, of people with leadership skills and ideas to transform day-to-day practice.

Towards the mid-1990s, having suffered several crises as a result of the co-optation of part of the discourse of the MRP by the educational administration, we can see a revival, which goes hand in hand with evolution 'towards theoretical and practical reflection on the function of critical pedagogy and implementation strategies in schools' (Martínez Bonafé, 1993). At this point we can say that the MRP had been transformed into base-level collective teacher groups which received the ideas of Action Research, introduced in Spain at that time.

The concepts of Action Research have gradually influenced both progressive teaching practice and theory in spain over time since 1982, the date on which the first Congress on Curriculum and Teaching was held in La Manga del Mar Menor, counting on the participation of John Elliott in place of the late Professor Laurence Stenhouse, as was his express wish. Not without difficulty and from a minority position, Action Research has slowly aroused growing interest from those teachers, professional groups and politicians involved in education who are concerned with and involved in the complex processes of pedagogical renovation in post-Franco schools.

In 1986, with Spain now a fully fledged democracy, the first Action Research training and work seminar was held in Malaga, developed by J. Elliott and Bridget Somekh. Subsequently, throughout the rest of the 1980s, seminars and workgroups proliferated and extended the ideas and practices of Action Research through other Spanish universities and regions. In 1986, the Wilfred Carr and Stephen Kemmis book *Becoming Critical* was published in Spanish, with great repercussions in the university sphere, and soon after Kemmis was invited to the University of Oviedo to attend a seminar.

In March 1992, the 2nd International Symposium on Critical Theory and Action Research was held in Valladolid, bringing together consolidated research groups from the universities of Barcelona, Málaga, Oviedo, Basque Country, Valencia and Valladolid, along with researchers and teachers from other regions. The Symposium saw the presentation of Action Research projects in diverse fields, such as children's education, primary education, teacher training (both initial and ongoing), adult education, classroom pedagogy for different subjects, social education, educational innovation, school curriculum and so on.

For the purposes of this work, the following conclusions of this Symposium are worth highlighting:

- Action Research and Critical Theory can be found in the customs and practice of the MRP, in certain 'reflexion' groups of some regions or university districts, and in certain teacher associations of different areas.
- The essence of Critical Theory resides not in adhering to any fashionable doctrine, which is susceptible to ideological imperialism, but rather in the analysis of economic, social, political and cultural reality, and in rigorous, systematic reflection with regards to the same and to liberating commitment, both personal and structural, to the situations observed.
- It would be a mistake for researchers to use Action Research techniques without first discovering the underlying principles of the approaches, where the revolutionary change of this paradigm operates: 'The simple radically reflexive practice, along with an open critical attitude, can constitute the fundamental essence of Critical Theory without any labels, since this

type of reflection excludes indoctrination, submission and manipulation' (Several Authors, 1995: 34).

- The attendees at the Symposium brought up the pressing need to take the discourse of Action Research, as it is currently found in the universities, to schools, since its presence amongst primary and secondary education teachers is marginal.

We shall now indicate how Action Research has brought about improvements in discourse, policies, rules and practices throughout the educational sphere in Spain.

THE INFLUENCE OF ACTION RESEARCH ON DISCOURSE AND THE DISCUSSION OF IDEAS

The idea of the teacher as a researcher who reflects upon his/her practice, the deliberation processes and the action/research programmes as instruments for the professional development of the teacher, the creation of educational communities, the epistemological critique of the different models of educational research and the proposed principles which should govern educational research are, amongst others, topical issues which, given their critical and suggestive nature, have provided suitable positions for educational practice and theory in Spain over the past 25 years (Mena, 2007). Over time, two main issues have been the centre of attention of AR work and studies carried out in our sphere:

- The professional development of teachers as researchers of their own practice, especially the relations between theory and practice.
- The construction of educational communities by way of participatory Action Research, especially cooperation in teaching and research into teaching.

Teachers as Autonomous Professionals Who Carry Out Research by Reflecting upon Their Own Practice

The predominant academic formula at the start of the 1980s extended the image of the teacher as a technician, applying pre-established routines to standardized problems. The image of teachers as researchers into their own practice came to re-affirm itself and take on special relevance in pedagogical theory and educational practice. The idea that the rational intervention of the teacher, as occurs in any other social practice, is always, to a certain extent, a true research process, began to be more widespread, at that time from the perspective of the practitioner.

For these social practices, impregnated with values, which do not have any strictly predictable consequences and whose results cannot be established clearly as they are open to individual and collective creation, the Action Research approach proposes deliberation as the most rational intervention method (Elliott, 1985).

Thus conceived, practical deliberation could be a similar process to that which Schön (1983, 1987) offers in his concept of practical knowledge, with an interesting accompanying nuance: the emphasis which Elliott places on the cooperative character of practical deliberation. The professional knowledge of teachers should form a complex and prolonged process of knowledge in action, 'savoir-faire' and of reflection in and about action 'action research'. Thus, relevant knowledge to orientate the practice of the teacher in the changing and uncertain world of the classroom appears when we propose facilitating the development of students' understanding, and is generated through reflection on the characteristics and processes of one's own practice, in all its aspects and dimensions: design, development and assessment. This conviction does not imply any devaluation of theory or accumulated knowledge, but rather allows positioning within a permanent process of confrontation and recreation from practice. As stated by Elliott (1985, 2004), teachers who develop their theories based solely on reflection on their own experiences, leaving aside the past and present reflections of others, end up reinventing the wheel.

This has been a topical dilemma in Spain over recent decades: the need to understand the accumulative character of the knowledge generated in reflection on practice, respecting the singularity of the processes and the hypothetical character of applications (Zeichner, 2007). Should the quality of the academic research and the quality of the Action Research be valued with different criteria? Should we maintain, as has happened in the international sphere and in particularly in the Spanish context, the classic separation between practitioner research, orientated mainly towards improving the practice of teaching, by those who participate in each specific teaching/learning situation, from traditional academic research, orientated mainly towards increasing theoretical knowledge of an area or field of study?

Maintaining this perverse dualism, which is deep-rooted in the Spanish academic sphere, only leads to stagnation in two extreme points of view, both of them inoperative. On the one hand is a positivist conception of the development of knowledge in social sciences, now clearly obsolete and questioned since Kuhn (1975), which, in education, has only achieved complex sets of sophisticated artificial plays, never replicable but always abstract and irrelevant (Nuthall, 2005) and which have distanced practitioners from the enrichment which the theories may offer. On the other hand are intuitive and anti-theoretical positions which renounce any procedure involving systematization and internal and external checking of the value and consistency of the propositions affirmed, legitimized only by the obscure affirmation of 'everything goes'? The scientific and cultural knowledge accumulated in the history of humanity in general and of the teaching profession in particular is an essential tool to support the reflection of teachers, not to replace it.

Moreover, it is evident that social practices show a clear trend towards a repetition of routine processes, and that the institutional character of educational practice restricts the possibilities of critical comparison and enriching dialogue. It is thus easy to understand that isolated reflection and practice by teachers can generate and reproduce a deformed self-understanding of reality, and that these deformations can be easily maintained and fed by the inertia of professional, institutional, cultural and environmental pressures. Much research on the evolution of the pedagogical knowledge, beliefs and attitudes of teachers coincides with highlighting the inexorable trend by the majority towards impaired thought, developing ever less flexible stereotypes which are ever more resistant to change, feeding off the tacitly or explicitly dominant ideology, the undiscriminating reproduction of professional tradition (Halkes and Olson, 1983; Pérez Gómez and Gimeno, 1988, 1992; Sola, 1999, 2000), the ritualized myths and routines of school culture (Nuthall, 2005; Russell, 2006; Loughrand, 2007) and the codes of classification and rigid structuring of the traditional teaching curriculum (Berstein, 1975).

> Teaching is a ritual that we all assimilate through at least 10 years of participation as students. Despite changing teacher education programs and many attempts to reform teaching methods, the core of the ritual remains largely unchanged, sustained by a 'stable web of beliefs and assumptions that are a part of the [wider] culture' (Stigler and Hiebert, 1999: 87) [...] Culture becomes so much a part of ourselves that we lose awareness of how it shapes our perceptions and organizes our lives [...] The problem is to find ways to stand outside the ritualized routines and myths to identify how they control what we perceive, believe, and do about reforming teaching and learning. (Nuthall, 2005)

Collaborative Action Research, which stimulates a process of contrasting one's views with others' and with the results of the action, is a powerful tool to understand the hidden influences which are present in school culture and which subtly permeate the thinking, feeling and practice of all those immersed in this culture, provided suitable procedures are established to break free from them and allow the appearance of new perspectives and different interpretations. The processes and cycles of AR provide a privileged tool to stimulate the complex integration of the two poles of the dilemmas which all innovative teachers, dedicated to their profession, face: commitment and distancing, emotions and rationality, oneself and others.

Perhaps this is the richest and most promising scenario in which teachers in the context of Spain currently find themselves. AR has opened up a promising horizon which is becoming ever more firmly established in the minds of the people concerned with improving teaching and learning practice, since it deals with specific problems, in real scenarios, whilst at the same time achieving a certain status of legitimacy amongst education politicians and even in the difficult sphere of the Spanish pedagogical academic environment (Mena, 2007). It is promising since it induces teacher researchers and teacher educators to deal with educational reality, carrying out research into our own practice, questioning the significance, utility and quality of our teaching, along with the effects which the educational contexts and strategies we lay out have on the learning processes and products of the students. As stated by Berry (2004: 1308), 'How can I be credible to those learning to teach if I do not practice what I advocate for them?'

Fortunately, AR in Spain, in a similar manner to the movement developed over the past decade in the United States known as Self-Study (Zeichner, 2007), is beginning to take shape as a relevant teaching strategy in teacher education university programmes, requiring the integration of action and reflection both in the development of students and the professional development of teachers and of teacher educators. Likewise, it is promoting the coming together of three spheres, which have traditionally been isolated in the history of education in Spain: practice, teacher education and academic research (Pérez Gómez et al., 1995).

Action Research for Teacher Training: An Illustrative Example from a Project

To illustrate this kind of learning partnership we draw on a project which combines training and teaching proficiency, both in initial and in ongoing training: *The Collective Creations for Change Project.* The primary school Nuestra Señora de Gracia is the key agency facilitating praxis and reflection for current and future primary school teachers and university teachers who are looking to give a common sense to their teaching and research practice.

A research and reflection group was established by the project to explore the pedagogical qualities of a kind of educational activity created by them and called *Collective Creations.* A group of eight primary school teachers was set up, plus two teachers and two students from the University of Malaga as external facilitators with support from Pedagogy, School Teaching and Social Education undergraduates at this university.

> With the activity **Think in colours with Picasso** there was a before and after in the life of the school. The motivation it brought about, the reflection processes it caused, the creativity it aroused in pupils, the frenetic level of activity in which the entire school was immersed … all led to significant changes in relations at the school [...] We discovered that these practices led to internal transformation processes in our children when it came to dealing with conflicts, along with a personal bond with the educational practice. (extract from the teachers' group research report)

However, not all the activities designed and developed have had the same impact on the lives and interests of the pupils. Which variables have had an influence? The focus of our reflections has been on analyzing and delimiting the characteristics of the *Collective Creations*, along with the possibility of introducing qualitative changes. Our concern has been to change the conditions and the relations and the learning of a group of pupils and parents who, given their highly disadvantaged social background, have remained on the edges of education with high levels of truancy and educational failure. We are submerged in an action research process in which we analyze different variables: communication and expression strategies, construction of personal identity, interpersonal relations, relations with knowledge, relations with surrounding spaces and the integration of families in the school education process.

The result is that university students not only observe educational practices in schools, but also collaborate with the teachers and students in order to understand, design and develop action plans for developing these educational practices.

Their diaries are useful not only for their university training, but also as a tool for analysis and comparison by this group of teachers. University teachers have a dual role in the reflection group: first, as external facilitators and second, as tutors in the practical training of university students; in other words, as with the primary school teachers and the pupils, they have the dual function of researching and practising.

Some conclusions from this work have allowed us to draw up new kinds of action: the *Collective Creations* have an overall purpose, but require each teacher to customize them and give them local meaning; they are flexible processes, involving opening the mind to the new, to the unexpected; they are processes which aim to enhance relations, produce knowledge and engender reflection; they are thus activities which generate change, but above all they are creative spaces and processes shared by different groups and levels. This work gradually leads to results which stimulate the process:

> our children actively take part in school dynamics; they go to school happy and feel they have a role as part of it; behaviour crises are less and less frequent and of lesser intensity; children's levels of reflection and acceptance of the rules, which they themselves have helped to draw up, are on the up. (2nd report of the teachers group of the school)

From the point of view of university students, the experiences and processes witnessed at Nuestra Señora de Gracia school have had a profound impact not only on a cognitive level, but also, more significantly, on an emotional level. This has led to the students relating to, stimulating and giving sense to their training and to their future, whilst the possibility of reflecting on and participating in an innovative experience and real research along with teachers from different educational sectors has led to a climate of partnership and a learning environment very different from those commonly found in university environments. The reflective process has enabled analysis of preconceptions, discovery of gaps and errors, and the construction of reflexive thought from practice, using theory as a tool for analysis, reflection and creation.

The Construction of Educational Communities through Participatory Action Research: Cooperation in Teaching and in Research on Teaching

Since the period of transition to democracy, it has also been possible to recognize in Spain several research developments with a participatory approach, Participatory Action Research (PAR), related to social action programmes, community development and institutional analyses promoted by different social movements, non-governmental organizations, neighbours associations and so on, associated in almost all cases with deprived sectors or close to workers movements. Thanks to his theory, practice and dissemination in Spain, the leading academic exponent has been Jesús Ibáñez (1979, 1985). The development of PAR has been associated fundamentally to social intervention and community development, and is only now beginning marginally to become incorporated into the sphere of education, especially in the practical training of social educators.

This, for example, has been the case at the University of Malaga, where the Curriculum and Teaching Department has participated actively in a community development project in an underprivileged district ('La Palmilla'), coordinated by Tomas Villasante, with the participation of students and teachers.

The emphasis on promoting and ensuring the participation of all the agents involved in a specific social context is the basic characteristic that determines the pedagogical value of Participatory Action Research. The action and reflexion cycles are diversified and take shape in the form of ever more elaborate techniques and procedures in order to encourage participation and try to overcome the inevitable (and apparently irresolvable) resistance and opposition. From the start of the analysis of needs, diagnosis of situations and definition of problems, attention is concentrated primarily on methodology for widen participation of everybody involved in that context in order to take on board the most diverse voices and interpretations, in particular those which are most unheard, marginal and out of sight. The relationship maps, the workgroups and the assemblies are decisive in the methodological basis of the PAR, as an outstanding tool to understand the complex network of human and social relations in each specific scenario.

Participatory social research as a form of collective knowledge construction, which promotes creativity in the networks of each context, can be applied in school scenarios. It is an outstanding tool to understand the complexity of the educational function in the information society, and also to uncover the routines, myths and rituals which make up the culture of schools as institutions. Furthermore, and more importantly, it allows us to understand and overcome any obstacles and possibilities we come across in the process towards change, discovery and construction of new teaching and learning relations, and to perceive the construction and application of knowledge in a new way.

The ultimate goal of PAR is the production of knowledge for transformation through the participation of all those involved. For this reason, the focus of the research is not only the problem to be resolved, but also the processes of change, the resistances and obstacles, and the procedures for the shared diagnosis and assessment of contexts, processes and products. As Villasante states (2000, 2002), PAR must lead to understanding, the application of the generated knowledge and the involvement or social mobilization of the agents involved in each scenario.

PAR thus has significant potential in the educational institutions change process, through building learning communities. We must not forget that for over 70 years Spanish schools have recruited teachers by way of a very bureaucratic procedure for the training, selection and appointment of public employees, who assume, as a result of a long historic tradition, that passing public entrance exams places them in unchangeable, lifelong work posts, which are beyond any control procedure or social assessment. In this manner, as the appointments in each school are made by way of seniority, it is very difficult to find conditions which are conducive to the development of work teams or professional life communities orientated towards shared projects and goals. PAR in education may contribute to the construction of learning communities, since universal participation promotes community integration and social cohesion by favouring open communication and constructive criticism of opinions and interests, as well as understanding of similar or differing interpretations.

Another project in which the authors of this chapter are involved and in which we bring together research and teaching in Social Education is the *Home Project*. This is a Participatory Action Research project for community development in an under-privileged district, dependent on the involvement of political leaders, social workers, university staff, university students and citizens.[1] An interesting line of development of this methodology is the recent initiative by researchers at the Sociology Department of La Laguna University (Canary Islands), in which Participatory Action Research methodology has been transferred to schools as a way of developing these supposedly educational environments into learning communities.

THE INFLUENCE OF ACTION RESEARCH ON POLICIES, RULES AND PRACTICE

The ideas from AR developed above have impregnated theory and practice, curricular and educational policy discourse and orientation, and the daily intervention of teachers, but have penetrated thinking more deeply about theory than about practice.

In 1984, the Socialist government started the transformation of schools by promulgating different laws on education. As of 1985 the regional government of Andalusia, perhaps influenced by a more intense participation of the MRPs and of academics close to AR, takes a different course. The most elaborate expression of the proposals upon which the experimental reform of primary education for ages 12–14 in Andalusia is based can be found in what has become known as the 'Carboneras Document', proposed in 1987 as the main pillar of the official reform. (Spain has a central government for the whole of the State, but is also divided into autonomous regions, of which Andalusia is one, which have responsibility for education. The result is that there is an education ministry, in addition to each autonomous region having its own regional ministry or department. This situation allows the autonomous regions certain levels of freedom when carrying out central directives.)

The Carboneras Document 'reflects the conclusions of the collective debate carried out around the experimental process by teachers, coordinators and advisers through different meetings and contacts' (p. 17) and constitutes an open curricular proposal for experimentation. In our opinion, the document should be considered a curricular proposal of unprecedented political, social and educational value in Spain, and shows the influence at the time of the penetration of the ideas of AR into the thinking of those who designed and implemented the reform in Andalusia. The influences can be found most clearly in the following aspects:

> **Research**, understood as a 'method to design and assess the curricular project' and a 'teacher's tool'. By converting research into this new meaning, we have been frontally attacking some of the most strongly held beliefs amongst professional teachers, who, up to this point, had unquestionably accepted the role of individual technical application which had been entrusted to them.

Assessment, understood as 'the research process in which explanations are obtained with regards to the working of the learning and teaching process, in order to subsequently introduce appropriate changes for improvement' (p. 92).

The teacher, understood as an independent and cooperative professional, who grows and develops by carrying out research into his/her own practice, facilitates, stimulates and orientates the autonomous learning of students.

In 1990 the LOGSE (Education Act) was promulgated, definitively abandoning the experimental line implemented around the Carboneras Document and bringing a return to 'precision' in curricular design and centralization of policy. Nevertheless, practically all the watchwords introduced in the beginnings can be found in the new law: autonomy, collaboration, research, reflection by teachers on their practice and so on. Action Research is no longer a model proposed for the majority, whilst its philosophy and methodology remain in the heart of minority groups with extensive discourse but a merely testimonial level of practice.

The panorama of in-service teacher education is quite different. Along with the MRPs, the Teacher Centres are the most important event in the recent history of ongoing teacher training in Spain. They are described as 'preferential instruments for teacher proficiency and the promotion of professionalism'. Ever since they were first set up, they have been entrusted with the ongoing education of teachers. Without renouncing models of a transmissive nature, it is worth highlighting the predominance of an autonomous model which places emphasis on self-education by teachers. With regards to Andalusia in particular, following a period of dependency, the 2nd Formative Plan (Several Authors, 2002) once again opened up perspectives and recovered with its declarations of interest in education focused on the problems, dilemmas and contradictions of daily practice, to which end annual meetings for research projects were created.

... research will be carried out to extend knowledge of the educational situation, based preferably on in-depth studies (case studies, biographies, observations, interviews and research). (Order of 2006)

THE CURRENT SITUATION

Although the practice of Action Research, both in teaching in general and in the teacher education system in particular, is not a generalized or predominant orientation, there are indeed many indicators which allow us to affirm its influence on the current Spanish educational system:

- Some quick details will allow us to support this proposition. In the region of Andalusia alone there are at least 12 subsidized Action Research projects under way at the time of writing, involving around 100 teachers (and many more without any official subsidy) with different topics, such as the understanding and improvement of school management (carried out by a group of head staff organized in a specific geographic area) and the analysis and elaboration of project methodology alternatives in three infant schools.

At the university level, the first international project using Action Research – Management for Organizational and Human Development (MOHD) (Somekh, 1997, 2006), which involved two Spanish universities (Málaga and La Coruña); different PhD theses; and one theoretical and empirical review of the 25 years of Action Research in Spain (Mena, 2007) should be mentioned.

• Moreover, groups of teachers in the Communication and Information Technologies centres are working intensely on the elaboration of materials,[2] with some using joint reflection and external observation cycles to improve the teaching of different materials and for the introduction of Communication and Information Technologies in the ordinary curriculum, constituting workgroups, which are very close to the most formalized Action Research.

• In 2004 the CARN Conference was held in Benalmadena, with the attendance of representatives of research groups from the universities of Granada, Las Palmas de Gran Canaria, Oviedo, Tenerife, Malaga, Almeria, Cadiz, Sevilla, Santiago de Compostela and Valladolid, presenting 18 Action Research papers which often involved teachers and students from primary and secondary schools.

• As an example, at Malaga University the authors of this work are participating in three Action Research initiatives. One of these, as we briefly mentioned before, is a Participatory Action Research initiative for the community development of an underprivileged district, counting on the involvement of both university staff and students and citizens. Another one has been implemented now for four years, in order to impart the teaching of a subject in primary school teacher education, counting on external observations, comments written by students, reflection sessions with students, consensual decision-making with regards to the action and so on. Finally, during the last year of the course, an online postgraduate programme is being carried out (Masters Degree + PhD), in which the action and reflection cycles take place with the active participation of the teachers involved, along with a large group of other colleagues, based on data provided by auto evaluation, an internal assessment carried out by a doctoral student and another external assessment carried out for this purpose.

• The 4th International Participatory Action Research Congress, with the collaboration of CARN, took place in Valladolid from 18th to 20th October 2007. The goals of this meeting included the official constitution of the Spanish-speaking CARN network, bringing together those who are now working on this line in Spain and numerous Latin American colleagues (Sverhlik, 2007).

Since the start of the 1980s, when Spain began to awake from a long period of lethargy, a very long road has been followed in terms of Action Research. This road which has not been exempt from difficulties, changing direction in line with the orientations of the National and Regional Governments and having to overcome the obstacles of professional thinking, which is plagued with ideological beliefs that are not subject to any form of reflexive scrutiny, and to the influence of the dominant social ideology, imbued with the need for immediate efficiency. AR, no longer unknown, neither an anecdotal nor marginal practice, has become an important theoretical and practical reference.

NOTES

1 Recently awarded the Josep Maria Priza by the Provincial Government of Barcelona.
2 Centres with a very large provision of Communication and Information Technologies, specifically computers with intranet and Internet connections.

REFERENCES

Several Authors (1987) *Por una enseñanza mejor. La Reforma del Ciclo Superior de EGB en Andalucía.* Junta de Andalucía. Sevilla.

Several Authors (1995) *Teoría Crítica e Investigación Acción.* Actas del II Simposio. Departamento de Didáctica y Organización Escolar. Universidad de Valladolid.

Several Authors (2002) *II Plan Andaluz de Formación Permanente del Profesorado.* Junta de Andalucía. Sevilla.

Several Authors (In press) *Report of a Action Research Experience: Creations Collectives.* Education Research Programs. Dirección General de Innnovación Junta de Andalucía. CEIP Nuestra Sra. De Gracia. Málaga. Spain

Bernstein, B. (1975) *Class Codes and Control.* Boston: Routledge & Keagan Paul.

Berry, A. (2004) 'Self-study in teaching about teaching', in J. Loughran, M.L. Hamilton, V. Laboskey and T. Russell (eds), *International Handbook of Self-study of Teaching and Teacher Education Practices,* Vol. 2. Dordrecht, The Netherlands: Kluwer Academic, pp. 1295–1332.

Carr, W. and Kemmis, S. (1986) *Becoming Critical: Education, Knowledge and Action Research.* London and Washington: Falmer Press.

Elliott, J. (1985) 'Facilitating Action-Research in schools: Some dilemmas', in R.G. Burgess (eds), *Field Methods in the Study of Education.* Hants: Falmer Press. Spanish edition in Elliott, J. (1990) *Investigación-Acci ón en Educación.* Madrid: Morata.

Elliott, J. (2004) 'Using research to improve practice: The notion of evidence-based practice', in C. Day, and J. Sachs (eds), *International Handbook of the Continuing Professional Development of Teachers.* Open University Press: Milton Keynes.

Halkes, R. and Olson, J.K. (1983) *Teacher Thinking: A New Perspective on Persisting Problems in Education.* Lisse: Swets and Zeitlinger.

Ibáñez, J. (1979) *Más allá de la sociología. El grupos de discusión: Técnica y crítica,* ed. Siglo XXI: Madrid.

Ibáñez, J. (1985) *Del algoritmo al sujeto: Perspectiva de la investigación social,* ed. Siglo XXI: Madrid.

Kuhn, T.S. (1975) *La estructura de las revoluciones científicas.* México: F.C.E.

Loughran, J. (2007) 'Researching teacher education practices: Responding to the challenges, demands, and expectations of self-studies', *Journal of Teacher Education,* 58: 2007.

Martínez Bonafé, J. (1993) 'Tecnocracia y control sobre el profesorado', *in Cuadernos de Pedagogía,* 211: 61–4.

Mena Marcos, J.J. (2007) *La investigación-reflexión-acción 25 años después. Una comparación entre lo que 'se sabe', 'se divulga' y 'se hace' a partir del análisis de documentos.* Tesis doctoral, Universidad de Salamanca.

Nuthall, G.A. (2005) 'The cultural myths and realities of classroom teaching and learning: A personal journey', *Teacher College Record,* 107 (5): 895–934.

Orden de 15 de mayo de (2006). Convocatoria de proyectos de investigaci ón educativa. Boja 113 de 14 de junio.

Pérez Gómez, A.I. (1988) El pensamiento práctico del profesor. Implicaciones en la formación del profesorado. En Villa, Aurelio. *Perspectivas y problemas de la función docente.* Madrid: Narcea.

Pérez Gómez, A.I., Barquin, J. and Angulo, J.F. (1995) *Desarrollo Profesional Docente: Política, Investigación y Práctica.* Akal: Madrid.

Pérez Gómez, A.I. and Gimeno Sacristan, J. (1992) El pensamiento pedagógico de los profesores: Un estudio empírico sobre la incidencia de los cursos de aptitud pedagógica (CAP), y de la experiencia profesional en el pensamiento de los profesores. *Investigación en la Escuela*. Octubre 1992.

Pérez Gómez, A.I. and Gimeno Sacristan, J. (1988) 'Pensamiento y acción en el profesor: De los estudios sobre planificación al pensamiento práctico', *Infancia y Aprendizaje*, 42: 37–63.

Russell, T. (2006) 'How 20 years of self-study changed my teaching', in C. Kosnik, C. Beck, A.R. Freese and A.P. Samaras (eds), *Making a Difference in Teacher Education through Self-Study: Studies of Personal, Professional and Program Renewal*. Dordrecht, The Netherlands: Springer, pp. 3–18.

Schön, D. (1983) *The Reflective Practitioner: How Professionals Think in Action*. Nueva York: Basic Books.

Schön, D. (1987) *Educating the Reflective Practitioner*. San Francisco: Jossey-Bass.

Sola Fernández, M. (1999) 'El análisis de las creencias del profesorado como requisito de desarrollo profesional', en Angulo Rasco, Barqu ín Ruiz y Pérez Gómez (coords.), *Desarrollo profesional del docente: Política, investigación y práctica*. Akal: Madrid, pp. 661–83.

Sola Fernández, M. (2000) 'La formaci ón de creencias ideol ógicas y su influencia en el Pensamiento Profesional', en Rivas Flores, I. (coord), *Profesorado y Reforma: ¿Un cambio en las prácticas de los docentes?* Aljibe: Málaga, pp. 73–80.

Somekh, B. (2006) 'Constructing intercultural knowledge and understanding through collaborative action research', *Teachers and Teaching: Theory and Practice*, 12 (1): 87–106.

Somekh, B. (1997) MOHD: *Management for Organisational and Human Development: Final Report*. Brussels, Belgium: European Union.

Sverhlick, I. (2007) *La investigación educativa: Una herramienta de conocimiento y de acción*. Noveduc: Buenos Aires.

Villasante, T., Montañ, S.M. and Martí, J. (2000) *La investigación social participativa. Construyendo ciudadanía 1*. Viejo Topo: Barcelona.

Villasante, T. and Garridof, J. (2002) *Metodologías y presupuestos participativos. Construyendo ciudadanía 3*. Iepala Editorial-CIMAS: Madrid.

Zeichner, K. (2007) 'Accumulating knowledge across self-studies in teacher education', *Journal of Teacher Education*, 58.

40

Popular Education and Action Research

Mary Brydon-Miller, Ismail Davids,
Namrata Jaitli, M. Brinton Lykes,
Jean Schensul, and Susan Williams

Mary's introduction: My fellow authors of this chapter represent five organizations that exemplify a commitment to community development and social justice through popular education and participatory action research among other strategies. As the diversity of these organizations makes clear, there is no single methodological model for how these goals are best achieved, nor a specific set of issues that can be addressed through popular education and action research. When Susan Noffke and Bridget Somekh approached me about writing this chapter, my thoughts immediately went to my co-authors, each of whom I know and respect for their contributions to action research and popular education. M. Brinton Lykes I have known for many years and admire both for her insightful scholarship and her unwavering commitment to working for positive social change. Namrata Jaitli and Susan Williams I have only just met within the past several months, although I have followed the work of their organizations for many years and count the founders of their organizations, Rajesh Tandon and Myles Horton, as among the most important influences on my own practice. Ismail Davids and Jean Schensul I have been fortunate to meet more recently and have been excited to have this opportunity to learn more about the important work they are doing.

In 2007 Highlander celebrated its seventy-fifth year, Society for Participatory Research in Asia (PRIA) did its twenty-fifth, while the Martín-Baró Fund, the Institute for Community Research, and the Foundation for Contemporary Research have all been in existence since the late 1980s. This combined 160 years of experience in using popular education as one approach to bring about social change demonstrates the important role these organizations fulfill in their communities and the energy and commitment of their founders, staff, and community partners.

My own experience of popular education and action research spans over 20 years as well, in a variety of settings from an independent living center where I worked with individuals with disabilities to address community accessibility, to a statewide elder health care advocacy network, to my more recent work in literacy programs with recently arrived refugee families. Currently I direct the Action Research Center at the University of Cincinnati, which, while based in an academic institution, includes community-based organizations as partners. But when Sue and Bridget asked me to consider writing this chapter, I wanted to bring together a set of authors whose combined experience would give you, our readers, a sense of the incredible range of possible applications of popular education. I invited each of my co-authors to respond to a set of questions I created that I hoped would generate common themes and provide specific examples of best practices as exemplified in the work of the organizations they all represent. Working from these responses as well as from published work by the authors and other materials describing these organizations, I put together a first draft of this chapter that was then circulated back to the authors for their feedback. This final version is the result of this iterative process of co-authorship. But it is impossible within the scope of a single book chapter to fully represent the extraordinary work of these organizations. We've tried here to capture a sense of how these organizations understand popular education, how they use these popular education strategies as a component of their action research practice, and how they have each developed distinctive strategies for enacting a shared set of values focused on democratic participation and social and economic justice. We've included citations that provide more in-depth descriptions of the history, mission, and specific projects of each organization and hope that you will be inspired to explore these materials and learn more about these organizations. Personally, I feel fortunate to have this opportunity to share the work of these thoughtful and committed innovators in the field of popular education and action research with the readers of this volume and I would like to express my gratitude to Susan and Bridget for making it possible for all of us to collaborate on this chapter.

ENTERING THE WORLD OF POPULAR EDUCATION AND ACTION RESEARCH

The Center for Mayan Ixil Education and Development, an organization funded by the Ignacio Martín-Baró Fund, works with youth and women to address issues of mental health and human rights in the rural town of Chajul, Guatemala, and its surrounding villages. Since the U.S. Central Intelligence Agency helped to topple the democratically elected government of the country in 1954, the 36-year civil war has left many Mayan women widowed and trying to care for their children despite crushing poverty and high rates of illiteracy. In one workshop 22 women gathered in a small schoolroom. The topic for the day was poverty. The workshop coordinator invited the women to work in small groups to assemble puzzle pieces forming the image of an insect or animal, and then to talk about the positive and negative characteristics of each creature: The cat scratches children and can be a nuisance, but it is quick and always captures what it hunts. The ant causes sorrow when it bites someone or destroys crops, but its strong system of mutual support enables it to both build and destroy. The workshop facilitator contributed traditional tales about these animals from Mayan folklore, and led the women in applying their characteristics to their own lives. One woman compared the women's need for community organization to the cooperative strategies used by bees and ants. The Mayan facilitator shuttled between traditional beliefs and contemporary problems, helping the women to rediscover their own and their community's strengths and traditions. The workshop was a context for learning, as one woman said, how to 'suffer less from the past'.

We begin with a brief introduction to each of our organizations, recognizing commonalities but at the same time acknowledging the broad range of locations, issues, and ways of engaging with our community partners. We then go on to examine in greater depth some of the common themes we've identified in comparing our philosophies and practices and discuss specific examples of issues we are addressing, both within our organizations as well as with community partners. Finally, we explore some of the challenges we face in continuing our efforts, including a discussion of the advantages and disadvantages of working with university-based researchers, ensuring the sustainability of our organizations, demonstrating the effectiveness of our work, and educating the broader public about the importance of the issues we are working on with our community partners and the impact our work is having in bringing about positive change.

AN INTRODUCTION TO THE ORGANIZATIONS

The Foundation for Contemporary Research (FCR) in Cape Town, South Africa, where Ismail Davids works as Executive Director, 'believes in a future where all South Africans are able to contribute to and benefit from the democratic culture and prosperity of our country through economic activity and social action' (Davids, 2005). Much of the work of FCR focuses on the areas of citizenship and participatory democracy, sustainable local economic development and community engagement in budgeting, and community capacity building and developmental partnerships. FCR was established in the late 1980s and was active in the struggle for democracy in South Africa. As such, the organization's community education program was specifically aimed at promoting democratic values and principles, thus highlighting the undemocratic nature of the then Apartheid government. At present, FCR's community education and action research interventions are broadly aimed at poverty reduction and deepening participatory democracy at the municipal or local level (Davids, 2006).

The Institute for Community Research (ICR) is an independent, community-based action research organization in Hartford, Connecticut, the state capital. Connecticut is one of the wealthiest states in the United States of America, but this wealth does not make its way into the cities which are among the poorest, most culturally diverse, and most segregated in the country. These disparities led to the articulation of the Institute's mission – to conduct research in collaboration with communities and other supportive institutions to promote justice and equity in a multi-ethnic world. Founded in 1987 by anthropologist Jean Schensul and a supportive intersectional board, ICR's mission responded to survival and growth needs of urban, racial/ethnic, and newly arrived cultural communities from around the world that were confronting a number of pressing health, education, and cultural representation issues and gaps. Currently ICR's work focuses on building larger community research partnerships that work on multiple levels to bring about sustainable change in the United States, India, and China. We are also involved in research to change structures and policies that have a negative effect on women, children, and vulnerable adults such as drug users. ICR has a long-term commitment to working with communities to support their cultural heritage through participatory ethnography and representation, and to continuing our program of work with youth that introduces ethnographic research and popular culture-based performance to advocate for equity and safe spaces throughout the state and nationally (Berg and Schensul, 2004; Schensul, 2005a, 2005b).

The Ignacio Martín-Baró Fund for Mental Health and Human Rights (MBF) is a small progressive fund established by psychologists, educators, and mental health workers, including M. Brinton Lykes, to further the goals to which Martín-Baró, social psychologist and Vice-Rector of the University of Central America, was dedicated. Martín-Baró, along with five of his Jesuit brothers, their housekeeper, and the housekeeper's daughter, was brutally murdered by soldiers of El Salvador's U.S. trained Atlacatl Battalion on November 16, 1989. A network of mental health workers in the U.S., Chile, and Argentina decided to form the Fund as one small effort to sustain the collaborative educational and social justice efforts in human rights and mental health that they had initiated together. Working under the auspices of the Funding Exchange, a progressive grantmaking network, MBF supports projects that use popular education and action research in addition to other strategies in their responses to state violence and war and in their struggles for social justice. MBF seeks not only to support progressive groups throughout the world in challenging institutional repression and confronting the mental health consequences of violence and injustice, but also to educate themselves and other potential allies about the existence and importance of this work (Lykes, 2001; Lykes et al., 2001).

The Society for Participatory Research in Asia (PRIA) based in New Delhi, India, is an international center for learning and the promotion of participation and democratic governance still led by its founding director Dr. Rajesh Tandon. Namrata Jaitli is on the staff of their new continuing education program. Their mission is to work toward the 'promotion of policies, institutions, and capacities that strengthen the voice and participation of the poor and the marginalized in improving their socio-economic status through democratic governance in society' (PRIA website). Over the past 25 years the organization's work has focused on a broad range of issues including natural resource management, voter education, gender awareness, occupational health and safety, and issues of local governance. Using a variety of educational strategies to promote their popular education campaigns, including citizen-centered workshops, video shows, exposure visits, and now an online continuing education curriculum, PRIA continues to develop innovative strategies for linking research to concrete action and for making educational opportunities more broadly available.(Bhatt and Tandon, 2001; Tandon, 2005).

The Highlander Research and Education Center, in New Market, Tennessee, where Susan Williams serves as Education Director, is in the southern Appalachian region of the United States. Highlander was founded as Highlander Folk School by Myles Horton, James Dombrowski, and Don West on the model of Danish Folk Schools and has been a regional center for popular education and community organizing since it was established in 1932. Highlander's mission is to work 'with people struggling against oppression, supporting their effort to take collective action to shape their own destiny. It creates educational experiences that empower people to take democratic leadership towards fundamental change' (Highlander website). Highlander's work is based at a rural residential workshop center, where people come to popular education workshops to analyze and strategize about issues affecting them. Highlander has been involved in major national and international social movements since its inception including labor organizing, civil rights, and immigration reform, as well as more local issues including landownership, mining safety, and the environmental impact of strip mining (Horton and Freire, 1991; Park et al., 1993).

SHARED VALUES AND THEORETICAL FOUNDATIONS

As these brief descriptions make clear, whether it is FCR's work to address the legacy of Apartheid, PRIA's efforts to promote greater educational opportunities for girls, or ICR's explorations of ways of integrating the arts and ethnography to strengthen urban adolescents' ability to address drug use, these organizations share a commitment to democratic practice, a respect for people's knowledge, and a conviction that together knowledge and collective action can bring about positive change.

In different ways each of our organizations reflects the commitment ICR states in its mission to 'education through praxis', or PRIA's motto, 'knowledge is power', or MBF's notion of 'education towards action'. As these statements suggest, our organizations all recognize the economic and political nature of knowledge and the ways in which educational opportunities continue to privilege some members of society over others. Popular education efforts such as those supported by our organizations are designed to address these inequities by building alternative approaches to education that enable those excluded from more traditional systems of schooling to take ownership of their own knowledge and experience, to connect it to broader realms of knowledge, and to use it in collaborative action research to engage in a struggle for social and institutional change. These beliefs and our understanding of the role of popular education as a means toward achieving social justice are reflected in the work of Paulo Freire (1970/1997) and other critical educators and activists whose theory and practice have shaped our own. Freire's work with Brazilian peasants and later with groups of adult learners around the world challenged the practice of 'banking education', traditional approaches to education in which students are expected to be the passive recipients of knowledge imparted by the teacher. In place of this Freire focused on the process of conscientization, the development of a critical consciousness and a problem-posing approach to educational practice which 'posits as fundamental that the people subjected to domination must fight for their emancipation' (Freire, 1970/1997: 67).

Freire's work links the practice of popular education with participatory action research. Participatory action research (PAR) has been defined as 'a process of research, education, and action to which all participants contribute their unique skills and through which all participants learn and are transformed' (Brydon-Miller 2001: 80; see also Hall, 1981). Orlando Fals-Borda and Rahman reflect this same emphasis on the central role of popular education as a critical component of participatory action research: 'it is useful to recall from the beginning that PAR is not exclusively research oriented, that it is not only adult education or only sociopolitical action' (1991: 3); rather it is the integration of these three practices that gives PAR its power to bring about positive and sustainable social change.

DEVELOPING EFFECTIVE PARTICIPATORY ACTION RESEARCH PROGRAMS USING POPULAR EDUCATION

Putting theory into practice, here we discuss a series of examples of projects in which our organizations are involved that are similar in focus but at the same time reflective of the distinct nature of the communities within which we work and the different political, economic, and cultural contexts which shape our practice

Landownership is a long-standing focus of both Highlander and PRIA. In the case of Highlander, this is an issue that crosses state borders across the Appalachian region. Highlander has brought together activists from communities across the region to share their concerns and to learn how to access and interpret tax records that can then be used to challenge large landowning interests which in many cases reap huge profits from mining and other activities, but pay little in the way of taxes that would support basic services to the people of the region (Horton, 1993). As Lewis notes, 'by controlling knowledge, the citizens were then empowered to confront the power structure' (2001: 360).

PRIA's involvement in landownership and displacement began with work in the area of natural resource management through a campaign to protect forests and the forest dwellers by educating the forest dwellers about their rights and by bringing them together with activists to explore issues of landownership and alienation with particular reference to tribal areas.

PRIA has also focused a great deal of attention on the issue of local self-governance and the development of community education programs aimed at strengthening citizen leadership especially among women, dalits,[1] tribals, and other minority groups. FCR has launched similar campaigns aimed at enhancing citizen capacity to participate in informing, drafting, and analyzing municipal budgets and final reports as well as development plans. In both cases these organizations challenge traditional systems of political power through citizen education designed to create opportunities for marginalized groups to participate in local and national democratic processes reflecting Freire's early work among Brazilian peasants.

ICR has taken a similar approach to democratize research together with marginalized groups including impoverished women, community economic development advocates, educators, and youth. As an example, for the past nearly 20 years, ICR has used a PAR approach to involve youth in their own research on issues of concern to them, by teaching them to utilize critical ethnographic methods including social mapping, digital photography and video, various types of face-to-face interviews, cognitive mapping, and other data collection techniques. Youth decide on their research topic, learn about themselves and each other, choose research methods, carry them out with their peers, and analyze the data for policy change and social advocacy. Since 1997, youth have done field research on topics, such as hustling, teen sexuality and pregnancy, dropping out of school, and most recently, racism, and used the results in education, advocacy through media and with political decision makers, and program planning with other youth to confront economic, sexual, and educational inequities.

The MBF has also supported projects designed specifically for young people, as was the case with the program in the Philippines titled *Children Braving the Storm: A Service-Advocacy Campaign for the Children of Mindanao and Payatas*. This project was launched in response to the devastating impact on children of the country's increasing militarization, its deteriorating economy, and the extreme poverty experienced by millions of squatters and relocatees in Manila and its surrounding area. The project uses play, artwork, storytelling, and drama to help the children to identify and express their feelings and thoughts about their experiences and to develop the capacity to advocate for their rights.

Highlander, too, has identified youth development as a critical focus area. The *Seeds of Fire* program which includes a yearly leadership development camp is designed

> to help young people to develop a shared power analysis, to understand the connections among oppressions and forms of exploitation, to become aware of the history of people's movements, to gain skills for cultural work, leadership, and organizing, and to bond together into a network that can both support its members and provide a powerful voice for youth issues. (Highlander website)

CREATING SUCCESSFUL ORGANIZATIONS THROUGH POPULAR EDUCATION AND ACTION RESEARCH

Beyond our efforts to put our values into practice in our community-based projects, we share a commitment to seeking effective means of reflecting these values within our own organizational policies and procedures. Recognizing the importance of addressing issues of gender inequity in the community, PRIA models this value by incorporating gender sensitivity in the organization's vision and mission statements, in institutional policies like human resources, in the sex ratio of the employees, and within the organizational working culture. To ensure that this commitment is translated into practice, PRIA has established a committee on gender awareness and mainstreaming which regularly manages any gender issues arising in the organization, such as sexual harassment, sex ratio of employees, and gender sensitivity in all the organization's policies.

Similarly, in seeking to support its commitment to justice and diversity, ICR has created hiring and personnel policies that support a multi-ethnic interdisciplinary staff, promote hiring, training and leadership of researchers from local communities in which we work, create, and sustain organizational practices that reinforce cultural and political self-awareness, and support social advocacy on issues that affect the lives of ICR staff. In other examples of strategies for developing organizational structures that reflect the values we espouse, the Martín-Baró Fund sees as a major part of its mission the education of its volunteer staff and donors and extending education for activism within the United States and so devotes time and energy within the organization to raising awareness of these issues. Highlander has worked hard to develop a democratically run center, with less hierarchy and less division between staff in different positions than is generally the case in more conventional organizations.

For anyone who has had the privilege of meeting people like Paulo Freire, Myles Horton, or Rajesh Tandon, it is clear that leading an organization dedicated to promoting positive social change requires a seemingly infinite source of energy and patience, a passion for the work, a deep respect for and engagement with their community partners, and a commitment to social justice. What may be less apparent is the joyfulness and sense of humor that each of these individuals and other organizational leaders we know bring to their work. Celebrating successes and having fun together are not viewed as afterthoughts or non-essential side activities, but are understood as a critical part of creating organizations that honor human relationships; and we have all learned that sharing food, telling stories, playing music, and dancing together are central to achieving our mission. Highlander has known this for years and draws upon the rich cultural heritage of the participants in their programs to draw people together. PRIA likewise incorporates music, dance, puppetry, and food into their celebrations – an irresistible invitation to join in. At the same time, fun has a serious purpose, as is the case with the MBF's yearly bowlathon which is used as a fund-raising event, and ICR's typical mix of community and heritage visual and performing arts and artists with serious social justice issues in its national conferences, and gallery and public programming events.

Operating a successful organization and enabling staff members to retain a sense of commitment despite the demands of our work also depends on effective management – creating opportunities for meaningful cross-staff engagement and communication, initiating successful approaches to problem resolution, developing careful hiring practices, and facilitating the development of positive relationships among the staffs and between staff and community partners are all critical aspects of a leader's work. Our organizations all strive to address these concerns and draw upon our understanding of popular education and participatory action research in these efforts.

MAINTAINING INDEPENDENCE AND DEVELOPING UNIVERSITY PARTNERSHIPS

Although some of us do hold university affiliations, all of the organizations described here exist successfully outside of formal educational settings. In fact, the longevity of these organizations would be enviable in most academic institutions and may be attributable in part to their independent status. Our feelings about developing potential partnerships between our organizations and university faculty and students are, to be honest, a bit ambivalent. We have all developed collaborations of one kind or another with university-based scholars, and some of us have been, or are now, university-based, and we recognize the potential advantages of developing partnerships with local university faculty who have the expertise and resources to make important contributions to our work. But the constraints placed upon university faculty in terms of hiring and tenure decisions, human subjects review processes that put the control of research decisions in the hands of a committee of academic scholars with little understanding of community-based research (Brydon-Miller and Greenwood, 2006), pressures to conduct more conventional forms of research and to publish for academic audiences all create barriers to effective and meaningful collaboration. At the same time, the sometimes arrogant attitude regarding the value of people's knowledge and the assumption on the part of some university-based scholars that community partners exist to train their students and participate in research on an academic schedule can drain the limited resources of organizations like ours while offering little by way of tangible benefits in return.

Despite these reservations, we believe that productive collaboration with university-affiliated researchers is possible and can serve the interests of our organizations and the communities we serve while providing important benefits to faculty and student partners as well. Such collaborations must begin with the development of long-term trusting relationships that demonstrate respect for the knowledge and experience of community partners and a genuine commitment to addressing critical social problems as they are defined by members of the community themselves.

This research must engage community members as equal partners and must result in practical outcomes that address these problems in concrete and sustainable ways. In exchange, students gain experience and understanding not available to them in the classroom, faculty have the opportunity to conduct meaningful research and to use their skills and their knowledge in productive ways, universities are able to fulfill their mandate to contribute in positive ways to their communities, and our general understanding of important issues is enhanced through research conducted in real-world settings rather than in sterile laboratories and lecture halls.

SUSTAINABILITY, FLEXIBILITY, AND LONGEVITY

Despite the longevity of organizations like Highlander and PRIA, long-term sustainability of our organizations remains a concern. Most of us are dependent on grants from governmental bodies and foundations to support our projects and to maintain our organizations. Support from individual contributors is also important to many of our organizations. Highlander's longevity would have been unlikely without a base of loyal individual supporters, who help the center survive and thrive over the long haul. Even for MBF, which is staffed entirely by volunteers, funding is still critical in supporting the community-based organizations and projects that depend on them for funding. One concern in partnering with universities, in fact, is that oftentimes there is the assumption that overhead costs will be paid to the academic institution without recognizing that our organizations have operating expenses as well. Partnerships which acknowledge the financial needs of independent organizations like ours, professional development opportunities in grant-writing and fund-raising, and a leveling of the playing field in terms of competition for funds would help to address these concerns.

Sustainability is also a matter of personal energy and dedication. The founding directors of our organizations, some of whom are included here as authors, all believed in the possibility of positive social change and in the responsibility of each individual to contribute to this effort; and they gathered around their staff members, volunteers, and community partners who shared their vision. However, constant demands of time and energy can lead to exhaustion, and our organizations all have needed to find ways to create new leadership and to create plans that will enable us to live beyond the time of our founders. In this Highlander can point the way as it celebrates its 75th anniversary in the company of dedicated supporters and with new initiatives and new partnerships on the horizon.

This ability to move beyond the issues that first inspired the founders to establish these organizations is another key to our sustainability. FCR continues to find new challenges in a post-Apartheid South Africa where the AIDS crisis threatens to overshadow all other concerns. ICR's fundamental mission calls for using research to promote social justice, and while the methodologies they use are consistent, the issues addressed and the partnerships they build may change.

Thus, the organization continues to use PAR in its work with new groups of youth and adults to expand HIV prevention from active drug users to older adults, female partners, and adolescents, to shift work on chronic health problems from Alzheimer's disease to autism research and advocacy in children of color, depending on the need. Also, MBF reaches out to new communities facing the aftermath of violence – unfortunately there never seems to be a shortage in this area. One distinct advantage our organizations have over traditional university-based research units that make this kind of maneuverability possible is that we are not constrained by the disciplinary boundaries that define the academy. We can respond to community concerns in more flexible ways, bringing to bear whatever kinds of resources and expertise are most appropriate for addressing the problem at hand

Two key challenges to sustainability of organizations like ours are in demonstrating the effectiveness of what we do to sometimes skeptical funders and in communicating what we have learned to our local partners and also to the broader public. The criteria by which our work is evaluated must simultaneously meet the standards of accountability and rigor demanded by granting agencies while at the same time addressing social problems in ways that our community partners find meaningful and compelling. ICR's *Vaccinate for Influenza Prevention* project targeted low income and minority older adults whose vaccination rates are only half that of the general population of older adults and who are more frequently hospitalized for flu-related problems. This project, a partnership between ICR staff and a committee of senior housing residents, showed scientifically sound outcomes including higher rates of vaccination among senior housing residents, and also resulted in an empowered group of residents who continued to hold flu clinics and to struggle with other public health issues in their building.

There is always the risk of challenging the status quo through these processes. Groups supporting this work have to be aware and able to weather the possibility of powerful institutions not being happy with people who are trying to change situations and systems. This work is really about creating a more just world, which will mean that people and institutions with resources and power will be challenged and will not be happy with change.

Successfully communicating the results of our projects and developing and disseminating effective educational materials to serve our community partners is also an important aspect of our work. One example is the publication *Voices from Below: Reflecting on Ten Years of Public Participation. The Case of Local Government in the Western Cape Province*, by Ismail Davids (2005). Integrating the theory and practice of participatory democracy, this volume tells the story of FCR's work in a manner that is at once rigorous and engaging. In this way it speaks to local partners and others concerned with increasing public participation in the region, while at the same time providing a case study that speaks to a broader audience interested in strategies for addressing these issues globally.

Finally, we understand sustainability as not simply the continued functioning of our individual organizations, but in terms of the ability of popular educators and community activists everywhere to address critical social and economic issues. To this end we believe in the importance of providing mutual support and in the value of collaboration, as evidenced by our work together on this chapter. Modern technology certainly contributes to our ability to support one another's efforts and to communicate with local partners as well as with educators and activists around the world about our work. Each of our organizations maintains a website (see links listed after the references) describing our programs, offering resources to local partners, and providing links to other organizations that share our commitments and concerns. At the same time, however, we recognize that caring and committed human relationships are the true key to our success and our longevity. We cherish our relationships with our community partners, with the volunteers and staff members of our organizations, and with one another. We are encouraged by the growing circle of people committed to promoting popular education and participatory action research for social change, and wait to welcome others to join us in this effort.

NOTE

1 The term dalit refers to members of the lowest, sometimes referred to as 'untouchable', caste in Indian society. This term was first coined by Dr. B.R. Ambedkar, an architect of the modern Indian constitution, and is generally preferred by human rights activists and members of this population.

REFERENCES

Berg, M. and Schensul J. (eds.) (2004) 'Youth-led participatory action research for social change', A special issue of *Practicing Anthropology*, 26 (2): 2–5

Bhatt, Y. and Tandon, R. (2001) 'Citizen participation in natural resource management', in P. Reason and H. Bradbury (eds.), *Handbook of Action Research: Participative quiring and Practice*. London: Sage, pp. 301–6,.

Brydon-Miller, M. (2001) 'Education, research, and action: Theory and methods of participatory action research', in D.L. Tolman and M. Brydon-Miller (eds.), *From Subjects to Subjectivities: A Handbook of Interpretive and Participatory Methods*. New York: New York University Press, pp. 76–89.

Brydon-Miller, M. and Greenwood, D. (2006) 'A re-examination of the relationship between action research and human subjects review processes', *Action Research*, 3 (1): 117–28.

Davids, I. (2005) *Voices from Below: Reflecting on Ten Years of Public Participation. The Case of Local Government in the Western Cape Province*. Cape Town, South Africa: Foundation for Contemporary Research.

Davids, I. (2006) *Learning about Local Government: A First Step towards Active Engagement*. Cape Town, South Africa: Foundation for Contemporary Research.

Fals-Borda, O. and Rahman, M.A. (eds.) (1991) *Action and Knowledge: Breaking the Monopoly with Participatory Action-Research*. New York: The Apex Press.

Freire, P. (1970/1997) *Pedagogy of the Oppressed*. New York: Continuum.

Hall, B. (1981) 'Participatory research, popular knowledge, and power: A personal reflection', *Convergence*, 44 (2): 6–17.

Horton, B. (1993) 'The Appalachian land ownership study: Research and citizen action in Appalachia', in P. Park, M. Brydon-Miller, B. Hall and T. Jackson (eds.), *Voices of Change: Participatory Research in the United States and Canada*. Westport, CT: Bergin & Garvey Press, pp. 85–102.

Horton, M. and Freire, P. (1991) *We Make the Road by Walking: Conversations on Education and Social Change*. Philadelphia: Temple University Press.

Lewis, H. (2001) 'Participatory research and education for social change: Highlander research and education center', in P. Reason and H. Bradbury (eds.), *Handbook of Action Research: Participative Inquiry and Practice*. London: Sage, pp. 356–62.

Lykes, M.B. (2001) 'Activist participatory research and the arts with rural Mayan women', in D.L. Tolman and M. Brydon-Miller (eds.), *From Subjects to Subjectivities: A Handbook of Interpretive and Participatory Methods*. New York: New York University Press, pp.183–99.

Lykes, M.B. in collaboration with the Association of Maya Ixil Women – New Dawn, Chajul, Guatemala (2001) 'Creative arts and photography in participatory action research in Guatemala', in P. Reason and H. Bradbury (eds.), *Handbook of Action Research: Participative Inquiry and Practice*. London: Sage, pp. 363–71.

Park, P., Brydon-Miller, M., Hall, B. and Jackson, T. (eds.) (1993) *Voices of Change: Participatory Research in the United States and Canada*. Westport, CT: Bergin & Garvey.

Schensul, J. (2005a) 'Strengthening communities through research partnerships for social change: The ICR perspective', in L. Hyland and L. Bennett (eds.), *Community Building in the Twenty-First Century* Santa Fe: School for Advanced Research (SAR) Press, pp. 191–218.

Schensul, J. (2005b) 'Sustainability in HIV prevention research', in E. Trickett and W. Pequegnat (eds.), *Community Interventions and AIDS*. Oxford: Oxford University Press, pp. 176–95.

Schensul, J. (2006) 'Life at the crossroads', *NAPA (National Association for the Practice of Anthropology) Bulletin*, 26: 163–90.

Tandon, R. (ed.) (2005) *Participatory Research: Revisiting the Roots*. New Delhi: Mosaic Books.

ORGANIZATIONAL WEBSITES

Action Research Center (ARC)	www.uc.edu/arc
Foundation for Contemporary Research (FCR)	www.fcr.org.za
Highlander Research and Education Center	www.highlandercenter.org
Ignacio Martín-Baró Fund (MBF)	www.martinbarofund.org
Institute for Community Research (ICR)	www.incommunityresearch.org
Society for Participatory Research in Asia (PRIA)	www.pria.org

41

Partnership Action Research for Social Justice: Politics, Challenges and Possibilities

Lew Zipin and Robert Hattam

MOBILIZING ACTION RESEARCH PARTNERSHIP TO PURSUE STRONG SOCIAL JUSTICE

Action research, as commonly defined, combines action and reflection with intent to change practice and theory (Carr and Kemmis, 1986). Whether the intent foregrounds, *socially just* change is, however, neither a common nor simple matter of definition, but depends on how social institutions are envisioned as 'just'. The action research project portrayed in this chapter mobilized a 'strong' social justice conception, defined by commitments to: (1) inclusive *recognition* of diverse cultures and identities; (2) empowered *participation* of diverse individuals and groups in democratic decisions about wider social arrangements affecting their lives; and (3) decent *distribution* of material well-being to meet needs and life-chance aspirations (Fraser, 2003). In the project discussed below, these justice commitments underpinned efforts to redesign curricula and pedagogies in schools of a 'disadvantaged' region, with further implications for school leadership and cultural ethos.

Vigorous school-change efforts inevitably meet acute obstacles. As the societal system for credentialed access to unequal statuses and rewards, mainstream schooling is a high-stakes competition, infused with norms and codes that favor, and so reproduce, cultural capital advantages of power-elite groups (Bourdieu and Passeron, 1977). Against such selective biases, social justice initiatives are necessarily tempered by 'pragmatic' reckoning with constraints (Boomer, 1999). As such, one must avoid proclaiming emancipation in advance of practice (McWilliam, 2004), but rather let ethics-invested practice lead where it can. *Practice*-led change is a methodological virtue of action research; however, projects do not easily muster the degrees of freedom needed to contest deeply institutionalized obstacles in *ethically* strong ways. Educational action researchers typically gain limited funding, time and infrastructural supports, usually under warrants of system-endorsed professional development agendas that encourage single-teacher projects with single-classroom focus on modest 'practical improvements'. Even when staff collaborate around whole-school change agendas, these tend to be captured within mainstream permissible limits.

School–university partnerships can bolster the ethical momentum of school-based projects. University sector norms of 'independent research and scholarship' allow greater relative autonomy for critical-ethical impulses (even in the currently unfavorable policy climate for social justice discourses). However, this often results in projects designed and driven largely by university partners who, workloaded and time-constrained, typically do not undertake sufficient dialogue with school staff to negotiate situated differences in perception, language and imagination about needed change – which tends to alienate school-based 'co-researchers' rather than enlist their agency (Davies et al., 2007).

Moreover, school–university projects still tend toward single-school 'case studies' that lack scale for tackling deeper systemic blocks to social justice: what Brennan (Chapter 16 in this volume) calls the 'intractable problems of schooling'. Gaining critical mass to challenge such impediments, argues Brennan, requires wider ambit; for example, by networking across multiple sites in which local projects share rationale, methodology and professional development. And if seriously chasing *socially just* change, such efforts need freedom from system compliance – not easily 'won' if governments are primary funding sources. The approach taken in the project discussed below was to form partnership across multiple stakeholder organizations that are closer than governments to 'the ground of change': a principals' network, an education union and a university research center. Each organization contributed funds as well as distinctive leverages within the educational field.

While pooling varied resources and political clout, such partnership also accumulates tensions across organizational elements that, within the complex relational ecology of an education system, each occupy distinctive positions, roles and functions, none 'purely' about justice, all incited by dynamics of power and pressure as well as by virtuous purposes. Each relates differently to local, national and global policy landscapes, with contingent vested interests and senses of constraint, often unexamined, that affect how each makes sense of ethical calls and methodological means to 'do justice' (Thomson, 2002).

In addition, multiple organizations may put teachers at further remove. In their direct teaching-and-learning relation with students, teachers are central in action research efforts to change schooling's formal 'message systems' (Bernstein, 1990) – curriculum, pedagogy and assessment – and informal 'hidden curricula'. Yet teachers lack organized leverage: they interact with, but do not drive, principal and union associations, whose exertions in project designs and processes may distance teachers' voice and agency.

To maximize potentials for socially just change, the dynamic complexities and tensions of such multi-organization collaborations need sociologically reflexive clarification (Bourdieu and Wacquant, 1992) among the partners. This chapter analyzes the complex inter-dynamics of one such action research project – Redesigning Pedagogies in the North (RPiN) – in which the authors were involved as university researchers. We thus narrate partnership dynamics from the standpoint of one element in the partnership. At the same time, we seek to place our 'university researcher' standpoint under critically reflexive examination.

GETTING TOGETHER AROUND MAKING A DIFFERENCE

RPiN was a three-year project (2005–2007) with a middle-years focus, located in the South Australian city of Adelaide's northern suburbs, among the most high-poverty regions in Australia, with a shifting demography involving increased itinerancy and cultural complexity. Secondary students, alienated by standardized curricula that lack resonance with their lives, typically leave school early or barely graduate, with uncertain future trajectories (Smyth and Hattam, 2004; Thomson, 2002). RPiN facilitated action research projects across all ten secondary schools of this region, aimed at (1) engaging learners by designing intellectually challenging curriculum units around funds of knowledge from students' local lifeworlds (Moll et al., 1992; Gonzalez et al., 2005); and (2) *enabling school achievement* through pedagogic scaffolds that bridge lifeworld-relevant curricula to learning of cultural capitals needed for mainstream academic success.

The RPiN partnership was primarily forged by a research team from the Centre for Studies in Literacy, Policy and Learning Cultures (LPLC), at the University of South Australia (UniSA), which won funding from the Australian Research Council as a Linkage project (LP0454869), matching funds committed by 'industry partners'. The latter comprised: (1) the Northern Adelaide Secondary School Principal's Network (NASSPN), through which each school contributed from professional development funds; (2) the South Australia branch of the Australian Education Union (AEU), which applied resources earmarked for their annual conference on middle schooling; and (3) the South Australian government's Social Inclusion Unit (SIU) as a 'silent partner' (providing some funds but with no hand in project operations). This partnership was novel in such Australian 'linkages', as the usual key 'industry' funding partner is a state education department that exerts considerable 'strings attached'.

The NASSPN principals also had a significant role in instigating RPiN, particularly through various conversations with LPLC members in which they raised attention to the *middle-years* as a crucial juncture when students begin self-selecting out of schooling as teaching and learning becomes more compartmentalized, content-driven and disengaged from students' lives – without 'compensation', as for 'more advantaged' learners, of a trajectory to decent life chances through academic success. RPiN thus aimed to *revitalize* middle-years curriculum and pedagogy by meaningful connection to students' *lifeworlds*.

In ensuing sections we gradually fold the RPiN partners into our narrative and problematize their interactions.

LPLC AND TEACHERS: A CO-RESEARCH INTERACTION

A Social Justice Methodo-Logic for Co-Research

LPLC members have extensive track records of co-research collaboration with teachers (see website: http://www.unisa.edu.au/hawkeinstitute/cslplc/default.asp) in varied projects that share a 'critical' focus on redressing power inequalities in and through schooling. Ethical commitment to 'strong' social justice is coupled with methodological orientations associated with 'critical' versions of action research: developing *theory-in-practice*; problematizing theory/practice in specific contexts; ownership of professional development by school staff; teacher and university researchers studying together; teacher collection and analysis of data; teachers (and students) as knowledge producers; and more. Such orientations assume schools as sites not only where privilege is reproduced but also where practitioners can 'make a significant contribution to an egalitarian society' (Smyth et al., 2000: 153). LPLC projects contribute internationally to a research *methodo-logic* that emphasizes teachers as proactive, 'the most important actors in the technology called schools', able to act as socially just change agents when reflecting critically on how '[their] own identities ... contend with the power relations that operate in schools and educational systems' (ibid.: 156–7).

In centralizing teachers as change agents, the RPiN project incorporated teacher capacity-building and professional renewal into its design (Noffke and Stevenson, 1995), creating a *professional learning community* across the 13 LPLC investigators and 32 teacher-researchers (roughly three from each school). During the project's first two years, LPLC and teacher co-researchers met in regularly scheduled roundtables (Brennan et al., 2001) to study toward, plan and evaluate project work. The LPLC team facilitated the roundtables, which focused on developing teacher capacities to design and implement curriculum units, negotiated with students, that make meaningful connection with students' localities of place: in effect putting learners to work as 'researchers' of their own lifeworld *funds of knowledge* (Moll et al., 1992; Gonzalez et al., 2005).

Professional learning in RPiN's first year, 2005, included activities to develop *ethnographic imagination* (Willis, 2000) about students' lives beyond school. Teachers learned how to learn from students: for example, by asking students to select, bring to class and 'teach' about cultural artifacts that carried significant identity resonances in their lives. Teachers also focused on aspects of their pedagogy, reflecting on what they might change in order to 'turn around' (Comber and Kamler, 2005) from deficit to asset views of students, seeing students as experts in their lived domains who can thus contribute lifeworld knowledge to revitalized curriculum. As such professional development provocations took root, teachers worked with LPLC members on designing curriculum units that could (a) 'make community curricular' by locating student work in their lifeworlds; and (b) produce artifacts that could be analyzed for funds of knowledge that future curriculum units might incorporate. Along with roundtables, LPLC researchers visited schools to work with teachers on the curriculum units.

The units were implemented in the last quarter of the 2005 school year. Teachers were asked to be systematic in researching their units, formulating research questions and plans to collect various kinds of data: teacher journals; student journals; video, audio and/or observer records of significant teaching moments; interviews with students; evidence of student engagement and learning (attendance data, test results, student writing and other artifacts); and assessment plans (assignments, learning contracts, etc). At year's end, teachers presented on their units at the AEU middle schooling conference and were interviewed by LPLC assistants. Some wrote formal accounts within master degree programs. In these ways teacher-researchers reflected on their efforts, in preparation to redesign new curriculum units – either refining the 2005 unit or developing a new one – for the 2006 action research cycle.

For the 2006 units (implemented in the second half of the school year), LPLC investigators emphasized more rigorous intellectual challenge, stronger curricular connection to students' lifeworld knowledge and assessments in which students perform their learning to school and local community audiences (thus giving knowledge 'back' to their communities). Efforts were also made to research how teaching-and-learning occurs in students' family/community sites (seeking lifeworld-based funds of *pedagogy* as well as *knowledge*). Teachers again presented at the year-end AEU conference, and were interviewed. In the third year, LPLC members worked with selected teachers from each school to develop accounts of their projects for an RPiN website-in-progress (http://www.ansn.edu.au/connecting_lives_and_learning).

Problematizing the LPLC-Teacher Interaction

As our account suggests, 'we' (the LPLC) drove professional development throughout RPiN. (We hereafter use the 'we' voice to signify our LPLC standpoint.) If teachers were foremost *action* researchers, we designed and pressed the *methodo*-logic of this action. Teachers' agency of course kicked in, shifting the logic in various ways (both in the tacit 'privacy' of their work with students and in 'public' RPiN dialogue). Yet teachers did not all invest in the RPiN methodo-logic to equal degrees. While some self-selected into the project with an informed sense (including some who had worked with LPLC researchers prior to RPiN), others were 'pushed' in by principals. Some strove for substantial curriculum connection to student lifeworlds; but others adapted this key logic of the project in 'lifeworld-lite' ways. While generally committed to serving 'disadvantaged' regions, RPiN teachers did not easily obviate tacit institutional habits of deficit thinking about learners from such regions. Even when such 'commonsense' was opened to critical reflection, underlying senses of its powerful institutional 'normality' were inhibiting (Ovsienko and Zipin, 2007).

We could apply similar sociological scrutiny to ourselves. Complex power dynamics of university workworlds weaken our capacities to enact (or even stay mindful of) our justice values in the face of tacit institutional norms, and habits they reinforce. However, we met with RPiN teachers in venues abstracted from our institutional contexts, wherein we felt and presented ourselves as bearers of 'strong justice' logics for changing *their* institutional workworlds. With sociological reflection, we can imagine this was confronting to teachers' work-situated senses of constraint. We of course presupposed that teachers would face systemic obstacles. In 'the thick of it', however, we could tend to forget – to 'personalize' more than 'sociologize' – in desiring that teachers take up our invested social justice methodo-logics for 'making a real difference'.

The key question, we suggest in hindsight, isn't whether lifeworld-connected curriculum and pedagogy can work if seriously practiced: we know of famous cases where learners from poverty and cultural minority positions 'beat the institutional odds' by such approaches (e.g. Wigginton, 1986; Gonzalez et al., 2005, among others). The question is how to mobilize *situated, strategically practical* logics for cutting through institutional *ideo*-logics that stack heavy odds against seriously implementing *methodo*-logics for socially just change. This is a *theory-in-practice* question, not addressable 'in theory alone'. Addressing it in an action research project, through the agency of all project actors, requires *sociologically reflexive* professional learning community built into the project design (we argue this point further in our conclusion).

Not that we didn't create worthwhile professional development: teachers generally enthused about the worth of the roundtables, where, like us, they were abstracted from workworld constraints. In an era of declining schooltime and space for professional dialogue, teachers are starved for it. We created four days yearly (some split into half-days) of Brigadoon-like occasions when teachers could talk seriously about their practice and how it could be otherwise. However, in returning from these sauna baths into their workworlds, teachers' insulated pores soon opened to cold institutional constraints. Robust engagement with RPiN methodo-logics could then appear 'romantic' and become difficult to keep in mind. Beyond 'usual' inhibitors – work-overload, system accountabilities and more – teachers encountered lack of sympathetic reinforcement from colleagues who signaled the standoffish message: 'I'm glad it's you and not me'. The *strong* social justice messages of their LPLC 'professional developers' could then be felt as 'coming on too strong' in the face of workworld 'realities'.

The problematics analyzed above are typical, we suggest, of university-teacher collaborations in which university agents push strong social justice. It gets more complicated when the fray is joined by project partners who, unlike teachers, bear organizational and funding presence as leverages within their positional standpoints of expectation, hope and doubt.

NASSPN AND LPLC: MIXING MESSAGES

If teachers are prime agents in changing practices and relations that directly shape learning, then principals are prime enablers of teacher agency to effect change. We hoped that, as an *organizational* partner, NASSPN might collectively reinforce principal leadership on behalf of RPiN within the schools. Yet our initial project design did not schedule any formal meetings between LPLC and NASSPN. Over the time of the project, we instigated two such meetings: one near the end of the second year to evaluate RPiN contributions to schools and consider ways to make them sustainable; the other at the end of the final year, with similar purpose. LPLC members occasionally visited NASSPN meetings to report on project developments. An oversight Management Team, which met four times yearly, comprised two NASSPN principals, three LPLC members and an AEU representative (no teachers, we must note). We also interviewed each principal once (before the first plenary meeting). Principals took no hand in RPiN roundtable or research processes. The interviews indicated that most were not greatly conversant with teachers' curriculum efforts and did little to create ways for RPiN teachers to make their project work known to colleagues.

In effect, we hesitated to 'ask too much' of NASSPN principals. Was this simply from a sense that principals, even more than teachers, are acutely timetabled and workloaded? We offer a deeper sociological analysis: that we sensed in principals a *habitus* (Bourdieu, 1990) – subjective dispositions tacitly embodied in their school-system positions – of wariness to take on *ambitious* change agendas, especially in the current policy climate. NASSPN formed partly in response to intensified 'market' competition – structured through accountability criteria set by governments holding purse strings – that wedge collegial relations among neighboring schools. Moreover, 'new managerialism' positions principals as *middle* managers in a 'line-management' hierarchy, wherein they are subject to squeeze-play pressures from demands of government departments 'above', needs of teaching staff 'below', and interests of diverse community groups surrounding schools, with varying degrees of leverage. Topping this, NASSPN principals cope with 'disadvantaged school' challenges (Thomson, 2002). Thus, complex synergies of plights induced collective association to communicate about them; and yet, some principals informally indicated to us that NASSPN 'professional community' was often a carefully guarded communication, since forming a network does not simply extricate principals from structural competition.

All these pressures, we argue, induced self-conserving (effectively 'conservative') reflexes regarding a project that, in its provocations toward *substantial* educational change, ran against principals' (dis)positional senses of *constraint*. If, among teachers, our 'strong justice' come-on evoked ambivalences, we gave them highly desired 'professional community' in the roundtables, which won us license to 'work our magic' on them – and some took up our prods to exceed constraints on behalf of 'justice'. By contrast, principals had their own NASSPN venue of peer colloquy; and their higher system-level status meant we were not positioned to offer to 'develop' their thinking about school 'leadership'.

Still, NASSPN *qua* organization, and its members *qua* principals, shared *ethical care* about 'less advantaged' learners; and in this they drew on their own 'social justice' impulses – albeit of more 'moderate' tilt than ours. As already discussed, the principals' main incentive for RPiN partnership was to redress middle-years student alienation and consequent momentum toward early school-leaving. Most of the schools had middle-years initiatives prior to RPiN. However, these tended less 'radically' than RPiN: we would locate them on the 'progressive' side of 'mainstream' – integrating some subject areas; team teaching; student exhibitions big on ICT display but small on curriculum innovation; and so on. 'Community' connection generally meant vocational or service placements with local or state businesses or governing agencies, rather than engaging students 'where they lived'.

Principals thus tended to deflect and dilute our pushes for strong curriculum connection with student lifeworld funds of knowledge, instead assimilating thematic bits of RPiN into what they were already doing. In the interviews, principals stressed real factors constraining middle-years curricular and pedagogic redesign: downward pressure from state-imposed standards for achieving the South Australian Certificate of Education (SACE) in senior years; time and resource limits; and much more. In their tones and accumulated emphases, however, we read subtexts less of pragmatism ('we need to find what works to make it happen') than skepticism ('we just can't do anything nearly as "radical" as you guys are after'). Variously expressed across interviews was an insistent 'defense' that RPiN is but one of many school initiatives; some are system-imposed; a school can only take up one or maybe two agendas demanding substantial effort; and, alas, RPiN cannot claim such priority.

And yet, in emergent interview moments some of the same principals voiced lyrical, even 'utopian' appreciations of RPiN ideas about engaging students through lifeworld-vitalized curriculum, wherein teachers learn from students, recognize their assets for learning and so transform pedagogic relations. Such contradictions make the analytic point that it was not RPiN's *ethical* logic that principals did not 'get'. Rather, it is difficult to 'get around' latent *dispositional senses of constraint* associated with the structural positions of the various partners. It is *these* that need sociological reflexivity, applied as much to LPLC as to teacher and principal standpoints. In perceiving principals' wariness and mixed messages, we tended to react with *psycho*-logical self-protectiveness, feeling that our ethical and methodological hopes were 'let down' by partners who were 'not taking seriously' their crucial roles. From the LPLC standpoint, tensions registered particularly late in the project, when our focus was on sustainability and further extension of what we hoped RPiN had set in motion in the schools. In arranging plenary meetings with NASSPN principals, we hoped to provoke them to take up the sustainability ball – with the strong social justice spins we'd put on it. The principals tended to let our tosses bounce past. If prodded, they threw back with comments about lack of time, lack of staff readiness, lack of infrastructure, and so on. If we coaxed further, suggesting that building readiness and infrastructure is part of 'leading', principals could throw back *hard*, suggesting that they were funding us, and it was our job to build.

Our analysis underscores that multi-organization partnership does not simply or automatically bolster strong pursuit of socially just change. Gaps and tensions are formidable when teacher and university co-researchers are the main interactors; they are compounded when multiple schools, and an organization of their principals, are added to the equation. Yet for a project to pursue substantive curricular and pedagogic changes, benefitting 'less advantaged' learners who face 'instractable' barriers of institutional schooling, significant principal leadership *is* vital (Lingard et al., 2003). We return to the question of how to enlist this vitality in our conclusion; but we first need to fold the union partner into our narrative.

THE AEU: A 'BIT PARTNER' WITH COMPLEX SUBTEXTS

In Australia, education unions historically have been active in educational reform, arguing that teachers' work conditions are inextricably tied to good teaching and learning, and that curriculum and pedagogy are core specifications of the labor process of teaching (Reid, 1998). Union-led teacher activism has provoked significant reforms to secondary schooling policy and practice, especially in the 1980s (Connell et al., 1991). The AEU also offers professional development (PD), joining debates over whether PD is union or employer business (currently topical given federal and state government reductions of PD funds, devolving responsibility to schools under imperatives to 'manage within budget'). The South Australia branch (AEU/SA) involves itself at the progressive edge of PD, promoting teachers as change agents, with the view to fill a crucial gap in times of conservative government-driven reforms. AEU/SA thus funds a Training and Development (T&D) unit, offering PD that includes action research. Most pertinent to this chapter, the T&D unit ran a two-year (2003–2004) *Community Capacity Building Project: Stronger Schools, Stronger Communities*, in which teacher teams from 'less advantaged' schools – some including a principal – conducted action research aimed at 'making local communities curricular' (Hattam and Howard, 2003). This project, facilitated by the authors of this chapter and the T&D Coordinator, was a significant antecedent to RPiN.

Within the RPiN partnership, AEU/SA was a small player, represented solely by the T&D Coordinator, who did not participate in roundtable or action research processes. Her main role was, in running the middle school conference (an annual AEU/SA event that preceded RPiN), to provide platform for RPiN teachers as featured presenters in 2005 and 2006. She also attended RPiN Management Team meetings, where she championed the methodo-logic of community-invigorated curriculum and pedagogy, on a few occasions urging the two principals on the Team that NASSPN should lead in enabling RPiN social justice goals and methods in the schools, and in extending them to more teachers.

In our observation (as participants in the meetings), both NASSPN principals responded reservedly. Words and body language suggested the T&D Coordinator was respected, and her invocations acceptable to them as individual agents; however, in representing NASSPN they held cards close to their chest. We think it notable that one principal was doing doctoral research (with LPLC supervisors) in which he used a critical social justice framework to analyze and model school governance. In his interview he expressed strong appreciation of RPiN's approach (but a *mea culpa* about not leading in his school, given time constraints). Yet in the Management Team setting he wore a NASSPN hat (or *habitus*), stressing un-readiness of the principals 'as a whole' and advising patient tact. Our interpretation, again, is that NASSPN, as an association of principals coping with complex positional pressures, cultures contradictory consciousness: principals subscribe to RPiN in progressive response to challenges; yet their self-conserving impulses dampen RPiN provocations.

However, the AEU, too, is a contradictory entity with which NASSPN principals engage in venues other than RPiN where industrial issues can put them at odds. For example, the SA government is currently maneuvering to give more say to principals in hiring staff. Despite government motives to shift accountability for 'capable staff' to principals, many want this change for varied reasons. Northern suburb principals hope for more agency to attract staff suited to teach 'disadvantaged' clientele (they also want policy incentives for such teachers to work in 'less advantaged' schools). However, the AEU opposes the move, with their own 'justice' warrants: to protect teacher members from potentially narrow positional interests of principals. Such contestations could confound AEU–NASSPN relations within RPiN: while 'personally respected', the T&D Coordinator still likely wears vestments of 'AEU' as a more complex signifier. This again speaks to relational power dynamics that call for critical sociological reflexivity across organizational elements of the RPiN partnership.

CONCLUSION: REFLEXIVE SOCIOLOGY FOR COMPLEX PARTNERSHIP

Our analysis finds that multiple partners bring multiplied complexities for challenging structural inequality in pursuit of strong social justice. Different partners embody distinctive and sometimes discrepant senses of what's at stake, what's possible, within what constraints – associated with their different relational positions within educational systems, and within equations of educational change. We have made a *social-epistemological* argument: that systemic pressures and inducements, as experienced from different social-*positional* standpoints, become *dis-positionally* internalized, subconsciously self-inhabiting: what Bourdieu (1990) calls *habitus*. Thus, agents from different partnership elements, when interacting and fielding each others' actions and perceived expectations, generate different tactics of self-protection and self-realization, different calculi of strategic possibility and constraint, which in some ways converge but in other ways clash.

This raises the need for what Bourdieu calls *reflexive sociology*: a 'reflexive vigilance' in which researchers critically analyze not just project data, but also project processes and interactions, unpacking the ways in which the researchers themselves 'are deeply invested' (Bourdieu in Bourdieu and Wacquant, 1992: 88). For action researchers, it means that, as they pursue an ethical logic of what they hope to change, and a methodo-logic of how to accomplish such change, they also sustain self-reflexive attention to 'the actual logic of practice ... of practice as the product of a *practical sense*, of a socially constituted "sense of the game"' (ibid.: 120–21; original emphasis). In complex partnership collaborations like RPiN, it entails *socio*-logical scrutiny of the partial perspectives of the distinct partnership elements, through *relational analysis* that discerns their interactive synergies and dissonances. It requires 'deconstructing the self-interested partialities of [all the] distinctive positions within the field' (Zipin, 1999: 37) – and especially one's own.

Action research is crucially about *reflexivity*: about theory-in-practice aimed at changing social practices and relations, provoking reflection on how well the change effort is working, followed by rethinking/re-practicing. To this reflexivity about the *pragmatic* (finding 'what works') impulse of change efforts, we suggest that action research partners would do well to join a reflexivity regarding their partnership interactions and dynamics. We thus argue for building strong sociological reflexivity into the partnership, with the purpose of furthering 'pragmatic-radical' pursuit (Boomer, 1999) – not abandoning the '*radical*' (furthering 'root values') impulse – of strong social justice. We suggest that reflexive sociology be built into a partnership's professional development, as something to which all partner agents commit, so as to raise their consciousness to their own situated, subconscious senses of possibility and constraint, their own strategic coping mechanisms, and how these interact with, and may sometimes counter and threaten, those of others in the partnership. Reflexive sociology could thus perform a kind of *pedagogic therapy* to strengthen understandings of self, other and relationships across partnership positions, and thus the viability of collaborative pursuit of the root-goal: social-educational *justice*. We advocate this 'therapy' when partnership is primarily among teacher and university co-researchers, and all the more when further players and organizations are involved.

We lack textual space to elaborate how sociological reflexivity for partnership action research might work. Given that this chapter's portrayal of the RPiN partnership is narrated from its authors' university-researcher standpoint, we conclude by suggesting that university agents should carry prime responsibility for seeing that the reflexive-sociological dimension of PD happens, both on pragmatic grounds – we are best positioned to do so; and on ethical grounds – we may be in most need of it. As our analytic narrative indicates, in partnerships aimed at changing *schools*, university agents in the partnership are abstracted – compared to teachers and principals – from their own work contexts. This remove makes it easier to press 'purely' and vigorously for strong justice and methodological pursuit, without contemplating the complexities and constraints that would inhibit our vigor if *our* institutional workworlds were the object of change-intending action research. Thus removed from our own contexts of 'the actual logic of practice', we can too readily rush to judge the cautions, dilutions, deflections and resistances that our partners strategically deploy. We thus need to take responsibility not only to encourage reflexivity across all partnership positions, but especially to scrutinize the partialities of our own positional exertions and 'blind spots' (Wagner, 1993).

ACKNOWLEDGMENTS

RPiN is an Australian Research Council funded Linkage Project. We thank our teacher co-researchers, industry partners (NASSPN, AEU/SA and SIU) and LPLC colleagues: Andrew Bills, Kathy Brady, Marie Brennan, Barbara Comber, Phillip Cormack, David Lloyd, Bill Lucas, Faye McCallum, Philippa Milroy, Helen Nixon, Kathy Paige, Brenton Prosser, Alan Reid, John Walsh and PhD student Sam Sellar. We particularly thank Sam Sellar, Marie Brennan and Andrew Bills for helpful conversations.

REFERENCES

Bernstein, B. (1990) *The Structuring of Pedagogic Discourse: Volume IV Class, Codes and Control.* London: Routledge.

Boomer, G. (1999) 'Pragmatic radical teaching and the disadvantaged schools program', in B. Green (ed.), *Designs on Learning: Essays on Curriculum and Teaching.* Canberra: Australian Curriculum Studies Association, pp. 49–58.

Bourdieu, P. (1990) *The Logic of Practice.* Stanford: Stanford University Press.

Bourdieu, P. and Passeron, J.C. (1977) *Reproduction in Education, Society and Culture.* London: Sage.

Bourdieu, P. and Wacquant, L. (1992) *An Invitation to Reflexive Sociology.* Cambridge: Polity Press.

Brennan, M., White, V. and Owen, C. (2001) *Year 9 Student Exhibitions Pilot Project.* Canberra: ACT Department of Education and Community Services.

Carr, W. and Kemmis, S. (1986) *Becoming Critical: Education, Knowledge, and Action Research.* London: Falmer Press.

Comber, B. and Kamler, B. (eds) (2005) *Turn-around Pedagogies: Literacy Interventions for At-Risk Students.* Newtown: PETA Press.

Connell, R., White, V. and Johnston, K. (eds) (1991) *Running Twice as Hard: The Disadvantaged Schools Program in Australia.* Geelong, VIC: Deakin University Press.

Davies, B., Edwards, J., Gannon, S. and Laws, C. (2007) 'Neo-liberal subjectivities and the limits of social change in university-community partnerships', *Asia-Pacific Journal of Teacher Education*, 35 (1): 27–40.

Fraser, N. (2003) 'Social justice in the age of identity politics: Redistribution, recognition, and participation, in N. Fraser and A. Honneth (eds), *Redistribution or Recognition: A Political-Philosophical Exchange*. London: Verso.

Gonzalez, N., Moll, L. and Amanti, C. (eds) (2005) *Funds of Knowledge: Theorizing Practices in Households and Classrooms*. Mahwah, NJ: Lawrence Erlbaum and Associates.

Hattam, R. and Howard, N. (2003) 'Engaging lifeworlds: Public curriculum and community building', in A. Reid and P. Thomson (eds), *Rethinking Public Education: Towards a Public Curriculum*. Flaxton: PostPressed.

Lingard, B., Mills, M., Christie, P. and Hayes, D. (2003) *Leading Learning: Making Hope Practical in Schools*. Buckingham: Open University Press.

McWilliam, E. (2004) 'W(h)ither practitioner research', *Australian Educational Researcher*, 31(2): 113–26.

Moll, L., Amanti, C., Neffe, D. and Gonzalez, N. (1992) 'Funds of knowledge for teaching: Using a qualitative approach to connect homes and classrooms', *Theory into Practice*, 32 (2): 132–41.

Noffke, S. and Stevenson, R. (eds) (1995) *Educational Action Research: Becoming Practically Critical*. New York: Teachers College Press.

Ovsienko, H. and Zipin, L. (2007) 'Making social justice curricular: Exploring ambivalences within teacher professional identity', *Australian Association for Research in Education*: http://www.aare.edu.au/06pap/code06.htm

Reid, A. (1998) 'Regulating the educational market: The effects on public education workers', in A. Reid (ed.), *Going Public: Education Policy and Public Education in Australia*. ACT: Australian Curriculum Studies Association, Inc, pp. 57–66.

Smyth, J. and Hattam, R. (2004) *'Dropping Out', Drifting Off, Being Excluded: Becoming Somebody without School*. New York: Peter Lang.

Smyth, J., Dow, A., Hattam, R., Reid, A. and Shacklock, G. (2000) *Teachers' Work in a Globalising Economy*. London: Falmer Press.

Thomson, P. (2002) *Schooling the Rustbelt Kids: Making the Difference in Changing Times*. Crows Nest, NSW: Allen & Unwin.

Wagner, Jon (1993) 'Ignorance in education research: Or, how can you not know that?', *Educational Researcher*, 22 (5): 15–23.

Wigginton, E. (1986) *Sometimes a Shining Moment: The Foxfire Experience*. Garden City, NY: Anchor Press/Doubleday.

Willis, P. (2000) *The Ethnographic Imagination*. Oxford: Polity Press.

Zipin, L. (1999) 'Simplistic fictions in Australian higher education policy debates: A Bourdieuan analysis of complex power struggles', *Discourse: Studies in the Cultural Politics of Education*, 20 (1): 21–39.

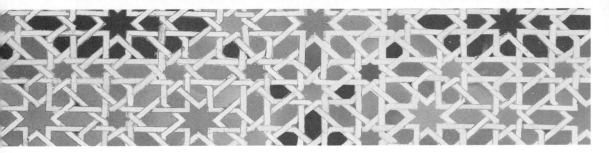

Conclusions

Bridget Somekh and Susan E. Noffke

The publication of this *Handbook of Educational Action Research* offers the opportunity to reflect on what has been achieved in the field. In no sense should it be seen as a definitive text which brings the work of the last 60 years to any kind of conclusion; yet it provides a marker of confidence, what one might call drawing on T.S. Eliot (1920) 'an objective correlative' through which we can appreciate the stature of action research as a methodology for *educational* research. It gives us all – readers, authors and editors – an opportunity to reflect on the breadth and complexity of current action research work and its educational trajectories.

The Handbook chapters cover a very wide range of topics, in many cases providing a dual lens that moves back and forth between a close focus on interpreting the detail of particular local action, and wider meaning making about educational issues and experiences through exploratory theorizing. They help us to see inter-connected struggles – between modes of research that seek to capture understanding/interpretation of 'the moment' and those that move towards change, using research as a form of 'trust' through which research-based actions, however contradictory, help us to move forward.

THE PROFESSIONAL, PERSONAL AND POLITICAL DIMENSIONS OF ACTION RESEARCH

The intention throughout the Handbook is to push out the boundaries of definitions and categories of what is valuable in action research. The search for what counts as quality remains at the core of the Handbook's purposes, together with an endeavour to illuminate variations and make space for minority approaches. In some cases the chapters within one Part or a sub-section of a Part reveal divergent views, as for example, in Part I the six chapters provide a wide range of potentially conflicting ideas on methodological orientations in action research. Yet, there is creative tension in the dissonance, and the impact of these six chapters can be seen as illustrating how important Harding's (1987) conceptualization of the distinctions between method, methodology and epistemology are to understanding the ways in which various iterations of action research differ or concur. Methods of data collection are much less important than the overall assumptions of what one does in the name of 'analysis', and how this is connected to both the aims of the research, and its understanding of what should count as 'valid' in both 'findings' and the actions that ensue from them.

The organization of the Handbook reflects the professional, personal and political dimensions of action research described in Noffke's (1997) earlier review of the international literature and elaborated by her in Chapter 1 (Noffke, this volume). None of the chapters can be wholly contained in any one orientation, but their groupings within the parts, and further within the sub-sections of each Part, invite their reading *in relation to* one another, throwing contrasts or similarities into relief to invite further attention. Thus the dimensions are important as a heuristic device to deepen our appreciation of the various orientations of action research represented in the chapters.

From readings of Parts II – IV, which focus in turn on the professional, the personal and the political, the purposes and achievements of work within each of the three dimensions clearly emerge. In Part II, the chapters provide abundant evidence that action research within the 'professional' dimension is a powerful means of educational transformation – for learners, for schools and colleges and for teachers and administrators. When the practice of education becomes action research-based, it becomes more wholly oriented towards learners through a transformational shift in relationships. Systematic inquiry brings a new process of action and investigation to the powerful model of bottom-up improvement for schools and practitioners are able to develop and learn through a meta-cognitive process focused directly on their own practice and relationships, leading to knowledge that is able to inform action. The professional status of educators is clarified through the public acknowledgement of teachers' knowledge and the development of new partnerships between teachers, administrators, parents, policy makers and university faculty.

In Part III, the chapters draw us into intensive engagement with interpretation and meaning making in relation to identity, social situations and activities, which characterizes the 'personal' dimension. Educational transformation in these chapters is observable in the enrichment of human experience through action research work that is informed by a strong theoretical or methodological base. The Handbook draws together for the first time a number of writers whose action research practice is explicitly informed by varied theoretical resources – psychoanalysis, complexity theory, existentialism, capability theory and Buddhism. Many of these chapters show how action research transforms theory itself by integrating theoretical exploration with inquiry into practice, taking into account the identity of the practitioner. They all deal very directly with ethical issues, working reflexively – from inside out and from outside in – so that the transformative impact of action research work on learners and educational organizations is respectful of difference and diversity.

In Part IV, the chapters open up the wide range of action research work with a strong social justice orientation that characterizes the 'political' dimension. Historically action research has often been aligned with social struggle, and action researchers have positioned themselves as allies in the struggle against oppressive practices. These chapters provide ample evidence of the passionate commitment of action researchers whose work is focused on the need to change organizations, communities and systems for the better. Some of the chapters are about creative, action-oriented resistance to oppression, others about strategic and political action to build on new opportunities at a time of national regeneration. Between them they demonstrate how action researchers engage as professionals and individuals with issues of class, gender, race or ideology to generate transformative action.

The permeable boundaries between the dimensions of the professional, the personal and the political are evident in Part I of the volume. In Parts II–IV, the inter-connections between dimensions are further indicated by sub-divisions of each part into chapters that are concerned with 'working with and for students and schools', chapters concerned with 'professional development, teacher voice and knowledge production' and chapters concerned with 'policy and change'. In Part I our attention is drawn to how methodological issues in action research span all three dimensions, and in Parts II – IV the arrangement of chapters in sub-divisions illustrates how each dimension in action research incorporates the other two. This is not merely an organizational device but rather a means of pulling out each dimension, as when two children play 'cat's cradle' with a looped piece of string, to show the variation possible in its breadth and depth. Each dimension can be seen as enhancing the others.

SO WHAT HAS THE HANDBOOK ACHIEVED?

The Handbook illustrates the diversity and flexibility of educational action research as its traditions have developed throughout the world. Its authors are drawn from 16 countries spanning all the continents except Antarctica, although – as is perhaps inevitable in a text published in English – the majority of its authors are drawn from the English-speaking world. Yet it is in non-English speaking countries that arguably action research has had the greatest impact as a means of intervention and regeneration, working opportunistically in the spaces created by political change in countries such as Spain (Pérez Gómez et al., Chapter 39 this volume) and South Africa (Robinson and Soudien, Chapter 38 this volume); aligning with the work of great educational thinkers and activists, such as Paulo Freire in Latin America (Flores-Kastanis et al., Chapter 37 this volume); focusing on the needs of local communities in developing countries (Brydon-Miller et al., Chapter 40 this volume).

The cultural range of the chapters is one of the Handbook's strengths. Action research is culturally embedded practice, taking somewhat different forms in different countries, positioned differently in relation to national manifestations of political oppression or opportunity. Where, as in the case of the chapters by Maguire and Berge, and Brydon-Miller et al., the authors come from different countries, the shaping of action research practices by local normative values becomes a focus of attention. In terms of the editorial work during the Handbook's production the double gaze created by collaboration between us – Sue and Bridget, an American and a 'Brit' – created numerous opportunities to be surprised by one another's insights. This has, we believe, helped us to interact more perceptively with the chapter co-authors – it has certainly turned the editorial work into a rich, collaborative learning experience.

The chapters show both the arbitrariness of the dimensions and also their importance. 'Professional' practice is clearly enhanced through action research in quite political ways, and the 'political' dimension is being reframed and clarified to expand our understandings of the ways in which power works both for and against children, teachers, schools and societies. A focus on the 'personal' allows one to look at the children and not just at the 'structures'; whereas without the personal orientation social justice may seem abstract, theoretical and not grounded in a concern with actual lives. Attention to the personal dimension is important because without it we may advocate for things that in the long run might not subvert the structures of oppression, but actually solidify them. In the end, without the *personal* commitment to children (their families, their communities), what is *educational* about action research?

The chapters also show how the attention of action researchers has turned more to 'methods', moving away from the unthinking adoption of techniques drawn from social science research towards a recognition that new kinds of methods are needed that fit with the principles of action research. Many authors pay careful attention to data gathering and analysis, and how these proceed towards differing understandings of knowledge claims, in particular towards thinking about the outcomes of action research as action and thought/reflection together. The chapters show, too, that action research is much more richly theoretical than it has traditionally been understood to be. The divergence of views in the chapters demonstrates that there is no one right way of conceptualizing action research. Its methodological base lies in the principles and values variously described in the chapters and not in prescriptions for clearly defined research methods and practices. Throughout the Handbook it is clear that action researchers engage in an exploratory way with a wide range of theories. Theories emanate from varied social contexts. They are engaged with and are interpreted in combination with other theories, used generatively to inform inquiry and action, and used to refine and reconstruct social situations through the core action research principle of *praxis* – action informed by knowledge and reflection.

SO, HOW DO WE MOVE ON FROM HERE?

The social context of educational action research looms strongly in the Handbook chapters. Action research is demonstrably a methodology for engaging with opportunities and constraints in local contexts, using academic and local theoretical understandings and reflexive sensitivities to create possibilities for varied understandings of the term 'improvement'. All of the chapters capture a sense of struggle and embody the kind of politics that is inherent in education. Whether it is an agenda of professional development – gaining a sense of greater understanding of practice; an agenda of personal fulfilment – gaining a greater sense of who we are and might be as practitioners and people; or of political engagement – the articulation of the meaning of injustice and the attempt to work towards its amelioration or indeed social transformation; all of the chapters engage with issues of power, personal and collective.

From here we have the opportunity to travel together. The making of this Handbook has been possible because of the well-established international networks of practitioner-scholars committed to educational action research practices. Some of these networks and alliances of action researchers go back to the 1970s, some are newly established; all are already inter-connected through overlapping memberships in organizations and personal relationships. There is already a sizable action research literature, comprising numerous books and journal articles, including those published in the specialist action research peer-reviewed journals. This Handbook invites a process of coalition building involving those whose contributions it contains and the many folks whose voices are, with great regret, not represented here. This is the first word in terms of 'handbooks', and an opportunity to lead in terms of building the field, and strengthening coalitions around professional, personal, and political dimensions of action research. It is our hope that this work will nurture that growth in the field and in the shared purpose of improving educational work.

REFERENCES

Eliot, T.S. (1920) *The Sacred Wood: Essays on Poetry and Criticism.* London: Routledge.
Harding, S. (1987) *Feminism and Methodology: Social Science Iissues.* Bloomington: Indiana University Press.
Noffke, S. (1997) 'Professional, personal, and political dimensions of action research', *Review of Research in Education',* 22 (1): 305–43.

Index

Figure in **Bold**, Tables in *Italics*

Accountability 15, 18, 44, 105, 115, 118, 227, 235, 258–259, 263–264. *See also* Social accountability

Action Learning, Action Research Association (ALARA) 3

Action research. *See* Educational action research

African American
  academic literature 6
  students 259–261, 435–436

Agency 94, 139, 162, 179, 185–186, 198, 235, 241, 252, 305, 307–308, 371, 378–379, 410, 421–423, 425, 487, 510, 513–514

Argentina 455–457, 498

Australia
  Aboriginal children in 229–230
  action research in 9, 12, 202, 204, 206, 228–230 (*see also* Educational action research)
  Australian Capital Territory (ACT) and 203, 211
  collaborations in 210–212
  curriculum in 203, 206, 208, 211, 230
  educational inequality in 226, 238
  education policy in 227, 239
  educational unions and 516
  Exhibitions project in 205–209
  Human Rights and Equal Opportunities Commission (HREOC) in 242
  Priority Actions Schools Program (PASP) in 239–247
  professional training in 203
  Redesigning Pedagogies in the North (RPiN) in 510–518
  schooling in 205–208, 226, 239
  school reform in 209–210, 409
  teacher research in 229, 410

Australian National Schools Network (ANSN) 203–204, 206, 210–211

Autism 125, 505

Autistic Spectrum Disorders 125–126

Autobiographical inquiry 40, 165, 251, 261, 351, 354

British Educational Communications and Technology Agency (BECTA), 189, 194, 199

Buddhist philosophy 251–252, 280–281, 283–288, 337–345

Bullying 282, 284, 415–417

Canada 12, 120, 203, 238, 252, 348, 352, 354–355

Capability 305–308, 310

Child development 55

Classroom(s)
  action research (*see* Classroom action research)
  activities 52
  community 51–52
  dialogue 58–59
  identity 184
  knowledge in 52, 170, 245
  research in (*see* Classroom action research)
  technology use in 192, 195–197, 377
  See also Teacher(s)

Classroom action research (CAR)
  challenges for 115–116
  collaboration and 107
  core principles of 51, 108–112
  impacts of 106, 113–115
  minority students and 106

Collaboration
  action research and 52–54, 90, 170–171, 256, 281–282, 284, 292, 336–339, 362, 488–490, 511
  best practices in 57, 18
  challenges of 56, 90
  educational institutions and 9, 40, 42, 52, 56, 101–102, 107, 166, 168, 174, 229, 503, 510, 514
  networked learning communities and 188

Collaborative Action Research Network (CARN) 3, 192, 396, 492

Colombia 454–457, 460

Commonsense
  affirmative culture and 448–450

Commonsense *(Continued)*
  context and 450
  schools and 444
  status quo and 451
  teachers and 447
Community
  development 186, 488–490, 492, 495, 501
  educational action research and 170–172, 426–429
  learning *(see* Learning: communities)
  networked learning 181 *(see also* Learning: networked; Primary School Learning Network)
  partners 107, 496–497, 502–506
  of practice 30, 34, 377
  school inquiry groups and 184
Compassionate meditation 284
Complexity theory
  action research and 365
  definition of 358–360
  history of 358, 365–366
  transphenomenality and 360–362, 367
Complicity 362, 364
Continuing professional development (CPD) 2
Corey, Stephen 9–10
Critique principles 325, **326**
Cross-cultural settings 166, 172–173, 524
Cultural capital 136–137, 375, 395, 423, 509–510
Cultural space 422–423, 425–426, 429
Curriculum
  in Australia 203, 206, 208, 211, 230
  innovation 194, 200, 204, 206, 468, 515
  schools and 44, 57–58, 206, 217, 423, 472, 483
  in South Africa 472–474, 476–477
  teacher research and 53
  technology and *220*
  in United Kingdom 31
  See also Humanities Curriculum Project

Democracy
  deliberative 78–80
  education and 308–309, 411, 445
  research and 86, 303, 325
Developing Inquiring Communities in Education Project (DICEP) 56–60
Dialectics 339–342
Dialogic inquiry 54–56
Diversity 19, 30, 90, 118, 209, *220*, 297–298, 350–357, 438, 502, 523
DuBois, W.E.B. 8, 11

Education
  achievement *(see* Educational achievement)
  action research in *(see* Educational action research)

boy crisis in 398, 400
change 31, 35, 37, 42, 46, 119, 166, 268, 383, 467, 469, 470–471, 515, 518
contestation in 27, 76, 78, 463, 517
democracy and 308–309, 411, 445
ethnicity and 239, 352, 399, 401–402, 420
gender equity in 12, 19, 72, 400–404
governance view of 223
human capability and 305–308, 310
policy 18, 75–76, 118, 205, 227, 239, 304, 307, 370, 400, 434, 480–482, 490–491
politics and 75–76
popular *(see* Popular education)
'pressure and support' in 221, 240–241
reform 17, 118, 149, 180, 222, 241, 398–399, 420, 516 *(see also* School reform)
research *(see* Educational action research; Research: educational)
rights 308
theories of 31, 35–36, 422, 439–440, 475
universities and 2, 167–168, 488
Educational achievement
  gap 144, 259, 400, 420–421
  identity 423
  improvement in 47, 106, 150, 179, 409, 435–436
  prediction 64, 242
Educational action research
  agency and 378–379
  'aims-talk' and 302–305
  alternatives to 442 *(see also* Educational poetics)
  autobiographical writing in 261, 279, 287
  Buddhism and *(see* Buddhist philosophy)
  on bullying 415–417 *(see also* Bullying)
  capability formation and 305–307, 309–310
  challenges to 205, 229, 258, 337
  as change paradigm 174–176 *(see also* Education: change)
  characteristics 89–90, 178–179, 347, 471, 521–522, 525 *(see also* Educational action research: definition)
  classroom and *(see* Classroom action research
  collaboration and 52–54, 90, 170–171, 256, 281–282, 284, 292, 336–339, 362, 488–490, 508, 511
  community and 170–172, 426–429 *(see also* Community)
  complexity theory and 365 *(see also* Complexity theory)
  critical reflection in 41, 162, 270, 342–343, 353, 355, 357, 401, 459, 513
  cross-cultural settings and 166, 172–173, 524
  definition 77, 82, 255, 340, 347, 508

Educational action research *(Continued)*
  dialectics and 339–342
  dimensions *(see* Educational action research
    dimensions)
  educational *(see* Educational action
    research)
  emancipatory 74, 77–80, 301, 349
  emotion and 270 *(see also* Emotion)
  ethics *(see* Ethics)
  ethnographic repertoires in 232–233
  existentialism and 252, 384–389 *(see also*
    Existentialism)
  feminism and 394, 398–399, 401–405, 407
    (see also Feminism)
  forms of 79–82
  gender and 14, 16, 94, 394, 399 *(see also*
    Gender)
  generative transformational self-realization
    and 317
  goals of 6–7, 20, 227, 303, 308, 313–315,
    317, 344, 349
  history of 2–3, 8–10, 12, 86, 105–108
  identity and 348–350
  innovation and 222–223 *(see also*
    Innovation)
  Israel and 167–176 *(see also* Israel)
  journals 3
  justification for 86, 315–317, 321, 325, 336
  large-scale 246–248
  loving detachment and 280–288
  memory and 270 *(see also* Memory)
  methodologies *(see* Research
    methodologies)
  narrative inquiry and 293 *(see also*
    Narrative inquiry)
  networks 120, 179–181, 183, 191, 226, 277,
    396 *(see also* Networking)
  organization creation and 502–506
  participatory *(see* Educational participatory
    action research)
  passionate inquiry in 278–280
  Pedagogies with E-Learning Resources
    Project and 190, 193–197, **197**,
    198–201, 377–378
  pedagogy in 192, *329*, 329–334, 434
  policies and 490–491
  popular education and *(see* Popular
    education)
  practitioner 155, 157–158
  pragmatics of 364–366, 518
  professional activities in 13, 524
  professional development and 337
    (see Teacher(s): professional
    development)
  psychoanalytical theory in 348, 353–354,
    356–357
  quality criteria for 158–159

reflexivity in 342–343, 518–519 *(see also*
    Reflexivity)
  second-order 168
  self in 348–350
  skill development and 10
  social justice and 6, 17, 20–21, 85–96, 206,
    259–261, 264, 325, 349, 394, 432,
    504, 508–510 *(see also* Social justice)
  in Spain 481–484, 491–492
  special education needs and 122–123,
    128–129, 233 *(see also* Special
    education needs)
  teacher development and 213–217, **215**
  teacher training and 487
  by teachers 108, 229–232, 234–235, 263,
    268, 484–487
  Teaching and Culture Project (TCP) in
    350–353
  volunteer groups and 221 *(see also*
    Volunteerism)
Educational action research dimensions
  analysis of 21
  capability 305–307
  development of 7–8
  personal 10–11, 14–16, 80–81, 144
  political 11–12, 16–17, 80–81, 93, 144
  professional 8–10, 13–14, 80–81, 144
Educational participatory action research
  (EPAR)
  capacity and 134–136
  definition 500
  educational community construction and
    488–490
  empirical sociology and 460–461
  Fals-Borda, Orlando 457, 460–461
  Freire, Paulo and 457–460
  in Latin America 453–457, 461–465
  political aspects of 454
  popular education and 500–501
Educational poetics 442, 450–451
E-learning 190, 193–194 *(see also* Pedagogies
    with E-Learning Resources Project)
Emotion 251, 262, 270, 272,
    280–286, 471, 479
England *(see* United Kingdom)
Episteme 29, 31
Epistemology 7, 21, 91, 321, 396, 465, 522
Ethics
  action research and 51, 255–257, 261–262
  boards 264–265
  educational challenges and 254
  of participation 457–460
  personal 469
  professional 309
  research 254
Ethnicity 92, 239, 352, 399, 401–402, 420
Ethnographic imagination 512

Ethnography 29, 498–499
Existentialism
    action research and 252, 384–389
    characteristics of 253
    in education 382–384
    personhood and 381–382
    professional 127

Feminism
    action research and 394, 398–399, 401–405,
        407
    exposure to 399
    inquiry 65, 400
    in Sweden 400
    theory 88, 398
Ford Teaching Project 9, 35, 349
Foundation for Contemporary Research (FCR)
    497, 499, 504–505
Future proofing 132–136, 138

Gender
    action research and 14, 16, 94, 394, 399
    equity 12, 19, 72, 400–404
    literacy and 228
    researchers and 261
    schools and 398, 405–406
    self-study and 11
General Teaching Council (GTC) 190,
    193–195, 198–200
Generic pedagogic framework (GPF), 196, **197**
Germany 144, 324, 329, 332

Highlander Research and Education Center
    11–12, 499–502, 504
Humanities Curriculum Project 9, 31, 190
Hypotheses 34–35
Identity theory 424–425

Ignacio Martín-Baró Fund for Mental Health
    and Human Rights (MBF) 498–499,
    501–502, 504–505
India 20, 397, 498
Information and Communication Technologies
    (ICT) 190, 194–200, 515
Injustice 66, 88, 134, 259, 282, 344, 397, 432,
    498, 525
Innovation
    action research and 222–223
    approaches for 219–222, *220*
    classroom 211, 216
    curriculum 194, 200, 204, 206, 468, 515
    institutionalization of **215**, 217–219, 221
    learning and 200, 482
    restructuring and 221
Institute for Community Research (ICR) 17,
    399, 495, 498, 501–502, 504
Institutional review boards 51, 250

Israel 101, 166–176
Justice
    as action research principle 251
    capabilities and 305
    economic 11, 496
    gender 399
    organizations for 17
    political functions and 79
    principles 325, **326**, 334
    social (*see* Social justice)
    See also Injustice

Kenya 295–296, 298
Knowledge
    action research and 9, 19–20, 89, 112, 120,
        250, 394
    claims 319
    in classrooms 52, 170, 245 (*see also*
        Knowledge producing schools)
    commonsense 29
    definitions of 15
    difficult 354–356
    economy 21
    educational 4, 26, 95, 165, 315, 318, 321
    generation 1, 9, 12, 15, 20, 26, 29, 41–43,
        45, 86, 100, 108, 137, **148**, 152, 172,
        174, 187, 202, 228, 233–235, 240,
        245, 272, 367, 371, 395, 451,
        461–462, 478
    industry 19
    modern culture and 32
    professional 19, 26, 156, 175, 213, 228,
        239, 245, 247, 292, 354, 394, 397, 485
    relational 66–68
    schools and (*see* Knowledge producing
        schools)
    self- 281, 285
    spectator theory of 30
    subjective 171
    teachers and 9–10, 26, 64, 95, 174, 211,
        215, 485
    teaching and 9–10
    theories of 26, 30
    work 133, 135–139
Knowledge producing schools 132, 134,
    136–140, 245

Language
    development 54–55
    learning and using 367
    research 42
    schools and 162
    second 106–107, 243, 355, 420
    self and 376
    vernacular 29
Leadership
    action research and 156

Leadership *(Continued)*
    district 105, 107
    school 122, 183, 194, 247, 508, 515
    teacher 46, 106, 108, 373
    youth 404, 426, 428
Learning
    adult 111
    communities 93–95, 101, 107, 121, 268,
        271, 489–490, 513
    group 129
    networked 101, 121, 179, 181, 184–185,
        187–188
    organizational 155, 157
    personal 27, 71, 133, 200, 251
    portfolios 102, 240–243
    school 55, 57, 136–137, 155, 247
    student 27, 41–42, 65, 68, 101, 112, 119,
        124, **143**, 147, 149–150, 169, 191–192,
        195, 198, 204, 239, 244, 247, 307,
        377, 478
    teacher 14, 44, 66, 110, 113, 150, 152, 207,
        216, 242, 258, 470, 478
    See also E-learning
Learning to Teach Collaborative 62
Lesson study
    definition 142, **143**
    examples of 144–147, **146**
    history 142–144
    mechanism of action **148**
    outcomes of 148–150
    texts 147–148
    unresolved issues in 151–152
Loving detachment 280–288

Marxist ideology 1
Meditation 284–286, 338–339
Memory 233, 270, 361, 377
Methodologies. *See* Research methodologies
Mexico 455, 456–457

Narrative inquiry
    action research and 251, 290, 292–293
    approaches to 292
    arguments for 291
    change from 293–296
    definition 290–291
    importance of 69–70
    resonant readings and 298
    teachers and 40
National College for School Leadership
    (NCSL) 194, 199
National Writing Project 181, 254, 399
Netherlands 15, 324, 329, 332
Networked learning communities 101, 121,
    179–180, 184–189
Networking 101, 178–179, 180, 182,
    379, 509

Networks *(see* Educational action research:
    networks)
North American Action Research Alliance
    (NAARA) 3

Objective subjectivity 251, 280, 285, 288 *(see
    also* Loving detachment)
Organizations
    community 110, 239
    educational 502–506, 523
    professional 13, 478
    social 462

Parent(s)
    action research and 40–41, 193, 256, 263
    choice 118
    educator views of 294–295
    school reform and 209
    teachers and 230, 232, 244, 294–295, 355,
        362–363, 368, 416
Pedagogies with E-Learning Resources Project
    (PELRS) 190, 193–197, **197**, 198–201,
        377–378
Pedagogy
    action research and 192, *329*,
        329–334, 434
    critical *329*, 331–332, 457, 483
    empirical-analytical *329*, 331
    frameworks for 324, **326**, **327**, 332–333
    Geisteswissenschafliche (humanistic) *329*,
        330–331
    goals 327
    history 329
    as human science 324, 326–328, 333
    normative/dogmatic 329–330, 329, *329*
    praxis 327
    principles *(see* Pedagogy: theories)
    student learning and 195
    teachers and 149, 240, 377
    theories 227, 324–327, **326**
Peer coaching 221
Phronesis 26, 29–30, 32–33, 36, 77
Policy. *See* Education: policy
Political theory 75, 77, 87, 432–433
Politics
    action research and 11, 83, 85
    definition 85
    of location 469, 473
    of participation 460–461
    of position 469, 475
    social justice and 87, 93
Popular education 458, 495–498, 501–503,
    505–506
Practitioner
    action research 155, 157–158 *(see also*
        Networked learning communities)
    inquiry 40–41, 497–500

Praxis 2, 26, 29–30, 33, 37, 46, 76–77, 79,
    251, 327–328, 334, 349, 397, 465, 487,
    499, 524
Primary School Learning Network (PSLN)
    181–183, 185–187
Priority Actions Schools Program (PASP)
    239–241, 245–247
Professionalism 325, **326**, 491
Psychoanalytical theory 348, 353–354,
    356–357
Pupil Autonomy in Learning with
    Microcomputers (PALM) 192, 196–197,
    372–373, 376
Pupils. *See* Student(s)

Qualifications and Curriculum Authority
    (QCA) 195, 200

Racial equality 12
Redesigning Pedagogies in the North (RPiN)
    510–519
Reflexive sociology 518
Reflexivity 2, 250, 252, 261, 342–343, 371,
    402, 515, 517–519
Research
    action (*see* Educational action research)
    data use in 433–435
    definition 7, 19
    educational 9, 15, 28–31, 39, 77, 107, 112,
        229, 314–317, 319, 366–367, 484 (*see
        also* Educational action research)
    goals of 6–7, 20, 51, 227, 303, 308,
        313–315, 317, 344, 349
    ideographic 28
    methodologies (*see* Research
        methodologies)
    narrative inquiry and (*see also* Narrative
        inquiry)
    nomothetic 28
    right to 19–20
    student 194, 196, 412–418, 437
    teacher (*see* Teacher research)
Research methodologies
    approaches to 92, 94–95
    critical discourse analysis
        161–163, 169
    critical incident analysis 161, 163, 281
    ethnographic 159, 498, 501
    narrative 161–161
    qualitative 159–161, 255
    quantitative 163–164, 255
    reciprocal interviewing 230–232
Respect 263–264 (*see also* Ethics: action
    research and)
Responsibility 257–259, 263–264 (*see also*
    Ethics: action research and)
REPRESENTATION project 376

School(s)
    changes in 217–218
    commonsense 444
    coordination in 219
    curriculum and 44, 57–58, 206, 217, 423,
        472, 483
    democratic processes in 11
    gender and 398, 405–406
    innovation in 213, 218
    inquiry groups and 184
    'intelligent' 245
    knowledge producing 132, 134,
        136–140, 245
    language and 162
    leadership 122, 183, 194,
        247, 508, 515
    learning and 55, 57, 136–137, 155, 247
    literacy levels in 229, 243
    reform (*see* School reform)
    systems 203, 206, 210–211, 219
School inquiry groups (SIGs) 181, 183
School Learning Portfolio 240, 245
School reform 17, 102, 155, 205, 207, 209,
    241, 409–414, 482. *See also* Education:
    reform
Self
    -identity 128, 348–350,
        371–373, 376–378
    -study 15–17, 40, 93, 162, 281, 287,
        386–387
Senior Leaders and ICT (SLICT) 199
Simplexity 363
Social accountability 313–314, 317, 319–321.
    See also Accountability
Social choice 36
Social class 18–19, 88–89,
    307–308, 350, 394, 420
Social identification 423–426
Social justice
    action research and 6, 17, 20–21, 85–96,
        206, 259–261, 264, 325, 349, 394,
        432, 504, 508–510
    agenda 12
    characteristics 89
    community education and 495–496
    education and 63, 71, 227, 307, 500
    inquiry and 318
    method-logic for 511–512
    political functions and 79, 85
    teachers and 228, 233, 434
Social theory 12, 42, 336, 395, 432–437,
    439–440
social transformation 215, 314, 319, 332,
    470–471. *See also* Social justice
Society for Participatory Research in Asia
    (PRIA) 498–499, 501–502, 504
Software 191–192, 194

South Africa
    action research and 301, 472–473 (*see also*
        Educational action research)
    curriculum in 472–474, 476–477 (*see also*
        Curriculum; School(s): curriculum and)
    educational challenges in 471, 474
    Foundation for Contemporary Research
        (FCR) 497
    lesson study and 144 (*see also* Lesson
        study)
    Revised National Curriculum Statements
        (RNCS) 472
    teacher development in 467, 474, 478 (*see
        also* Teacher(s): development)
South Australian Certificate of Education
    (SACE) 515
Spain
    action research in 481–484, 491–492
    civil war in 482
    Pedagogic Renovation Movements (MRPs)
        in 482, 490–491
    Teacher Centres ('CEPs') in 482
Special education needs (SEN)
    action research in 122–123, 128–129, 233
    demand for 119
    ethical issues and 127–128
    mainstream schooling and 118, 121–122,
        129
    in UK 120–122, 125
Stance 44–46
Standardized achievement tests 18, 228
Story constellations 296–297
Student(s)
    African American 259–261, 435–436
    agency 185–186
    as change agents 186–187
    bullying and 282, 284, 415–417
    consultation with 186
    cultural space of 422 (*see also* Cultural
        space)
    development 423–424
    economically disadvantaged 229, 244
    educational decisions and 446
    ethnicity 260, 435 (*see also* Ethnicity)
    feminism and 405–407 (*see also* Feminism)
    identity 424–425
    minority 106 (*see also* Ethnicity)
    performance 123, 213, 259, 421, 423–424
    physical education 434, 437–439
    researchers 194, 196, 412–418, 437
    school reform and 17, 241, 409–414 (*see
        also* School reform)
    social skills of 395, 424–425,
        435–437, 444
    special education needs and 123, 233 (*see
        also* Special education needs)
    standardized achievement test and 18, 228

technology and (*see* Technology)
troubled 226
underachievement 123, 213, 259, 421,
    423–424
Sweden 394, 399–401
Teacher(s)
    action research by 108, 229–232, 234–235,
        263, 268, 484–487 (*see also*
        Educational action research; Teacher
        research)
    challenges for 37, 132, 136
    as change agents 511, 514
    classroom identity 184
    common sense and 447 (*see also*
        Commonsense)
    demographic shifts in 229
    development 46–47, 57, 213–217, **215**, 396,
        467–471, 477–476
    education 4, 10, 14–16, 40, 43, 66, 112,
        149, 159, 166–68, 214, 297–298,
        350–354, 386–387, 482–483, 486,
        491–492
    feminism and 405–407 (*see also* Feminism)
    knowledge and 9–10, 26, 64, 95, 174, 211,
        215, 485
    leadership and 46, 106, 108, 373
    learning 14, 44, 66, 110, 113, 150, 152, 207,
        216, 242, 258, 470, 478
    motivation 326
    narrative inquiry and 40
    parents and (*see* Parent(s): teachers and)
    pedagogy and 149, 240, 377
    professional development 46–47, 64, 192,
        223, 227–228, 235, 328, 435, 467–470,
        512–513
    research (*see* Educational action research;
        Teacher research)
    self-identity in 349, 447 (*see also* Self: -
        identity)
    social justice and 228, 233, 434
    technology and 132 (*see also* Technology)
    training (*see* Teacher(s): education)
    unions 13, 67, 239, 241, 245, 456,
        468, 510, 516
    voice 101–102, 251, 260, 395, 468,
        477–478, 523
    writing and 269
Teacher research
    classroom action research and (*see*
        Classroom action research)
    cross-generational 229, 233
    curriculum and 53
    definition 40, 43, 263
    development 213–217, **215**, 269
    dialectic of 43–44
    equity issues in 399
    goals of 39

Teacher research *(Continued)*
 inquiry stance and 44–46
 local knowledge and 45
 networks 35, 226
 self-reflection and 484–487
 theory and 42–43, 45
 as a Way of Knowing 44
Teaching and Culture Project (TCP) 350–353
Teaching and Higher Education Act (1988) 193
Techne 32–33, 36
Technology
 classroom use of 101, 192, 195–197, 321, 373, 377
 curriculum *220*
 home use of 192–193, 196
 research use of 274
 social spaces and 379, 422–423
 See also Information and Communication Technologies
Theoria 32
Transphenomenality 360–362, 367

Unions *(see* Teacher(s): unions)
United Kingdom
 action research in 96, 372–376
 curriculum in 31
 educational policy in 238, 370, 470
 General Teaching Council (GTC) in 190, 193–195, 198–200
 Initial Teacher Education and New Technology Project (INTENT) 373
 school reform in 409
 special education needs in 120–122, 125

United States
 action research in 259, 469 *(see also* Educational action research)
 educational policy in 164, 238, 434
 inclusive education in 118
 Madison, Wisconsin School District (MMSD) 105–110 *(see also* Classroom action research)
 school reform in 409
 teacher researchers in 348–349 *(see also* Teacher research)
Universities
 collaboration with 9, 17, 40, 47, 56, 100–101, 107, 112, 148, 151, 198, 210–211, 228–229, 263, 394, 397, 503–504, 509, 513
 faculty of 11, 40, 268
 power dynamics of 513
 research and 2, 10, 40–43, 167–168, 198, 434 *(see also* Educational action research)

Volunteerism 179–180, 221

Writing
 autobiographical 261–262, 287
 days 181–182
 as inquiry tool 267, 271–275
 phases of 271–275
 significance of 250, 275
 teachers and 269
 workshops 234

Youth. *See* Student(s)